IR

Fourth Edition

For Brandy, Nita, and Melanie

Sara Miller McCune founded SAGE Publishing in 1965 to support the dissemination of usable knowledge and educate a global community. SAGE publishes more than 1000 journals and over 600 new books each year, spanning a wide range of subject areas. Our growing selection of library products includes archives, data, case studies and video. SAGE remains majority owned by our founder and after her lifetime will become owned by a charitable trust that secures the company's continued independence.

Los Angeles | London | New Delhi | Singapore | Washington DC | Melbourne

IR

Seeking Security, Prosperity, and Quality of Life in a Changing World

Fourth Edition

James M. Scott

Texas Christian University

Ralph G. Carter

Texas Christian University

A. Cooper Drury

University of Missouri

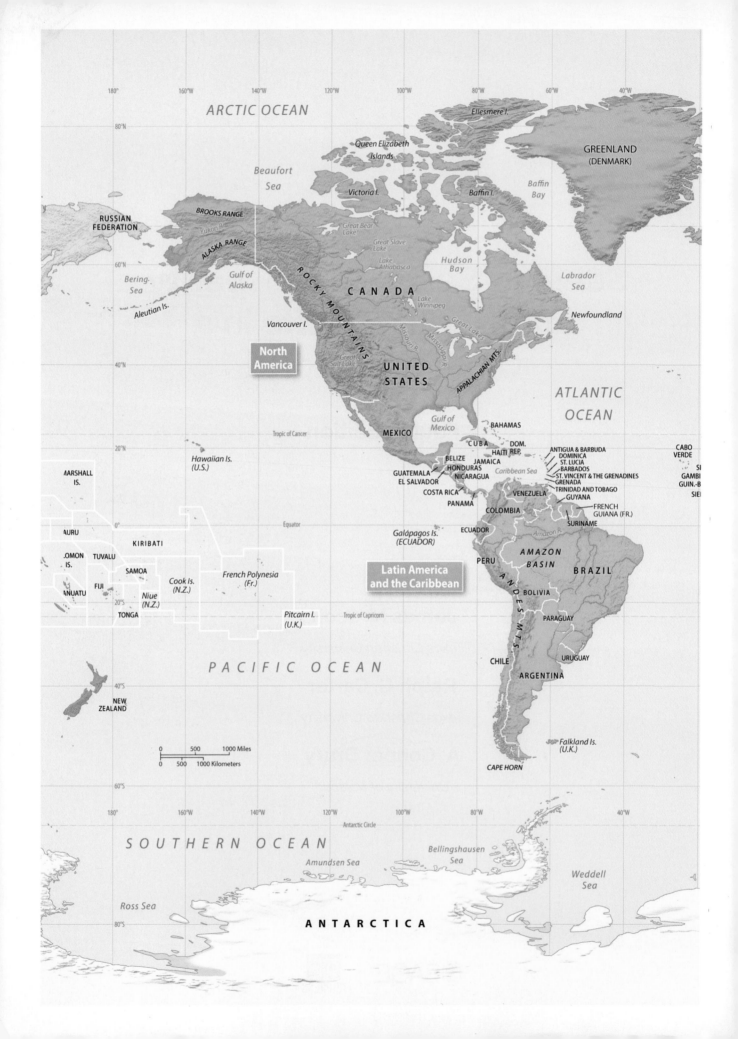

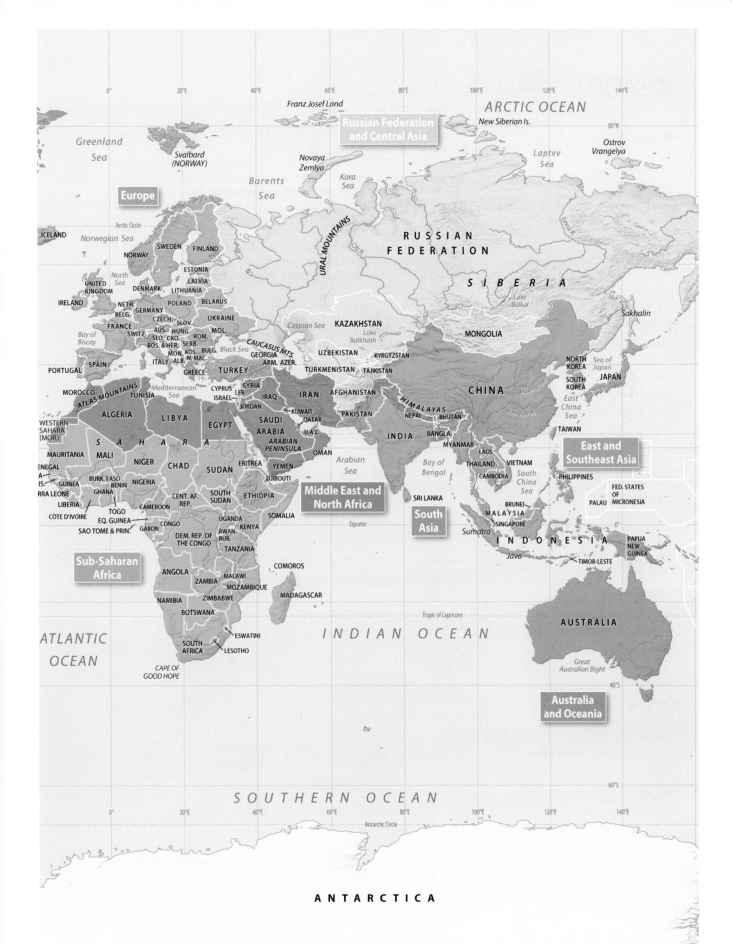

FOR INFORMATION:

CQ Press

An imprint of SAGE Publications, Inc.

2455 Teller Road

Thousand Oaks, California 91320

E-mail: order@sagepub.com

SAGE Publications Ltd.

1 Oliver's Yard

55 City Road

London EC1Y 1SP

United Kingdom

SAGE Publications India Pvt. Ltd.

B 1/I 1 Mohan Cooperative Industrial Area

Mathura Road, New Delhi 110 044

India

SAGE Publications Asia-Pacific Pte. Ltd.

18 Cross Street #10-10/11/12

China Square Central

Singapore 048423

Acquisitions Editor: Anna Villarruel

Editorial Assistant: Lauren Younker

Production Editor: Bennie Clark Allen

Copy Editor: Laureen Gleason

Typesetter: C&M Digitals (P) Ltd.

Proofreader: Larry Baker

Indexer: Integra

Cover Designer: Scott Van Atta

Marketing Manager: Jennifer Jones

Printed in Canada.

Library of Congress Cataloging-in-Publication Data

Names: Scott, James M., 1964- author. | Carter, Ralph G., author. | Drury, A. Cooper, 1967- author.

Title: IR : seeking security, prosperity, and quality of life in a changing world / James M. Scott, Texas Christian University, Ralph G. Carter, Texas Christian University, Cooper Drury, University of Missouri.
Other titles: International relations

Description: Fourth edition. | Thousand Oaks, California : CQ Press A Division of SAGE, [2022] | Includes bibliographical references and index.

Identifiers: LCCN 2020034339 | ISBN 9781544381619 (paperback) | ISBN 9781544381664 | ISBN 9781544381633 (epub) | ISBN 9781544381640 (epub) | ISBN 9781544381626 (pdf)

Subjects: LCSH: International relations—Textbooks.

Classification: LCC JZ1242 .S38 2022 | DDC 327—dc23
LC record available at https://lccn.loc.gov/2020034339

21 22 23 24 25 10 9 8 7 6 5 4 3 2 1

BRIEF CONTENTS

Preface xvii

Acknowledgments xxi

About the Authors xxv

CHAPTER 1. **World Politics: Seeking Security, Prosperity, and Quality of Life in a Complicated and Connected World 2**

Part I. Theory and Practice

CHAPTER 2. **The Players and the Playing Field: Anarchy, States, and Non-state Actors 20**

CHAPTER 3. **Powerful Ideas: Realism, Liberalism, and Constructivism 50**

CHAPTER 4. **Alternative Perspectives on International Relations 82**

Part II. International Security

CHAPTER 5. **Understanding Conflict: The Nature and Causes of Conflict and War 112**

CHAPTER 6. **Seeking Security: Managing Conflict and War 146**

CHAPTER 7. **Building Peace: Structures of Cooperation 180**

Part III. Economic Security

CHAPTER 8. **The Pursuit of Economic Security: Trade, Finance, and Integration 222**

CHAPTER 9. **Economic Statecraft: Sanctions, Aid, and Their Consequences 254**

CHAPTER 10. **International Development: Relations Between the Haves and Have-Nots 286**

Part IV. Human Security

CHAPTER 11. **Human Rights: People, Human Security, and World Politics 320**

CHAPTER 12. **Managing the Global Commons: Whose Responsibility? 352**

CHAPTER 13. Transnational Advocacy Networks: Changing the World? 382

Appendix of World Maps 424

Glossary 433

References 443

Index 450

Part V. Looking Ahead

CHAPTER 14. Security, Prosperity, and Quality of Life in the Balance: Future Directions and Challenges 406

DETAILED CONTENTS

Spencer Platt/Getty Images

Preface   xvii

Acknowledgments   xxi

About the Authors   xxv

CHAPTER 1. World Politics: Seeking Security, Prosperity, and Quality of Life in a Complicated and Connected World   **2**

Learning Objectives   3

Opening Vignette: The Challenge of Security, Prosperity, and Quality of Life in World Politics   3

Introduction: Making Sense of World Politics   3

1-1 A Complex World Connected to You   3

   1-1a World Politics and You   4

   1-1b Geography and the Small-World Phenomenon   5

   ● The Revenge of Geography: The Shrinking World   6

1-2 The Challenge of Security, Prosperity, and Quality of Life in World Politics   7

   1-2a The Nature of Security   7

   1-2b Fundamental Challenges: Anarchy, Diversity, and Complexity   8

   ● Foreign Policy in Perspective: Shifting Ways of Seeking Security   9

1-3 The Levels of Analysis and International Relations   10

1-4 Explaining the Patterns of World Politics   11

1-5 Dilemmas of Cooperation in International Relations: The Prisoner's Dilemma and the Stag Hunt   12

   1-5a The Prisoner's Dilemma   12

   1-5b The Stag Hunt   13

   1-5c Considering the Implications of the Prisoner's Dilemma and the Stag Hunt   13

   ● Theory in Action: Defeating the Prisoner's Dilemma and Getting a Stag, Not a Rabbit   14

Conclusion: Seeking Security and Contending With Challenges   15

Key Concepts   15

Key Terms   16

Review Questions   16

Think About This   17

For More Information . . .   17

Part I. Theory and Practice

CHAPTER 2. The Players and the Playing Field: Anarchy, States, and Non-state Actors   **20**

Learning Objectives   21

Opening Vignette: A Look at the Players: Conflict and Violence in Syria   21

Introduction: The IR Game Board   22

2-1 The Search for International, Economic, and Human Security in a Changing World   22

   2-1a Anarchy and Interdependence   23

   2-1b The Security Dilemma   24

2-2 The Pre-Westphalian System (Pre-1648)   25

2-3 The Westphalian System (1648–1989)   26

   2-3a States and Their Characteristics   26

   ● Foreign Policy in Perspective: The US Military and Its Impact on Global Armaments   29

   ● Spotlight On: Diplomatic Immunities   30

   2-3b Nations and Other Players   30

   2-3c The Evolution of the Westphalian System   31

   ● The Revenge of Geography: Ethnic Geography and Conflict in Afghanistan   **32**

2-4 The Neo-Westphalian System (1990–Present)   **35**

   2-4a The Development of Non-state Actors   36

   2-4b The Rise of Non-state Actors   37

   2-4c Globalization and Its Effects   40

Muhammed Said/Anadolu Agency via Getty Images

Bob Rives/Getty Images

2-4d New Stresses on States 41

2-4e The Changing Meaning of Sovereignty 43

● Theory in Action: Responsible Sovereignty and Humanitarian Interventions 44

Conclusion: Same Players but a Changing Field? 45

Key Concepts 46

Key Terms 46

Review Questions 47

Think About This 47

For More Information . . . 48

CHAPTER 3. Powerful Ideas: Realism, Liberalism, and Constructivism **50**

Learning Objectives 51

Opening Vignette: Will a "Democratic Peace" Persist? 51

Introduction: Powerful Ideas 52

3-1 Theory and International Relations 52

3-1a Thinking Theoretically 52

3-1b The Analytical Uses of Theory 52

3-1c Theory and Causation: The Components of Theory 53

3-1d Concluding Thoughts on Theory 54

● Theory in Action: The Democratic Peace and Democracy Promotion 55

3-2 The Realist Perspective on World Politics 56

3-2a Realism and the Nature of the International System 57

● Spotlight On: Variants of Realism 58

3-2b Realism and the Relevant Actors in International Relations 58

3-2c Realism and the Important Resources in International Relations 59

3-2d Realism and the Central Dynamics of International Relations 60

● The Revenge of Geography: Geography and Power 61

● Spotlight On: Military Power and World Politics 62

3-3 The Liberal Perspective on World Politics 63

3-3a Liberalism and the Nature of the International System 64

● Spotlight On: Variants of Liberalism in World Politics 65

3-3b Liberalism and the Relevant Actors in International Relations 66

3-3c Liberalism and the Important Resources in International Relations 67

3-3d Liberalism and the Central Dynamics of International Relations 68

3-4 The Constructivist Perspective on World Politics 69

3-4a Constructivism and the Nature of the International System 70

● Spotlight On: Variants of Constructivism 71

3-4b Constructivism and the Relevant Actors in International Relations 71

● Foreign Policy in Perspective: Russia and Its Neighbors 72

3-4c Constructivism and the Important Resources in International Relations 73

3-4d Constructivism and the Central Dynamics of International Relations 74

Conclusion: Dueling Theories? 77

Key Concepts 78

Key Terms 79

Review Questions 79

Think About This 80

For More Information . . . 80

CHAPTER 4. Alternative Perspectives on International Relations **82**

Learning Objectives 83

Opening Vignette: Confronting Iraq 83

Introduction: Alternatives to Realism, Liberalism, and Constructivism 84

4-1 Foreign Policy Analysis 84

4-1a Individual Explanations of Foreign Policy 85

AHMAD AL-RUBAYE/AFP via Getty Images

Spencer Platt/Getty Images

4-1b Group Explanations of Foreign Policy	87
● Theory in Action: Personality and Policymaking: Donald Trump in Context	88
4-1c Societal Explanations of Foreign Policy	89
4-1d Regime Explanations of Foreign Policy	90
4-1e Foreign Policy Analysis as the Foundation for International Relations	91
4-2 Marxism and Marxist Theory	**91**
4-2a Marxist Theory and International Relations	92
4-2b Marxist Theory as an Alternative Lens	94
● Foreign Policy in Perspective: Brexit: The UK Withdrawal From the European Union	95
4-3 World Systems Theory	**96**
● The Revenge of Geography: Zones of Wealth and Peace?	99
4-4 Feminism	**100**
4-4a The Impact of Women on International Relations Theory	101
4-4b The Impact of Women on International Relations	102
● Spotlight On: Women and World War C	103
4-4c The Impact of International Relations on Women	106
4-4d Half of the Population but Not Half of the Input	107
Conclusion	**107**
Key Concepts	**108**
Key Terms	**109**
Review Questions	**110**
Think About This	**110**
For More Information . . .	**110**

Introduction: International Conflict	**113**
5-1 The Nature of Armed Conflict	**114**
5-1a War and Its Types	114
● Spotlight On: Defining War Empirically	117
5-1b Terrorism	118
● Spotlight On: ISIS and Modern Revolutionary Terrorism	120
5-2 The Nature and Evolution of War in World Politics	**121**
● Spotlight On: Terrorism in 2018	123
5-2a Increasing Deadliness	123
5-2b More Limited Wars	124
5-2c War in the Developing World	124
5-2d More Civil War	126
5-2e More Unconventional War	126
● Spotlight On: Fourth-Generation War	128
5-3 Why Wars Begin	**129**
5-3a The Causes of War: Factors Leading to Conflict	130
5-3b The Causes of War: Explaining the Patterns	131
● Foreign Policy in Perspective: Losing the Lead?	133
● Spotlight On: Rational Actors and Bargaining Theories of War	135
● Theory in Action: Constructing the Democratic Peace	136
● The Revenge of Geography: Location, Interests, and Conflict	139
Conclusion: The Consequences of Wars	**141**
Key Concepts	**142**
Key Terms	**143**
Review Questions	**143**
Think About This	**144**
For More Information . . .	**144**

Part II. International Security

CHAPTER 5. Understanding Conflict: The Nature and Causes of Conflict and War   112

Learning Objectives	113
Opening Vignette: A Coming War Between the United States and China?	113

CHAPTER 6. Seeking Security: Managing Conflict and War   146

Learning Objectives	147
Opening Vignette: Responding to Russian Missiles?	147

iStock/rusm

Spencer Platt/Getty Images

Introduction: Managing Conflict and
Seeking Security   147
6-1 The Challenge of International Security   148
    6-1a The Security Dilemma   148
    6-1b The Challenge of Power   148
6-2 Realist Approaches to Security and Conflict 149
    6-2a Weapons   150
    ● Spotlight On: China's Military Spending   151
    ● The Revenge of Geography:
       Security and Geography   154
    6-2b Alliances   157
    6-2c Balance of Power   159
    6-2d Using Force   160
    ● Spotlight On: Deterrence After
       the Cold War?   163
6-3 Liberal Approaches to Security and Conflict 165
    6-3a Arms Control and Disarmament   165
    ● Theory in Action: Arms, Arms Control,
       and War   166
    ● Spotlight On: Iran and Nuclear Proliferation 170
    6-3b Collective Security   170
    6-3c Security Communities and the Democratic
       and Capitalist Peace   173
    ● Foreign Policy in Perspective:
       China's Pursuit of Security   175
Conclusion: Seeking Security   176
Key Concepts   177
Key Terms   177
Review Questions   178
Think About This   178
For More Information . . .   178

7-2 Diplomacy: Negotiation in World Politics   183
    7-2a The Nature and Role of Diplomacy   183
    ● Spotlight On: Who Represents the
       United States Abroad?   184
    7-2b The Art of Diplomacy   185
    7-2c The Forms of Diplomacy   186
7-3 International Law: Norms and Rules
Without Central Authority   187
    7-3a The Nature of International Law   189
    7-3b The Sources of International Law   189
    ● Spotlight On: The Just War Tradition
       and International Law   190
    7-3c Compliance and Enforcement   192
    ● Theory in Action: The United States
       and the World Court   193
    ● Foreign Policy in Perspective:
       The Marshall Islands, International Law,
       and the World Court   195
7-4 International Organizations: The European
Union, the United Nations, and Many Others 196
    7-4a Why Do International Organizations Exist? 196
    7-4b Types of International Organizations   197
    7-4c Key International Organizations in World
       Politics   201
    7-4d The European Union: The Most Powerful
       Regional Organization   203
    ● The Revenge of Geography:
       Can Europe Unite?   209
    7-4e The United Nations   210
    ● Spotlight On: The Basic Purposes
       of the UN   212
    ● Spotlight On: Who Pays for All of This,
       Anyway?   215
Conclusion   217
Key Concepts   218
Key Terms   218
Review Questions   219
Think About This   219
For More Information . . .   220

CHAPTER 7. Building Peace: Structures of Cooperation   180

Learning Objectives   181
Opening Vignette: A New World Order?   181
Introduction: Achieving Cooperation   182
7-1 Cooperation and Its Challenges   182

Saul Loeb/AFP/Getty Images

AP Photo/Mark Lennihan

Part III. Economic Security

CHAPTER 8. The Pursuit of Economic Security: Trade, Finance, and Integration   **222**

Learning Objectives   223

Opening Vignette: The Global Economy and the Resurgence of Nationalist Economics   223

Introduction: Money Is Power   224

8-1 Money, Power, and Security   224

    8-1a Complex Linkages in International Relations   224

    ● Spotlight On: Levels of Interdependence and Integration   225

    8-1b Markets and Governments: A Sometimes Tense and Codependent Relationship   226

8-2 The National Economy Era: Colonialism and Mercantilism   226

    ● The Revenge of Geography: Why Did the Europeans Colonize Asia, Africa, and the Americas, Not the Other Way Around?   228

8-3 The International Economy Era: Free Trade, Liberalism, and Marxism   229

    8-3a World (Trade) War   229

    ● Theory in Action: Should Countries Pursue Free Trade?   230

    8-3b Marxism   232

    8-3c Marxism Implemented   232

    8-3d From International to Global Economy Eras: The Liberal International Economic Order After World War II   233

8-4 The Global Economy Era   236

    8-4a The Modern Economy   237

    8-4b Globalization and the Global Economy   240

    ● Foreign Policy in Perspective: Free Trade Under Threat?   247

Conclusion   249

Key Concepts   250

Key Terms   251

Review Questions   251

Think About This   251

For More Information . . .   252

CHAPTER 9. Economic Statecraft: Sanctions, Aid, and Their Consequences   **254**

Learning Objectives   255

Opening Vignette: Carrots and Sticks?   255

Introduction: Using Wealth to Influence Other Countries   255

9-1 Economic Statecraft   256

    ● Spotlight On: Iran, Nuclear Weapons, and Sanctions   257

    9-1a The Long History of Economic Statecraft: Money as a Carrot and a Stick   259

9-2 Economic Sanctions   259

    9-2a The Types of Economic Sanctions   259

    9-2b Total Sanctions   262

    9-2c The Many Purposes of Sanctions   263

    9-2d The Failure of Economic Sanctions   264

    ● Theory in Action: Leverage, Sanctions, and LGBTQIA Rights   265

    ● Foreign Policy in Perspective: Are Sanctions on North Korea Finally Working?   266

    ● Spotlight On: Women and Economic Sanctions   268

    9-2e The Costly Consequences of Sanctions   269

9-3 Foreign Aid   270

    9-3a Development Aid   270

    ● Spotlight On: US Development Aid in Perspective   271

    ● The Revenge of Geography: Did the Berlin Wall Fall on Africa?   272

    9-3b Military Aid   276

    9-3c Aid for Democracy   278

    9-3d Humanitarian Aid   280

Henry H. Herrmann/ullstein bild via Getty Images

iStock/rusm

Conclusion 282
Key Concepts 282
Key Terms 283
Review Questions 283
Think About This 283
For More Information . . . 284

CHAPTER 10. International Development: Relations Between the Haves and Have-Nots 286

Learning Objectives 287
Opening Vignette: A Tale of Two Economies 287
Introduction: The Differences Between the Rich and the Poor 288
10-1 The Wealth Gap 288
   10-1a Our Understanding of the Rich and the Poor 289
   10-1b The Countries That Have Wealth and the Countries That Don't 290
   10-1c The Distribution of Wealth and Development Within Countries 292
10-2 Why Are Some Countries Rich and Others Poor? 295
   10-2a Natural Resources 295
   10-2b Colonial History 297
   ● The Revenge of Geography: Does Being in the South Make You Poor? 298
10-3 Development Theories and Policies 299
   10-3a Modernization 299
   10-3b Dependency Theory 300
   ● Spotlight On: Climate, Climate Change, and Economic Development 301
   10-3c World Systems Theory 302
   10-3d Import Substitution Industrialization 304
   10-3e Export-Led Growth 305
   10-3f The Washington Consensus 306
   ● Spotlight On: Democracy and Economic Growth 307
   10-3g The Millennium Development Goals and Beyond 308
   ● Theory in Action: Women in International Development 309
10-4 International Organizations and Development 310
   10-4a The International Monetary Fund and the World Bank 310
   ● Foreign Policy in Perspective: Debt Forgiveness 311
   10-4b The World Trade Organization 313
   10-4c The United Nations 313
Conclusion 315
Key Concepts 315
Key Terms 316
Review Questions 316
Think About This 316
For More Information . . . 317

Part IV. Human Security

CHAPTER 11. Human Rights: People, Human Security, and World Politics 320

Learning Objectives 321
Opening Vignette: Fleeing Civil War in Syria 321
Introduction: Redefining Sovereignty From Protecting Borders to Protecting People 322
11-1 The Evolution of Human Rights 322
   11-1a Individual Rights 322
   11-1b Societal Rights 323
   11-1c Group Rights 324
   ● The Revenge of Geography: Turmoil in the African Great Lakes Region 328
11-2 The Human Rights Regime: From Norms to Rules 329
   ● Foreign Policy in Perspective: The United States and Human Rights 332

Hristo Rusev/NurPhoto via Getty Images

NOAA

11-3 The Challenge of Implementation and
Enforcement 334
  11-3a State-Based Initiatives 334
  11-3b International Organization–Based Initiatives 340
  ● Spotlight On: The Issue of Femicide 341
  11-3c NGO-Based Initiatives 344
  ● Theory in Action: Protecting Human Rights:
    NGOs and Humanitarian Intervention 347
Conclusion: The Evolving Human Rights Regime 348
Key Concepts 348
Key Terms 349
Review Questions 349
Think About This 349
For More Information 350

CHAPTER 12. Managing the Global Commons: Whose Responsibility? 352

Learning Objectives 353
Opening Vignette: The Great Pacific Garbage
  Patch 353
Introduction: Managing the Global Commons
  and the Consequences of Human Actions 353
12-1 The "Tragedy of the Commons"
  Illustrated in the Environment 354
  12-1a Pollution 354
  12-1b Deforestation 355
  12-1c Desertification 357
  12-1d Global Climate Change 357
  12-1e Biodiversity Challenges 361
12-2 The Evolving Environmental Regime and
  the Challenges of Sustainable Development . 363
  12-2a State Actions 363
  ● Spotlight On: Sustainable Development Goals 365
  12-2b Public and Nongovernmental
    Organization Actions 366
  ● Theory in Action: Which Non-state Actors
    Matter Most in the Environmental Arena? 367

  12-2c International Organization Actions 368
  ● Spotlight On: Sea Shepherd 369
  ● Foreign Policy in Perspective: A Lonely
    "Leader"? The US and Climate Change 371
12-3 The Challenge of Fostering Sustainable
  Development 372
  12-3a Poverty Reduction 372
  12-3b Sustainable Economic Development 372
  ● The Revenge of Geography: What's Up
    With Mountain Societies? 373
  12-3c Resource Preservation 374
12-4 Emerging Arenas of Competition and
  Cooperation 374
  12-4a Maritime Developments 374
  12-4b Cyberspace as a New Arena
    (and Outer Space as a Revisited One) 375
  12-4c Human Migration 376
  12-4d Pandemic Diseases 377
Conclusion: Managing the Global Commons 377
Key Concepts 378
Key Terms 379
Review Questions 379
Think About This 380
For More Information 380

CHAPTER 13. Transnational Advocacy Networks: Changing the World? 382

Learning Objectives 383
Opening Vignette: Why Do People Still Get Polio? 383
Introduction: A New Form of International Actor? 384
13-1 What Are Transnational Advocacy
  Networks? 384
13-2 How Do Transnational Advocacy Networks
  Affect Human Security? 385
  13-2a Popularizing Ideas 385
  ● The Revenge of Geography: Do TANs
    Reflect Their Home Cultures? 387
  13-2b Influencing States 387

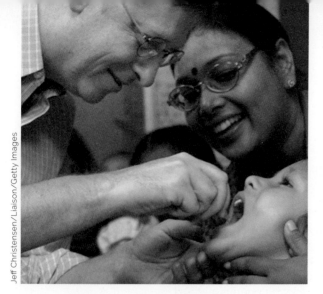

Jeff Christensen/Liaison/Getty Images

iStock/chaofann

● Foreign Policy in Perspective: The Case of the Nigerian Schoolgirls 389

13-2c Encouraging and Enabling Cooperation 390

13-3 The Diverse World of Transnational Advocacy Networks 391

13-3a Self-Oriented TANs and What They Do 391

● Spotlight On: How Do Criminal TANs Develop? 393

● Spotlight On: Trafficking in Human Organs 394

13-3b Other-Oriented TANs and What They Do 395

● Spotlight On: Al-Qaeda and ISIS: Global Jihadist Networks 396

13-3c Evaluating TANs 400

Conclusion: Transnational Advocacy Networks and the Global Future 400

● Theory in Action: Evaluating TANs in the International System 401

Key Concepts 402

Key Terms 402

Review Questions 403

Think About This 403

For More Information . . . 403

Part V. Looking Ahead

CHAPTER 14. **Security, Prosperity, and Quality of Life in the Balance: Future Directions and Challenges 406**

Learning Objectives 407

Opening Vignette: How Big a Problem Is North Korea? 407

Introduction: Interpreting How the World Works 408

14-1 Anarchy, Diversity, and Complexity in World Politics 409

14-1a These Challenges Are Pervasive 409

14-1b These Challenges Are Changing 410

14-1c These Challenges Are Connected 412

14-1d These Challenges Are Not Insurmountable 413

14-2 Seeking Security 414

14-2a Traditional Military Security Concerns Continue but Are Evolving 415

14-2b Economic Security Concerns Gain Importance and Are Shaped by Globalization and Interdependence 416

14-2c Human Security Issues Are Increasingly Central and Connected to Both Economic and Military Security 417

14-2d All Security Issues Have Heightened Effects on Women and Children 417

14-3 The Road Ahead 418

14-3a From State-Centric to Multi-centric System 418

14-3b Emerging Challenges and Dilemmas 418

14-4 Theory in Action, Geography, and Foreign Policy in Perspective 419

14-4a Theory in Action 419

14-4b Revenge of Geography 420

14-4c Foreign Policy in Perspective 420

Conclusion 421

Key Concepts 421

Review Questions 422

Think About This 423

For More Information . . . 423

Appendix of World Maps 424

Glossary 433

References 443

Index 450

PREFACE

Making sense of the complicated events and interactions of world politics is enormously challenging. As students of world politics, we want to develop familiarity with the events and details, but we also want to see the larger patterns and develop explanations for them. Our challenge is thus to blend an engaging discussion of issues and events with a thematic and conceptual approach that helps place them in context and helps develop better understanding of their meaning, causes, and implications. In short, we want to engage together as students of world politics, not just to think about **what** happens but also to understand **why** and **how** it happens.

IR: Seeking Security, Prosperity, and Quality of Life in a Changing World is our effort to do just that. This textbook offers an introduction to international relations that can fit a typical course term, while also supplying a rich array of relevant, enriching features that illustrate the concepts, bring home the ideas to students, and aid the professor in stimulating discussion and interest in the topic. We anchor our effort by writing the book in an accessible, conversational tone to engage students. International relations can be a daunting arena to which some students cannot relate, but we believe it is a compelling subject that can and should be approached as an exciting conversation that is engaging in the same way that a good movie draws in the viewer. As students read and think, they will find us asking them questions, pausing for reflection, presenting problems and puzzles, and working through ideas and issues with them.

To achieve the goal of addressing events and issues in the context of broader patterns and explanations, we consistently weave together treatment of issues with theory and real-world policy concerns. Rather than introducing the theories of international relations in extensive chapters and thick descriptions in the first section of the text and then ignoring theory in the remaining text, as many books do, we try to present theory and concepts clearly and thoroughly in the first section and then (a) apply the theoretical lenses throughout the book and (b) explicitly incorporate applications of how theories and concepts influence real-world behavior and policy. We also stress a problem- and theme-based approach throughout, not only to unify the chapters but also to provide extensive pedagogical and discussion opportunities focused on understanding explanation, meaning, and implications of the events and issues of world politics. In addition, we direct significant attention to who the players are, what they want, and how they behave to keep the roles and policy behavior of key actors—both states and non-states—central to our investigation of how and why international relations unfolds as it does. Consequently, *IR* is balanced in coverage, combining timeless theoretical understanding and analysis with descriptive elements of contemporary international realities.

THE SEARCH FOR SECURITY IN A CHANGING ENVIRONMENT

This book is organized around the idea of security, but we define security broadly to include international security, prosperity (i.e., economic security), and quality of life (i.e., human security). In most social interactions, humans seek order and predictability, and those goals cannot be reached without adequate security. This desire for security is far more important across the globe than who is politically in charge, what form of governance is followed, or what economic system is used. Our emphasis on the various elements of security—issues of war and peace, wealth and prosperity, and the quality-of-life concerns of humans—provides a unique grounding in what is most important in the lives of most people on the planet. As the players of international relations seek international, economic, and human security, the world in which they do so has evolved and changed, affecting what they seek, how and why they seek it, and how they interact. Thus, we place our discussions of each related area of security in the context of change and ask our students to think about how the evolving context of world politics affects things like war and peace, wealth and prosperity, and the quality-of-life concerns of humans.

To lend focus and structure, throughout all our chapters, we introduce and apply three fundamental challenges that condition the behavior, interactions, and processes of world politics.

> First, the **anarchy** of the international system—the fact that there is no central authority—has pervasive effects on the nature of international conflict and the prospects and forms of international cooperation.

> Second, the **diversity** in the international system—the many players, ideas, cultures, and political structures—has similar consequences for international interactions.

> Finally, the **complexity** of international interactions—involving multidimensional issues, state and non-state actors, national and transnational processes, and other factors—generates challenges for all the players as they pursue their preferred outcomes.

The anarchic structure of the international system is a foundational element for understanding and managing conflict and war, and it conditions global economic interactions and the pursuit of wealth, as well as the prospects for a human rights regime and environmental cooperation. Diversity of identity, values, and culture is a critical issue for human rights and human security, while also affecting conflict and economic relations. The complexity of the global political system complicates global economic interactions and coordination, and it affects the pursuit of international security and human security. Throughout the text, we raise questions about these challenges to encourage critical thinking, analysis, and reflection.

ORGANIZATION

Our emphasis on the security theme and these three central challenges unifies the textbook and enables us to place description, events, and interactions into a context for explanation and interpretation. To investigate world politics and the pursuit of broadly defined security, we organize the book into four relatively equal and balanced parts, bracketed by introductory and concluding chapters. **Chapter 1** introduces our text's themes: international, economic, and human security; the challenges of anarchy, diversity, and complexity; levels of analysis; and both the prisoner's dilemma and stag hunt concepts.

In **Part I**, we present three chapters that lay out the playing field or game board of world politics, introduce the players and broad trends, and present the theoretical lenses that make up our theoretical toolbox. **Chapter 2** provides a historical overview of the international system and major actors. In the Westphalian international system (1648–1989), anarchy reigns and state actors hold their sovereignty inviolate; non-state actors are secondary players in most cases. In the neo-Westphalian international system, globalization has put some parameters on anarchy and some limits on sovereignty; non-state actors are rising in importance and rival state actors in many instances. **Chapter 3** examines how realist, liberal, and constructivist theories see, understand, and explain world politics. **Chapter 4** presents alternative lenses, including foreign policy analysis and critical approaches such as feminist and Marxist theories, and discusses their contributions and challenges to realist, liberal, and constructivist approaches. With these theoretical and conceptual tools in hand, we then turn to the substantive core of the book—three sections examining different arenas for the pursuit of security.

Part II focuses on security and conflict. ***Chapter 5*** investigates conflict and its nature, causes, and consequences. ***Chapter 6*** focuses on efforts to manage conflict and war, including arms, deterrence and alliance formation, collective security, arms control and disarmament, and others. ***Chapter 7*** explores efforts to build structures and institutions of cooperation that facilitate the pursuit of security through international law and international organizations.

Part III shifts attention to prosperity and economic security. ***Chapter 8*** emphasizes the pursuit of wealth and prosperity and discusses international trade and the goals and instruments of international finance and monetary relations. It also delves into globalization and its consequences, costs, and benefits. ***Chapter 9*** devotes attention to economic statecraft and the tools states and others use to pursue economic security. Topics include sanctions and aid and the use of these tools as threats and punishment or as incentives and rewards. ***Chapter 10*** concentrates on relations between richer and poorer countries and explores the nature and causes of development, the inequalities between and within states, and paths to economic development and security in this context.

Part IV turns to quality of life and human security. ***Chapter 11*** focuses on human rights. Topics covered include civil, political, economic, and social rights; tensions between externally evaluated human rights and national sovereignty; and efforts at the protection of human rights by states, international organizations, international tribunals, and nongovernmental organizations. ***Chapter 12*** concentrates on transnational issues in managing the global commons and multiple challenges with which the world must grapple. Topics covered include the challenges facing the physical environment (e.g., pollution, deforestation, desertification, global climate change); the quest for sustainable development; and new, emerging arenas of conflict and cooperation (e.g., maritime issues, cyberspace, human migration, and pandemic diseases) and the international responses to them by individuals, states, international organizations, and nongovernmental organizations. ***Chapter 13*** takes up transnational advocacy networks, collections of nongovernmental actors crossing traditional borders and boundaries. Topics covered include the types, activities, and impact of transnational advocacy networks active in international politics—religious, terrorist, humanitarian, economic, and others.

Chapter 14 concludes our text by reflecting on the pursuit of security in the future and discussing the directions and challenges of world politics. In this chapter, we synthesize our preceding discussions and draw some ideas and questions for reflection that build on our main theme (seeking security) and the three core challenges the players of world politics face as they pursue it and interact with each other.

FEATURES AND PEDAGOGY

On a practical level, this textbook is explicitly organized for the instructor's convenience for term structure and testing. The four major sections are of roughly equal length and lend themselves to be used with either four sections/exams for the class or the more traditional midterm/final in which two sections would be covered for each test. Further, we provide a series of features that involve either (a) critical thinking or (b) interpreting evidence. The exercises in these features provide the professor with considerable flexibility in how the class is run. For example, a large class with discussion sections could rely on these exercises for the separate discussions, while a smaller class could use them to illustrate concepts during a regular lecture, thereby making the lecture itself more interactive. We regard these as "features that teach," and each chapter includes six complementary types:

Chapter Openers. We begin each chapter with an opening vignette or puzzle that frames the chapter topics and themes. With each, we provide some reflection questions for use in and out of the classroom.

Spotlight On. These boxed features raise topics that may need more explanation and highlight interesting cases. Each of them presents a closer look at relevant concepts and issues that tie the topic back into the chapter and book themes.

Theory in Action. International or world politics is the result of real people making decisions and choices. Thus, the importance of how ideas (e.g., beliefs, values, preferences, motivations) shape our decisions, choices, and actions is important to emphasize. These boxed features demonstrate how ideas are directly translated into policy and action, and each ends with a set of critical thinking questions. For students, these can take the mystery out of why they are expected to learn the underlying theories of international politics like liberalism, realism, constructivism, and other critical theories (e.g., Marxism, world systems theory, feminism).

The Revenge of Geography. As globalization has caused national boundaries to mean less and less, the physical realities of geography retain their importance. These boxed features (named after Robert D. Kaplan's 2009 *Foreign Policy* article of the same title) incorporate maps, mapping exercises, and discussion questions alongside a case demonstrating how geography can influence international relations. For example, in a map of Africa, we show the states and ethno-linguistic groups of the continent. Along with discussion questions, this map engages students in thinking about how competing forces (political borders and ethnic borders) shape international politics.

Foreign Policy in Perspective. We bring student focus on how the dynamics of international relations translate into policy and behavior with boxed features that explore how certain actors—states (big and small) and non-states—pursue international, economic, and human security in particular contexts. These boxes include examples drawn from many perspectives that allow students to think about what the players of world politics seek and how and why they do so. Each ends with a set of critical thinking questions.

Think About This. We close each chapter with a problem or puzzle drawn from and relating to the chapter contents. These problems are grounded in the relevant concepts and present opportunities to apply theoretical lenses and analysis and extract evidence and information from the chapters to make arguments and explanations. Each of these chapter-enders includes a short paragraph framing a problem and culminates in a question or puzzle to "solve."

TEACHING RESOURCES

This text includes an array of instructor teaching materials designed to save you time and to help you keep students engaged. To learn more, visit sagepub.com or contact your SAGE representative at **sagepub.com/findmyrep**.

A FINAL NOTE

Underlying all our efforts is our fundamental philosophy, organized around student engagement and active learning, and around efforts to facilitate subject mastery and the development of critical and analytical thinking generated when students ask "why" questions and formulate answers. We have been gratified by the warm reception our text has received from students and instructors since its inception, and we have made every effort to strengthen and improve this most recent edition. Although our overall approach and outline remain consistent, we have revised this edition substantially to ensure its continued relevance and success. We hope you find it helpful as you engage with your students to make sense of international relations and think about how the world works.

ACKNOWLEDGMENTS

We would like to thank the following instructors for their and their students' invaluable feedback as we wrote the book:

Olayiwola Abegunrin, Howard University

Dilshod Achilov, University of Massachusetts Dartmouth

Duane Adamson, Brigham Young University

Yasemin Akbaba, Gettysburg College

Joan Serafin Andorfer, Frostburg State University

Joseph Avitable, Quinnipiac University

Sangmin Bae, Northeastern Illinois University

Kelly Bauer, George Washington University

Svetla Ben-Itzhak, Kansas State University

Koop Berry, Walsh University

Patricia Bixel, Husson University

Patrick Bratton, Hawaii Pacific University

Marijke Breuning, University of North Texas

Courtney Burns, Georgia Southern University

Charity Butcher, Kennesaw State University

Jetsabe Caceres, University of Toledo

Joseph Chaikel, Salisbury University/ UMES

Thomas Chioppa, Brookdale Community College

Robert Chisholm, Columbia Basin College

Renato Corbetta, University of Alabama at Birmingham

Eric Cox, Texas Christian University

Bruce Cronin, City College of New York

Carrie Currier, Texas Christian University

Suheir Daoud, Coastal Carolina University

Ursula Daxecker, University of Amsterdam

Michael Deaver, Sierra College

Brian Dille, Mesa Community College

Agber Dimah, Chicago State University

Polly Diven, Grand Valley State University

John A. Doces, Bucknell University

Tom Doleys, Kennesaw State University

Pedro G. Dos Santos, Luther College

Oya Dursun-Ozkanca, Elizabethtown College

Andrew Essig, DeSales University

William Felice, Eckerd College

Femi Ferreira, Hutchinson Community College

Amanda Cook Fesperman, Illinois Valley Community College

Paul Frank, Sacramento City College

Brian Frederking, McKendree University

Daniel Fuerstman, State College of Florida

Caron Gentry, University of St. Andrews

Gigi Gokcek, Dominican University of California

David Goldberg, College of DuPage

Simon Peter Gomez, Reinhardt University

Robert Gorman, Texas State University

Anna Gregg, Austin Peay State University

Paul Haber, University of Montana

Maia Hallward, Kennesaw State University

Tracy Harbin, Seminole State College

Brooke Harlowe, Lock Haven University

Andrea B. Haupt, Santa Barbara City College

Paul Hensel, University of North Texas

Uk Heo, University of Wisconsin–Milwaukee

Eric Hines, University of Montana–Missoula

Aaron Hoffman, Purdue University

Leif Hoffmann, Lewis-Clark State College

Claus Hofhansel, Rhode Island University

Aart Holtslag, Shepherd University

Cale Horne, Covenant College

Michael Huelshoff, University of New Orleans

Mir Zohair Husain, University of South Alabama

Kate Ivanova, Ohio State University–Newark

Steven F. Jackson, Indiana University of Pennsylvania

Mike Jasinski, University of Wisconsin–Oshkosh

Thomas Johnson, University of Jamestown

Harry Joiner, Athens State University

Michael Kanner, University of Colorado-Boulder

Julie Keil, Saginaw Valley State University

Phil Kelly, Emporia State University

Brian Kessel, Columbia College

Richard Kiefer, Waubonsee Community College

Damir Kovačević, University of Wisconsin–Eau Claire

Richard Krupa, William Rainey Harper College

Paul Labedz, University of Central Florida

Daniel R. Lake, State University of New York–Plattsburg

Ritu Lauer, Peninsula College

Christopher Lawrence, Middle Georgia State University

James Leaman, Eastern Mennonite University

Anika Leithner, California Polytechnic State University

Michael Lerma, Northern Arizona University

Christopher Leskiw, University of the Cumberlands

Yitan Li, Seattle University

Timothy Lim, California State University–Los Angeles

Timothy Lomperis, Saint Louis University

Stephen Long, University of Richmond

Mary Manjikian, Regent University

Khalil Marrar, Governors State University

Matthias Matthijs, Johns Hopkins University

Philip Mayer, Three Rivers Community Technical College

Julie Mazzei, Kent State University

Mary M. McCarthy, Drake University

Paul T. McCartney, Towson University

Autumn McGimsey, Cape Fear Community College/University of North Carolina Wilmington

Elizabeth McNamara, University of North Carolina, Greensboro

John Miglietta, Tennessee State University

Wesley Milner, University of Evansville

Jonathan Miner, University of North Georgia

Kristine Mitchell, Dickinson College

Sara Moats, Florida International University

Jason J. Morrissette, Marshall University

Carolyn Myers, Southwestern Illinois College

Michael Nelson, Wesleyan University

Gabriella Paar-Jakli, Kent State University

Robert Packer, Pennsylvania State University–University Park

James Pasley, Park University

Clint Peinhardt, University of Texas–Dallas

Dursun Peksen, University of Memphis

Jeffrey Pickering, Kansas State University

Marco Pinfari, American University in Cairo

Marc S. Polizzi, Murray State University

Dave Price, Santa Fe College

William Primosch, Montgomery College/ Northern Virginia Community College

Steven Redd, University of Wisconsin–Milwaukee

Andrew W. Reddie, Dominican University of California

Dan Reiter, Emory University

James Rhodes, Luther College

Lia Roberts, Mount Saint Mary's University

Joanna Sabo, Monroe County Community College

Chris Saladino, Virginia Commonwealth University

Maria Sampanis, California State University–Sacramento

Brent Sasley, University of Texas–Arlington

Kanishkan Sathasivam, Salem State University

Brian Schmidt, Carleton University

Francis Schortgen, University of Mount Union

Lou Schubert, City College of San Francisco

Susan Sell, George Washington University

John Shively, Metropolitan Community College–Kansas City

Michael Snarr, Wilmington College

M. Scott Solomon, University of South Florida

Mark Souva, Florida State University

James Sperling, University of Akron

Seitu Stephens, Delaware County Community College, Lincoln University

Robert Sterken, University of Texas at Tyler

Feng Sun, Troy University

Richard Tanksley, North Idaho College

Moses Tesi, Middle Tennessee State University

Clayton Thyne, University of Kentucky

Jaroslav Tir, University of Georgia

Peter Trumbore, Oakland University

Krista Tuomi, American University

Brian Urlacher, University of North Dakota

Brandon Valeriano, Cardiff University

Adam Van Liere, University of Wisconsin–LaCrosse

Alex Von Hagen, NYU Shanghai

Geoff Wallace, University of Washington

James Walsh, University of North Carolina at Charlotte

David Watson, Sul Ross State University

Robert Weiner, University of Massachusetts–Boston

Robert E. Williams, Pepperdine University

Byungwon Woo, Hankuk University of Foreign Studies

Ashley Woodiwiss, Erskine College

David Yamanishi, Cornell College

Yi Edward Yang, James Madison University

Min Ye, Coastal Carolina University

Jeremy Youde, Australian National University

Tina Zappile, Stockton University

Dana Zartner, University of San Francisco

ABOUT THE AUTHORS

James M. Scott is Herman Brown Chair and Professor of Political Science at Texas Christian University. His areas of specialization include foreign policy analysis and international relations, with particular emphasis on US foreign policymaking and the domestic sources of foreign policy. He is author or editor of nine books (including this one); more than 50 refereed articles, chapters, and essays in highly reputable outlets; and more than 100 review essays, chapters, conference papers, and other works. He has been conference organizer and president of both the Foreign Policy Analysis section of the International Studies Association and the International Studies Association–Midwest, and he has served on several governing committees in each association. He has been a two-time winner of the Frank J. Klingberg Award for Best Paper Presented by a Faculty Member at the ISA–Midwest annual meeting. Since 1996, he has received more than three dozen awards from students and peers for his outstanding teaching and research, including his institution's highest awards for research in 2000 and 2001 and for research mentoring in 2002. He is the recipient of the 2012 Quincy Wright Distinguished Scholar Award and the 2018 Excellence in Teaching and Mentoring Award from the ISA–Midwest. From 2005 to 2014, he was director of the Democracy, Interdependence and World Politics Summer Research Program, a National Science Foundation Research Experience for Undergraduates. He was associate editor of *Foreign Policy Analysis* from 2009 to 2015, was coeditor of *Political Research Quarterly* from 2015 to 2018, and is currently lead editor of *International Studies Perspectives*.

Ralph G. Carter is Piper Professor of 2014, Professor, and former Chair of the Department of Political Science at Texas Christian University. His areas of specialization include international relations and comparative foreign policy analysis, with a particular emphasis on the domestic sources of foreign policy. He is the author, coauthor, editor, or coeditor of six books and more than 50 articles, book chapters, review essays, monographs, and other professional publications. He has been an invited scholar to universities in the United States, Canada, and the United Kingdom. In addition to serving on the Executive Committee and chairing other committees of the International Studies Association, he also served as president of ISA's Foreign Policy Analysis section, president of the International Studies Association–Midwest, and associate editor of *Foreign Policy Analysis*, as well as on the editorial boards of *Foreign Policy Analysis* and *International Studies Perspectives*. He also served the American Political Science Association as a member of its Program Committee. In addition to over three dozen teaching awards and recognitions, in 2006, he became the first person from an undergraduate department to receive the Quincy Wright Distinguished Scholar Award from the ISA–Midwest. In 2012, *Princeton Review* named him as one of *The Best 300 Professors* in the US, and in 2013, the "Ralph G. Carter Excellence in Political Science" Scholarship was created at TCU. In 2014, he was named one of 10 Piper Professors of Texas and received the TCU Chancellor's Award for Distinguished Achievement as a Creative Teacher and Scholar.

A. Cooper Drury is Senior Associate Dean of the College of Arts and Science and Professor of Political Science at the University of Missouri. He earned his BA and MA from Michigan State University (1990, 1992) and his PhD from Arizona State University (1997). His primary research and teaching interests focus on foreign policy and international political economy. Specifically, he studies the causes, outcomes, and consequences of economic sanctions. Professor Drury has authored or coauthored two books and over two dozen articles and chapters. He is the three-time winner of the Frank J. Klingberg Award for Best Paper Presented by a Faculty Member at the International Studies Association–Midwest conference. Professor Drury has trained more than two dozen doctoral students at the University of Missouri. In 2006, he received the University of Missouri's Gold Chalk Award for excellence in graduate education and mentoring. He has received the 2013 Quincy Wright Distinguished Scholar Award and the 2016 Excellence in Teaching and Mentoring Award from the International Studies Association–Midwest. He is also the recipient of the 2019 Distinguished Scholar Award from the Foreign Policy Analysis Section of the International Studies Association. Professor Drury is very active in the profession. He was editor-in-chief of *Foreign Policy Analysis*, served as the program co-chair for the 2016 ISA conference, was co-chair of the 2014 WISC/ISA conference, and is a past president of both the Foreign Policy Analysis section and ISA–Midwest.

The UN Security Council in an early 2020 meeting
What issue could the countries represented here be discussing?

Spencer Platt/Getty Images

1

World Politics

Seeking Security, Prosperity, and Quality of Life in a Complicated and Connected World

Learning Objectives

After studying this chapter, you will be able to . . .

1-1 Summarize the complex arena of world politics.

1-2 Identify the nature and challenges of security, prosperity, and quality of life in international relations.

1-3 Define the levels of analysis in the study of international relations.

1-4 Describe the challenges of cooperation among the actors of international relations.

1-5 Assess the dilemmas of cooperation illustrated by the prisoner's dilemma and stag hunt scenarios.

Chapter Outline

1-1 A Complex World Connected to You

1-2 The Challenge of Security, Prosperity, and Quality of Life in World Politics

1-3 The Levels of Analysis and International Relations

1-4 Explaining the Patterns of World Politics

1-5 Dilemmas of Cooperation in International Relations: The Prisoner's Dilemma and the Stag Hunt

The Challenge of Security, Prosperity, and Quality of Life in World Politics

Let's begin with a brainstorming exercise. Considering what you know right now about world politics and the interactions that make up international relations, *what does it mean to be secure?* Jot down some ideas, perhaps drawing on current events, previous classes you have taken, and even your own experiences. Now, think about the kinds of things that threaten security as you have just characterized it, and make a list of some of the most important factors, forces, situations, and so on that reduce or diminish security. Finally, consider the kinds of things that improve or enhance security as you have defined it and draw up another list of the most important factors, forces, and situations that make countries and their citizens more secure in world politics.

INTRODUCTION: MAKING SENSE OF WORLD POLITICS

Your brainstorming probably produced a relatively complicated collection of ideas. This is no surprise. In fact, it is to be expected. Making sense of world politics can be a daunting task. Although the study of **world politics** once concentrated almost exclusively on the political relationships between the countries of the world, today it involves a much broader range of activities and interactions—political, economic, and social— among these states and a wide variety of non-state actors, such as international organizations, non-state national and ethnic groups, transnational corporations, nongovernmental organizations, and individuals. As time has passed, world politics has evolved to include an increasingly diverse set of states from the developed and developing worlds; a rich array of cultural perspectives and values held by states, nations, and individuals; and a great variety of non-state actors. Important resources have changed, as have the nature and characteristics of power, while the traditional issues of world politics have expanded to include a more complex variety of international and transnational matters.

1-1 A COMPLEX WORLD CONNECTED TO YOU

>> **1-1 Summarize the complex arena of world politics.**

Today there is simply no end to the stream of events and activities that constitute international relations, and, at first blush, there often seems to be no rhyme or reason to them, either. Consider, for example, a few select items from just one 90-day period in 2020:

....

world politics: political, economic, and social activities and interactions among states and a wide variety of non-state actors, such as international organizations, non-state national and ethnic groups, transnational corporations, nongovernmental organizations, and individuals.

- The United Arab Emirates and Israel negotiated normalized relations in the Abraham Accord.

- Fighting between Armenia and Azerbaijan risked regional stability, with Turkey supporting Azerbaijan and Russia supporting Armenia.

- The United States imposed new sanctions against Iran for its nuclear programs but failed to persuade the UN Security Council to vote to do the same.

- International piracy increased, spurred by the global pandemic and its economic repercussions.

- Russian president Vladimir Putin engineered constitutional changes and a national referendum to allow him to stay in power until 2036.

- A World Trade Organization report condemned US imposition of sanctions against China as a violation of WTO and free trade rules, despite the US argument that China was engaging in the theft of US technology and intellectual property.

- The UN Security Council condemned the Islamic State for acts it labeled as possible war crimes, crimes against humanity, and genocide in Iraq.

- In Rome, Pope Francis i"sued his third encyclical— "Brothers All"—calling for love to transcend geography and distance. The Pope articulated opposition to tribalism and xenophobia in global society and highlighted the dangers posed by social media.

- The global pandemic caused by the new coronavirus (SARS-CoV-2) continued to expand around the world, with more than 45 million cases and over a million deaths. The US led the way, with nearly 9 million cases—including the US President—and 225,000 deaths.

- All the while, thousands around the globe continued to die from malnutrition and disease because they did not have access to potable water, food, and basic medicine.

As this brief list suggests, the range of issues and events extends across many areas and in many directions—from conflict to cooperation, and from traditional security issues to concerns about wealth and prosperity, quality of life, and even basic human survival. Detecting the patterns and forces at work and explaining their causes and consequences appear overwhelming and impossible. What, if any, underlying factors or forces drive such a disparate set of events?

1-1a World Politics and You

At the same time, it can be difficult to connect the dots between events and developments on the world stage and our lives. Students frequently wonder what impact developments such as those we have just introduced have on them personally. World politics can seem like an abstract, far-off realm of movie-like events that appear to have little bearing on our lives. Textbooks such as these frequently go to some lengths to connect students in classrooms to events on the world stage. Frankly, although it can appear distant, international relations affects our daily lives in many ways, from the trivial to the profound. Let's consider a few examples:

- More than 150 million deaths have occurred because of war over the past five centuries, with the vast majority happening in the 20th and 21st centuries (e.g., Beer 1974; Levy 1983; Pettersson and Öberg 2020). Have you, a family member, or a friend served in the armed forces? Do you live near a military base of some kind? What characteristics and issues of world politics lead countries like the United States to maintain sizable military

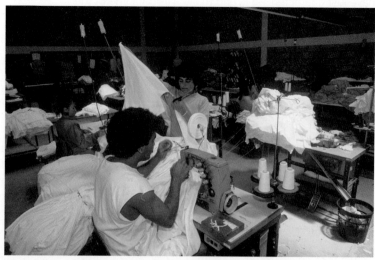

Workers in the clothing industry from around the world
Where are your clothes from, and what does this suggest to you about international relations?

Universal Images Group via Getty Images

and security establishments and send their soldiers into harm's way?

- Have you been frustrated by long lines and security delays at airports in recent years? What about having to remove your shoes and belt, take your laptop out of your carry-on bag, and so on? What world politics issues and events do you suppose are behind such inconveniences?

- Take a look at the clothing you are wearing today. How many countries do you represent in your wardrobe alone? Which ones are represented? What impact and issues do you think this list indicates?

- You did some things in 2020 that you never seriously considered before—staying at home, maintaining at least six feet from other people, and wearing a mask in public. How did the global COVID-19 pandemic, which began in China and rapidly spread throughout the world, affect you?

The world is increasingly interconnected, which means events that might appear relatively obscure can have dramatic effects on the lives of individuals far away. For example, think about how the conflicts in Iraq and Syria and the rise of the Islamic State have affected those countries, the region, and countries all over the world through violent conflict, humanitarian crises generated by the displacement of refugees and civilian deaths, and terrorist actions in places such as Paris, Brussels, Manchester, London, San Bernardino, and elsewhere. Or consider how events in a relatively obscure area of China have affected the entire world, including your own hometown.

What about the examples of several of the economic crises of the past 20 years or so? In 1997, economic problems in the relatively tiny economy of Thailand exploded into a global financial crisis that seriously affected countries all over the world, including the United States. About a decade later, in 2008, a similar dynamic occurred in the United States, stemming from ballooning real estate prices coupled with risky—and ultimately failed—gambles on complicated debt instruments. The ensuing global financial crisis, the so-called Great Recession of 2008–2010, put more than 10% of the US labor force out of work and heavily affected the lives of citizens around the world. About a decade after that, the economic consequences of the global COVID-19 pandemic shook the world, causing economic downturns and pushing hundreds of millions of people out of work in every country of the world. As these examples suggest, the interconnections between countries often mean that problems

A family fleeing the violence in Mosul
What would it be like to live in the middle of a civil war?
Gail Orenstein/NurPhoto via Getty Images

in one place can quickly become problems for many places!

1-1b Geography and the Small-World Phenomenon

It also helps to understand how spatially connected states are in the contemporary international system. Consider basic geography for a moment. In the Western Hemisphere, we typically see the world as shown in Map 1-1 (see "The Revenge of Geography: The Shrinking World"). Starting from this view, let's take the example of two large countries—Russia and the United States. It is easy to think of these two countries as far apart, but doesn't that really depend on how we look at things? Based on a Pacific-centered perspective, as in Map 1-2, the two states look closer together. They look even closer together from the perspective of the North Pole, as shown in Map 1-3. Now consider that modern technology means you can visit the Russian Federation's official website in a matter of seconds and travel between New York and Moscow by airplane in less than 11 hours. An intercontinental ballistic missile can make the trip in 30 minutes—a primary concern during the Cold War, but now Russian hackers can attack the computer and information systems of Western democracies almost instantaneously, without leaving the comfort of their own offices. Finally, have a look at Map 1-4, which presents the world from a perspective that, though not as familiar to most of us, more accurately represents the size and location of most countries. How does this alter your view of the relationship between countries?

Increasingly, what happens around the world and in the relations between countries and other important players has real-life and significant consequences for ordinary citizens going on about their lives. So understanding and explaining the patterns and forces

The Shrinking World

As world politics has evolved, and the technologies of information, communication, and transportation have developed, the geographic landscape of the world has taken on new meaning. One way to begin to understand the changing nature, opportunities, and constraints of geography for world politics is to reflect on the meaning and implications of different perspectives.

Consider Map 1-1, a common image of the world that shows the vast distances between countries such as Russia and the United States, while also illustrating the close proximity of other countries to each other. Now consider Map 1-2: How does this image change your perspective on the possibilities of conflict, cooperation, and interaction between countries?

What if we adopted the perspective shown in Map 1-3? Which countries are neighbors now? What difference, if any, would this perspective make to your sense of which countries are most likely to interact with each other?

Now, look at Map 1-4, which presents roughly the same perspective as Map 1-1 but with the perspective corrected to more accurately reflect the relative geographic size and location of the continents and countries of the world. What does this image suggest to you about world politics and the relationships among its major players?

How do these different perspectives change the way you understand the relationships between countries? ●

MAP 1-1

Political Map of the World

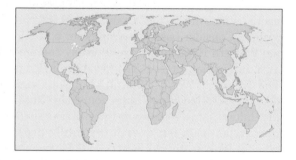

Source: WikiCommons.

MAP 1-2

An Alternative Perspective of the Political World

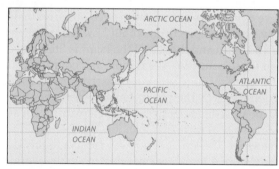

MAP 1-3

Polar Projection Map

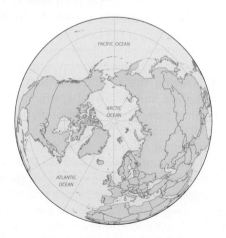

MAP 1-4

The Peters Projection of the World

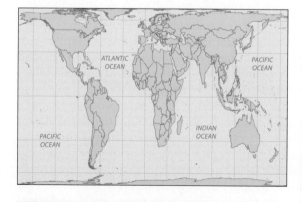

Source: WikiCommons.

at work in world politics is increasingly important. In this textbook, we try to bring some order and focus to the complex arena of world politics and help you develop a better understanding of its dynamics. We blend descriptive content with a conceptual toolbox and practical applications as a foundation for understanding and explaining international interactions.

1-2 THE CHALLENGE OF SECURITY, PROSPERITY, AND QUALITY OF LIFE IN WORLD POLITICS

>> **1-2** **Identify the nature and challenges of security, prosperity, and quality of life in international relations.**

Because world politics is such a complex arena, there are many approaches to its study. In this textbook, we approach world politics as a search for security, but we define security very broadly to include traditional, economic, and human dimensions that give us insight into the traditional security, global economic, and quality-of-life matters of international relations. This overarching theme helps provide focus and coherence to our efforts to make sense of the subject. In our perspective, the key to understanding events, such as those we listed at the start of the chapter, is to consider the broad meaning of security in its traditional, economic, and quality-of-life—or human—dimensions and its pursuit by both states and non-state actors in world politics. We hope that by the time you have worked through this text, you will be able to return to those examples—and a wide range of other current events—and provide context and explanation for what drives them.

1-2a The Nature of Security

At its core, **security** is a relatively simple concept: It refers to survival and safety. As one political scientist has characterized it, seeking security involves the "pursuit of freedom from threat" (Buzan 1991: 18). To achieve this, states and other actors in world politics try to maintain their independent identity and functional integrity, while addressing a substantial range of concerns about the conditions of existence (Buzan 1991: 18–19). However, in our perspective, the idea of security has a much broader meaning than it is often given, and understanding its broad scope is critical for understanding world politics.

Traditionally, in world politics, the term *security* has referred principally to the military, intelligence, and law enforcement arenas, with special emphasis on conflict, violence, and war. These are clearly central issues in world politics, but we define security more broadly. In most social interactions, humans seek order and predictability, and those goals cannot be reached without adequate security. One way or another, most of what the players in world politics—states, international institutions, nongovernmental organizations, and other transnational actors—seek in their interactions with one another involves the desire to be safe and to survive and thrive, broadly speaking.

We prefer to think about international relations as the search for security, prosperity, and quality of life by using a broad conception of security as encompassing three arenas or dimensions. The first—*national and international security*—is the most common and what people usually think of when discussing security. This dimension involves issues related to national defense, conflict and war, and arms control and disarmament. So, for example, when countries build up their armed forces, deploy military forces to defend themselves or to disrupt terrorist networks, place restrictions on visits by citizens of other countries, and negotiate arms control agreements with other countries, they are seeking national and international security. Recently, we have seen this aspect of security reflected in uses of force in Afghanistan and Iraq, the conflict in Ukraine, the escalation of violence in Israel and the Palestinian Territories, efforts to counter the Islamic State insurgency in Syria and Iraq, and actions to prevent the spread of nuclear weapons to countries such as Iran and North Korea.

The second arena or dimension is *economic security*. When countries, corporations, and others seek wealth and prosperity through profitable economic relations and exchanges, they are ultimately seeking economic security. In the current context, we observe this aspect of security reflected in trade and trade competition among countries, cooperation to ensure economic recovery in the wake of the global recession of recent years, efforts to deal with debt crises for both developed and developing countries, and the ways countries are grappling with the challenges of globalization.

The third arena or dimension is *human security*. This dimension fundamentally concerns the quality of life that people experience. So when the players of world politics grapple with issues of health and disease, such as the global COVID-19 pandemic, or environmental threats, such as climate change, pollution, and deforestation, or when they try to promote and protect human rights, they are seeking human security. In recent years, this aspect of security has been

....

security: survival and safety, typically referring to the military, intelligence, and law enforcement arenas but also including economic and human dimensions.

seen as countries wrestle with appropriate responses to public health crises and their extensive implications, in the growing problem of climate change, as people throughout the world rebel against their governments in pursuit of greater participation and protection for human rights, and as some states and organizations, such as the US and the North Atlantic Treaty Organization (NATO), use force to intervene in Libya to support rebels seeking the overthrow of Muammar Gaddafi or in Syria in response to alleged uses of chemical weapons by the Assad regime against its citizens. Thus, as we stress the general pursuit of security—freedom from threat—that underlies world politics, we direct our attention to national and international security, economic security, and human security, as depicted in Figure 1-1. As you will see, we have organized our text to address these dimensions of security into Part II (international security), Part III (economic security), and Part IV (human security).

1-2b Fundamental Challenges: Anarchy, Diversity, and Complexity

In world politics, the search for security is quite complicated (see "Foreign Policy in Perspective: Shifting Ways of Seeking Security"). As we devote our attention to the players of world politics and their interactions in pursuit of this multifaceted objective, we focus on three fundamental challenges that influence world politics: anarchy, diversity, and complexity. As we will see throughout our text, these challenges are linked together as well (Figure 1-2).

- *The anarchy of the international system.* There is no central, authoritative government over the players of world politics, both states and non-states. This absence of central authority has pervasive effects on the nature of world politics across almost every issue, from international conflict to the prospects and forms of international cooperation. Formal anarchy does not mean chaos or disorder, or that there are no **norms**, that is, regular patterns of behavior in world politics. Neither does it necessarily mean that there is always conflict and war. It means, simply, that *there is no central government*. Unlike established countries, world politics does not have authoritative central bodies to make, enforce, and adjudicate laws. The international institutions that do exist—such as the United Nations and the World Court—are dependent on their member states and have only the very limited authority those states willingly give them. Formally, there is no authority above the nation-state, and this structural fact has enormous implications for conflict,

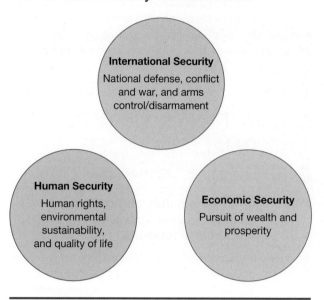

FIGURE 1-1

The Pursuit of Security in Three Arenas

International Security
National defense, conflict and war, and arms control/disarmament

Human Security
Human rights, environmental sustainability, and quality of life

Economic Security
Pursuit of wealth and prosperity

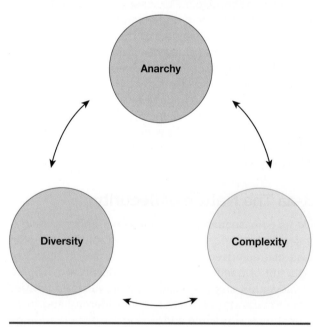

FIGURE 1-2

The Fundamental Challenges of World Politics

Anarchy

Diversity

Complexity

economic relations, and efforts to meet transnational problems and challenges, such as human rights and the environment.

- *The diversity in the international system.* World politics is characterized by myriad players. About 200 states and many thousands of

----

norms: commonly held standards of acceptable and unacceptable behavior.

Shifting Ways of Seeking Security

During presidential campaigns, and quite often after being elected, US presidents talk about how to achieve national security—how to make the country safe from harm. They want to both reassure US residents and warn others not to trifle with US national security interests. These national security interests rarely change when a new president enters office, but presidents often differ in how they want to approach attaining their national security goals. They also often like to differentiate themselves from their predecessors.

When President Barack Obama entered office, he wanted to differentiate his approach from that of his predecessor—George W. Bush. Obama found Bush's approach too unilateralist. President Bush often said he was going to do what he thought was right to make the US safe, even if other states or organizations such as the UN disagreed. Bush's decision to topple the regime of Saddam Hussein by invading Iraq in 2003 was one example of a "go it virtually alone" approach that Obama rejected. For his part, Obama sought to engage other world leaders often and become part of a more multilateral, cooperative effort to achieve shared international goals. While involving others makes any resulting decisions have more international legitimacy and potential significance, it also slows the process and can lead to outcomes that fall short of one's desires. Critics of Obama's approach accused him of

indecisiveness and of abandoning the leadership role long played by the US in the Western world.

Just as presidential candidate Obama sought to differentiate his approach from that of President Bush, presidential candidate Donald Trump sought to differentiate his approach from that of Obama. Trump saw an international system rife with dire threats to US security interests, threats that had increased on Obama's watch. His approach was to emphasize an independent United States, reducing multilateral commitments while increasing military power, and regularly threatening to use it, to deter others from taking actions that jeopardized US interests. Trump said that by doing so, he would put "America first" and "make America great again." By acting decisively and swiftly, he said he would make other countries both respect and fear US power. Based on these examples, consider the following questions:

1. How do the assumptions about security vary in each approach?

2. What interests does each of these approaches best achieve, and what problems might each cause?

3. What effects do these changes in US security approaches have on other relevant international actors? ●

---

nationalities are involved, as are hundreds of international organizations and thousands of nongovernmental organizations. Businesses of various shapes and sizes—including transnational corporations whose production facilities and reach extend across borders and regions—interact with each other, with the governments of countries, with international organizations, and with groups and individuals all over the world. The diversity of these players is staggering. States come in different shapes and sizes and are differentiated by size (geographic and population), wealth (from the very rich to the very poor), type of economy, and regime type (from the many flavors of both democratic and non-democratic systems). But widely differing ideas, religions, cultures, and subcultures divide the players in world politics as well. Such diversity has important consequences for international interactions.

• *The complexity of international interactions.* In part due to the many different players and values just described, world politics is an extraordinarily

complex arena. The players of world politics are increasingly connected and interdependent, with many linkages stretching across and between them. World politics involves multidimensional issues, state and non-state actors, national, international, and transnational processes, and many other factors, all connected in ways that can confound the players as they seek international, economic, and human security. Imagine playing a game of chess but on a system of boards arranged in multiple levels, so that players make their moves in multiple channels with multiple linkages (see Nye 2005). This is what the "game board" of world politics approaches. These connections and linkages may create problems and complications, but they also often reduce the impact of anarchy by enabling—and sometimes forcing—the players of world politics to work together.

These three challenges permeate our examination of world politics in the chapters that follow. For example, the anarchic structure of the international system is a foundational element for understanding and managing conflict and war, and it affects global economic interactions, the pursuit of wealth, the prospects for protecting human rights, and environmental cooperation. Diversity of identity, values, and culture is a critical issue for human rights and human security, while also having a great impact on conflict and economic relations. The complexity of the global political system often forces the players of world politics together, sometimes leading to cooperation on problems that transcend borders, and sometimes leading to conflict. Complexity can facilitate global economic interactions and coordination to address such problems as the economic and financial crises of the past 20 years or so, but it can also trigger clashes among players with different preferences or values and make it difficult to pursue international security, economic security, and human security at the same time.

1-3 THE LEVELS OF ANALYSIS AND INTERNATIONAL RELATIONS

>> 1-3   **Define the levels of analysis in the study of international relations.**

By now you have almost certainly gained some appreciation for how complicated it is to make sense of world politics. The search for security across international, economic, and human dimensions and the three central challenges (anarchy, diversity, and complexity) of world politics involve a dizzying array of actors and events, but they can still be understood if we have the right tools. For analytical purposes, these things can be organized into **levels of analysis** that help us comprehend the interactions, causes, and consequences of world politics.

The broadest of these levels is the **systemic or international level**, where attention is directed to the broad patterns and interactions among the players of world politics, and emphasis is placed on the impact of the structural characteristics of the international system itself—including anarchy, the distribution of

power, interdependence, globalization, and others—on those interactions.

At the **state or national level**, attention is directed to the states—or units—themselves, and emphasis is placed on the attributes of countries and nations, such as the type and processes of government or the economy, culture, or other national attributes, and how these factors shape policy goals and behavior and the interactions among the players.

At the **individual level**, attention is directed to people—policymakers, business CEOs, and other influential persons. This level of analysis emphasizes the personalities, perceptions, and preferences of individual decision makers and their effects on policy and interactions. This includes leaders, such as Donald Trump (United States), Angela Merkel (Germany), Vladimir Putin (Russia), Hassan Rouhani (Iran), Xi Jinping (China), and Pope Francis (Vatican), and other individuals from the non-state actor arena, such as investors and philanthropists George Soros and Warren Buffett, U2 singer and African aid activist Bono, actress and Special Envoy for the UN High Commissioner for Refugees Angelina Jolie, Nobel Peace Prize winner and founder of the International Campaign to Ban Landmines Jody Williams, Microsoft founder and foundation head Bill Gates, and Aga Khan of the Aga Khan Development Network.

Thinking in terms of levels of analysis points us to certain kinds of issues and events but also prompts different kinds of questions and explanations. Table 1-1 summarizes these levels of analysis and identifies some explanations at those levels that you will find in upcoming chapters. As you review the table, note the last column, which includes some very simple explanations at each level of analysis for the case of Russia's interventions into Ukraine. At the system level, the emphasis for explanation might be on the challenge posed by Russia as a rising power seeking to regain lost power and influence in the areas around its border. The state level might stress the impact of alleged threats by Ukrainian nationalists against ethnic Russians living in Ukraine and the impact that had on the Russian public back home, whereas the individual level might emphasize the worldview of Russian President Vladimir Putin, who saw the breakup of the Soviet Union as one of the greatest catastrophes of the 20th century. Each of these perspectives may help explain the interventions, even if they differ in their focus.

These levels of analysis serve at least two important purposes in the study of world politics. First, they offer useful guides for organizing information, events, and the factors that shape them so that we can make distinctions between them. Second, they guide explanation, helping us organize cause-and-effect relationships, ask different kinds of questions, and be aware

----

levels of analysis: different perspectives from which international relations may be examined.

systemic or international level: locating the causes of behavior and outcomes in the nature and characteristics of the international system.

state or national level: locating the causes of behavior and outcome in the nature and characteristics of states and nations.

individual level: locating the causes of behavior and outcomes in the nature and characteristics of people.

TABLE 1-1

Levels of Analysis and World Politics

LEVEL	FOCUS	KEY VARIABLES	SAMPLE EXPLANATIONS FOUND IN UPCOMING CHAPTERS	EXAMPLE: RUSSIAN INTERVENTIONS IN UKRAINE
System	Structural characteristics of the international system are central to explaining patterns of behavior in world politics.	Anarchy Distribution of power Interdependence Globalization	Balance of power Power transition theory	Rising power Russia seeks greater power and influence in the region and challenges declining Western powers (the US and NATO).
State	Characteristics of countries (national attributes) are central to explaining patterns of and variations in behavior in world politics.	Regime type Nationalism Subnational groups	Democratic peace Group identity Fascism	Authoritarian Russia behaves aggressively, alleges threats to Russian-speaking Ukrainians by non-Russian-speaking Ukrainians, and alleges fascist threat to Russian speakers, invoking memories of World War II.
Individual	Characteristics of individuals are central to explaining the foreign policy behavior of states and other players in world politics.	Personality Psychology Individual worldviews and preferences Perceptions and misperceptions	Aggressive versus nonaggressive leaders Leadership style and worldviews Cognitive processes	President Vladimir Putin says the demise of the Soviet Union was the most catastrophic event of the 20th century, feels threatened by Western encroachment in Russia's traditional sphere of interest, and acts quickly before the West can react.

of interactions and explanations that link up across the levels of analysis.

One simple and recognizable illustration may help clarify these contributions. Consider a serious traffic jam in a heavily populated area. Observing and explaining its causes and effects might take place from the perspective of the helicopter that sees the jam from above and can describe and explain its broad pattern and consequences. This is similar to the system level of analysis focusing on the broad structure that affects behavior (in this case, road networks and traffic patterns). But one might also focus on two cars that collided and examine their unique characteristics, actions, and role in the traffic jam, which would be similar to focusing on state-level factors in world politics. Finally, one can consider the individual drivers and their decisions, such as the person texting a friend instead of paying attention to driving, and explain things at that level, which is similar to the individual level of analysis. One thing to note is that the kinds of questions that can be asked and the kinds of explanations that can be offered from each perspective are different, but all of them shed light on the phenomenon to be explained (in this case, the traffic jam). Look again at Table 1-1 and examine it carefully

to be sure you are comfortable with the level of analysis concept before you move on.

1-4 EXPLAINING THE PATTERNS OF WORLD POLITICS

>> **1-4 Describe the challenges of cooperation among the actors of international relations.**

As we work together to build a better understanding of the dynamics of world politics, focusing on the pursuit of security in the face of the three fundamental challenges described previously, we want to improve our ability to explain the patterns of world politics that we encounter and identify. In such a complex arena, this requires the use of theoretical and conceptual shortcuts that focus attention on critical cause-and-effect relationships. **Theories** are essential tools for the explanation of complex realities, and they help

theories: tools for explaining cause-and-effect relationships among often complex phenomena.

us strategically simplify the world to bring important features into clearer relief. One way to understand theories of world politics is to think of them as lenses, such as those you might find in a good pair of sunglasses. Such lenses might come in a variety of colors, and each shade filters out some portion of the light in order to improve vision. Theory is like that: A good theory simplifies reality to reduce the white noise and sharpen the clarity of key factors, which aids in the explanation of patterns and the prediction of likely developments.

As we discuss in Chapters 3 and 4, the pursuit of security in world politics can be interpreted in a variety of sometimes complementary and sometimes contradictory ways. In these chapters, we present a number of theoretical paradigms or frameworks with which to examine world politics to make sense of how the world works:

- *Realism*, which revolves around the issues of conflict and power and stresses the role of states pursuing their self-interests

- *Liberalism*, which tends to emphasize cooperative approaches and includes the role and influence of non-state actors

- *Constructivism*, which builds on the social construction of reality and stresses the role of the identity, ideas, culture, norms, and interactions of people

- *Foreign policy analysis*, which emphasizes the individuals and groups who make decisions and the processes and policies that they produce

- *Marxism*, which stresses class-based economic interests and the role of wealth and who controls it as the key to behavior

- *Feminism*, which focuses on gender issues and approaches and asks what the world would be like if it were not historically dominated by men

Each of these broad paradigms grapples with the meaning and consequences of anarchy, diversity, and complexity differently and, therefore, presents different versions of the nature and dynamics of world politics. After we present these theories and concepts clearly and thoroughly in Chapters 3 and 4, we then (a) apply the theoretical lenses throughout the remainder of the book and (b) explicitly include in each chapter discussions and "Theory in Action"

boxes considering how theories and concepts influence real-world behavior and policy.

In the context of these theories, we also draw attention to what we believe are two of the most important current trends in world politics. First, the current world is experiencing great uncertainty because of the changing power and roles of key states. The US, which has enjoyed dominance in the international system for at least several decades, is struggling with the costs of leadership, while other countries such as China and Russia are increasingly asserting themselves and challenging the US. As realist theorists and others suggest, such potential power transitions are moments of great importance in world politics. Second, the current world is greatly affected by the forces of globalization, which generates integration and connections across borders but also prompts tension and conflict within and between states because of its impact on international, economic, and human security. We highlight the nature and impact of these two critical developments in each part and chapter, calling attention to the opportunities and challenges they pose and applying the theoretical lenses to understand their causes and consequences.

1-5 DILEMMAS OF COOPERATION IN INTERNATIONAL RELATIONS: THE PRISONER'S DILEMMA AND THE STAG HUNT

>> **1-5 Assess the dilemmas of cooperation illustrated by the prisoner's dilemma and stag hunt scenarios.**

Let's bring this first chapter to a conclusion by considering two ideal-type situations often introduced to highlight some of the patterns and challenges of world politics.

1-5a The Prisoner's Dilemma

The first situation is known as the **prisoner's dilemma**. Imagine two individuals who are suspected (for good reason) of being involved in a crime, say, a major theft. The authorities isolate the two suspects in separate rooms so that they cannot communicate. Both suspects know that if they remain silent, they will be charged for lesser violations and receive minor punishment and very short jail time, due to lack of evidence for their more serious offense. However, in their separate rooms, each

prisoner's dilemma: a situation in which two prisoners must decide whether to collaborate with each other or not.

TABLE 1-2

The Prisoner's Dilemma

		SUSPECT B	
		CONFESS	**REMAIN SILENT**
Suspect A	Confess	Suspect A—10 years Suspect B—10 years	Suspect A—free Suspect B—20 years
	Remain Silent	Suspect A—20 years Suspect B—free	Suspect A—1 year Suspect B—1 year

is informed that if they confess and betray the other suspect, the one who confesses will receive immunity for cooperating with law enforcement and go free, while their partner will be prosecuted and punished for the crime. If both confess, they both go to jail (with somewhat reduced terms for cooperating with the authorities). Realize that even if both thieves do not want to rat out their partner and are willing to split the loot evenly, they must think defensively. It's not just what one suspect might gain from confessing but what they would lose if they keep quiet and their accomplice confesses. What do you think will happen? What would you do? This situation is represented in Table 1-2.

1-5b The Stag Hunt

The second situation is known as the **stag hunt** and was described by the political philosopher Jean Jacques Rousseau in the 18th century. Imagine a village, a hunting society, organizing a hunt to bring down a great stag that will feed the whole village and provide other benefits, such as its hide. To bring down this stag, the hunters plan an approach that depends on each hunter collaborating with the rest by covering a specific area, so that the stag will be trapped and killed. However, while the hunt is proceeding, one of the hunters flushes a rabbit. The hunter immediately recognizes that pursuing and killing the rabbit means that he or she will be fed. But the rest of the hunters will end up losing the stag because it will escape through the area vacated by the hunter who is abandoning the hunt and chasing the rabbit. What do you suppose happens? Put yourself in the place of the hunter who sees the rabbit. What would you think? What would you do?

1-5c Considering the Implications of the Prisoner's Dilemma and the Stag Hunt

Together these two stories highlight several key issues about the nature of world politics. Both of them suggest there are important structural obstacles to cooperation between states, and other players, in world politics. In particular, these scenarios illustrate the tension between pursuing self-interest and broader collective interests. They also suggest that the conditions of the game provide powerful incentives for the players to see things through the lens of self-interest rather than more broadly. In the prisoner's dilemma, for example, it is logical for the suspects to confess, even though they each could derive greater mutual benefits through cooperation. By confessing, they give up the best mutual outcome, but they avoid the worst outcome—being held solely responsible and serving a long jail term. The opposite is true in the stag hunt, where it is easier to cooperate and bring down the stag rather than grab the rabbit.

In world politics, a similar result can be seen in arms races, where two countries give up the best outcome (mutual cooperation to avoid them and control armament), instead choosing to build up their weaponry so that they are not victimized if the other country cheats and builds up its own while the first does not. Perhaps neither really wants to continue to arm itself (best outcome), but both choose to do so (less desired) to avoid being vulnerable if the other one does (worst outcome). Even if we all want our leaders to be honest and not break the promises they make in international treaties, the prisoner's dilemma suggests otherwise. Imagine if all the states with nuclear weapons agreed to eliminate all those weapons. Might the world be considered a safer place? Let's say that the United States went along with this agreement, but the Russians did not. Instead, they kept a secret stockpile of nuclear weapons but only for defensive purposes. Would that make you feel safe? What if other countries cheated on the agreement? Do you think that, just in case, it would be a good idea for the United States to cheat as well—just for defensive purposes? Do you think the United States would be irresponsible if it didn't cheat? Notice how something as simple and good as maintaining the defense of one's country can make cooperation so difficult.

The prisoner's dilemma isn't just about conflict, however. For example, few people would dispute that pollution is a bad thing, or that cars significantly contribute to the world's pollution. If everyone agreed to cut back driving by simply riding a bike for any trip

stag hunt: a situation in which hunters must decide whether to collaborate with each other or act on their own.

Defeating the Prisoner's Dilemma and Getting a Stag, Not a Rabbit

The paradox of the prisoner's dilemma (PD) is that what is mutually best for the two people or states involved is not best for the individual person or state. If more than two people or states are involved in a PD-type situation, it is referred to as a **collective action problem.** Whether 2 or 20 actors are involved, individually reasonable choices lead to bad outcomes for all. But not all PD situations end in the default outcome; sometimes the involved states cooperate with each other so that they attain the mutually beneficial outcome (in the PD story, cooperation means that neither prisoner confesses). For example, during the Cold War, the US and the Soviets came to several nuclear arms control agreements that limited the number of nuclear weapons in the world, and as discussed in Chapter 8, states have generally not engaged in trade wars after World War II. So how can the prisoner's dilemma be overcome?

The first solution is an actor that has the power to force other countries to follow the rules. In the PD story, this would be the case if both suspects worked for an organized crime syndicate, such as that headed by the fictional Vito Corleone of the *Godfather* film trilogy. If the prisoners ratted each other out, they would face serious consequences from the mob boss, such as "sleeping with the fishes," as the saying goes. In the international arena, this solution is difficult because only a few times in history has one state been powerful enough to enforce cooperation. That is one of the keys to anarchy—there is no world government or police to keep states from misbehaving.

The second solution is referred to as a tit-for-tat strategy. The idea behind this strategy is to begin by trusting the other actor, but if the other actor betrays you, then punish it by not cooperating. Of course, this strategy works only if the PD situation is one that repeats over and over. In that situation, you can switch between cooperating and not cooperating, depending on what the other actor does. If the other actor does the same thing, then both actors will cooperate with each other over time. For the PD story, imagine two criminals who worked together for most of their lives and trust each other implicitly—they would not rat on each other.

This cooperative situation does not spring up out of nowhere, however. During the Cold War, the United States and the Soviet Union initially had great distrust of one another as they found themselves competing and conflicting over issue after issue in Europe and around the world. With time and repeated interactions in settings such as the UN, the two states began to trust each other enough to attempt an arms reduction treaty. Forums such as the UN provide an important place for states to interact on a public stage so that they can build

cooperative or hostile reputations. As the United States came to realize that the Soviets were not as aggressive after Premier Joseph Stalin's death as they had been under Stalin's rule, and as the Soviets realized that the United States could also be trusted, they negotiated ways to "trust but verify," the phrase used by President Ronald Reagan during the arms negotiations with Soviet President Mikhail Gorbachev.

The solution to the stag hunt (SH) is both easier to attain but also less clear than the PD situation. In SH situations, the hunter who sees the rabbit must decide between sure individual gain and likely collective gain. If she trusts her fellow hunters, it is an easy decision: Hunt the stag because there is more meat, and everyone will benefit. However, if she does not completely trust her fellow hunters, then she must decide how likely it is that the other hunters will go after the stag or after a rabbit if they see one. So how can she be sure the other hunters won't go after a rabbit?

First, if the hunters, or states, are all part of a cohesive group, then trust has already been developed. For example, the Canadians and the British are close allies with the United States. These states are unlikely to betray each other, so cooperating is easy. The less positive, cooperative history a pair of states shares, the less able they will be to cooperate.

Second, if there is a way that the actions of all the hunters can be seen by each other, then no one can chase the rabbit without the others knowing. Because all hunters prefer the stag and can see each other, they know no other hunter will go for the rabbit. Imagine hunting on a grassy plain where each hunter can see the other. In the international context, this means the actions of all states must be transparent. For example, the best way to compel North Korea to curtail its nuclear program is for the powerful states in the region (China, Japan, Russia, South Korea, and the United States) to place unified pressure on North Korea. Together these states would have more influence than if they acted alone (which is why North Korea continues to object to multistate talks). Given that for any one of these states to back away from the unified talks would be a public act, they can trust that each of the other states will not back down from the unified position. Solving the SH situation is both as easy as trusting each of the other actors and as hard as developing that trust.

1. Summarize the factors discussed previously that could enable the participants in a prisoner's dilemma to cooperate. What other factors might also contribute?

2. What factors best enable the participants in a stag hunt situation to trust each other and cooperate?

3. What are the short- and long-term implications of the actions associated with the stag hunt scenario? ●

collective action problem: a condition in which the uncoordinated actions of individuals lead to less than optimal outcomes because, although many individuals would benefit from cooperative action(s), few incentives lead any particular individuals to assume the costs of such action(s).

within two miles of their home (that's 40% of all trips), pollution would be reduced significantly. If everyone did this, we would all enjoy cleaner air, but if everyone did this *except* you, you would still get clean air—and the convenience of driving a car (particularly when it's raining, snowing, extremely hot, etc.). Thus, by cheating on the agreement, you would get all the benefits and none of the costs. The problem, of course, is that few people would ride a bike and give up the convenience with only the hope that the rest of the world will eventually do the same.

Similarly, the two scenarios suggest that part of the underlying issue is trust. In the study of world politics, this is often referred to as a **commitment problem**—countries have a hard time committing to cooperative courses of action that assure their partners that they will keep their end of the deal for mutual benefit and forgo the possibility of their own short-term gains (see "Theory in Action: Defeating the Prisoner's Dilemma and Getting a Stag, Not a Rabbit"). In the stag hunt, for example, the individual hunter must choose between cooperating for the good of all or defecting for selfish gain. But each hunter must also consider the possibility that another member of the hunting party might be faced with a similar choice and must consider the consequences of cooperating with the group if another member does chase the rabbit.

In this case, the game between the players isn't a competition like it is for the prisoners. Instead, this is a coordination and reassurance game. The hunter who chooses not to chase the rabbit will also get her dinner from the stag. Further, by going after the rabbit, the hunter will betray the society and make it very likely that she will be kicked out of the village. Thus, there are plenty of reasons for the hunter to stay the course and go after the stag. However, all the hunters need to know that they are equally committed to the stag hunt, so that a rabbit will tempt none of them. What would ensure that the hunter continued the stag hunt?

CONCLUSION: SEEKING SECURITY AND CONTENDING WITH CHALLENGES

The tensions revealed in the prisoner's dilemma and stag hunt scenarios are rooted in the very same challenges we introduced in this chapter: anarchy, diversity, and complexity. Contending with them forms a major part of world politics and the interactions among the various players. Furthermore, these are not merely abstract questions: There are potentially enormous consequences for countries and other players as they grapple with the dilemmas of self-interest and mutual interest, between doing what is best for oneself and what is best for the group, and between short-term and long-term perspectives. As we bring this introductory chapter to a close, let's return once more to our initial question about how you thought about security. Consider again the ideas you brainstormed at the outset. Given some of the ideas discussed in the chapter, how would you revise your thinking about the meaning of security in light of the challenges of anarchy, diversity, and complexity? ●

commitment problem: countries have a hard time committing to cooperative courses of action that assure their partners that they will keep their end of the deal for mutual benefit and forgo the possibility of their own short-term gains.

KEY CONCEPTS

1-1 Summarize the complex arena of world politics.

The study of world politics involves more than the political relationships among the countries of the world. It also includes the activities and interactions—political, economic, and social—among states and a wide variety of non-state actors, such as international organizations, non-state national and ethnic groups, transnational corporations, nongovernmental organizations, and individuals. The range of issues extends across conflict to cooperation and from basic security issues to quality-of-life concerns, so identifying the patterns and forces at work and explaining their causes and consequences is difficult. What happens in world politics has real-life consequences for ordinary citizens everywhere, so understanding and explaining the patterns and forces at work in world politics is increasingly important.

1-2 Identify the nature and challenges of security, prosperity, and quality of life in international relations.

In world politics, security involves three arenas or dimensions:

- National and international security, which involves issues related to national defense, conflict and war, and arms control and disarmament

- Economic security, which involves the pursuit of wealth and prosperity by countries, corporations, and others

- Human security, which concerns the quality of life that people experience and includes issues such as human rights and the global environment

As the players in world politics seek security in these three arenas, they grapple with three fundamental challenges:

- Anarchy, which is the absence of a central, authoritative government over the players of world politics, both states and non-states

- Diversity, which is the myriad differences among the players of world politics

- Complexity, which refers to the multidimensional issues, players, connections, and interactions of world politics

1-3 Define the levels of analysis in the study of international relations.

Levels of analysis help us comprehend the interactions, causes, and consequences of world politics. The broadest of these levels is the systemic or international level, where attention is directed to the structural characteristics of the international system itself—including anarchy, the distribution of power, interdependence, globalization, and others—and their impact on the broad patterns and interactions among the players of world politics. The state or national level directs attention to the states—or units—themselves and their attributes, such as the type and processes of government or the economy, culture, ethnic groups, or other state or national attributes, and how these factors shape the goals, behavior, and interactions of the players. The individual level directs attention to people—policymakers, business CEOs, and other influential persons—and how their personalities, perceptions, and preferences affect policy and interactions.

1-4 Describe the challenges of cooperation among the actors of international relations.

It would make sense for countries to cooperate in order to control the costly acquisition or dangerous spread of weapons, but often they do not cooperate, even when doing so would be in their mutual best interest. Attempts at mutually beneficial collaboration to promote economic growth and development and to protect the environment are frequent, but these attempts also frequently fail.

1-5 Assess the dilemmas of cooperation illustrated by the prisoner's dilemma and stag hunt scenarios.

Stories of the prisoner's dilemma and the stag hunt highlight the tension between pursuing self-interest and broader collective interests. They also suggest that the conditions of the game provide incentives for the players to see things through the lens of self-interest rather than more broadly. In the prisoner's dilemma, it is logical for the suspects to confess, even though they each could derive greater mutual benefits from cooperation. By confessing, they give up the best mutual outcome, but they avoid the worst outcome—being held solely responsible and serving a long jail term. The opposite is true in the stag hunt, where it may be easier to cooperate and bring down the stag rather than grab a rabbit, but fear of betrayal by others can lead to individual pursuit of the rabbit anyway.

KEY TERMS

world politics 3

security 7

norms 8

levels of analysis 10

systemic or international level 10

state or national level 10

individual level 10

theories 11

prisoner's dilemma 12

stag hunt 13

collective action problem 14

commitment problem 15

REVIEW QUESTIONS

1. What does it mean to be secure in international relations?

2. How might anarchy, diversity, and complexity pose challenges for the pursuit of security in international relations?

3. What are levels of analysis through which we can attempt to understand and explain international relations?

4. What are the key challenges for cooperation in international relations?

The Cooperation Puzzle in World Politics

At first glance, the benefits of cooperation seem obvious and compelling. They can be observed at almost any level of interaction. In fact, we all engage in cooperation when we obey traffic laws when driving—if we didn't, there would be traffic accidents all over the place, many of them lethal. Yet in world politics, cooperation appears less often and is more difficult to attain than we might expect. It would make sense for countries to cooperate in order to control the costly acquisition or dangerous spread of weapons, but often they do not, even when cooperating would be in their mutual best interest. Attempts at mutually beneficial collaboration to promote economic growth and development and to protect the environment are frequent, but these attempts also often fail. The players of world politics work together to establish institutions, norms, and rules to shape behavior in mutually beneficial and predictable ways, but those efforts are often incomplete and episodic or fleeting. And although most states are at peace with most other states most of the time, many observers would argue that conflict and war happen regularly enough to be the rule and not the exception in world politics. All countries are not necessarily "engaged in, recovering from, or preparing for war," as Professor Hans Morgenthau, a famous international relations scholar, once argued, but certainly war happens persistently enough to make us wonder why countries do not cooperate to prevent it more often.

Why is cooperation so hard in world politics, and what conditions make it most likely?

FOR MORE INFORMATION . . .

Booth, Ken, and Nicholas Wheeler. (2007). *The Security Dilemma: Fear, Cooperation and Trust in World Politics.* New York, NY: Palgrave-MacMillan.

Buzan, Barry, and Lene Hansen. (2010). *The Evolution of International Security Studies.* Cambridge, UK: Cambridge University Press.

Ferguson, Yale, and Richard Mansbach. (2012). *Globalization: The Return of Borders to a Borderless World?* New York, NY: Routledge.

Flint, Colin. (2012). *Introduction to Geopolitics.* New York, NY: Routledge.

Lauren, Paul Gordon, Gordon A. Craig, and Alexander George. (2006). *Force and Statecraft: Diplomatic Challenges of Our Time.* New York, NY: Oxford University Press.

Nye, Joseph S., Jr. (2011). *The Future of Power.* New York, NY: Public Affairs Press.

Reveron, Derek, and Kathleen Mahoney-Norris. (2011). *Human Security in a Borderless World.* Boulder, CO: Westview.

PART I

Theory and Practice

CHAPTER 2.
The Players and the Playing Field: Anarchy, States, and Non-state Actors

CHAPTER 3.
Powerful Ideas: Realism, Liberalism, and Constructivism

CHAPTER 4.
Alternative Perspectives on International Relations

Hundreds of thousands dead, millions driven from their homes

Why have so many international actors allowed the Syrian civil war to continue?

Muhammed Said/Anadolu Agency via Getty Images

2

The Players and the Playing Field

Anarchy, States, and Non-state Actors

Learning Objectives

After studying this chapter, you will be able to . . .

2-1 Summarize how the search for international, economic, and human security has evolved in a changing international system.

2-2 List the major types of actors and relationships of the pre-Westphalian international system.

2-3 Differentiate the major types of actors and relationships of the Westphalian international system.

2-4 Recognize the major types of actors and relationships of the neo-Westphalian international system.

Chapter Outline

2-1 The Search for International, Economic, and Human Security in a Changing World

2-2 The Pre-Westphalian System (Pre-1648)

2-3 The Westphalian System (1648–1989)

2-4 The Neo-Westphalian System (1990–Present)

A Look at the Players: Conflict and Violence in Syria

The wave of change in the Arab world known as the Arab Spring of 2011 was a watershed event. Long-standing regimes fell in Tunisia, Egypt, and Libya. However, the Bashar al-Assad regime in Syria managed to push back at its domestic challengers, prompting a ten-year civil war with hundreds of thousands of dead and more than 13 million driven from their homes. By 2020, with Russian help, the Assad regime steadily defeated its challengers and asserted its control over most of Syria.

When faced with domestic protests, both Syrian police and security forces turned on the protesters, but the protesters fought back, prompting harsher reprisals from the regime's defenders. Soon elements of the Syrian military who objected to killing their own citizens defected and created the Free Syrian Army to fight against the regime. Other anti-Assad rebel groups also formed, often with the support of outsiders. The Islamic Front was supported by Saudi Arabia; the al-Nusra Front was an al-Qaeda-linked group; and the Syrian Democratic Forces comprised militias of Syrian Kurds, Turkmen, Assyrians, and Armenians, along with other Syrian Arabs. The group known as the Islamic State, the Islamic State in Iraq and Syria (ISIS), or the Islamic State in Iraq and the Levant (ISIL), or simply by its Arab initials Da'esh, sought to carve out an Islamic-ruled territory in Syria as well. Further, the United States provided technical support to some rebel groups seen as

moderates in the conflict. How did the Assad regime manage to stay in power in the face of so many opponents?

There are two immediate answers to that question. First, the Assad regime has not held back its military in attacking Syrian rebels and rebel-held civilian areas. In violation of international law, the regime has used chemical weapons and antipersonnel barrel bombs against civilian areas more than once. President Assad seems willing to do anything to stay in power. Second, he's had a lot of help. Iran, its al-Quds special operations forces, and its client Hezbollah forces from Lebanon have waded into the war on the regime's side because of a religious connection. The Assad regime is dominated by Alawites, an offshoot of Shi'a Islam, and Iran is a Shi'a-based theocracy. Syrian Alawite militias have joined in as well in defense of the regime—and of themselves. Syrian Christians have formed their own militias in support of the regime, as they too fear an Islamic-themed regime in the future. Further, Russia has intervened significantly in the conflict, supporting Assad's military actions and using its air force to pound rebel targets. Russia has long been a military backer of the Assad regime, has both a naval base and an air base in Syria, and is thought to have millions if not billions of dollars in commercial contracts with the Assad regime—which could disappear if the regime falls.

There's also a broader reason the war has gone on so long. The Assad regime and its defenders want it to stay in power, but the opposition forces have different goals. Some simply want the Assad family and its entourage gone and a secular or democratic regime installed. Others want to create an Islamic regime. The United States attacked a Syrian air base in retaliation for chemical weapons attacks and wants the Assad regime gone. The US also wants the Islamic State exterminated. Turkey too wants the Islamic State exterminated, but it wants Kurdish militias operating near the Turkish border to be eliminated as well, some of which are US allies. Indeed, Turkey aggressively intervened in northern Syria against the Kurds, one of the most effective groups opposing Assad. Iran wants the Islamic State defeated because it sees the group as a Saudi-backed agent, so it cooperates with the United States on that goal, but it pushes back when the US military targets Assad's forces. Russian air forces strike at the Islamic State, but they also strike at rebel forces that the US backs. Turkey even shot down a Russian jet that crossed its border. Finally, after 2017, the US sharply curtailed its activities in support of Syrian rebels as well.

The result is a prolonged conflict like something out of *Game of Thrones*, in which you can't tell the players without a scorecard. The UN, the US, and Russia have all tried to negotiate cease-fires, but none of the attempts have worked. The results have been devastating for the Syrian people and surrounding countries.

1. What types of international actors are involved in this conflict?
2. Which are the most significant actors?
3. What is the basis of their power in this regional conflict?

INTRODUCTION: THE IR GAME BOARD

The complex patterns and dynamics of international relations take place on an evolving "game board." The players in this game engage in an international system that both shapes, and is shaped by, their actions and interactions as they seek security in its international, economic, and human dimensions. In this chapter, we take a broad look at this game board, or playing field, to lay out and assess its main features, the key types of players involved, and the patterns and trends that characterize both over time. As we set this context, we will see that the system, the players, and their roles and interactions have developed through three historical periods.

Nuclear arsenals

Why is it okay for some states to have nuclear weapons but not others?

2-1 THE SEARCH FOR INTERNATIONAL, ECONOMIC, AND HUMAN SECURITY IN A CHANGING WORLD

>> **2-1 Summarize how the search for international, economic, and human security has evolved in a changing international system.**

You are probably familiar with different types of international actors. You're a citizen of a country (or a *state*, as we say in international politics), you may be a member of the local Amnesty International chapter on your campus, and someone you know may work for a multinational corporation. These examples represent different types of international actors in world politics. The playing field for such actors is the international system, which consists of the players and the relationships between them. Both the players and the relationships matter. In the modern era, the players, or international actors, are of several broad types. States—such as France or Japan—are typically easy to identify, as they occupy defined spaces on maps. There are about 200 such states; the newest one is South Sudan, which became a recognized state in 2011. There are also non-state actors. Some non-state actors are actually made up of states. Examples include the United Nations (UN), the European Union (EU), or the African Union (AU). These are typically termed international organizations (IOs). Other non-state actors are organizations that allow individuals to join, such as Amnesty International, Greenpeace, or the

Red Cross. These are usually called nongovernmental organizations (NGOs). Some are commercial business entities, such as General Motors, British Petroleum (BP), or Bayer, which are commonly referred to as multinational or transnational corporations (MNCs or TNCs) when their production facilities and transactions cross the boundaries of several countries. Others are transnational advocacy networks (TANs), such as al-Qaeda. Local or subnational actors can be identified, too. These might include *individuals* who change the world around them, like the Dalai Lama or Bono, or wealthy people who take action in world politics, such as Bill Gates or George Soros. Other subnational actors may be *governmental units* within a state that influence world politics with their actions, such as when the Spanish city of Barcelona sends a trade mission to China. As you can see, the numbers and types of international actors are numerous, and we take a closer look at them later in this chapter.

The **international system** includes the ongoing relationships among these actors as well. International actors do not just bump up against each other randomly. There are expectations about what actors should do in certain situations. There are both written rules and unwritten norms that condition how these actors behave. For example, the United States may still be the most powerful state in the international system at this point, but that does not mean it can do anything it wants. Other international actors prefer order, and thus they want to be able to anticipate what actors like the United States will do whenever possible. The presence of expectations, rules, and norms makes anticipating such actions somewhat easier. As you'll see, both the actors and their relationships matter.

2-1a Anarchy and Interdependence

Let's begin with the international system and its key characteristics. One of the defining structural characteristics of the international system is anarchy. As we said in Chapter 1, formal anarchy does not mean chaos. Anarchy simply means the lack of a central, overarching authority that governs world politics and the actors involved in it. In the anarchic international system, the main players—states—have **sovereignty**, which means they govern themselves. There is no equivalent of the cop on the corner to make sure that rules and norms are followed or that expectations are met, and there is no central authority to govern the members of the system. International actors, particularly states, will often pursue their own interests with seemingly little concern about how their actions affect others, in part because no one has the responsibility, authority, and power to make them behave, and

in part because the anarchic structure of the international system makes **self-help** a core motivation. In such circumstances, some international actors behave as if the only law is the law of the jungle—the survival of the fittest. Of course, among these actors, power differences exist, and such asymmetries can be important elements of what states do and how they interact. China has more options regarding what it does than do states like Moldova or Haiti.

However, anarchy is not the only significant structural characteristic. The fact that most international actors do not behave in a purely self-interested fashion suggests that anarchy is not the law of the jungle. Other features of the international system help create order. One of these important structural characteristics is **interdependence**, which refers to the mutual connections that tie states and other players to each other. No state is fully independent and able to provide for all its needs and manage all its problems, and the mutual dependencies that exist and grow link players together. Not all these dependencies are equal, and interdependence between different actors varies, but the bottom line is that what one state does often affects other states. This interdependence—in varying levels and degrees—creates significant connections between the players that force them to interact with each other and often result in greater cooperation than would otherwise be expected. Therefore, although formal anarchy is an essential feature, it does not mean that states or other players are not connected.

Similarly, although there are no authoritative central bodies—those that can enforce laws—to govern the international political system, formal anarchy does not mean there is no order, organization, or meaningful institutions in world politics. In part due to interdependence, but also due to common goals and common problems, the international system has many international organizations whose members are the sovereign states of the anarchic system. These organizations, such as the United Nations, the World Bank, the International Monetary Fund, and many others, provide forums for members to coordinate efforts to solve common problems. Moreover, although these organizations' authority is severely constrained by their members, they often play important roles,

....

international system: the constellation of international actors and the relationships between them.

sovereignty: having supreme authority over people and territory.

self-help: the idea that individual actors are responsible for making themselves secure and protecting their own interests.

interdependence: mutual connections and reliance between international actors.

help develop norms and rules, and frequently have resources (provided by their members) to address problems. The international system is anarchic, but a level of structure and order exists within it, and these IOs can mitigate the effect of anarchy to some degree.

Furthermore, even for major powers such as the United States, China, Russia, or Germany, there are costs to be paid for not meeting others' expectations or not following well-established rules and norms. International actors are often concerned with reciprocity—the practice of behaving toward others as they behave toward you—and therefore follow these rules and norms to help ensure that others do as well. Violating rules and norms can result in costs ranging from international scorn to economic or military punishment. Despite the formal anarchy of the system, the international system is like a society in some ways. Those who repeatedly choose to act outside its rules, norms, and expectations are typically seen as outlaws. So when North Korea is called out for failing to follow the rules of the system, spokespersons for the regime react to such labels because those words sting. In the anarchic international system, diplomatic communications can lessen or inflame tensions between actors as well as clarify or obscure an actor's intentions; sometimes words are substitutes for actions, and at other times they trigger the very reactions they are trying to prevent (Trager 2010). So how do we protect ourselves?

2-1b The Security Dilemma

The most tempting response to the question of how we protect ourselves is the simplest one. As "Rule 2: Double-Tap" in *Zombieland* reminds us, in anarchy, you'd better have a gun. In an anarchic system, self-help is the norm, as states must depend on themselves to provide for their own security and protect their own interests. But how does one society increase its own security without threatening the security of others? This consequence of self-help is the **security dilemma**: Often, the things that a state does to make itself secure threaten—or at least appear to threaten—the security of other states, who respond in ways that end up creating or expanding threats to the first state. This dilemma represents a central dynamic in world politics.

When we think of rivals such as India and Pakistan or Israel and Iran, the dangers involved in the security dilemma become self-evident. India

The Walking Dead, an American horror drama television series
What happens when there is no central government to provide order?

Atlaspix/Alamy Stock Photo

and Pakistan share a border; they have fought three major wars since 1947, all of which India has won; and they have minor border clashes virtually each year. In 1998, India detonated a series of nuclear devices, and Pakistan did the same just a few weeks later. There seems no doubt that rivals like these two adjoining states would benefit from more cooperation. Yet as the prisoner's dilemma in Chapter 1 showed, cooperation is hard to achieve. The gains that come from both sides' cooperation are attractive, but the risks to one side if it cooperates and the other doesn't are profound—literally life-and-death in this case! Prudence suggests that each country should continue to arm itself and watch the other closely. That means the next war could be fundamentally more deadly.

For their part, Israel and Iran have not fought each other directly, but former Iranian President Mahmoud Ahmadinejad has called for the destruction of Israel. More to the point, Iran has been a primary financier of the Hezbollah militia in Lebanon, which Israeli forces were unable to defeat following a series of border clashes in 2006. Israel's government is troubled by Iran's nuclear programs, fearing it will acquire nuclear weapons that would threaten Israel, but Israel is reputed to have 100 to 200 nuclear weapons itself. Each of these rivals watches the other's actions closely. A strike by Israel against Iran, or by Iran against Israel, could happen, and the state that launched the attack would probably claim it acted in self-defense.

Although core features of the international system such as the role of anarchy and the security dilemma are persistent, their nature and effects change over time. To best understand international politics, the key turning point in history came in 1648 with the **Treaties of Westphalia** that ended the Thirty Years' War and began the modern state system. Given this starting point, we can divide the international system's history into three periods: the pre-Westphalian

---

security dilemma: the steps that states take to make themselves secure often result in threats to other states, whose reactions to those threats make the first state less secure; thus, what a state does to gain security can often make it less secure.

Treaties of Westphalia: two treaties in 1648 that ended the Thirty Years' War and created the modern international system.

A meeting between Iranian and European Union officials in Vienna, Austria, in 2015 to discuss issues regarding the Iranian nuclear program

Why are agreements like these so hard to make and keep?

Hasan Tosun/Anadolu Agency/Getty Images

system, the Westphalian system, and the neo-Westphalian system.

2-2 THE PRE-WESTPHALIAN SYSTEM (PRE-1648)

>> **2-2   List the major types of actors and relationships of the pre-Westphalian international system.**

For most of human history, geography limited people's contact. Oceans, rivers, mountain ranges, dense forests, and deserts divided peoples and limited their interaction. Individuals might live their whole lives without traveling more than a few miles from their place of birth. Over time, innovations like domesticating plants and animals led to larger communities and thus larger political organizations. Year-round agriculture and constantly occupied communities began approximately 7,000 years ago with the Sumerian culture in ancient Mesopotamia (Kramer 1988). Around the globe, monarchies and empires rose and fell, but *modern international politics arose out of European history*. The combination of Europe's advantages—temperate climate, adequate rainfall, arable land, natural resources, navigable rivers, and multiple maritime linkages—allowed its inhabitants to expand and dominate others (Diamond 1999). Thus, we can say that the international system is Eurocentric.

The Romans used both military force and technological innovations, such as a superior system of roads, to knit together much of Europe. After the fall of the Roman Empire, a weak monarchy system evolved. That system was dominated by **feudalism**, a socio-economic-political system in which rulers would grant land to the local aristocracy in return for their loyalty and support. In return for the landowners meeting their material needs, peasants would work the land. As monarchs became militarily stronger, the territories they controlled grew larger and better integrated, becoming the bases of modern states—and modern state rivalries.

The **Thirty Years' War** (1618–1648) was the watershed event in modern international politics. It began as a religious conflict between Protestants and Catholics in the Holy Roman Empire when the pope tried to force Protestant rulers to return to Catholicism. Because the Holy Roman Empire stretched across all of Central Europe, over time virtually every European power became involved. The Danes, Dutch, Swedes, Spanish, French, and others sequentially entered conflicts that became more about power—and who would rule where—than about religion alone. When the wars finally ended with the Treaties of Westphalia, many of Europe's modern states had broken free from the Holy Roman Empire, and a new international system was created based on sovereign states and the principle of nonintervention into their domestic affairs (see Map 2-1). In short, within a state's borders, the religion of both the people and their ruler was their business, not the business of outsiders, and the modern state system was born.

feudalism: a socio-economic-political system in which rulers granted land to the local aristocracy in return for their loyalty and support, and others worked the land in return for food, shelter, and protection from the local aristocracy.

Thirty Years' War: a series of wars (1618–1648) that created many modern European states.

MAP 2-1

Europe After the Treaty of Westphalia, 1648

Source: Wikicommons, Europe on the 24th of October 1648, after the Peace of Westphalia. https://commons.wikimedia.org/wiki/File:Europe_24_October_1648.svg. Licensed under CC BY-SA 3.0, https://creativecommons.org/licenses/by-sa/3.0/deed.en.

2-3 THE WESTPHALIAN SYSTEM (1648–1989)

>> **2-3**   **Differentiate the major types of actors and relationships of the Westphalian international system.**

The idea of borders as barriers to political interference from outside was very important in the Westphalian

....

state: a political-legal unit that (a) has an identifiable population, (b) is located within defined borders recognized by others, and (c) has a government with sovereignty.

system, and, as we'll see, within those borders different types of governing regimes developed.

2-3a States and Their Characteristics

States were the primary actors in the Westphalian international system. A **state** is a political-legal unit that meets three conditions: (a) It has an identifiable population; (b) it is located within defined territorial borders recognized by others; and (c) its government possesses sovereignty, which means it is self-governing. States have great diversity in their form of government, from presidential and parliamentary democracies of many kinds to authoritarian regimes centered around individual leaders, parties, the military, and combinations of these rulers. However, one core idea of the Westphalian system was that these states all possessed sovereignty. In **Westphalian sovereignty**, *within a state's borders there is no higher authority* than the government of the state itself. Each state—regardless of its size or form of government—rules over its own territory and domestic affairs as it sees fit, and states are entitled to noninterference by other states in their domestic affairs, a principle included in Article 2 of the UN Charter in 1945. Westphalian sovereignty also has an external component. Sovereign states are free to choose their own courses of action in the world beyond their borders, and with that freedom comes the opportunity to succeed or to fail.

The roughly 200 states in the international system vary widely across many dimensions. As shown in Table 2-1, they can be large or small, rich or poor. States also vary widely in how much freedom their citizens experience. As Map 2-2 shows, states can be politically free, partly free, or not free based on their regime type and protection of political rights and civil liberties.

As Table 2-2 shows, some of the states with the strongest nonnuclear militaries may surprise you. Did you expect to find India, Egypt, or Brazil on the list? Almost certainly the presence of the United States as the number-one conventional military power did not come as a surprise, but what does this number-one ranking mean? How strong is the US military, and how do others react to it? Those questions are addressed in the box "Foreign Policy in Perspective: The US Military and Its Impact on Global Armaments."

An interesting exception to the sovereignty principle can be found in the foreign embassies in a state's capital city. **Embassies** are properties that house the permanent diplomatic missions of other countries. They have the benefit of **extraterritoriality**. For example, that meant when WikiLeaks founder Julian Assange stepped into the Ecuadorian Embassy in London, he left the United Kingdom and entered Ecuador. While Ecuador allowed him to stay there—until 2019—the British could not execute an arrest warrant issued by Sweden against him for the alleged sexual assault of two of his Swedish volunteers or extradite him to the US to face espionage charges brought against him there. Thus, extraterritoriality explains why some people accused of wrongdoing may seek asylum in the embassies of other states. The key officials working in these missions are professional diplomats—individuals occupying positions in the foreign policy establishments of states or the management of other organizations who represent

TABLE 2-1

The Range of States in the International System

FIVE LARGEST STATES (IN SQUARE MILES)[a]	FIVE SMALLEST STATES (IN SQUARE MILES)[b]
1. Russia (6.6 million)	1. Vatican City (0.2)
2. Canada (3.9 million)	2. Monaco (0.7)
3. United States (3.71 million)	3. Nauru (8.5)
4. China (3.70 million)	4. Tuvalu (9)
5. Brazil (3.3 million)	5. San Marino (24)
FIVE LARGEST STATES (EST. POPULATION 2016)[c]	**FIVE SMALLEST STATES (EST. POPULATION 2016)[c]**
1. China (1,373,541,278)	1. Vatican City (1,000)
2. India (1,266,883,598)	2. Nauru (9,591)
3. United States (323,995,528)	3. Tuvalu (10,959)
4. Indonesia (258,316,051)	4. Palau (21,347)
5. Brazil (205,823,665)	5. Monaco (30,581)
FIVE WEALTHIEST STATES (WORLD BANK 2018 GROSS DOMESTIC PRODUCT IN MILLIONS)[d]	**FIVE POOREST STATES (WORLD BANK 2018 GROSS DOMESTIC PRODUCT IN MILLIONS)[d]**
1. United States ($20,544,343,456,936.5)	1. Tuvalu ($42.5)
2. China ($13,608,151,864,637.9)	2. Nauru ($125.6)
3. Japan ($4,971,323,079,771.9)	3. Kiribati ($188.3)
4. Germany ($3,947,620,162,503)	4. Marshall Islands ($221.3)
5. United Kingdom ($2,855,296,731,522)	5. Palau ($284.0)

Sources: [a]Infoplease, "The Top Ten: Largest Countries," https://www.infoplease.com/top-ten-largest-countries; [b]ThoughtCo., "The World's Smallest Countries," https://www.thoughtco.com/the-worlds-smallest-countries-1433446; [c]US Central Intelligence Agency, "Country Comparison: Population," *The World Factbook*, https://www.cia.gov/library/publications/the-world-factbook/rankorder/2119rank.html; [d]World Bank, http://databank.worldbank.org/data.

Westphalian sovereignty: the idea that within a state's borders there is no higher authority than the government of the state itself.

embassies: properties that house the permanent diplomatic missions of other countries, typically located in the capital city of a state.

extraterritoriality: the principle that one is exempt from prosecution of the laws of the state, typically applied in the case of an embassy.

MAP 2-2

Map of Freedom, 2020

Do any of these classifications of free, partly free, or not free states surprise you?

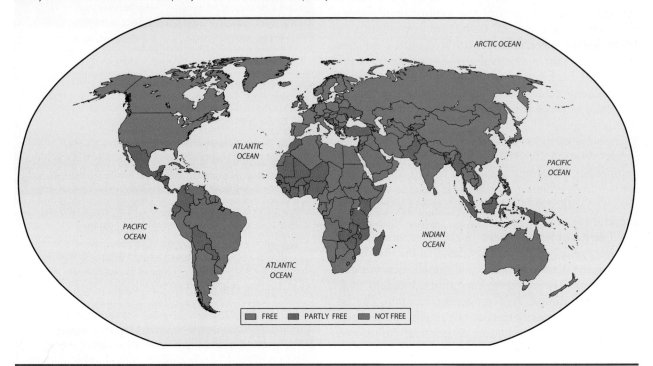

FREE   PARTLY FREE   NOT FREE

Source: © Freedom House/*Freedom in the World.*

TABLE 2-2

Ten Strongest Conventional Military Powers in the World (comparing nonnuclear forces only, 2020)

1.	United States
2.	Russia
3.	China
4.	India
5.	Japan
6.	South Korea
7.	France
8.	United Kingdom
9.	Egypt
10.	Brazil

Source: GlobalFirepower.com, "2020 Military Strength Ranking," http://www.globalfirepower.com/countries-listing.asp.

and negotiate on behalf of their country or employer. Even when they leave the grounds of the embassy, accredited diplomats are still largely exempt from the laws of the state in which they work. Thus, if an accredited diplomat (or even an immediate family member of one) is accused of a crime, typically the most a state can do is to expel the diplomat or person from the country. Of course, the other state involved may expel one of the first state's diplomats in retaliation, as indicated in the box "Spotlight On: Diplomatic Immunities."

Diplomatic immunity is a pragmatic adjustment to the sovereignty principle based on reciprocity: If countries are to sustain communication—even in times of violent conflict—and try to resolve disagreements, they must have confidence that their official representatives and negotiators will be able to engage in diplomacy safely. Yet embassies and embassy officials are increasingly the targets of state and nonstate actors. For example, in 2015 and 2016, attacks resulting in deaths occurred in foreign embassies

The US Military and Its Impact on Global Armaments

In the Westphalian system, states were clearly the most powerful international actors. Because power was measured in military terms, it was rational for states to seek to increase their military power. The more power, the better, right? From that perspective, what does the case of the United States demonstrate?

As Table 2-2 shows, the United States has the most powerful conventional military in the world, but that does not convey the degree of dominance of the United States in the military arena. The United States leads the world in not only conventional but also nuclear weapons. During the Cold War, the United States had more than 12,000 strategic nuclear warheads (those with the range to be launched from one continent and hit targets on another). By 2011, the New START Treaty had restricted the United States and Russia to no more than 1,550 deployed strategic nuclear warheads per side. However, only strategic nuclear warheads were restricted. The United States also has tactical nuclear weapons with shorter ranges. Estimates of the number of these that have been deployed vary, but currently they total about 500 deployed and undeployed, according to the Federation of American Scientists and the Arms Control Association. Russia has more tactical and strategic nuclear warheads than the United States, but its ability to deliver those weapons pales in comparison to the US ability to use long-range missiles, shorter-range missiles, submarine-launched missiles, and bombers to do so. No other state can rival the United States when it comes to the combination and numbers of nuclear weapons and the multiple ways to deliver them, which may be why Russia recently began to reintroduce intermediate-range nuclear missiles to Europe despite the Intermediate-Range Nuclear Force (INF) Treaty's banning of such weapons. This step led the US to abandon the INF Treaty in 2019 (and may also have influenced the US decision to abandon the Open Skies Treaty in 2020). The fact that the United States has not used nuclear weapons since 1945 does not change the fact that it is the only state in the world that has done so.

However, the United States has also amply demonstrated its willingness to use conventional military force. From 1945 to 2000, the United States used military force 383 times, thereby averaging about seven uses of force per year. How many times has the United States used military force since then? The fact that US military spending accounts for almost 40% of all global military spending further indicates that the United States is committed to maintaining its dominance over others. Does this pursuit of military power make the United States more secure? The security dilemma suggests that other states must consider how to protect themselves from the military might possessed by the United States. How do they do that?

Some states will rely on the development of their own nuclear forces—like North Korea, India, and Pakistan. Others, like China and Iran, invest heavily in the acquisition of modern submarine forces and anti-ship missiles to keep the US Navy at arm's length. While presumably hoping to avoid a nuclear confrontation, Russia and China have sought to develop fifth-generation combat jets to compete with US F-22s and F-35s (the Russian Su T-50 and the Chinese Chengdu J-20). Finally, Russia, China, and North Korea have been long suspected in the thousands of online hacking attacks that target the US military each year.

Thus, in the neo-Westphalian system (see Section 2-4), states still face pressures to defend themselves and their borders, as illustrated by the security dilemma. Consider the following questions:

1. How powerful does a state need to be to defend itself?

2. Do higher levels of US military spending at some point become counterproductive, in that they encourage potential rivals to increase their military spending?

3. How much military spending can the United States afford? ●

Sources: William G. Howell and Jon C. Pevehouse, *While Dangers Gather: Congressional Checks on Presidential War Powers* (Princeton, NJ: Princeton University Press, 2007); Nikolai Sokov, "Issue Brief: Tactical Nuclear Weapons (TNW)," *Nuclear Threat Initiative*, May 2002, http://www.nti.org/analysis/articles/tactical-nuclear-weapons/; Amy F. Woolf, "U.S. Strategic Nuclear Forces: Background, Developments, and Issues," CRS Report for Congress, Congressional Research Service, July 14, 2009, https://fas.org/sgp/crs/nuke/RL33640.pdf.

SPOTLIGHT ON

Diplomatic Immunities

Diplomats are normally exempted from prosecution for violating local laws in the host state, because laws vary considerably across states and—considering that diplomats represent another sovereign state—how they are treated can be seen as sending a message about that state. But what happens when diplomats or their family members do bad things? The offenses could be minor. For example, during the Cold War, Soviet diplomats had a reputation for shoplifting underwear at fine department stores. Those crimes were typically ignored. By contrast, in 1997, a Georgian diplomat drove drunk and killed a 16-year-old girl in Washington, DC. With the permission of the Georgian government, that diplomat was prosecuted, convicted of manslaughter, and served time in both US and Georgian prisons.

In December 2013, India's deputy consul general in New York City—Devyani Khobragade—was arrested and indicted for visa fraud and making false statements to law enforcement officials. The visa fraud involved Khobragade's claim that she was paying her Indian housekeeper $4,500 per month, but the housekeeper said she was actually paid less than the US minimum wage. Upon her arrest, Khobragade was treated like any other criminal suspect, which included being strip-searched before being escorted to her jail cell. Incensed at her treatment, Indian officials upgraded her diplomatic assignment to the Indian Embassy, where she had full diplomatic immunity. At that point, the State Department ordered her to leave the country; she did, and subsequently a US diplomat was ordered to leave India. Lost in this exchange were any concerns about the housekeeper or her allegation that she was not allowed by her employer to return home to India.

Was this a case of India being insulted by the United States or of a human trafficking case going unpunished? How could this matter have been handled better? ●

---

or missions in Afghanistan, Egypt, Iraq, Kyrgyzstan, Libya, and Somalia. When diplomats are targets of violence, what implications do you think this holds for the conduct and future of diplomacy—especially given that these attackers are principally non-state actors?

2-3b Nations and Other Players

States are not the only way people organize and identify themselves in world politics. Another clarification is appropriate now. Typically, one will hear the terms *country* and *state* used interchangeably. *State* is the more legal term in international politics, but there is no real harm in using these as synonyms. However, the terms *nation* and *state* are often used interchangeably in casual conversation, and that usage is inaccurate. The word **nation** is a sociocultural term for a group of people who possess a collective identity that is a product of multiple factors. It can be something as basic as a sense of shared values that lead people to identify with each other, but in most states, collective or national identity is generally based on more visible factors, like shared ethnicity, religion, language, culture, history, and the like. In any event, the nation concept is fundamentally about distinguishing "us" from "them." When a state's population comprises largely members of one nation, the term **nation-state** is most accurate. So Armenia, Cuba, and Japan may fairly be called nation-states, because nearly all their population share a common ethnicity. By contrast, Kuwaitis and Qataris do not constitute even a bare majority of the populations of Kuwait and Qatar, respectively, so the term *nation-state* is much less accurate in such cases.

Challenging cases come from around the world. In the Balkans, the former Yugoslavia dissolved amid violence driven by ethnic nationalism among a number of groups. In the Middle East, a vexing issue of competing nationalisms involves the Israelis and the Palestinians. They essentially claim the same territory known as Palestine, but both cannot have it. Since 1948, the Israelis have controlled most of the territory; thus, the Palestinians have been a nation without a state. Here we have one territory with two nations.

A different example is represented by the Kurds. Kurds share a common language and history and see themselves as a single nation. However, as Map 2-3 shows, the area in which they would constitute the majority of the population—a potential Kurdistan—overlaps the boundaries of Iran, Iraq, Syria, Turkey, and,

---

nation: an identifiable group of people who share a collective identity typically formed around bonds based on factors such as shared language, culture, and the like.

nation-state: a state in which nearly all of the population are members of the same nation.

MAP 2-3

Kurdistan

How many states would lose territory and people if Kurdistan became independent?

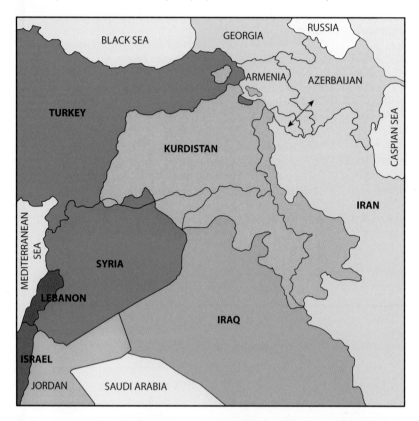

to a small extent, Armenia. Thus, we have one nation that spans multiple states but still does not have a state of its own. Afghanistan is another example, just as complicated (see the box "The Revenge of Geography: Ethnic Geography and Conflict in Afghanistan").

An even more compelling illustration of the differences between nations and states is found in Africa. Former imperial powers established borders based on convenience or the amount of territory they could control. Those borders rarely corresponded with the national groupings of the indigenous people. Because African states maintained their former colonial borders when they became independent, it is little wonder that many of those states continue to suffer from a lack of a collective identity on the part of their citizenry. Map 2-6 shows how little correspondence there is between state borders and groups based on national ties.

States were not the only actors in the Westphalian system; non-state actors developed as well and existed alongside states. However, state actors were clearly the preeminent actors in the state-centric Westphalian international system. Non-state actors

became more important and influential in the neo-Westphalian system, which we discuss in Section 2-4.

2-3c The Evolution of the Westphalian System

Over the 341-year sweep of the Westphalian era, states developed and gained strength. Some got so strong that by the latter half of the 20th century, the Cold War risked the threat of global annihilation. The ending of the Cold War brought this system to a close.

The Empowerment of States

From a European-based system in the 17th century, the Westphalian system expanded globally mostly via European **imperialism**—the colonization and exploitation of other territories by European states, which is why a European-based regional system is now the basis of world politics. The American and French Revolutions introduced the initial development of a **democracy** norm to the system. Over time, more and more states gave their citizens a meaningful role in choosing their leaders, or, if not, they at least tried to call themselves democracies. For example, North Korea's official name may be the Democratic People's Republic of Korea, but that regime is unlikely to be confused with a real democracy anytime soon. In fact, no country with the word *democratic* in its name is actually a real democracy.

A norm that really began in the French Revolution and spread through the Westphalian system is **nationalism**—the emotional connection of the mass public with the state. By the early 20th century, most citizens were emotionally invested in their state, taking pride in its accomplishments and being offended by any perceived slights by others. Nationalistic rivalries and ties played an important role in the origins of World War I. When a Serb assassinated Austria-Hungary's Archduke Franz Ferdinand and his wife Sophie in 1914, the result was a war that spread rapidly. Austria-Hungary couldn't fail to respond to this

imperialism: control and exploitation by one state of the economy, culture, and/or territory of others, usually called colonies.

democracy: a form of governance in which the people have a meaningful choice in selecting their rulers.

nationalism: the emotional connection of the mass public to their state.

Ethnic Geography and Conflict in Afghanistan

Afghanistan has long been difficult to govern. Part of that difficulty is physical, because mountain ranges crisscross the country, separating inhabitants from each other. Outside the major cities, Afghans tend to be suspicious of strangers, as they tend to live fairly isolated lives. But the complicated cultural identities are even more important to these challenges.

As shown by Map 2-4, Afghanistan is a land of many nations. The largest group of Afghans is the Pashtuns, at about 42% of the population, followed by Tajiks (27%), Hazaras and Uzbeks (9%), the Aimaks (4%), Turkmen (3%), and Balochs (2%). About half of the Afghan population speaks Dari—an Afghan form of Persian— and the Pashtuns speak Pashto. Both Dari and Pashto are considered the official languages of Afghanistan.

So who speaks for Afghanistan? The leaders have traditionally been Pashtuns, because they are the largest single group, but there are more combined non-Pashtuns in Afghanistan than Pashtuns. Complicating this is the fact that there are many more Pashtuns; they just happen to live across the border in Pakistan. As Map 2-5 shows, if Pashtunistan was a nation-state, it would encompass much of Afghanistan and Pakistan. Plus, we cannot ignore the fact that the Afghan Tajiks may have emotional bonds to Tajikistan next door, that Afghan Uzbeks may have similar ties to Uzbekistan, that Afghan Turkmen may look to Turkmenistan, and that even Afghan Balochs may look with yearning eyes toward the Balochistan provinces in southeastern Iran and southwestern Pakistan.

MAP 2-4

Afghanistan's Tribal Areas

With these different nationalities included, is it any wonder that Afghanistan is hard to unite, much less govern?

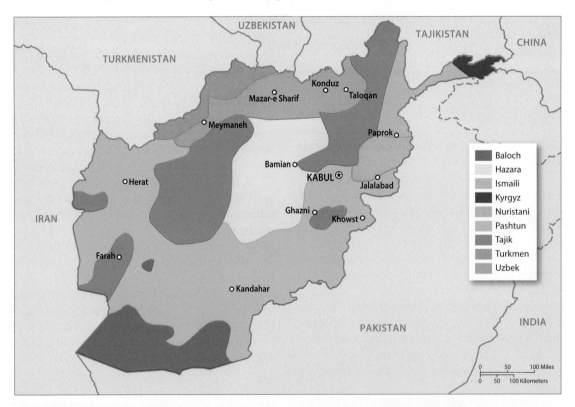

Source: Maps of World, www.mapsofworld.com.

MAP 2-5

Pashtunistan

If Pashtunistan were an independent state, what would that mean for Afghanistan and Pakistan?

Source: US Central Intelligence Agency, "Afghanistan," *The World Factbook,* https://www.cia.gov/library/publications/the-world-factbook/geos/af.html.

1. What role might ethnic geography play in conflict and instability in Afghanistan?

2. What are the implications of this ethnic geography for efforts to manage conflict and instability in the region? ●

---

slight, Serbia couldn't afford to knuckle under, and the Russian czar couldn't afford to disappoint the Russian public that wanted to protect their Slavic cousins in Serbia. The war quickly got out of hand, and its massive cost in lives and treasure led to an armistice in 1918 and the subsequent **Treaty of Versailles** in 1919, a peace treaty with lasting consequences.

Nationalism reached a new high point in the 1930s. Opposition to **communism** arising in the new Soviet Union led to the most extreme application of nationalism: the rise of **fascism** in Italy and Germany. Italy's Benito Mussolini and later Germany's Adolf

Hitler both rose to power in part based on their violent opposition to local communists, but their fascist ideology glorified violence and viewed successes

....

Treaty of Versailles: the treaty in 1919 that ended World War I, imposed heavy penalties on Germany, and created the League of Nations.

communism: the anticapitalist economic philosophy created by Karl Marx that promoted centralized control of a country and its economy for the equal redistribution of resources to the country's citizens.

fascism: a political ideology that glorifies the state over the individuals it comprises and that relies on nationalism and violence to bond the citizenry to the state.

MAP 2-6

Murdock Ethnic Map (1959)

Given the divergence between state borders and the borders of human communities, is it any wonder that internal violence plagues much of the African continent?

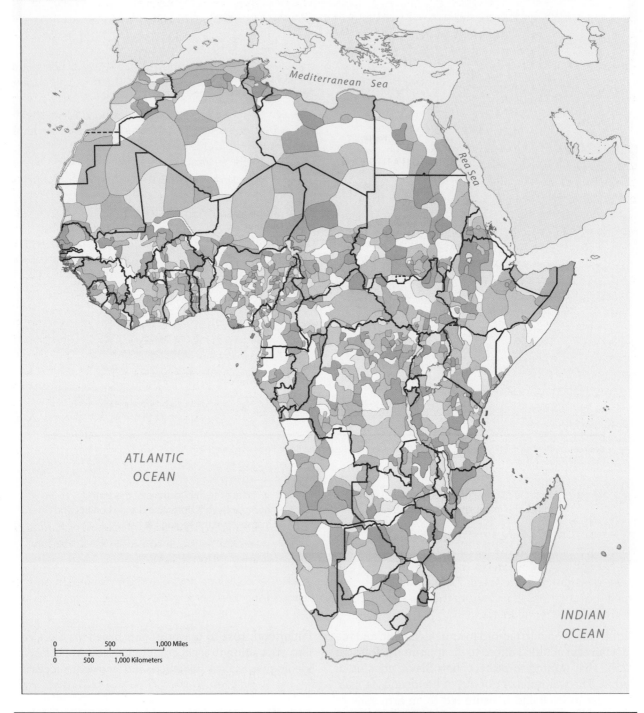

Source: George P. Murdock, *Africa: Its Peoples and their Culture* (New York, NY: McGraw-Hill, 1959).

on the battlefield as proof of the superiority of their respective nations (Steger 2008). Such nationalist ambitions by Japan and Germany led to World War II, which in some ways started as early as 1931 when Japan invaded the Chinese province of Manchuria. In 1939, war began in Europe with the German invasion of western Poland and the later Soviet invasion of eastern Poland and Finland. The war did not end until the Germans surrendered in May 1945, and following the US detonation of atomic bombs over the Japanese cities of Hiroshima and Nagasaki, the Japanese surrendered in August 1945.

The Cold War

The last major phase of the Westphalian system was the **Cold War**, a period of intense rivalry and competition between two large blocs of states—an anti-communist bloc led by the United States and a pro-communist bloc led by the Soviet Union—which lasted from 1947 until 1989. Each bloc had its own primary military alliance: the US-led **North Atlantic Treaty Organization (NATO)**, which bound together the United States, Canada, and most Western European states, and the Soviet-led **Warsaw Pact**, which bound together the Soviet Union and its Eastern European allies. Although the two superpowers never directly engaged each other, confrontations involving the superpowers or their client states erupted around the world.

In 1947, communist involvement in the Greek civil war led the US to proclaim the Truman Doctrine—the policy that the US would help states resisting communist expansion. In 1948, Soviet leaders tried to shut off Western access to the jointly occupied city of Berlin, the former German capital. The US and Western powers responded with the Berlin Airlift, which resupplied West Berliners with food and supplies, and the crisis abated in 1949. Also in 1949, the Soviets detonated their first nuclear bomb, and the Chinese Communist Party took control of the Chinese mainland. In 1950, the communist regime in North Korea launched a surprise invasion of South Korea. The Korean War ended in a tie in 1953, but it also led to the establishment of NATO and the rearmament of the US to a war-footing. In 1961, Berlin was the focus again as the Soviets built a wall separating the two halves of the city to prevent East Europeans from using defection to West Berlin as a way to escape communist control. The United States responded by sending more troops to West Berlin and with a presidential visit to West Berlin by President John Kennedy.

In 1962, the Soviets challenged the United States by putting short- and medium-range missiles in Cuba, which was a new communist ally after the revolution led by Fidel Castro. These missiles posed the threat of a nuclear attack on the southeastern portion of the United States with only a few minutes' notice. By placing US military forces on global alert and imposing a naval embargo against Cuba, the US was able to pressure the Soviets to remove their missiles. Six months later, the US removed similar missiles facing the Soviet Union from bases in Turkey. This nuclear brinksmanship led the two superpowers, along with the British, to agree to a treaty limiting nuclear testing, which served as a building block for the later nuclear nonproliferation regime.

Still, proxy wars between superpower clients continued in Vietnam in the 1960s and early 1970s, in Angola in the 1970s, and in Nicaragua and El Salvador in the 1980s. By the late 1980s, the Soviet Union's economy began to fail as it reached the limits of what a command economy could order people to produce. Furthermore, the Soviet Union could not keep up with the US defense rearmament program under President Ronald Reagan, and it was shaken by the challenge to Soviet supremacy by the Polish people and Pope John Paul II and the costs of fighting a decade-long war in Afghanistan. In 1989, Soviet President Mikhail Gorbachev announced that Soviet client states in Eastern Europe would be allowed to determine their own policies, and East Germans quickly knocked holes in the Berlin Wall. At that point, the Cold War was over, and a new international system—the neo-Westphalian system—emerged.

2-4 THE NEO-WESTPHALIAN SYSTEM (1990–PRESENT)

>> **2-4** **Recognize the major types of actors and relationships of the neo-Westphalian international system.**

After the Cold War ended and the Soviet Union collapsed into 15 relatively weak states, new pressures

Cold War: a period of intense rivalry and competition from 1947–1989 between the United States and its allies on the one hand and the Soviet Union and its allies on the other.

North Atlantic Treaty Organization (NATO): a military alliance structure created following the outbreak of the Korean War in 1950 and led by the United States.

Warsaw Pact: the military alliance created by the Soviet Union as a response to the 1955 addition of West Germany into NATO.

emerged in the international arena. The result is an international system in which the states remain the central actors, but they are now buffeted from within and without by other actors, networks, and problems that readily span national borders. Although sovereign states are still the most powerful international actors, in the current system some non-state actors possess a considerable amount of power and influence in world politics. Wars between states (interstate wars) are less commonplace, but internal conflicts within states (intrastate wars) and between states and non-state actors are more frequent and often far more destructive, at least for those involved. Thus, we can say we have moved into a neo-Westphalian system, a new, modified version of the previous Westphalian system. As we said earlier in the chapter, non-state actors existed in the Westphalian system, but their enhanced roles are really at the heart of the shift to the neo-Westphalian system.

2-4a The Development of Non-state Actors

States were the dominant actors in the Westphalian system, but they were not the only actors. **Non-state actors** were plentiful but played secondary roles. Significant nongovernmental organizations (or NGOs) early in this period were as diverse as the Catholic Church and the Dutch and British East India Companies. The leaders of the Catholic Church tried to influence what states did and how they did it. For their part, large commercial organizations such as the East India Companies often acted as agents for their respective states in the economic realm, and state leaders typically prevailed if the interests of these companies and their home governments diverged.

By the 20th century, improvements in global transportation and communication enabled the number and importance of non-state actors to rise. One significant type of non-state actor that rose in numbers and influence was the **multinational corporation (MNC), or transnational corporation (TNC).** Such corporations, with names ranging from Apple

....

non-state actors: international actors that are not states; they may include international organizations, nongovernmental organizations, multinational corporations, and individuals.

multinational corporations (MNCs): companies that have subsidiaries (other companies) in multiple countries; also known as *transnational corporations (TNCs)*.

nongovernmental organizations (NGOs): organizations whose membership is not restricted solely to states.

international organizations (IOs): international organizations whose membership is restricted to states.

subnational actors: international actors typically seen as subparts of a state, such as individuals or local governmental entities.

to ZTE (a Chinese smartphone manufacturer), became increasingly notable players in the international system. **Nongovernmental organizations (NGOs)** were another significant type of non-state actor, and they were often devoted to particular issues. Indeed, for almost any problem you can think of in international relations—poverty, injustice, women's rights, the environment, and any other—NGOs arose to address it. Some NGOs were so successful at humanitarian work that they won the Nobel Peace Prize, including the American Friends Service Committee and the Friends Service Council, the International Committee of the Red Cross and the League of Red Cross Societies, Amnesty International, International Physicians for the Prevention of Nuclear War, the International Campaign to Abolish Nuclear Weapons, and the Organisation for the Prohibition of Chemical Weapons.

As transportation linkages improved and international interactions became more routine, other **international organizations (IOs)** arose. Many of these IOs focused on a narrow range of international cooperation. For example, the Universal Postal Union began in 1874 to handle international mail. In 1930, the Bank for International Settlements was created to coordinate routine transactions between the central banks of sovereign states. The **League of Nations** was formed in 1920 with a broader mission: to keep the peace and institutionalize cooperation following World War I.

However, since 1945, the most prominent IO has been the United Nations (UN). Like its predecessor the League of Nations, the UN was created in 1945 to keep the peace and institutionalize international cooperation. Its principal organs are the UN General Assembly, UN Security Council, UN Economic and Social Council, UN Secretariat, and International Court of Justice (or World Court). We discuss the United Nations and its principal organs in Chapter 7, where you will also find an organizational chart that shows its many agencies and offices. There are also transnational advocacy networks (TANs), which may include individuals, social movements, NGOs, and at times state actors, and these are discussed in detail in Chapter 13. They may also include other **subnational actors**, like individuals or other political entities, as discussed in Chapters 11 and 12. Table 2-3 recaps the types of non-state actors that have become prominent in the neo-Westphalian system.

The shift to the neo-Westphalian system has been marked by (a) the rising importance of non-state actors, (b) globalization, (c) a subsequent relative weakening of states as actors, and (d) a new principle of responsible sovereignty. Let's address each of these changes in turn.

TABLE 2-3

Types of Non-state Actors

TYPE OF NON-STATE ACTOR	IDENTIFYING ELEMENT	EXAMPLES
International governmental organizations (IOs)	Only states may be members	United Nations European Union World Trade Organization
Nongovernmental organizations (NGOs)	Members include at least some non-state actors	Amnesty International Aga Khan Development Network International Red Cross
Multinational corporations (MNCs)	Commercial entities dedicated to making a profit whose subsidiaries span multiple states	Samsung General Motors Unilever
Transnational advocacy networks (TANs)	Networks of groups that press on behalf of their agendas; cannot comprise solely state actors	Refugee Research Network International Campaign to Ban Landmines al-Qaeda
Subnational actors	Those that normally fall within a state	Ricky Martin City of Barcelona, Spain State of California

TABLE 2-4

The Top 10 Multinational Corporations in 2016 and Their Closest State Comparisons (by revenues and GDP, in billions of dollars, respectively)

MNCS	STATES
1. Walmart ($482)	23. Poland ($470)
2. State Grid (China; $330)	31. Egypt ($336)
3. China National Petroleum ($299)	36. Singapore ($297)
4. Sinopec (China; $294)	39. Ireland ($294)
5. Royal Dutch Shell ($272)	41. Colombia ($282)
6. ExxonMobil ($246)	42. Chile ($247)
7. Volkswagen ($237)	43. Finland ($237)
8. Toyota ($237)	43. Finland ($237)
9. Apple ($234)	43. Finland ($237)
10. BP ($226)	44. Bangladesh ($221)

Sources: State data: "GDP Ranking," World Bank, July 2017; MNC data: "Revealed: The Biggest Companies in the World in 2016," *The Telegraph*, July 20, 2016.

2-4b The Rise of Non-state Actors

In the neo-Westphalian system, states are still the most powerful actors, but non-state actors have increasingly become important players in international politics, at times even rivaling some states for influence.

One example is the rise of multinational corporations. As Table 2-4 shows, if one compares the largest MNCs by their annual sales revenues to states by their gross domestic product (GDP; their annual output of goods and services), the top MNC in 2016—Walmart—produced more revenue (about $482 billion) than all but 24 of the 189 states ranked by the International Monetary Fund. It is thus no exaggeration to say that large MNCs now rival many states in terms of their *economic* clout.

It might not seem surprising that six of the 10 largest corporations in the world are energy companies (oil companies China National Petroleum, Sinopec, Royal Dutch Shell, ExxonMobil, and BP, and the Chinese electric company State Grid), but note that only three of the top 10 are US corporations (Walmart, ExxonMobil, and Apple), and three of the top four are Chinese. So the rise of MNCs is a truly global phenomenon. Not only do these firms have considerable financial clout; at times they also face a growing set of global rivals that have the power of states behind them: **sovereign wealth funds**. Such funds that invest money provided by the government of their state are not new, but they have grown rapidly in the neo-Westphalian era. As Table 2-5 indicates, each of the top 10 sovereign wealth funds has assets in excess of $295 billion; four of these are from China, four are from the Middle East, one is from Norway, and one is from Singapore. When you compare Tables 2-4 and 2-5, it is clear that in a globalized economy, wealth is spreading far beyond North America and Europe.

sovereign wealth funds: investment funds owned by states.

TABLE 2-5

Top 10 Sovereign Wealth Funds in 2016 (by billions of dollars in assets under management)

SOVEREIGN WEALTH FUND	STATE	ASSETS
1. Government Pension Fund—Global	Norway	$1,200
2. China Investment Corporation	China	$940
3. Abu Dhabi Investment Authority	United Arab Emirates	$697
4. Kuwait Investment Authority	Kuwait	$592
5. Hong Kong Monetary Authority Investment Portfolio	China–Hong Kong	$540
6. Government of Singapore Investment Corporation	Singapore	$440
7. SAFE Investment Company	China	$418
8. Temasak (Singapore)	Singapore	$375
9. Qatar Investment Authority	Qatar	$328
10. National Social Security Fund	China	$325

Source: Based on Sovereign Wealth Fund Rankings, SWF Institute 2020.

Besides the examples cited here, other NGOs provide a variety of services in the global community. These include the following types:

- Humanitarian relief programs (such as the France-based Doctors Without Borders or British-based Oxfam)

- Economic development programs (such as the US-based Bill and Melinda Gates Foundation or the Switzerland-based Aga Khan Development Network)

- Educational programs (such as Belgium-based Education International or the Switzerland-based Foundation for Education and Development)

- Civil society development programs (such as US-based groups like the Global Fund for Women or the Civil Society Development Foundation)

- Human rights empowerment and protection programs (like UK-based Amnesty International or US-based Human Rights Watch)

- Environmental protection programs (like Friends of the Earth International or Greenpeace)

Many of these NGOs are able to accomplish things states cannot do well, or sometimes cannot do at all. For example, the use of the Internet has expanded so rapidly that state bureaucracies would have difficulty keeping up with the technological changes required to manage domains and route messages. Thus, a series of NGOs has arisen to handle these matters, including the Internet Society, the Internet Architecture Board, and the Internet Engineering Task Force. Sometimes states that need help are reluctant to accept help from or be indebted to other states for political or status reasons. However, there seems to be far less stigma linked to accepting assistance from an NGO. Aid from NGOs may be seen as having fewer strings or conditions attached. For example, communist North Korea has faced famine multiple times in the neo-Westphalian period. It will not readily accept food aid from capitalist states, so food aid must be funneled through NGOs or the United States in order to be acceptable to the North Korean regime.

Individuals can be influential non-state actors as well, particularly when they work with international organizations. Celebrities can carry a lot of media attention to an issue, such as when Bono raises money for African economic development, George Clooney raises money for victims of the violence in Darfur, or Richard Gere presses for better treatment of Buddhists by China. Angelina Jolie brings media attention to the plight of many living in camps through her role as a special envoy of the United Nations High Commissioner for Refugees, much like Audrey Hepburn did before her as a special ambassador for UNICEF. Religious leaders also get involved as key individuals, such as the Dalai Lama pressing the case for Tibetan independence from China or Pope John Paul II supporting Polish independence from Soviet control in the waning days of the Cold War.

Yet one does not have to be a celebrity to help change the world. Jody Williams was a teacher and an aid worker before she joined the International Campaign to Ban Landmines, and both she and the group won the Nobel Peace Prize. Norman Borlaug was an agronomist working in Mexico who pioneered new types of high-yield, disease-resistant wheat to help feed the world; he also won the Nobel Peace Prize.

Finally, some individuals become famous, or even infamous, for their impact on others.

Ricky Martin delivers aid to victims of Hurricane Maria in Puerto Rico

What can a global celebrity do to affect world politics?

Gladys Vega/Getty Images

Pope (now Saint) John Paul II meeting with the communist leader of Poland as the Cold War neared its end

How did a pope help bring down a communist regime?

ph/Luciano Mellace/Getty Images

Osama bin Laden was just another wealthy young Saudi until he heard the call to go to Afghanistan and join the **mujahideen** to fight the Soviet invaders of that country in the 1980s. The mujahideen's victory over the Soviets led him to believe that, if Allah willed it, even superpowers could be defeated by the devout. Thus, when the United States failed to heed his calls to leave Saudi Arabia and end its support for Israel, his transnational network **al-Qaeda** initiated a series of terrorist attacks on the United States that ultimately left

nearly 3,000 dead on September 11, 2001. Bin Laden subsequently became the "most wanted" man in the world, and many around the world were relieved (and some were joyful) when he was killed in Pakistan in 2011. Before his death in 2019, Abu Bakr al-Baghdadi gained notoriety as the leader of the Islamic State, the terrorist organization formed after the US invasion of Iraq that is at the center of much of the violent conflict in Iraq and Syria.

Networks of these non-state actors, along with some state actors, can play important roles as well, some for public goods and some for private gain/purposes. As we discuss in Chapter 13, transnational advocacy networks help create and disseminate principles and norms that contribute to the structures and institutions of cooperation. Such networks provide particularly good opportunities for non-state actors to affect diplomacy and world politics because they are so public and high profile, they gain so much media attention, and they constitute situations in which states are probably more open to the input of non-state actors.

One final feature of the neo-Westphalian system has been the general rise in the importance of identity politics—reacting to politics based on one's perceived group identity. The groups could be large, as in Christians in Europe or the United States reacting

mujahideen: those who fight to liberate Muslims or traditionally Muslim lands from control by nonbelievers; the insurgency resisting the Soviet invasion of Afghanistan is the most widely known example.

al-Qaeda: translated as "the base," this is a fundamentalist Islamic transnational terrorist organization, responsible for many attacks on Western countries and moderate Islamic countries; most infamously, it organized, funded, and perpetrated the September 11, 2001, attacks in the United States.

to Muslim immigrants, often creating a backlash and a move to more populist appeals to the majority community. They could also be relatively small, as in specific nations or groups of people questioning state authority. In 2017, two independence referendums passed—one in the Catalonia region of Spain and the other in the Kurdistan region of northern Iraq. Other examples have been seen in places ranging from Mexico and Guatemala (with Mayan peoples) to China (with Tibetans). But the rise in the relevance of non-state actors is not the only characteristic of the neo-Westphalian system. There are three others.

2-4c Globalization and Its Effects

Along with the relative rise of these non-state actors, a second characteristic of the neo-Westphalian system is the phenomenon called **globalization**. Globalization refers to the increasing integration of global society through economic, technological, political, and cultural means. As suggested earlier, this global integration can strengthen some non-state actors, challenge traditional state identities and loyalties, and produce instances of populist backlash on the part of majority communities. Think of how the Islamic State is able to recruit violent converts globally through social media. Used by many to share their experiences with friends, social media has enhanced the Islamic State while leading some citizens to use violence against their own countries. It can also help tie actors together in new and more meaningful ways. For example, citizens in China and Japan crave South Korean soap operas, a desire that brings these peoples just a little closer together. In short, it can have both positive and negative effects, depending on the situations and the actors involved.

Although trade has long tied states together, these ties have become stronger in recent years, making states and peoples more interdependent on each other than ever before. Multinational corporations long ago realized that setting up subsidiaries in other states where they did business made considerable sense, so now US autoworkers might be making vehicles for BMW, Honda, Hyundai, Mazda, Mercedes-Benz, Mitsubishi, Nissan, Subaru, or Toyota, not for Chrysler, Ford, or General Motors.

Restaurant chains are another good example of global economic connections. Just stroll Paris's Avenue des Champs-Élysées from the Arc de Triomphe to the Place de la Concorde. On arguably the most famous street in France, one finds Pizza Hut and Kentucky Fried Chicken franchises. Then there's the

tale of the little Japanese girl getting off the airplane from Tokyo, walking into Los Angeles International Airport, and saying, "Look, Mommy, they have McDonald's here, too!" That story might be apocryphal, but consider the facts. In 2017, McDonald's had more foreign franchises (21,914) than US franchises (13,344). KFC had almost four times more franchises abroad (15,029) than in the US (4,391). Domino's sells curry pizza in India and tuna pizza in Japan. Dunkin' Donuts has locations in 30 countries and will sell you a seaweed donut in China or a mango chocolate donut in Lebanon (Dazkowski 2017).

Recent technological innovations spurred the rate of such global interconnections. For more than 100 years, transportation technologies were essentially limited to how fast trains could run or ships could sail. With the development of modern jet air travel, now one can go from one side of the world to the other in about a day. Even when flying to and from non-hub airports, travel time is still considerably faster than ever before. For example, flying from Lincoln, Nebraska, to Kinshasa, Democratic Republic of the Congo, can be done in as few as 22.5 hours—with the right flight connections—or it can take as long as 42 hours. Still, getting from the middle of the United States to the middle of Africa in less than two days would shock 19th-century travelers.

Perhaps even more important than air travel is the lower cost of moving freight on a global basis. This was first noticeable with the development of larger and larger oil tanker ships, and these were followed by the development of modern container ships. Carrying preloaded containers of a standard size lowered the cost of shipping by making it easier and faster to load and unload such cargo vessels, and the less time ships are in port, the more time they are at sea making

A woman in rural India with her mobile phone
Is there anywhere mobile phones aren't found?

Exotica.im/Universal Images Group via Getty Images

---

globalization: the increasing integration of global society through the spread of technology, foreign trade, transportation, cultural exchange, political institutions, and social connections.

money. As transoceanic transport ships increased in size and speed, the cost of doing business around the world dropped significantly, and firms found it increasingly cost-effective to locate their operations and sell their products in many different countries.

Communication has also been transformed. Improvements in mobile phone technologies have lowered the cost to communicate over wide distances, so most people on the planet can now afford to own mobile phones. The global population is now more than 7 billion, and there are about 5 billion mobile phones in the world, about three quarters of which are smartphones (that's 3.5 billion, or half the world's population). Thus, it is nearly as common to see mobile phone usage in urban areas of developing states as it is in the richest societies on the planet.

Information technologies have also evolved. With the advent of cable and satellite television, viewers can watch channels from all over their country, the region, or the world. For example, a family in Beirut with a satellite dish might watch daily news programming from the Qatar-based al Jazeera network, family programming on French channel Cinépop, and American movies on HBO or Showtime, while the teens might slip into another room to watch videos on MTV, VH1, or YouTube.

Then there are the movies. With only a few exceptions (like India's "Bollywood" or China's film industry), moviemakers now go after the global market. According to *Paste Magazine* (Jackson 2019), the top 10 movies in 2019 all had more gross revenues outside the US than inside it. These are, in descending order, *Avengers: Endgame, The Lion King, Toy Story 4, Captain Marvel, Spider Man: Far From Home, Aladdin, Us, John Wick: Chapter 3, Hobbs and Shaw,* and *How to Train Your Dragon: The Hidden World.* Thus, when people in non-Western societies complain about foreign ideas and values undermining their culture, the effects of movies and television are often cited as examples.

The Internet clearly plays into this argument as well. In 1990, there were only 2 million Internet users worldwide, but by 2019, more than 4 billion users—over 53% of the world—were online (International Telecommunications Union 2020). A consequence of this openness is that regimes have less control over information than before. In 2011, Egypt's military-dominated regime learned that populist revolutions can be organized via online social media, and China and Google have repeatedly struggled over the Chinese regime's desire to put parts of the Internet off-limits to Chinese users.

The combination of satellite television and the Internet has revolutionized global information sharing. Now very few places can be considered remote. International news channels, whether using broadband or satellite transmissions, can show riots in Greece or Thailand or terrorist attacks in Paris, Brussels, Manchester, or London in real-time streaming video. English-language newspapers are available online for all regions of the world and most individual states. The Westphalian emphasis on borders and preventing interventions into one's own domestic affairs has been rendered far less relevant by these technological innovations.

In short, globalization means that international interactions are easier and far more commonplace. As a result, international interdependence is clearer than ever to see. What happens in one state or region of the world influences others in ways that are hard to ignore, and vice versa. The Westphalian distinction between foreign and domestic becomes harder to discern. Yet evaluating globalization from a normative perspective is difficult, as it produces effects that are both positive and negative. As the Global Policy Forum (n.d.) notes:

> The globalized world sweeps away regulation and undermines local and national politics, just as the consolidation of the nation state swept away local economies, dialects, cultures and political forms. Globalization creates new markets and wealth, even as it causes widespread suffering, disorder, and unrest. It is both a source of repression and a catalyst for global movements of social justice and emancipation. The great financial crisis of 2008–09 has revealed the dangers of an unstable, deregulated, global economy but it has also given rise to important global initiatives for change. (para. 2)

In 2020, some of the negative properties of globalization were on full display, as the highly interconnected world experienced a global pandemic that originated in Wuhan Province, China, and quickly spread throughout the world. By late 2020, more than 43 million people were infected globally, with more than 1.1 million deaths and counting.

2-4d New Stresses on States

The third major characteristic of the neo-Westphalian system is an increase in the numbers and types of stresses on states. Borders drawn on maps become less meaningful, as groups within states identify more with others based on geography, tribe, clan, or religion. In many European states, immigrants from Africa and the Middle East get pushed into ghettos and are often criticized for failing to assimilate. Their visible presence leads populist or nativist politicians and groups to push back at what they see as the

"Muslimization of Europe." In France, Corsicans press for autonomy for their island. In Russia, Chechen and Dagestani suicide bombers attack subways and train stations, seeking independence or revenge for loved ones lost in Russian counterterrorist operations. Aided by Russia, Ukraine's Crimea reunited with Russia, and Russian-speaking Ukrainians in the eastern provinces are largely autonomous from Kiev's control. In the eastern fringes of the Democratic Republic of the Congo (DRC), Tutsi militias attack non-Tutsi communities, killing or enslaving the innocent, which prompts elements of the Rwandan army to intervene in the DRC in search of the Tutsi militants. Muslim militias target Christians in both Nigeria and Central African Republic, prompting Christian militias to respond in kind. In Iraq, Sunni groups rebel against the Shiite-dominated regime and target Kurdish populations in the north, while in Syria, factions supporting the Assad regime, the Islamic State, Kurds, and other anti-regime groups are engaged in conflict. In Israel and the Palestinian territories, violent struggle continues between Israelis and Arabs. Finally, across the board, Islamist groups inspired by or networked with al-Qaeda or the Islamic State launch attacks in the United States, United Kingdom, France, Belgium, Spain, Saudi Arabia, Yemen, Iraq, Syria, Pakistan, Afghanistan, the Philippines, Indonesia, Kenya, Nigeria, and elsewhere.

Beyond such violence, internal economic threats arise as non-state actors pursue their own agendas. In 2005, the government of the Iraqi province of Kurdistan signed a contract with Norwegian oil company DNO to develop oil fields there, even though no laws had yet been passed determining who had the legal rights to develop Iraq's oil reserves. The contract was subsequently cancelled by the national government in Baghdad, and DNO was forced to pay damages to Iraq (Gibbs 2010). In the United States, investment firms seeking to maximize their profits in real estate and real estate derivative securities minimized or hid the risks from investors. Although a number of these firms made impressive profits, the resulting housing collapse of 2008 undermined the national and global credit markets, created the Great Recession of 2008–2010, and put both the national and the global economies in danger. Seeing oneself as a victim of economic actions taken by others can lead to more extremist political positions—and actions.

In the neo-Westphalian system, external pressures buffet states as well. Economic crises often force states to turn to the International Monetary Fund (IMF) to stop runs on their currency, as did several Asian states in 1997 and Greece (as well as other European countries, including Spain, Italy, and Portugal) several times since 2010. Not only are these loans that must be repaid; they also come with conditions on what the recipients must do to put their economies on a sounder footing—steps that often generate widespread opposition at home. In Asia, the IMF ultimately put together aid packages totaling more than $100 billion to bail out the currencies of Indonesia, South Korea, and Thailand, which were rapidly becoming worthless. In 1998, the IMF lent $22 billion to Russia to stop a similar run on its currency. In Greece, the IMF coordinated with the European Union and the European Central Bank to extend multiple loans totaling hundreds of billions of euros to address the Greek financial crisis. These lenders forced painful budget cuts in return for financial bailouts. Across the EU, resulting domestic protests over the social impact of slashing government budgets contributed to changes to the parties in power in eight states (Greece, Ireland, Italy, Portugal, Spain, Slovenia, Slovakia, and the Netherlands).

External pressures on states may be political as well as economic. For instance, Amnesty International is often successful precisely because it focuses unwanted attention on states that incarcerate political prisoners. According to Amnesty International, for example, in 2015, the top 10 worst attacks on human rights were carried out, in alphabetical order, in China, Egypt, Hungary, Israel, Gambia, Kenya, Pakistan, Russia, Saudi Arabia, and Syria. All were said to be guilty of widespread violations of basic human rights, up to and including extrajudicial killings (Withnall 2016). Two years later, the Amnesty International annual report added Venezuela, Yemen, Turkey, and Myanmar, among others, to its list of human rights hotspots. Although sovereignty means that states can technically ignore outside pressures, in reality, shaming by such organizations matters and often leads to changes in a state's behavior.

Even well-intentioned acts can pressure states. For example, most in the West would assume that

Spanish protestors against Vladimir Putin's homophobic policies
What can human rights activists do to influence the behavior of states?

Denis Doyle/Getty Images

free and fair elections and the creation of *civil society* organizations represent positive advancements in a society. However, many regimes take a very different view of these groups. For example, recently in both Russia and Turkey, foreign observers to elections and organizers of civil society organizations have been harassed or arrested as enemies of the regime. In Russia, the local offices of well-known Western NGOs as well as UN-related organizations have been raided or shut down and some of their personnel ordered out of the country. In Turkey, reporters for Western media outlets have been detained or exiled, while thousands of Turks have been arrested as potential threats to the regime's survival. What Westerners see as democracy and local empowerment can be seen by authoritarian regimes as external efforts at forcible regime change, and such regimes will take extreme measures to stay in power.

2-4e The Changing Meaning of Sovereignty

A fourth and final hallmark of the neo-Westphalian system is a fundamental change in what sovereignty means. Westphalian sovereignty was clear. Inside one's borders, there was no higher authority than the state. States had no right to intervene in other states' internal affairs. However, the results of World War II opened the door to seeing sovereignty differently. How Germany treated Jews, Roma peoples, LGBTQIA individuals, and others was sufficiently horrible to lead others to say that such actions were wrong, regardless of whether they occurred within a state's borders or not. Later events at the dawn of the neo-Westphalian period would reinforce this idea.

For example, in 1990, Iraq invaded and occupied Kuwait. When Iraqi forces were expelled from Kuwait, Iraqi Shi'ites and Kurds tried to break free from Saddam Hussein's Sunni-based Iraqi regime. Iraqi military forces turned on those Iraqi citizens, as Iraqi forces had previously done in the 1988 Anfal campaign in which conventional and chemical warfare attacks killed at least 50,000 Kurds and possibly as many as 180,000 ("Timeline" 2006; Wong 2006). Even though this Iraqi use of force was inside its own borders, the international community acted. In 1991, the United Nations passed UN Security Council Resolution 688, which authorized the UN and its members to intervene in Iraq to protect Iraq's citizens from their own government. That same year, the government of Somalia was overthrown; a civil war resulted, and no group was able to govern the country. Civilian refugees needed international aid to survive, and in 1992, the UN Security Council passed a number of resolutions authorizing a military intervention into Somalia to ensure that humanitarian supplies reached

those refugees. In 1992, war broke out in the former Yugoslavian territory of Bosnia-Herzegovina, and **ethnic cleansing** ensued, whereby one ethnic group (be it the Bosnian Serbs, the Bosnian Croatians, or the Bosnian Muslims) would purge or "cleanse" an area of its rivals by forced expulsion, violence, or death. Again, the UN declared this practice to be illegal under international law, thereby justifying intervention by outsiders. The **genocide** in Rwanda in 1994, which resulted in at least 800,000 deaths and possibly hundreds of thousands more, just contributed to this momentum (Verpoorten 2005). In short, in the early 1990s, it became increasingly clear that populations at times needed protection their government could not provide or even protection from their own government. These operations were termed **humanitarian interventions**.

As the UN Secretary-General's Special Representative for Internally Displaced Persons, Sudanese diplomat Francis Deng (1995) first coined the idea of **responsible sovereignty**. He argued that the Westphalian idea of sovereignty as a state's responsibility to control its borders and protect its territory had to give way to the idea of sovereignty as the responsibility of a state to protect its citizens (**neo-Westphalian sovereignty**). At the 2005 UN General Assembly meeting, world leaders agreed that if states did not meet their responsibility to protect their own public from war crimes, genocide, and the like, then others should step in and do so. Over time, the idea of protecting one's citizens evolved past physical protection from violence in the form of international security; to some, it also implied protecting one's citizens from other common threats—like economic deprivation, environmental threats, and so on—or economic and human security, as we call them in this text (Jones, Pascual, and Stedman 2009). Although some states, such as Russia and China, continue to resist this modification of Westphalian sovereignty, the broader concept of responsible sovereignty became more firmly entrenched as a norm of the neo-Westphalian system. In short, states could no longer do whatever they wanted within their own borders without eliciting potential interventions from others in the international system.

....

ethnic cleansing: a form of violence in which an ethnic group purges or "cleans" a territory of its rival ethnic groups, by forced expulsion, violence, or death.

genocide: the deliberate killing of a religious, ethnic, or racial group.

humanitarian interventions: military or nonmilitary interventions into a state by outside groups for the purpose of protecting endangered people and meeting the needs of the state's residents.

responsible sovereignty: the idea of sovereignty as a state's responsibility to protect its citizens.

neo-Westphalian sovereignty: *see* responsible sovereignty.

Responsible Sovereignty and Humanitarian Interventions

The theory of responsible sovereignty is a radical departure from prior notions of sovereignty. Under Westphalian sovereignty, state borders were to be clear demarcations separating the domestic and international arenas. As noted earlier, Article 2 of the UN Charter reaffirms that states are not to intervene in the domestic affairs of any other states. However, the end of the Cold War coincided with a number of instances in which state regimes preyed on their own people or could not protect their people from becoming victims of violence within their borders. Although a limited multinational effort helped protect some Iraqi Kurds from the Iraqi military from 1991 to 1997, the international community had little response to genocidal violence in the Bosnian civil war from 1992 to 1995 or the Rwandan genocide in 1994. As a result, in 1995, Francis Deng proposed that states should intervene when regimes will not or cannot protect their citizens.

Yet the number of successful humanitarian interventions since 1995 arguably seems quite small. The United States and NATO intervened in Yugoslavia in 1999, Australia intervened in East Timor in 1999, the United Kingdom intervened in Sierra Leone in 2000, the African Union intervened briefly in the Darfur and Burundi conflicts in 2003 and again in Darfur in 2008 as part of a joint AU/UN force, the United States intervened briefly in Haiti in 2004, and one might consider the US-led effort to change regimes in Iraq in 2003 a successful humanitarian intervention in the sense that some saw it as a way to protect the Iraqi people from a brutal regime.

By contrast, the number of instances where citizens go unprotected and either no one intervenes or the intervention is unsuccessful seems quite large. Cases could be made for the need for humanitarian interventions in a variety of places since 1995. A partial list would include the DRC, Central African Republic, Burundi, Sudan, Uganda, Zimbabwe, Libya, and Somalia in Africa. It could also include Afghanistan, Pakistan, Myanmar, and North Korea in Asia and Haiti again in Latin America. The list could also include specific troubled regions of otherwise stable states—like the northern Caucasus region of Russia (in Chechnya and Dagestan, for example) or northern Mexico, where the government has lost control of some areas to violent drug cartels. Certainly, with the violence, destruction, and displacement of people in Syria, the actions of the Assad regime against its own people, and the refugee crisis across the region and the world that these developments have caused, a strong case can be made for broad intervention in that situation.

So what is stopping such interventions? IOs cannot intervene unless their members provide the military personnel and are willing to pay the costs of the operation. States with the wealth and military power to do so often do not define these situations as vital to their national interests, and, as such, they are largely unwilling to act. Simply put, these situations are not deemed to be worthy of their cost in lives and treasure. In select instances, the state that would be the target of the intervention rejects what it sees as external interference, as would be the case in Russia, for example.

1. Should nationalism (and national interests) trump our humanitarian impulses?

2. What is our responsibility to others?

3. Does the value of human life depend on who or where people are?

4. Is responsible sovereignty a concept whose time has not yet come?

We'll see in Chapters 3 and 4 that your answers may depend on which international relations theories make the most sense to you. ●

Source: James Kurth, "Humanitarian Intervention After Iraq: Legal Ideals vs. Military Realities," *Orbis* 50 (2006): 87–101.

The bottom line is that some issues are clearly transnational now. International security, economic security, and human security matters now often transcend national boundaries. As we will see in Part IV of the text, issues in the global commons—those areas not controlled by any one state and shared by all—confound the ability of single actors to deal with them. Issues such as disease, international terrorism, crime, pollution, and humanitarian protection present complex challenges to the global community.

In essence, the neo-Westphalian system has been transformed and is still being transformed, by significant changes in the norms or rules by which international politics is conducted. For example, views on the use of force have changed. In the early 20th century, US President Theodore Roosevelt could champion speaking softly but carrying a big stick. Those who possessed sufficient force routinely threatened its use or actually used it. Today, force is viewed as a legitimate state action only if used in self-defense or as a last resort when stakes are high. Otherwise, those who violate these norms risk being viewed as aggressors, who might then face punishment from others in the international system. Consider how US President Dwight Eisenhower talked about using nuclear weapons and tried to employ a strategy of "brinksmanship" to escalate crises in an effort to force an enemy to back down. Such nuclear saber-rattling is now seen as highly irresponsible and dangerous, and most regard the use of nuclear weapons as something to be avoided. Deciding how to respond to situations in which people are at risk often depends on the theoretical approaches that decision makers employ, as the box "Theory in Action: Responsible Sovereignty and Humanitarian Interventions" suggests.

Other norms that arose during the Westphalian era have taken on new importance in the neo-Westphalian system. For example, **supranational regimes** (IOs whose rules can override those of their member states in limited circumstances) are becoming somewhat more commonplace. For example, the **Nuclear Nonproliferation Regime** is a set of rules for how states develop, maintain, and regulate nuclear power and nuclear materials. Those who have signed and ratified the **Nuclear Nonproliferation Treaty** agree not to develop nuclear weapons if they have not previously done so and also agree to spread nuclear technology only under rules specified by the International Atomic Energy Agency. Another example of a supranational regime is the **World Trade Organization (WTO)**, which supports and develops the free-trade regime in world politics. To promote and support free trade and more open economies, the WTO makes the rules of trade for its 164 state members, administers those rules, and authorizes penalties against states that violate its rules. While supranational regimes like these deal with a limited set of issues, others deal with an array of issues across a specified geographic jurisdiction. A good example is the **European Union (EU)**, an IO that can make decisions on a variety of issues that constrain its 27 member states. It is this ability to override state sovereignty that led, in part, to the United Kingdom's 2016 decision to withdraw from the EU (known popularly as "Brexit"), which was finally completed in 2020.

CONCLUSION: SAME PLAYERS BUT A CHANGING FIELD?

By and large, the same *types* of actors found in prior periods are found in the current neo-Westphalian international system: states and non-state actors like IOs, NGOs, MNCs, TANs, and individuals. However, their numbers and political significance have changed. States are still the most significant actors, but in relative terms, their ability to dominate the international system has decreased somewhat as the power of non-state actors has increased. IOs, NGOs, MNCs, TANs, and notable individuals are rapidly rising in both numbers and influence, and at times they rival the power of some states. Under certain circumstances, non-state actors can do things that states cannot or will not do, and thus they supersede states in influence at times.

Perhaps more noticeable are the changes in relationships that constitute the international system. Norms have changed, with new restrictions on the actions of states. It is no longer acceptable for the strong to push around the weak. Genocide or crimes against noncombatants are not acceptable just because they happen inside a state's borders. States have increasingly been held responsible for protecting their populations and for meeting their minimum human needs; thus, the concept of responsible sovereignty now exists alongside and often in contradiction to traditional Westphalian notions of sovereignty. States see benefits in joining supranational organizations that may, at times, tell them they cannot do what they want. The end of the Westphalian international system opened the door to numerous changes in how international politics is routinely conducted and in how security is defined and protected.

So what do such changes suggest regarding the roles played by anarchy, diversity, and complexity in the current international system? How you make sense of these changes—and their meanings—may depend on the degree to which you see these events through realist, liberal, constructivist, feminist, or other lenses, the topic to which we turn next. ●

....

supranational regimes: international organizations or sets of rules that can bind states even against their will.

Nuclear Nonproliferation Regime: a formal treaty and its related rules set by the International Atomic Energy Agency regulating how states may develop, maintain, and use nuclear power and nuclear materials.

Nuclear Nonproliferation Treaty: a treaty prohibiting those with nuclear weapons from providing them to others and those without nuclear weapons from seeking them.

World Trade Organization (WTO): a supranational organization established in 1995 that promotes free trade between member countries; it sets the rules for international trade, administers them, and authorizes penalties for states that violate them.

European Union (EU): a regional supranational organization with 27 member states.

KEY CONCEPTS

2-1   Summarize how the search for international, economic, and human security has evolved in a changing international system.

The formal anarchy of the international system means that there are no authoritative bodies above the players themselves. In such circumstances, some international actors behave as if the only law is survival of the fittest. In an anarchic system, self-help is the norm, as states must depend on themselves to provide for their own security and protect their own interests. The consequence is a security dilemma, in which the things that states do to make themselves secure often threaten—or at least appear to threaten—the security of other states. However, other features of the international system help create order and cooperation among the actors and their actions. One of these characteristics is interdependence among actors, the mutual connections that tie states and other players to each other. Others include common goals and/or values, shared norms and rules, and common problems to be solved. These features can lead to greater cooperation among the players, as well as the establishment of international organizations whose members are the sovereign states of the anarchic system. These organizations, such as the United Nations, the World Bank, the International Monetary Fund, and many others, provide forums for members to work together to solve common problems.

2-2   List the major types of actors and relationships of the pre-Westphalian international system.

The pre-Westphalian world was dominated by feudalism, a socio-economic-political system in which rulers would grant land to the local aristocracy in return for their loyalty and support. In return for the landowners meeting their material needs, peasants would work the land. The monarchies were weak; thus, the major actors were non-state actors—like the Catholic Church and local elites. As monarchs became stronger, the territories they could control grew larger and better integrated, becoming the basis of modern states—and modern state rivalries. The Thirty Years' War (1618–1648) marked a major transition. When the wars finally ended with the Treaties of Westphalia, a new international system emerged based on sovereign states and the principle of nonintervention into their domestic affairs. The power of the church was reduced, and within a state's borders, the religion of both the people and their ruler was its own business, not the business of outsiders. Thus, the modern state system— and the Westphalian era—was born.

2-3   Differentiate the major types of actors and relationships of the Westphalian international system.

States were the primary actors in the Westphalian international system. A state is a political-legal unit that meets three conditions: (a) It has an identifiable population, (b) it is located within defined territorial borders recognized by others, and (c) it has a government that possesses sovereignty. According to Westphalian sovereignty, within a state's borders, there is no higher authority than the government of the state itself. States were not the only actors in the Westphalian system; non-state actors developed as well and existed alongside states. However, states were the preeminent actors in the state-centric Westphalian international system. Over the 341-year sweep of the Westphalian era, states continued to develop and gain strength. Some states got so strong that by the latter half of the 20th century, the Cold War risked the threat of global annihilation. The end of the Cold War brought this system to a close.

2-4   Recognize the major types of actors and relationships of the neo-Westphalian international system.

As the Cold War ended and the Soviet Union collapsed, new pressures emerged in the international arena. States remained the most powerful international actors, but in the neo-Westphalian system, non-state actors grew in power and influence in world politics. Wars between states (interstate wars) have become less commonplace, but internal conflicts within states (intrastate wars) and conflicts involving other non-state actors have become more frequent. Nations, groups of people who share a collective cultural and ethnic identity, clash when their territories do not correspond with state borders. The neo-Westphalian system is marked by a comparative rise in the importance of non-state actors such as multinational corporations, nongovernmental organizations, international organizations, and others. The phenomenon of globalization has also weakened states with new problems and pressures. A new principle of responsible sovereignty—the idea of sovereignty as a state's responsibility to protect its citizens—has emerged to challenge traditional state sovereignty.

KEY TERMS

international system 23

sovereignty 23

self-help 23

interdependence 23

security dilemma 24

Treaties of Westphalia 24

feudalism 25

Thirty Years' War 25

state 26

Westphalian sovereignty 27

embassies 27

extraterritoriality 27

nation 30

nation-state 30

imperialism 31

democracy 31

nationalism 31

Treaty of Versailles 33

communism 33

fascism 33

Cold War 35

North Atlantic Treaty Organization (NATO) 35

Warsaw Pact 35

non-state actors 36

multinational corporations (MNCs) 36

nongovernmental organizations (NGOs) 36

international organizations (IOs) 36

subnational actors 36

sovereign wealth funds 37

mujahideen 39

al-Qaeda 39

globalization 40

ethnic cleansing 43

genocide 43

humanitarian interventions 43

responsible sovereignty 43

neo-Westphalian sovereignty 43

supranational regimes 45

Nuclear Nonproliferation Regime 45

Nuclear Nonproliferation Treaty 45

World Trade Organization (WTO) 45

European Union (EU) 45

REVIEW QUESTIONS

1. What are the major types of actors in the international system?

2. What do key terms like *anarchy, interdependence, the security dilemma*, and *globalization* mean?

3. What made the Westphalian system different from the pre-Westphalian system and the neo-Westphalian system?

4. Why have states managed to be the most significant international actors for hundreds of years, and how might that be changing?

5. What major events or developments mark each of these three international systems over time?

THINK ABOUT THIS

Are States Still the Most Important Players in World Politics?

Scholars studying world politics have long focused on the sovereign state as the main, even only, important actor in the international system. Well-known modern realist theorists such as Hans Morgenthau, Kenneth Waltz, and John Mearsheimer place the state at the center of all that really matters in world politics. However, in the past several decades, other scholars have seen things differently. People such as Richard Rosecrance questioned the basis of state power, and others such as

Robert Keohane and Joseph Nye, Margaret Keck and Kathryn Sikkink, and Alexander Wendt have increasingly focused on the role and influence of non-state actors.

Now that you have read and thought about our discussion of the playing field and actors in world politics, as well as the trends and evolution that have occurred, what do you think?

In what ways are states still the most important players in world politics, and in what ways are they limited and challenged by non-state actors?

FOR MORE INFORMATION . . .

International Organizations

See the list provided by the staff at the Northwestern University library, available at http://libguides.northwestern.edu/IGO.

Multinational Corporations

See at least a partial listing of MNCs at http://en.wikipedia.org/wiki/List_of_multinational_corporations.

Nobel Peace Prize Recipients

See the listing at http://nobelprizes.com/nobel/peace.

Nongovernmental Organizations Associated With the United Nations

See the listings and links available at https://www.nobelprize.org/prizes/lists/all-nobel-peace-prizes.

States

Try the CIA's *The World Factbook*, which includes basic information on all states and a number of other specific territorial units (for example, Hong Kong), available at https://www.cia.gov/library/publications/the-world-factbook/index.html.

NOTE

1. Not all territories identified on maps are diplomatically recognized as sovereign by all other states. Examples include Kosovo, Taiwan, Transnistria, Ossetia, and Abkhazia. Others still have an active association with their former imperial power— like Puerto Rico (United States) or the Falkland Islands (United Kingdom), for example.

Muhammed Said/Anadolu Agency via Getty Images

Members of the 325th Airborne Infantry Regiment
Brigade Combat Team board a Continental
Airlines jet bound for Kuwait in 2003 at Pope Air
Force Base, in North Carolina

What explains the dynamics of cooperation and
conflict in international relations?

3 Powerful Ideas

Realism, Liberalism, and Constructivism

Learning Objectives

After studying this chapter, you will be able to . . .

3-1 Identify the nature and use of theory and describe the components of theory.

3-2 Explain the foundations of the realist approach in terms of its conception of (a) the nature of the international system, (b) its relevant actors, (c) important resources, and (d) central dynamics.

3-3 Explain the foundations of the liberal approach in terms of its conceptions of (a) the nature of the international system, (b) its relevant actors, (c) important resources, and (d) central dynamics.

3-4 Explain the foundations of the constructivist approach in terms of its conception of (a) the nature of the international system, (b) its relevant actors, (c) important resources, and (d) central dynamics.

Chapter Outline

3-1 Theory and International Relations

3-2 The Realist Perspective on World Politics

3-3 The Liberal Perspective on World Politics

3-4 The Constructivist Perspective on World Politics

Will a "Democratic Peace" Persist?

Since 1945, empirical evidence presents some intriguing findings regarding regime types, the outbreak of war, and the resulting casualty counts. First, democracies have been involved in, and have even started, wars with nondemocratic countries. For example, the United States used military force 383 times between 1945 and 2000 (Howell and Pevehouse 2007). The United Kingdom and France have been involved in militarized conflicts with other nations more than any other state, and they are two of the three oldest democracies in the world. Second, wars involving at least one democracy tend to produce more battle deaths than wars between two nondemocracies. That is, a war between two autocracies is usually much less bloody than a war between an autocracy and a democracy. Third, nondemocratic countries have warred with each other regularly.

Yet two stable democracies do not appear to have ever gone to war with each other (Russett and Oneal 2001). In addition to not fighting with each other, democracies seem less likely to even threaten each other with the use of force, and they tend to settle their disputes more peacefully and quickly. Thus, there seems to be something to the idea of a **democratic peace**. But things appear to be changing, and new tensions between democracies such as the US and European countries have emerged.

1. What factors might explain these patterns?

2. If democracies are more peaceful, then why are their wars with autocracies so bloody?

3. Will democracies remain peaceful with each other?

....

democratic peace: a state-level theory of war stating that institutional and normative characteristics of democratic regimes lead them to peaceful relations with each other.

INTRODUCTION: POWERFUL IDEAS

The playing field of world politics is complicated, as we explained in Chapter 2. It combines a number of structural characteristics, a wide variety of actors, and a broad range of activities into a complex mix that is often hard to comprehend. How is one to make sense of the complex international system, international actors, and interactions—by doing more than merely describing events that occur? The short answer is through the use of theory—an analytical tool essential for the explanation of complex realities.

3-1 THEORY AND INTERNATIONAL RELATIONS

>> 3-1   **Identify the nature and use of theory and describe the components of theory.**

A theory is simply a way to explain the world around us. Theorizing is something we all do every day, whether we know it or not. Truly, facts—or, in the case of international relations, the behavior of international actors—have little meaning without an explanation (a theory) to connect them. For example, Russia's actions to annex Crimea, part of Ukraine, in 2014 are simply fact. However, those facts mean something more if one understands that states compete with each other in the international arena, or that Russia has long sought to maintain friendly regimes and control over countries around its periphery, or that eastern Ukraine and the Crimea region are heavily populated by people of Russian descent. In short, explaining Russia's actions—and even predicting its next steps—demands that we think about cause-and-effect relationships.

This is theory—an explanation of how events and actions fit together. Theorizing is essential to any effort to understand why international actors behave the way they do, why the events and actions that make up world politics occur, and what they mean. In this chapter and the next, we consider a number of theoretical perspectives that offer explanations for the complicated dynamics of world politics. In this chapter, we compare three central approaches— realism, liberalism, and constructivism—and in the next, we examine several alternatives—foreign policy analysis, Marxist-based theories, and feminist international relations theory. These perspectives highlight different aspects of world politics and provide sometimes complementary but more often contending explanations for the behavior, patterns, and outcomes we observe in the international system.

3-1a Thinking Theoretically

To begin, let's first consider the meaning of theory and theorizing. As we have suggested, theory is an explanation for connecting events, actions, behaviors, and outcomes. More specifically, it is a set of analytical tools for understanding the cause-and-effect relationships between phenomena. For example, as you considered the topic of democratic peace at the beginning of this chapter, you engaged in theorizing about world politics. Indeed, people theorize every day, sometimes explicitly, more often implicitly, sometimes naively, and sometimes with great sophistication. Why didn't I do better on a test? Why did an innocent comment hurt someone's feelings?

Policymakers also rely on and are influenced by theories of various kinds. For example, when the United Nations authorizes economic sanctions against Iran or when NATO implements sanctions against Russia, they do so hoping that the economic pressure from the sanctions will lead those countries to change their behavior. Similarly, when the US deploys military force in response to North Korean nuclear weapons tests or threats of Iranian efforts to destabilize parts of the Middle East, those actions reflect ideas about how the threat and use of force can deter or coerce another state, as well as even broader theories about how states influence each other or how to gain and sustain security. Each of these policy actions is based on a theory.

3-1b The Analytical Uses of Theory

As analysts, we depend on theory to explain the choices of policymakers and the consequences of policies they enact. Why did the Soviet Union seek a nonaggression pact with Nazi Germany before World War II when the two countries appeared to be rivals— maybe even outright enemies—up to that point? Why did leaders believe the United States, Canada, and Mexico would all benefit from a free-trade agreement linking their economies? Why do Israeli leaders keep building residential settlements in areas claimed by Palestinians, knowing that such construction will alienate Palestinians and their supporters? Why did the Russians deploy troops into Ukraine and annex Crimea in 2014? Why did the UK withdraw from the European Union in 2020? We cannot answer these questions without relying on theory.

As we discussed briefly in Chapter 1, theory is a way to explain the patterns of world politics—or any other subject area, for that matter—and theories help us make strategic simplifications of the world to bring important features into clearer focus. Think of theories as lenses, such as those you might find in a good pair of sunglasses. If it is too bright, you can't see very well, but with good sunglasses, you can see and understand the world around you. Moreover, sunglass lenses come in different colors, and each shade filters out a different portion of the light in order to sharpen and improve vision, so each pair lets you see the same world around you in a different way. In effect, theory simplifies reality to reduce the "glare of the sun" and to sharpen the clarity of key factors. This aids in the explanation of the most important behavior and even the prediction of likely developments.

Consider another metaphor: You're sitting in a very loud restaurant. Perhaps there is loud music, crying babies, or, worse, both. The noise is so loud that you cannot hear your friends talk. The white noise in the restaurant is like a bunch of irrelevant facts. To understand the strong relationship between the United States and Canada, does it help to know that both flags have white and red or that the Canadian flag has a maple leaf on it, while the American flag has stars? Of course not—while factual, that information is simply white noise. Theory simplifies reality by cutting out all of that unneeded information so that we can better understand the important forces at work in the world, just like turning down the music and quieting the unhappy babies in the restaurant would let you hear your friends better.

As a simplifying device intended to improve understanding of complex reality, theory has particular meaning for the study of the empirical—or real—world. Contrary to popular usage (e.g., "oh, that is just a theory . . ."), which often casts theory as something fictional or unrelated to "reality," empirical theory is really just a cause-and-effect explanation of real or observable phenomena in the world that addresses "why" questions, not "what happened" questions. For example, let's go back to our opening puzzle about peace between democracies. Theory is the explanation we offer in response to the question of *why* democratic countries apparently do not go to war with each other. **Empirical theory** links important aspects of the world to outcomes, specifies the mechanisms that link the two, and ends in hypotheses—if-then statements about empirical behavior. Importantly, empirical theory allows us to test those explanations/hypotheses against the events that happen in the real world to gauge the theory's utility or value. Thus, empirical theory differs from **normative theory**, which seeks to advocate how the political world *should be* and is often referred to as political philosophy.

3-1c Theory and Causation: The Components of Theory

Empirical theory aims at explaining *causal* relationships and patterns among the phenomena being studied. This is a difficult task because of the complexity

of the world, and unlike theory in other sciences, it is difficult, even impossible, to create and manage laboratory experiments that allow us to isolate cause and effect as one might do in a study of disease or nuclear physics. And one can almost never repeat an experiment to retest empirical findings in world politics—imagine the absurdity of attempting to rerun the 2008 war between Georgia and Russia!

With these difficulties in mind, social scientists stress three fundamental requirements that increase our confidence when we claim causality in the social world. Think in terms of two factors, A (cause) and B (effect), which you think are related:

- A and B must change together, or you cannot claim that one causes change in another—this is called *covariance*.

- A must come before B in time because causes must come before effects, or they cannot be causes—this is called *temporal order*.

- Other plausible or likely causes of B (say, C, D, E, and F) must be eliminated or accounted for as best as possible in order to isolate the true effect of A on B—this is called *nonspuriousness*.

There are other considerations that affect the quality and utility of a theory, but these three requirements are essential.

Cause and effect

Sometimes a causal chain is simple, and other times it is very complex.

iStock.com/pxel66

empirical theory: a theory based on real-world observations and explanations.

normative theory: a theory based on prescription and advocacy of preferred outcomes.

With these essentials for a causal argument in place, theory identifies a set of concepts (e.g., democratic governments, war), specifies their interrelationships (peaceful relations), and, most important, *explains the reasons* for those relationships. As such, theory involves three central elements: description, explanation, and prediction. Theory also usually offers a basis for prescription, but we regard that as a by-product of these three main components. Let's briefly consider each of these elements.

Description

Theory directs attention to particular aspects of the world that are most important to the phenomenon in question. It tells us which facts are important. As such, it offers a descriptive element, but it is not mere description. Indeed, as one of our former professors used to emphasize to us, "facts without theory are trivia." They are dots without connections. To theorize is to move up the ladder of abstraction from simple description to *selective* description of those aspects of reality that are most important. In part, this requires observers to see individual events as part of classes or types of events in order to gain perspective on the enormously complicated world around us.

Explanation

Theory provides cause-and-effect explanations of the linkages between those aspects of the world on which it focuses, which is the most important role theories play. As such, theory explains how and why those descriptive concepts are linked. For example, the mere statement that democracies do not go to war with each other is not a theory. A theory would be constructed if you said: (a) "In democracies leaders are constrained by and answerable to the people who elect them," and (b) "consequently, when two democratic countries are in a dispute, both leaders are constrained by their electorates and less able to go to war." In the first case, we simply offered a description of an empirical observation, but in the second, we provided a potential explanation for why democracies do not fight one another.

Prediction

Theory provides a basis for anticipating future events and developments. This aspect of theory is really a derivative of the first two—knowing what to observe and understanding how things are connected. If, for example, you theorize that key characteristics of democratic government, such as an informed electorate, lead countries with such regimes to settle their disputes peacefully, you should be able to predict what will happen in the future if (a) two democratic governments with informed electorates have a dispute (then they are unlikely to fight) or (b) democratic governments with informed electorates spread throughout the world (then there should be fewer wars worldwide). Conversely, if you theorize that the peace between democracies since World War II is a function of other factors, such as the existence of a common major enemy or high levels of trade between democratic states or the presence of a free press in democratic countries, then you would base your predictions on those things.

A Basis for Prescription

Theory may also provide a basis for prescribing behavior or policy—that is, it may lead to normative conclusions about what *should* be. Because theory tells us what to observe, why things are connected, and what will happen in the future, we might be able to shape the future if we are able to control or alter certain things. For example, medical researchers have shown that moderate, regular exercise helps lower blood pressure, cholesterol, and excess body fat and increase heart and lung function—all things that increase health and life expectancy. From that we can predict that people who engage in moderate exercise will generally be healthier and live longer. This might lead a government to prescribe a policy for physical education in school, or businesses might find ways to encourage their employees to exercise more often in order to lessen their health care costs or reduce absences.

The evidence and theory that link democratic governance and peaceful relations between countries provide a good example. If democracies do not fight each other, then a policy prescription for achieving a more peaceful world might be to support and promote democratization in other countries. If more countries are democratic, then there should be more peaceful relations in the world. In fact, many US and European leaders have argued exactly this idea in recent decades (see the box "Theory in Action: The Democratic Peace and Democracy Promotion"). Many other examples abound, and you can probably generate interesting policy prescriptions based on the exercise at the beginning of this chapter.

3-1d Concluding Thoughts on Theory

Let's wrap up this overview with a few concluding thoughts. First, theory should be tested against empirical evidence to gauge its accuracy and utility. For example, we might theorize that countries with McDonald's restaurants never fight each other (the "Golden Arches" theory described by the author

The Democratic Peace and Democracy Promotion

The belief that democracies are more peaceful in their relations with one another has long motivated democratic leaders to advocate the spread of democratic institutions to other countries. In the United States, for example, President Woodrow Wilson, in his influential "Fourteen Points" speech of 1918, advocated the spread of democracy and self-determination for all nations to make the world safer and more peaceful. More recently, every US president since Jimmy Carter in the 1970s has made a similar appeal. President Carter advocated protecting and promoting human rights and democratic governance, and President Ronald Reagan called for a "crusade for freedom" on behalf of democracy.

As the Cold War ended, subsequent administrations placed even greater emphasis on promoting democracy. President George H. W. Bush expanded US democracy promotion with such actions as the use of US military force in Panama in 1989 and with special aid to the countries of Eastern Europe (the 1990 Support for Eastern European Democracy—or SEED—Act) and the former Soviet Union (the 1992 Freedom Support Act). When Bill Clinton assumed office, the United States expanded its efforts even further. According to President Clinton, in his 1995 State of the Union address, "ultimately, the best strategy to ensure our security and to build a durable peace is to support the advance of democracy elsewhere."

Twenty-first-century presidents have continued the commitment. As George W. Bush stated in his 2005 inaugural address, "the best hope for peace in our world is the expansion of freedom in all the world. . . . So it is the policy of the United States to seek and support the growth of democratic movements and institutions in every nation and culture." At a major speech in Cairo in June 2009, Barack Obama expressed his "unyielding belief that all people yearn for certain things: the ability to speak your mind and have a say in how you are governed; confidence in the rule of law and the equal administration of justice; government that is transparent and doesn't steal from the people; the freedom to live as you choose. These are not just American ideas; they are human rights. And that is why we will support them everywhere." Only the election of Donald Trump reversed this trend, with the Trump administration taking numerous steps to reduce US support and assistance for democratization substantially after 2017.

Yet support for democracy promotion is not exclusive to the United States. One study examined the foreign policies of 40 countries between 1992 and 2002 and concluded that they engaged in substantial and widely varying commitments and efforts to promote democracy in other countries (Herman and Piccone 2002). Overall, these efforts by the United States and others included such things as diplomatic approaches, economic efforts such as the provision of foreign aid, and even military intervention to protect or establish democratic regimes.

1. What cause-and-effect assumptions are policymakers drawing on when they prescribe such policies?

2. What happens when democracy spreads in the world? What about when it declines?

3. What happens when support for democracy is reduced? ●

Thomas Friedman about twenty-five years ago), but until we test this theory with evidence, we won't know if there is any value to it. In fact, this particular argument does not stand up well to empirical scrutiny. There have been a number of instances since 1989 in which militarized disputes between countries with McDonald's restaurants occurred, including Pakistan and India over decades and Russia and Ukraine over the past few years, and there are almost certainly other factors at work that determine both the presence of McDonald's and peaceful relations between countries. Can you think of some?

Second, many scholars embrace the principle of **parsimony** in their efforts. Parsimony holds that the simplest explanations should be preferred over more complicated ones, all other things being equal. Detail and complexity for their own sake are of no advantage to explanation unless they really offer better explanations of how, when, and why something happens.

Third, theorizing can take place in a given level of analysis (e.g., explanations that stress system-level, state-level, or individual-level factors), or it can link explanations across levels of analysis. But good theory is clear about which approach is being utilized.

parsimony: the principle that simple explanations are preferable to complex explanations when other things are equal.

Russians eat at McDonald's in 1997 in Moscow, Russia
What are the implications of the spread of McDonald's to countries around the world?

Andres Hernandez/Liaison/Getty Images

Finally, try to remember that theories are tools to be used. They are simply an explanation of the relevant facts. It may be that one theoretical approach or another is preferable in some situations but not others. You do not necessarily have to choose one theoretical approach and ignore others. Instead, you might treat theory like tools in a toolbox: Which ones are most helpful for given situations? After all, hammers are great for pounding nails but lousy for cutting boards.

3-2 THE REALIST PERSPECTIVE ON WORLD POLITICS

>> **3-2   Explain the foundations of the realist approach in terms of its conception of (a) the nature of the international system, (b) its relevant actors, (c) important resources, and (d) central dynamics.**

Almost 2,500 years ago, the Greek historian Thucydides wrote about the conflict and competition among Greek city-states led by Athens and Sparta. According to Thucydides, at the heart of the conflict was "the growth in Athenian power and the fear which this caused in Sparta." In a memorable episode of this contest between Athens and Sparta, the Athenians

demanded surrender from the tiny island of Melos and threatened invasion and devastation if Melians refused. When the Melians pleaded for justice and fairness, the Athenian commander told them they were wasting their time. In matters of such import, he asserted, "The strong do as they will, and the weak suffer what they must."

From this episode, Thucydides tied the conflict between Athens and Sparta to the core of what we now know as realist theory: their competition for power and influence and the security dilemma it prompted between them. In the Melian tale, Thucydides reasoned that ideals such as justice and fairness were irrelevant to the relations between states. Instead, leaders must focus on security and survival—the accumulation of power needed to protect their interests. Thus, the Melians should have joined the Athenians to ensure their future security. Instead, they did not join Athens, and as a result, the Athenian military destroyed Melos to demonstrate its power and prevent the Melians from aligning with Athens's key rival, Sparta.

Thucydides was one of the first realist writers, and although **realism** is the oldest theory of international relations, it is still widely accepted and used today. Realism is accepted not only as a way to understand the world but also as a policy guide. That is, the theory explains how states act in the international system, and like the story of Athens and Melos, it also offers guidance on how states *should* act. Thucydides tells the story of Melos to explain what happened and, just as important, to teach leaders how to avoid the fate that befell Melos. He points out that they should have sided with Athens (or called on Athenian enemy Sparta for an alliance), regardless of whether it was the just or fair thing to do; it was the choice that would have saved their lives.

Thus, realism acts as both an explanation and a guide or prescription for policy. Particularly since World War II, realism has been the predominant approach to international relations around the world. States such as China, Russia, and the United States all tend to act as realists. We say "tend" to act as realists because complexity is everywhere in international relations. As you will see when we discuss liberalism, no state follows a strictly realist-type foreign policy.

The realist perspective traces back to thinkers and scholars such as Thucydides, Sun Tzu, Shang Yang, Niccolò Machiavelli, and Thomas Hobbes. The theory is rooted in a pessimistic view of human nature. Hobbes famously characterized the

realism: a major theoretical approach to international relations emphasizing the competitive, conflict-ridden pursuit of power and security among states in world politics.

state of nature—a hypothetical situation where there was no government—as "solitary, poor, nasty, brutish, and short." He argued that if there were no government to constrain people from their worst impulses, then there would be no functioning society. Perhaps the best way to imagine Hobbes's state of nature is to think of apocalyptic-style movies, television shows, and books, such as *The Road*, *28 Days Later*, *The Walking Dead*, and *Snowpiercer*. In these stories, humans almost universally turn on each other in horribly violent ways and cooperate only out of fear. That is the world that Hobbes saw if it were not for governments to constrain people and force them to behave.

Building on these foundations, the more modern-day roots of realism include E. H. Carr, whose *Twenty Years' Crisis: 1919-1939* describes how the realities of power politics destroyed what he characterized as idealistic hopes and plans for peace and cooperation after World War I and led to World War II. They also include Hans J. Morgenthau, whose *Politics Among Nations* stresses "the national interest defined in terms of power" as the main factor motivating states in international politics.

Realism is the simplest of theories of world politics, which contributes to its power and pervasiveness. It rests on a parsimonious leveraging of a few key aspects of the international system and its parts to explain broad patterns of behavior and interaction. Although there are many variants and flavors of realist theory, they tend to be unified around a common core of ideas and assumptions. Many thousands of pages have been devoted to developing and articulating realist theories of international relations, but we can focus on a number of core elements to gain a working familiarity with the perspective and its descriptive, explanatory, predictive, and prescriptive applications.

At the risk of simplifying the nuances and subtleties, let's consider what realism offers for (a) the nature of the international system, (b) its relevant actors, (c) important resources, and (d) central dynamics. We will adopt this scheme in our discussion of liberalism and constructivism as well to make it easier to compare and contrast these three major approaches. Because we discuss and apply these theories further in subsequent chapters, our purpose here is to provide a foundation for our efforts to explain and understand the patterns and interactions of world politics.

3-2a Realism and the Nature of the International System

According to realists, a central characteristic of the international system overshadows all others and forms the foundation of the explanations the perspective offers. That characteristic is *anarchy*—which quite simply means the absence of central authority, not chaos, as we discussed in Chapter 2. Although the international system is more complicated than this simple portrayal suggests, realists tend to argue that other aspects of the system are less significant and can be ignored as secondary factors, for the most part. For realists, the absence of a central government to establish order and wield power and authority establishes a fundamentally Hobbesian world in which the main players of world politics must rely on themselves and themselves alone to protect their interests and accomplish their goals. In this *self-help* world, power is both a central instrument and a primary objective to ensure survival and security. Indeed, according to realists, the anarchy of the international system makes it the domain of power, not law, morality, society, or institutions. And according to realists, this main structural aspect of the international system ensures that conflict is always possible—and is the central problem of world politics.

Anarchy as the central feature of the international system has several other consequences for the system. First, because anarchy means there is no higher governing authority above states, these main political units are sovereign—possessing the sole authority to govern within their borders. In combination with self-help, sovereignty also means that states are responsible for securing their own interests and, at least in principle, that they are not obligated to follow rules or decisions made by others unless they so choose or are coerced into doing so by a more powerful state.

Second, the international system is stratified, with different levels of resources, wealth, and power possessed by different states. Realists tend to differentiate between great or major powers and other powers, with some also identifying middle powers. This **stratification** is important for realists for at least two reasons. First, realists argue that states with different levels of power act distinctly due to their position in the anarchic system, with great powers having the greatest freedom of choice and action, as well as the most influence. Second, realists argue that states seek to preserve or gain power—to move up this hierarchy—as a way of securing their interests and influence. The central ingredient of these differing levels of power and state efforts to be powerful is military might, which we discuss later in the chapter.

Finally, as we discussed in Chapter 2, the anarchic international system, with its self-help characteristic, establishes persistent security dilemmas. Simply put, because states are responsible for their security

....

state of nature: a hypothetical condition before the advent of government.

stratification: unequal distribution of power, influence, and/or other resources.

Variants of Realism

As a theoretical perspective, realism comes in many flavors:

- *Classical realism.* This variant of realism finds its roots in the political philosophy of Thomas Hobbes and emphasizes the aggressive, power-seeking, and selfish nature of human beings as the ultimate source of state behavior. As well-known classical realist Hans Morgenthau (2005) wrote, the first principle of classical realism is that "politics, like society in general, is governed by objective laws that have their roots in human nature" (p. 4). In world politics, the state is the collective reflection of individual human nature carrying out the pursuit of power.

- *Neo-realism.* This variant, by contrast, focuses on the nature of the international system rather than human nature. According to leading neo-realist theorists such as Kenneth Waltz, the anarchic structure of the international system causes the units in the system (states) to seek their own security through the accumulation of power, thus leading to balance-of-power politics. Thus, it is not greed or a selfish nature that pushes states to do what they do—instead, the system makes them do it.

- *Neo-classical realism.* This variant has been advocated by theorists such as Gideon Rose and Randall Schweller and attempts to bridge the divide between the first two variants by starting with the structure of the international system to explain broader international outcomes and patterns, and then adding in state- and individual-level factors to help explain the differing foreign policies of particular states.

We can also distinguish between defensive and offensive orientations of realism:

- *Defensive realism* stresses that states are interested in being secure from threats but are faced with security dilemmas that generate fear and uncertainty. As key advocates such as Robert Jervis and Stephen Walt suggest, defensive realists do not argue that states always seek to maximize their power or seek dominance; they contend that there are conditions in which states can be more or less secure.

- *Offensive realism,* advocated by such theorists as John Mearsheimer, by contrast, stresses that states (especially great or aspiring-to-be-great powers) always seek power and dominance. As Mearsheimer (2001) put it, "States pay close attention to how power is distributed among them, and they make a special effort to maximize their share of world power. . . . Given the difficulty of determining how much power is enough for today and tomorrow, great powers recognize that the best way to ensure their security is to achieve hegemony now, thus eliminating any possibility of a challenge from another great power" (pp. 34–35). In the course of these efforts, great powers naturally come into conflict with each other.

Think about how each of these variants reflects the central core of realism, as well as how they differ from each other. What are the strengths and weaknesses of each variant? How might each one capture and explain important parts of world politics? ●

and survival, they must take action to protect themselves. However, the actions that states take to secure themselves frequently appear potentially threatening to other states, which naturally take steps to protect their own security. The results often produce situations of greater potential danger, so the dilemma is clear: The actions a state takes to secure itself often wind up making it even less secure because of the action–reaction cycles they produce. Realists express a variety of views on this feature of international politics, from those who argue that some states have good, essentially defensive intentions to those who assert that most states prefer dominance and actively seek it. In either case, security dilemmas arise and spur conflict and competition (see the box "Spotlight On: Variants of Realism").

3-2b Realism and the Relevant Actors in International Relations

Within the anarchic system of world politics, not surprisingly, realists concentrate on the state as the central, and usually only, actor of consequence in the international system. It is not that realists fail to recognize that other players—many of which we discussed in Chapter 2—exist. Instead, realists assert that non-state actors are either of secondary importance or are derivative of states. Yes, a realist would say, there are international organizations such as the UN, but such organizations are creations of states, they serve the interests of states, and they reflect the preferences of the most powerful states. To realists, the states are the primary players.

As we suggested previously, in the realist simplification of world politics, these states are sovereign and self-help oriented, which means they are basically self-interested and self-regarding. As in the stag hunt example from Chapter 1, realists portray states as fundamentally selfish actors seeking their own security. That does not necessarily mean that cooperation among them is impossible. It suggests, however, that such cooperation will be highly dependent on calculations of self-interest and benefits, and thus will be temporary and highly constrained by suspicion and mistrust, because no state can really count on another to forego opportunities for advantages. For realists, states may join together to counter a common enemy or prevent another state from becoming too powerful, but they are unlikely to sustain that cooperation once the common threat has been addressed. Thus, the British and Americans were unable to sustain their cooperation with the Soviets after the defeat of Germany in World War II, and the United States and NATO, on the one hand, and Russia, on the other, saw opportunities and momentum for cooperation after the Cold War deteriorated in the face of competing and conflicting national goals.

Moreover, it is common for realists to simplify even further about states. Rather than consider how societal forces, complex governments and processes, different regime types, or different political parties and individual leaders affect states, many realists prefer to treat the state as a **unitary actor** (i.e., like a billiard ball, a single moving part) that responds rationally to the structures and dynamics of the international system. Treating states as unitary actors lets us see them as if they are single rational entities. In effect, states such as North Korea and the United States think and act as single actors: North Korea "decides," the United States "negotiates," the two countries "threaten." That way we don't need to know about the particular leaders or groups and their preferences inside the countries. These rational actors calculate their national interests and goals and take action accordingly.

Thus, in this realist simplification, states are also fundamentally undifferentiated, except for power and capabilities. That is, realists filter away much of the descriptive detail of states (type of government, culture, leader characteristics, which party controls government, and the like) and assume that all states want the same things and are affected by the international system in similar ways, with the only significant difference being how much power and capability they have to act. Those states with greater power and capabilities have more opportunity to act than those without such resources. As Thucydides suggested, strong states pursue their interests, and weaker states have little choice but to go along, one way or another. When China and the Philippines claim ownership of the same islands, for example, realists distinguish these states from each other by their power and resources. What is not relevant are differences in type of government, the personalities of a single leader, and other such details.

As we describe in the box "Spotlight On: Variants of Realism," different schools of thought within realism exist, of course. Neo-classical realists place greater emphasis on the individual leaders and states, their interests, and the ways their choices and actions then shape the resulting international system. Neo-realists, by contrast, stress the structure of the system and its central role in shaping the general behavior and interactions of states. However, all variants tend to treat the state as a rational, self-interested actor seeking power and influence in the pursuit of security.

3-2c Realism and the Important Resources in International Relations

In the anarchic system of sovereign states seeking their own interests, realists stress the importance of power and capabilities. As Hans Morgenthau (2005), an early and influential realist theorist in the 20th century, put it, states pursue "the national interest defined in terms of power." Realists contend that the anarchy of the international system makes it the domain of power and capabilities. To put it simply, according to realists, power rules in world politics. States seek it and wield it. Its distribution affects how states act and the likelihood of conflict. But what is power?

There are many definitions, but a very simple starting point captures the realist concept of power very well: **Power** is the ability to get what you want. For realists, power in world politics is both an instrument and a goal (i.e., states seek it as both a means and an end), and its acquisition and use are part of the basic fabric of state behavior and interactions. As Morgenthau's statement indicates, the realist concept of power is that states must seek it to secure themselves and their interests in an anarchic world.

At least three key features of power dominate the realist perspective. First, power is relative and relational. It makes little sense to discuss power except in terms of relationship. Your power compared to whom? At its heart, the realist notion of power turns on the view that what matters most is how power is distributed

....

unitary actor: the simplified conception of a state as a single entity or actor.

power: the ability to get what you want.

and how gains in power by one state compare to those of another. In effect, a realist determines power not by assessing what a state has (e.g., 100 nuclear missiles or 5 aircraft carrier battle groups) so much as what one state has compared to another (100 *more* nuclear missiles, 5 *more* carrier battle groups) and how the advantage (or disadvantage) is changing (growing, shrinking, remaining stable). This leads to what realist theorists discuss as the **relative gains** problem: States are more (or, at least, as much) concerned with the growth of their own power resources compared to another's than they are with **absolute gains**, or how much of the resource they have or gain on its own. Think of it this way: A concern for relative gains suggests that a state would rather increase its power by 5 points per year if its rival gains only 3 points per year, instead of gaining 10 points if its rival gains 12 points. To a realist, the first scenario means a relative gain of two, and the second means a relative loss of two.

Second, realists view power in a *hierarchical* fashion, with military power the most important and essential for the ability to get what one wants in world politics. Realists acknowledge that power has many sources and that many resources are necessary for a state to be powerful. As Table 3-1 shows, these sources and resources include underlying factors such as geographic and territorial characteristics and attributes, natural resources, and other factors that realists often characterize as *potential* sources of power (see the box "The Revenge of Geography: Geography and Power"). Factors such as wealth, industrial or technological capacity, and the like are also important. But a realist would say that they are important ultimately as a means by which a state can develop and deploy military power in pursuit of security and influence. As Robert Art, a realist scholar, has stated, force is, ultimately, the final judge of world politics. From this perspective, there is a good reason why virtually all states—and all major powers—devote considerable resources to developing their military forces (see the box "Spotlight On: Military Power and World Politics").

Furthermore, realists tend to treat power as **fungible**, meaning that power resources can be converted into influence easily, just as a dollar can be quickly and easily turned into many things: food, iTunes downloads, legal services, and so on. Realists see power similarly: States with power—especially military might—can turn it into positive outcomes across many issue areas, including diplomatic negotiations and trade relations. The more (military) power a state has, the more likely it is to get its way on a whole host of issues.

relative gains: the comparative effect of a decision or situation on an actor relative to those of another actor.

absolute gains: the total effect of a decision or situation on an actor.

fungible: the ability to use one type of power for multiple purposes.

TABLE 3-1

Resources of Power in World Politics

RESOURCE	EXAMPLES
Geographic resources	Size of territory; defensible borders
Natural resources	Arable land; raw materials
Economic resources	Wealth; industrial capacity; technological leadership and development
Military resources	Quantity and quality of armed forces; advanced military technology; military leadership
Human resources	Population; education and skills; leadership; national image and morale

One way to understand this power equation is shown in Figure 3-1. In this depiction, the application of power begins with resources like those we have already discussed. These resources are harnessed and converted into actual capabilities, which depends heavily on the abilities of society and the leaders making the decisions. Once converted, these capabilities are applied as foreign policy instruments. We can broadly classify such instruments into three categories: (a) diplomacy (which involves bargaining and negotiation, as we discussed in Chapter 2), (b) economic instruments (which involve aid, trade, and sanctions, as we discuss in Chapter 9), and (c) military instruments (e.g., the use of force, as we discuss in Chapter 6). For realists, although each of these instruments is important, ultimately military power trumps all.

3-2d Realism and the Central Dynamics of International Relations

From these foundations, the last element of the realist approach is easy to understand. In an anarchic world characterized by insecurity, self-help, and security dilemmas, states seek power to protect their interests and ensure their survival. Because power is relative and ultimately based on military strength, states cannot ever really have enough or trust others to be satisfied in an environment where *conflict is the norm.* As Hans Morgenthau (2005) once famously argued, "All states are either preparing for, recovering from, or engaged in war." Viewed through this lens, world politics is a conflict-ridden arena where states compete with one another for power and influence. In this arena, powerful states assert themselves and seek advantage over one another, while weaker states

Geography and Power

MAP 3-1

Islands of Security? The Geographic Location of the United States, United Kingdom, and Japan

Does the world seem safer for countries mostly surrounded by water?

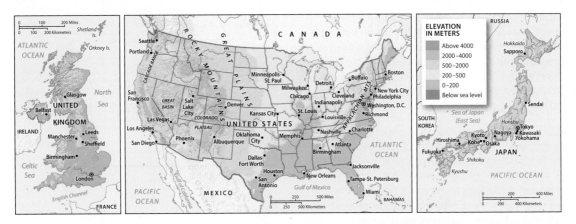

The geographic location and characteristics of a country can be a significant source of power and of perceptions of safety or vulnerability. Look at Map 3-1 and the locations of the United Kingdom, the United States, and Japan. These three states share one feature in common: All three are effectively island states bounded by water from most or all of their neighbors. Although not an island, for the United States, the presence of two large bodies of water like the Atlantic and Pacific Oceans separating it from other major powers in Europe and Asia has long offered a degree of protection and security, as well as freedom of movement and easy access to trade routes via the oceans. Behind these two vast moats and easy transportation avenues, the geographic size and relatively abundant natural resources of the US have also contributed to its potential power and ability to be secure. The UK and Japan both enjoy the protection of water separating them from others, as well as offering avenues for trade and economic activity. But in the case of these two countries, that separation—especially from potentially major rivals in Europe and Asia—is more limited and, in combination with their smaller size and natural resource endowments, can contribute to isolation and feelings of vulnerability as well.

Contrast the geographic locations and implications of these virtual island states with the geography of other countries. China, for example, is surrounded by other countries and must consider what power is needed to defend its borders on all sides. China can consider neither Russia nor North Korea to be a trustworthy friend, and China's border with India has been the site of numerous but limited military clashes in recent years. Japan's navy and air force also must be watched carefully by the Chinese. Israel and the Palestinians cannot agree on their borders with each other, and Syria wants the Golan Heights back from Israel. What other states have geographic locations with significant implications for their power and security? What about states with mountainous borders or large deserts separating them from their neighbors? How about countries such as Egypt and Panama, whose geography and location provide transportation links between bodies of water (i.e., in the Suez and Panama Canals)? What consequences derive from these features? What about those without any obvious geographic features marking their territory?

1. How do geographic features add to and detract from power and security?

2. What power advantages have countries like the United States enjoyed because of their location and ocean borders?

3. How have changing technology and globalization affected the significance of geography for power and security? ●

Military Power and World Politics

Both realists and liberals argue that military power is important to world politics. However, for most realists, military power is the sine qua non of world politics—the essential ingredient for any state's power and security. The website GlobalFirepower.com collects data on the military power of countries of the world (45 categories of information) and then ranks countries from most to least powerful. Table 3-2 presents their ranking of the top six military powers in the world, with their figures on military personnel and defense spending drawn from their ranking system for 2020. All six of these countries have increased their military forces and spending over the past three years. Japan and South Korea have also recently surpassed the UK and France and taken their places on the list.

After looking over this information, think about the measure of power represented, but also think about the ranking of these countries as the top six most powerful countries. If realists are right, that means these should be the most powerful countries in the world. How well does this list represent power and influence in world politics? Who is not on this list that you think should be? ●

TABLE 3-2

The Most Powerful Countries in the World in 2020?

COUNTRY	ACTIVE MILITARY PERSONNEL	DEFENSE BUDGET
United States	1.4 million	$750 billion
Russia	1.01 million	$48 billion
China	2.2 million	$237 billion
India	1.4 million	$61 billion
Japan	247,000	$49 billion
South Korea	580,000	$44 billion

Source: GlobalFirepower.com, "2020 Military Strength Ranking," http://www.globalfirepower.com/countries-listing.asp.

FIGURE 3-1

The Application of Power

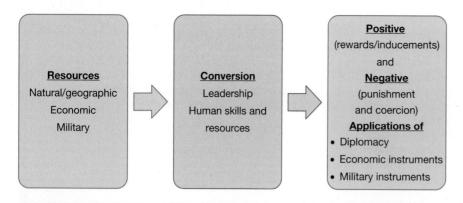

cope with the consequences. So states are much like billiard balls colliding with each other on a regular basis as they pursue and protect their national interests and seek and wield power. As the philosopher Thomas Hobbes wrote in *Leviathan*, in the absence of "a common power to keep them all in awe, they are in that condition which is called war; and such a war is of every man [or state] against every man [or state]."

In this world, realists generally view international politics as **zero-sum** situations. Building on their emphasis on relative gains, realists tend to argue that virtually all scenarios result in a winner and a loser, so that a gain by one state necessarily means a loss by another. For instance, in the example of the difference between absolute and relative gains, the two-point gain by the first state by definition means a two-point loss (in relative terms) by the other, not gains by each (one greater, one lesser). This tendency to see power and other interactions in zero-sum terms reflects the realist presumption of conflictual or competitive relations in world politics. As realist theorist John Mearsheimer (2001) argues, in this context the

zero-sum: a condition in which one party's benefit or gains require comparable losses by another party.

central aim of powerful states is to dominate at least their region and potentially more.

According to realists, which states, and particularly how many of them, have power greatly shapes the general patterns of world politics. Some **distributions of power** contribute to more conflict and war, some to less, while all distributions are subject to change as those out of power seek more of it and those in power seek to preserve it. As we discuss in more detail in Chapter 5, when we discuss conflict and causes of war, realists often categorize particular periods of international relations by identifying the number of great powers, often referred to as poles, or *polarity*, in the international system. The international system can be **unipolar**, with one great power; **bipolar**, with two; or **multipolar**, with more than two. Some realists discuss **tripolar** systems as an intermediate state between bipolar and multipolar systems. According to realists, each of these distributions creates different patterns, constraints, and opportunities for states seeking power and security, although there is disagreement over which distribution is more or less prone to conflict. In one example, *The Tragedy of Great Power Politics*, John Mearsheimer (2001) explains the frequency and likelihood of war as a function of the distribution of power. According to Mearsheimer, unipolar or hegemonic systems experience the fewest wars. Rigid bipolar systems, where most states are tightly aligned with one or the other of the two major powers, are more violent, but loose bipolar systems are even more prone to war. Multipolar systems, with many major powers competing for influence and security, are the most war prone. It is easy to see the central dynamic stressed by realists at the heart of explanations such as this—the competition for power and security among self-interested states.

This quite naturally leads to a central dynamic of world politics that realist theorists typically emphasize: **balance-of-power politics**. We discuss this dynamic in more detail in Chapter 6, but let's note here that this term generally refers to the pattern of activity that occurs as states take action to make themselves secure by seeking power, countering the efforts of real or potential rivals to gain power advantages, and using power to counter security threats from others. According to realists, states monitor their security environment and take actions to meet perceived threats from others by seeking power. According to many realists, because all states make these kinds of calculations and take these kinds of steps, the balance of power is much like the magic of the market in capitalism: As each state pursues its self-interests in this way, balances tend to emerge.

In sum, realism directs our attention to the pursuit of power and security in an anarchic and conflict-ridden world, highlighting the role of states and their national interests (see Table 3-3 for a summary).

TABLE 3-3

Summary of Realism and World Politics

KEY FEATURES	REALIST INTERPRETATION
Nature of the international system	Anarchic; self-help
Relevant actors	States
Important resources	Power, especially military
Central dynamics	Conflict; zero-sum calculations
Anarchy	Fundamental structural condition generating fear, uncertainty, and conflict
Diversity	States have different levels of power and competing interests
Complexity	Generated from stratification of power and competing self-interests of states

Yet realism is not the only theoretical approach to consider. Let's now take up its primary competitor.

3-3 THE LIBERAL PERSPECTIVE ON WORLD POLITICS

>> **3-3** Explain the foundations of the liberal approach in terms of its conceptions of (a) the nature of the international system, (b) its relevant actors, (c) important resources, and (d) central dynamics.

Like realism, **liberalism** has a lengthy intellectual history, from thinkers such as Hugo Grotius, Baron de

distribution of power: a characteristic of the international system emphasized by realists based on the number of great or major powers and how power is distributed among them in a given period of time.

unipolar: a distribution of power in the international system in which there is one great power.

bipolar: a distribution of power in the international system in which there are two great powers.

multipolar: a distribution of power in the international system in which there are more than two great powers.

tripolar: a distribution of power in the international system in which there are three great powers.

balance-of-power politics: patterns of shifting alliances, force, and counterforce among states as they seek power, counter the efforts of rivals, and confront security threats.

liberalism: a major theoretical approach to international relations emphasizing the role of individuals, norms, and institutions to explain patterns of cooperation and conflict in world politics.

Montesquieu, and Immanuel Kant to the present day. To be sure, the term *liberal* means different things in different contexts, but in international relations theory, it is used quite differently than in domestic politics, so it is important not to confuse the meanings. In contrast to realism, liberalism rests on a much more optimistic view of human nature and progress. Rather than the Hobbesian view of a violent state of nature, liberal theorists are more likely to embrace John Locke's view. For Locke, the state of nature (i.e., the world without central government) depicted an uncertain and often insecure world in which conflict was possible but in which reason and reciprocity often led to cooperation, albeit cautious cooperation. As E. H. Carr described it in *The Twenty Years' Crisis*, liberalism builds on the conception of mutual interests among states that can suffer from suspicion, misunderstanding, or ineffective institutions but that can be overcome by reason, education, communication, institutions, and law.

Just as Thucydides illustrates realist thinking, Immanuel Kant provides a good depiction of liberal thinking. According to Kant in *Perpetual Peace*, states could overcome conflict and establish lasting cooperative relationships by embracing a series of norms to guide behavior. Most important, the combination of "republican" or democratic government in states, international institutions to help coordinate and guide them, and a cosmopolitan law ensuring "hospitality" and commercial relations among the states and their citizens would overcome the threat of war and establish the "state of peace" (Doyle 1986; Russett and Oneal 2001).

As Kant's prescriptions suggest, liberal theory takes a more complicated approach to world politics that directs attention to more concerns than does realism. In fact, many liberals object that realism is not very "realistic" because it oversimplifies world politics too severely and overlooks key factors and broad patterns of behavior. Some liberal theorists point out that war is, in fact, a relatively rare occurrence when one considers the number of states, their many interactions, and the potential conflicts among them. Liberal theorists also argue that *cooperation is much more common* than realism suggests. Although early liberalism was heavily committed to prescriptions for peace, more recent liberal theory has emphasized explanations for the patterns of cooperation and conflict in world politics. To do so, liberal theory relaxes each of the central assumptions of realism and offers a less parsimonious set of explanations. However, liberal theory tends also to be more fragmented because it directs our attention to many more factors in world politics than does realism (see the box "Spotlight On: Variants of Liberalism in World Politics"). To better understand this, let's consider the four elements

A monument to German philosopher Immanuel Kant

What leads liberal theorists like Kant to believe in the possibility of "perpetual peace"?

Smith/ullstein bild via Getty Images

of our comparative framework where liberalism is concerned.

3-3a Liberalism and the Nature of the International System

Most liberal theorists accept that the international system is basically anarchic and that this structural characteristic has important consequences for international relations. However, they typically object to the realists' emphasis and definition. To liberal theorists, it makes more sense to discuss the *formal* anarchy of the system, acknowledging the absence of a formal, authoritative, central government in world politics. However, unlike realists, liberal theorists usually point to one or more of several additional features of the international system that also play important roles in world politics and reduce the consequences of formal anarchy.

Variants of Liberalism in World Politics

Like realism, as a theoretical approach, liberalism has a number of flavors. Because liberal theorists see a more complex international system and a broader variety of actors who matter in world politics, they also point to a variety of moving parts that drive the patterns of behavior—cooperation and conflict—in which states and non-state actors engage. Let's consider four variants:

- *Political liberalism.* This variant stresses the importance of regime type, especially democracy, on relations between states. A good representation is the democratic peace theory, which attributes peaceful relations between democracies to the democratic characteristics of the governments and societies. Advocates point to the absence of war between democracies over time and often stress the fact that countries that have fought with each other in the past have stopped doing so once they shared democratic regime types.

- *Economic/commercial liberalism.* This variant stresses the importance of trade and economic exchange to relations between states. This tradition goes back a long way, to Adam Smith in the 18th century, as well as to Norman Angell in the early 20th century, who argued (ironically, just before the outbreak of World War I) that trade had grown so important to European countries that war was unthinkable. More recently, scholars such as Erik Gartzke have advanced a capitalist peace argument. US presidents such as Bill Clinton and George W. Bush have reflected this variant of liberalism when advocating for extending and deepening trade with China to help maintain peaceful relations between the two countries.

- *Institutional liberalism.* This variant stresses the importance of international institutions and organizations such as the United Nations for cooperative relations between states and other actors in world politics. Advocates of this variant emphasize the role of institutions in promoting communication, building norms, and facilitating cooperation and predictability in world politics. Scholars such as Bruce Russett and John Oneal have argued that more significant institutional linkages between countries serve as a good predictor of peaceful relations. A good example is the role of international financial institutions such as the International Monetary Fund and the World Trade Organization in promoting cooperation and coordination on economic policy to help avoid the escalation of economic conflict into violence between states, as occurred during the 1920s and 1930s when such institutions did not exist. The development and role of the European Union in integrating the conflict-ridden states of Europe into a peaceful community is often pointed to as a good example as well.

- *Societal/ideational liberalism.* This variant of liberal theory stresses the role of shared identity, culture, norms, and societal connections in relations between societies. For example, many observers interpret the EU as an international organization created on the basis of post–World War II cooperation that was forced upon Europeans by the United States in return for Marshall Plan aid. Yet the degree of cooperation that now marks this union of states willing to cede some of their sovereignty to the larger entity seems unlikely had there not already been some shared bonds based on similar religious, cultural, and linguistic ties. ●

First, liberal theorists point to the presence of **international norms** and mutual interests among states that mitigate the effects of anarchy. As Hedley Bull stressed in *The Anarchical Society*, these shared norms and common interests create opportunities and expectations for cooperation and understanding. They also condition and temper the self-help impulses that realists ascribe to the anarchic structure. Thus, states may have the right to meet their energy needs by developing nuclear power, but a relatively sophisticated set of norms exists—called the nonproliferation regime—regarding how states should do so and how they should allay the fears of others as they develop nuclear power resources. Most states observe those norms; when states violate them, virtually the entire international system reacts negatively toward their actions—just ask Iran or North Korea.

Second, liberal theorists point to interdependence among states as an important characteristic. As Robert Keohane and Joseph Nye (2011) describe in *Power and Interdependence*, states are connected by mutual dependencies to one degree or another, so that no state is truly self-sufficient or able to go it

international norms: unwritten rules or expectations of acceptable behavior.

alone. The deeper these connections are—in terms of economic interactions like trade and investment, political connections, and societal and cultural linkages—the more consequences there are for state behavior and interactions. According to liberal theorists, more interdependent states are less likely to engage in violent conflict, more likely to collaborate to resolve problems, and more likely to behave as partners because they have a greater stake in getting along with others. States that are less connected with others—like North Korea or Myanmar—have less to lose if they challenge norms of cooperation; there is less stopping them from becoming violent. Hence, interdependence reduces the effects of the anarchic structure of world politics.

Third, liberal theorists point to **institutions** as important characteristics—as well as players (see the next section, on relevant actors)—of the international system. Although liberal theorists agree that international institutions are constrained and incomplete, they typically argue that such institutions still matter and thus place greater emphasis on them than realists. According to liberal theorists, international institutions dampen and moderate the effects of anarchy by providing arenas for cooperation and communication, norm building, coordination, and problem solving. Although few liberal theorists would characterize international institutions as more powerful, more authoritative, or more important than the governments of states (especially the most powerful and influential ones), they typically see institutions as playing a more significant and independent role in world politics than do realist theorists and seek to incorporate the influence of these institutions into explanations of world politics.

In Chapter 6, for example, we discuss collective security, which has its foundations in liberal theory as an institutional mechanism for states to manage and prevent conflicts. As we discuss in detail in that chapter, the basis of collective security is that states form an organization like the League of Nations or the United Nations and commit themselves to joining together to respond to any attack by one member on any other member. This approach is a method for managing power and responding to threat by pooling resources to bring a preponderance of power to bear on an aggressor. As such, it places great emphasis on the role that the collective security organization can play in shaping the behavior of states and reducing the effects of formal anarchy by promoting communication and cooperation and offering something other than stark self-help scenarios to states.

....

institutions: structures, patterns, and mechanisms for establishing norms, rules, order, and cooperation in world politics.

As a consequence of this general liberal view of the international system, which adds a number of potentially important characteristics to the formal anarchy emphasized by realists, liberal theorists see more opportunities for cooperation and peace in world politics. In particular, system-level dynamics such as the security dilemma tend to be viewed more as trust and communication problems than as fundamental and unalterable consequences of anarchy. For liberal theorists, norms, interdependence, and institutions can all reduce, or even eliminate, security dilemmas.

3-3b Liberalism and the Relevant Actors in International Relations

Liberal theorists also depart from their realist counterparts on the question of which players are important. As Keohane and Nye suggested, liberals relax the two main assumptions of realist theorists when it comes to players. First, many liberal theorists relax the assumption of states as unitary and undifferentiated actors. Instead, liberal theorists often see the importance of individuals, governmental institutions and agencies, and societal forces in shaping state behavior and interactions. Liberal theorists are far more likely to study the effects on world politics of personality and decision-making factors and processes, different types of regimes and governments, cultural variations, interest groups and corporations, and other subnational players and factors.

Second, liberal theorists tend to relax the assumption of the state as the only important actor as well. Non-state actors, such as those reviewed in Chapter 2—international organizations (IOs) such as the United Nations and the World Trade Organization; nongovernmental organizations (NGOs) such as Amnesty International, Greenpeace, and the International Red Cross; multinational or transnational corporations (MNCs/TNCs) such as Nike, Toyota, IBM, and Siemens; and transnational advocacy networks (TANs) such as the International Red Cross and Red Crescent Movement, the Refugee Research Network, the Islamic State, or al-Qaeda—are also considered significant. Many liberal theorists argue that such players are potentially important actors on a wide range of issues and frequently influence states and affect behavior and outcomes in ways that go far beyond the realist treatment of them as secondary, derivative, and mostly unimportant players. For liberal theorists, leaving these non-state actors out of explanations frequently produces incomplete or misleading conclusions. The question for liberal theorists is when and how do these players play important roles? Hence, for liberal theorists, a much greater concern for the diversity of the actors in world politics both complicates

Hard power

What conception of power does this image suggest?

iStock.com/guvendemir

Soft power

What kind of power does this image suggest?

Mustafa Kamaci/Anadolu Agency/Getty Images

and enriches explanations of the patterns of world politics.

3-3c Liberalism and the Important Resources in International Relations

Liberal theorists are also concerned with power as a critical resource in world politics. However, liberal theorists depart from realists on the nature and characteristics of power and influence. At least three key differences have great importance in liberal explanations of world politics.

First, the liberal lens stresses the *multidimensional* nature of power. Much more than realists, who acknowledge the great range of power resources but stress military power as the essential and central component, liberal theorists recognize the importance of military power but argue that there are many sources of power and influence in world politics. Military might is one, and it is important in many situations. However, other sources and types of power can also be critical, and because many of the players in world politics do not possess military power at all (e.g., NGOs, IOs, MNCs/TNCs) but still exert influence, the sources of their power are also important. Even some states have greater influence than their military power would suggest. For example, liberal theorist Richard Rosecrance has stressed the rising importance of "trading states" (e.g., Germany, Japan) and "virtual states" (e.g., Japan, South Korea, Singapore) since the mid-1980s, whose power and influence is important but fundamentally unrelated to territory and military might. Thus, for liberal theorists, economic resources, natural resources, human resources (such as skills and education), and ideas can all be important elements of power in their own right, and not merely as contributors to a state's military capabilities.

Reflecting this liberal emphasis on the multidimensional nature of power, Joseph Nye (2005) has differentiated between **hard power** and **soft power** in world politics. Where hard power includes the realist conceptions of "the ability to get what you want" through coercive means such as military force, soft power involves "the ability to get what you want through attraction rather than coercion." It depends more on ideas, appeal, cooperative relations with allies, and productive connections between countries. In particular, image and credibility, reputation, and the appeal of ideas enable a state or other actor to exercise power over preferences, not just power over actions. Effective soft power results in "the ability to get another to want what you want." According to Nye, military power (hard), economic power (hard and soft), and ideas/reputation (soft power) are all important.

Building on the multidimensional nature of power, liberal theorists tend to reject the realist emphasis on its hierarchical nature as well. Instead, the liberal lens tends to view power as *situation specific* or *context dependent*. No single power resource is paramount in every situation. Instead, as Keohane and Nye (2011) argue in *Power and Interdependence*, there are multiple hierarchies of power determined by the issue at hand and other contextual factors. Having the world's largest and most powerful military may have been the most significant source of power in the conflict between the United States and Saddam Hussein's Iraq in 2003. It may not be the only or even the most important factor in relations between China and the United States or in countering the threat of transnational terrorism. It may be

hard power: power based on coercive means, such as military force.

soft power: power based on attraction and persuasion rather than coercion.

completely irrelevant to the threat of a pandemic like COVID-19, global climate change, or trade disputes between countries. Similarly, the economic power and influence of Germany or China may be central to shaping global economic relations or global climate change but largely unrelated to confronting pirates in the Gulf of Aden.

Even military power itself can be seen as context dependent. How else can one explain the failures of the United States in Vietnam and the Soviet Union in Afghanistan, both situations in which the world's superpowers confronted substantially weaker, poor, developing countries but were unable to translate their clear advantages in military power into success? Similarly, despite more than a decade of effort and all the military and economic resources deployed and expended by the US over that time, violence and rebellion continued in Iraq, even escalating after then as insurgents challenged the US-backed regime and seized territory. Or as liberal theorists would argue, military power is largely irrelevant to resolve issues of economic competition and trade relations between the United States and China, to prevent certain countries from unsustainable whaling practices, to convince Brazil to protect its rain forest from further destruction, or to respond effectively to the threat of a global pandemic. Hence, liberal theorists are much more skeptical about the fungibility of power, preferring to treat issue areas separately.

3-3d Liberalism and the Central Dynamics of International Relations

From these foundations, the general orientation of liberal theorists emerges: In a formally anarchic world in which states and other actors share (a) some common interests and goals, (b) varying levels of interdependence, and (c) connections through institutions and other channels, conflict is possible, but it is not the norm. Some situations and issues promote cooperation and reduce the likelihood of conflict, especially violent conflict. States are important actors, but their behavior and interactions are shaped by the individuals, groups, organizations, and institutions that make up their country and government and by non-state actors in the international system. Power is multifaceted and wielded in a variety of ways. Unlike realists, who tend to see the dynamics of world politics as the unfolding of similar behavior in cycles, liberals see the dynamics of world politics more in terms of progress and change that unfolds over time in a more linear fashion.

A relatively recent example that illustrates this point is the debate over the future of Europe and

NATO after the end of the Cold War in 1989. Realists such as John Mearsheimer predicted that the end of the Cold War would trigger a return of conflict and competition in Europe and the likely end of the NATO alliance, because the common threat posed by the Soviet Union was the reason for the cooperation (both between countries such as France and Germany and between European states and the United States in general). With the disappearance of that common threat, Mearsheimer expected the return of former patterns of conflict as the enduring forces of world politics asserted themselves. As Mearsheimer (2001) colorfully put it, "We will soon miss the Cold War."

By contrast, liberal theorists such as Stanley Hoffman, Robert Keohane, Bruce Russett, and Thomas Risse countered that many things have changed since World War II. The spread of democracy, the development of norms against war among European countries, influential and cooperative institutions such as the EU, and shared interests and benefits from cooperative practices have all fundamentally changed relations among European states such as France and Germany and relations between Europe and the United States as well. With such changing dynamics and progress, these theorists argued, a return to violent conflict is highly improbable. About three decades later, which perspective has been more accurate? Are shifts in power and interests generating tensions among NATO allies and signaling its decline? Or do the institutions, interdependence, and norms connecting NATO allies provide the glue that preserves their cooperation?

For liberal theorists, when conflict occurs, it can typically be traced to factors such as misunderstanding, miscommunication, cultural differences, bad regimes, and other such causes. Leaders, decisions, processes, regimes, and institutions shape the general patterns of world politics. So liberal theorists are especially interested in explaining the patterns of cooperation that characterize much of world politics, while also accounting for the exceptions of violent conflict.

However, and in large part as a consequence of the liberal conception of power (i.e., its multidimensionality and situation-specific nature) and the international system, liberal theorists tend to see world politics as a **positive-sum** game rather than a zero-sum game. Because of mutual interests and goals, the possibilities of trade-offs across issue areas, and the multidimensional nature of power and influence, liberal theorists see many more possibilities for win-win scenarios and often argue that focusing on absolute gains rather than relative gains is the relevant perspective for most actors most of the time. The 2015 Iran nuclear deal provides an example of a seemingly win-win scenario. Major powers like the US, the UK,

positive-sum: a condition in which all parties to an issue can benefit or "win."

France, Russia, China, and Germany were concerned with the prospect of Iran's nuclear energy program being used clandestinely to produce a nuclear weapon. Iran's unwillingness to allow international inspections of its nuclear facilities fed those concerns. For its part, Iran wanted to have a nuclear program and wanted access to significant financial assets frozen in foreign bank accounts. A deal was struck. The other countries (known as the P5+1) secured Iran's agreement to delay for some years its ability to produce a nuclear weapon (by sending 98% of its enriched nuclear fuel abroad, getting rid of about two thirds of its centrifuges used to enrich nuclear fuel, and allowing limited international inspections, along with other concessions). In exchange, Iran received international recognition of its right to have a peaceful nuclear program and regained access to about $100 billion of its own money in frozen accounts. Just three years later, the US walked away from the deal. From a liberal perspective, can you explain why a superpower like the US would abandon a cooperative treaty like this?

Table 3-4 summarizes the key features of liberalism.

3-4 THE CONSTRUCTIVIST PERSPECTIVE ON WORLD POLITICS

>> 3-4 **Explain the foundations of the constructivist approach in terms of its conception of (a) the nature of the international system, (b) its relevant actors, (c) important resources, and (d) central dynamics.**

Constructivist theories of international relations find their foundations in the field of sociology and thinkers such as Émile Durkheim and Max Weber. Nicholas Onuf may have been the first international relations scholar to use the term *constructivism*, arguing that we live in "a world of our making," but Alexander Wendt is probably best known for this approach, which sees "facts" as "socially constructed." In other words, ideas and facts mean what we as members of a social group agree they mean. This perspective challenges the basic assumptions of both realism and liberalism by asking fundamental questions about such concepts as anarchy or the nature and meaning of power and by linking ideas and shared understanding of them to actions and relationships in world politics. For example, is the international arena like the violence portrayed in *Westworld* or *The Walking Dead*, the school playground without teachers, or a large family just trying to get along?

TABLE 3-4

Summary of Liberalism and World Politics

KEY FEATURES	LIBERAL INTERPRETATION
Nature of the international system	Formal anarchy, with interdependence, shared norms, and international institutions linking the players
Relevant actors	States and non-state actors (e.g., international institutions, multinational or transnational corporations, international nongovernmental organizations, transnational advocacy networks)
Important resources	Multidimensional and situation-specific power; hard and soft power
Central dynamics	Cooperation, competition, and conflict; positive-sum calculations
Anarchy	Meaningful characteristic of the international system, generating security dilemmas and complicating cooperation and coordination
Diversity	State and non-state actors, with different perspectives, values, institutions, and preferences struggle to cooperate and communicate
Complexity	Webs of connections between states and societies create both opportunity and challenges for world politics

Both realism and liberalism make several assertions about the international arena. They both claim, for example, that anarchy—the absence of central government—is the prevailing condition in the world. Realism asserts that states are the primary actors. Liberalism also emphasizes states, but it expands the list of actors to include non-state actors. What do these assumptions mean? Does the anarchy that defines the international system necessarily mean a violent, fearful environment like Hobbes described or an environment more like a troop of chimpanzees where there is real structure, cooperation, and altruism? In contrast to realism and liberalism, constructivism directs our attention to the meanings behind ideas and actions and the ways in which interactions shape expectations and behavior.

....

constructivism: a major theoretical approach to international relations emphasizing the importance of ideas, collective identities, and the social construction of reality.

3-4a Constructivism and the Nature of the International System

As we have said, anarchy does not mean chaos; it simply means the absence of central government. Even in anarchy, we see both order and structure in world politics, and the existence of institutions such as the United Nations, the World Trade Organization, and others makes that clear. But what about the world Hobbes described? Think about the way Hollywood movies depict the American West during US territorial expansion. Almost universally, everyone either carries a gun or lives in fear of subjugation by those with guns. The Old West is often depicted as a true Hobbesian world in which everyone lives in fear of others and life is "nasty, brutish, and short," at least until the hero saves everyone by killing the villain. The moral is quite simply that one must provide for one's own security (i.e., self-help). This depiction is generally how realists see the world. States must defend themselves or be subjugated by more powerful states. Certainly, during the era of colonial expansion, imperial wars, and gunboat diplomacy, this description appeared accurate. Powerful countries like the United Kingdom took over weaker countries like India, and the powerful countries fought with one another (e.g., the UK and France). Is this how the world works today?

According to prevailing international norms, outright military conquest is no longer acceptable, at least for the purposes of owning another country. That is why Russia's annexation of Crimea in 2014 was so contentious: The Crimeans voted to join Russia while disguised Russian troops stood by. (Was that a "free and fair" election?) Further, Russian troops have been found in the eastern Donbass region of Ukraine, which remains beyond the control of the government in Kiev. By contrast, the 2001 US invasion of Afghanistan (authorized by the UN for collective security) and the 2003 US invasion of Iraq were officially aimed at removing an international threat. In neither case was the US goal to retain control of the territory. Neither was colonized the way it might have been before the middle of the 20th century.

So what has changed? The international system is still formally anarchic. There is no world government with a true enforcement mechanism, and the UN does not have any authority that is not first granted to it by individual member states. Yet what is considered acceptable behavior by states is different now than it was just 60 years ago. Instead of the Wild West, the international system seems to be more like a somewhat unruly family. Some members of the family get along very well (e.g., the United States and Canada),

others misbehave (e.g., North Korea, Iran), but generally most of the family members cooperate with each other at least to some degree. States do not, as suggested by realism, constantly engage in conflict or preparation for conflict. In fact, as several observers have argued, as a practice, large-scale war is a social institution that has become steadily less acceptable and more abhorrent to more and more states as societal values have changed and states have learned war's true costs over time (see Mueller 1989).

This change in perspective and behavior is at the heart of what constructivists emphasize in their explanations of the patterns of world politics. Thus, rather than treat anarchy as a given condition, political scientist Alexander Wendt (1992) provided the constructivist view, arguing that "anarchy is what states make of it" (p. 395). That is, anarchy is socially constructed, not determined by the environment. **Social construction** simply means that a concept is created by the ideas and interactions within a society. For example, fashion is a social construction. The clothes worn in the 1970s were considered very good-looking then, but jokes were made about them in the 1980s (and today, for that matter). There is nothing about the clothes that are or are not inherently fashionable. Instead, society's opinion changed and redefined what was fashionable, and, as important, those ideas led to behavior and actions (what clothes are made and sold and what people wear). Something that is not a social construction is rain. The environment, specifically the level of moisture in the sky, determines whether or not it will rain. Society's opinion has no influence over the rain. Realists and liberals see anarchy like rain—something that is determined by the environment. Social constructivists like Wendt see anarchy like fashion—something that the actions and opinions of a society create. Of course, like realism and liberalism, constructivism is a complex approach with many varieties (see the box "Spotlight On: Variants of Constructivism"), but constructivists generally share a commitment to examining how social practices and identities are "constructed" by human agency (Fearon and Wendt 2005).

According to Wendt, we can identify three ideal types of anarchy, each with very different implications for action:

- In *Hobbesian anarchy*, the system is much like realists depict, where states are adversaries and conflict is a normal part of their competition for power and survival.

- In *Lockean anarchy*, the system is more like liberals describe it, with states viewing each other as rivals but in which cooperation, competition, and conflict occur.

- In *Kantian anarchy*, states see each other as friends and no longer fear each other or

social construction: creation of a concept by the interactions and ideas within a society.

Variants of Constructivism

Just as realism and liberalism come in different varieties, many scholars identify different variants of constructivism as well. International relations scholars James Fearon and Alexander Wendt (2005) divide constructivist approaches into three categories:

- *Positivist constructivism.* Knowledge claims about social life can be made, and causal explanations are appropriate in social inquiry. In other words, we can observe and explain accurately international relations.

- *Interpretivist constructivism.* Knowledge claims about social life can be made, but causal explanations are *not* appropriate in social inquiry. In this case, our observations can

be accurate, but we are unable to explain the causes of those observations accurately because our explanation is only one of a multitude of perspectives.

- *Postmodern constructivism.* Knowledge claims about social life are simply part of discursive power (see Section 3-4c), and causal explanations are *not* appropriate in social inquiry. This variant suggests that our own perspective affects both what we observe and how we explain it; thus, neither claims about facts nor causes are valid. Instead, only descriptions of power dynamics can be argued. ●

Source: Fearon and Wendt (2005).

consider using force against each other. Instead, they find peaceful ways to settle their disputes and support each against other threats. Thus, "anarchy" itself is what states make of it, and it does not determine state behavior.

If a central characteristic like anarchy is something that is constructed by the actions and opinions of states and non-state actors in the international system, then the meaning and characteristics of anarchy can change over time. During the colonial era, it was acceptable to conquer small states and thus make war for profit. In the current, postcolonial era, war for profit is not considered acceptable. This change is the result of a different social construction of what anarchy means. Just as fashions have changed over the years, so have the rules that states generally follow. Thus, the patterns of behavior that stem from "anarchy" in world politics will evolve and change and will be different for different groups. For example, anarchy means something very different for the states of the European Union or the NATO alliance than it does for the states of Africa, the Middle East, or South Asia. In the first set of groups, anarchy does not mean self-help, security dilemmas, and competition at all, but in the other groups, it often does.

3-4b Constructivism and the Relevant Actors in International Relations

Like liberalism, the constructivist perspective sees a more complicated array of players in world politics.

Of course, constructivists pay attention to the state as a major player—some, like Wendt, treat world politics as an essentially state-centric system. But constructivists tend to see states more like liberals than realists: as complicated, multifaceted entities rather than as unitary, rational actors. Moreover, because constructivists emphasize the role of norms and ideas, they tend to stress the importance of people, groups, and cultural factors within states as very important. These are where the ideas come from and are held.

Like liberals, constructivists see significance in a variety of non-state actors and organizations, including international institutions, nongovernmental organizations, and transnational advocacy networks. Moreover, constructivists pay close attention to cultural groups in world politics—nations or ethnic groups and their experiences, ideas, and values. Finally, constructivists emphasize the importance of the identities and interests of the players as central to understanding their behavior. As we have just described, though, these aspects of the relevant actors are also socially constructed. Hence, what "Russia" means to the United States is shaped by US culture and experience but also by the patterns of interactions and shared experiences between the two countries. "Russia" meant something particular during the Cold War between the two countries (rival, enemy), something else in the post–Cold War environment (vanquished? partner?), and something else again (back to rival? enemy?) in the wake of the aggressive actions taken against neighboring states such as Georgia (2008) and Ukraine (2014) and interference in the elections of the United States and other

Russia and Its Neighbors

In recent years, Russia has increased its efforts to exert influence in its geographic neighborhood. For example, in 2008, Russia used military force against its neighbor Georgia to support breakaway provinces of South Ossetia and Abkhazia, which it has occupied since. In 2014, Russia used force and other methods to accomplish the annexation of Crimea, part of Ukraine, and to support the rebellion of Russian-speaking groups in eastern Ukraine. Russia has also engaged in political interference in many other countries around its perimeter over the past decade or so, trying to manipulate elections and support pro-Russian parties and leaders. Finally, Russia has interfered in the democratic processes of the US, countries in Europe, and elsewhere to divide them, cause civil strife, promote more Russia-friendly leaders, and weaken the core supporters of the liberal international order, among other things.

In January 2015, Russia led some of its partner states of the former Soviet Union, Belarus and Kazakhstan, to establish the Eurasian Economic Union, building on and extending existing trade agreements to further integrate the countries of the region along a variety of dimensions, including labor, investment, and energy. Kyrgyzstan and Armenia also joined, and Moldova became an official observer in 2017. The Eurasian Economic Union is open to other states around Russia's perimeter as well, most of whom are being actively courted by Russian President Vladimir Putin.

Motivated by President Putin's vision of a trade and political bloc capable of challenging the United States, China, and the European Union, the Eurasian Economic Union is characterized by some observers as "a new geopolitical force capable of standing up to Russia's competitors on the world stage" (Neyfakh 2014). According to Putin (then prime minister) in 2011, when the foreign policy initiative was first announced, "We suggest a powerful supranational association capable of becoming one of the poles in the modern world" (Putin 2011). The implications of this foreign policy

Russia's Prime Minister Vladimir Putin rides a horse in southern Siberia's Tuva region on August 3, 2009

REUTERS/RIA Novosti/Pool/Alexei Druzhinin

initiative were not lost on Western leaders. Then US Secretary of State Hillary Clinton characterized it as the possible "re-sovietization" of the region in December 2012. Western concerns increased after the Russian annexation of Crimea from Ukraine in 2014 and other aggressive actions in the years since.

In light of the theoretical perspectives discussed in this chapter, how should Russia's actions in its neighborhood and, in particular, the formation of the Eurasian Economic Union be interpreted and explained?

1. Why would Vladimir Putin seek to establish a new Eurasian Economic Union?

2. How would realists, liberals, and constructivists explain the initiative and its likely consequences?

3. What foreign policy responses from the United States, China, and the states of the EU are most likely, according to these three theoretical perspectives? ●

European allies in recent years. (See the box "Foreign Policy in Perspective: Russia and Its Neighbors" for more on Russia's actions.)

For example, constructivist scholars such as Michael Barnett and Martha Finnemore stress the importance of state identities and interests and the way the norms of the international society shape them. In particular, Finnemore argues that these norms are shaped, supported, and spread by international organizations that help guide states toward particular behavior and understandings of their interests. Constructivist scholars like Peter Katzenstein emphasize how domestic culture and groups within states shape their identities and interests and the norms and behavior they embrace. Finally, constructivist scholars such as Margaret Keck and Kathryn Sikkink point to the role of transnational actors in shaping state interests about a variety of things, often serving as

A Titan II missile in its silo

Does what this missile represents depend on which country owns it?

Courtesy of the US Department of Defense

"norm entrepreneurs" who advance particular values and expectations and influence state behavior (see our discussion of transnational advocacy networks in Chapter 13).

3-4c Constructivism and the Important Resources in International Relations

Like liberal theorists, constructivists take a more complex and multidimensional view of power. Constructivists accept some of the material or tangible aspects of power that both realists and liberals stress, but they push further than both of those perspectives to stress the **ideational** aspects of power and influence. In effect, they push the conception of soft power even further than liberals. In this conception, ideas, norms, identities—ways of thinking about yourself and others—and statements are an important part of what constitutes power and influence. Constructivists call this *discursive power* and stress that the meaning of things is an important element of power as well as the empirical nature of things. According to constructivists, discursive power works by producing and reproducing shared meanings, which shape how people understand the material world, their own and others' identities, and their relations with others. Thus, the nature of power and the relevant resources of power are also understood through social construction. To constructivists, the basis of power is not in the material power of states or institutions but rather in the ideas that people believe in and the shared understandings they develop. It is not that the material world and tangible resources of power do not matter, but their meaning depends on shared ideas, norms, and interpretations.

Consider nuclear missiles, for example. To a realist, these missiles are a tangible example of the most important aspect of power—military strength. To a liberal, the missiles may represent power and influence, but they are not likely to be relevant in the relations between the United States and Canada or between the US and Japan. To a constructivist, social construction does not mean there is a question about whether or not there are missiles. Instead, the meaning of the missiles depends on the players' identity, interactions, and interests. So such missiles, when possessed and deployed by the United Kingdom, are not a threat to the United States and are not even particularly relevant to the relationship between the US and the UK. However, these same missiles, when deployed by Iran, North Korea, and even Russia or China, take on an entirely different meaning for the power and security of countries such as the US, South Korea, and Japan, and they result in a very different pattern of actions and interactions.

Indeed, most Americans probably think that it's okay that the United States, the United Kingdom, and France have nuclear weapons. During the Cold

....

ideational: emphasizing the centrality of ideas and norms in shaping behavior and interactions.

War, nuclear weapons in the hands of the British and French were not viewed in anything like the same way as those controlled by Soviet leaders; instead, they were interpreted as contributing to American power. Now, since the end of the Cold War, some people may also be comfortable with Russia and China having such weapons. Further, most people outside of North Korea probably think it's not okay that North Korea has a nuclear weapon. What about the nuclear arsenals of India, Pakistan, and Israel?

If you live in Iran or another predominately Muslim state in the Middle East, you probably think it's really bad that the Israelis have nuclear weapons. If you are Israeli, you probably think it is not only a good thing but also necessary for your survival and that the real negative scenario would be the possession of nuclear weapons by neighboring states. Why else would the Israelis conduct military strikes on suspected nuclear program sites in countries such as Iraq (1981) and Syria (2007 and 2017)? On the surface, one can understand why these two different views can exist. In effect, Syria and Israel are historically enemies, and each side would see the other as threatening. Iran and Israel similarly view each other with great suspicion and hostility. That is exactly the point of constructivism. Security is defined or constructed by each country. Thus, although Iran may see itself as a good state that has a bellicose and nuclear-armed neighbor, Israel probably sees itself as a good state whose neighbors—although militarily weaker—threaten its survival and can't be allowed to possess such weapons.

3-4d Constructivism and the Central Dynamics of International Relations

Because a central idea behind constructivism is that all social relationships are constructed by people and therefore are subject to change, it follows that the central dynamics of world politics are subject to great variation over time and among different pairs or groups of states. The historically intense hatred between the Protestants and Catholics in Northern Ireland provides a useful example. Northern Ireland has been a part of the United Kingdom since 1921, and in 1971, civil violence broke out between the Protestant-controlled government and the Catholic Irish Republican Army (IRA). For decades, the violence raged between these two groups, and the division between Protestants and Catholics widened. Like all conflicts, the causes are complex and multiple. Economic disparities between the two groups and a lack of political representation by the Catholics contributed to the divisiveness. However, it is also important to realize that the hatred between the two groups was fostered by a social construction. There were no visible differences between these two groups. They spoke the same language. They lived in the same country. Within the Irish Catholic community, however, there was the belief—created by the Irish Catholic community—that the Protestants were not really Irish and should not be governing Northern Ireland; further, they thought Northern Ireland should be reunited with the Republic of Ireland. Conversely, the Irish Protestants believed that the Catholics were

Paramilitary members of the Protestant "Ulster Defense Association" barricade a street

If the title didn't tell you who the combatants were, would you know if they were Catholic or Protestant?

David Lomax/Keystone/Hulton Archive/Getty Images

trying to drive them from their homes and would stop at nothing to rid Northern Ireland of their presence. To be sure, there was some truth to both of these beliefs—the IRA and the Northern Ireland government (and British armed forces) were fighting. However, if there had been a reason for the hatred beyond their partially misinformed beliefs, such as the enslavement of one group by the other, then compromise would not be possible. In that case, the two sides would prefer to continue fighting until one side lost.

Instead, a peace process slowly began in 1994 and ended with an agreement that provided for a governing body based on **consociational democracy**—that is, guaranteed representation for both Protestants and Catholics. Although problems continue, there has been a shift in the social construction of the two sides. They are no longer bitter enemies but perhaps cordial opponents. The shift involved years of diplomatic debate but also a change in how the two communities perceived or socially constructed their views of each other.

You might ask if the peace in Northern Ireland is simply the result of the two sides getting tired of fighting. If that were the case, you might expect only a **negative peace**, the mere absence of fighting. Instead, there is real cooperation in Northern Ireland, suggesting that there is a **positive peace** between the two groups. Also, if groups that defined themselves as enemies simply grew tired of fighting, then how could we explain the continual fighting in the Middle East between the Israelis and their Arab neighbors? To end a conflict and build peace, the two sides must no longer define each other as enemies.

Another sad example that highlights the constructivist view of the central dynamics of world politics is Rwanda, home to two main ethnic groups: the Hutus and the Tutsis. The two groups date back approximately 2,000 years and were perceived by colonial powers to have slightly different physical features. Supposedly, Hutus were shorter, and Tutsis had a narrower nose. After a long history as a German colony, Rwanda came under Belgian control after World War I. In 1935, Belgium issued identity cards identifying each Rwandan as either Hutu or Tutsi—considered by the Belgians to be different races. After almost 2,000 years, however, lineage was difficult to determine (can you trace your relatives back that far?). So the Belgians based the identity of the two races on physical differences, and when that was not apparent, the number of cattle owned by the family would determine their race (families with more cattle were determined to be Tutsi; Chretien 2003).

Unfortunately, determining a person's ethnicity based on his or her economic status had fatal consequences. The 1935 identity cards artificially constructed two groups that competed for political

A pair of friends in Rwanda, one Hutu and the other Tutsi
These two people are friends, but a few years before this picture was taken, they were bitter enemies willing to murder each other with a machete. How can such "enemies" be friends?
AP Photo/Ben Curtis

and economic power and left the smaller group, the Tutsis, in control of the country. Over the years, the competition intensified to the point of open conflict and revolt. In 1994, the Hutu-controlled government and militias began murdering both Tutsis and politically moderate Hutus on a massive scale. In the end, the Rwandan genocide claimed the lives of approximately 800,000 people, many of them hacked to death by their neighbors using machetes.

The root of the genocide was the socially constructed race division put in place by the Belgians. To be sure, the genocide was preceded by a conflict that took years to develop and in which both sides played a part. For the Belgians' part, they did not anticipate such a horrendous outcome. However, the division was socially constructed, and it killed almost a million people. For a chilling representation of the Rwandan genocide, watch the film *Hotel Rwanda* (2004) or, alternatively, the documentary *The Ghosts of Rwanda* (2004). Both films will leave you horrified.

The relationship and interactions between the United States and Russia offer another example of the importance of changing social constructions and their effects on the central dynamics of world politics. Consider what happened in 2010, when 10 people were arrested by US authorities who suspected them of spying for Russia. During the worst days of the Cold War (say, in the 1950s or early 1960s), such a scandal would have provoked much attention and a

....

consociational democracy: a form of government that guarantees representation to the different ethnic or religious groups within the country.

negative peace: a lack of conflict between two countries or groups.

positive peace: a situation between two countries that is not simply a lack of conflict but rather a mutual affinity for each other.

serious confrontation. But in 2010, then Russian Prime Minister Vladimir Putin (a former career Soviet intelligence officer with the KGB) denounced the arrests as "unfounded" on the day they were announced in the press, but the Russians said and did nothing much beyond issuing that statement. Less than two weeks later, Russian and American airplanes met on the tarmac of a Vienna airport, where the 10 individuals arrested in the United States were swapped for four Russians previously imprisoned on charges of spying for the United States or the United Kingdom.

Why didn't these matters provoke a more serious confrontation? Perhaps the answer lies in changes in the relationship between the two countries after the end of the Cold War. In 2010, US President Barack Obama and Russian President Dmitry Medvedev communicated frequently and sought to find ways for their states to cooperate and put past rivalries behind them as best they could; we can say they created a new social construction of friendship and cooperation. Thus, "friends" might minimize their reactions to negative situations such as spy scandals, but "rivals," "enemies," or "opponents" will not. Neither Medvedev nor Obama was willing to let a minor espionage case sabotage an emerging positive relationship.

Now think about the more recent situation. Since 2010, Russia has engaged in aggressive actions against Ukraine, including annexation of Crimea and the use of military power to support rebellion in the eastern part of that country. Russia has also aggressively interfered in democratic processes in the US and other European countries. For example, the US concluded that Russia hacked into computer systems and engaged in information warfare designed to influence the 2016 presidential election. These interactions have raised the prospect that the "rival" or "enemy" construction of the relationship will return. How would a spy scandal like the one in 2010 be treated today?

Yet another good example of the power of social construction came in 1967. During the **Six-Day War** pitting Israel against Egypt, Jordan, and Syria, a US naval vessel was attacked. The USS *Liberty* was in international waters north of the Sinai Peninsula where Israeli and Egyptian forces were fighting when it was attacked by Israeli aircraft and torpedo boats. The ship was heavily damaged, 34 on board were killed, and 170 were injured. Had this involved an attack by the Soviet Union or one of its allies during this Cold War era, severe military reprisals would have resulted, perhaps even leading to World War III. Yet

The USS *Liberty* after Israeli patrol boats and aircraft attacked it, killing 34 US sailors

What if the Soviets had done this to a US ship during the Cold War?

Bill Ray/The LIFE Picture Collection via Getty Images

in this case, the Israelis said it was an honest mistake in wartime, President Lyndon Johnson did not question that explanation, and the Israelis ultimately paid $14.5 million in compensation to the families of the dead and injured and for damages to the ship itself.

It may have been an honest mistake on Israel's part, but it also may have been intentional. The *Liberty* was a spy ship operated by the US National Security Agency (NSA) and was engaged in eavesdropping on battlefield communications during the war. The Israelis may have simply wanted to prevent others from having access to that intelligence information. Had President Johnson not seen the Israelis as "friends," their explanation might not have been accepted, and the more sinister motive might have been attributed to them. In hindsight, it seems highly likely that the social construction of the US–Israeli relationship as one of "friends" rather than of "rivals," "competitors," or even "enemies" made a considerable difference in the US response.

....

Six-Day War: the 1967 war between Israel, Egypt, Jordan, and Syria. Israel won the war and took control of the occupied territories (the Gaza Strip, West Bank, and Golan Heights).

These examples show the power of the social construction of ideas as a way to explain the dynamics of world politics (see Table 3-5). Political realism would be unable to explain these episodes, due to its emphasis on states as unitary actors rationally pursuing their national interests defined largely in terms of military power. Liberalism recognizes that **substate actors** exist and can matter but would be unequipped to explain the intrastate violence in Northern Ireland or Rwanda or the lack of interstate violence between the United States and Israel. Social constructivism provides a different lens through which these real-world situations can be explained.

CONCLUSION: DUELING THEORIES?

Each of the three major approaches to understanding and explaining international relations simplifies international reality, although the approaches do so in different ways, highlighting different features and elements of the international system, its relevant actors and their resources, and the major patterns and dynamics that emerge (see Table 3-6). Recent events

TABLE 3-5

Summary of Constructivism and World Politics

KEY FEATURES	CONSTRUCTIVIST INTERPRETATION
Nature of the international system	Socially constructed, dynamic anarchy
Relevant actors	States, organizations, people, ideas
Important resources	Determined by social construction
Central dynamics	Conflict, cooperation, but changing patterns from state to state
Anarchy	Structure of the international system that is determined by ideas, interactions, and statements
Diversity	Different social definitions of the world and other actors
Complexity	Fashioned by the changing social constructions of the world

substate actors: groups within a state, such as political parties, insurgents, or ethnic groups.

TABLE 3-6

Comparing the Theories

FEATURE	REALISM	LIBERALISM	CONSTRUCTIVISM
Nature of the international system	Anarchic; self-help	Formal anarchy, with interdependence, shared norms, and international institutions	Socially constructed, dynamic anarchy
Relevant actors	States	States and non-state actors	States, organizations, people, ideas
Important resources	Power, especially military	Multidimensional and situation-specific power; hard and soft power	Determined by social construction
Central dynamics	Conflict; zero-sum calculations	Cooperation, competition, and conflict; positive-sum calculations	Conflict, cooperation, but changing patterns from state to state
Anarchy	Fundamental structural condition generating fear, uncertainty, and conflict	Meaningful characteristic of the international system, generating security dilemmas and complicating cooperation and coordination	Structure of the international system that is determined by ideas, interactions, and statements
Diversity	States have different levels of power and competing interests	State and non-state actors, with different perspectives, values, institutions, and preferences struggle to cooperate and communicate	Different social definitions of the world and other actors
Complexity	Generated from stratification of power and competing self-interests of states	Webs of connections between states and societies create both opportunity and challenges for world politics	Fashioned by the changing social constructions of the world

since the turn of the century appear to pit the three perspectives against each other once again. Realism, liberalism, and constructivism have been cast as contenders and as complementary explanations for different situations. Consider what you now know about theory in general and these three major theoretical approaches in particular: Is the current context an example of the consequences of **hegemony** (the dominance of one state), with rivals and challenges to the

....

hegemony: domination of the international system by one country.

dominant power (the United States) emerging? Or is it an example of the dynamics of liberalism, with zones of peace and zones of turmoil in the world? Could it be that the ideas, interests, and interactions that shape the behavior of states have developed to establish new norms and patterns of behavior? Or are elements of all three perspectives at work at the same time? At the end of the day, we must theorize to arrive at answers. But hold on: If you find these theoretical approaches to be a bit inadequate, there are others to consider, and they are the focus of the next chapter. ●

KEY CONCEPTS

3-1   Identify the nature and use of theory and describe the components of theory.

Theory involves a set of concepts, specifies their interrelationships, and, most important, explains the reasons for those relationships. A theory links these concepts, relationships, and explanations with hypotheses: "if . . . then . . ." statements about particular relationships and outcomes that should be observable in reality if the explanation is useful. Theory involves description, explanation, and prediction. It usually offers a basis for prescription as well.

3-2   Explain the foundations of the realist approach in terms of its conception of (a) the nature of the international system, (b) its relevant actors, (c) important resources, and (d) central dynamics.

For realists, anarchy—the absence of a central government to establish order and wield power and authority—establishes a fundamentally Hobbesian world in which sovereign states, the main players of world politics, must rely on themselves to protect their interests and accomplish their goals. In this self-help world, power—the ability to get what you want—is both a central instrument and a primary objective to ensure survival and security. Realists assume that all states want the same things, with the only significant difference among them being how much power and capability they have to act. Because power is unequally distributed, the international system is stratified, with different levels of resources, wealth, and power possessed by different states. Realists view power as relative and hierarchical, with military power the most essential for the ability to get what one wants in world politics. Because power is relative and ultimately based on military strength, states cannot ever really have "enough" or trust others to be satisfied in an environment where conflict is the norm. The distribution of power among countries affects how they act and the likelihood of conflict. Realists generally view international politics as zero-sum situations and consider conflict to be the normal dynamic in an anarchic system.

3-3   Explain the foundations of the liberal approach in terms of its conceptions of (a) the nature of the international system, (b) its relevant actors, (c) important resources, and (d) central dynamics.

Liberal theorists begin with the formal anarchy of the system, acknowledging the absence of formal, authoritative central government in world politics. But liberal theorists also recognize the importance of one or more additional features of the international system that reduce the impact of formal anarchy, such as international norms, mutual interests among states, interdependence, and institutions. Because these characteristics tie states together, liberal theorists see more opportunities for cooperation and peace. System-level dynamics such as the security dilemma tend to be viewed more as trust and communication problems that can be reduced by norms, interdependence, common identity, and institutions rather than as unalterable consequences of anarchy. Liberal theorists also view differences in states—in type of government and other features—as important for state behavior, and they see the importance of individuals, governmental institutions and agencies, non-state actors, and societal forces in shaping state behavior and interactions. The liberal lens stresses the multidimensional nature of power, recognizing the importance of military power but arguing that there are many sources of power and influence in world politics. Liberals differentiate between hard power and soft power and tend to reject the realist emphasis on the hierarchical nature of power. Instead, they tend to view power as situation specific or context dependent. In a formally anarchic world in which states and other actors share some common interests and goals and are interdependent and connected through institutions and other channels, cooperation, competition, and conflict are all possible. Conflict, however, is not the norm, and world politics is often a positive-sum game. Progress and change are both possible and likely.

3-4 Explain the foundations of the constructivist approach in terms of its conception of (a) the nature of the international system, (b) its relevant actors, (c) important resources, and (d) central dynamics.

States do not, as suggested by realism, constantly engage in conflict or preparation for conflict. Social construction simply means that a concept is created by the identities and interactions of societies. Anarchy is the absence of central government, but what it means for state behavior varies according to the players' ideas and shared experiences and interactions. For constructivists, states are important, but they consist of people with identity and values. Other actors are also important, including international institutions, nongovernmental organizations, and transnational advocacy networks. Moreover, constructivists pay close attention to cultural groups in world politics—nations or ethnic groups and their experiences, ideas, and values. To constructivists, the basis of power is not in the material power of states or institutions but rather in the ideas that people believe in and the shared understandings they develop. It is not that the material world and tangible resources of power do not matter, but their meaning depends on shared ideas, norms, and interpretations. Because a central idea behind constructivism is that all social relationships are constructed by people and therefore are subject to change, it follows that the central dynamics of world politics are subject to great variation over time and among different players in world politics.

KEY TERMS

democratic peace 51

empirical theory 53

normative theory 53

parsimony 55

realism 56

state of nature 57

stratification 57

unitary actor 59

power 59

relative gains 60

absolute gains 60

fungible 60

zero-sum 62

distribution of power 63

unipolar 63

bipolar 63

multipolar 63

tripolar 63

balance-of-power politics 63

liberalism 63

international norms 65

institutions 66

hard power 67

soft power 67

positive-sum 68

constructivism 69

social construction 70

ideational 73

consociational democracy 75

negative peace 75

positive peace 75

Six-Day War 76

substate actors 77

hegemony 78

REVIEW QUESTIONS

1. What is theory, and what are its central purposes?

2. What are the main areas of agreement and disagreement between realists, liberals, and constructivists in their conception of the international system?

3. What are the main areas of agreement and disagreement between realists, liberals, and constructivists in their conception of the relevant actors in international relations?

4. What are the main areas of agreement and disagreement between realists, liberals, and constructivists in their conception of power and influence in international relations?

5. What are the main areas of agreement and disagreement between realists, liberals, and constructivists in their conception of the major patterns of behavior and interaction in international relations?

THINK ABOUT THIS

Peace in Europe After 1945

For centuries Europe was among the most violent places in the world. In the early 20th century, this pattern of persistent warfare culminated in the two largest wars of world history, World Wars I and II. However, since World War II's end, this region has enjoyed persistent peace. Large-scale warfare appears a thing of the past, and much of Europe is now united and cooperating in the European Union. In 2012, the EU was awarded the Nobel Peace Prize, an act that would likely have been unimaginable less than a century before. Consider this dramatic change in fortune for Europe before and after 1945 in light of the three theoretical perspectives we discussed in this chapter.

How would realists, liberals, and constructivists explain peace in Europe after World War II? Which explanations help us understand recent developments the most?

Anubis3Medal: Gustav Vigeland/ Public domain/Wikimedia Commons

FOR MORE INFORMATION . . .

Burchill, Scott, Andrew Linklater, Richard Devetak, Jack Donnelly, Terry Nardin, Mathew Paterson, Christian Reus-Smit, and Jacqui True. (2013). *Theories of International Relations,* 5th ed. New York, NY: Palgrave-Macmillan.

Doyle, Michael W. (1997). *Ways of War and Peace: Realism, Liberalism and Socialism.* New York, NY: Norton.

Drezner, Daniel. (2015). *Theories of International Politics and Zombies,* rev. ed. Princeton, NJ: Princeton University Press.

Dunne, Tim, Milja Kurki, and Steve Smith. (2020). *International Relations Theories: Discipline and Diversity,* 5th ed. London, UK: Oxford University Press.

Sterling-Folker, Jennifer, ed. (2013). *Making Sense of International Relations Theory,* 2nd ed. Boulder, CO: Lynne Rienner.

Viotti, Paul R., and Mark V. Kauppi. (2011). *International Relations Theory,* 5th ed. New York, NY: Longman.

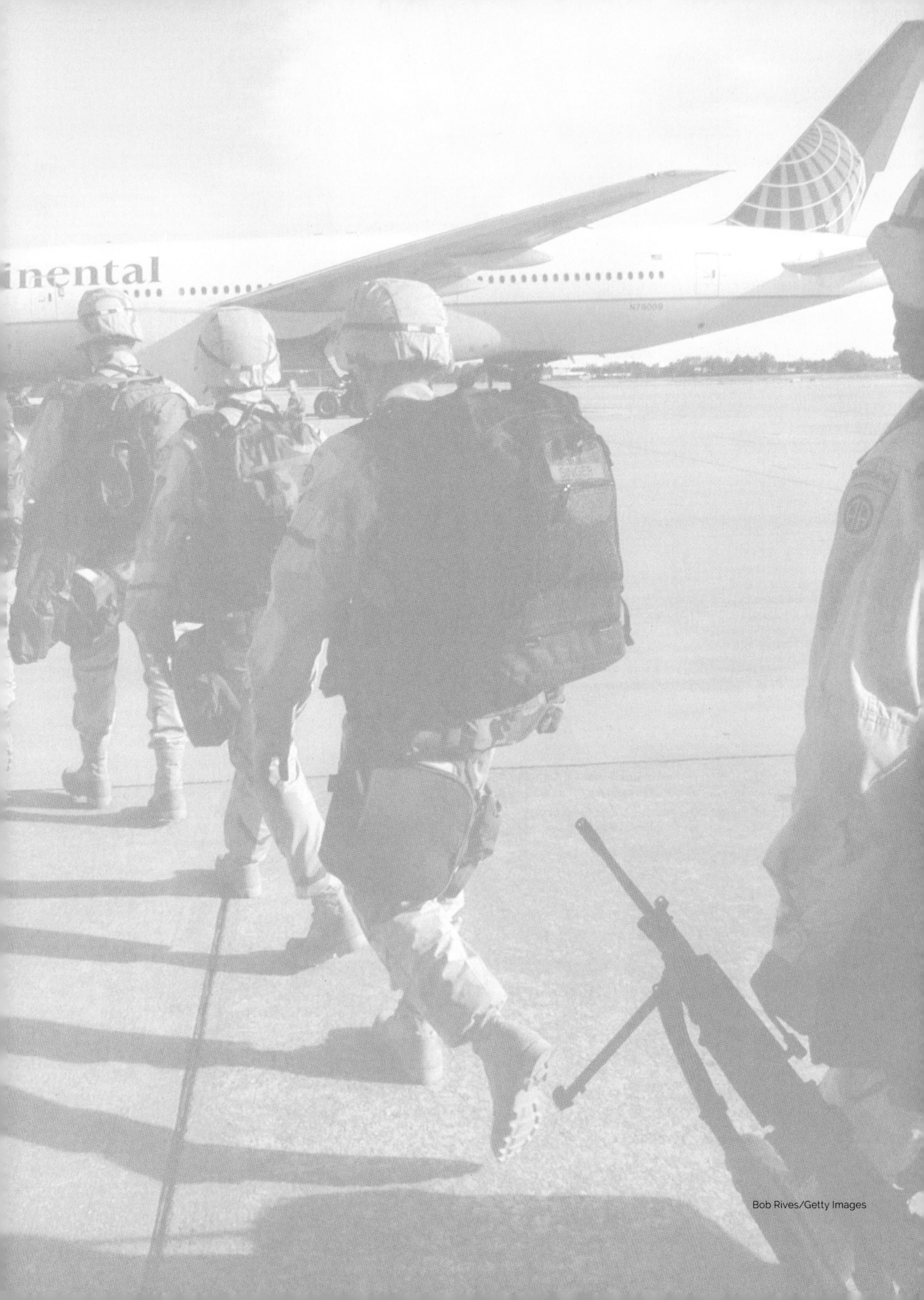

Bob Rives/Getty Images

Iraqi counterterrorism forces stand guard in front of the US embassy in Baghdad in January 2020

Why did the United States decide to use force in what now seems an interminable conflict in Iraq?

AHMAD AL-RUBAYE/AFP via Getty Images

4

Alternative Perspectives on International Relations

Learning Objectives

After studying this chapter, you will be able to . . .

4-1 Understand how the foreign policy perspective provides a foundation for international relations.

4-2 Explain how economic class as used by Marxist theory can be the driving force for how nations interact with each other.

4-3 Describe the different aspects of world systems theory and how they explain international relations.

4-4 Outline the ways in which gender affects and is affected by international relations.

Chapter Outline

4-1 Foreign Policy Analysis

4-2 Marxism and Marxist Theory

4-3 World Systems Theory

4-4 Feminism

Confronting Iraq

By the end of 2020, US involvement in the Iraq War reached its 17th year. Its costs exceeded $2 trillion in military and related spending on aid and reconstruction and veterans' care/benefits, making it second only to World War II in expense. About 4,600 US military personnel have been killed and close to 32,000 wounded in the military action. Estimates of total casualties range from about 100,000 to more than a million for all participants, when military and civilian casualties are included. Yet violence and instability continue. US military personnel returned to Iraq in 2014, and the Trump administration dispatched another 4,000 in mid-2017, adding more than 3,500 to a deployment to Kuwait in 2020 in the wake of a US military operation that killed General Qassem Soleimani, the commander of Iran's secretive Quds Force. Although advocates of the US invasion assured the public that it would be short, decisive, and relatively inexpensive, the reality has been very different. Why did the seemingly endless war occur?

About a year and a half after the al-Qaeda attacks on the United States in September 2001, the US unleashed a military attack on Iraq in March 2003. Unlike the previous use of force in Afghanistan in 2001, which was related directly to the terrorist attacks and aimed at confronting al-Qaeda and its benefactors—the Taliban regime—in Afghanistan, the invasion of Iraq was much more controversial. The administration of US President George W. Bush justified the action on several grounds, attempting to link Iraq to the global war on terror and warning against the dire prospects of Iraq's efforts to develop weapons

of mass destruction (WMD), even though Iraq was not involved in the 2001 terrorist strikes, and evidence of its WMD programs was highly doubtful at best. Why would the US engage in such a controversial—and ultimately costly and counterproductive—military action? How do you think realist, liberal, and constructivist theorists would explain this "war of choice"?

Perhaps other explanations might be in order. Some analysts point to the personal characteristics of President George W. Bush or to the dysfunctional decision processes that the US president and his advisers followed. Others might direct our attention to issues of economic power and security and argue that asserting American dominance in the global pecking order and gaining control and influence over Iraq's oil were at the heart of the choice. Still others might approach this action in the context of the underlying and pervasive effects of a world in which women are omitted and subordinated in global politics and foreign policy decisions. Some might emphasize how racial differences drive such decisions. How might understanding and explaining the 2003 war benefit from these perspectives?

1. Do realist, liberal, and constructivist theories adequately explain the 2003 Iraq War?

2. How might the characteristics of leaders and decision-making processes shed light on the decision and its aftermath?

3. Are there insights from the structures and processes of the global capitalist system, or from the gendered nature of world politics, that might help explain the war?

INTRODUCTION: ALTERNATIVES TO REALISM, LIBERALISM, AND CONSTRUCTIVISM

In Chapter 3, we discussed the three most commonly used theories of how the world works. Each theory has a different view of how states interact and what is required for them to cooperate. This chapter presents three different challenges to those three dominant theories. First, **foreign policy analysis** switches the focus of understanding how states behave in the international arena to the people and groups who make the foreign policy decisions within each country. Instead of simply saying a state seeks security in the international system, foreign policy analysis examines how a dictator might try to increase his or her security or how a legislature might constrain a leader's attempt to strengthen the state's military power. Second, critical economic theories like **Marxism** and **world systems theory**—a theory inspired by Marxism—argue that the world is divided into economic zones (by their level of development) and that these zones determine how states interact, with wealthier countries exploiting poorer countries. Marxist-based perspectives therefore suggest that realist, liberal, and constructivist assumptions are somewhat misguided and that the key factor to understanding interstate behavior is wealth and who controls it. Finally, **feminist international relations theory** suggests that we should look through a different lens to see what obstacles women face in world politics, what the world would look like if it were not historically dominated by men, and what issues we would pay attention to if our views of world politics

were not so gendered. How would things be different if women played a more equal role in world politics?

Throughout the chapter, we present the perspectives each of these theories brings to explaining international relations; the key forces and patterns they direct our attention to as alternatives to realism, liberalism, and constructivism; and some of their limits. It is important to understand, however, that we do not have to either accept or reject these perspectives categorically. Instead, we can learn from each of them and adapt our views of international relations so that we better understand the world around us. The goal of this chapter is not to suggest that the theories discussed in Chapter 3 are wrong but to provide a range of ways to look at states and their behavior. By understanding the many different lenses available, we are able to select and adapt the ones that make the most sense to us and apply them to the issues and circumstances in which they are most useful.

4-1 FOREIGN POLICY ANALYSIS

>> **4-1   Understand how the foreign policy perspective provides a foundation for international relations.**

The first perspective to deviate from realism, liberalism, and constructivism is foreign policy analysis, though scholars of international relations use different terms for this approach. The study of foreign policy is best understood by its **agent-centered approach**. According to this approach, to understand how states interact, we must focus on agents—the individuals and groups who make decisions within the state.

For realism, states are assumed to be unitary, rational actors. In Chapter 3, we discussed the idea of a *unitary actor*. The notion of the state as a rational actor underlies realist and some of liberal theorizing as well. This **rational actor model** simplifies our understanding and explanation of the behavior of states by assuming a common, unified approach to decisions, as summarized in Figure 4-1. Though there are many versions of this approach, they commonly simplify the decision process to assume that actors respond to problems by rank-ordering their goals, identifying available options, and weighing the costs and benefits of each. Then the actor selects the option expected to provide the greatest benefits at the lowest costs, in light of the specified rank-ordered goals, and carries out the decision, observing the outcome so that adjustments can be made if needed.

For example, a realist would describe the 2014 Russian intervention in Crimea and eastern Ukraine

---

foreign policy analysis: a theoretical approach that focuses on the process and outcomes of foreign policy decisions made by the people and groups who determine a state's actions in international relations.

Marxism: an argument developed by Marx and Engels that asserted all politics was determined by social class and that the world would progress through historical economic epochs.

world systems theory: a Marxist-based theory that explains international politics as the rich core states exploiting the semi-periphery and the periphery states, the semi-periphery states exploiting the periphery states, and the periphery states being exploited by both.

feminist international relations theory: a feminist approach to understanding international relations that focuses on the role of women and gender and how historically the world has been dominated by men.

agent-centered approach: understanding and explaining international relations by focusing on the individuals and groups who make decisions within the state.

rational actor model: a model in which, as unitary actors, all states make decisions according to a rational process in which goals are ranked, options identified and evaluated, and selections made to maximize benefits according to the goals of the actor.

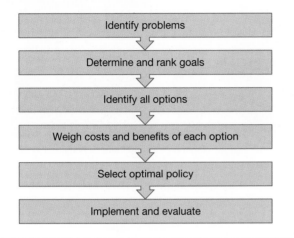

FIGURE 4-1

The Rational Actor Model

- Identify problems
- Determine and rank goals
- Identify all options
- Weigh costs and benefits of each option
- Select optimal policy
- Implement and evaluate

in simple terms: Russia decided to take Crimea from Ukraine in order to increase its security and power. For explanatory purposes, the rational actor model therefore presumes purposive and goal-oriented behavior consistent with the idea of maximizing benefits and minimizing costs. It also assumes that *all actors behave the same*, simplifying away differences in individuals, groups, decision processes, societal factors, and regime characteristics so that those things do not have to be considered when explanations for international relations are offered.

These are precisely the characteristics to which foreign policy analysis pays attention. Returning to the 2014 Russian intervention in Ukraine, foreign policy analysis would explain it quite differently, focusing on the agents involved. For example, a foreign policy analysis approach might focus on Russian President Vladimir Putin. Thus, the invasion might be explained as driven by Putin's aggressive beliefs about international relations and his desire to regain control of lost territories. Can you think of additional examples in which you might try to explain a country's actions in world politics by connecting them to leader personality and beliefs?

Both of these explanations could be correct—or useful—depending on the situation, but sometimes looking at the agents who make foreign policy is a necessary part of the explanation. For example, President Obama declared a "red line" in Syria in 2012 after evidence indicated that the Assad regime had used chemical weapons. When he did so, he implied that the United States would intervene with military force. It therefore seemed clear that the US would attack the Syrian government. However, perhaps in an attempt to back down from his threat, in 2013

President Obama asked the US Congress to authorize a military strike. The House of Representatives was strongly opposed to the idea of military intervention. As a result, the United States did nothing. To understand this episode, we need to look at the agents involved—in this case, the president and members of Congress—and the processes involved in the decisions. A constructivist might say that Congress socially constructed the reality involved, but a realist or a liberal would not be able to explain these events except to say that the US did not intervene in Syria after the discovery that chemical weapons were used.

Agents can be people or groups. In the preceding examples, we discussed individuals, Putin and Obama, and a group or governmental institution, Congress. There is no correct answer to the question of what a state's agent or agents are. In some cases, individual characteristics are important to consider. Donald Trump's volatile narcissism; Vladimir Putin's aggressive, expansionist personality; Angela Merkel's cautiousness and conservatism; Hugo Chávez's anti-American focus; and Kim Jong-un's ruthlessness, self-indulgence, and ambition are all examples of specific individual characteristics that might affect a state's foreign policy.

Most of the time, however, it makes more sense to think of groups of leaders. President Trump and Chancellor Merkel have advisers and cabinet ministers who help them make decisions. Similarly, President Xi Jinping of the People's Republic of China works with the Politburo Standing Committee of the Chinese Communist Party to make decisions. Thus, whether in a democracy or an authoritarian regime, the agent of the state—the key decision maker—is usually a group of individuals.

Other groups that can be considered agents are interest groups, the media, and even public opinion. Foreign policy analysts can also consider the regime or government itself an agent. Unlike realists, however, they understand that a state's government is not the entire state, and unlike liberals, they realize that there may be multiple leaders within a society. Thus, for example, they can think of the US government, but any decisions it makes are made in the context of American public opinion, interest groups, the media, and so on. Thus, foreign policy analysis might focus on individuals, small groups, bureaucratic organizations, legislatures, domestic or societal forces such as interest groups and public opinion, and different regime types.

4-1a Individual Explanations of Foreign Policy

When we focus on individuals as the key agent in foreign policy decision making, there are many different possible approaches. The common characteristic is that they all show how individual preferences or human characteristics affect how leaders make decisions. Political scientist Herbert Simon wrote about how humans make decisions. He suggested that there are those who are rational decision makers, making decisions like a computer, perfectly logical and with no emotion (much like a Vulcan from *Star Trek*). On the other end of this spectrum are the emotional decision makers, those who make decisions without any consideration for reality. Most leaders—and most people—fall in between these two opposites in what Simon called **bounded rationality**. This concept means that leaders try to be rational or logical when making decisions, but there are limits or bounds on our ability to be rational.

For example, have you ever taken an immediate dislike to someone after meeting him or her? Even without interacting with someone, we can have a negative reaction to that person. Why? It's not logical or rational to have a "gut feeling" and distrust someone without getting to know the person, but most people have had this experience. Now imagine that you are the leader of a country. What if you have that reaction to another leader? Will that affect how you negotiate with that leader? What if it's the other way around—for some reason, you just trust the other leader for no other reason than a "gut feeling." Would you be more willing to make a trade deal or sign a treaty with that leader? Thus, our emotions, personality, and preferences limit our ability to be perfectly rational.

To put this idea of bounded rationality to work, scholars developed different theories for how leaders make decisions. One theory, **operational code analysis**, argues that leaders have a tendency to (a) prefer either conflict or cooperation and (b) believe they are either very effective or limited in their ability to control others. This does not mean that leaders who prefer conflict are immoral warmongers; it just means that they believe the world is a conflictual place and often one must use force to protect oneself. Similarly, a leader preferring cooperation will still go to war; such a leader's preference only means that a cooperative strategy might be tried first, if possible.

Stephen Walker developed a way to measure a leader's conflict/cooperation and effective/limited

Russian President Vladimir Putin and Chinese President Xi Jinping
What difference does an individual leader make?
Ramil Sitdikov/Sputnik via AP

beliefs from a distance. Because leaders such as Putin, Merkel, and Trump aren't likely to take personality tests for researchers, Walker created a way to measure their beliefs from their speeches. By coding what and how leaders say things in scores of their speeches, scholars are able to see how much they prefer conflict or cooperation, how much control they believe they have, and how they learn over time. For example, US President Jimmy Carter started his time in the White House preferring cooperation and believing he had considerable ability to affect other leaders. After the Soviet invasion of Afghanistan and the Iranian hostage crisis, his beliefs were nearly identical to those of Ronald Reagan—he believed that the world was conflictual and chaotic and that leaders must use force to protect their countries.

Another individual explanation of foreign policy is **prospect theory**. According to scholars such as Rose McDermott and Jack Levy, this theory argues that humans are rational, but that changes depending on the situation. The best way to describe this is through a simple exercise:

- In Scenario 1, you are presented with two choices: Option 1—80% chance of winning $1,000—or Option 2—40% chance of winning $2,500. Most people choose Option 1. It's almost a "sure thing," and even though Option 2 has a greater utility (the payoff multiplied by the probability), people prefer to be risk averse in these conditions.

- In Scenario 2, you are also presented with two choices: Option 1—80% chance of losing $1,000—or Option 2—40% chance of losing $2,500. In this case, most people go with Option 2. They are willing to risk more money with the hope that they won't lose anything.

----

bounded rationality: the idea that leaders want to make rational or logical decisions but are limited by their lack of knowledge or other human factors.

operational code analysis: the idea that leaders have a tendency to (a) prefer either conflict or cooperation and (b) believe they are either very effective or limited in their ability to control others.

prospect theory: the idea that humans are rational but their rationality is situationally biased; that is, they are more risk averse when things work in their favor and more risk taking when things aren't going well.

In the first scenario, you are in what prospect theory calls the domain of gains. That is, you're ahead and less willing to take risks. In the second scenario, you are in the domain of losses and much more willing to accept risky options. Here's another way to think of it: Would you work harder to get a promotion or to keep your job if it was threatened? The promotion is in the domain of gains, whereas getting fired is clearly in the domain of losses. Most people would fight hardest to keep their job.

So how does prospect theory relate to foreign policy analysis? Leaders will find themselves in these domains and act accordingly. For example, in 1960, an American U-2 spy plane was shot down over the Soviet Union. President Eisenhower found himself in the domain of losses because the United States had been caught violating Soviet airspace and illegally gathering photos. Instead of admitting the spying, Eisenhower took the far riskier option and denied it. Once the Soviets showed the world the incontrovertible evidence, Eisenhower was caught not only spying but also lying to the public. The fallout included the Soviets canceling an important summit meeting with Eisenhower, an event that was meant to top off his legacy as president, and difficult negotiations to get the captured pilot returned (depicted in the film *Bridge of Spies*).

In perhaps the most "individual" of theoretical perspectives, what if some people are genetically more prone to violence? Peter Hatemi and Rose McDermott (2012) are leading the study of this phenomenon and its consequences for international relations. These analyses show that a small portion of all populations carry this gene, but it is activated only when the person experiences extreme violence or hardship during the early stages of life. This experience could be surviving a famine, being a refugee, living in a war zone, or even experiencing a military intervention. In these cases, the gene is likely to be activated. As a result, in countries suffering from severe economic hardship and violence, there are more people willing to commit extreme violent acts. As the number of violent events increases, such as suicide bombings, the environment continues to activate the gene in children and young adults, creating a vicious cycle.

The connection to international relations should be clear—violent states are likely to continue to produce violent individuals—but there is also a perverse impact. Imagine that a country is experiencing a moderate level of famine and civil unrest, and the UN authorizes a humanitarian military presence to keep the peace and help secure food deliveries. That military intervention, though intended to be humanitarian, may spark increased tensions that activate the gene in the younger generation. Thus, the humanitarian intervention may actually lead to more violence

in the future. The increased future violence activates more of these genes, creating a downward spiral.

This research is very much on the frontier of what we know about genetics and violence, and it has potential for expanding our understanding of conflict around the globe. Still, this work is in its early stages and should be viewed with a careful eye. The implications of this research are both good and bad. For example, if we could identify the gene carriers, we might be able to provide counseling that reduces their penchant for violence, but governments could also simply jail them or even kill them. What do you think about this line of research? Does it potentially cross a line that could be dangerous?

Without getting into each person's genetic code, individuals still vary by personality, and that can affect their decision making. The box "Theory in Action: Personality and Policymaking: Donald Trump in Context" delves into this more deeply.

4-1b Group Explanations of Foreign Policy

In his famous study of the Cuban Missile Crisis, Graham Allison (1971) showed that leaders in the US government held different opinions on how to deal with the Soviet missiles in Cuba based on the organization in which they worked. Army commanders recommended that President Kennedy order an invasion, the Air Force recommended bombing to destroy the missiles, and the Navy suggested a blockade. In a classic example of "where you stand is determined by where you sit," each commander's solution was a reflection of the job he held. This is a classic example of the **organizational/bureaucratic politics model** of foreign policy.

The bureaucratic politics approach rests on three characteristics of bureaucratic organizations (which every state has) that affect the process of decision making: hierarchical structure, specialization, and routinization. Bureaucratic organizations are hierarchically structured, with divisions of authority from top (most authority) to bottom (least authority). Specialization means that organizations are established to attend to particular tasks, and within organizations, offices exist for increasingly specific responsibilities as you move down the hierarchy. At the same time, the further down the hierarchy you go, the more routine behavior becomes, as bureaucratic personnel are increasingly likely to follow "standard operating procedures" to do their jobs.

....

organizational/bureaucratic politics model: a model in which foreign policy decisions are the products of large bureaucratic organizations doing what they know to do or see as in their organizational interest.

Personality and Policymaking: Donald Trump in Context

Donald Trump's volatile and domineering style and approach to politics have generated a great deal of attention. Sympathetic observers applaud his blunt and unconventional approach, while critics highlight his impetuousness, thin skin, and grandiose sense of his own importance.

In a recent analysis, Allesandro Nai, Ferran Martinez i Coma, and Jürgen Maier (2019) assessed Trump's personality in the context of more than 100 other political leaders around the world. According to their personality assessment, Trump is extremely extroverted; extremely low on agreeableness; extremely low on conscientiousness; extremely neurotic (low emotional stability); and extremely high on narcissism, psychopathy, and Machiavellianism. Compared to the scores of other leaders in the study, Trump's scores on agreeableness, conscientiousness, and emotional

stability were the lowest, and his scores for narcissism and Machiavellianism were the highest.

The authors also concluded that Trump's negative tone and appeals to fear were comparatively high. As they summarize, "Trump's off-the-charts personality and campaigning style suggest that even when compared with other abrasive, narcissistic, and confrontational political figures, he stands out as an outlier among the outliers" (Nai, Martinez i Coma, and Maier 2019: 609). This assessment is broadly consistent with those of other analysts (e.g., Immelman, 2017; McAdams 2016; Sherman 2015).

1. What do you think these personality traits might mean for foreign policymaking?

2. What aspects of world politics might be most affected by leader personalities? ●

Because of these basic characteristics, foreign policy decision making is affected by bureaucratic politics and processes. At the top of the bureaucratic organizations, agency leaders tend to approach foreign policy problems with information, perspectives, and policy preferences that reflect their organizational viewpoints and specialization. Often, competition over policy options among agencies and their personnel occurs, and as Allison and Zelikow (1999) note, the result is frequently "political bargaining, coalition building, and compromise" (p. 255).

Further down in the organizations, agencies and personnel tend to follow their own routines and stress their own responsibilities and perspectives as well. Each bureaucracy develops its own organizational missions and standard operating procedures. As a consequence, organizational behavior tends to be "incremental" in nature, where members of organizations act very similarly from one day to the next. Bureaucratic policymaking also tends to reflect established bureaucratic repertoires and routines, with standard operating procedures for addressing a recurring set of issues.

Another aspect of organizations and their influence on how we think concerns budgets. In addition to influencing how we see the world and what policy options we develop, we associate our future with the organization. As a consequence, people want their

organization to succeed. For example, when President Carter authorized Operation Eagle Claw to rescue the hostages in Iran, each of the armed services wanted to be involved. There was infighting between the Navy, Army, and Marines about the roles each would play in the mission. That infighting, driven by a desire to be part of the action and justify future budgets, contributed to the failure of the operation.

Finally, bureaucratic agencies can pursue contradictory policies as each organization pursues its own course within its jurisdiction. All of these characteristics of bureaucratic culture and processes affect the foreign policy behavior of the state in significant ways, and this approach focuses on these behaviors to understand why a certain state engages in particular foreign policy behavior on a specific issue or problem, rather than assuming a coherent, unitary, and rational process.

Foreign policy decisions are affected not only by which organizations are involved in a leader's decision but also by how the leader structures his or her **advisory group**. Studies show that the more restricted the flow of information within an advisory group, the more extreme the state's foreign policy will be. Thus, leaders who allow only the most senior advisers to speak directly to them tend to be more likely to use military force compared to an open or collegial advisory system. In the more open group, senior and junior advisers openly share ideas and often arrive at more inventive policies short of using military force.

advisory group: the set of individuals from whom leaders seek decision-making assistance.

There are many good examples of the impact of advisory group structure and process. For instance, foreign policy theorists such as Charles Duelfer and Stephen Dyson (2011), Dina Badie (2010), Chris Dolan and David Cohen (2006), and David Mitchell and Tansa George Massoud (2009) have all argued that George W. Bush's advisory structure and processes led to a series of decision-making problems during the 2003 Iraq War decision making, resulting in the invasion of Iraq. Kevin Marsh (2014) explains the 2009 decision to "surge" American forces in Afghanistan to the nature of the advisers, advisory structures, and processes during the Obama administration. And numerous recent accounts attribute the nature and outcomes of many foreign policy decisions in the Trump administration to its disorganized structures and processes and the nature of advisory groups and their relationships.

Whether it's called an advisory group or something else, small-group decision-making dynamics matter. Have you ever been in a group where everyone agrees on what to do, but it still turns out to be wrong? Maybe other opinions should have been heard. What about that group you were in where no one seemed to agree on anything? Nothing got done. Think of small-group decision-making processes as a continuum. At one end there's the process known as **groupthink**, which occurs in groups where everyone seems to want to get along. Here, one choice seems to gain traction with few or no objections. If members have doubts about that choice, they may not voice them, or if they do, the others may discount or ignore the doubts. Groups with these dynamics seem likely to make major mistakes, as psychologist Irving Janis argued when he named the phenomenon. At the other end of the continuum is the group where so many options are pushed that it becomes difficult to reach any agreement. Alex Mintz and Carly Wayne (2016) call this process **polythink**. Of course, the objective would be to have a group with dynamics that fall somewhere between these two extremes. You want enough differing inputs to ensure that relevant information is considered, but you don't want so much input that decision making becomes paralyzed. Finding this optimal process can be difficult in real life, particularly during crises.

Group politics can also affect foreign policy in a democracy based on the size of the leader's majority. In the United States, the president appoints top executive branch officials. Thus, the secretary of state and the secretary of defense work directly for the president. In a parliamentary democracy with **proportional representation**, most governments are coalitions. That is, they are a coalition of cooperative political parties. So, for example, a government could be composed of a pro-union party, a socialist party, and an environmental party. Research by Juliet Kaarbo and Ryan Beasley (2008) shows that these coalition governments engage in more extreme foreign policies compared to single-party governments, like those in the United States and the United Kingdom. The reason for this is twofold. First, coalitions often include more extreme parties, and these political parties can demand more extreme policies, effectively hijacking a state's foreign policy. Second, because there are multiple parties in the government, it is hard for the public to determine who is to blame for a policy. In the US, this is impossible because only one party—the party of the president—is held responsible for foreign policy. In other democracies, however, it is not uncommon to have more than three parties in the government. If that were the case, who would you blame for a problem?

4-1c Societal Explanations of Foreign Policy

Another approach to understanding international relations from a foreign policy perspective is to look at the interest groups within a country. The most famous of these interest groups within the United States are typically tied to a specific country, so they lobby the government for more favorable policies toward their preferred country. For example, for years the Cuban American National Foundation was a well-organized interest group that focused pressure on the Castro regime in Havana; it virtually dominated US policy toward Cuba in the 1980s and 1990s. Another well-organized group is the American Israel Public Affairs Committee (AIPAC), a pro-Israel interest group. AIPAC lobbies US leaders for favorable policies toward Israel, such as the selling of military weapons technology and sanctions on Iran. Its influence is so significant that other groups try to counter it (like the group J Street, for those who think Israel should compromise more in the hope of peace) or mimic it (like the American India Public Affairs Committee).

These groups certainly have an influence on US foreign policy, but their focus is limited to one country (Cuba, Israel, or India) or region (the Middle East). As you will see in Chapters 8 and 13, there are other international groups that can have an impact on a

---

groupthink: characteristics of some decision groups that result in a shared viewpoint or preference that leads the group to ignore relevant information and exclude dissenters from that viewpoint in order to protect it.

polythink: characteristics of some decision groups that result in so many options and preferences being introduced that agreement on any one becomes unlikely, if not impossible.

proportional representation: a democratic system in which parties or factions get approximately the same percentage of legislative seats as votes they received in the most recent election.

country's foreign policy that is not limited to a single country. Groups focused on human rights and multinational corporations focused on profits can affect how a state makes its foreign policy. Groups like Amnesty International can push even the most powerful countries to levy economic sanctions on states that violate human rights or push states to intervene in humanitarian crises, while multinational corporations spend countless dollars on influencing policies about interstate trade and finance.

All of these groups can have a big impact on a country's foreign policy, but perhaps the most powerful influence is simply public opinion. In a democracy, leaders must satisfy their public's demands or be voted out of office. As a result, leaders try to either figure out what their public wants or lead the public to what the leader wants. For example, following the Battle of Mogadishu in 1993, when 18 American soldiers were killed, President Clinton feared that there would be a public backlash against him, partly because of media coverage of the event. Consequently, he announced the withdrawal of US forces from Somalia. Though such a backlash did not occur, Clinton's belief that it would led him to shift US foreign policy. In this case, Clinton followed his perception of what the public wanted.

The importance of public opinion is so strong that scholars argue that leaders will engage in conflicts just to divert the public's attention away from other problems. Called *diversionary theory* (see Chapter 5 for more discussion of this idea), there is some evidence that leaders are more likely to use the military when they face domestic economic crises, domestic criticism, or, worse, a scandal. A classic example is President Clinton's bombing of sites in Sudan and Afghanistan after the intern with whom he had an affair—Monica Lewinsky—testified before Congress. Perhaps the most outrageous illustration is the movie *Wag the Dog*, in which the president's "fixer" hires a Hollywood producer to create a fictitious war with Albania after the president was caught in a sex scandal. Whether or not leaders consciously use the military when they are facing political attacks at home is not clear, and fiction like *Wag the Dog* is clearly just that, fiction. There is, however, a slight preference for leaders to be more active during these periods.

4-1d Regime Explanations of Foreign Policy

Thus far, we have examined individual and societal theories of foreign policy. Most of these theories

suggest that human nature is not purely rational or logical. Instead, they argue that personality characteristics or preferences bound or limit rational decision making. Thus, although leaders are mostly rational, their human nature can get in the way. Another group of foreign policy scholars assume that leaders are rational, but they still take an agent-centered approach to understanding foreign policy.

An influential example of these theories was developed by Bruce Bueno de Mesquita and his colleagues in a 2003 book titled *The Logic of Political Survival*. The political survival theory is quite simple and applies to all types of regimes—from democratic to autocratic. The theory argues that leaders want to stay in power, and to do so, they must satisfy at least half of the people who are in the **selectorate**, the group that selects the leader. In a democracy, the selectorate are the people who are eligible to vote. To become a leader in a democracy, then, you must get half of the voters to choose you. That half is called the **winning coalition**.

In an authoritarian country, clearly the selectorate is not the voters. Instead, it is the powerful elites whose support the leader needs. These elites are usually military generals, the wealthiest business people, and perhaps political party leaders. Even in a state like North Korea, Kim Jong-un must have the support of generals and those who control the state-owned industries. This does not mean it is democratic; it just means that leaders cannot rule by sheer force of will. They must have the support of some people.

Thus, the key difference between a democracy and an autocracy is the size of the selectorate, and that has a dramatic effect on how the leader makes foreign policy. In a democracy, the leader must satisfy most of the public and, therefore, must provide "peace and prosperity." That means a healthy economy and either no war or at least a successful war. Democratic leaders who have a bad economy or lose a war are

US President Donald Trump and North Korean Leader Kim Jong-un have cast each other as villains and as rational counterparts

What motivates leaders to direct their people's attention to other countries and global issues in one way or another?

Kyodo via AP Images

selectorate: those in a state who provide the power base for a leader.

winning coalition: the half of the voters whose support you must have to win an election.

unlikely to be reelected—just look at Presidents Johnson and Carter. The former withdrew from the 1968 election because of the failures in Vietnam, and the latter was soundly defeated in 1980 because of the poor economy.

In an autocracy, however, the leader needs to satisfy only a few people. Therefore, the economy can be in poor condition as long as the leader pays off his or her supporters. Further, such a leader can engage in wars and even lose, as long as the generals are satisfied, which can mean launching occasional attacks and using or testing their newest weapons.

What does this mean for our understanding of international relations? Democratic leaders will tend not to engage in conflict, because they fear becoming entangled in a war that leads to their electoral defeat. If they do go to war, however, they will go "all in," so to speak, because they must win the war to stay in office. Authoritarians will engage in limited wars and prefer not to go "all in" because that would hurt their military, which could lead to a coup d'état by one or more of their dissatisfied generals. Although the political survival theory of foreign policy does not give us details about the individuals involved and human nature, it does provide a clear and concise way of understanding how the agents who make foreign policy balance their domestic political constraints and international pressures.

4-1e Foreign Policy Analysis as the Foundation for International Relations

If we do not consider these different perspectives, foreign policy theorists argue, we are missing out on important details that realists, liberals, and constructivists ignore. Further, foreign policy theories provide answers to why states are not always rational—why they do not always follow what a realist or liberal theorist might expect. An invasion of Cuba during the missile crisis would almost surely have resulted in the launch of the operational nuclear missiles in Cuba. Nuclear war would have followed. This was not the goal of the US military, but an invasion made the most sense from their perspective. What if President Kennedy had chosen the invasion and nuclear war had followed? How would a realist, a liberal, or a constructivist explain this outcome?

The other important benefit that foreign policy theories provide is the foundation for understanding international relations. Realists assume that states are unitary—that their actions are the actions of a single decision maker. Liberals and constructivists may focus on leaders and society, respectively. Foreign policy analysis looks deeper and explains how those decisions are made within the state, often down to the group and individual level.

4-2 MARXISM AND MARXIST THEORY

>> **4-2** **Explain how economic class as used by Marxist theory can be the driving force for how nations interact with each other.**

We turn now from the foreign policy analysis focus on the agents of foreign policy to an economic approach to understanding world politics. Marxist theory is very different from realism, liberalism, and constructivism because it starts from a very different view of the world, one in which economic class rather than power is the driving force.

"The history of all hitherto existing society is the history of class struggles" (Marx and Engels 1848). This quote from the beginning of *The Communist Manifesto* sums up the Marxist theory approach to international relations. In its most basic form, the approach asserts that all actions by people and states are driven by economic desires rather than desires for power, security, and so on. The radical departure from realism, liberalism, and constructivism comes from the idea that states do not seek security; they seek to make their capitalist class—that is, the wealthiest individuals in the country—wealthier.

The theory laid down by Karl Marx and Friedrich Engels was part theory, part historical interpretation, and part policy prescription. We will focus on the theory and later discuss a spin-off of Marxism. The theory actually focuses on the individual and class rather than on the state, but what it says about individuals very much involves states. Marxist theory sees the state of nature not at all like the realists and liberals; it asserts that humans like to be productive, and if unconstrained by society and government, they will live peacefully and happily with each other, working, building, and creating. The obstacle to this utopia is the misguided pursuit of wealth that develops through human history.

The theory suggests that after leaving the most primitive tribes, humans developed a society with two economic classes: workers and the wealthy. Those classes exchanged labor for money, but at no point in history has that exchange been equal. Instead, the wealthy class takes wealth from the workers by paying them less than their labor is worth, a process of exploitation that began with feudalism during medieval times. The wealthy class (royalty or lords) owned all land and resources, while peasants (serfs) owned nothing and worked on the lord's land in exchange for the right to live there, the right to eat some of the food produced on the land, and protection from harm. The serfs were not free to leave, but they were not slaves. In return for working his land, the lord provided law and order for the peasants.

Statue of Karl Marx and Friedrich Engels in Berlin, Germany
When these two men were alive, many considered them to be radicals and troublemakers. How are they viewed today, and how have their ideas affected the way we understand politics and economics?

Eye Ubiquitous/Universal Images Group via Getty Images

With the development of specialized skills (e.g., metalworking, weaving), the economy and society industrialized. This change in the economy led to the end of feudalism and the birth of **capitalism**. In capitalist societies, workers (also called the **proletariat**) were free and could sell their labor to the **capitalist class or bourgeoisie**, who were typically not willing to pay what the workers' labor was worth. The capitalist class thus profited from the laborers' effort and did no work themselves.

....

capitalism: an economic system of complete or near complete free markets in which market forces determine what is purchased and what is sold. There are variations of capitalism, but the emphasis is on limited government involvement in and regulation of the economy.

proletariat: the working class that sold its labor for less than its value to the capitalists.

capitalist class or bourgeoisie: the owners of businesses, factories, and the like, who profit from the work of laborers but do not work themselves.

Marx and Engels theorized that, eventually, the proletariat would rise up and revolt against the capitalists, overthrow them, and take control of the government. The new government would take complete ownership of the economy for the proletariat, and it would begin to break down the old capitalist institutions. Part of this process would be to reeducate everyone so that they understood humans are happier as workers, not as wealthy individuals living off the work of others. This government would be considered socialist. After reeducating everyone and destroying the old capitalist institutions, over time the government itself would wither away and society would become truly communist, a utopia where everyone cooperated, and the human vices inspired by capitalist greed and envy would be eradicated. As a well-known quote from Marx (who borrowed it from others) states, this utopia would thrive as wealth/production was cooperatively and collectively gained "from each according to his ability, to each according to his need."

4-2a Marxist Theory and International Relations

You may be asking yourself what this has to do with international relations. Where are the states, the diplomats, the armies, the non-state actors? There are two connections that make Marxist theory more than an economic explanation of society and relate it directly to international relations.

First, unless a state was socialist, its motives were to promote the wealth of the capitalist class. According to the theory, the capitalist class controlled the government, and thus all policies, foreign and domestic, were made to benefit the capitalists. Marxist theory asserts that wars are not fought for territory or security but for the profit they will bring the wealthy class. For example, a communist interpretation of World War II would assert that a newly wealthy class within Germany was attempting to gain access to markets, resources, and more labor. By attempting to conquer other colonies and annex territory in Europe, the Nazi Party was acting on behalf of German capitalists who wanted to expand their wealth beyond Germany's borders. The German economy had been suffering badly prior to the military buildup and war preparations. Once Adolf Hitler took control of the country, he began building up the economy. Marxist theory would cite this as evidence that Hitler was trying to rebuild and expand the wealth of the capitalists rather than create a master race that would last thousands of years.

It is worthwhile to stop for a moment and think about this interpretation and what it means. Marxist theory would argue that Hitler really didn't care about the Jews or his Aryan master race. Instead, he was simply rebuilding the economy and eliminating a portion of the wealthy capitalist class. Thus, it was simply a fight over wealth. This same argument would be applied to other genocides, such as Rwanda. Instead of race being the motivating factor, it was the competition for money that was simply disguised as a racial issue. Thinking back to our opening puzzle, consider how this perspective might explain the 2003 Iraq War. What do you think of this argument? In what ways does it help explain these examples, and what are its limitations and weaknesses?

Another example comes from the first leader of the first communist state, the Soviet Union. Vladimir Lenin argued that relatively rich and powerful countries such as Britain and France needed colonies to continue expanding the wealth of their capitalist class and to delay the inevitable socialist revolution. In *Imperialism: The Highest Stage of Capitalism*, Lenin argued that these wealthy states might be nearing the brink of a revolution, but by conquering new colonies, they could extract more wealth from the colonies and pay off the workers within the home state. For example, to keep British workers from revolting, Great Britain needed to acquire more and more colonies to extract wealth for the capitalists and pay the British proletariat more so that they would not overthrow the government. According to Lenin, capitalist states would compete for such colonial acquisitions (empires) and would engage in war with each other as a consequence. In fact, Lenin predicted that once the entire world had been colonized, the big imperial powers would turn on each other, and the final conflict would end in their destruction and a series of successful socialist revolutions. Lenin explained World War I as a function of this imperialism pattern.

The second connection between Marxist theory and international relations concerns the process of societies shifting from capitalism to **socialism**. The theory asserted that socialism would spread worldwide. Marx and Engels saw the spread of communism to be an inevitable, evolutionary process, but other communist leaders such as Stalin interpreted Marx and Engels to mean that a socialist state was obligated to compel **regime change** in other states. That is, it was the responsibility of socialist countries to promote socialist revolutions in other countries. Not all socialist countries followed this philosophy, nor did many have the ability to actively promote social revolts. The Soviet Union, however, very actively promoted social revolution around the world. In the years between World Wars I and II, some limited support was given to the Chinese Communist Party led by Mao Zedong, and in 1949 the Chinese Communists prevailed in their civil war and came to power in Beijing. After World War II, beginning with the division of Germany into East and West components and continuing through Eastern Europe, the Soviet Union provided significant support, mostly in the form of military aid, to communist insurgents and politicians. It also put significant pressure on the United States, the United Kingdom, and France to withdraw any objections to the Soviet influence in Eastern Europe.

In many cases, the Soviets were successful, and in others they were not. In Hungary, Czechoslovakia, Bulgaria, Romania, and Poland, the Soviet Union was successfully able to install socialist governments under its control. Although the Soviets had to intervene in Hungary and Czechoslovakia at different points during the Cold War, these countries remained socialist until the fall of the Soviet Union.

The Soviets also failed in many cases. They supported the communists in Greece during its brief civil war following World War II, but the British and Americans threw their support behind the anti-communist elements. In Italy, the Soviets gave support to communist candidates, but the United States secretly provided significant funding to the anti-communist candidates in the national elections. The anti-communist parties generally prevailed as a result. In Yugoslavia, the Soviets were unable to control the socialist government led by Josip Tito. Yugoslavia was socialist, but Tito did not want to follow the edicts from Moscow. He continued to build a socialist economy, but he developed closer ties with Western Europe and the United States to counter pressure from the Soviets.

As the Cold War went on, the Soviets continued to support communist insurgents around the globe. They supported Fidel Castro in Cuba, Ho Chi Minh in Vietnam, Mengistu Haile Mariam in Ethiopia, the Popular Movement for the Liberation of Angola in (you guessed it) that country, and Daniel Ortega in Nicaragua, to name just a few. This pressure by the Soviets was often countered by US support of anti-communist factions in these countries and others.

The point to draw from these historical examples is that Marxist theory is directly tied to international relations. The theory was often interpreted to prescribe an activist foreign policy, and thus it had a profound impact on world politics. Although there are realist, liberal, and constructivist interpretations of the Cold War, the Marxist perspective is that socialism was supposed to spread, by force if need be, across the globe. Understanding this goal certainly provides

....

socialism: an economic-political system in which the government controls the economy and redistributes wealth to create economic equality in the country.

regime change: the change of a country's government or type of government.

Cuban leaders Raúl and Fidel Castro

Fidel Castro was in power for longer than 10 US presidents, succeeded after his death by his brother Raúl. What will happen to Cuba now that Raúl has stepped down as the Cuban president?

Francois LOCHON/Gamma-Rapho via Getty Images

one explanation of why the Soviets and Americans fought the Cold War.

4-2b Marxist Theory as an Alternative Lens

Marxist theory and its adaptations provide an alternative and non-mainstream perspective on international relations. **Colonies** were certainly an economic gain for the country that controlled them; states like the United Kingdom profited handsomely from colonies such as India. Imperial powers often fought for the control of colonies. To this day, states often act to secure greater resources, such as oil. One can argue that oil is a strategic resource needed for security, but it also fuels the economy. The global socialist revolution never occurred, but the perspective offered by Marxist theory gives us a different and often helpful perspective on international relations. In a world in which economic globalization is a major force, transnational corporations and international investors and financiers are major players, and economic inequality is worsening, what insights might the Marxist approach offer? Although the search for security is key to understanding international relations, wealth is still a powerful motive, and economic security may at times override international security.

Thus, for Marxist theory, the capitalist drive for wealth determines behavior—often in a crude way. For example, rich states might colonize poor societies.

---

colonies: territories that are legally owned and controlled by another country, typically called the imperial power.

dependency theory: a theory of development that argues that the dominance and exploitation of poor countries by rich countries prevents progress and development in the poor countries and makes them dependent on the wealthy countries.

One effort to build an international relations theory from Marxist foundations emphasizing the drive for wealth is **dependency theory**. Dependency theory divides the world into classes: a "core" of wealthy capitalist states and a "periphery" of less-developed countries. In world politics, the rich core does not have to take over the poorer or weaker societies of the periphery by force. Instead, core countries simply have to control the wealth or resources found in the poorer or weaker societies and shape or control the governments of those countries. That can be accomplished via one-sided economic relationships and structures of trade that keep periphery countries tied to the core as suppliers of key products and resources. The box "Foreign Policy in Perspective: Brexit: The UK Withdrawal From the European Union" examines these economic relationships when the conflict is between core countries.

In the Middle East, the economic relationship might be centered on oil. For years, states such as the United Kingdom, France, and the United States used their oil corporations to try to control certain Mideast regimes. By finding the oil, producing it, and paying royalty fees to the local elites in charge of those Mideast states, Western corporations enriched local elites beyond their prior expectations. As a result, the local power structure had financial incentives to remain loyal to the needs of the states enriching them. For their part, the wealthy states now had reasonably certain access to a needed resource at an attractive price. Yet because initially the local elites rarely had the engineering, technical, or managerial expertise to run their own oil industries without outside help, they often were constrained to take whatever offer the wealthy outsiders made them because their alternative was to do without that new source of wealth. Thus, local elites became dependent on wealthy states, and the wealthy states could often manipulate this dependency to get what they wanted from the poorer states.

Oil was the focus of such dependency relationships in the Middle East, but in other states it might be different vital natural resources—like bauxite ore (for making aluminum) or copper ore in Chile, gold in the Democratic Republic of the Congo, diamonds in Sierra Leone, and so on. Oftentimes, multinational corporations were the agent that accomplished the wealthy state's goal of creating dependency relationships. In fact, one of the main tenets of the dependency perspective is that such corporations were key instruments of the core.

A good example came from one company in Guatemala. In the 1950s, the United Fruit Company practically owned Guatemala. It was the largest single landowner in the state and the largest single employer, and it owned the only railroad line and only telephone company in Guatemala. At some

Brexit: The UK Withdrawal From the European Union

As the governing Conservative Party sought reelection in 2015, its leader—Prime Minister David Cameron—faced unrest from a faction within his party expressing concerns about the social and economic costs of European Union membership. At the same time, the right-wing UK Independence Party was gaining public support for its nationalist, anti-EU, and anti-immigrant platform, threatening to bleed votes away from the Conservative Party. Hoping to fortify his own party support and get the right-wing voters to join the Conservative Party, Cameron endorsed a future referendum on EU membership in an effort to secure control of Parliament in the election. When the Conservative Party unexpectedly gained an outright majority of seats in Parliament in its 2015 election victory, the Conservative Party scheduled a national referendum on EU membership for June 2016. With a majority of the public supporting continued membership, albeit with some changes and safeguards for national control of some issues, Cameron and the mainstream portion of his party did not expect the referendum (to leave the EU) to succeed.

After a hotly contested campaign pitting "stay" advocates against "leave" proponents, the surprise results ended in a 51.9% to 48.1% victory for those advocating "Brexit," or British exit from the EU. Highly controversial, and potentially very costly for the UK, Europe, and perhaps others in the global economy, the divisive vote pitted rural against urban areas, the working class against professionals, and England and Wales, which voted to leave, against Northern Ireland and Scotland, which voted to stay (see Map 4-1). The UK had joined the forerunner to the European Union in 1973 and the expanded EU in 1992. Twenty-five years later, it elected to withdraw.

Shocked, Prime Minister Cameron immediately announced his resignation and was replaced by Theresa May. Leaders of the anti-EU faction of the Conservative Party were elevated to key positions in the government, including Boris Johnson (former mayor of London) as head of the UK's Foreign Office. As the new prime minister, May began the process of British withdrawal from the EU in early 2017, invoking Article 50 of the Treaty on the European Union to begin the process for Brexit. As Brexit proceeded, the UK faced the challenge of renegotiating all of its trade policies with Europe (imagine if California seceded and had to negotiate trade policy with the US, as if it were a foreign country like Mexico or Canada). The very serious difficulties in doing so caused multiple delays and failures during 2018 and 2019, eventually leading to Theresa May's resignation and her replacement by Boris Johnson. Johnson negotiated a revised agreement with the EU, and after a national election

MAP 4-1

Voting Areas for the European Union Membership Referendum

Source: Map of the United Kingdom showing the voting areas for the European Union membership referendum, 2016. https://commons.wikimedia.org/wiki/File:United_Kingdom_EU_referendum_2016_area_results.svg#/media/File:United_Kingdom_EU_referendum_2016_area_results_2-tone.svg. Licensed under licensed under CC BY-SA 4.0 http://creativecommons.org/licenses/by-sa/4.0.

in December 2019 kept him in office, he secured ratification by the parliament in January 2020. The UK formally exited the EU at the end of that month.

1. Why would the British seek withdrawal from the EU in 2016?

2. Do realism, liberalism, and constructivism explain the Brexit decision?

3. Might leaders and domestic politics play a role? What about the impact of globalization, identity, and inequality? ●

First Arabian American oil company well in Saudi Arabia

For more than 70 years, the United States has been involved in the Middle East because of its valuable oil. How fair was this relationship in the 1950s? What about now?

Three Lions/Getty Images

Workers in Guatemala deliver bananas

Although your bananas may cost only a few dollars for a bunch, fruit is big business in Latin America. How much do you think these workers benefit from the wealth they help produce?

AP Photo/Rodrigo Abd

point, whatever the US-owned United Fruit Company wanted in Guatemala, it tended to get from the Guatemalan government. When the Guatemalan regime led by President Jacobo Árbenz chose to stand up to United Fruit in 1953–1954, the company appealed to the US government for help. Given that US Secretary of State John Foster Dulles and his brother Allen Dulles, the director of central intelligence at the time, had previously worked for the Wall Street law firm of Sullivan and Cromwell that represented United Fruit and that John Foster Dulles was a member of United Fruit's board of directors, the company had sympathetic ears at high levels of the US government. Thus, it seems unsurprising that the CIA organized a military coup that toppled the offending Árbenz regime and replaced it with one more friendly to United Fruit's corporate interests. As a reward, the new Guatemalan government led by Carlos Castillo Armas was showered with increased levels of US foreign aid, so long as it continued to do what the United States and United Fruit wanted it to do. The regime consequently became increasingly dependent on the economic goodwill of the United States to remain in power.

Dependency theory argued that in addition to the local ruling elites being dependent on wealthy corporations, poor states were dependent on the wealthy to develop, modernize, and grow their economies. Because corporations like United Fruit (now Chiquita Brands International Sàrl) could extract all of the profits from Guatemala's fruit plantations, the Guatemalans themselves were left only with enough money to survive—not enough to develop and grow. The theory argued that such foreign investment and ownership of property and resources in the poor countries made it impossible for them to develop into modern economies. So Guatemala continued to produce low-cost bananas but not higher-cost manufactured items, like automobiles or computers. However, empirical evidence showed that foreign direct investment did help grow the economies of these poor countries, suggesting that the theory, while intuitive, was factually inaccurate. Considerable debate continues to surround the idea of poor states' dependence on wealthy states. In countries where the foreign investment is well managed and regulated by the local government, considerable economic advancements have been made. However, there were many cases similar to Guatemala in the 1950s. Many countries were once part of the big colony known as French West Africa. Are West African states rich yet?

4-3 WORLD SYSTEMS THEORY

>> **4-3**   **Describe the different aspects of world systems theory and how they explain international relations.**

Using the foundations created by Marx and Engels and the innovations of the dependency argument from the 1960s, scholars in the 1970s developed an alternative economic theory of international relations.

World systems theory (WST) took the idea of unequal exchange between the classes that was the basis for Marxist theory and applied it to the international system. The theory asserts that instead of a universal capitalist class ruling the world, each state acts according to its position in the economic system. Like structural realism, state behavior according to WST is very much determined by the state's economic characteristics relative to other states in the world.

It is easy to understand this theorizing—which can become rather dense if you are not careful—by looking at the way WST describes the world. WST asserts there are three zones or types of states. The first zone is the **core**. Core states are the wealthiest, most powerful, and most industrialized, and they basically call the shots in the world economy. These countries make the most profitable and advanced products of the particular time, they have the strongest and most efficient governments, they are often at the forefront of technological innovation, and they have the greatest influence in world politics. A good example of a core state is the United States. It produces goods and services such as military weapons, computers, pharmaceuticals, software, and financial and legal services. Like other core states, its economy is diversified, so it also sells a great deal of agricultural products and heavy equipment. The US government is large, and—despite what you might think if, say, you often have trouble with your student loans—it is very efficient compared to other countries. Other examples of core states are Germany, France, Japan, Australia, the United Kingdom, Norway, and Sweden.

The second economic zone is the **semi-periphery**. Semi-peripheral states tend to produce goods and services and do not rely solely on the export of raw materials (e.g., lumber, food, oil) for their economy. However, those goods and services are not as profitable as the core country's products. For example, semi-peripheral states will tend to export textiles, household items, some types of industrial equipment, and so on. The economy will be industrializing and developing toward that of the core, but it will be at least one generation behind core-country products. The government will be stable and relatively efficient but still developing toward the goal of the core-zone level of efficiency. These states will have a strong voice in the world but not compared to the core states.

A good example of a semi-periphery country is India. It has a strong, stable democracy, although the government does have efficiency issues. It exports textiles, rugs, jewelry, and drilling equipment, as well as (refined) fuel oil, steel, chemicals, vehicles, and both information technology services and information technology software engineers. India has significant influence in the world, but not when compared to the United States, Japan, Germany, or the United Kingdom. Other semi-peripheral states include Mexico, China, South Africa, Chile, Brazil, and Russia.

The last zone is the **periphery**. These states have weak governments, tend to sell only raw materials or cheap labor, and have almost no influence in world politics. Examples of these states are unfortunately plentiful. Bangladesh, Vietnam, most of sub-Saharan Africa, and most of Central America and the Caribbean are peripheral states. They make very small profits from their raw materials and cheap labor, their governments tend to be the most unstable and corrupt in the world, and they have almost no voice on the world stage.

Before you read any further, think of a few states we haven't discussed thus far and see if you can identify which zone they occupy. Is a wealthy state like Saudi Arabia in the core, semi-periphery, or periphery? What about Spain, Singapore, or South Korea? China represents an interesting puzzle in this as well. A state's zone isn't always determined by wealth but rather by what its economy produces and consumes, as well as how wealthy and educated its residents are. Map 4-2 depicts the classification of countries into the three zones. Do you find any surprises?

These three zones operate in a hierarchical fashion. Like Marx's view of the capitalist class, the core dominates and extracts profits from the semi-periphery and periphery, the semi-periphery dominates and extracts profits from the periphery, and the periphery is simply left in relative poverty. Like Marxist theory, WST argues that wars are fought between the different zones to enforce the world order. For example, WST explains the US-led invasion of Iraq in 2003 as the leading core state attacking a periphery state because the core state (the United States) believed that the periphery state (Iraq) was attempting to gain considerable power with weapons of mass destruction and, perhaps, to preserve the hierarchical relationship and control of an importance resource—oil. In another example, the Cold War is explained as a war between two rival economic systems—capitalism and communism. WST asserts that it is not security that the United States and the Soviet Union sought but dominance over the economic system.

Like Marxist theory, WST is appealing in many of its descriptive elements, and it may be particularly interesting in the globalizing world. However, WST

....

core: the economic zone composed of wealthy countries producing high-end products.

semi-periphery: the economic zone composed of middle-income countries that produce secondary products.

periphery: the economic zone composed of poor countries that primarily export raw materials.

MAP 4-2

The Countries of the Core, Semi-Periphery, and Periphery

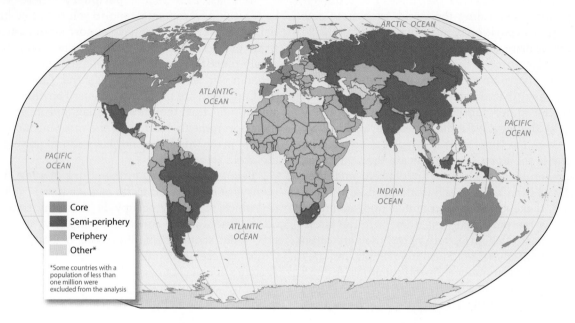

Core
Semi-periphery
Periphery
Other*

*Some countries with a population of less than one million were excluded from the analysis

Source: Wikicommons.

also has limits in the power of its predictions and explanations. Part of the reason for this is that the theory, again like Marxism, also advocates and predicts social change. Realism, liberalism, and constructivism make fewer and more limited predictions, none as bold as the fall of capitalism. Marxist theory and WST both take that risk, so to speak, but it does not pay off. By removing the politicized aspect of both theories, you can see the explanatory benefits: the importance of economic conditions, wealth as a motive, and so on. When applying these theories to the world, however, it is important to realize that both WST and especially Marxist theory are ideologies in addition to theories.

Critics also note that WST tends to consider the zones—and the class structure that underlies them—as more important than the actual states that compose them. Like Marxist theory, the state is not emphasized relative to the three zones. Some observers—realists and liberals, for instance—may consider this problematic, but it is valuable to consider how certain characteristics may transcend state boundaries. Economic connections across zones or classes may be one of those characteristics. Wealthy states, corporations, and individuals very often have similar

World Economic Forum: a forum held in Switzerland every year that brings together wealthy individuals, corporate leaders, industry leaders, and heads of government to coordinate economic policies and initiatives.

preferences and work together to attain their mutual goals. A good example is the **World Economic Forum** held in Davos, Switzerland, every year, which brings together wealthy individuals, corporate and industry leaders, and heads of government of selected core states to coordinate economic policies and initiatives. However, those same states, corporations, and individuals often have competing goals, and conflict arises from that competition.

So does the World Economic Forum provide evidence that WST is right or wrong? What does it say about Marxist theory? What about other examples, like the G20 meetings in which the leaders of the 20 largest economies meet to discuss matters of common concern? Which one of these theories (and don't forget about realism, liberalism, and constructivism) is most helpful? Like the rest of international relations, the answer is not simple. WST and Marxist theory have a point that economic interests cross state borders, but governments are typically not simply an illusion covering up economic struggle. Instead, we should consider the power of economic interests when we also consider the politics of international relations. Ultimately, as students of international relations, we should consider all possibilities and not limit ourselves to one perspective or theory. Other implications of these geographic zones are explored in the box "The Revenge of Geography: Zones of Wealth and Peace?"

Zones of Wealth and Peace?

Looking at Map 4-3, do you notice any particular patterns? The wealthiest states tend to be north of the equator, with the most notable exception being Australia. Notice also how the poor and rich states are clustered around each other (see Chapters 8 and 10 for a discussion of this pattern).

MAP 4-3

World Map Showing GDP per Capita and Internal Violence

Why do poorer countries have greater rates of civil violence? Why aren't the poorest states more violent?

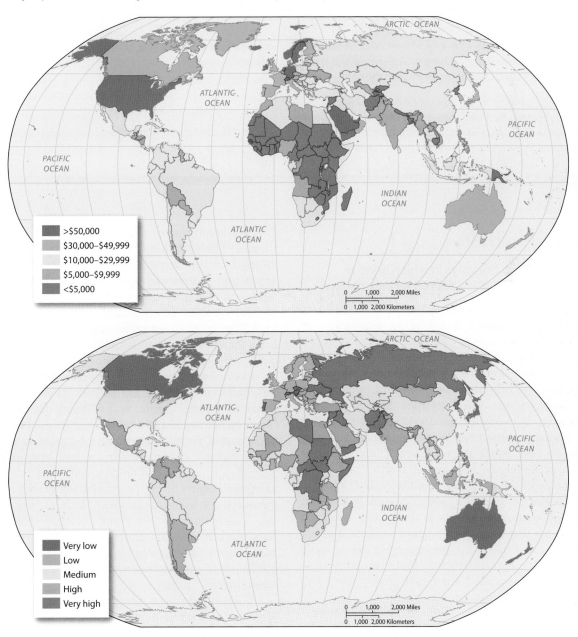

> \>$50,000
> $30,000–$49,999
> $10,000–$29,999
> $5,000–$9,999
> <$5,000

> Very low
> Low
> Medium
> High
> Very high

(Continued)

(Continued)

Now also note how violence tends to occur in the same groups of countries that are also poor. Just being born in a country like Somalia means your life would be completely different than if you were born in Germany. The average German lives to be 81 years old, but the average Somali lives to only 55. Perhaps this is the first revenge geography has on humans—quite simply, the country in which you were born.

Looking at these two conditions—poverty/violence and wealth/peace—how does Marxist theory explain these patterns? If all conflict is based on economic classes, are there fewer classes in wealthy countries? Shouldn't there be conflict, according to Marxist theory, in all non-socialist countries? What about world systems theory? Using WST terms, why is the periphery so much more violent than the core?

These theories would likely point out the unequal relationship between the wealthy states and the poor states. Both theories might assert that the wealthy states extract surplus from the poor countries to pay off the middle and lower classes in their own countries. To extract the surplus, the wealthy states instigate conflict in the poor states to keep them from fighting back. That is why, according to these theories, there is little conflict in wealthy states but considerable violence in poor states.

Constructivists might suggest that in poor countries, the difference between rich and poor people is so extreme that many of the poor feel deprived and believe that violence is the only rational option to improve their condition. In wealthier countries, the poor are better off, and the difference between them and the wealthy is not usually so extreme. Thus, the violence could be the result of a socially constructed view emphasizing deprivation.

1. Does one of these explanations make more sense to you? Why?

2. What might be done to help solve this poverty–conflict nexus? ●

4-4 FEMINISM

>> **4-4** **Outline the ways in which gender affects and is affected by international relations.**

Like the constructivist and Marxist approaches to international relations, the feminist approach offers a different perspective from liberalism and realism. In fact, feminism often uses a constructivist approach to explain the role of women in world politics and the consequences world politics has specifically for women. Like Marxist theory, it suggests not just an explanation of international relations but also a goal to seek equality for women. The similarities with Marxist theory, however, end with the alternative nature of the approach and the desire for social change. Marxist theory, as we discussed, focuses on class and economic conflict. It does not leave room for the idea that men and women are different or act differently and that there are consequences specific to men and women. It suggests that if economic disparities are eliminated, then men and women will be equal, but it sees gender inequality as only a side effect of economic inequality. The idea that fundamental differences exist in the behavior and outlook of men and women is one of the assumptions that some feminists use in their approach to international relations.

The feminist approach can be divided into three themes. The first theme is the narrowest and most focused on the impact of gender on how we think about and understand world politics. This form of feminism asks whether our entire view, our entire way of thinking about international relations, is masculinized. That is, all of the realist and liberal thinkers—at least at first—were men. Perhaps the development of our theories themselves is gender biased and should be reexamined, because our ways of thinking about international relations are biased. Even now, as a study by Dion, Sumner, and Mitchell (2018) notes, "accumulated evidence identifies discernible gender gaps across many dimensions of professional academic careers including salaries, publication rates, journal placement, career progress, and academic service. Recent work in political science also reveals gender gaps in citations, with articles written by men citing work by other male scholars more often than work by female scholars. . . . [Thus,] women's research is viewed as less important or their ideas are attributed to male scholars, even as a field becomes more diverse" (p. 312).

The second theme raises the question of whether world politics would be different if women held more or most leadership positions in states. This theme addresses how women may behave differently from men in a political environment and how that different behavior would shape world politics. For example, would war be less common if women represented half (or more) of the world's leaders? Unlike the first theme, this approach suggests we may be thinking about international relations correctly—we just need more women involved.

The third theme reverses the focus of the first theme. Instead of looking at what impact women may or could have had on theory development or world politics, this branch of feminist international relations focuses on the impact world politics has on women. For example, do women suffer economically more than men during a war? In this strand of thinking, we are encouraged to consider a different set of problems that tend to be "hidden" by the gendered nature of world politics and international relations theory.

4-4a The Impact of Women on International Relations Theory

In addition to the practical idea that more women leaders could change the world, an even more fundamental argument about gender and international relations exists. We have discussed international relations theorists such as Thucydides, Machiavelli, Hobbes, Morgenthau, and others. Each of these thinkers has a common characteristic—with few exceptions, they are all men. What if all of our theories about international relations are gender biased? Those theories are read and often studied by all world leaders, even before they rise to power. That means that those theories guide how leaders—men and women—act in the international arena. But what if these theories are wrong or at least are biased toward masculine traits, such as competitiveness and aggression?

Many feminist scholars ask this question. Could the international system not be as competitive and dangerous as we think, or perhaps it is but doesn't have to be? What if we instead thought of other nations as friends or partners? What if instead of coercion, diplomacy and negotiations were given longer to work? It certainly seems reasonable to think that war would be less likely and that the international system would be more peaceful.

Another problem with defining the world as hostile and women as peaceful is that doing so helps exclude women from the study and practice of international relations. For example, J. Ann Tickner (1992) argues that by defining world politics in masculine terms—dangerous, hostile, competitive, and so on—women have been considered irrelevant. If women are good at peace, but international relations is about conflict, then what do women have to offer? Tickner points out that we must consider alternative definitions of the international system that include feminine viewpoints. Only then can we both include more

women in the study and practice of foreign affairs and better understand the world in which we live.

You may be thinking that much of this discussion sounds similar to constructivist ideas about anarchy, and you would be right. The idea that our understanding of the international system is gender biased is based on the idea that it is socially constructed. In the world dominated by men—particularly in centuries past—women rarely helped construct the international system. If they had, concepts such as security, anarchy, and sovereignty might have very different meanings today.

We can't go back in time to change our theories and practices, but we can be aware of them as we try to figure out how the world works. As students of international relations, we should take time to question the assumptions that create the foundation for realism and liberalism. For example, is the idea of self-help purely masculine? If it is, how would the international system function if we had a gender-balanced view of anarchy that better included the perspectives of men and women? Perhaps anarchy would mean less self-help and more collective action that would root out aggressive states and reform them.

Although not directly related to gender, studies of baboons by Robert Sapolsky show that troops in which there are no aggressive males tend to be more peaceful (surprise!), but when outside aggressive males join the troop, they are quickly taught the non-aggressive norms of the troop. Perhaps a gender-balanced international system would work the same way: Conflict would be rare, and aggressive states would be ostracized until they became less bellicose. States are not like baboons, but we should be proactive in that kind of questioning and thinking when we examine the world.

New Zealand Prime Minister Jacinda Ardern speaks to media during a press conference in May 2020
How does gender really matter?

Hagen Hopkins/Getty Images

4-4b The Impact of Women on International Relations

Women make up just under half (49.6%) of the world's population, but less than 10% of the world's countries are currently led by women. Although as many as 24 states had a woman as chief executive in recent years, by mid-2020, only 22 women held the top leadership position of their countries, out of 196 countries in the world (see Table 4-1). In fact, most of the world's countries have never had a woman leader (only about 70 countries have at some time). To be sure, there are many other women in leadership positions, such as three of the last seven US secretaries of state: Madeleine Albright, Condoleezza Rice, and Hillary Clinton. Women have also played important political roles and occupied important political positions outside of head of government as well, including such individuals as Nancy Pelosi, twice Speaker of the House of Representatives in the US; Britain's Princess Diana, who tirelessly campaigned against land mines and pushed the British royal family into more philanthropic roles before her untimely death; and Tarana Burke, who started the Me Too movement. Even considering these women, the number of women in any political leadership role is still well below half. This gender imbalance in world leaders begs the question: If half or more of the world's leaders were women, would there be a difference in international relations? For just one example, see "Spotlight On: Women and World War C."

TABLE 4-1

Women Country Leaders, 2020

HEAD OF STATE OR GOVERNMENT	COUNTRY	YEARS IN OFFICE
Chancellor Angela Merkel	Germany	14
Prime Minister Sheikh Hasina	Bangladesh	11
Prime Minister Erna Solberg	Norway	6
Prime Minister Saara Kuugongelwa	Namibia	5
President Bidhya Devi Bhandari	Nepal	4
State Counselor Aung San Suu Kyi	Myanmar	4
President Kersti Kaljulaid	Estonia	3
Prime Minister Ana Brnabic	Serbia	3
President Tsia Ing-wen	Taiwan	3
President Halimah Yacob	Singapore	3
President Paula Mae Weekes	Trinidad and Tobago	2
Prime Minister Katrín Jakobsdóttir	Iceland	2
Prime Minister Jacinda Ardern	New Zealand	2
Prime Minister Mia Mottley	Barbados	2
President Sahle-Work Zewde	Ethiopia	2
President Salome Zurabishvili	Georgia	1
President Zuzana Čaputová	Slovakia	1
Prime Minister Mette Frederiksen	Denmark	1
Prime Minister Sophie Wilmès	Belgium	1
Acting President Jeanine Áñez	Bolivia	1
Prime Minister Sanna Marin	Finland	1
President Katerina Sakellaropoulou	Greece	1

Note: Figures are through August 2020. President of the Swiss Confederation Simonetta Sommaruga is a member of the Swiss Federal Council, which serves collectively as head of state and head of government.

Women and World War C

In 2020, as the novel coronavirus COVID-19 swept across the world in a global pandemic, country after country scrambled to respond to the public health crisis. Globally, leaders undertook a wide variety of measures to protect their citizens. While some delayed and denied the seriousness of the problem, others took early efforts to manage and minimize the devastating effects of the virus. What did the countries with the best responses to COVID-19 share in common?

According to Avivah Wittenberg-Cox (2020), the countries of Iceland, Taiwan, Germany, New Zealand, Finland, Norway, and Denmark distinguished themselves with their effective responses. Their common future: women in the role of chief executive. Angela Merkel (Germany), Tsai Ing-wen (Taiwan), Jacinda Ardern (New Zealand), Katrín Jakobsdóttir (Iceland), Sanna Marin (Finland), Erna Solberg (Norway), and Mette Frederiksen (Denmark) all led their countries to swift, decisive, aggressive, and effective responses that dramatically mitigated the damage of the pandemic, putting their countries well ahead of most in managing the effects of the virus and positioning

their societies for speedier recovery. As Wittenberg-Cox stated, they constitute "case study sightings of the seven leadership traits men may want to learn from women" (para. 10).

Contrast the experiences of these seven countries with others. Wittenberg-Cox (2020) put it starkly:

> Now, compare these leaders and stories with the strongmen using the crisis to accelerate a terrifying trifecta of authoritarianism: blame-"others," capture-the-judiciary, demonize-the-journalists, and blanket their country in I-will-never-retire darkness (Trump, Bolsonaro, Obrador, Modi, Duterte, Orban, Putin, Netanyahu . . .). (para. 9)

Do you think the pattern of women leaders saving more lives in their countries is just a coincidence, or could it be that they prioritize life, human security, and quality-of-life issues over personal power issues? Could this be due to their gender or perhaps norms about appropriate gender roles? ●

Some theories argued that there would in fact be differences. Following the basic stereotypes of men and women, some feminist scholars argued that women would be more peaceful and cooperative leaders than men. Instead of being realists, women would tend to be more liberal in their approach to international relations. They would be less concerned with national and international security, for example, and more concerned with economic and human security—and economic security would be defined partly as economic equality. Instead of being coercive, women leaders would engage other countries with aid and diplomacy. More important, they would interact with countries not to gain power but to develop a better relationship that would focus on peace, equal development, and, perhaps, the environment. The result would be a more peaceful planet.

This perspective is often ascribed to **difference feminists**. This feminist perspective sees men and women as different in their basic nature. These differences can be attributed to genetic or hormonal differences (e.g., estrogen versus testosterone) and/or socially constructed differences (e.g., more boys play competitive contact sports than girls). These basic differences mean that women would be better at negotiating a peace treaty, whereas men would be

better at fighting a war. Both can be considered as important and needed, but both must also be considered equal. That is, difference feminists argue that only male traits are values in international relations, so there is more conflict in the world. If more women were in leadership roles, then there would be greater balance and peace in the international system.

A potential problem with this perspective is that, in many instances, as women ascended to lead different countries, they tended to act much like their male counterparts. That is, women were no less coercive and tough than men when leading a country. For example, Margaret Thatcher, the prime minister of the United Kingdom from 1979 to 1990, was referred to as the "Iron Lady," not because she was engaging, nurturing, and peaceful but because she talked and acted very tough. Thatcher engaged the Soviets with very harsh diplomacy but then convinced her close ally, President Ronald Reagan, that the new Soviet leader, Mikhail Gorbachev, was someone with whom they could negotiate. Up to that point, Thatcher had no intention of negotiating with the Soviets. In 1982,

difference feminists: proponents of the feminist perspective who argue men and women are fundamentally different in their abilities, particularly in their approach to conflict.

early in Thatcher's tenure, Argentina invaded the Falkland Islands, British-owned and populated islands approximately 300 miles off the coast of Argentina. Thatcher led a successful and short (74-day) war to reclaim the islands. She made it clear from the start of the invasion that she would not negotiate with the Argentinians at all. It was also widely reported at the time that Thatcher urged George H. W. Bush to take a hard-line, aggressive approach to Iraq's invasion of Kuwait in 1991.

Thatcher may be an archetypal example, but she is by no means the only one. Indira Gandhi of India, Golda Meir of Israel, Benazir Bhutto of Pakistan, Angela Merkel of Germany, Theresa May of the United Kingdom, and others have held the leadership position of their countries. As more and more (although it is clearly still very few) women held those positions, they proved to behave more like than different from the men who preceded them. They were tough, did not shrink from conflict, and certainly did not fit an older stereotype of women as peaceful, nurturing mothers who feared conflict. So perhaps women—when leading a country—really do not behave any differently from men?

There are at least two potential responses to the conclusion that the gender of the leader does not matter. First, even though women and men are obviously different, the leadership position—whether it is president, prime minister, or autocratic leader—requires that both men and women act the same way to be successful. Consider women leaders in the developing world: Should we expect their gender to lead to different behavior, or should we expect factors such as poverty and ethnic divisions to cause them to act

no differently than the male leaders of the developing world? Some would argue that, regardless of the personal characteristics and preferences of the leader, they must act pretty much like all other leaders or cease to be effective and thus cease being the leader. For example, imagine that a pacifist was elected to a country's presidency. If that leader did not stand up to the pressures of other leaders, including showing a willingness to use the military when appropriate, either that leader could be replaced by another leader or the country could eventually be taken over by more aggressive states. Thus, to stay in power and maintain the integrity of the state, the leader—man or woman—would have to forgo his or her own pacifism and act assertively, even coercively, like other leaders.

This response is based in part on the self-help characteristic of the international system. If one leader tried to be engaging rather than coercive, passive rather than assertive, other states would quickly take advantage of that state. No one was going to help Margaret Thatcher retake the Falkland Islands, and the Argentinians were not responsive to engagement. She had to take the islands back by force.

A second response to the idea that women leaders are no different from their male counterparts is based on the tiny number of state leaders who are women. The idea is that in the current self-help, anarchic system, we should not be surprised that women behave in the same manner as men. They are simply following the rules of the game. However, would those rules be different if half of the leaders in the world were women? What if half of the leaders of Europe had been women in 1648 when the self-help system was born? If the leadership had been gender balanced

Heads of the wealthiest states meet at the 2019 G7 Summit

German Chancellor Angela Merkel stands out among the world's most powerful leaders. Would the world be different if half (or more) of the leaders were women?

AP Photo/Andrew Harnik, Pool

in 1648, perhaps the system would have evolved into a more cooperative, less competitive system. Instead of self-help, perhaps "responsible sovereignty" would have formed more than 370 years ago.

The problem with this response is that it is speculative. It asserts that because the world system (anarchy, self-help) is constructed or conceived by men, it is necessarily competitive and aggressive. It also asserts that women are simply not as aggressive as men. But is this the case? There is no way to know, because we cannot go back in time and fundamentally change the structure of European society in 1648. We can speculate what the world would be like if men and women shared power hundreds of years ago. So what would the world look like? Would there be sovereign states? Would there be more or less war? Would there be more or less poverty?

There is, however, empirical research on the impact of women in other organizations—businesses and corporations, agencies, and even legislative bodies—that suggests that the mere presence of women in those organizations has an impact and that those with significant numbers of women exhibit a different decision-making style and pursue different agendas (McGlen and Sarkees 1993, 1995, 2006). For example, legislatures with more women tend to consider and debate social policy (e.g., medical coverage and regulation) more than economic policy (e.g., tax rates). Some evidence indicates that corporations and other types of organizations with more women in top positions tend to practice more cooperative, participatory, and consensus-based approaches to decision making. In other words, men and women may prioritize issues differently and thus pursue different agendas when given the opportunity.

When do such opportunities arise for women? One interesting hallmark of this research suggests that there is a sort of critical mass or threshold (about 30%) that must be reached. In organizations in which women constitute less than 30% of the personnel (or leaders), little difference can be identified. In those with more than 30%, some research finds that this critical mass empowers a kind of solidarity in which women's different style, approach, and preferences are evident. In effect, where there are few women, those in power or leadership tend to conform to the male-dominated context, but where there is a critical number of women, they do not (Dahlerup 1988; Kanter 1977; Phillips 1995; see the UNWomen.org website for more information).

This perspective is promoted by **liberal feminists**. This feminist view does not require there to be a fundamental difference between the politics of men and women. Instead of suggesting that both men and women should be in equal leadership roles because they bring different abilities to the table, liberal

President Bidhya Devi Bhandari, the first woman president of Nepal

Not all women leaders are from powerful countries. Elected in 2015, President Bhandari is the chief executive in a traditionally male-dominated country. What would it be like to be the first woman leader of a male-dominated country?

AP Photo/Manish Swarup

feminists suggest that simply having more women in leadership roles is important and will make a difference. The women may lead in the same way that men do, but if there is an equal number of men and women, different issues will likely be discussed (e.g., human security issues might matter more and international security issues less), different perspectives will be incorporated into discussion, and, most important, there will be gender equality for women.

It is important to note the difference between these two perspectives. Liberal feminists see an equal number of women and men in leadership roles as important because it promotes overall gender equality, which is a good thing. Difference feminists go further and suggest that women are more peaceful and less aggressive than men, and thus more women leaders will create an environment in which there will be more peace.

Some fascinating research in this area has begun to tell us what effects gender equality might have on international relations. For example, whether or not women are in leadership positions, do countries that have higher levels of respect for women act differently from those that discriminate against them? The answer is yes—when a country has greater gender equality, it is less likely to initiate a war, although it may still be attacked by other countries. Further, countries with greater gender equality tend to be less likely to have civil wars (Hudson, Ballif-Spanvill, Caprioli, and Emmett 2017). Thus, whether women directly influence international politics, or whether

....

liberal feminists: proponents of the feminist perspective who argue men and women can approach issues such as conflict the same way but that it is important to have equal representation of the two genders.

countries that treat women equally indirectly influence international affairs, the status of women matters when one is trying to understand international relations.

4-4c The Impact of International Relations on Women

Having discussed whether our theories of international relations are gender biased and how women might affect international relations, we must turn to how world politics affects women. Generally speaking, women do not hold an equal status in countries around the world. If they did, in 2010 the UN would not have felt the need to create the United Nations Entity for Gender Equality and the Empowerment of Women (or UN Women). Some examples may be useful to illustrate the situation. Holding a job means a greater level of independence and worth. But according to World Bank data for 2016, women compose only 46% of the workforce in the United States and in Germany, 47% in the United Kingdom, and 48% in France. Globally, the median share of women in the workforce is 39%. Although Germany has a woman chancellor, Angela Merkel, only about 31% of the parliament (the Bundestag) is made up of women. That percentage might seem low until you consider that in 2020 a record high of just under 24% of the members of the US House of Representatives were women. The US ranks 76th (out of nearly 200 countries) on this measure.

Women in developing countries have it much worse. In a fundamentalist theocracy such as Iran, women have few rights and protections relative to men. Severe religious restrictions require women to cover their bodies and hair while in public, and when they do not, the punishment can include death. In Iran, as of 2020, only 19.5% of the workforce was made up of women. That does not give women much independence or worth.

When the Taliban controlled Afghanistan, women older than 11 years of age could not leave their homes unless accompanied by their husband or a close male relative. If a woman was widowed and had no male relatives in the area, she could literally starve to death in her own home.

In China, boy babies are considered to be more valuable than girls, and more baby girls are aborted than baby boys. Sex-selection abortions have become so rampant that for every 100 girls born, there are 120 boys born. Even more horrific, newborn girls are regularly found in dumpsters, abandoned and left for dead by their parents ("The Truly Inspiring Story . . ." 2012).

Because women are often at a disadvantage in a country, particularly in poor and developing countries, they tend to be hurt more than men when there is upheaval in a society, and few events cause more upheaval than international war and civil war. When a country slips into conflict—whether with another state or through civil war—potential violence, higher levels of stress and anxiety, and severe economic disruption are likely results. In the United Kingdom during World War II, there was food and fuel rationing and curfews. In non-democratic countries, the restrictions are usually more severe. Beyond rationing and curfews, any dissent toward the government is likely to lead to forced relocation, forced labor, and severe punishment. In this climate, violence against women is more common. The stresses of war and the new restrictions initiated by the government make domestic violence against women more likely. The likelihood of rape increases when a civil war is being fought in the country, as soldiers and insurgents often use rape as a way to punish their enemy indirectly. Moreover, as Hudson, Ballif-Spanvill, Caprioli, and Emmett (2014) have argued, women's systemic insecurity affects the well-being and security of all, with societies having more gender equality and greater protections for women's rights more likely to flourish.

Wars often mean that men are drafted to fight, leaving women to work to support the war effort. The new employment for women can create new independence for them, but wars often cause economic recession as well. The economic downturn creates pressure within the society, and higher levels of unemployment can lead to domestic violence as families try to cope with less money.

Unlike war, globalization has differing effects on the status of women. Globalization in the form of foreign trade and investment often means more employment opportunities, especially for women who have traditionally had less access to education and training in developing countries. These jobs give women greater worth and more autonomy. On the negative side, many of these jobs are criticized for being sweatshops where employees work long hours for little pay and no job security. However, considerable evidence indicates that the more empowered and successful women are in a society, the better that society performs in the global economy.

The jury is still out, so to speak, on the effects of globalization on women, but recent studies show that economic sanctions—often considered a more peaceful and humane method of coercing a state—have harmful effects on women. Economic sanctions cause a country's economy to shrink. As a consequence, unemployment increases, and in developing countries, women lose their jobs first. Even though women usually earn less than men in these countries, they are still fired from their positions before men. The stress from the shrinking economy also causes more domestic violence and a lower respect for women in poorer countries. Although this effect is smaller compared to the violence against women during wars, it highlights how vulnerable women can be to world events—events that are completely outside of their control.

4-4d Half of the Population but Not Half of the Input

What can be concluded about the feminist perspective on international relations? First, feminism takes a constructivist approach to the world. Given that the primary argument is that the social system tends to place men in positions of power and those positions shape international relations, the construction of the social system has had a huge if not sole defining impact on world politics. There is no biological reason that men would hold most of the positions of political leadership, so constructivism provides the best way to explain the current situation.

Second, because men dominate the positions of leadership, it is hard to know if women would act any differently. However, as our box on "Women and World War C" suggests, women in leadership may behave distinctly. Although many of the arguments about women being different leaders are hypothetical, we do know that legislatures such as the German Bundestag, in which women hold more than 30% of the seats, tend to prioritize some issues differently. Only the future will tell us how different women may act when they hold more leadership positions. In the near term, we may look at leaders like Germany's Angela Merkel or the recently elected women leading Georgia, Slovakia, Denmark, Belgium, Bolivia, Finland, and Greece. Last and certainly not least, we know that women, particularly in less-developed countries, are subject to far worse conditions and treatment than men. Wars, sanctions, economic decline—all of these factors hurt women more than men. Even worse, in many countries, women do not have basic rights, such as freedom to choose their spouse, where they live, or how many children they have; the list goes on.

We should take from this discussion the importance of considering the feminist viewpoint. We cannot forget that when a war starts, it is bad for everyone but particularly bad for women. We also need to ask ourselves this question: Must international relations work "this way," or could it change if the leaders of the world were more evenly balanced between men and women?

Arrested members of the local tribal council who ordered a 15-year-old girl killed because she helped a couple elope in Pakistan in 2016

What might this girl have achieved if allowed to live, and why did these men think it was acceptable to order her death?

SHAKEEL AHMED/AFP via Getty Images

CONCLUSION

So when are the alternatives described in this chapter most useful? Or are realism, liberalism, and constructivism more helpful approaches to understanding international relations? The answer to this question is threefold.

First, we must evaluate each of the perspectives. To do this, we want the same qualities found in a good answer to an exam question: completeness and succinctness. The best perspective is the one that offers the most complete explanation without containing useless information. For example, the predictions of Marxist theory are not helpful for understanding international relations, but its singular focus on economic relationships does provide a lot of information. Foreign policy analysis provides details about how individual agents behave, but is that too much information? Table 4-2 summarizes each of the theories we discussed in this chapter. For each theory, you should ask yourself if it tells "the whole truth and nothing but the truth." Do you think the theory tells you what you need to know to understand the main cause-and-effect relationships, without telling you more than you need to know?

Second, we must answer this question: When is each theory most helpful? These theories each make compelling arguments as to how the world operates. Although Marxist theory often made incorrect predictions, there is certainly truth in some of its characterizations of how people and states relate to each other. Money matters! Foreign policy analysis shows us how leaders can make irrational or illogical decisions, but aren't many of their decisions rational and logical? Feminism shows us that anarchy is socially constructed and does not have to mean competition and conflict, but does that mean there isn't a lot of competition and conflict in the world today? To answer that question, simply look at the conflicts in Iraq, Afghanistan, Syria, Libya, Ukraine, Yemen, and so on. So perhaps feminists are right, but so are realists? What we must do at the end of the day is decide how we as citizens of the world think the world works. Armed with the knowledge of these different perspectives, we can better see the patterns that exist and persist in international relations.

Third, we need to ask this question: Why pick just one theory? There are definitely aspects of these theories that do not fit together. Marxist theory invalidates the ideas of feminism. Foreign policy analysis rejects the idea of a unitary state. However, the idea that economic class is a powerful driving force seems pretty intuitive. So does the evidence that states will follow less aggressive foreign policies if they have greater gender equality. Perhaps the best way to understand international relations is to consider all of these approaches. When carpenters build a house, they use more than just a hammer. For us, each theoretical lens we have considered in this chapter, and in Chapter 3, may help us gain insights on particular problems and situations. Like the carpenter, perhaps we should use all of the tools at our disposal to understand the complex world around us. ●

TABLE 4-2

Summary of Foreign Policy Analysis, Marxist Theory/World Systems Theory, and Feminism

KEY FEATURES	FOREIGN POLICY ANALYSIS	MARXIST THEORY/WORLD SYSTEMS THEORY	FEMINISM
Nature of the international system	Anarchy	Hierarchical	Anarchy, historically dominated by men
Relevant actors	Agents (individuals, groups, societal groups)	Economic classes/states	States, organizations, people
Important resources	Decision-making power/influence	Wealth, military/economics to gain wealth	Power
Central dynamics	Small-group decision making	Class conflict/predatory economics	Conflict as defined by male-dominated history
Anarchy	Exists in the lack of central supranational organizations	Exists in the competition between the wealthy classes in different states/wealthy versus poor states	Lack of central authority, historically defined as conflictual by male leaders
Diversity	Differences in leadership structures/paths to legitimacy	Differences in economic classes/states constitute the only meaningful diversity	Historically low because of a lack of women leaders, now changing
Complexity	Created by the need to satisfy multiple constituency or elite groups	Created by the single driving force of economic class/state economic status	Shaped by the differences that women leaders bring to the world

KEY CONCEPTS

4-1 Understand how the foreign policy perspective provides a foundation for international relations.

The study of foreign policy is agent centered, focusing on the individuals and groups who make decisions within the state in order to understand what states do and how they interact. Thus, foreign policy analysis focuses on individuals, small groups, bureaucratic organizations, legislatures, domestic/societal forces such as interest groups and public opinion, and different regime types. When the focus is on individuals, the emphasis is on how individual preferences or human characteristics affect how leaders make decisions. When the focus is on small groups or bureaucratic organizations, the emphasis is on how group dynamics, organizational perspective, and organizational processes affect preferences, decisions, and policy behavior. When the focus is on societal forces, the emphasis is on how interest groups, public opinion, and other factors affect decision makers and their decisions. Regime-type explanations focus on how different types of governments and political processes affect the foreign policy choices and behavior of states. Thus, foreign policy explanations look inside the state and explain how and why decisions are made, often down to the group and individual levels.

4-2 Explain how economic class as used by Marxist theory can be the driving force for how nations interact with each other.

Marxist theory sees economic class rather than power as the driving world force. In its most basic form, the approach asserts that all actions by people and states are driven by economic desires rather than desires for power, security, and the like. In this dynamic, class differences—between those who control wealth (capitalists) and those who do not (proletariat)—drive behavior and, in world politics, lead to efforts to enrich the wealthy class, usually at the expense of the others. Marx and Engels theorized that, within countries, eventually the proletariat would rise up and revolt against the capitalists, overthrow them, and take control of the government. The new socialist government would take ownership of the economy for the proletariat, and it would begin to break down the old capitalist institutions. Over time, with the destruction of the old capitalist institutions, the government itself would wither away and society would become truly communist—a utopia where everyone cooperated and the human vices inspired by capitalist greed and envy had been eradicated. Chiefly an explanation of processes within countries, Marxism is relevant to world politics in at least two ways. First, unless a state was socialist, its motives were to promote the wealth of the capitalist class, which controlled the government, and thus all foreign and domestic policies were made to benefit the capitalists. Marxist theory asserts that wars are not fought for territory or security but for the profit they will bring the wealthy class. Second, the theory asserted that socialism would spread worldwide. Marx and Engels saw the spread of communism to be an inevitable, evolutionary process, but other communist leaders such as Stalin interpreted Marx and Engels to mean that a socialist state is obligated to compel regime change in other states.

4-3 Describe the different aspects of world systems theory and how they explain international relations.

World systems theory applies the ideas of Marxism and class differences to international relations. Using the concept of class, WST asserts there are three zones or types of states. Core states are the wealthiest, most industrialized, and most powerful in the world economy. Semi-peripheral states tend to produce goods and services and not rely on the export of raw materials (e.g., lumber, food, oil) for their economy. However, those goods and services are not as profitable as the core country's products. Periphery states have weak governments, tend to sell only raw materials or cheap labor, and have almost no influence in world politics. According to WST, each type of state has particular interests and behavior that are determined by its position in the economic system. The core dominates and extracts profits from the semi-periphery and periphery, the semi-periphery dominates and extracts profits from the periphery, and the periphery is simply left in relative poverty. WST argues that wars are fought between the different zones to enforce the world order and within the semi-periphery and periphery over scarce resources, injustice, and other matters.

4-4 Outline the ways in which gender affects and is affected by international relations.

Feminist international relations theories address one or more of three main themes. One theme asks whether our entire way of thinking about international relations is masculinized because most international relations theorists—at least at first—were men. A second theme raises the question of whether world politics would be different if women held more, or most, leadership positions in states. Generally speaking, women do not hold equal status in countries around the world and are severely underrepresented in government positions. A third theme is more empirical and reverses the focus of the first theme, examining the impact of world politics on women. War, economic downturns, and economic sanctions, among many issues of world politics, have particularly harmful effects on women. Women are at a particular disadvantage in poor and developing countries, where they often have fewer rights and protections relative to men. Globalization, however, often means more employment opportunities for women.

KEY TERMS

foreign policy analysis 84

Marxism 84

world systems theory 84

feminist international relations theory 84

agent-centered approach 84

rational actor model 84

bounded rationality 86

operational code analysis 86

prospect theory 86

organizational/bureaucratic politics model 87

advisory group 88

groupthink 89

polythink 89

proportional representation 89

selectorate 90

winning coalition 90

capitalism 92

proletariat 92

capitalist class or bourgeoisie 92

socialism 93

regime change 93

colonies 94

dependency theory 94

core 97

semi-periphery 97

periphery 97

World Economic Forum 98

difference feminists 103

liberal feminists 105

REVIEW QUESTIONS

1. What alternatives to realism, liberalism, and constructivism exist, and which of them are the most compelling?

2. What does studying individuals, groups, and institutions and their role in decision making add to our understanding of world politics?

3. How important is economic class? Can the struggle between the classes explain all international relations?

4. What does Marxist theory do to explain how nations interact?

5. How are women treated in the world? Do world events have a different impact on women compared to men?

THINK ABOUT THIS

The Value of Additional Lenses

For centuries, scholars and other careful observers relied on realism to make sense of international relations. Later, liberalism—and then constructivism—arose as a way to interpret world events and make sense of them. For most of the modern era, explanations swung between those theories like a pendulum. Yet obviously they were insufficient tools in some instances, or others would not have developed the more recent approaches we now refer to as foreign policy analysis, Marxist theory, and feminism.

In light of Chapter 3 and our discussion in this chapter, which "corrections" to realism, liberalism, and constructivism presented by foreign policy analysis, Marxist theory, world systems theory, and feminism are most helpful to explaining world politics? Which are least helpful?

FOR MORE INFORMATION . . .

Feminism

Hudson, Valerie, Bonnie Ballif-Spanvill, Mary Caprioli, and Chad Emmett. (2014). *Sex and World Peace*, rev. ed. New York, NY: Columbia University Press.

Runyan, Anne Sisson, and V. Spike Peterson. (2013). *Global Gender Issues in the New Millennium*, 4th ed. Boulder, CO: Westview Press.

Tickner, J. Ann. (2014). *A Feminist Voyage Through International Relations*. New York, NY: Oxford University Press.

Foreign Policy Analysis

Aldon, Chris, and Amnon Aran. (2016). *Foreign Policy Analysis: New Approaches*, 2nd ed. London, UK: Routledge.

Brummer, Klaus, and Valerie M. Hudson, eds. (2015). *Foreign Policy Analysis Beyond North America*. Boulder, CO: Lynne Rienner Publishers.

World Systems Theory

Wallerstein, Immanuel, Charles Lemert, and Carlos Aguirre Rojas. (2013). *Uncertain Worlds: World-Systems Analysis in Changing Times*. New York, NY: Great Barrington Books/Routledge.

PART II

International Security

CHAPTER 5
Understanding Conflict: The Nature and
Causes of Conflict and War

CHAPTER 6
Seeking Security: Managing
Conflict and War

CHAPTER 7
Building Peace: Structures of Cooperation

Turkish soldiers with US-made M60 tanks drive through a town in Syria

Why do wars persist as a problem in world politics?

5

Understanding Conflict

The Nature and Causes of Conflict and War

Learning Objectives

After studying this chapter, you will be able to . . .

5-1 Identify the nature and forms of armed conflict.

5-2 Describe the evolution of and trends in armed conflict.

5-3 Assess the causes of interstate and intrastate war at the (a) system, (b) state, and (c) individual levels of analysis.

Chapter Outline

5-1 The Nature of Armed Conflict

5-2 The Nature and Evolution of War in World Politics

5-3 Why Wars Begin

A Coming War Between the United States and China?

Recently, political scientist Graham Allison wrote that China and the US were stuck in a "Thucydides trap" (Allison 2017b; see also Allison 2017a). According to Allison (2017b),

> as China challenges America's predominance, misunderstandings about each other's actions and intentions could lead them into a deadly trap first identified by the ancient Greek historian Thucydides. As [Thucydides] explained, "It was the rise of Athens and the fear that this instilled in Sparta that made war inevitable." The past 500 years have seen 16 cases in which a rising power threatened to displace a ruling one. Twelve of these ended in war. (para. 3)

In such a Thucydides trap, when power shifts and a challenger catches up to a dominant leader, even their most basic interactions become more dangerous, and flashpoints or crises can easily spin out of control, leading to military conflict even if neither the challenger nor the dominant leader would have chosen such a course.

China's rapid rise, dramatic economic growth, increasing military might, and growing influence in world politics all make it look like a challenger quickly catching the top dog. Indeed, in 2019, the University of Sydney's (Australia) United States Studies Centre went so far as to say, "The U.S. is no longer the dominant power in the western Pacific and would struggle to win a conflict against China. . . . [In fact], the U.S. could lose a war before it starts if, for example,

China were to launch a wide-scale, coordinated missile attack against U.S. and allied bases" (Shinkman 2019). When the challenges facing US leadership in world politics are considered, the picture appears even bleaker. Because many observers note that both the US and China consider their position in the world to be unique and exceptional, warranting leadership and influence, it might be even harder to imagine that one would defer to the other.

1. What factors make a future war between the US and China likely?

2. What other factors do you think work against the outbreak of war between the two?

3. What theoretical perspectives underlie each explanation?

INTRODUCTION: INTERNATIONAL CONFLICT

Conflict and war have long been regarded as *the* central problems of international relations. It is no wonder these issues have occupied center stage. In Chapter 3, we quoted a well-known statement by the realist international relations theorist Hans Morgenthau, whose words are especially relevant here: "All states are either preparing for, recovering from, or engaged in war." The traditional approach to security in world politics has long emphasized the survival and safety issues connected to conflict and war as the most important matters of world politics. In this approach, security typically means power and survival, territorial integrity, and political independence, with the state as the primary focus and other non-state actors such as terrorists, freedom fighters, and international

Syrian men carrying babies make their way through rubble in Aleppo in 2016

With the human toll of war so high, why does it continue?

AMEER ALHALBI/AFP via Getty Images

organizations as secondary. This is the traditional arena of interests and military power, emphasizing the problem of conflict and war between and within states and often involving other non-state actors.

War of various kinds is a persistent feature of world politics over the centuries. Its implications for the survival of states and its enormous costs in lives and treasure have combined to keep it at the center of attention for policymakers and for international relations scholars seeking to explain it, predict it, prepare for it, and prevent it. Conflict and war have exacted monumental costs—lives, material, wealth, and power—from those states, groups, and individuals it has involved. For the United States, for example, participation in war has cost some $7 trillion (and counting) and more than 2.5 million in dead and wounded over its history as an independent country. Some estimates place global casualties from war at close to 4 billion when both direct and indirect casualties are included.

In Part II of our text, we examine the arena of international security. This chapter focuses on understanding conflict and war—especially the nature and causes of these security issues—which are central challenges in the international security arena. We begin with an overview of conflict and war and its various forms and then discuss the changing patterns of armed conflict over time. We then turn to the causes and consequences of war. In Chapter 6, we focus our attention on the strategies states and other actors have used to manage conflict and achieve security. Finally, in Chapter 7, we consider efforts to gain security and manage conflict through structures of cooperation.

5-1 THE NATURE OF ARMED CONFLICT

>> **5-1   Identify the nature and forms of armed conflict.**

Even the most optimistic observer would have to concede that conflict and war are persistent patterns of world politics. It is (happily) true that most conflicts among the players of world politics are resolved without resorting to violence. However, even though war is relatively rare (thank goodness) given the number of states and national groups in world politics that could be fighting with each other at any given time, armed clashes of varying scope and size have been a regular feature in international relations, and armed conflict continues to occur around the world. According to John Keegan (2011), in *A History of Warfare*, while the particular features and practices of war have varied according to the historical and societal contexts in which it occurred, it is a universal phenomenon crossing space and time. By some accounts, close to 15,000 violent clashes between different groups have occurred over recorded history, with about 600 significant wars taking place since the year 1500. As Map 5-1 and Figure 5-1 show, since World War II, and at present, armed conflicts have involved countries and peoples from all over the globe.

5-1a War and Its Types

In the simplest account of this persistent and important phenomenon of world politics, the self-interests of

MAP 5-1

Active State-Based Conflicts, 2018

What do the locations and occurrences of conflict around most of the world indicate?

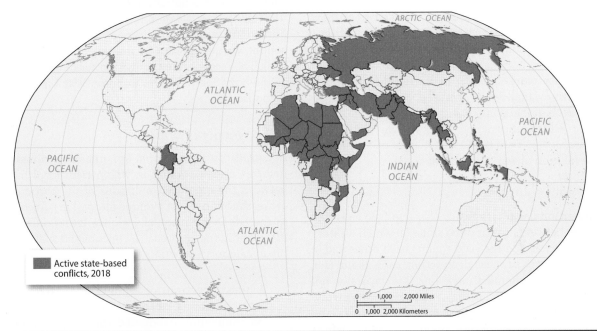

Source: Data from Uppsala Conflict Data Program, https://ucdp.uu.se/downloads/charts.

FIGURE 5-1

Armed Conflict by Region, 1946–2018

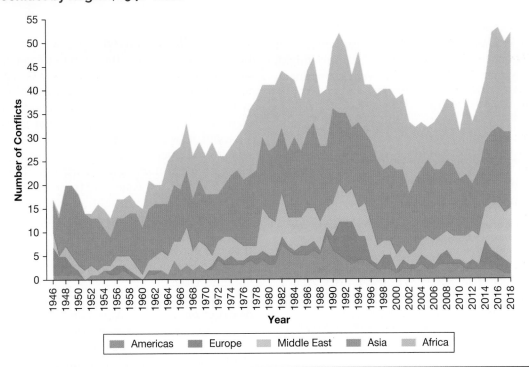

Source: Data from Uppsala University Research, Uppsala Conflict Data Program *UCDP Conflict Encyclopedia*, http://www.pcr.uu.se/digital Assets/595/c_595102-l_1-k_region_jpg.

players clash, and violence sometimes erupts. **War**—organized, violent (i.e., military) conflict between two or more political actors—occurs when the participants engage in armed struggles to gain or defend territory, resources, influence, authority, and other things of high value. The participants can involve two or more states (**interstate war**), two or more groups within a territory (intrastate or **civil war**), or a combination of states and non-state groups (**extra-systemic or extra-state war**). Such armed struggles obviously range from small-scale, localized disputes to large-scale, even global conflicts.

To better understand war, we can distinguish between a variety of types, which leads us to consider the evolution of war over time as well.

Conventional War

Conventional war is typically characterized as armed conflict between two or more states in which military forces of each side are used against each other and in which weapons of mass destruction, such as nuclear, biological, or chemical weapons, are typically not used. Conventional wars may be *general wars*, involving multiple participants seeking to conquer and control the territory of their opponents and in which the full range of the available arsenal of conventional weapons is used against military targets and against the infrastructure of a country. Such large-scale warfare is exemplified by World Wars I and II. From the early 17th century, major powers increasingly resorted to general war until the incredible devastation of the two world wars in the 20th century ushered in changes. *Limited wars* involve the use of conventional weapons (i.e., not weapons of mass destruction) but do not involve the participants' full military might, nor do they seek complete victory over the opponent;

....

war: organized, violent (i.e., military) conflict between two or more parties.

interstate war: armed conflict between two or more states.

civil war: armed conflict between competing factions within a country or between a government and a competing group within that country over control of territory and/or the government.

extra-systemic or extra-state war: armed conflict between a state and a non-state entity, such as colonial wars and wars with non-state national or terrorist groups.

conventional war: armed conflict between two or more states in which military forces of each side are used against each other and in which weapons of mass destruction, such as nuclear, biological, or chemical weapons, are not used.

unconventional war: armed conflict in which civilian and nonmilitary targets are emphasized, forces used include nontraditional forces outside organized militaries, and a wide array of weaponry, including weapons of mass destruction, may be employed.

weapons of mass destruction: nuclear, chemical, and biological weapons.

instead, they have a smaller, more limited goal. In the 1991 Gulf War, for example, the United States and its allies deployed a portion of their military capabilities for limited goals (expelling Iraqi forces from Kuwait) and did not conquer and occupy Iraq once its forces were defeated. In short, such wars may be limited in terms of their geographic scope, goals sought, or the amount of military force brought to bear. The facts on the ground matter in defining war, as the box "Spotlight On: Defining War Empirically" demonstrates.

Unconventional War

In contrast to conventional war, **unconventional war** involves armed conflict in which traditional battles between the organized militaries of the participants are less prominent (or avoided altogether). According to the US Department of Defense (2011), instead of these traditional approaches, unconventional war is a broad category involving

> a broad spectrum of military and paramilitary operations, normally of long duration, predominantly conducted through, with, or by indigenous or surrogate forces who are organized, trained, equipped, supported, and directed in varying degrees by an external source. It includes, but is not limited to, guerrilla warfare, subversion, sabotage, intelligence activities, and unconventional assisted recovery. (p. 490)

Typically, unconventional warfare not only involves targeting civilian populations much more directly, as well as other nonmilitary targets; it also means that the forces involved are not traditional organized military forces. Two examples of this type of warfare may be helpful here. First is the war in Vietnam, in which the guerrilla Viet Cong forces—considered insurgents by today's definition—first engaged in military conflict with the French until 1954 and then with American troops after the United States began its intervention. Second, when the Soviets occupied Afghanistan in the 1980s, they battled the mujahideen, a guerrilla or insurgent force that did not fight the Soviets head-on but instead launched harassing attacks against Soviet troops in outlying areas.

Since the introduction of **weapons of mass destruction** in World Wars I and II, the use of such weaponry has been characterized as unconventional warfare as well. This complicates the definition of war because both world wars are usually considered conventional, yet unconventional weapons were used in both. It is still correct to consider both of those

Defining War Empirically

War may fall into the category of "I know it when I see it" for many, but concepts like this must be carefully defined in empirical terms. Political scientists have employed several standards in their efforts.

Correlates of War

In the well-established Correlates of War data project, an empirical threshold of 1,000 battle deaths distinguishes war from other, smaller armed disputes. The Correlates of War data define a *militarized interstate dispute*—or MID—as the threat, display, or use of military force short of war (less than 1,000 battle deaths) by one member state explicitly directed toward the government, official representatives, official forces, property, or territory of another state. This is a relatively restrictive definition that excludes some military engagements, including US military operations in Iraq since 2003.

Uppsala Conflict Data Program

The Peace Research Institute of Oslo (PRIO) defines war empirically in the same way (an armed conflict reaching a cumulative total of 1,000 battle deaths, and then an annual total of 1,000 battle deaths each subsequent calendar year) in its Uppsala Conflict Data Program. PRIO also defines a *major armed conflict* as one in which a cumulative total of 1,000 battle deaths has been reached, with at least 25 battle-related deaths occurring each subsequent calendar year. A *minor armed conflict* involves 25 battle-related deaths prior to reaching the 1,000 battle-death total.

1. Given these definitions, was the US invasion of Iraq a war? What about the subsequent occupation and "state-building" in Iraq?

2. Are the current conflicts in Afghanistan, Iraq, Libya, Ukraine, and Syria wars by these definitions? ●

Sources: Correlates of War website, www.correlatesofwar.org; Uppsala Conflict Data Program website, www.pcr.uu.se/research/ucdp.

conflicts conventional, but today, if weapons of mass destruction were *widely* used in a conflict, it would certainly be considered unconventional.

Civil War

Conventional war means armed conflict between two or more states, but civil war involves armed conflict between competing factions within a country or between an existing government and a competing group within that country over control of territory and/or the government. Civil wars come in various sizes and shapes, from expansive general wars, like the American Civil War of the 1860s, to more limited or unconventional conflicts, like those in Syria after 2011. Table 5-1 lists most of the civil wars since the end of World War II. Civil wars may initially pit factions within a country against each other, but they frequently become internationalized. As we discuss later in this chapter, this may occur as the conflict or its consequences spill over the country's borders or if external parties become involved in the conflict. Good examples include the recent conflicts in Libya (2011, ongoing) and Syria (ongoing), which not only involved home-grown resistance to the dictators in each country (Colonel Muammar Gaddafi in Libya and President Bashar al-Assad in Syria) but soon attracted intervention by others. In Libya, US and NATO forces, along with limited support from other states in the region, intervened to help overthrow Gaddafi, and in Syria, Russia, the US, Iran, and others have engaged in the conflict.

Asymmetric War

Directly related to unconventional war, **asymmetric war** pits two or more groups of very different military size or power against each other. To overcome the disadvantages stemming from this imbalance of power and technological superiority, the smaller or weaker participant often resorts to unconventional tactics rather than engage in an almost certainly futile attempt to fight a traditional battlefield war. These may include those described by the US Department of Defense earlier, such as guerrilla warfare, subversion, and sabotage, including the development of **improvised explosive devices (IEDs)** to use against

....

asymmetric war: armed conflict between two or more groups of very different military size or power.

improvised explosive device (IED): a homemade bomb, often placed on roadsides and other sites, fashioned from an explosive device and a detonator, and usually triggered by remote device or "booby trap" mechanism.

TABLE 5-1

Select Civil Wars Since 1945

Greek Civil War, 1946–1949	Tajikistan Civil War, 1992–1997
Paraguayan Civil War, 1947	Burundi Civil War, 1993–2005
Palestinian Civil War, 1947–1948	Yemen Civil War, 1994
Costa Rican Civil War, 1948	First Chechen War, 1994–1996
Vietnamese Civil War, 1954–1975	Iraqi Kurdish Civil War, 1994–1997
Congo Civil War, 1960–1966	First Congo War, 1996–1997
Guatemalan Civil War, 1960–1996	Nepalese Civil War, 1996–2006
North Yemen Civil War, 1962–1970	Albanian Rebellion, 1997
Dominican Civil War, 1963	Cambodian Civil War, 1997–1998
Rhodesian Bush War, 1965–1980	Republic of the Congo Civil War, 1997–1999
Nigerian Civil War, 1967–1970	Guinea-Bissau Civil War, 1998–1999
Cypriot Civil War, 1967–1974	Kosovo War, 1998–1999
Cambodian Civil War I, 1970–1975	Second Congo War, 1998–2003
Pakistani Civil War, 1971	Second Liberian Civil War, 1999–2003
Lebanese Civil War, 1975–1990	Second Chechen War, 1999–2009
Mozambican Civil War, 1975–1992	Côte d'Ivoirian Civil War, 2002–2007
Angolan Civil War, 1975–2002	Darfur (Sudan) Civil War, 2003–2009
Cambodian Civil War II, 1978–1993	Haitian rebellion, 2004
Nicaraguan Civil War, 1979–1990	Colombian Civil War (1964, ongoing)
Salvadoran Civil War, 1979–1991	Afghan Civil War (1978, ongoing)
Peruvian Civil War, 1980–2000	Ugandan Civil War (1987, ongoing)
Sudanese Civil War, 1983–2005	Somali Civil War (1991, ongoing)
Sri Lankan Civil War, 1983–2009	Iraq Civil War (2003, ongoing)
First Liberian Civil War, 1989–1996	Chad Civil War (2005, ongoing)
Rwandan Civil War, 1990–1993	Libya Civil War (2011, ongoing)
Georgian Civil War, 1991–1993	Syria Civil War (2012, ongoing)
Algerian Civil War, 1991–2002	Ukraine Civil War (2014, ongoing)
Sierra Leonean Civil War, 1991–2002	Yemen Civil War (2015, ongoing)

the more powerful adversary. These tactics may also involve attacks that turn the technology of the adversary on itself in improvisational approaches. Take, for example, the September 11, 2001, attacks on the US by al-Qaeda terrorists. They seized control of four US airliners and flew them into the World Trade Center towers in New York and the Pentagon in Washington, DC. (The fourth plane crashed in Pennsylvania after passengers struggled with the hijackers to regain control of the plane.) In these dramatic and devastating attacks, which resulted in the deaths of nearly 3,000 people, no explosives were even used—the "bombs" were the high-tech airliners themselves and the flammable fuel they contained. In a somewhat similar

2016 attack in Nice, France, the Islamic State claimed credit when a Tunisian rented a 19-ton truck and drove it down a crowded street that had been turned into a pedestrian walkway for Bastille Day celebrations. Nearly 90 innocents died in the attack, and scores more were injured. In such warfare, traditional measures of "success" and "victory" like capturing enemy territory or their national capitals are obviously much less important, if not completely irrelevant.

5-1b Terrorism

No up-to-date discussion of conflict and war can ignore the problem of **terrorism**. Clearly, terrorism is a form of unconventional and asymmetric war. Definitions of terrorism are more difficult than might be expected (yet another example of "I know it when

....

terrorism: indiscriminate violence aimed at noncombatants to influence a wider audience.

I see it"). As a label, the term *terrorism* has often been attached to violence perpetrated by groups the observer does not like. This calls to mind the old cliché that "one man's terrorist is another man's freedom fighter." As noted terrorism expert Bruce Hoffman (1999) has argued,

> terrorism is a pejorative term. It is a word with intrinsically negative connotations that is generally applied to one's enemies and opponents, or to those with whom one disagrees and would otherwise prefer to ignore. . . . If one identifies with the victim of the violence, for example, then the act is terrorism. If, however, one identifies with the perpetrator, the violent act is regarded in a more sympathetic, if not positive (or, at the worst, an ambivalent) light; and it is not terrorism. (p. 32)

How, then, can we understand this form of violence? There is no single, universally accepted international definition of terrorism to guide us. There are, however, plenty of definitions to consider. According to Walter Laqueur (2001), there are more than 100 major definitions that emphasize a wide variety of things. Common factors often cited in these definitions include emphasizing the targeting of civilians or other noncombatants for the purpose of creating terror in a society for political purposes, but many definitions get far more complex as they try to categorize the motives behind actions.

Rather than getting lost in motives or other considerations, perhaps political scientist Peter Sederberg (1989) provides a useful approach to defining the term. In *Terrorist Myths: Illusions, Rhetoric and Reality*, he urges us to focus on the act first, and then consider who might be engaged in it. In his view, this might help us salvage the concept—in effect, anyone engaging in the act is engaging in terrorism. So what defines the act of terrorism according to Sederberg? As Figure 5-2 shows, if we distinguish between targets (combatants or noncombatants on the vertical axis) and means (discriminate or indiscriminate on the horizontal axis), we can place terrorism in one of the four resulting cells and identify it as the combination of *indiscriminate* violence (e.g., a suitcase bomb left on a subway platform, which does not discriminate among its victims—anyone who happens to be there is hurt or killed) directed at *noncombatants* (civilians not part of the armed forces or national command/leadership). The remaining cells in the figure help us differentiate other forms of violence, such as murder, limited war, and general war. Supplementing this, we might draw on elements of the preceding definitions to distinguish between the victims of the violence (those injured by the bomb blast) and the audience

Terrorist attacks on the World Trade Center, September 11, 2001
How can a country defend against the use of such "weapons"?
AP Photo/Carmen Taylor

FIGURE 5-2

Defining Terrorism by Means and Targets

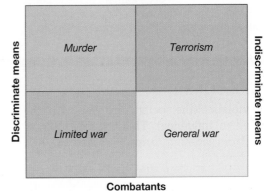

Noncombatants

	Discriminate means	Indiscriminate means
	Murder	Terrorism
	Limited war	General war

Combatants

ISIS and Modern Revolutionary Terrorism

In recent years, the most conspicuous revolutionary terrorist organization has been based in Syria and Iraq. Whether we call it ISIS, ISIL, the Islamic State, or its Arabic acronym Da'esh, it has sought to create a new Islamist caliphate—a state ruled by an extreme interpretation of Islam. Not only did it create a footprint of territory it controlled in Syria and Iraq; it also accepted like-minded branches in other Islamic regions and encouraged its "soldiers" to commit attacks against Western targets.

ISIS was founded in Iraq in 1999 by Abu Musab al-Zarqawi, a Jordanian who, after a short career as a thug and petty criminal, embraced a rigid form of Islam while in a Jordanian prison. He became a Salafi, one of those who want to return Islam to the purity of its first 100 years in the late 7th and early 8th centuries. After release from prison, he journeyed to Afghanistan to join al-Qaeda, but its leaders later found him hard to control. They suggested he take his campaign against Western ways elsewhere, so he created the Organization of Monotheism and Jihad, better known as al-Qaeda in Iraq. Not only did his organization resist the US occupation of Iraq; it later launched attacks on Iraqi Shi'as and Shi'a religious sites. Zarqawi's professed goal was to create a sectarian war within Islam so that the "heretic" Shi'as (as he saw them) could be eliminated and a Sunni caliphate created that would spread across the world. His violence against other Muslims was too much for al-Qaeda, and it disavowed any connection to his group. Ultimately, al-Zarqawi was killed by a US air strike in 2006 (Warrick 2016).

After al-Zarqawi's death, the organization went through internal turmoil and several leadership changes, but in 2014, an Iraqi, Abu Bakr al-Baghdadi, announced the creation of an Islamic state in Syria and Iraq with himself as its caliph or leader. The announcement came from Mosul, the second largest city in Iraq, which ISIS had recently captured. Al-Qaeda in Iraq had morphed into ISIS, which now had a foothold in northern Syria and in the western, Sunni-dominated region of Iraq. After a quick expansion of its territory at the expense of the Syrian and Iraqi governments, it began to suffer setbacks, and by 2020, ISIS lost control of Mosul, Raqqa, and virtually all the territory in Iraq and Syria it previously held for years.

Rather than concede defeat, ISIS issued calls for like-minded Salafis to attack hostile targets wherever possible, and its "soldiers" complied. By 2016, more than 1,200 people had been killed in ISIS-directed or ISIS-inspired attacks. Attacks against tourists on the beach in Tunisia killed 39 and wounded 39 more. Attacks on concertgoers and others in Paris killed 130 and wounded nearly 400 more. In Nice, 84 pedestrians died after being run over by a man driving a truck, and more than 300 were injured. Attacks also took place in Algeria, Canada, Australia, Denmark, Egypt, San Bernardino, Brussels, Orlando, and New York City. Also attacked were non-Western targets in Egypt, Yemen, Kuwait, Turkey, Lebanon, and Bangladesh. Some attacks killed one or two people, others killed dozens, and some killed hundreds (Yourish, Watkins, Giratikanon, and Lee 2016). In late 2019, after the US withdrew most of its forces in Syria, where it had been engaging in and supporting anti-ISIS operations, and Turkey unleashed a cross-border intervention against Kurdish forces, which had been an essential part of the anti-ISIS efforts, signs pointed to a resurgence of ISIS activities. According to the US Defense Intelligence Agency, "ISIS exploited the Turkish incursion and subsequent draw-down of U.S. troops to reconstitute capabilities and resources within Syria and strengthen its ability to plan attacks abroad" (Hennigan and Walcott 2019).

Clearly, killing Abu Musab al-Zarqawi and Abu Bakr al-Baghdadi did not make al-Qaeda or ISIS go away. Branches have expanded to Afghanistan, Algeria, Egypt, Indonesia, Mali, Nigeria, the Philippines, Saudi Arabia, and Yemen. Like magnets, failed states, or those with ungovernable spaces, draw terrorists like ISIS to them. Moreover, as long as there are marginalized people in Western states—the children of Muslim immigrants who don't feel like they fit in, young people desperate for a group identity that they believe will give their life meaning, or even career criminals, for example—ISIS will continue to find converts. It's hard not to foresee a "whack-a-mole" situation in which success in one location will simply drive terrorists to new places. ●

---

of the violence (the society or government the act is intended to influence). This approach allows us to refrain from labeling terrorists based on their goals or purposes.

state-sponsored terrorism: terrorism that includes covert and overt repression of and violence against civilian populations and more extreme acts such as genocide, supported or perpetrated by the state.

Who, then, engages in terrorism? Many definitions from the political and academic world exclude governments, focusing on non-state actors. However, it is quite possible for states to be engaged in terrorism if they employ violence in certain ways. Such **state-sponsored terrorism** includes covert and overt repression of civilian populations, and more extreme acts such as genocide (which we discuss in more detail in Chapter 11; Sederberg 1989). State-sponsored terrorism also includes states that fund, arm, or aid terrorist groups, such as Iran's arming of Hezbollah in Lebanon and Hamas in the Palestinian Gaza Strip over the past several decades or the Pakistani military's alleged funding and support for al-Qaeda as well as for Lashkar-e-Taiba's attacks on India's parliament in 2001 and its attacks in Mumbai in 2008. Such state-sponsored terrorism would also include those times when the terrorist attack is conducted by agents of the state itself, such as North Korea's 1983 bombing of a diplomatic meeting in Burma that killed a number of South Korean government representatives.

For non-state terrorism, which is of particular importance in our discussion of types of conflict and war, there are several ways to classify those who resort to such tactics. According to Cindy Combs (2010), one simple distinction is between "crazies" (emotionally disturbed individuals who resort to terrorism), "criminals" (individuals using terrorism for personal gain), and "crusaders" (individuals using terrorism in pursuit of a collective cause).

According to Sederberg (1989), a useful classification scheme has four categories:

1. *Criminal terrorists.* Individuals and groups using terrorism for financial gain. Examples would include the narcoterrorism of drug cartels or, perhaps, the violence employed by various organized crime groups.

2. *Nihilist terrorists.* Individuals and groups using terrorism for the destruction of order without an agenda for its replacement. Examples would include the Red Army Faction or Baader-Meinhof gang in Germany, the Red Brigades in Italy, and, perhaps, the Weather Underground in the United States.

3. *Nationalist terrorists.* Individuals and groups of particular ethnic/cultural identity who engage in terrorism in pursuit of the interests of their ethno-nationalist groups. Such groups typically target the governments ruling them and seek autonomy and independence. Examples include the Irish Republican Army, the Palestinian Liberation Organization, Basque separatists (Spain), Chechen separatists (Russia), and others, including, perhaps, Hamas.

4. *Revolutionary terrorists.* Individuals and groups who engage in terrorism in pursuit of broader regional or global transformations of the social and political order. Examples would include some revolutionary Marxist organizations during the Cold War and, more recently,

groups such as Hezbollah, al-Qaeda, and the Islamic State (see the box "Spotlight On: ISIS and Modern Revolutionary Terrorism").

As a form of violence—even warfare—and as a problem for world politics, terrorism is not new. It has always been a tactic of weaker and disadvantaged groups in conflict with others. However, experts on the matter generally date the modern era of terrorism at about 1968, when members of the Popular Front for the Liberation of Palestine hijacked a plane from Israel's El Al Airlines and held its passengers hostage, seeking the release of Arab terrorists jailed in Israel (the prisoners were released in order to get the hostages back). Since then, it has become more salient as an international issue. Of course, the dramatic attacks on the United States on September 11, 2001, increased attention to the importance of the problem as well. The empirical evidence suggests that as a form of violence and war in the modern world, incidents of terrorism ranged from a low of about 6,700 to high of more than 14,000 between 2005 and 2018 (see Table 5-2, Figure 5-3, and "Spotlight On: Terrorism in 2018" for recent statistics).

Terrorism involves a variety of tactics, including bombing, hijacking, kidnapping, and many others. Suicide attacks have been employed with greater frequency in recent decades as well. Responding to these attacks is challenging, in part because the tactic can be quite simple, like ramming a group of people with a truck, and changes constantly. Like other unconventional fighters, terrorists are more difficult to locate and target. They don't wear uniforms or identification badges. In general, addressing this challenge has some combination of the following efforts: reducing vulnerability through national and international security measures (e.g., strengthening airport security), increasing information and intelligence on potential threats so that they can be countered, enhancing cooperation across national and international jurisdictions, disrupting financial transfers, dissuading enemies from attempting attacks, disarming and eliminating attackers through coercion, and reducing recruits and terrorist havens and harbors.

5-2 THE NATURE AND EVOLUTION OF WAR IN WORLD POLITICS

>> 5-2 **Describe the evolution of and trends in armed conflict.**

Not surprisingly, the nature of war has evolved over time. A simple way of illustrating some of the changes is to think about the depiction of warfare in

TABLE 5-2

Incidents of Terrorism Worldwide

	2005	2006	2007	2008	2009	2010	2011	2012	2013	2014	2015	2016	2017	2018
Attacks worldwide	11,023	14,443	14,435	11,725	10,969	11,641	10,283	6,771	9,707	13,463	11,774	11,072	8,584	8,093
People killed, injured, or kidnapped as a result of terrorism	74,327	74,616	71,856	54,653	58,711	49,928	43,990	34,033	53,458	76936	75,837	74,900	47,151	58,571
People worldwide killed as a result of terrorism	14,482	20,515	22,736	15,727	15,310	13,193	12,533	11,098	17,891	32,727	28,328	25,600	18,753	32,386
People worldwide kidnapped as a result of terrorism	35,050	15,787	4,981	4,869	10,750	6,051	5,554	1,283	32,577	34,781	35,320	15,500	8,937	3,534

FIGURE 5-3

Terrorist Attacks Since 1971

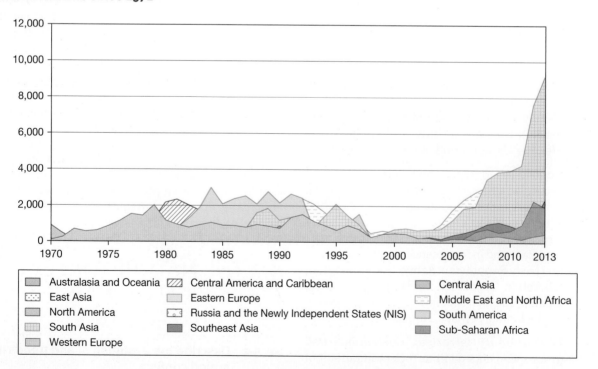

Source: National Consortium for the Study of Terrorism and Responses to Terrorism (START). (2016). Global Terrorism Database [data file]. Retrieved from http://www.start.umd.edu/gtd/features/GTD-Data-Rivers_20090522.aspx.

Terrorism in 2018

In 2018, a total of 8,093 terrorist attacks occurred worldwide in 84 different countries, resulting in almost 33,000 deaths and nearly 23,000 injuries. In addition, 3,534 people were kidnapped or taken hostage. The total number of attacks worldwide continued to decline, dropping another 6% from 2017. However, the number of deaths surged by almost 73% from 2017.

Although these attacks occurred worldwide, they were heavily concentrated geographically. More than half of all attacks (4,157 attacks, or 51.4%) occurred in just five

countries: Iraq, Afghanistan, Syria, India, and Nigeria. Similarly, more than 80% of the fatalities occurred in just five countries: Afghanistan, Syria, Nigeria, Yemen, and Somalia. The highest number of attacks and fatalities occurred in Afghanistan (1,294 and 9,961, respectively), replacing Iraq, which had been at the top of the list every year since 2013. ●

Source: US State Department, *Annex of Statistical Information: Country Reports on Terrorism 2018*, October 2019, https://www.state.gov/wp-content/uploads/2019/10/DSG-Statistical-Annex-2018.pdf.

---

the well-known imagery of film. Consider the battle scenes of *Braveheart* (1995), which depicts the armed struggles between Scotland and England in the 13th century, in which axes, swords, pikes, and archery were deployed in largely hand-to-hand battles. Fast-forward to the battle scenes shown in the movie *The Patriot* (2000), depicting the American Revolution of the late 18th century, where muskets and cannon dominated, or those of *Glory* (1989), set in the American Civil War, in which artillery, longer-range (though still inaccurate) rifles, and other weaponry appear. Now, fast-forward to the battle scenes of *All Quiet on the Western Front* (1930) or *Gallipoli* (1981; World War I) or *Saving Private Ryan* (1998) or *Dunkirk* (2017; World War II), which show the impact of technological advances in weaponry, such as automatic weapons, air power, and armored vehicles. *Platoon* (1986), set in the Vietnam conflict of 1960s, shows the complications of military clashes between less-developed indigenous forces and modern armies. Depictions of war in *Black Hawk Down* (2001), *Jarhead* (2005), *13 Hours* (2016), *Sand Castle* (2017), *The Outpost* (2020), and the documentary *Restrepo* (2010) depict modern conflicts on the battlefields of the late 20th and early 21st centuries, highlighting the contrasts and complications of technologically advanced militaries in conflict with unconventional forces. The 2016 Showtime documentary *Zero Days* describes the emergence of war in cyberspace utilizing computers, software, and many other aspects of information technology. This string of films also nicely illustrates the shifts from the traditional battlefields of the past to the often highly ambiguous contexts of current armed struggles.

5-2a Increasing Deadliness

The images of war depicted in these films highlight a number of trends. At least five of these are especially

interesting and provide a good context for our focus on the causes of war in this chapter. First, war has become increasingly destructive and deadly over time. Consider that from the time of Rome to 1899, the average period of time necessary for 1 million people to die in war was about 50 years. Since 1900, that period has been one year. According to political scientist Jack Levy (1983), from 1500 to 1975, there were 589 wars exacting some 142 million deaths. Four times as many of those deaths (80% of the total) occurred in the 20th century than in the four centuries leading up to it. The imagery in the films illustrates the technological advances in weapons and changes in the war-fighting organizations that have combined to help drive this trend. In one sense, human beings have been extremely efficient in developing ever-expanding abilities to kill each other in great numbers. What other factors help explain the increasing deadliness of war over this time period?

Picks and spears

How does this kind of military technology shape warfare?

Pictorial Press Ltd/Alamy Stock Photo

Muskets and cannon

How does this kind of military technology shape warfare?

Patrick Ward/Alamy Stock Photo

Advanced weaponry

How does this kind of military technology shape warfare?

AF archive/Alamy Stock Photo

5-2b More Limited Wars

A second trend appears counterintuitive to the first in some ways: Since 1945, by several measures, wars have become more limited. This is especially true for the major powers of the post-1945 era, which have largely refrained from the large-scale conflict with each other of the first half of the 20th century. The advent of the nuclear age and the incredible destructive power of nuclear weapons have contributed to this trend, as major powers have refrained from the use of the most destructive of modern weapons available to them and from wars that might result in their use. The development of increasingly precise smart weapons and smart technology has also played a role. It also appears that war has become less deadly, in the sense that there has been a decline in battle deaths since 1945, as shown in Figure 5-4. What other factors help explain these shifts? As we discuss later, some observers have argued that, for the developed world at least, major war has become obsolete (e.g., Mueller 1989). As Figure 5-5 shows, wars between major powers are sharply down over time.

5-2c War in the Developing World

A third trend is that wars have increasingly been located in the second tier, or the developing world, since 1945 (see Map 5-2). It is an interesting empirical fact that *all wars* since 1945 have occurred in the less-developed parts of the world, and they have either pitted a developed country (or countries) against forces from the less-developed world (e.g., the US–Vietnam conflict, 1954–1973; the USSR–Afghanistan conflict, 1979–1989; United Kingdom–Argentina, 1982; or the first and second US–Iraq conflicts of 1991 and 2003) or have involved two or more forces from the developing world (e.g., the Cambodia–Vietnam War, 1975–1989; the Iran–Iraq War, 1980–1988; and the Second Congo War, 1998–2003). Unless one counts the conflicts between Russia and first Georgia (2008) and then Ukraine (2014) or the fighting between Serbia, Croatia, Bosnia, and other parts of the former Yugoslavia—which was really a civil war—no conflicts since 1945 have been between two developed countries. Another way to look at this is to compare the most fragile and most stable states in the world, as we show in Table 5-3. Again, what do you make of this

FIGURE 5-4

Deaths From War After World War II

State-based battle-related deaths per 100,000 since 1946, 1946 to 2016

Only conflicts in which at least one party was the government of a state and which generated more than 25 battle-related deaths are included. The data refer to direct violent deaths per 100,000 of world population. Deaths due to disease or famine caused by conflict are excluded. Extra-judicial killings in custody are also excluded.

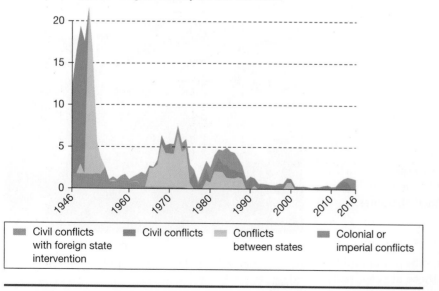

Civil conflicts with foreign state intervention   Civil conflicts   Conflicts between states   Colonial or imperial conflicts

Source: Max Roser, "War and Peace," 2020, https://ourworldindata.org/war-and-peace.

FIGURE 5-5

Percentage of Years in Which the Great Powers Fought One Another, 1500–2015

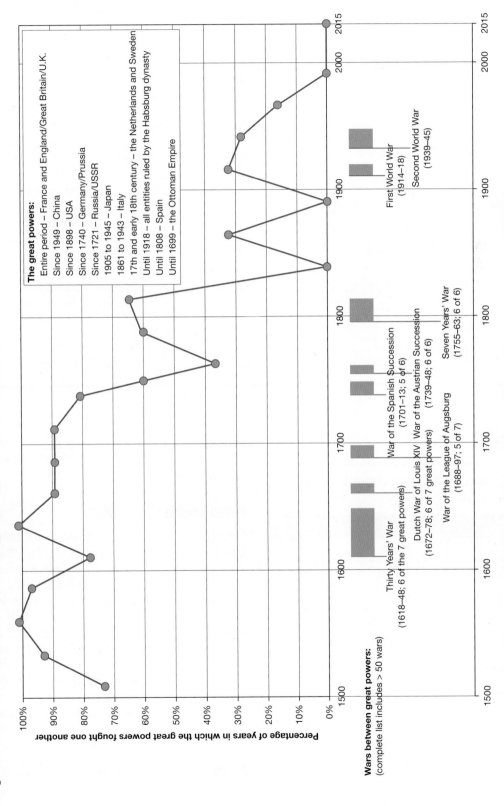

Wars between great powers:
(complete list includes > 50 wars)

Thirty Years' War
(1618–48; 6 of the 7 great powers)

Dutch War of Louis XIV
(1672–78; 6 of 7 great powers)

War of the League of Augsburg
(1688–97; 5 of 7)

War of the Spanish Succession
(1701–13; 5 of 6)

War of the Austrian Succession
(1739–48; 6 of 6)

Seven Years' War
(1755–63; 6 of 6)

First World War
(1914–18)

Second World War
(1939–45)

The great powers:

Entire period – France and England/Great Britain/U.K.
Since 1949 – China
Since 1898 – USA
Since 1740 – Germany/Prussia
Since 1721 – Russia/USSR
1905 to 1945 – Japan
1861 to 1943 – Italy
17th and early 18th century – the Netherlands and Sweden
Until 1918 – all entities ruled by the Habsburg dynasty
Until 1808 – Spain
Until 1699 – the Ottoman Empire

Source: Max Roser, "War and Peace." 2018. https://ourworldindata.org/war-and-peace. Licensed under CC BY-SA by the author Max Roser.

MAP 5-2

Map of Major Conflicts Since World War II

What parts of the world has conflict most affected since World War II?

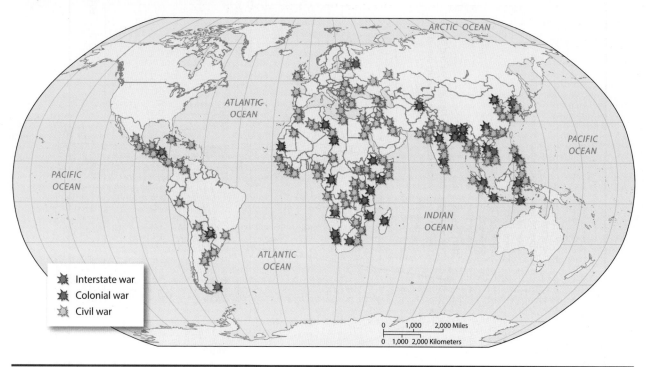

Legend:
- Interstate war
- Colonial war
- Civil war

Source: Data from "Conflict Map," https://www.nobelprize.org/educational/peace/conflictmap/conflictmap.html.

TABLE 5-3

Most Fragile and Most Stable States in the World, 2019

MOST FRAGILE STATES	MOST STABLE STATES
Yemen	Finland
Somalia	Norway
South Sudan	Switzerland
Syria	Denmark
Congo	Australia
Central African Republic	Iceland
Democratic Republic of the Congo	Ireland
Chad	Canada
Afghanistan	New Zealand
Iraq	Luxembourg

Source: The Fund for Peace, Fragile States Index (https://fragilestatesindex.org/wp-content/uploads/2019/03/9511904-fragilestatesindex.pdf).

comparison, and what it might mean for conflict? Also, consider what factors might help explain the more general and very interesting empirical trend.

5-2d More Civil War

Fourth, over time, and especially since 1989, war has become increasingly internal, as civil war has become the most common form of warfare. Figure 5-6 illustrates this phenomenon, highlighting the growth of civil and internationalized civil wars and the decline—almost disappearance—of interstate and extra-systemic (e.g., colonial) wars. According to the Uppsala Conflict Data Project, 90% or more of the armed conflicts since 1989 have been intrastate conflicts. In no period of history since the emergence of the state system in the 17th century has the difference between these two types of conflict been so dramatic. What factors might help explain this post-1989 shift?

5-2e More Unconventional War

The last fundamental trend worth noting is the shift from conventional to unconventional war over the last half of the 20th century and early 21st century. Although unconventional war is related to civil and extra-state

FIGURE 5-6

Military Conflicts by Type, 1946–2018

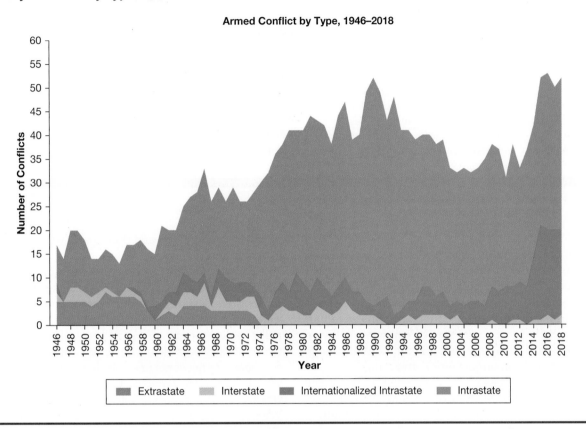

Source: Uppsala Conflict Data Program, http://www.pcr.uu.se/digitalAssets/595/c_595102-l_1-k_type_jpg.

war, its distinguishing characteristics involve participants, tactics, and weaponry. Hence, this shift has been illustrated perhaps most dramatically in the rise of terrorism and the images of commercial airliners crashing into buildings in New York City and Washington, DC, on September 11, 2001; the train bombings in Madrid, Spain, in 2004; the sequence of attacks against tourists and civilians in Mumbai, India, in 2008; and the terrorist strikes in France, Belgium, and the United Kingdom in 2016–2017. According to the famous 19th-century study *On War* by Carl von Clausewitz, war was depicted as a state-centered concept with specific distinctions between governments, military forces, and populations. In this conception, as von Clausewitz wrote, war was "the continuation of politics by other means" and fundamentally tied to the policies and interests of states. Increasingly since 1945, however, armed struggle has involved non-state actors and has blurred, ignored, or rendered irrelevant the distinctions between government, military forces, and population. Weaponry increasingly involves more than typical military arsenals. The civil wars, insurgencies, and terrorism of the post-1945 period are

quite different: much more unconventional, involving irregular forces and non-state actors that pose significant challenges because of their nature (see "Spotlight On: "Fourth-Generation War"). What force and factors underlie this shift, and what implications does it have for explaining and managing conflict in world politics?

In the current context, cyberwarfare is one of the most important and challenging aspects of unconventional warfare. In 2010, as Iran pursued its covert nuclear weapons program, its facilities, especially the Natanz uranium enrichment plant, began experiencing widespread and unusual failures in the centrifuges used to enrich uranium for weapons development. Not long after, other computer networks in Iran began experiencing strange patterns of failure and unexplained shutdowns. Soon, signs of malicious files began to appear on computers around the world. Ultimately, these problems were attributed to a computer worm called Stuxnet, developed by the US and Israel as apparently the world's first digital weapon and unleashed against the Iranian industrial targets to disrupt and impede the country's nuclear weapons program. Taking advantage of a flaw in the

Fourth-Generation War

First used in the 1980s by the US Department of Defense, the term *fourth-generation war* blurs the distinctions between state and non-state participants, war and politics, combatants and non-combatants (civilians), and battlefields and non-battlefields (see Terriff, Karp, and Karp 2008). At the core of the idea is the decline of the nation-state's monopoly on the means and uses of force, with non-state actors such as terrorists, insurgents, and guerrilla armies increasingly engaged in more unconventional warfare. Fourth-generation warfare is also often highly asymmetric, usually with weaker, non-state participants relying on strategies and tactics that target civilians, nonmilitary infrastructure, and other more vulnerable targets to avoid direct battlefield combat with a state's military forces. In addition, fourth-generation war can involve a wide variety of mostly nonmilitary tactics, including cyberwar and internet trolling, propaganda, misinformation and disinformation, and other actions. ●

Windows operating system, the worm penetrated computers controlling the operations and caused Iranian centrifuges to malfunction. Unfortunately, Stuxnet soon spread outside its targeted range and was identified on many computer networks around the world, although its harmful operations were narrowly targeted to a precise set of computer software and hardware configurations, and it did little damage outside its Iranian targets (see Zetter 2014).

In the high-speed, interconnected world of the digital age, this new form of warfare has emerged. **Cyberwarfare** is the attempt by one state or nation to cause disruption, discord, damage, death, or destruction by using computers and other digital devices to carry out digital attacks on the computer systems of another. Hacking and hackers are at the core of cyberwarfare, but the concept refers to the actions of states/nations, or directed by states/nations, rather than those in which individual hackers or criminal groups might engage. However, non-state actors such as terrorist groups may also engage in cyberwarfare.

Most experts regard cyberwarfare as a highly likely component of future conflicts. Such attacks may be directed at government information systems, military and industrial targets, commercial networks and institutions, universities and hospitals—which are especially vulnerable—and infrastructure such as power/electricity, water, and gas. As you might already conclude, most developed and developing economies depend on information systems, computers, and computer networks for everything from governing and infrastructure to transportation and communications—think about all that happens when you purchase an item on Amazon, from the order to payment to shipping—and thus are very vulnerable to cyberwarfare.

The weapons of cyberwarfare are quite sophisticated. They include such things as phishing attacks and ransomware designed to gain access to computer hardware, accounts, and information systems; viruses and malware designed to corrupt and control computer systems and networks; denial-of-service attacks that make computers or networks unavailable to users; and use of what is known as "zero-day" vulnerabilities or exploits, which are bugs or flaws in software (such as Microsoft's Windows operating system or Office software or Adobe's Flash software) that are unknown to the manufacturer and/or public and are thus open for exploitation because they have not been patched. The intelligence agencies of many countries amass an evolving suite of such weapons and employ them in what seems to be constantly evolving, adapting, and sophisticated ways.

As many as 30 to 60 countries are currently developing cyberwarfare capabilities, according to the US intelligence community. Leading players in the cyberwarfare arena include Russia, China, Iran, and North Korea, along with the US and its friends and allies, such as the UK and Israel. The US Defense Department has annually identified China's increasing defense spending on cyberwarfare capabilities as a point of great concern, and Iran and North Korea have developed significant cyberwarfare capabilities and have launched disruptive attacks against such targets as the US financial system (Iran, in 2012–2013) and Sony (North Korea, in 2014). In fall 2017, the US Department of Homeland Security and the FBI warned of a serious and expansive North Korean cyber campaign they called HIDDEN COBRA, through which North Korea was targeting the US aerospace, telecommunications, and finance industries through malware attacks designed to penetrate computer networks and exploit access (US-CERT 2017).

---

cyberwarfare: the attempt by one state or nation to cause disruption, discord, damage, death, or destruction by using computers and other digital devices to carry out digital attacks on the computer systems of another.

Russia is a major player as well, with a highly advanced cyberwarfare strategy and capabilities that it has deployed aggressively against its neighbors, European countries, and the US, as Map 5-3 shows (Greenberg 2019). For example, one of the earliest cyberattacks came in 2007 when Estonia announced its plans to remove a Soviet-era monument to Red Army troops from the center of the capital city to a cemetery on the outskirts of town. As anti-Estonian protests ignited, fueled by false information disseminated by the Russian media, Russia launched cyberattacks against Estonia that interrupted banks, disabled ATMs, shut down e-mail, and disrupted government and private communications networks through denial-of-service attacks in which websites and networks were overwhelmed by the volume of phishing attempts and ping floods by large numbers of botnets (McGuinness 2017). More recently, the US intelligence community and the US Senate Intelligence Committee confidently concluded that Russia organized and directed cyberattacks and cyberwarfare against the US in its attempts to sow chaos and influence the 2016 election and has continued to press cyberattacks of a variety of kinds through 2020. Through Facebook, the Russians were even able to create right-wing extremist protests without entering the US themselves. In late 2017, British Prime Minister Theresa May and UK intelligence officials publicly accused Russia of using information warfare and cyberattacks to interfere in British elections and attack media, telecommunications, and energy sectors. Learning from the Russian cyberattacks during the US presidential campaign, the French successfully countered similar Russian cyberattacks in support of far-right candidate Marine Le Pen in the 2017 French presidential election. As one part of its effort, the French government created thousands of false websites that attracted many of the Russian cyberattacks away from more legitimate targets.

For the US, cyberwarfare has recently been elevated to the status of a special unified combatant command, to take its place alongside similar commands for the Middle East (Central Command), Pacific (Pacific Command), the Americas (Southern Command), Europe (European Command), and other geographic regions. The leading agency in the intelligence community responsible for much of the cyberwarfare capabilities in the US is the National Security Agency (NSA), located in Fort Meade, Maryland. Currently, Cyber Command, the theater command for US cyberwarfare, is housed on the top floor of the NSA, and the director of the NSA also serves as the head of Cyber Command, to ensure that the operational role of the command is closely connected to the NSA's technical capabilities.

MAP 5-3

Russian Meddling in Europe

Taken together, these five trends suggest that we can distinguish between three, or perhaps four, general eras of warfare since the emergence of the state system in the 17th century:

- The Era of Great Power War, 1648–1945
- The Era of Limited War, 1946–1989
- The Era of Civil War, 1989–2001
- The Era of Unconventional War, 2001–present

Let's now turn to explanations of conflict to better understand what causes war.

5-3 WHY WARS BEGIN

>> 5-3 Assess the causes of interstate and intrastate war at the (a) system, (b) state, and (c) individual levels of analysis.

Now that we have a sense of the evolution of conflict in world politics and the aspects of both continuity and change that are apparent, we turn to explanations for the causes of war in world politics. To do so, we need to think both practically and theoretically to build a better understanding of the problem of conflict. Indeed, comprehending broad explanations is essential for making sense of particular cases and a critical aspect of understanding patterns.

Even a moment's reflection on the overarching patterns just discussed might lead you to conclude that the problem of conflict in world politics is what we might call *overdetermined*. That is, there would seem to be a great variety of possibilities for explaining conflicts, any one of which appears convincing as an explanation. And yet it is certain that conflict is multicausal and that no one explanation is sufficient, either for explaining one particular war or for understanding a pattern of conflict. To consider the question of what causes war, let's reflect on two dimensions: (a) the factors over which conflict occurs and (b) the explanations of why war occurs.

5-3a The Causes of War: Factors Leading to Conflict

Take a moment and reflect on the examples of wars that we have considered to this point. What would you identify as the main purposes for which these wars were fought? What key issues generate international conflict?

Chances are that *territory* is at the top of most lists and for good reason. Most studies of war identify territory as the most significant source of conflict among all the actors of world politics. For example, according to political scientists John Vasquez and Marie Henehan (2010), of all the issues that spark conflict, territorial disputes have the highest probability of escalating to war. A study by K. J. Holsti (1991) concluded that more than half of the wars over the past three centuries involved conflict over territory. States and others fight over territory for a variety of reasons, including access to and control of important resources; strategic features or locations such as defensible borders (e.g., mountains, rivers, and other bodies of water), transportation routes and chokepoints, and others; or cultural features related to the race/ethnicity of a population, history or traditions, and other similar considerations. Geography and territory matter in another way: States and others that are in closer proximity to one another are more likely to engage in armed conflict. Simply put, if two countries are next to each other, it is easier for them to fight than if they are on opposite sides of the world.

Holsti's study of conflict from the Westphalian to the neo-Westphalian period provides a good guide to other key factors. As you consider this list, remember that conflicts and wars can arise from multiple issues and rarely have just one source:

- *Nation-state creation.* The "search for statehood" and independence has been a powerful motivator for conflict and war and has become increasingly important over the past 300 years.

- *Ideology.* According to Holsti, ideas have been increasingly important to world politics and international conflict. Good examples include the 20th-century wars over fascism and communism (World War II, the Cold War) and, perhaps, the impact of democratic governance on peaceful relations among regimes sharing that type of government.

- *Economics.* Many conflicts and wars in the earlier parts of the Westphalian era involved competition for economic resources, markets, and/or transportation. According to Holsti, such issues have become much less central to war over the past 100 years or so as interdependence, international norms, and international regimes have worked against outright warfare over them. Still, key economic resources have been identified as issues underlying a number of recent conflicts, including the 1991 Gulf War and, perhaps, the 2003 US intervention in Iraq.

- *Human sympathy: ethnicity, religion, and war.* According to Holsti, acting on behalf of others out of sympathy—particularly to protect perceived religious and ethnic kin abroad or for humanitarian purposes—has often been an important factor behind international conflict. India's intervention in East Pakistan (now Bangladesh) in 1971 and the US-led multilateral operations in Kosovo (1999) and Libya (2011) are good examples of such instances.

- *Predation and survival.* This issue involves an effort to eliminate another state (usually for territorial or identity reasons). According to Holsti, this issue has been behind conflict and war most commonly in the 20th century.

- *Other factors.* States have (occasionally) gone to war to defend allies and to defend or restore the balance of power. However, these factors are more important to understanding why states join ongoing wars rather than why the wars begin in the first place.

Holsti's study is certainly not exhaustive or definitive, but it does help identify key issues that often motivate war. Overall, he concludes that "relatively abstract issues—self-determination, principles of political philosophy and ideology, and sympathy for kin—have become increasingly important as sources of war while concrete issues such as territory and wealth have declined" (p. 321). If Holsti is correct, there is at least one potentially very important implication to this pattern: Issues related to territory and wealth are more open to compromise and much more easily resolved through nonviolent approaches than are issues involving statehood, ideology, and identity.

What other issues can you think of that lead to war between and among the players in world politics? In particular, given our earlier discussion of key trends in the evolution of war, have the conflicts since Holsti concluded his study in 1989 reinforced these findings, or do you see important differences?

5-3b The Causes of War: Explaining the Patterns

Let's examine the causes of war more theoretically. A good way to organize thinking about the causes of war is to rely on the levels of analysis we introduced earlier in the textbook: system, state, and individual. Theorists from the realist, liberal, and alternative perspectives offer explanations at each of these levels to help make sense of why conflict and war are persistent and recurring patterns in world politics. Contending, and sometimes complementary, explanations at each level of analysis highlight particular cause-and-effect relationships and focus on particular mechanisms to shed light on the problem of war. As we consider each level of analysis, you might think back to the opening account of the potential Chinese challenge to the United States and consider how explanations at each level help us understand the potential causes of a future conflict.

System-Level Explanations

The broadest category of explanations focuses on attributes of the international system to explain recurring patterns of conflict and war. As we discussed in Chapter 1, at this level, realists, liberals, and others direct our attention to broad patterns in the interactions among the players of world politics, and emphasis is placed on the impact of the structural characteristics of the international system itself on such matters as the frequency and likelihood of conflict. Such characteristics include anarchy, the distribution of power, interdependence, and others.

In Chapter 3, our discussion of realist theory described that perspective's emphasis on international anarchy and its consequences for world politics. This is a good entry point to system-level explanations of conflict and war. Remember that the core of this argument stressed how anarchy—the absence of central government in world politics—creates a variety of consequences, including self-help and self-interested behavior, power seeking, and security dilemmas. For realists, then, this essential structural characteristic is at the root of international conflict because it establishes conditions in which competition, mistrust, and clashing interests are frequent—the normal state of affairs in world politics. In effect, the anarchic system creates conditions of insecurity and competition in which conflict is all too common. This is at the heart of what Hans Morgenthau meant when he asserted that "all states are either preparing for, recovering from, or engaged in war." Realist theorist John Mearsheimer (2001) goes even further, arguing that the structural conditions stemming from anarchy "create powerful incentives for great powers to think and act offensively with regard to each other" (p. 32).

Could the violence-producing nature of anarchy simply be a social construction? Why can't anarchy be peaceful? A lack of governance does not have to equate with violence. Would you wantonly commit murder if you could get away with it? Other reasons to act violently must exist, and many social constructivists point to the fact that most leaders and scholars believe in the *idea* that anarchy is violent. Violence becomes self-fulfilling: We believe that anarchy is violent, so we act in a way that makes anarchy violent.

This system-level argument is helpful, but as you can see from the constructivist perspective (and the question about committing murder), it is limited. International anarchy is a constant condition, but conflict and war vary considerably. War happens more or less frequently over time and involves some states but not others. Generally, mostly unchanging conditions like anarchy, self-help, and the security dilemma provide little explanation of this variance. Moreover, conflict and war occurred long before the modern international system emerged in the 16th and 17th centuries, so other factors must be involved.

System-level explanations address the first issue (are there structural configurations that are more prone to conflict?), whereas explanations at other levels are more helpful in the second (when systemic characteristics don't change, how do we explain the occurrence of conflict?). Let us consider some further system-level explanations that stress attributes of the international system that do vary. One of these is that particular distributions of power are more or less conflict prone. The distribution of power refers to the number of major powers that exist at a given moment and how power is distributed among them. According to many realist theorists, the frequency of war is largely determined by this structural factor. In fact, a lively debate over whether bipolar (systems with two major powers) or multipolar (systems with more than two major powers) distributions are more or less war prone has long existed among theorists. Table 5-4 summarizes some of the arguments on either side of this debate. What do you think it means for this kind of theorizing that a good case can be made for both sides of the argument?

An example of a systemic argument based on the distribution of power comes from John Mearsheimer. He argued that bipolar distributions—situations with two dominant powers—are the least conflict prone, in large

TABLE 5-4

Bipolarity, Multipolarity, and War

BIPOLARITY	MULTIPOLARITY
More Stable	**More Stable**
Two major powers create a solid balance.	More actors increase opportunities for peaceful interactions.
War anywhere could become war everywhere.	More actors increase the number of states who could oppose an aggressor.
Certainty and calculation are easier.	
Control over allies is easier. Conflict is only likely between the two major powers.	More actors mean more mediators to moderate conflicts.
	More actors may slow the rate of arms races.
Balance of power is easier to identify and achieve.	States cannot focus on only one adversary.
Shifts in the power of most states do not matter.	Hostility is diffused.
	Ambiguity, uncertainty, and unpredictability increase with more actors and complexity.
Less Stable	**Less Stable**
Levels of hostility are very high.	Opportunities for conflict increase.
There are no mediators to moderate conflict between the major powers.	Diversity of interests increases.
Conflict anywhere can draw in the major powers.	Misperception and miscalculation increase in situations of greater complexity and uncertainty.
Stalemate between major powers may enable conflicts in peripheral areas.	More states mean that unequal distributions of resources are more likely.
Clarity and certainty might lead to war.	

measure because there is less fear among major powers over the prospect of attack. Multipolar systems—more than two great powers—are more conflict prone than bipolar systems because there are more axes of potential conflict and the great powers are less sure of who

....

hegemonic stability theory: a theory holding that the international system is most stable when one state (the hegemon) dominates.

power transition theory: a systemic theory holding that wars are most likely when changes in power distributions occur.

cyclical theories of war: conflict based on the rise and relative decline of leading powers in the international system in which stability occurs as the victors in major wars assert themselves, and war occurs as a function of the subsequent and inevitable rise of challengers to those dominant powers.

hegemon: a country that is an undisputed leader within its region or the world. After World War II, the United States was considered the world hegemon.

their allies are. However, Mearsheimer (2001: chap. 9) distinguishes between two types of multipolar systems: *Balanced multipolar systems* (those without a potential dominant hegemonic state) are less warlike than *unbalanced multipolar systems* in which a potential hegemon exists and generates considerable fear among the other major powers. Other realists argue that unipolar "moments," periods when there is only one dominant power, tend to be the most stable distributions of power. Indeed, **hegemonic stability theory** argues that the international system is most stable when one state (the hegemon) dominates. However, these moments tend to be brief because other states prefer not to be dominated (see our discussion of power transitions and long cycles below). Such unipolar moments are likely to prompt challengers and balancing efforts by others who seek to avoid or curtail domination.

Other theorists point to structural characteristics related to power to advance additional arguments. For example, some stress the **power transition theory**, which asserts that wars are most likely when *changes* in power distributions occur—when some states are relatively rising in power (and thus want to demonstrate their power or others want to stop them) or when others are falling in power (and thus want to prove that they are still powerful or become targets of opportunity for other more powerful states). This is the central basis for the "Thucydides trap" argument that we introduced at the outset of the chapter. The outbreaks of both World Wars I and II also fit this theory (Organski 1968; Organski and Kugler 1980). In 1914, Germany was a rising power aligned with a falling power—Austria-Hungary. Austria-Hungary wanted to demonstrate its remaining power by putting Serbia, a minor but rising power, in its place. In World War II, the United Kingdom was falling in power while Germany was again rising. In Asia, Japan was a rising power that desired its place among other major powers. In each of these cases, the rising power challenged the existing/falling power for control of the region or the international system. Both Germany and Japan wanted greater or complete control of their regions, and war was the result. A more recent example is Russia's conflict with Ukraine—could that be the result of Russia seeing itself as a rising power and Russia's perception of NATO and the United States as falling powers? Of course, as the opening puzzle of the chapter indicates, the rise of China in world politics over the past three decades or so probably presents the most compelling example—and challenge. To return to that example, the implications of this current power transition suggest that conflict between China and the US is very likely at some point.

Still others argue for **cyclical theories of war** based on the rise and relative decline of leading powers in the international system (**hegemons** found in

Losing the Lead?

"The coronavirus pandemic has put US global leadership at stake" (Burrows and Engelke 2020). As the global pandemic rapidly spread in 2020, US decisions and responses left many—both friends and adversaries—more concerned and skeptical about US leadership than ever before. The delayed and ineffective response, unilateral actions such as closing borders to travel from Europe taken without consulting allies, failure to engage in efforts to coordinate and contribute to global responses, and attacks on international organizations such as the World Health Organization were among the many areas of concern and resentment from the rest of the world. To many other countries, it appeared as though the US was withdrawing from the international order.

The US decisions and non-decisions led European countries to express frustration, disappointment, and the intention to take their own steps to address the problem for themselves and the rest of the world. Asian friends and partners also found the "America First" approach of the US troubling and in stark contrast to what might be expected from an engaged leader in the Pacific region. Other parts of the world keenly felt the lack of attention and leadership as well.

And then there is China. While its domestic response to the virus was draconian and authoritarian, it effectively stopped the spread within China's borders. More important, as a result of China's efforts to position itself as more successful, more responsible, and more engaged in leadership and assistance to others during the global pandemic, China's global position stands to benefit, perhaps substantially (Campbell and Doshi 2020). Ahead of the US in its recovery and consistent in its defense of its own actions, China is positioned to reap benefits, both in its economic competition with the US and in its relationship with others in the global economy. Countries in Asia, generally more successful in controlling the pandemic and poised to emerge from its devastation more quickly, may find reasons to pivot toward China. Countries in other regions such as Africa, already the beneficiaries of rapidly expanding foreign aid from and economic ties with China, may do the same. Europe, despairing of the "America First" approach of the US and facing the China challenge, might take their own course to address it.

On many fronts, US influence has suffered from the effects of the global pandemic and the consequences of its own policy choices, not least in its "soft power" to persuade and attract followers.

1. How much do you think the US has hurt its world standing?

2. What do you think the consequences of declining US influence and leadership might be for potential conflicts around the world?

3. What might this potential power transition moment mean for conflict and war involving major powers? ●

---

unipolar power distributions). In these arguments, stability occurs as the victors in major wars assert themselves, and war occurs as a function of the inevitable rise of challengers to those dominant powers over time (Gilpin 1991; Goldstein 1988; Modelski 1978; Thompson 1988). Both power transition and cyclical theories rest on the premises of realist approaches to world politics, especially the idea that states seek power and security for themselves first and foremost. For more on this, see "Foreign Policy in Perspective: Losing the Lead?"

These arguments share a common emphasis on realist structural factors—the competition for power and security in an anarchic world. However, other system-level explanations are offered by liberal theorists and radical theorists. For liberal theorists, a key systemic characteristic central to the causes of war (or, more accurately, the reduction of its frequency) is interdependence—the mutually dependent linkages between the players of world politics. Some liberal theorists argue that conditions of greater interdependence among players in the international system result in significantly reduced instances of war among them. Such interdependence may be economic (increased trade or investment, for example) or political (increased ties through international institutions). These factors, according to liberal theorists, reduce the effects of formal anarchy and create greater cooperation and peaceful relations (Mansfield and Pollins 2003; Russett and Oneal 2001). By contrast, theorists advocating the world systems approach we discussed in Chapter 4 argue that the capitalist structures of the international system generate competition for resources and markets between developed states and also generate conflict between the developed and developing states that often leads to war and subsequent subjugation of the developing state (Wallerstein 1974, 2004).

Feminist theory provides another alternative theoretical approach that operates at the level of the international system. Although this may also be interpreted as an individual-level explanation, some view this as systemic, so we can consider it here as well. For many feminist theorists, wars occur primarily because most states are entities dominated by men. From this perspective, wars are likely because men are more inclined (biologically and culturally) to rely on violence to resolve disputes than are women, who are more inclined to rely on verbal tools to resolve differences (Sjoberg 2013; Tickner 1992). As women leaders become more numerous in the international system, will wars become less commonplace? Time will tell.

System-level explanations are potentially powerful and attractive because they are relatively simple. For example, see the box "Spotlight On: Rational Actors and Bargaining Theories of War." However, they are often very general and more successful at explaining broader patterns, such as systemic conditions under which war is more or less frequent (or more or less intense). They are generally less helpful in explaining the participants of wars or particular wars. For help in these areas, we turn to state-level and individual-level explanations.

State-Level Explanations

Unlike explanations at the system level, which emphasize attributes of the international system (as the name implies), state-level explanations direct attention to the states—or units—themselves. Emphasis is generally placed on various attributes of countries and nations, such as the type and processes of government, economy, or culture, and how these factors affect the behavior and interactions of the participants in conflict. The argument at this level is that particular qualities of some states lead them to be more (or less) conflict prone or warlike. Although a central point of realist arguments at the systemic level is that war is normal and always possible in an anarchic international system, state-level arguments are quick to point out that states and other actors are not equally violent. In fact, between 1816 and 1980, about 50% of the members of the international system never participated in any international war (Ikenberry 2002). State-level arguments thus grapple directly

with the question of which states are the most likely participants in war.

Among the **national attributes** that state-level analysts point to in order to explain why some states are more warlike than others, five attributes are most commonly identified (Mearsheimer 2001):

- *Type of government.* Certain regime types seem more warlike, whereas others are less so. Democracies are often believed to be more peaceful than authoritarian regimes, at least in the sense of initiating war with other democracies. Given that democratic governments are accountable to the populace and to legal/institutional constraints—whereas authoritarian regimes are not, or are less so—democracies should be less war prone. Thus, a democratic peace based on a joint democracy effect appears to exist (Ikenberry 2011). See the box "Theory in Action: Constructing the Democratic Peace."

- *Type of economy.* Could the type of economy or other economic characteristics be connected to the war-proneness of states? Some liberal theorists have argued that capitalist economies are more peaceful than others because of their emphasis on trade, wealth, and profit (Angell 1910; Gartzke 2007). One does not shoot one's customers, as the saying goes; it's bad for business. By contrast, alternative theorists such as John Hobson (1965) and Vladimir Lenin (1939) argued precisely the opposite, holding that capitalism motivated states to compete with each other for resources and markets and resulted in wars between them, especially as imperialism drove them to try to control other parts of the world. Socialist states, by contrast, would be more peaceful because they would not be motivated by this need.

- *Demographic, cultural, physical, or geographic attributes.* This rather broad cluster of explanations is more of a grab bag than a unified argument. Realists, for example, have long argued that larger, more powerful states are more likely to engage in war than other states (Bremer 1980; Small and Singer 1970). Others have argued that population pressures such as growth, overcrowding, and lateral pressure generated by rising demands for resources lead some states to engage in war (Choucri and North 1975). Borders may create points of friction that often result in war, so states with more borders, or contested borders, engage in war more frequently than those without such contiguity issues (Cashman 1993).

- *Level of political instability.* Another common state-level condition often associated with war is the *scapegoat* or **diversionary theory**. Popularized by movies such as *Wag the Dog* and *Canadian Bacon*, this explanation holds that states suffering from poor economic conditions (like high inflation,

national attributes: features of states or nations such as regime type, type of economy, culture, geography, resources, and the like.

diversionary theory: the idea that states suffering from poor economic conditions or internal strife are more likely to resort to force outside their borders in efforts to divert attention from those internal problems or to rally the public behind their leadership.

Rational Actors and Bargaining Theories of War

The connection between politics and war goes back a long time, with Carl von Clausewitz's connection of war to the policies and interests of states acting as a good example. In recent decades, some scholars have extended this general approach to develop a "bargaining model of war" that treats war as part of the range of behavior—from diplomacy to military force—in which states (and other actors such as ethnic groups) engage as they compete and struggle over scarce resources. In the bargaining model of war, war itself is just a continuation of bargaining as states try to gain favorable outcomes for themselves. As Dan Reiter (2003) has characterized it:

> Fighting breaks out when two sides cannot reach a bargain that both prefer to war. Each side fights to improve its chances of getting a desirable settlement of the disputed issue. The war ends when the two sides strike a bargain that both prefer to continuing the war, and the outcome is literally the bargain struck. Finally, the duration of peace following the war reflects the willingness of both sides not to break the war-ending bargain. (p. 29)

Many scholars have applied this theory to the explanation of decisions to go to war, how and how long wars are fought (as states gain information about costs, benefits, and bargaining positions), when they end, and what consequences they produce. At the heart of this model is the conception of states as rational actors calculating preferences, costs, and benefits on the basis of the information they have and gain (about themselves and their opponents) through their actions.

This approach to explaining war does not consider the role that state-level factors such as regime type, culture, or the psychological trauma a war can visit on the people of a country play in the causes of war. Nor does it consider the role of individual leaders and their personalities and psychological characteristics emphasized by the individual-level explanations we discuss in this chapter. It only considers war as a policy option available to a rational, unitary state. Thus, your openness to this approach to understanding war may depend on the degree to which you think war is a rational act or states are rational actors! ●

Source: Dan Reiter, "Exploring the Bargaining Model of War," *Perspectives on Politics* 1, no. 1 (2003), 27–43.

---

unemployment, or economic recession or depression) or other internal strife (generated by ethnic or other divisions) are more likely to resort to force outside their borders in efforts to divert attention from those internal problems and generate unity in the face of some external enemy. In the flipside of this argument, states with such conditions may be attractive targets for attack by others as well (Cashman 1993).

- *Previous war involvement.* Additional explanations based on national attributes stress prior experiences with war. A **war weariness** argument explains that states that have most recently experienced a significant, costly war are more peaceful in the aftermath because of the impact of those costs and experiences on the population, public opinion, and leaders. For example, after the costly and protracted Vietnam conflict, the United States was often said to be reluctant to commit American troops to another conflict. This "Vietnam syndrome" continues to receive attention and may have been reinforced by subsequent experiences in Somalia (1993), Iraq (2003–present), and Afghanistan (2001–present). In particular, American leaders appear to be significantly more constrained in their decisions to introduce ground forces into

potentially long-term operations (Kalb and Kalb 2011; Mueller 2005). In *The Retreat From Doomsday: The Obsolescence of War*, John Mueller introduces another variant of this argument, pointing to a learning function for developed states that have participated in the major wars of the 20th century. According to Mueller, by the middle of the 20th century, virtually all of Europe, North America, and the developed world elsewhere had recognized this through the experiences of World Wars I and II, and by 1990, this recognition had spread even further. Thus, just as with social conventions such as slavery and dueling, societies learned through experiences that practices like these, and war, were costly, unacceptable, and just plain wrong.

Although the empirical evidence in support of these various explanations is mixed, the theories provide insights into state-level attributes that may contribute to our understanding of why some states participate in war more or less often than others. Yet explanations of war at the state level are less helpful in explaining why

....

war weariness: the idea that states that have most recently experienced a significant, costly war are more peaceful in the aftermath because of the impact of those costs and experiences.

Constructing the Democratic Peace

The joint democracy effect, or "democratic peace thesis," contends that institutional and normative characteristics of democratic regimes lead them to peaceful relations with each other. As we noted at the outset of Chapter 3, a significant body of empirical evidence supports this theory: While democracies have engaged in war with non-democracies and non-democracies have warred with each other, *two liberal or consolidated democracies have never gone to war with each other* and are also much less likely to threaten or use force short of war with each other. Thus, there seems to be something to the idea of a democratic peace.

Policymakers in democracies have embraced the main outlines of this international relations theory. Motivated by the idea that democracies are more peaceful in their relations with each other, many democratic countries have implemented policies of democracy promotion to spread democracy more widely throughout the international system. According to one study of the foreign policies of 40 countries between 1992 and 2002, there were substantial, although widely varying, commitments and efforts toward this end through individual and multilateral approaches (Herman and Piccone 2002). For the United States, as Allison and Beschel (1992) suggested shortly after the end of the Cold War, "the democratic revolutions of 1989, coupled with the retreat of authoritarian regimes in Latin America and parts of Asia and Africa, have prompted a resurgence of interest throughout the

U.S. government and society at large in promoting democracy" (p. 81).

Until recently, US interest in the promotion of democracy and better human rights practices transcended ideological differences. Presidential administrations from the first Bush and Clinton to the second Bush and Obama proclaimed support for democracy promotion and implemented policies—from diplomacy and economic aid and trade to sanctions and military intervention—to do so. However, after 2016, the Trump administration sought to reduce US efforts to support and promote democracy, cutting aid budgets and shifting policy rhetoric decidedly away from this purpose.

Consider the nature and evolution of conflict and war and the connection between the international relations theory and the policies of the United States and others who have embraced democracy promotion.

1. What are the strengths and weaknesses of translating this theory on the causes of war and peace into foreign policy?

2. What policy actions might be adopted, and what are their potential positive and negative consequences?

3. What happens if democratic countries stop supporting and promoting democracy in other countries? ●

---

particular wars occur. It is to the individual level that we turn for help in that type of explanation.

Individual-Level Explanations

In many ways, the third level of analysis is the least abstract set of explanations because this level directs our attention to people and their attributes. In some individual-level explanations, emphasis is on general aspects of **human nature**. Other individual-level explanations focus on the specific characteristics of individual leaders, including their personalities, perceptions, psychology, and policy preferences. In effect, then, explanations at this level focus either on the nature of humans in general or on the nature of some humans in particular.

....

human nature: innate characteristics of human beings, said by some to be a cause of war.

Explanations emphasizing human nature generally focus on arguments that humans are inherently aggressive. From philosophers such as St. Augustine, Thomas Hobbes, and Reinhold Niebuhr to psychologists and sociobiologists such as Sigmund Freud, Konrad Lorenz, and Edward O. Wilson, scholars have often attributed national violence in the form of war to innate characteristics of human beings. For example, there are a variety of explanations that trace the causes of war to biological factors. In ethology—the study of animal behavior—researchers attribute war to human aggressive and territorial instincts that developed through biological evolution (Ardrey 1966; Lorenz 1966). In effect, war occurs as a function of human instincts and satisfies some basic human needs. Sociobiologists such as Edward O. Wilson combine ethological studies with other biological factors as well as psychology, anthropology, and sociology to explain war—and its variations—as a consequence of the interaction between genes and the cultural environment, emphasizing the centrality of aggression in this complex mix. However, such arguments suffer from the same limits as the system-level argument about anarchy: If human nature is aggressive, why is war not constant? Why are some people and some societies peaceful? How, in short, do we explain peace?

One answer to this is the feminist approach that suggests the rules and patterns of the international system were established by men. We introduced this argument at the system level, but it can also be considered as an individual-level argument in some forms. Because men are often considered to be more aggressive, the rules are very competitive (e.g., self-help) rather than cooperative. Because the rules are established, it doesn't matter if a leader is a man or a woman, but the ultimate cause of conflict is the set of rules created and dominated by men. What if instead of a competitive game, the rules inspired cooperation? This explanation, however, suffers from the same issue as war being innate to human beings.

Perhaps, then, the individual-level explanations stressing the particular characteristics of *some* individuals—national leaders—and their individual makeup provide helpful insights into what causes war. In particular, perhaps explanations at this level shed light on specific wars and the decisions to engage in them. There are dozens of approaches to this level of explanation, including, according to Cashman (1993), "differences in willingness to take risks, different perceptions (and misperceptions) of the environment and of one's opponents, different images of the world and operational codes, difference in ability to change or adjust present images, different psychological needs, different personality traits, and differences in ability to deal with stress" (p. 75). One line of explanation has stressed **psychological needs** and the possibility that some individuals are more power oriented or compensate for low self-esteem by acting more aggressively. Other studies emphasize **personality traits** such as dogmatic, domineering, or authoritarian personalities that might lead individuals with such traits to be more likely to advocate the use of force in particular situations. Similarly, studies suggest that extroverts seek more cooperative outcomes than introverts and that narcissism is usually associated with hostility, aggression, and power-seeking behavior. Finally, another line of explanation focuses on cognition and the propensity for misperception and miscalculation.

Factors such as these are almost certainly interconnected and almost certainly play out in varying ways in the small-group contexts of most foreign policy decisions. For example, the groupthink argument suggests that the characteristics of some decision groups turn the particular mix of personalities and group structure into a situation in which the participants get locked into a single way of thinking and ignore relevant information. In certain situations, this phenomenon can lead to decisions to use force. A good example of this is US decision making on Vietnam under President Lyndon Johnson and his advisers, and it may characterize the US decision to go to war in Iraq in 2003 under George W. Bush as well. In both cases, scholars argue that the presidents and their advisers were convinced that war was the only logical choice and refused to consider seriously other options (Badie 2010; Janis 1972; Scott and Rosati 2021). Moreover, different regime types probably connect to these factors as well, with individual characteristics of leaders probably more important to understanding war in regimes in which such individuals are more powerful and less constrained by structures and processes of accountability.

Explaining Civil Wars

Before we leave this section, we should take some time to address the causes of civil wars that, as we have seen, are an increasingly important aspect of international conflict. In his classic work *Why Men Rebel*, political scientist Ted Robert Gurr (1970) offers a **frustration-aggression theory** for rebellion and civil war. According to Gurr, although frustration over lack of fairness, repression, inequality, and other matters does not necessarily lead to violence, it can do so if it is persistent and intense. **Relative deprivation** is critical to understanding when that threshold is crossed. Relative deprivation is the discrepancy between what people think they deserve and what they actually think they can get. According to Gurr (1970), "the potential for collective violence varies strongly with the intensity and scope of relative deprivation among members of a collectivity" (p. 24). It is therefore a subjective phenomenon (even rich people can feel relative deprivation), and frequently the sense of relative deprivation depends on the awareness of the opportunities and conditions of others.

More specifically, civil wars can arise from population-related issues, from the pressures on scarce resources (such as land) generated by population growth to issues related to diversity and identity (as

....

psychological needs: essential emotional and psychological requirements of humans, said to be hierarchical by theorists such as Maslow.

personality traits: varying characteristics of individuals, some of which may lead to more aggressive behavior and preferences.

frustration-aggression theory: the idea that people resort to violence under conditions of persistent denial of expected treatment, for example, fairness and equality.

relative deprivation: the discrepancy between what people have and what they think they deserve based on what others have.

MAP 5-4

Ethno-linguistic Map of Ukraine

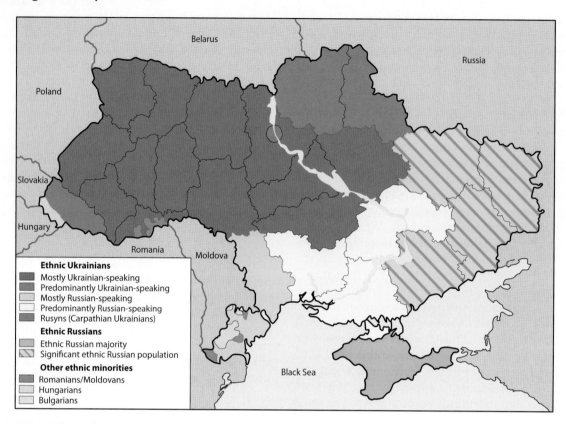

Source: Ethno-linguistic map of Ukraine by Wikipedia user Yerevanci, https://commons.wikimedia.org/wiki/File:Ethnolingusitic_map_of_ukraine.png. Licensed under CC BY-SA 3.0, https://creativecommons.org/licenses/by-sa/3.0/legalcode.

ethnic groups motivated by nationalist sentiment within a state seek greater autonomy). Repression and other government policies may be at the heart of civil war, prompting disaffected groups to rebel. In recent years, identity issues related to what some characterize as "ancient ethnic hatreds" have been offered as explanations for intrastate conflict and war as multiethnic states have struggled to sustain themselves (e.g., see Kaplan 1994). Legacies of colonialism may also be related to civil war. One prime example we introduced in Chapter 2 is the legacy of state boundaries in Africa drawn largely by European colonizers that fit poorly with the **ethnic geography** of the continent, resulting in a wide array of pressures on regimes and borders, including **irredentist claims**

(or irredentism) to territory with people of similar ethnic identity, kinship rallying, minority-group status, and a variety of others. Issues related to resources are also behind civil wars, with groups seeking to gain control of key areas, resources, and the government to ensure benefits. One example from another region is the conflict in Ukraine since 2013, which has not only pitted the Russian-speaking people from the eastern and southern regions of the country against the regime in Kiev and the Ukrainian-speaking regions but also involved intervention by Russia (see Map 5-4). Some arguments even link environmental issues such as deforestation to pressure for civil war (Homer-Dixon 1999). Regime behavior, including repression, corruption, illegitimacy, and poor economic performance, can also contribute to civil war.

As we noted earlier, ethnic conflict has become increasingly violent and all too common since World War II and especially since the end of the Cold War. One classification of the origins of ethnic conflict uses three general categories of explanation (Freeman 1998; Jesse and Williams 2010; Lake and Rothchild 1998).

....

ethnic geography: the spatial and ecological aspects of ethnicity (e.g., where groups live in relation to one another), which affect the culture, politics, and social practices of states, nations, groups, and individuals.

irredentist claims (or irredentism): claims to territory in another state based on historical control or the presence of people with common ethnic identity.

Location, Interests, and Conflict

Realtors often repeat the phrase "location, location, location" to explain the value of one home over another. Can something that simple also help explain a country's interests in world politics or shed light on likely conflicts? Consider the examples of Russia and China. As a territorial state, Russia is fundamentally landlocked and has historically been intensely interested in the nature of the countries around its borders, as well as trying to maintain access to transportation routes that do not involve navigating the frozen Arctic. As Map 5-5 shows, in the decades after the end of the Cold War, the buffer of friendly regimes around Russia's European border has shrunk dramatically as NATO has expanded to the east. According to George Friedman (2017b):

the retreat of Russian forces back to the line separating the country from the European Peninsula was unprecedented. Since the 18th century . . . Russia's border had not been that close to Moscow. . . . The West absorbed the Baltics into NATO, bringing St. Petersburg within a hundred miles of a NATO country. . . . The fact that this scenario leaves Russia in a precarious position means that . . . Russia does not have the option of assuming that the West's interest in the region comes from good intentions. At the same time, the West cannot assume that Russia—if it reclaims Ukraine—will stop there. Therefore, we are in the classic case where two forces assume the worst about each other,

MAP 5-5

The European Peninsula and Russia

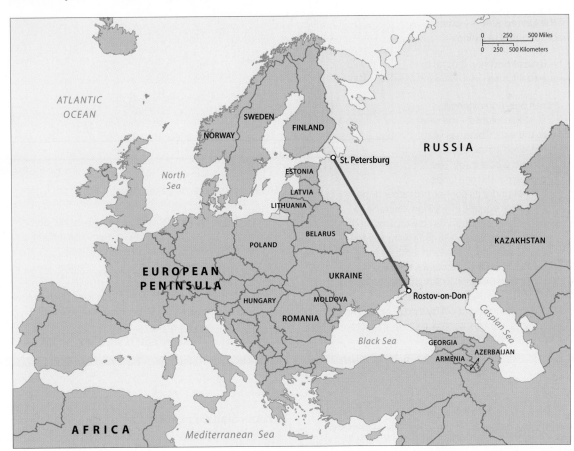

(Continued)

(Continued)

but Russia occupies the weaker position, having lost the first tier of the European Peninsula. It is struggling to maintain the physical integrity of the Motherland. (para. 34–41)

Now consider China and Map 5-6. Although it is not as obviously landlocked as Russia, China also faces a location problem, as its most heavily populated, developed, and economically prosperous centers are clustered along its eastern borders, which meet the South China, East China, and Yellow Seas. There, however, it faces similar concerns as Russia, as other countries such as Japan, Indonesia, the Philippines, and Taiwan—all longtime friends of the United States—control access routes to China.

This leads Friedman (2017a) to argue that China

has only one external strategic interest—the seas to the east. China has vital maritime interests built around global trade. The problem is the sea lanes are not under its control, but rather under American control. In addition, China has a geographic problem. Its coastal seas are the South China Sea, south of Taiwan, and the East China Sea, to its north. Both seas are surrounded by archipelagos of island states ranging from Japan to Singapore with narrow passages between them. These passages could be closed at will by the US Navy. The US could, if it chose, blockade China. (para. 20–21)

MAP 5-6

The Seas Off China's Coast

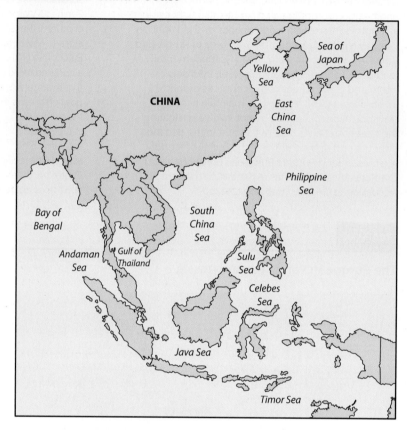

Think about these two examples.

1. How does "location, location, location" color the Russian and Chinese views of themselves, their neighbors, and their interests?

2. How does geography affect conflict?

3. Could these geographic locations push Russia and China closer together or cause conflict between them? ●

....

primordialism: an explanation of ethnic conflict that stresses the fundamental bonds of kinship and identity that establish ethnic differences that divide people and often generate ancient ethnic hatreds.

instrumentalism: an explanation of ethnic conflict that stresses the role of leaders who emphasize and exacerbate ethnic differences (and commonalities) as a means to their own ends.

Primordialism stresses the fundamental, psychological bonds of kinship and identity that establish ethnic differences that divide people and often generate "ancient ethnic hatreds." Essentially, historical feuds between groups continue and ferment into active civil violence today. **Instrumentalism** stresses the role of leaders who emphasize and exacerbate ethnic differences (and commonalities) as a means to their own ends. For example, Slobodan Milošević rose to power partly on his campaign against the ethnic Albanians in Kosovo—using the historical divide between the Muslim Albanians and Orthodox Christian Serbs as a means to gain support and power. Some research even suggests that leaders order campaigns of rape and violence against women of other ethnic identities to dehumanize them and increase the sense of identity and cohesion among the soldiers committing the crimes (Cohen 2013). **Constructivism** emphasizes the social construction of identity and the ways that social interactions define ethnicity for groups of people. When an ethnic identity is defined as being in opposition to another ethnic group, conflict is more likely. For example, being an Irish Catholic might mean you don't like Irish Protestants, or being an Arab might mean you don't like Jews. These identities can be historical or recently constructed, making the conflict between them difficult to manage.

Another way to think about this distinguishes between "greed-based" (mostly in the instrumentalism and primordialism categories) and "grievance-based" (mostly in the primordialism and constructivism categories) explanations of civil war that point to internal factors or causes of civil conflict. In addition, there are external factors that influence the onset and nature of civil wars. Such external factors include the geographic location (see the box "The Revenge of Geography: Location, Interests, and Conflict"), the presence of conflict in neighboring countries (which may spill over or drag in a neighbor), and intervention in the form of military support for armed groups by major regional or global powers (which may hasten or prolong the violence). These external connections help make civil war a significant issue in world politics.

In the end, the issues underlying civil war parallel those for interstate war: territory, resources, identity, and others. And the underlying causes mirror those for interstate war as well, with multiple levels at work. For world politics, understanding civil war is critical for at least three reasons. First, it is the most common form of conflict in the contemporary global context. Second, it has exacted enormous costs from the societies it has affected. The most heinous instances of mass violence seen on the world stage in the past several decades—genocides—have all stemmed from internal conflicts: in the Sudan, the former Yugoslavia, Rwanda, Cambodia, Congo, Syria, and elsewhere. Finally, as Figure 5-4 showed, civil wars are increasingly internationalized, whether by drawing in external parties, spilling over into neighboring countries, or through proxy warfare.

CONCLUSION: THE CONSEQUENCES OF WARS

War is a costly enterprise. It is, most certainly, a social and political phenomenon, one perpetrated by humans against each other. It is persistent and resilient, affecting people across time and space from the beginning of recorded history to the present. Springing from many sources, whatever its issues and causes, it has exacted a ghastly toll on the world.

Indeed, the political, economic, social, environmental, and human costs are extensive. Obviously, war exacts costs in the form of direct and indirect casualties. By some estimates, close to 4 billion people have been casualties of war over time—which is nearly half of the earth's current population. Enormous amounts of money have been spent preparing for, engaging in, and recovering from war. Beyond these direct costs are other less direct ones. Economically, for example, the consequences of war include the hardships of hunger, refugees and forced migration, and degradation of essential public services (such as potable water), as the example of the ongoing conflict in Syria illustrates. The public health consequences of war are extensive. Casualties from hunger and disease and other indirect consequences of war usually exceed the immediate casualties (Stewart and FitzGerald 2001). In the case of Syria, WorldVision (2020) estimates that approximately 6 million Syrians have fled or been forced from Syria as refugees, with about the same number displaced within the country. Half of those affected are children, and more than half of the country's population (22 million, pre–civil war) need humanitarian assistance.

War also disrupts the economies of both victor and vanquished in a serious fashion. Environmental costs are also often very steep. For instance, Vietnam lost 20% of its forests and one third of its mangrove swamps to the extended conflict in the middle of the 20th century. In 1991, the Gulf War resulted in one of history's largest oil spills when withdrawing Iraqi troops destroyed and set fire to Kuwaiti oil wells. War-torn societies also suffer from significant degradation of human rights and gender equality. In short, armed conflict has affected human well-being and diminished the quality of life of billions of people over time.

The costs of war extend to both winners and losers. For example, the cost of winning a war may deplete a society's resources. Look at some of the World War II winners: Britain, France, and the Soviet Union. The British and French were essentially bankrupt after

....

constructivism (and ethnicity): an explanation of ethnic conflict that emphasizes the social construction of identity and the ways in which social interactions define ethnicity for groups of people.

Casualties of war

We know entire generations can be profoundly affected by a war. What will the impact be on these children's generation?

Samir Tatin/Anadolu Agency/Getty Images

World War II, and the Soviets had much of their country destroyed. Further, winners of major wars often find themselves at the heart of struggles to define and maintain a new international order, which can place great burdens on both those states with such responsibilities and those states affected by them (Ikenberry 2000, 2012). Losing wars can also exact serious political costs on the leaders responsible for the decisions to engage in fighting. Elected officials in democratic states may face punishment at the ballot box on election day, and authoritarian rulers may face efforts to overthrow or assassinate them (Bueno de Mesquita and Siverson 1995; Bueno de Mesquita, Siverson, and Woller 1992; Debs and Goemans 2010; Goemans 2000). Not surprisingly, these political consequences often have important effects on the decisions of a leader on whether to go to war, how hard and how long to fight, and when to quit. Finally, losing wars can cast long shadows over countries and their subsequent decisions and behavior in world politics. Think about the consequences of World War II for German and Japanese politics, for instance. Or consider the long shadow the Vietnam War cast over American politics and military strategy (Kalb and Kalb 2011).

War has changed over time, but it persists. It is fought for many purposes and has many causes. Indeed, conflict is endemic to a world characterized by anarchy, diversity, and complexity, and states and non-state actors grapple with persistent conflicts in the pursuit of security. In Chapters 6 and 7, we examine efforts to manage conflict and provide security. Before we move on, we might consider again the forces that work against efforts to manage and reduce conflict and war, as well as those areas of potential. Reflect on the causes of war we have reviewed here and consider what avenues they suggest for the successful management of conflict and achievement of security in world politics. ●

KEY CONCEPTS

5-1 Identify the nature and forms of armed conflict.

War is a regular—though rare—and highly costly event in world politics. War occurs when the participants engage in armed struggles to gain or defend territory, resources, influence, authority, or other things of high value. The participants can involve two or more states (interstate war), two or more groups within a territory (intrastate, or civil war), or a combination of states and non-state groups (extra-systemic or extra-state war). Such armed struggles obviously range from small-scale, localized disputes to large-scale, even global conflicts. Conventional war generally involves armed conflict between two or more states in which military forces of each side are used against each other and in which weapons of mass destruction, such as nuclear, biological, or chemical weapons, are generally not used. Unconventional war involves armed conflict in which civilian and nonmilitary targets are targeted, forces used include nontraditional forces outside organized militaries, and/or weapons of mass destruction may be employed. Civil war involves armed conflict between competing factions within a country or between an existing government and a competing group within that country over control of territory or the government. Asymmetric war pits two or more groups of very different military size or power against each other, in which the weaker participant often resorts to unconventional tactics rather than engage in traditional battlefield war. Terrorism is a form of unconventional and asymmetric war.

5-2 Describe the evolution of and trends in armed conflict.

War has become increasingly destructive and deadly over time. Since 1945, wars have become more limited and increasingly have been located in the developing world. Over time, and especially since 1989, war has become increasingly internal, as civil war has become the most common form. There has been a shift from conventional to unconventional war over the last half of the 20th century and early 21st century.

5-3 Assess the causes of interstate and intrastate war at the (a) system, (b) state, and (c) individual levels of analysis.

War has been waged over territory; the "search for statehood" and independence; ideology; competition for economic resources, markets, or transportation; sympathy or humanitarian reasons, particularly to protect perceived religious and ethnic kin abroad; predation and survival; and to defend allies and to defend or restore the balance of power. System-level causes include anarchy, self-help, security dilemmas, distribution of power, structural characteristics related to power, interdependence, and states dominated by men. State-level causes include type of government; type of economy; demographic, cultural, physical, or geographic attributes; level of political instability; and previous war involvement. Individual-level causes include human nature, psychological needs, and personality traits. Civil wars can arise from population-related issues, from the pressures on scarce resources (such as land) to issues related to diversity and identity. Repression and other government policies may be at the heart of civil war, prompting disaffected groups to rebel. There are "greed-based" (mostly in the instrumentalism and primordialism categories) and "grievance-based" (mostly in the primordialism and constructivism categories) explanations of civil war. External factors such as the presence of conflict in neighboring countries and intervention by major regional or global powers also influence the onset and nature of civil war.

KEY TERMS

war 116

interstate war 116

civil war 116

extra-systemic or extra-state war 116

conventional war 116

unconventional war 116

weapons of mass destruction 116

asymmetric war 117

improvised explosive device (IED) 117

terrorism 118

state-sponsored terrorism 120

cyberwarfare 128

hegemonic stability theory 132

power transition theory 132

cyclical theories of war 132

hegemon 132

national attributes 134

diversionary theory 134

war weariness 135

human nature 136

psychological needs 137

personality traits 137

frustration-aggression theory 137

relative deprivation 137

ethnic geography 138

irredentist claims (or irredentism) 138

primordialism 140

instrumentalism 140

constructivism (and ethnicity) 141

REVIEW QUESTIONS

1. What is war, and what are its major forms?

2. What is terrorism, and why is it a challenging form of warfare?

3. How has war evolved over time? What are the main elements of change and continuity? What factors best explain the changes?

4. What are the main explanations for the causes of war at the system level of analysis? In what ways are these explanations most useful?

5. What are the main explanations for the causes of war at the state level of analysis? In what ways are these explanations most useful?

6. What are the main explanations for the causes of war at the individual level of analysis? In what ways are these explanations most useful?

7. Why are civil wars now so commonplace?

THINK ABOUT THIS

The Future of War

Consider the changing nature of armed conflict over the past few centuries and the major explanations of its causes. Some perspectives and explanations—for example, those of major realist thinkers such as John Mearsheimer or individual-level analyses stressing human nature—seem to suggest that war is likely to persist as a major problem for world politics. Others—for example, those of major liberal thinkers such as Michael Doyle and advocates of the democratic peace theory—seem to offer more optimistic assessments. One—John Mueller—even argues that major war is now obsolete. Given what you have learned about the trends in and explanations for war, reflect on the problem of war and its nature and impact in future world politics, focusing particularly on the possibility that major wars can be controlled, reduced, or, indeed, even eliminated as a problem in world politics.

Can major wars be made a thing of the past?

FOR MORE INFORMATION . . .

Cashman, Greg. (1993). *What Causes War? An Introduction to Theories of International Conflict.* Lanham, MD: Lexington Books.

Combs, Cindy. (2010). *Terrorism in the 21st Century*, 6th ed. Englewood Cliffs, NJ: Prentice Hall.

Jesse, Neal, and Kristen Williams. (2011). *Ethnic Conflict: A Systematic Approach to Cases of Conflict.* Washington, DC: CQ Press.

Lake, David, and Donald Rothschild. (1998). *The International Spread of Ethnic Conflict.* Princeton, NJ: Princeton University Press.

Levy, Jack, and William Thompson. (2010). *The Causes of War.* New York, NY: Wiley-Blackwell.

Waltz, Kenneth. (2001). *Man, the State, and War.* New York, NY: Columbia University Press.

AREF TAMMAWI/AFP via Getty Images

A convoy of nuclear missiles in a military parade rehearsal on Red Square, Moscow

What best explains the role and consequences of weapons such as nuclear missiles?

iStock.com/rusm

6 Seeking Security
Managing Conflict and War

Learning Objectives

After studying this chapter, you will be able to . . .

6-1 Identify the challenges of seeking international security in world politics.

6-2 Describe and evaluate power-based approaches to international security embraced by realists, including military might, alliances, and the uses of force.

6-3 Describe and assess cooperation-based approaches to international security embraced by liberals, including arms control and disarmament, collective security, and security communities.

Chapter Outline

6-1 The Challenge of International Security

6-2 Realist Approaches to Security and Conflict

6-3 Liberal Approaches to Security and Conflict

Responding to Russian Missiles?

In early 2017, US General Paul Selva, the vice chairman of the Joint Chiefs of Staff, testified that the Russians had deployed intermediate-range nuclear missiles in violation of the 1987 Intermediate-Range Nuclear Forces Treaty between the United States and Russia, which banned the testing, production, and deployment of such weapons. According to General Selva, "the system itself presents a risk to most [US] facilities in Europe. . . . And we believe that the Russians have deliberately deployed it in order to pose a threat to NATO and to facilities within the NATO area of responsibility" (Gordon 2017: 8).

Beginning in 2013, the US raised concerns over these missiles as they were being produced and tested, but the deployment dramatically raised the stakes. Moreover, because Russian military spending increased by more than a factor of four since 1998 and Russian forces had engaged in military actions in Georgia (2008) and Ukraine (2014), the context of the controversial missile deployment was even more troubling. The US first formally alleged a treaty violation in 2014. In the fall of 2018, after years of formal complaints, the Trump administration announced its intention to terminate the treaty because of Russian noncompliance. In August 2019, the US withdrew from the agreement.

1. Why would Russia develop and deploy intermediate-range nuclear missiles in violation of a standing agreement?

2. What should the US and NATO countries do to address the challenges of increased Russian military spending, use of military force, and missile deployments now that the treaty is dead?

3. What does this situation suggest about the pursuit of security in world politics?

INTRODUCTION: MANAGING CONFLICT AND SEEKING SECURITY

In the pursuit of international security, states and other players frequently come into conflict. The combination of the anarchy of the international system, the diversity of the players and their perspectives and interests, and the complexity of issues and interactions these players face almost ensures that clashes will occur. As we saw in Chapter 5, all too frequently those clashes can become violent and result in armed conflict, large or small. Managing this challenge—seeking security and dealing with conflict—is therefore one of the most critical concerns the players of world politics face.

States and other players have a variety of ways to seek international security in world politics. In this chapter we consider the particular challenges of attempting to manage conflict while also providing security. We begin by reviewing the essential context of the challenge the players in world politics face, highlighting the main features of the security dilemma, the pursuit of power, and the potential for conflict. We then turn to fundamentally realist-based approaches to conflict and security, involving weapons, alliances, and the use of force. Then we discuss liberal alternatives, involving arms control and disarmament, collective security, and the development and maintenance of a democratic and capitalist peace. We conclude with some enduring challenges before moving on to discuss the structures and institutions of cooperation in Chapter 7.

6-1 THE CHALLENGE OF INTERNATIONAL SECURITY

>> 6-1 Identify the challenges of seeking international security in world politics.

The players in world politics—both states and non-state actors—seek security. They want to protect themselves from threats to either their survival or essential interests, and they want to be physically safe from attack from other actors. For states, the protection of **political sovereignty** and **territorial integrity** is especially important in a world without central government. Traditional views of international security emphasize the ability of a state to protect itself from threats against its welfare and survival, usually through the accumulation of military power. International security can also be viewed more cooperatively to emphasize areas of common interest that link states as they address shared concerns for safety and well-being. As we will see in Parts III and IV, challenges to economic security and human security also motivate the players of world politics.

However, the enduring problem of war, discussed in Chapter 5, and the persistent efforts of states to seek power and acquire military arsenals suggest that the pursuit of security often results in insecurity, arms races, conflict spirals, and, sometimes, war. The interests and objectives of states and other players are often different, leading to disagreement, fear, uncertainty, and conflict. The absence of authoritative central institutions in world politics often makes coordination and cooperation difficult, prompting fear from the players that their interests will not be protected unless they take action themselves. Hence, the core elements of the security challenge stem from the combination of anarchy, diversity, and complexity in world politics. At the foundation of this fundamental challenge are the security dilemma and the challenge of power.

6-1a The Security Dilemma

As we explained in Chapters 2 and 3, security dilemmas stem from the paradoxical situation in which the

political sovereignty: the principle that a state has authority and independence to rule without interference within its own borders.

territorial integrity: the principle that other actors should not violate the territory or boundaries of a state.

things one does to be secure often end up creating even greater insecurities. This dilemma rests in large part on the anarchic structure of world politics. As we described in Chapter 2, any society, even an international one, without a central coercive authority will pose dangers as the members try to figure out how to protect themselves from real and potential threats. In such systems, self-help is the norm, as states must depend on themselves to provide for their own security and protect their own interests. They cannot turn to a cop on the corner for protection. Unfortunately, as states engage in self-help, the consequence is a security dilemma. How does one society increase its own security without seeming to jeopardize the security of others? This dilemma is made even more serious by the diversity of the players in world politics. Differences in size and influence, culture, and perspective often lead to very different interpretations of the nature and meaning of actions and events. Add in the problem of complexity—in which multidimensional issues; state and non-state actors; national, international, and transnational processes; and many other factors are linked together—and it is easy to see how choosing actions to gain security and manage conflict might wind up producing the opposite result.

Whatever approach to world politics one takes—realist, liberal, constructivist, Marxist, or feminist—conditions can generate action–reaction cycles. Whether one thinks all states seek power and domination (realists), some states behave aggressively (liberals), states misunderstand and miscommunicate (liberals and constructivists), core states dominate peripheral states (world systems theorists), states are driven by constructed identities and interactions (constructivists), or state behavior is masculinized by the dominance of men in leadership positions (feminists), conflict and sometimes war are often the logical result of the security dilemma. Each state may take actions it sees as defensive and nonthreatening, but such actions often alarm others and could cause exactly what each is trying to avoid. This, then, is a central challenge facing the players of world politics as they seek security and try to manage the conflict that appears inevitable because of anarchy, diversity, and complexity.

6-1b The Challenge of Power

Think back to our discussion in Chapter 3, where we noted that power is often considered the currency of world politics: Those players who have power generally are more able to get what they want than those who do not. Of course, this simple conception hides a great deal of complexity. We have already reviewed how power is seen differently through different lenses and how a great variety of resources—from raw military might to the appeal of ideas—are involved. In terms of security and conflict, the focus of this chapter, the context of the security dilemma involves a corresponding power dilemma: How do states and other players accumulate and apply power in pursuit of international security?

Several challenges are at the heart of this dilemma. First, whether power is viewed as zero-sum or positive-sum is a major issue. We introduced these concepts in Chapter 3, where we also described them in terms of relative and absolute gains. In terms of the pursuit of power and security, the zero-sum approach—in which there must be a winner and a loser, so that advantages for one generally mean disadvantages for another—presumes conflictual or competitive relations in world politics and efforts by states to accumulate power for themselves to ensure their safety and survival. In contrast, the positive-sum approach—in which mutual interests provide opportunities for win-win situations—sees possibilities for collaborative efforts to establish mutual security and cooperative efforts to manage conflict.

A second challenge of power stems from the significant disparities among states and other actors in world politics. As anyone can easily see, and as realists are quick to point out, power is not evenly distributed throughout the international system—and probably can never be. These disparities in power between the haves and have-nots create challenges for all concerned because they generate uncertainty, fear, threats, and competition. Moreover, larger, more powerful states are often forced to view security more broadly than simply their own narrow welfare and survival, taking interest in the problems and conflicts of others, while less powerful states are often forced to contend with the actions and concerns of the more powerful. For example, a recurring tension of the post–Cold War era has been Russia's desire to dominate a sphere of influence around its borders and the resulting efforts by affected countries such as Georgia, Poland, Latvia, Lithuania, Estonia, and Ukraine to resist those Russian pressures.

Overall, managing the challenges of anarchy, diversity, and complexity in the pursuit of security leads to a number of typical strategies. Virtually every state seeks to build military power of some kind for security reasons, and many states actively use military might to gain security and resolve conflict. States also form alliances to expand their power and protect themselves against common threats or enemies. Throughout history, states have also engaged in a variety of efforts to control the accumulation, spread, and use of military might, and they have attempted to work together and pool power to gain security and manage or reduce the likelihood of conflict. Communities of states with similar interests, identities, and other common linkages have sought to harmonize relations with each other in security communities as well.

At the same time, a range of non-state actors have been engaged in activities and interactions that both enhance and complicate the management of conflict and the pursuit of international security. Let's consider these efforts to gain security, categorizing them in terms of realist approaches (military power, alliances, and use of force) and liberal approaches (arms control and disarmament, collective security, and security communities).

6-2 REALIST APPROACHES TO SECURITY AND CONFLICT

>> **6-2** Describe and evaluate power-based approaches to international security embraced by realists, including military might, alliances, and the uses of force.

An ancient Roman scribe once wrote, "If you want peace, prepare for war" (*si vis pacem, para bellum*).

US troops deploying to the Middle East in January 2020
How do states use military might to gain security?

For centuries, this saying has summarized realist approaches to security and conflict. In a dangerous world, the argument goes, states must accumulate military capabilities to deter potential attackers, defend against attacks, and extend power and influence. States generally have two basic options: building their own military might and forging alliances to increase military capabilities.

6-2a Weapons

Most states expend considerable resources on military and security forces. With the exception of very small microstates, such as many of those in the Pacific Ocean, virtually every country in the world maintains military forces. (Exceptions are Costa Rica, which abolished its armed forces in 1948, and Grenada, which has not maintained its own armed forces since 1983. Both of these countries still maintain small internal security forces.) To understand this approach to international security, let's consider the expenditures states make and key characteristics of military might. We will consider the uses of military force later in this section.

Buying Security?

As realists are quick to point out, most countries devote considerable sums of money to building their military forces, and this has been a relative constant in world politics. Over time, states—especially major powers—have engaged in the accumulation of military might and the development of ever more capable weaponry. In Chapter 5, we noted how the evolution of warfare could be nicely illustrated through the imagery of popular films. The same is true of military technology, from the swords and spears of films such as *Gladiator* (2000) and *Vikings* (2013) to the high-tech weaponry depicted in *Eye in the Sky* (2015), *Body of Lies* (2008), or *The Hurt Locker* (2008). The development and accumulation of such increasingly capable weaponry have been a central story in world politics, and the major arms race of the Cold War period between the US and the Soviet Union was merely a more modern version—albeit with the potential to be an increasingly deadly one with the development of nuclear weapons—of an age-old dynamic.

States continue to acquire weapons. Although global military spending declined between 1988 and 1998 in the wake of the Cold War, it rose steadily after that, with a brief dip in 2013–2014. Table 6-1 shows the top 10 countries by their military expenditures in 2018. Not surprisingly, the list contains what most observers would regard as the most powerful countries in the world, and the United States is at the very top, as it has been for decades. Indeed, as Figure 6-1 shows, at 36%,

---

TABLE 6-1

Top 10 Countries in Military Spending, 2018

COUNTRY	US$ (BILLIONS), CONSTANT 2017 $
United States	649
China	250
Saudi Arabia	67.6
India	66.5
France	63.8
Russia	61.4
United Kingdom	50.0
Germany	49.5
Japan	46.6
South Korea	43.1

Source: Nan Tian, Aude Fleurant, Alexandra Kuimova, Pieter D. Wezeman, and Siemon T. Wezeman, *Trends in World Military Expenditure, 2018*, Stockholm International Peace Research Institute, April 2019.

FIGURE 6-1

Top 15 Countries and Their Share of Global Military Expenditures, 2018

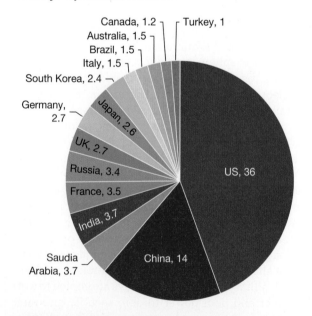

Source: Constructed by the authors with data from Nan Tian, Aude Fleurant, Alexandra Kuimova, Pieter D. Wezeman, and Siemon T. Wezeman, *Trends in World Military Expenditure, 2018*, Stockholm International Peace Research Institute, April 2019.

China's Military Spending

China is the largest country in the world by population, second largest by size of economy, and fourth largest by territory. According to the US Department of Defense, which publishes an annual report specifically on China's military might (and that alone should tell you something about the importance of the issue), China increased its military spending between 1996 and 2018 by more than 11 times, as Figure 6-2 shows. As military experts are quick to point out, China's estimates of its expenditures, and even those of the US Defense Department, underestimate actual expenditures, which probably now exceed $250 billion. At least as interesting as these overall figures are the priorities China is emphasizing in its efforts to increase its military power. These include ballistic and cruise missiles, submarines, electronic warfare (including cyberwarfare) capabilities, high-tech weapons such as stealth aircraft, and increasingly sophisticated information technology and command, control, and communications

capabilities. China also commissioned its first aircraft carrier in 2012 and put it into action in 2016, much sooner than was previously estimated. China's second aircraft carrier underwent initial sea trials in 2020.

China faces internal security concerns and continued tension over the future of Taiwan, as well as confrontations with Japan, the Philippines, and Vietnam over maritime claims in the South and East China Seas. However, it is not involved in any wars, nor does it have an extended system of global alliances, and it has only one foreign military base to fund.

- Why would China devote so much of its resources to such a dramatic increase in military might?

- What consequences might this steady expansion of military capabilities have in the region and in the world? ●

FIGURE 6-2

China's Defense Spending, 1996–2018

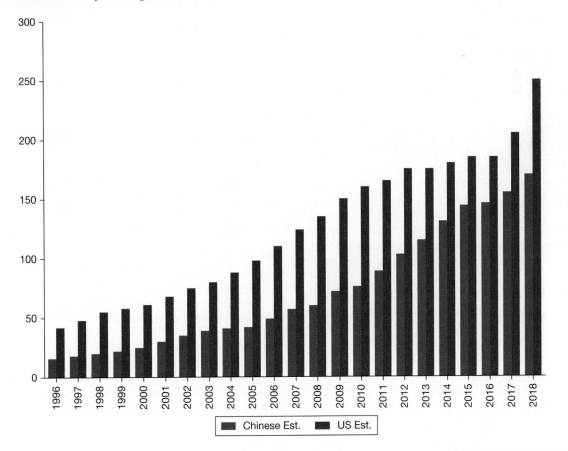

Source: Pentagon Reports on China's Military, 2010–2020, US Department of Defense.

the US share of global military spending is almost three times that of its closest competitor (a percentage that has fallen from about a decade ago, when the US alone made up over half of the world's spending on the military). Since 2000, the United States has more than doubled its annual military spending. In the same time frame, China and others have also dramatically increased their military spending. However, even with these changes, the US still spends almost three times more on the military than China (see "Spotlight On: China's Military Spending") and 10 times more than Russia.

Of course, large states have more resources to allocate to military spending. Table 6-2 shows the countries that spend the most of their available resources on the military. Ranking military spending as a percentage of gross domestic product—or as defense burden—presents a very different view: Poorer, often conflict-ridden countries are high on this list. Indeed, it is hard to avoid the conclusion that the countries least able to afford to spend their resources on the military still do so, at quite high rates.

According to realists, states devote these resources to their militaries to counter threats and to gain or maintain power. However, given their rather bleak view of the prospects for peace and security, realists contend that, despite amassing military might, conflict is still likely. In fact, they often argue that military power is necessary to deal with the inevitable conflicts that arise in the dangerous, anarchic world they see. In their view, failing to accumulate power leaves a state vulnerable, severely limiting its ability to preserve its national, economic, and human security. Before moving on, stop and reflect for a moment: How do you think this perspective affects the security dilemma?

Military Forces

Traditionally, much of the money spent on defense has gone to building larger and larger armed forces. Indeed, the number of military personnel in a given state has long been an important measure of military might, and over the centuries states have assembled ground, naval, and (for the past 100 years or so) air forces to wield the weaponry they have accumulated. Table 6-3 shows the overall size of the military forces for a number of countries. Major powers such as the United States and China maintain the largest forces in sheer numbers, while mid-sized powers such as the European states of France, Germany, and the United Kingdom field smaller, but still sizable, forces. Other key countries such as India and Pakistan field sizable militaries as well. Indeed, the numbers in Table 6-3 illustrate the realist perspective that security concerns lead most countries, both major powers and smaller

TABLE 6-2

Top 25 Countries in Military Spending as a Percentage of GDP, 2018

COUNTRY	PERCENTAGE
Saudi Arabia	8.8
Oman	8.2
United Arab Emirates	5.7
Algeria	5.3
Israel	5.1
Kuwait	5.1
Lebanon	5.0
Jordan	4.7
Armenia	4.3
Pakistan	4.0
Uzbekistan	4.0
Yemen	4.0
Russia	3.9
Ukraine	3.8
Azerbaijan	3.8
Bahrain	3.6
Colombia	3.5
Namibia	3.4
Singapore	3.4
Kyrgyz Republic	3.2
United States	3.2
Morocco	3.1
The Gambia	3.0
Burma	2.9
Cuba	2.9

Source: Data are from the World Bank, "Military Expenditure (% of GDP)," 2018, http://data.worldbank.org/indicator/MS.MIL.XPND.GD.ZS?year_high_desc=true.

states, to desire and seek militaries of significant size. That major powers would do so is not terribly surprising, but why do smaller states devote such substantial shares of their obviously limited resources to this purpose? Can you think of other factors that might be at work? (See the box "The Revenge of Geography: Security and Geography.")

TABLE 6-3

Estimated Size of Top 10 Current Military Forces, 2020

COUNTRY	APPROXIMATE ACTIVE MILITARY FORCES
China	2.18 million
India	1.44 million
United States	1.4 million
North Korea	1.28 million
Russia	1.01 million
Pakistan	654,000
South Korea	580,000
Iran	523,000
Vietnam	482,000
Saudi Arabia	478,000

Source: Data are from http://www.globalfirepower.com/active-military-manpower.asp.

Increasingly, however, sheer numbers are misleading. They do not account for such factors as military technology or less tangible factors such as troop quality and training, leadership, and morale. For example, at the time of the 1991 Gulf War, Iraq had the world's fourth largest army—that did Iraq little good as the technologically superior forces led by the United States quickly overwhelmed the poorly trained and unenthusiastic Iraqi forces. Images of Iraqi troops surging from their fortified positions with their hands up to surrender in the early moments of the 1991 military operations are among the most striking of the war. Some Iraqi troops even surrendered to Western journalists. In the second war in Iraq in 2003, although the Iraqi army of about 375,000 troops significantly outnumbered US forces, those numbers again did little good in the face of US military technology and tactics. However, the vast technological superiority of US military forces in the Vietnam War was insufficient to overcome the will and commitment of the Vietnamese forces fighting against them. So military force is the combination of numbers of troops, their quality of training and leadership, the quality and quantity of armaments, the ability to project that military power elsewhere, and the troops' willingness to fight.

High-Tech: The Revolution in Military Affairs

The most advanced militaries are less distinguished by the sheer size of their forces and more defined by the technology they deploy. Over the past several decades in particular, significant advantages have accrued to those countries able to harness advances in weaponry and information technology. Major powers have always sought advances in weaponry to provide advantages on the battlefield, and the history and evolution of warfare are full of situations in which revolutionary equipment and tactics delivered advantages that often resulted in very one-sided victories. Examples include the incredibly devastating effects of the English longbow on the heavily armored French cavalry in the battles of Crécy (1346) and Agincourt (1415), the success of the German Panzer armies and blitzkrieg tactics in the early years of World War II, and, as noted, the US successes in 1991 and 2003 in Iraq. Consequently, as realists would predict, major powers regularly seek to develop and obtain the most advanced and powerful weaponry to gain advantage over real and potential rivals.

A stunning revolution in the technology of war occurred with the beginning of the nuclear age in August 1945. After the United States used two atomic bombs against Japan at Hiroshima and Nagasaki, developing and deploying nuclear weapons became a significant aspect of military power with dramatic consequences. States deploying nuclear arsenals are automatically more likely to be regarded as military powers. However, the existence of nuclear weapons transformed the ways strategists thought about war. As US strategist Bernard Brodie (2008) stated shortly after World War II, "thus far the chief purpose of our military establishment has been to win wars. From now on its chief purpose must be to avert them. It can have almost no other useful purpose" (p. 205).

The prospect of nuclear annihilation transformed great-power war by making it far riskier (a state, in particular its civilian population, can be destroyed without being defeated on the battlefield), so direct military confrontations between countries deploying

The revolution in military affairs: high-tech weapons

How has the advance of military technology affected conflict and security?

JOHANNES EISELE/AFP/Getty Images

Security and Geography

Since 1815, Switzerland has managed to sit out Europe's wars without amassing a sizable military or forging alliances with powerful states. As of 2020, the Swiss military totaled only about 241,000 troops, of which only 21,000 were active-duty. At the same time, Switzerland has firmly established itself as a neutral player in world politics, even while hosting a significant range of international organizations and institutions and being heavily engaged in the international economy.

Contrast the Swiss experience with that of Poland, which has spent a great deal of the Westphalian era trying to avoid invasion or attempting to cope with conquest and occupation. Situated on the great northern plain of Europe, Polish territory has long

MAP 6-1

Borders in Europe

How do defensible borders change a country's security?

been a route for and location of invasion and battles. Polish history is replete with occupation, conquest, and efforts to find security through alliances with countries like France and Britain to help overcome its vulnerability. It has been attacked, dominated, occupied, and dismembered by Prussia, Germany, Russia, the Austro-Hungarian Empire, and the Soviet Union.

Why was Switzerland more successful than Poland at avoiding attack and maintaining its independence and security? Part of the answer is geographic (see Map 6-1). Poland's experiences in world politics are driven in large measure by its location between other powerful states, along with its relatively indefensible borders along the northern plains of Europe. There are few physical barriers between Poland and its neighbors to the east, west, or south, and being located directly between competing great powers is not an ideal spot. Switzerland, by contrast, not only has the advantage of being out of the vortex of great powers; it also has the incredible advantage of having its borders secured by some of the most rugged mountain ranges in Europe. The simple physical location and attributes of these two countries dramatically color their sense of and experiences with security and the security dilemma.

Now consider the geographic locations of both Russia and China. Both are major powers, but both have insecure borders. Russia's western border is hemmed in by European states no longer under Moscow's control. Its southern borders bump up

against the Islamic world. In the east, Russia confronts a long border with rising power China. In all three directions, no serious barriers to the invasion of Russia exist. For its part, China could try to expand at Russia's expense in Siberia, and Chinese business owners have already begun to operate in Russia's underpopulated eastern territories. China confronts a restive Islamic population in its western provinces and has a more-than-50-year border conflict with India, which has flared up recently and continues to be a concern. China's lifeline in trade runs through maritime routes with chokepoints controlled by other countries and international trade routes China is now trying to control through the creation of new islands in the South China Sea.

Think about the examples of Switzerland, Poland, Russia, and China and consider how similar factors affect other states and their perspectives on security as well.

1. How does the geography and location of the United States, separated from Europe and Asia by two vast oceans, affect its sense of security?

2. How does the geography and location of Israel affect its sense of security and its relations with its neighbors?

3. How might geography affect the strategies that states like Poland, Russia, and China adopt to ensure their security? ●

---

nuclear arsenals diminished considerably. In spite of the high-stakes tensions of the Cold War, for example, the United States and the Soviet Union never directly confronted one another militarily, and the fear of a nuclear war during the 1962 Cuban Missile Crisis drove home the potential consequences of this technological revolution.

Thus, a series of new concerns arose with respect to nuclear might. First, states with nuclear arsenals felt the need to possess weapons in quantities and with capabilities (explosive power, accuracy) sufficient to ensure the ability to retaliate against an attack. Ensuring a second-strike capability became critical, and the action–reaction cycle of arms competition between the major nuclear powers ensued. Second, acquiring nuclear capabilities became important to other countries. Britain, France, and China followed the United States and the Soviet Union to each develop their own nuclear arsenals, in

part to ensure that they could deter nuclear strikes themselves with the threat of retaliation, and in part to ensure that they had a seat at the table with the major powers. These five states were the first official nuclear weapons states, but they have been joined by India (1974) and Pakistan (1998), which publicly tested nuclear devices, and Israel, which has not publicly acknowledged possession of nuclear weapons but is widely believed to have an arsenal of between 100 and 200 weapons. North Korea first tested nuclear weapons in 2006 and has done so multiple times since then. It is suspected of possessing sufficient material for about 20 to 30 nuclear weapons and in 2017 claimed to have achieved the ability to make warheads small enough to be placed on missiles. Finally, preventing the spread of nuclear weapons and weapons materials to other states has become a major issue as well (see Map 6-2). In addition to efforts to construct international agreements and institutions

MAP 6-2

Nuclear Weapons States, 2017

Is this too many, or too few, nuclear weapons states?

a.

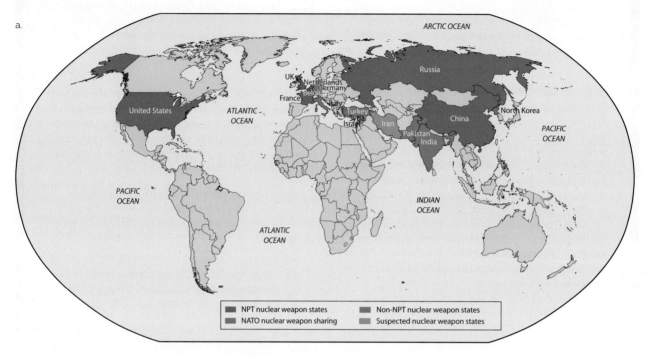

b.

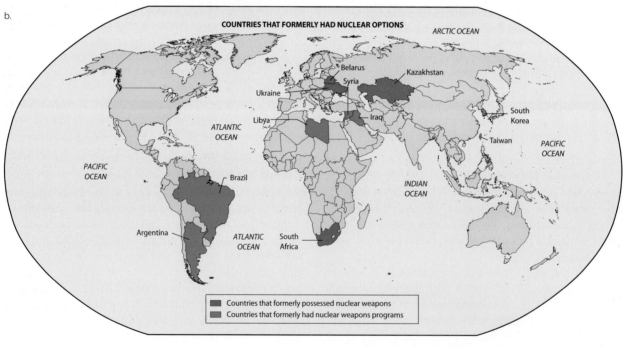

such as the Nuclear Nonproliferation Treaty (1968), the Comprehensive Nuclear Test-Ban Treaty (1996), and the International Atomic Energy Agency (1957), a variety of efforts—from the offering of benefits and rewards to more coercive measures, including military operations—have been undertaken to prevent other states from gaining nuclear capabilities.

The technological revolutions affecting military power have also involved efforts to build better, more capable, and more efficient weapons (e.g., faster, more heavily armored tanks or more lethal bombers and fighter jets) as usual, but also through new advances in battlefield technology and tactics. The so-called **revolution in military affairs** stresses the "evolution of weapons, military organizations, and operational concepts among advanced powers [and] focuses on the changes made possible by advancing technology" (Galdi 1995: 1). Embraced by both major powers and many others, the recent transformation emphasizes the combination of intelligence; surveillance and reconnaissance capabilities (driven by technologies such as satellite imagery and unmanned remote-operated vehicles in the air and on the ground); command, control, and communications capabilities (driven by advances in information technology, including battlefield computers); and precision weaponry and forces (including highly accurate missiles and artillery, highly efficient firepower, and stealth technology that hides military assets more effectively). Because of the high cost of developing and deploying such weaponry, wealthier states have a significant advantage in the acquisition and use of these weapons.

The United States, in particular, has a significant edge over both its friends and potential rivals. However, other countries have not stood still while the US has developed its capabilities. China has drastically expanded its military spending, with significant portions devoted to more advanced technology, tactics, and capabilities. As the 2019 US Department of Defense report on China's military and security policies states, China is committed to an extensive military modernization and expansion program that includes the ability to fight and win "'informatized local wars'—regional conflicts defined by real-time, data-networked command and control (C2) and precision strike" (Office of the Secretary of Defense 2019: ii–iii).

Russia too has paid attention to these matters. For example, in 2014, as it used its force to pressure Ukraine and annex Crimea, Russia relied on a much more modern and nuanced set of strategies and tactics that indicated its progress in the revolution in military affairs. Its operations relied on a skillful blend of modern, well-equipped and trained rapid-reaction forces, special forces, technology, information and communications technology, and cyberwarfare

to isolate Ukrainian forces from their command and control centers (Gordon 2014). Since 2008, Russia has pursued a "New Look" military strategy targeted at modernizing its defense industry: replacing three quarters of its military equipment; expanding its military forces and capabilities, personnel, and 70% of its military equipment by 2020; increasing the number of enlisted personnel; and overhauling the defense industrial base.

These examples help highlight another important consequence of the acquisition of weaponry in pursuit of power and security: the regular appearance of **arms races** between states. These are peacetime competitions among rivals to outdo one another in terms of weapons acquisition or capabilities; they can be driven by fear or by design. Whether it is competition to field the most capable and largest army of heavily armored knights on horseback during medieval times, the naval arms races before and after World War I, the nuclear arms race between the United States and the Soviet Union during the Cold War, or the high-tech weaponry and cyberwarfare competition of the present (which we discussed in Chapter 5), as states have sought weapons to provide for power and security, they have engaged in competition to field the biggest and the best weaponry. Such races tend to be interdependent: The efforts and decisions of each state to develop and deploy specific types of weapons are dependent on the parallel decisions of the rival state(s). Military spending tends to be reciprocal and driven by action–reaction or stimulus–response processes. Empirical evidence to date suggests that many arms races escalate to war, although most wars are not preceded by arms races, and, indeed, a great many arms races do not end up in war, either. In the current context, the competition among states such as the United States, China, and Russia in high-tech weaponry, strategies, and tactics is a good example of these arms-racing tendencies. What are the implications of arms races, and of the underlying effort to acquire weaponry, for security itself?

6-2b Alliances

Realists also emphasize the efforts of states to forge **alliances** with other states to counter threats and increase strength. The logic of this approach is

---

revolution in military affairs: the transformation of weapons, military organizations, and operational concepts for military force that leverages the information and communications revolutions of the latter 20th and early 21st centuries.

arms race: peacetime competition in armaments by two or more states driven by conflict interests, fear, and suspicion.

alliance: a formal commitment between states to cooperate for specific purposes, such as mutual defense.

relatively straightforward: When there are common interests between states, such as a common enemy, they agree to cooperate militarily to meet the threat. Alliances in general involve offensive commitments to join together in military operations (think of the Soviet–German pact prior to the outbreak of World War II) or the more common defensive commitments to come to each other's aid in the event of an attack (good examples include the NATO alliance, especially during the Cold War). Such alliance commitments first have a deterrent purpose, intended to ward off a potential attack, and then a defensive purpose, intended to enable the allied states to defeat such an attack if it were to occur.

We can identify at least three essentially realist approaches to alliances. First, such alliances might be driven by **protection** dynamics. In this approach, a small state might engage in an alliance with a larger, more powerful state to gain its help and protection from a dangerous neighbor or adversary. It may seek out a powerful state, as when Poland sought an alliance with both Britain and France before the outset of World War II. Even countries like Costa Rica and Grenada, which have eliminated their militaries, engage in alliances to help secure themselves. In fact, it is largely because of its relationship to the United States that Grenada was able to dismantle its military forces.

Second, **bandwagoning** might drive such alliances. In this approach, a state allies with a powerful state after deciding that the benefits of siding with the more powerful state are greater than the costs of doing so (Waltz 1979; Wright 1942). Bandwagoning may result from the calculation that opposition to the more powerful state (by itself or by others) is unlikely to succeed or from the calculation that the opportunity to share in the benefits of the stronger state's pursuit of power is compelling, whether those benefits involve payoffs from the stronger state or a share of any spoils of war that might ensue. A good example is the behavior of central European states, such as Hungary and Romania, in the years around the start of World War II, when they joined with Nazi Germany. A more recent example was the several smaller European states that sided with the US-led invasion of Iraq in 2003 in direct opposition to Germany and France. Bandwagoning involves *unequal exchange* because the smaller and more vulnerable state makes concessions to the larger power and

accepts a subordinate role (Walt 1987: 282). Map 6-3 illustrates the military alliances and agreements to which the United States was a party in early 2017.

Finally, such alliances might be driven by **balancing** dynamics. In this approach, a state allies with other states to counter the power or threat of another (Walt 1987; Waltz 1979). In this dynamic, alliances are most likely to form when power imbalances emerge. As one state's power grows, it presents a potential threat to others, which may join together to counter the first and more (or potentially more) powerful state. Shared concerns over the possible threat posed by the growing power of the first state lead the others to *balance* against it by making an alliance. The alliance between France and Russia in the years before World War I reflected their concern with the rising power of Germany, as did the British decision in the same period to abandon its historical role as offshore balancer to join France and Russia to counter the rising challenge of Germany. Similarly, one interpretation of the NATO alliance uniting the United States, Canada, and most Western European states emphasized the need to counter the Soviet threat in Europe.

However, realists are not the only ones who turn to alliances. Liberals also embrace this approach but differently. Realists tend to view alliances as temporary arrangements that states should be willing to quickly make and break in order to meet threats. Liberals tend to see them as more enduring and based on cooperation, common values and identities, and mutual interests. The NATO alliance provides a nice illustration. For realists, NATO was fundamentally an alliance made necessary by the need to counter the Soviet Union during the Cold War. Liberals, by contrast, point to NATO's continued existence and expansion after the Cold War's end (when the threat against which it formed had disappeared) and stress the cooperative links and shared values and interests that have helped it persist and evolve. In recent years, American leaders such as President Donald Trump and Secretary of Defense Robert Gates have publicly called into question the usefulness and effectiveness of NATO, a position that might appear questionable in light of Russia's increased assertiveness, the conflict between Russia and Ukraine, and the corresponding heightened tension between NATO and Russia since 2014. What do you think? Will NATO continue, or will it fade away and dissolve?

The effect of alliances is unclear. Some historical evidence suggests that most alliances are followed by war, and that wars involving alliances are larger and involve more states (which might appear to be self-evident), but the same evidence shows that most wars are not preceded by alliances. Furthermore, the impact of alliances on conflict (and thus in providing security) depends heavily on the nature and

---

protection: in alliances, an arrangement by a small state to gain help from a larger state.

bandwagoning: in alliances, siding with a rising power to gain benefits.

balancing: in alliances, forming coalitions to counter the rising power and threat of a state.

MAP 6-3

US Alliances

Why does the United States have so many alliances?

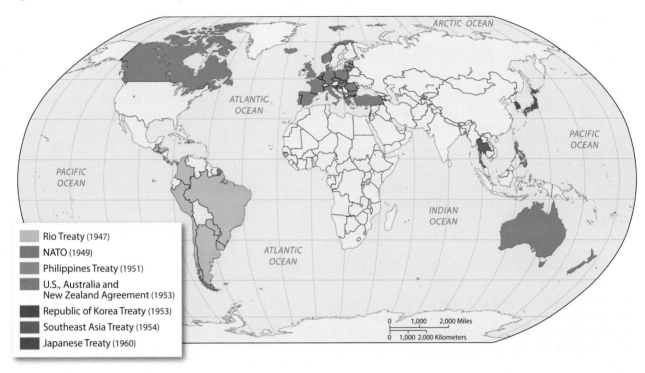

Rio Treaty (1947)
NATO (1949)
Philippines Treaty (1951)
U.S., Australia and
New Zealand Agreement (1953)
Republic of Korea Treaty (1953)
Southeast Asia Treaty (1954)
Japanese Treaty (1960)

credibility of the alliance commitments themselves. In principle, the more credible the commitment, the more likely the alliance is to deter the potential attack. Firm alliance commitments are more credible, but they also serve to encourage more risky and confrontational behavior by alliance partners, which may trigger armed conflict rather than prevent it. Given this mixed record, what types or characteristics of alliances do you think are likely to be most successful in the pursuit of security?

6-2c Balance of Power

Together, these two approaches to security—arms and alliances—form the core of balance-of-power politics. Although this term is used in a variety of ways in world politics (see Table 6-4), the broadest meaning refers to the pattern of activity that occurs as states take action to make themselves secure by seeking power, countering the efforts of real or potential rivals to gain power advantages, and using power to counter security threats from others. According to realists, states monitor their security environment and take actions to meet perceived threats from others by seeking power. **Internal balancing** occurs when states

independently build up their military might, as we discussed earlier. **External balancing** occurs when states join with others in alliances to combine their might to meet a common rival or threat. Such arrangements are likely to be temporary and short lived: According to realists, as the conditions that give rise to the alliances change, we should expect alliances to appear and disappear relatively fluidly. To paraphrase the words of Lord Palmerston, a 19th-century British statesman, countries have no permanent friends or enemies, only permanent interests. According to many realists, because all states make these kinds of calculations and take these kinds of steps, the balance of power is much like the magic of the market in capitalism: As each state pursues its self-interests in this way, balances tend to lend themselves to periods of stability, however brief.

Balance-of-power dynamics may occur at the level of the whole international system, as the Cold War contest between the United States and the Soviet

internal balancing: countering the power of a rival by increasing one's own power and military might.

external balancing: countering the power of a rival by forming coalitions with other states.

TABLE 6-4

Balance of Power

BALANCE OF POWER AS . . .	MEANING
Description	A snapshot of the distribution of power in the world at any given moment
Equilibrium	A condition in which power is roughly balanced among the world's major powers so that no one has a significant edge
Dynamic	A pattern of behavior by states seeking to compete in anarchy and manage security through internal (arms) or external (allies) efforts to counter real or potential rivals and gain power advantages

Union after World War II illustrates, or at the regional level. In the latter, we might observe the patterns of balance-of-power dynamics in Asia, Africa, the Middle East, Latin America, and so on. Realists emphasize that states are likely to prefer internal balancing because they have more control in that approach, especially because alliances among self-interested states (as realists would characterize them) are likely to be rather unreliable and subject to change.

6-2d Using Force

Of course, realists are quick to point out that in a dangerous and anarchic world, force will be used, and relatively frequently. States wishing to be secure must have power to secure themselves, and power, to realists, depends on the ability to use military force. Two leading theorists put it well: To one, military force "is the most important material factor making for the political power of a nation" (Morgenthau 1973: 29), and to the other, "force serves, not only as the *ultima ratio* [or final argument], but indeed as the first and constant one" (Waltz, in Art 1999: 5–6).

Applying Military Force

In pursuit of security, states may use force in a variety of ways. According to the Militarized Interstate

. . . .

deterrence: persuading a potential adversary to refrain from attacking through the threat of costly retaliation.

direct deterrence: the use of retaliatory threats to discourage attacks against the state making the deterrent threat.

Dispute data (Jones, Bremer, and Singer 1996) often used by political scientists who study war and the use of force, these uses include the following:

- *Threats of force*—including threats to blockade, to forcibly occupy territory, to declare war, and to use force, including nuclear weapons or other weapons of mass destruction

- *Displays of force*—including placing forces (including nuclear forces) on alert; mobilizing armed forces; public displays or operations of land, air, or naval forces in or outside a state's territory; and purposeful border violations with military forces (without combat)

- *Uses of force*—including blockades, occupation of territory or seizure of material or personnel, small-scale military clashes or raids (with less than 1,000 total battle deaths), and declarations of war

- *Interstate war*—involving sustained military combat resulting in more than 1,000 total battle deaths

Strategies Linking Force to Security

How can states apply their military power through these means to obtain security? In general, we can identify at least four main uses that may translate military power into security.

Deterrence   Over the centuries, states have long sought to amass military might to keep adversaries from attacking them. This is the essence of **deterrence**, the possession of sufficient military might so that would-be adversaries understand that any potential gain from attacking would involve costs so high that the attack is just not worth it. Deterrence says, "Don't attack, or else." This use of force has a long history, but its role and significance increased considerably after World War II with the advent of the nuclear age.

Led by strategists such as Bernard Brodie and Thomas Schelling, among others, deterrence is commonly understood to rest on three components. First, for a state to be able to deter a potential aggressor, it must have the necessary military capability to retaliate in a damaging way. Second, a state must make a commitment in order to deter. That is, a state must issue a threat that a certain action will result in retaliation. Third, a state must somehow demonstrate its will—to convince the target that such a retaliation would be carried out if necessary. Hence, both capability and credibility are central to successful deterrence.

Military strategists often distinguish between direct and extended deterrence and between immediate and general deterrence. **Direct deterrence**

Part of the US nuclear deterrence triad, the Navy's newest and largest nuclear submarine, the Ohio-class, carries 24 missiles—more than any other submarine currently deployed in the world

How do such deterrent forces contribute to security?

US Navy/Public domain/Wikimedia Commons

involves the use of retaliatory threats to discourage attacks against the state making the deterrent threat, while **extended deterrence** involves retaliatory threats to discourage attacks against allies and friends of the state making the deterrent threat. **Immediate deterrence** involves the threat to retaliate against attackers who are believed to be actively considering specific military operations against the target, which is readying itself to respond. **General deterrence**, by contrast, involves threats to retaliate in a context of underlying politico-military competition, but when there is no active military conflict generating the need to respond.

After World War II, nuclear deterrence was a central part of the defense strategies of both the United States and the Soviet Union. Not only did these countries build increasingly large and powerful arsenals for direct deterrence of each other; they also made commitments to extend their nuclear umbrellas to important allies. For the United States, for example, Europe, Japan, and others were included in the extended deterrence commitment, while the Soviet Union included its allies in Eastern Europe and elsewhere.

Immediately after World War II, when the United States was the sole nuclear power, and even after the Soviet Union had acquired nuclear weapons but could not use them against US territory, the United States could make nuclear threats more freely. As the nuclear arms race accelerated and the Soviet Union expanded its nuclear arsenal to match and, in some ways, to exceed that of the United States, **brinkmanship** and the underlying strategy became far too risky to maintain. From the early 1960s to the end of the Cold War,

the basis of deterrence for both sides became what was known as **mutually assured destruction (MAD)**.

This approach was pretty simple: It amounted to a "you shoot, I shoot, and we are both dead" threat that established a basic nuclear stalemate and made conflicts very dangerous. In terms of deterrence, MAD rested on the ability of both sides to field a secure, second-strike capability of sufficient size to destroy a significant portion of the other side's society, usually in what was known as counter-value targeting (or targeting cities and industrial centers), no matter what kind of attack was directed against them. That is, even if one side unleashed a counterforce strike designed to destroy nuclear arsenals and other war-fighting abilities, the other side would still be able to retaliate with a devastating second strike in return. Clearly, therefore, MAD depended on an arsenal and the ability to fire the weapons (command and control) even in the face of a nuclear strike.

....

extended deterrence: retaliatory threats to discourage attacks against allies and friends of the state making the deterrent threat.

immediate deterrence: the threat to retaliate against attackers who are believed to be actively considering specific military operations against the target.

general deterrence: threats to retaliate in a context of underlying politico-military competition, but when there is no active military conflict generating the need to respond.

brinkmanship: the strategy of escalating conflicts or crises to nuclear threats in order to force the other side to back down.

mutually assured destruction (MAD): the ability of both sides to field a secure, second-strike capability of sufficient size to destroy a significant portion of the other side's society.

At its heart, the nuclear arms race that dominated the Cold War was an action–reaction cycle of competition to ensure that no weapons gains of the other side could eliminate this fundamental second-strike, or MAD, capability. Both the United States and the Soviet Union developed increasingly powerful and accurate nuclear weapons, deploying them on land (intercontinental ballistic missiles, or ICBMs, as well as medium- and short-range missiles), through the air (as gravity bombs and, later, cruise missiles), and across the sea (as submarine-launched ballistic missiles, or SLBMs). The Anti-Ballistic Missile Treaty (ABM) of 1972 was even concluded to limit the ability to defend against missiles in order to help ensure the stability of a second strike.

Deterrence represents a so-called peaceful use of force because it rests on the threat, not the actual use of force. Indeed, if the retaliatory act is necessary, deterrence has failed. It is far easier to succeed, because successful deterrence requires an adversary to refrain from doing something; that is, behavior change is not really necessary. At the same time, it is much more difficult to know if deterrence is succeeding because it is hard to know whether the potential attack was ever really going to happen. For example, did US deterrence policy prevent the Soviet Union from attacking the United States (or vice versa) during the Cold War? There were no direct attacks, so it must have, right? But did the United States or the Soviet Union ever really intend to attack the other? Finally, if the possession of nuclear weapons meant that the United States and the Soviet Union could not fight with each other out of fear of mutual annihilation, doesn't that logic suggest that many, most, or even all states should have nuclear arsenals? (See the box "Spotlight On: Deterrence After the Cold War?" for more on deterrence since 1989.)

Defense Just like it sounds, the defensive use of force means having the ability to fight off an attack, to deny an attacker a victory. **Defense** involves deploying and using military force to protect oneself, ward off an attack, and minimize damage from the attack to the greatest extent possible (Art 1980). The key to gaining security in this strategy is to build sufficient, usable military capabilities to fight off an attack. Defensive force can also contribute to deterrence, as the more substantial, clearer, and more obvious the

Deterrent threats

Does the B-2 Stealth Bomber act as defense, prevention, compellence, or all three?

Courtesy of the US Department of Defense

defensive capabilities are, the greater the likelihood that a potential attacker will refrain from attacking in the first place. And yet in the event of an imminent or actual attack, defensive force improves a state's ability to be secure by fighting off the attack.

Prevention and Preemption The preventive and preemptive uses of force are related to defense in many ways. The central idea behind both is that there is a threat facing the state, against which it is best to strike first before an attack can be unleashed. Preventive and preemptive uses of force are based on the view that, in some situations, the best defense is a good offense. What is the difference between preemption and prevention? The strategies are not very precisely defined and are highly controversial and subject to political argument as well. In general, **preemption** occurs when the threat of attack is *imminent*, that is, expected within a matter of weeks, days, or even hours; **prevention** occurs when the threat is seen as *inevitable*, that is, expected sometime in the more distant future (Art 1980: 6). Both preemptive and, especially, preventive uses of force are highly controversial because they involve using force first, which is sometimes hard to distinguish from outright aggression.

For example, in June 1967, Israel watched while its neighbors (Egypt, Syria, and Jordan) mobilized their forces in preparation for military operations against it. Rather than wait for the imminent attacks, Israel struck first in what came to be called the Six-Day War, with a series of devastating preemptive strikes that savaged its adversaries' military forces. Did Israel engage in a justifiable preemptive strike in the face of imminent attacks by its foes, as its defenders assert, or did it engage in aggression against its neighbors, as its critics claim? Does it matter?

Fast-forward to 1981, when Israel sent fighter jets into Iraq to bomb the Osirak nuclear reactor (purchased

---

defense: deploying and using military force to fight off an attack.

preemption: the use of military force to strike first when an attack is imminent to blunt the effectiveness of the impending attack.

prevention: the use of military force to strike first when an attack is inevitable to take advantage of a more favorable balance of forces, rather than wait for an adversary to gain the advantage from which to strike.

Deterrence After the Cold War?

Many scholars and policymakers credit the Cold War nuclear standoff between the United States and the Soviet Union for what diplomatic historian John Lewis Gaddis called the "long postwar peace." However, questions arose about nuclear deterrence and its role in the new post–Cold War context.

First, as Map 6-4 shows, the nuclear weapons "club" is getting more members. As of 2017, the Arms Control Association estimates that nine states control about 15,000 nuclear warheads. Few seem to worry about the arsenals of the US, UK, France, or China, as these states have vested interests in the international system as currently comprised. Russia, however, seems to be on an expansionary trajectory at the expense of its neighbors, North Korea believes only nuclear weapons and missiles can protect its regime from the US, and regional rivalries make the arsenals of Israel in the Middle East and India and Pakistan in South Asia a cause of concern.

Some scholars and practitioners pointed to the logic of deterrence to advocate the spread of nuclear weapons to new states. Realist theorists John Mearsheimer and

Kenneth Waltz, among others, essentially argued that the logic of deterrence would prevail and more countries with nuclear weapons would result in more stability among them, as they would find themselves in the same kind of stalemate as the United States and Soviet Union did during the Cold War. Others like Scott Sagan argued that proliferation would greatly increase the possibility of nuclear accidents, theft of nuclear weapons, or other purposeful uses of the weapons. Given such fears, most states and the United Nations adopted policies designed to prevent the spread of nuclear weapons. Still, a lively debate over theories of deterrence continued.

Second, another shift in deterrence after the Cold War is the increasing concern for ways to deter smaller-scale attacks. In the post–Cold War context, states seek ways to deter or protect themselves from smaller attacks, such as a single bomb or missile. This has led some countries— principally the United States—to continue to develop the capability to shoot down incoming missiles. This capability is referred to as either **national missile defense** or **theater missile defense**, depending on whether the system protects the entire country or surrounds a specific

MAP 6-4

Nuclear Warhead Inventories, 2019

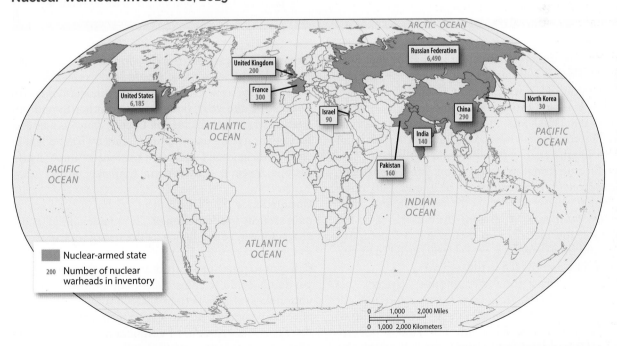

Source: Arms Control Association.

(Continued)

(Continued)

theater or area, such as the East Asian region containing the Koreas. The effectiveness of these systems is not particularly good, and, in fact, it is not clear how well they might perform. However, all the powerful states in the world watch carefully when the United States performs tests of the system.

In the post–Cold War world, deterrence is not just about nuclear deterrence. It applies to conventional weapons as well. Taiwan maintains a strong military with powerful defensive capability to deter the Chinese from invading the island state. The United States and South Korea maintain a large military presence on the border with North Korea, along with a large minefield designed to deter the North Koreans from launching an attack on the South. In fact, any country that has an opponent or enemy or even potential enemy must deter those threats. Can you think of any country that doesn't face some threat from the international system? (*Hint*: There are a few . . . sort of.)

Another significant area of concern about deterrence stems from the dramatic rise in the salience of civil war, unconventional war, and asymmetric war—and the related increase in the importance of non-state actors in conflict (see Chapter 5)—which calls into question the continued relevance—and even possibility—of meaningful

national missile defense: the capability to protect a country from nuclear attack by shooting down incoming missiles.

theater missile defense: the capability to protect a specific or limited geographic area from nuclear attack by shooting down incoming missiles.

deterrence. Perhaps the most dramatic aspect of this issue is terrorism. The basic idea behind deterrence is that if attacked, the state can counterattack and hurt badly the original attacker. Of course, this fundamental equation depends on the attacker having what amounts to an identifiable return address!

That is the key difficulty when deterring terrorism: Terrorist organizations hide and are often not directly connected to a single country. Therefore, it's hard to deter a group that you can't counterattack. North Korea isn't likely to attack South Korea, because if it does, the South Korean and US militaries will retaliate. North Korea can't really hide; everyone knows where it is, and it cannot be moved. The same cannot be said for terrorist groups such as al-Qaeda or even the Islamic State. If they attack, where does the victim counterstrike? If states can't legitimately threaten a counterstrike, deterrence is difficult, if not outright impossible.

Changes in the international context since the end of the Cold War thus raise a number of interesting questions:

1. Would the spread of nuclear weapons into the hands of more states extend the logic of deterrence and promote stability, or would it create a more dangerous world?

2. How can states deter terrorists and other non-state actors? Is it even possible?

3. Is large-scale nuclear war a threat, or are smaller nuclear exchanges more likely between such places as Pakistan and India or Israel and Iran? ●

from France) under construction near Baghdad. Both Iraq and France maintained that the reactor was part of a 20-year-old Iraqi program intended for scientific research and the peaceful production of nuclear energy, but Israel was convinced it was intended to manufacture nuclear weapons. Rather than wait for Iraq to acquire such capabilities and any benefits that might accrue from their possession, Israel dispatched a squadron of American-made F-15 and F-16 fighters, which passed through both Jordanian and Saudi airspace (without permission) during the raid and destroyed the reactor. Was this attack a preemptive strike and thus defensive, or was Israel striking first to maintain its dominance in the region?

In 2007, Israel conducted another airstrike, this time against Syria, targeting a suspected nuclear site believed to be in development with the help of the North Koreans. Although the Israeli government refrained from public comment, this attack was

compellence: the use of military force to stop a foe from doing something it was already doing or to force it to start doing something it was not yet doing.

apparently to prevent the development of a nuclear reactor the Israelis feared would lead to the ability to produce fissile material for making nuclear bombs. In 2013, 2015, and 2017, Israel bombed other Syrian targets, destroying missiles the Israelis said were bound for Lebanon to be used against Israel by Hezbollah. In each of these cases, these are preventive force justifications, however controversial they may be.

Compellence The fourth strategy for using force to gain security is **compellence**. Thomas Schelling (1966) characterized compellence as the use of military force to stop a foe from doing something it was already doing or to force it to start doing something it was not yet doing. To do so, the state engaging in compellence undertakes military actions that will stop only when its adversary engages in the desired response.

A classic example of compellence is the US use of force in the 1962 Cuban Missile Crisis. In October 1962, faced with the discovery that the Soviet Union was placing nuclear missiles in Cuba, the United States mobilized forces and employed a naval blockade, while preparing for further military action, to persuade the Soviet Union to dismantle and withdraw its missiles. After 13 very tense days, nicely dramatized by the 2000 film *Thirteen Days*, the Soviet Union backed down and the crisis passed. As then–Secretary of State Dean Rusk characterized it, the United States and the Soviets were "eyeball to eyeball" with military action, even nuclear war in the balance, but they averted the crisis by blending force and diplomacy. It is for this reason that compellence is often labeled **coercive diplomacy**.

Compellence may be the easiest strategy to evaluate in terms of success, but it is the hardest strategy to use. It is successful when the adversary (target) stops (or starts) doing what was demanded by the state deploying the force. However, because compellence requires the target to act, usually very publicly, in response to a combination of threat and punitive action, it also tends to trigger concerns about prestige, reputation, and losing face. Consequently, it may trigger resistance and escalation or even strategic withdrawal followed by future challenges that threaten a state's security in new, even more serious ways.

For realists, pursuing security consistently involves some combination of these approaches: acquiring military might, forging alliances, and using force to protect oneself, one's friends, and one's interests. As Robert J. Art (1980) aptly summarized:

> The efficacy of force endures. For in anarchy, force and politics are connected. By itself, military power guarantees neither survival nor prosperity. But it is almost always the essential ingredient for both. Because resort to force is the ultimate card of all states, the seriousness of a state's intentions is conveyed fundamentally by its having a credible military posture. Without it, a state's diplomacy generally lacks effectiveness. (p. 35)

To return to the words of that Roman scribe we mentioned earlier, "If you want peace, prepare for war." But what happens if everyone behaves this way?

6-3 LIBERAL APPROACHES TO SECURITY AND CONFLICT

>> **6-3** Describe and assess cooperation-based approaches to international security embraced by liberals, including arms control and disarmament, collective security, and security communities.

If realists are fond of the saying that those who want peace should prepare for war, liberal theorists might well embrace the view of early-20th-century peace advocates that "those who want peace should agree to keep it" (*si vis pacem para pactum*). As you might expect, the more liberal approaches to security and conflict management emphasize cooperation and coordination. Let's be clear: It's not that liberal theorists do not see a dangerous world or that they see no role or use for military power. Liberals agree on the utility of deterrence and the need for self-defense capabilities in a dangerous world. However, they tend to temper their views with concerns over the impact of military competition and the efficacy of the use of force, and they tend to see greater opportunities for cooperation based on mutual interests. Because of these perspectives on how the pursuit of security can lead to undesirable outcomes, liberals often advocate for other solutions, including arms control or disarmament, collective security, and security communities.

6-3a Arms Control and Disarmament

Liberal approaches tend to view the security dilemma as driven by uncertainty and, ultimately, problems with trust and understanding. Consequently, it is no surprise that a central approach to international security from a liberal perspective is the construction of agreements to control or eliminate weapons. Such agreements help resolve the security dilemma, reduce uncertainty, and avoid arms races and the threats that arise from the accumulation of military might. In contrast to realists, who look to power and capabilities to ensure security, liberals see such dynamics as one of the main reasons for insecurity and the escalation of conflict into violence. In effect, if your rival doesn't have a gun, your rival can't shoot you, and if *both* of you aren't engaged in efforts to accumulate weapons, you are less likely to feel threatened or be threatening. In such a context, your mutual interests might be more obvious, and your ability to manage conflicts and disagreements peacefully when they occur might be improved.

Arms control and disarmament are related but distinct approaches to security and conflict. **Disarmament** stresses the elimination (or, at least, the drastic reduction) of weapons; **arms control** generally stresses restraint or regulation of the amount, type, positioning, or use of weapons. The two overlap

....

coercive diplomacy: a strategy that combines threats and the selective use of force with negotiation in a bargaining strategy to persuade an adversary to comply with one's demand.

disarmament: the elimination of arsenals or classes or types of weapons.

arms control: regulation of the amount, type, positioning, or use of weapons.

Arms, Arms Control, and War

Seeking security through the acquisition of arms or through arms control and disarmament depends in part on whether one views weapons as a cause of war. *Spiral theorists* believe that the anarchic environment of world politics leads otherwise peaceful actors to arm themselves out of fear and uncertainty (Lamb 1988: chap. 10). As the security dilemma suggests, others react by arming themselves, leading to increased tension and an action–reaction cycle in which arms are acquired in greater amounts. Eventually, this cycle "spirals out of control and some incident touches off a war no one really wanted" (Lamb 1988: 181). *Aggressor theorists*, by contrast, believe that some states are naturally warlike, requiring other states to be prepared to fight to protect themselves and punish the aggressor (Lamb 1988: 183).

Spiral theorists thus argue that arms cause war by contributing to misperception, fear, and insecurity. Arms control and disarmament are therefore vital, as they promote communication and cooperation and help prevent or break the spirals that lead to war. The most extreme spiral theorists will advocate unilateral disarmament measures as signals of peaceful intentions. For aggressor theorists, such actions are foolish. Instead, they argue that military strength is a necessary deterrent to aggressors. Arms control is undesirable, even dangerous, because it may create vulnerability or a false sense of security. Spiral theorists view shows of strength by aggressors as escalatory steps in the conflict spiral, while aggressor theorists view conciliatory actions like disarmament as dangerous acts of appeasement likely

only to encourage aggressors (Lamb 1988: 1184–1185). In some ways, this argument is not that different from the debate over allowing guns to be carried on college campuses; some see that as inherently dangerous, and others see it as necessary to protect oneself from evildoers.

Arms control policies are heavily influenced by the particular theories state leaders embrace, whether they recognize it or not. British Prime Minister Neville Chamberlain was driven by a simple spiral theory in his efforts to head off war in Europe before World War II, while other European leaders tended to be influenced by aggressor theories in the run-up to World War II, competing with each other to demonstrate resolve and deploy military force. One or the other of these approaches have guided American presidents (and probably their Soviet, then Russian, counterparts) for the past 50 years. Often disputes among leading diplomats and foreign policy advisers based on these competing perspectives have resulted in challenges, delays, and even failures in efforts to negotiate. What do you think?

1. Do arms cause war or ensure peace?

2. What is the role of arms control and disarmament in providing security?

3. Should states make arms control treaties?

4. Can any kinds of arms control and disarmament satisfy both spiral and aggressor theorists? ●

when such efforts target specific types of weapons for elimination, which could be characterized as either targeted disarmament or qualitative arms control (see the next section). However, most advocates of arms control believe that general disarmament is an unrealistic (and, perhaps, undesirable) outcome. At the same time, many advocates of disarmament argue that arms control is a half-measure at best that fails to address the moral imperatives of disarmament.

In part, both arms control and disarmament rest on the premise that controlling weaponry and the competition to acquire it will make states more secure and better able to manage conflict. Arms control, in particular, is committed to establishing limits and stability in the military competition between countries, to reduce uncertainty and promote trust and cooperation (Lamb 1988: 20). Controlling the escalatory spiral of weaponry in this fashion should thereby lead to better management of the security dilemma (see

"Theory in Action: Arms, Arms Control, and War" for a short discussion of contending perspectives). Let's consider arms control first, then turn to disarmament.

Arms Control

Table 6-5 lists major arms control agreements since World War I, and Table 6-6 shows the basic aspects of arms control, identifying the key features of participants, purposes, and types. In terms of participants, arms control can be unilateral, although instances in which a single state voluntary refrained from acquiring weapons are highly unusual and often only temporary. Bilateral agreements between rivals and competitors are more common but are frequently limited in their impact. Unless the world is essentially bipolar, as during the Cold War between the United States and the Soviet Union, the broader effect of bilateral agreements can be limited. Multilateral

TABLE 6-5

Major Arms Control Treaties Since World War I

TREATY	YEAR ENTERED INTO FORCE	FOCUS	MEMBERS
Washington Naval Agreements	1922	Limits major naval vessels	Multilateral
Geneva Protocol on Chemical and Biological Weapons	1925	Bans use of chemical and biological weapons	Multilateral
Antarctic Treaty	1959	Bans military activity in Antarctica	Multilateral
Limited Test Ban Treaty	1963	Bans nuclear tests except underground	US, UK, USSR; others joined later
Outer Space Treaty	1967	Bans nuclear weapons in space	US, UK, USSR; others joined later
Treaty of Tlatelolco	1967	Establishes nuclear weapons–free zone in Latin America and the Caribbean	Multilateral
Nuclear Nonproliferation Treaty	1970	Bans acquisition of nuclear weapons by nonnuclear states	Multilateral
Strategic Arms Limitation Treaty I	1972	Limits nuclear weapons arsenals	US, USSR
Anti-Ballistic Missile Treaty	1972	Limits strategic missile defense systems (terminated in 2002)	US, USSR
Seabed Arms Control Treaty	1972	Bans nuclear weapons on ocean floor	US, UK, USSR; others joined later
Threshold Test Ban Treaty	1990 (1974)	Limits size of nuclear tests	US, USSR
Biological Weapons Convention	1975	Bans all biological weapons	Multilateral
Strategic Arms Limitation Treaty II	(1977) never ratified	Limits nuclear weapons arsenals	US, USSR
Treaty of Rarotonga	1986	Establishes nuclear weapons–free zone in South Pacific	Multilateral
Intermediate-Range Nuclear Forces Treaty	1988	Bans intermediate-range nuclear forces from Europe (terminated in 2019)	US, USSR
Treaty on Conventional Armed Forces in Europe	1992	Limits key categories of conventional weapons for NATO and Warsaw Pact forces	NATO; Warsaw Pact
Strategic Arms Reduction Treaty I	1994	Reduces nuclear arsenals (expired in 2009)	US, Russia
Comprehensive Nuclear Test-Ban Treaty	(1996) not in force	Bans all nuclear explosions (not in force)	Multilateral
Treaty of Bangkok	1997	Establishes nuclear weapons–free zone in Southeast Asia	Multilateral
Ottawa Treaty on Anti-Personnel Mines	1999	Bans land mines	Multilateral
Treaty on Open Skies	2002	Protects unarmed aerial surveillance	Multilateral
Treaty of Moscow	2003	Limits number of deployed nuclear warheads	US, Russia
Treaty of Semipalatinsk	2008	Establishes nuclear weapons–free zone in Central Asia	Multilateral
Treaty of Pelindaba	2009	Establishes nuclear weapons–free zone in Africa	Multilateral
Convention on Cluster Munitions	2010	Bans cluster bombs	Multilateral
New Start (Strategic Arms Reduction Treaty)	2011	Reduces existing active nuclear arsenals by 50%	US, Russia
Arms Trade Treaty	2014	Regulates international trade in conventional weapons	Multilateral: 130 signatories, 89 ratifications

TABLE 6-6

Participants, Purposes, and Types of Arms Control

PARTICIPANTS OF ARMS CONTROL	PURPOSES OF ARMS CONTROL	TYPES OF ARMS CONTROL
Unilateral Bilateral Multilateral	Reduces likelihood of conflict and war Reduces likelihood of uncontrollable war Reduces resources devoted to armaments Controls proliferation of weapons of mass destruction Establishes and reinforces restraints on violent behavior Contributes to progress toward disarmament	Rules of war Communication and administration Confidence-building measures Geographic agreements Quantitative limitations Qualitative limitations Horizontal proliferation control

Source: Adapted and summarized from Chapters 2 and 3 in Christopher Lamb, *How to Think About Arms Control, Disarmament and Defense* (Englewood Cliffs, NJ: Prentice Hall, 1988).

agreements, which range from just a few participants to arrangements involving most states, are potentially more far-reaching (depending on the number of participants) but are also much more difficult to achieve because of the multiple perspectives and interests involved, as well as the difficulty in monitoring and verifying compliance.

Let's focus on the types of agreements and consider a few examples:

- *Rules of war.* Societies have long had concerns with trying to find limits on the occurrence and acceptable practices of war. For example, in 1928 the Kellogg-Briand Pact tried to outlaw war, and the treaty establishing the League of Nations also banned aggression among its members. The Geneva Conventions of 1864, 1906, 1929, and 1949 are examples related to acceptable practices, establishing rules for the treatment of wounded and captured soldiers, as well as civilians, during times of war. The Hague Conventions of 1899 and 1907 established a variety of limits on the use of weapons and war crimes (see also our discussion of this topic in Chapter 7).

- *Communication and administration.* Arms control agreements of this type focus on measures to improve cooperation and communication to reduce tension between participants. A central example is the conclusion of the 1962 "Hot Line" agreement to establish a direct and dedicated communications link between the United States and the Soviet Union—often seen as a bright red phone in the White House in movies and television—in the aftermath of the Cuban Missile Crisis, which was updated in the 1980s to include more modern communications and the establishment of nuclear crisis centers in both countries. The tenuous links between leaders during the incredible tension of the missile crisis in 1962 was the prime motivator in this accord.

- *Confidence-building measures.* This type of arms control agreement usually refers to much more specific arrangements for transparency and information sharing on military matters to reduce the fear and uncertainty that often occur. Agreements to share information on military exercises and troop movements, allowing inspections and observers, and a variety of other restraints that promote openness, transparency, and predictability are at the core of this type of agreement. In the 1970s and 1980s, for example, the Conference on Security and Cooperation in Europe and its successor, the Organization for Security and Cooperation in Europe, established agreements to provide for advance warning of military exercises by rival NATO and Warsaw Pact forces and to allow observers from the other side, all in order to lessen the tension between the two blocs.

- *Geographic agreements.* This type of agreement limits or bans military activities and arms competitions in specific locations. Generally, these agreements are straightforward. For example, in 1959 the United States, the Soviet Union, and others agreed to the complete demilitarization of Antarctica to avoid competition and conflict over military bases and activities there. Similarly, the 1967 Tlatelolco and Outer Space Treaties banned the placement of nuclear weapons in Latin America and in outer space, respectively, and the 1971 Seabed Arms Control Treaty did the same for the ocean floor. At present, there are five agreements establishing nuclear-weapons-free zones throughout the world: Latin America, as noted; the South Pacific (the Treaty of Rarotonga); Southeast Asia (the Treaty of Bangkok); Africa (the Treaty of Pelindaba); and Central Asia (the Treaty of Semipalatinsk). However, only the Latin America treaty has the full compliance of all the official nuclear powers: The United States has not agreed to the South Pacific or Africa agreements, and none of the nuclear powers has agreed to the Southeast Asia or Central Asia accords.

- *Quantitative limitations.* Just as their name implies, these agreements establish some numerical limitation on some or all arsenals. For example, the Washington Naval Agreements of 1922 and the London Naval Treaty of the next decade set limits for Britain, France, Italy, Japan, and the United States on the number of battleships and cruisers allowed to each party, based on tonnage limitations. The Strategic Arms Limitation Talks (producing SALT I in 1972 and SALT II in 1979) set limits on the number of nuclear weapons delivery vehicles that the United States and the Soviet Union could develop. The Strategic Arms Reduction Talks (START) initiated in the 1980s by US President Ronald Reagan and Soviet President Mikhail Gorbachev resulted in a 1991 agreement (START I) that limited the two sides to 6,000 total nuclear warheads and 1,600 total delivery vehicles (e.g., intercontinental ballistic missiles, submarine-launched ballistic missiles, and bombers). In 2010, the United States and Russia concluded and ratified the so-called New START treaty, which reduced nuclear delivery vehicles by half, to 800, and limited deployed nuclear warheads to 1,550.

- *Qualitative limitations.* This type of agreement controls types of weapons, not just numbers. The 1987 Intermediate-Range Nuclear Forces (INF) Treaty between the United States and the Soviet Union eliminated an entire class of nuclear weapons from the two sides' arsenals. Similarly, the 1997 Chemical Weapons Convention prohibited the development, production, acquisition, stockpiling, retention, transfer, or use of chemical weapons by its 190 members.

- *Horizontal proliferation control.* Agreements of this type seek to limit the spread of weapons and weapons technology beyond states that currently possess them (see "Spotlight On: Iran and Nuclear Proliferation" for discussion of one example). The best-known example of this type of agreement is the 1968 Nuclear Nonproliferation Treaty (NPT), which was extended indefinitely in 1995. This agreement, which currently has 190 members, limits nuclear weapons to the five official nuclear weapons states (United States, Russia, Britain, France, and China) and establishes procedures for the peaceful use of nuclear energy by the non–nuclear weapons states. Four non-members of the NPT are known or believed to have nuclear weapons: India, Pakistan, North Korea, and Israel. North Korea, which was initially a member of the NPT, withdrew in 2003 and has aggressively pursued a nuclear weapons program ever since. Efforts to complete a Comprehensive Nuclear Test-Ban Treaty (adopted by the UN in 1996) are also geared toward preventing the spread of nuclear weapons. More than 160 states have ratified the treaty, and another 34 have signed, but not ratified, it (including the United States, Iran, China, Israel, and Egypt).

Disarmament

Although some advocates of arms control see it as an opportunity to make progress toward more general disarmament, historically disarmament movements have tended to involve the public, social movements, and nongovernmental organizations more often and more extensively than states themselves. There are instances of involuntary disarmament, in which a state is forced to relinquish its arsenals by those who have defeated it in war. For example, after military victories, Rome famously forced disarmament on Carthage in a 3rd-century agreement. Similarly, Napoleon forced Prussia to disarm in an 1806 treaty. Following both World War I and World War II, the victorious Allies forced disarmament on their defeated foes as well. However, in all these cases, the forced outcomes were short lived, and the defeated states soon found ways to rearm (and, in fact, often to retaliate against those who forced the disarmament on them).

In the late 19th and early 20th centuries, efforts in The Hague conferences (1899 and 1907) and the world disarmament conference of the 1930s embraced disarmament goals but produced few results. The Hague conferences mostly restricted the use of certain kinds of weapons, and the 1930s endeavor collapsed under the tensions of that period and the rise of German power. Indeed, German withdrawal from the conference in 1933 effectively destroyed any prospect of success.

The advent of the nuclear era gave some new impetus to disarmament efforts. The devastating power and destructiveness of nuclear weapons led many to push for their elimination. Right after World War II, the United States proposed a nuclear disarmament pact known as the **Baruch Plan**, which proposed to establish a UN Atomic Development Authority (ADA) to take control of all nuclear energy activities. The Soviet Union insisted that the United States disarm first before the ADA was established. Both sides refused to accept the other's proposal, and the plan failed. Subsequent official efforts toward nuclear disarmament generally followed suit.

Still, nuclear disarmament efforts have been led by the publics of various states, social movements, and nongovernmental organizations within and across national boundaries. For example, it was significant public pressure in the United States and Europe, in part by mothers concerned about contaminated

---

Baruch Plan: a nuclear disarmament proposal authored by US statesman Bernard Baruch after World War II to place nuclear weapons and energy activities under the control and authority of the United Nations.

Iran and Nuclear Proliferation

In 2015, the US led the so-called "P5+1"—the United States, the United Kingdom, Russia, France, and China, plus Germany—and the European Union to an agreement with Iran. In the Joint Comprehensive Plan of Action (JCPOA), the parties agreed to end Iran's development of nuclear weapons and establish supervision and monitoring of Iran's nuclear power industry, in return for which the US, the other parties, and the UN Security Council would lift economic sanctions in place on Iran for its nuclear programs.

Just two years later, the US signaled its unwillingness to abide by the agreement. Despite efforts by the other parties to persuade it otherwise, and despite confirmation by the JCPOA, European allies, the UN, the International Atomic Energy Agency (IAEA), and the state, defense, and intelligence agencies of the US itself that Iran was in compliance, in May 2018, the US withdrew from the agreement and took steps to reestablish harsh economic sanctions on Iran.

About a year later, Iran began a series of steps to abandon the 2015 accord, announcing in May 2019 that "it would reduce compliance with its obligations every 60 days until its demands on sanctions relief are met" (Davenport 2020). In January 2020, Iran abandoned the final constraint in the agreement, ending its adherence to the limits on uranium enrichment. In early March 2020, the IAEA reported that Iran was approaching the necessary nuclear material to make a nuclear weapon, estimating it was about a year away if it so chose. As one observer noted (Ward 2020), these developments meant that "the US and Iran could be facing a dangerous military confrontation—the exact scenario many experts warned could very likely happen" if the US abandoned the 2015 agreement. What does this episode highlight about nuclear weapons and efforts to control their spread? ●

milk, that led the Soviet Union, the United States, and Britain to conclude the 1963 Partial Test Ban Treaty, which eliminated testing in the atmosphere and seas.

Another good example is the antinuclear movement that spread in the early 1980s. Prompted by increased tension between the United States and the Soviet Union and plans to expand nuclear arsenals and the deployment of missiles in Europe, as well as the collapse of arms control talks, antinuclear demonstrations erupted in the United States and across Europe. Citizens, scientists, and religious organizations (including the Catholic Church) advocated for control, reduction, and eventual elimination of nuclear weapons. In the United States, the nuclear freeze and nuclear disarmament movements conducted large-scale demonstrations and lobbied American policymakers to take steps to curtail the nuclear arms race. In Germany, antinuclear groups pressured the government to oppose the expanded deployment of American nuclear missiles. Although unsuccessful in achieving their central goals, these and other groups brought pressure to bear that contributed to the resumption of arms control talks between the United States and the Soviet Union and the conclusion of the INF Treaty in 1987.

Even more recently, the 60th anniversary of the United States' use of atomic bombs against Japan in 1945 prompted public demonstrations calling for nuclear disarmament. In 2008, Norway convened an International Conference on Nuclear Disarmament; in 2009, US President Barack Obama called for a nuclear-free world; and in the wake of the 2011 Fukushima nuclear disaster in Japan (see Chapter 12), some renewed efforts for nuclear disarmament occurred as well. However, states thus far have resisted nuclear—or any other type of—disarmament. Arms control remains the more productive result.

6-3b Collective Security

A second major liberal approach to security and conflict is **collective security**. In many ways, this approach is the liberal answer to balance-of-power politics. Indeed, it was frustration with the results of balance-of-power politics—which many blamed for the start of World War I—that led to efforts to construct a collective security system in the period between the two world wars. This highlights a significant point: Although balance-of-power politics happen on their own, collective security has to be constructed (Claude 1988). Collective security requires a concerted effort at cooperation and coordination and the establishment of institutions.

Collective security can be summarized in the simple phrase "an attack on one is an attack on all."

collective security: an approach to security and conflict in which states join together into an organization, ban the use of force by its members, and commit themselves to joining together to respond to any attack by one member on any other member.

The basis of collective security is that states form a community to maintain peace among its members. All members of the community agree to respond together to an attack by one or more member states on any other members. This approach is a method for managing power and responding to threat by pooling resources to bring a preponderance of power to bear on an aggressor. Improved security is thus gained in three ways. First, the collective security institution provides a forum for multilateral diplomacy and negotiation to promote understanding and communication and to resolve conflicts and disagreements before they escalate to more serious levels. It establishes norms, rules, and procedures that stress peaceful conflict resolution. Second, the threat of collective action should deter most potential aggressors, who should calculate that the promise of an overwhelming response by the community would negate the potential benefits of any attack. Third, in those instances in which the collective security regime fails to resolve the issue or deter the potential attacker, the pooling of might in response (often, but not necessarily always, military) should be sufficient to defeat and punish the attacker and defend the victim. This demonstration should, in itself, provide important signals and lessons to future potential attackers.

A collective security system thus depends on several key components:

- *Universal membership.* Collective security is meant to keep peace among the members of the arrangement, unlike alliances, which typically involve an agreement to defend each other in the event of an attack from another state outside the alliance. It is important for collective security that all major states are members.

- *Agreement to renounce the use of force.* The members of a collective security system must agree that they will not use force against each other to resolve their disagreements.

- *Commitment to respond to the use of force.* The members of a collective security system must agree that they will respond to the use of force by any member of the system against any other member of the system by joining together to punish the attacker and defend the victim.

These basic requirements are more complicated than they initially appear. They require that aggression be definable and identifiable so that an attacker can be punished. They also require that the pooled might of the community exceeds the might of any individual member so that a collective response can be successful. Furthermore, they require that all members be prepared and *willing* to commit their resources in defense of any other state, no matter which state or how small, and no matter which state the attacker might be. Finally, a collective security system probably requires a central organization that can coordinate discussion and decisions for the community.

Three attempts at some form of collective security have occurred in the modern state system. In the 19th century, the major powers in Europe (Britain, Russia, Austria, Prussia, and eventually France) joined in the **Concert of Europe**, which operated from 1815 to 1854. The concert rested on a shared commitment to the peace settlement of 1815 (the Congress of Vienna). It also included the principle that any change to the territorial status quo embodied in that agreement would be arranged through negotiation among the members of the concert, or the instigator of the change would face punitive action by one or more members of the concert. Although the Concert of Europe helped preserve peace in Europe for 40 years, it eventually failed for at least three reasons: (a) The commitment to the status quo among the members of the concert deteriorated, leading to increasing conflict and pressure for change to the 1815 agreement; (b) changes in power among member states and rising states outside the concert, combined with the exclusion of minor states from the concert, led to the inability of the concert to manage conflict; and (c) the lack of a central organization made it difficult to manage the complex discussions and negotiations necessary to preserve the peace, as well as to facilitate coordinated responses to states challenging the 1815 agreement.

After World War I, the victorious states established the League of Nations explicitly to construct a collective security system for multilateral and collective efforts to provide security and keep peace and to avoid a repeat of the devastating war that had just ended. The members of the league committed themselves to refrain from aggression against other members and to support the principle that any act of aggression against any member was an act of war against all members. Unlike the Concert of Europe, the league included a wide variety of members, both large and small. In the event of aggression, the members agreed to impose diplomatic and economic sanctions against the aggressor and, with the unanimous recommendation of the league's executive council, to contribute military resources to a military action in response.

However, the League of Nations proved ineffective in the face of the increasingly severe conflict of the 1920s and 1930s. One problem was that key

....

Concert of Europe: a 19th-century multilateral organization composed of Great Britain, Russia, Austria, Prussia, and France to promote stability, cooperation, and multilateral diplomacy.

states were not included in the league, including the United States (which refrained from joining) and the Soviet Union (which was excluded until the 1930s). Moreover, the league's effectiveness suffered because some states—such as Italy, Japan, and Germany— were considerably less committed to the status quo than others. Perhaps most important, the league failed when its members proved unwilling or unable to punish countries such as Japan and Italy when they engaged in military actions in Manchuria and Ethiopia, respectively. Key members of the league proved reluctant to expend their resources in defense of smaller states, and other calculations of interest (e.g., the concern that Italy might be needed to help resist Germany) increased their unwillingness to confront the aggression.

After World War II, the victorious powers again sought to construct a collective security system to manage conflict and keep peace, establishing the United Nations and, in particular, the UN Security Council in 1945 for that purpose. The members of the UN pledge to refrain from the use of force against each other and to use the UN for help in resolving conflict that might arise between them. The UN Charter empowers the UN Security Council—made up of five permanent members (the United States, Russia, China, France, and the United Kingdom), each of which holds veto power over any resolution, and 10 rotating members—to identify threats to peace and acts of aggression and to take action in the form of diplomatic or economic sanctions or the use of force to restore international peace and security.

Like its predecessor, the UN has proven less effective as a collective security organization than its creators hoped. During the Cold War, the veto power possessed by the United States and the Soviet Union effectively paralyzed the Security Council and prevented collective security actions. The only exception occurred in the case of the Korean War in 1950, when the UN Security Council authorized military action by members to help South Korea repel the invasion by North Korea. This authorization was possible only because the Soviet Union was boycotting UN Security Council meetings in protest over the refusal of the United States and other members to seat the new communist regime in mainland China as the official representative of that country.

During the paralysis of the UN Security Council caused by the Cold War conflict between the United States and the Soviet Union, the UN developed a **peacekeeping** role as an extension of its collective

security purpose. The first UN peacekeeping operation was the United Nations Truce Supervision Organization sent in 1948 to Israel to help sustain a cease-fire between that newly established state and its Arab neighbors. In total, 71 UN peacekeeping missions have been authorized all over the globe, at a total cost of about $70 billion.

In the first generation of peacekeeping operations, the UN typically provided a small multinational force—occasionally called blue helmets for the UN-provided headgear they wear—to help keep peace by providing a buffer between parties in conflict, often along a border or an agreed-upon cease-fire line. Usually very lightly armed, and never intended to engage in combat, these peacekeeping forces were drawn from the military forces of neutral states or smaller powers that were not aligned with any of the major parties to the conflict. In general, first-generation peacekeeping required three levels of agreement: (a) agreement among the parties of the conflict to accept the peacekeeping (that is, there should be a peace to *keep*; these forces did not *make* peace), (b) agreement among the major powers to fund the peacekeeping operation, and (c) agreement from other states to provide the peacekeeping forces. These forces monitored the peace and helped the parties to the conflict refrain from the temptation to restart hostilities. In this sense, they served as a basic deterrent to continued fighting.

After the Cold War's end, there was optimism that the UN could take up its collective security role, and the initial authorization of military action to repel Iraq from Kuwait after its 1990 invasion fueled that hope. However, in the conflicts of the post–Cold War period, the 1991 Gulf War proved the exception rather than the rule. In part due to the changing nature of conflict and war during this period (especially the rise of intrastate conflict), which we discussed in Chapter 5, and in part because member states found that they continued to have competing interests in the new environment, the post–Cold War world did not provide any greater incentives for successful collective security actions. Additionally, if the states did not have an interest in the conflict, they were often unwilling to put any of their troops in harm's way. The unwillingness or inability to act in the face of such conflicts as Somalia, Bosnia, Rwanda, Darfur, Kosovo, and others showed that the will to engage in collective security was still lacking. Hence, traditional collective security peace operations continued to languish.

In contrast to traditional collective security operations, the UN made much more significant contributions in its peacekeeping operations. From 1948 to 2017, the UN engaged in 71 peacekeeping operations around the world. The vast majority of these operations have occurred since 1990 and the end of the Cold War. After

....

peacekeeping: the provision of third-party forces from the UN or other regional organizations to help keep peace by providing a buffer between parties in conflict, often along a border or an agreed-upon cease-fire line to monitor and maintain the peace.

UN peace operations

What does this image of first-generation peacekeepers suggest about their role and capabilities?

RAVEENDRAN/AFP via Getty Images

UN peace operations

What does this image of second-generation peacekeepers suggest about their changing role and capabilities?

PASCAL GUYOT/AFP via Getty Images

the end of the Cold War, second-generation peacekeeping developed, in which the peacekeeping forces were much more substantial and much more complex. In 2019, 14 peacekeeping operations were active (see Map 6-5), involving just over 88,000 troops and almost 13,000 civilians from 124 different countries. These second-generation peace operations differed from their first-generation predecessors in some significant ways.

As we noted, first-generation peacekeepers, who generally relied on a preexisting cease-fire and the consent of the parties involved in the conflict, were lightly armed and very rarely authorized to use force in anything other than direct self-defense. Second-generation peacekeeping forces, such as those deployed in Somalia, the former Yugoslavia, and elsewhere around the world, are typically larger, more complex (involving both military and civilian personnel), and more capable. They are also engaged in a broader range of military, security, political, and humanitarian activities, and they are frequently authorized to use military might to make or enforce peace. In fact, their operations are often authorized under the UN Charter's Chapter VII authority, which allows the UN Security Council to take military and nonmilitary action to "restore international peace and security." Indeed, although the evolution did not start there, in many ways the failure of the more traditional peacekeepers initially deployed to help defuse the violent conflict in the former Yugoslavia helped spur the shift to more muscular and capable peace operations and forces. Finally, because these second-generation peace operations often occur in complicated civil war situations, the consent of the parties involved is not always a prerequisite—which also means the peacekeepers are more likely to face hostility and have to engage in more dynamic peacemaking, peacekeeping, and peace-enforcing activities.

These characteristics of second-generation peace operations helped increase their capabilities and their impact. Indeed, many evaluations of these operations agree that they make important contributions to peace and security, especially in civil wars. However, these same characteristics also ensure that their tasks are more difficult, because they often involve ongoing conflicts and tenuous cease-fires. Moreover, as you might expect, the kinds of conflicts that gain UN attention and subsequent peacekeeping forces are often the most difficult and intractable conflicts, which makes success even more challenging.

Collective security faces formidable challenges. In addition to the need to establish a central organization to facilitate decision making and coordination, the three cases introduced here suggest that major powers must also share common interests and a general commitment to peace, and probably the status quo, for collective security to work effectively. Moreover, major powers must be willing to expend resources on behalf of others in pursuit of common interests. Aggression must be identifiable, and the collective action problem must be overcome so that members of the organization cannot stand aside and hope that some other state will take up the burden. In the end, a realist might ask, if these conditions existed, would a collective security system be necessary?

6-3c Security Communities and the Democratic and Capitalist Peace

The final liberal approach to security is probably the most indirect but perhaps the most effective as well. Inspired in part by the ideas of the philosopher Immanuel Kant, its emphasis is on developing a network of ties between states and other actors that link states together in a web of connections and shared interests

UN Peacekeeping Operations

MAP 6-5

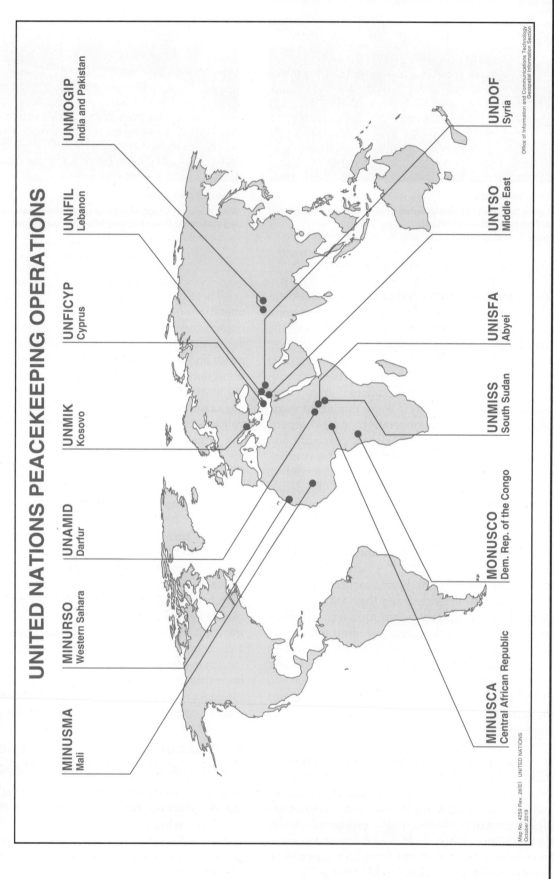

UNITED NATIONS PEACEKEEPING OPERATIONS

MINUSMA
Mali

MINURSO
Western Sahara

UNAMID
Darfur

UNMIK
Kosovo

UNFICYP
Cyprus

UNIFIL
Lebanon

UNMOGIP
India and Pakistan

MINUSCA
Central African Republic

MONUSCO
Dem. Rep. of the Congo

UNMISS
South Sudan

UNISFA
Abyei

UNTSO
Middle East

UNDOF
Syria

Map No. 4259 Rev. 26(E)   UNITED NATIONS
October 2019

Office of Information and Communications Technology
Geospatial Information Section

Source: United Nations. "Peacekeeping Operations Factsheet." January 2019. https://peacekeeping.un.org/sites/default/files/pk_factsheet_01_19_eng.pdf.

China's Pursuit of Security

China is a rising power whose role and influence in world politics is swiftly expanding. Its purposes and foreign policy actions therefore garner a great deal of attention from its neighbors in the region, especially Taiwan and Japan, and leading powers such as the United States. According to the US Defense Department, which reports annually on Chinese military capabilities and strategies:

> China's leaders have benefited from what they view as a "period of strategic opportunity" during the initial two decades of the 21st century to develop domestically and expand China's "comprehensive national power." Over the coming decades, they are focused on realizing a powerful and prosperous China that is equipped with a "world-class" military, securing China's status as a great power with the aim of emerging as the preeminent power in the Indo-Pacific region. (Office of the Secretary of Defense 2019: i)

A central component of this effort is dramatically increased military spending and an extensive modernization program, with the goal of complete overhaul by 2035. As the US Defense Department notes:

> PLA modernization includes command and force structure reforms to improve operational flexibility and readiness for future deployments. As China's global footprint and international interests have grown, its military modernization program has become more focused on investments and infrastructure to support a range of missions beyond China's periphery, including power projection, sea lane security, counterpiracy, peacekeeping, humanitarian assistance/disaster relief, and noncombatant evacuation operations. (Office of the Secretary of Defense 2019: iii)

As China's power has increased, and its interests, role, and influence in the world have grown, Chinese leaders have steered military spending toward high-tech transformations consistent with the revolution in military affairs, extending its ability to project power well beyond its own territory and borders. Naval power is a core aspect of this commitment. According to the US Defense Department, China's navy

> is the largest navy in the region with more than 300 ships and continues to undergo rapid modernization to multi-role platforms. China's first domestically-built aircraft carrier will likely join the fleet in 2019, and China began construction of its second domestic aircraft carrier in 2018. (Office of the Secretary of Defense 2019: 35)

As noted earlier, that second aircraft carrier underwent its initial sea trials in 2020. Beyond its navy, China is boosting spending on its air force and its cyberwarfare capabilities as well.

What does China's efforts to build up its military power in these ways mean? According to one analysis, China's military power has expanded so greatly that it is now the dominant power in the Western Pacific and could well win a war with the US (Shinkman 2019).

Consider the perspectives on the pursuit of security discussed in this chapter, as well as the relevant ideas from previous chapters.

1. What best explains Chinese actions?

2. In what ways do these actions contribute to and challenge China's security?

3. What might other countries think about China's foreign policy behavior, and how might they react? ●

(Kant 1996). In such a **security community**, traditional security concerns among members are transformed because people are bound by a sense of community and common interest, such that war becomes virtually unthinkable. Constructivist scholars also embrace this argument, stressing the shared identities and interests and complex interactions that transform the relationships between societies (Adler and Barnett 1988).

What strategies help establish security communities? Liberals generally look to a cluster of interlinked approaches. First, many advocates of this approach stress building common identity and understanding

security community: a group of states bound by shared identities and interests and complex interactions among which security threats are virtually nonexistent.

among states. Efforts to foster societal contact and exchanges and to promote democracy are good examples of such approaches. Fostering **cultural exchange** reduces the distance between peoples and builds understanding. Programs such as the United States' Fulbright educational exchange program are meant to foster the "promotion of international good will through the exchange of students in the fields of education, culture and science." **Democracy promotion** leads to shared political practices and is premised on the fact that democratic countries are much less likely to go to war with each other and much more likely to resolve conflicts peacefully (see discussions of the democratic peace in Chapters 3 and 5 and of democracy promotion in Chapter 9).

Second, advocates of this approach have attempted to "build peace in pieces" by promoting transnational cooperation on economic and social problems that grow to link societies together (Mitrany 1966). Based on theories of **functionalism and neo-functionalism**, this approach stresses specific technical cooperation on economic and social issues that build linkages and shared interests among societies. As these linkages deepen and become more routine, they expand to more areas, leading to even greater cooperation and institutional connections. A good example of this can be seen in the development of the European Union. Beginning as the European Coal and Steel Community in the 1950s, the integrative approach inspired by functionalism and neo-functionalism led to stronger and more extensive linkages as the early organization grew into the EU of today, with its extensive institutions and single common currency for many of its members. Along the way, it helped transform European relations from the highly conflict-ridden patterns that preceded the two devastating world wars in the 20th century to the peaceful security community we see today. Could this success be duplicated in other regions of the world?

Third, and related to the previous point, advocates of this strategy emphasize the cultivation of interdependence and institutions that help states coordinate their actions as they develop mutual interests. One aspect of this involves economic ties, with the argument that developing and deepening economic relationships such as trade and financial networks contributes

to a "capitalist peace" that dramatically reduces the potential for violent conflict (Gartzke 2007). Another aspect, which motivated a large portion of post–World War II institution building, stresses the development of international institutions to help coordinate and govern economic policy and interactions (discussed in Chapter 8). Part of the logic of the post–World War II international institutions such as the International Monetary Fund and the World Bank, as well as less formal institutions—such as the G7, G8, and now G20—is that the norms, rules, and decision procedures that promote economic coordination within these institutions help reduce conflict and foster a sense of community. International institutions of other kinds to address social problems such as the environment, health, and a variety of other issues produce similar effects. Still, some states, such as China, will trust both international norms and increasing their own militaries to ensure their security (see the box "Foreign Policy in Perspective: China's Pursuit of Security").

In the end, advocates argue, strategies such as these build community and transform the security calculations of states and societies. According to their advocates, they transform and redefine the security dilemma and reduce the situations in which conflict erupts into violence. By trying to create and spread zones of peace, these strategies contend with the challenges posed by anarchy, diversity, and complexity by reducing uncertainty and fear and building common interests and cooperation. What do you think of the long-term prospects of such efforts to transform relations among states and societies?

CONCLUSION: SEEKING SECURITY

National and international security remains an elusive, central issue in world politics. Although power-based and cooperation-based approaches have been advocated and embraced over time, security challenges remain, conflict persists, and violence still erupts far too often. However, as we saw in Chapter 5, there has been an evolution to the nature of conflict and to the nature of security as well. Few observers would argue that security is not a challenge in the current world, nor would many argue that conflict and war have disappeared. Yet security issues have changed. The French no longer harbor fears of war with Britain or Germany, or vice versa. The prospect of direct military conflict between major powers has declined over many decades. Optimists might argue that even the rapid military growth of China and growing Russian aggressiveness should not unduly alarm the EU or the United States, as both countries face constraints on their military power and have sizable trade interactions with the

....

cultural exchange: programs involving the exchange of citizens—students, teachers, scientists, artists, and others—between countries to foster cultural understanding and cooperation.

democracy promotion: a cluster of activities, ranging from diplomacy to aid to intervention, designed to foster and support democratization in other countries.

functionalism and neo-functionalism: technical cooperation on economic and social issues that build linkages and shared interests among societies and expand to more areas, leading to even greater cooperation and institutional connections.

EU and the United States, which may make any future war with them look less appealing. But military spending continues at significant levels, and force continues to be used to resolve conflicts. Are people and states more secure today or less? And what strategies and actions have contributed to that condition?

Finally, now that you have considered major arguments on the causes of war (see Chapter 5) and approaches to security (this chapter), think back to our initial discussion of the prisoner's dilemma in Chapter 1. Remember that the essence of the prisoner's dilemma is that each prisoner ends up choosing a course of action that provides less benefit in order to avoid suffering a greater cost. Which of the approaches to security we have discussed here do you think is most likely to produce the optimal outcomes, and under what conditions? And which ones are most likely to produce less beneficial outcomes? ●

KEY CONCEPTS

6-1 Identify the challenges of seeking international security in world politics.

The players in world politics seek security—to protect themselves from attack by other actors and guard their essential interests. The protection of political sovereignty and territorial integrity is especially important in a world without central government. The pursuit of security often results in insecurity, arms races, conflict spirals, and, sometimes, war. The absence of authoritative central institutions in world politics often makes coordination and cooperation difficult, prompting fear from the players that their interests will not be protected unless they take action themselves. The core elements of the security challenge stem from the combination of the anarchy, diversity, and complexity of world politics. At the foundation of this fundamental challenge are the security dilemma and the challenge of power. Security dilemmas arise as a state takes actions it sees as defensive and nonthreatening, but such actions alarm others, and the result may be exactly what each is trying to avoid, which may produce even greater insecurities. The disparities in power between the haves and have-nots create challenges because they generate uncertainties, fears, threats, and competition.

6-2 Describe and evaluate power-based approaches to international security embraced by realists, including military might, alliances, and the uses of force.

Realists stress that the dangerous world of international relations requires states to accumulate military capabilities to deter potential attackers, defend against attacks, and extend power and influence. States generally have two basic options: building their own military might and forging alliances to increase military capabilities. According to realists, states devote resources to their militaries to counter threats and to gain or maintain power to deal with the inevitable conflicts that arise in a dangerous, anarchic world. Realists also emphasize the efforts of states to forge alliances with other states to counter threats and increase strength. When there are common interests between states, such as a common enemy, they agree to cooperate militarily to meet threats. Such alliances might be driven by protection, bandwagoning, or balancing dynamics and are usually relatively temporary. Realists stress that in a dangerous and anarchic world, force will often be used. States wishing to be secure must have power to secure themselves, and power, to realists, depends on the ability to use military force through deterrence, defense, and more proactive applications of force.

6-3 Describe and assess cooperation-based approaches to international security embraced by liberals, including arms control and disarmament, collective security, and security communities.

Liberal approaches to security and conflict management emphasize cooperation and coordination. They tend to view the security dilemma as driven by uncertainty and problems with trust and understanding. Consequently, liberals stress the construction of agreements to control or eliminate weapons. Disarmament emphasizes the elimination (or the drastic reduction) of weapons, while arms control generally promotes restraint or regulation of the amount, type, positioning, or use of weapons. In part, both arms control and disarmament rest on the premise that controlling weaponry and the competition to acquire it will make states more secure and better able to manage conflict. A second major liberal approach to security and conflict is collective security, the liberal answer to balance-of-power politics. In collective security, states join together into a community and commit to respond to any attack by one member on any other member. The final liberal approach to security is the development of security communities. A security community is a group of states bound by shared identities and interests and complex interactions among whom security threats are virtually nonexistent.

KEY TERMS

political sovereignty **148**

territorial integrity **148**

revolution in military affairs **157**

arms race **157**

alliance **157**

protection **158**

bandwagoning 158

balancing 158

internal balancing 159

external balancing 159

deterrence 160

direct deterrence 160

extended deterrence 161

immediate deterrence 161

general deterrence 161

brinkmanship 161

mutually assured destruction (MAD) 161

defense 162

preemption 162

prevention 162

national missile defense 163

theater missile defense 163

compellence 164

coercive diplomacy 165

disarmament 165

arms control 165

Baruch Plan 169

collective security 170

Concert of Europe 171

peacekeeping 172

security community 175

cultural exchange 176

democracy promotion 176

functionalism and neo-functionalism 176

REVIEW QUESTIONS

1. Why is security such a challenge in world politics?

2. According to realists, how do arms and alliances contribute to security?

3. How can military force be used to produce security?

4. According to liberals, how can arms control and disarmament contribute to security?

5. How does collective security address the problem of security and conflict, and what are its strengths and weaknesses?

6. What is a security community, and how is it developed?

THINK ABOUT THIS

Weapons, Force, and Security

Realists from Thomas Hobbes to John Mearsheimer have long argued that military power and the use of force are the essential ingredients for survival and prosperity. Liberal theorists from Immanuel Kant to Robert Keohane and Joseph Nye have argued that military power and the use of force involve consequences that often outweigh their advantages and thus contribute to insecurity as often as not. Consider the role of military power in the approaches to security discussed in this chapter and the relative strengths and weaknesses of each approach.

Do weapons and military arsenals contribute to security or insecurity in world politics?

FOR MORE INFORMATION . . .

Art, Robert J., and Kelly Greenhill. (2015). *The Use of Force: Military Power and International Politics,* 8th ed. New York, NY: Rowman and Littlefield.

Claude, Inis L. (1962). *Power and International Relations.* New York, NY: Random House.

Cohen, Eliot. (2017). *The Big Stick: The Limits of Soft Power and the Necessity of Military Force.* New York, NY: Basic Books.

Kay, Sean. (2015). *Global Security in the 21st Century: The Quest for Power and the Search for Peace,* 3rd ed. New York, NY: Rowman and Littlefield.

Larsen, Jeffrey, and James Wirtz, eds. (2009). *Arms Control and Cooperative Security.* Boulder, CO: Lynne Rienner.

Morgan, Patrick. (2006). *International Security: Problems and Solutions.* Washington, DC: CQ Press.

UN Secretary-General António Guterres addresses the UN General Assembly at the United Nations headquarters in New York

What gives the leader of the UN influence?

Spencer Platt/Getty Images

7 Building Peace
Structures of Cooperation

Learning Objectives

After studying this chapter, you will be able to . . .

7-1 Identify the underlying challenges to cooperation in pursuit of security.

7-2 Explain the nature and forms of diplomacy.

7-3 Describe the nature and functions of international law.

7-4 Evaluate the nature and functions of international organizations.

Chapter Outline

7-1 Cooperation and Its Challenges

7-2 Diplomacy: Negotiation in World Politics

7-3 International Law: Norms and Rules Without Central Authority

7-4 International Organizations: The European Union, the United Nations, and Many Others

A New World Order?

In 1990, Iraq invaded the neighboring state of Kuwait. American President George H. W. Bush addressed a joint session of the US Congress, and in his speech, he argued that

> out of these troubled times . . . a new world order . . . can emerge: a new era—freer from the threat of terror, stronger in the pursuit of justice, and more secure in the quest for peace. An era in which the nations of the world, East and West, North and South, can prosper and live in harmony. . . . A world where the rule of law supplants the rule of the jungle. A world in which nations recognize the shared responsibility for freedom and justice. A world where the strong respect the rights of the weak.

Thereafter, a UN-sanctioned, US-led military coalition drove Iraqi forces from Kuwait. Less than a week after the successful conclusion to the first Gulf War, President Bush stated:

> Now, we can see a new world coming into view. A world in which there is the very real prospect of a new world order. In the words of Winston Churchill, a "world order" in which "the principles of justice and fair play . . . protect the weak against the strong." A world where the United Nations, freed from cold war stalemate, is poised to fulfill the historic vision of its founders.

Three decades later, one would be hard-pressed to find similar optimism for this "new world order" or the role of the United Nations. Conflict and violence continue, and a world based on law and cooperation remains elusive. The UN and the world failed to prevent the brutal deaths of 800,000 Rwandans in 1994. They have struggled to respond effectively to armed conflict and violence in Syria since 2011 and in Ukraine since 2014. North Korea has developed more nuclear weapons and ballistic missiles to deliver them. Europe faced a refugee crisis caused by drought in North Africa and the violence of the 2011–2012 Arab Spring. Many states welcomed refugees, but some, like Hungary and more recently the US, tried to deny refugees any haven, and the British left the European Union in part over the issue. Little global cooperation occurred to address the challenge of COVID-19 and the global pandemic and economic downturn it generated. All the while, intrastate violence marked much of central Africa, the Middle East, and South Asia. Instead of greater cooperation to meet these challenges, states struggle now more than ever to cooperate. The elusive quest for a world of cooperation in which international law and international institutions establish justice and peace continues. We haven't "passed that test" yet.

1. Why are the structures of peace and cooperation so hard to achieve in world politics?

2. Why isn't the rule of law the norm in relations between countries?

3. What might contribute to progress in these areas?

INTRODUCTION: ACHIEVING COOPERATION

Cooperation to achieve international peace and security is often challenging. Although the benefits of cooperation seem pretty obvious, achieving it is almost always harder than it initially appears. States and non-state actors cooperate extensively across a wide variety of matters—from the mundane to the life threatening—to achieve common goals and to manage conflicts and disagreements without resorting to violence. And yet in many situations, countries simply fail to cooperate at all, regardless of the stakes involved. Cooperation is both commonplace and hard, as contradictory as that seems.

For example, a set of rules for how the high seas and its resources will be governed is codified in the **Law of the Sea Convention**. The United States signed the convention and follows its rules, but the US Senate never formally ratified it. Some Senate critics said approving the convention would undermine US sovereignty and freedom of action. Yet in addition to helping ensure freedom of operation by the US Navy in and around the world's oceans and key transit points, the convention also includes rules about handling piracy on the high seas, protecting commercial fishery stocks, and regulating deep-sea mining of rare minerals—just to cite three examples. All of these issues are clearly in the interests of the United States, but as long as some leaders and elites see cooperation as "giving something up," it will be hard to accomplish. So even though cooperation is smooth for some issues, the road to gaining cooperation and institutionalizing it can be long and bumpy, and not all concerned will want to come along for the ride.

In Chapters 5 and 6, we focused our attention on understanding the nature and causes of conflict and war and on the strategies state and non-state actors use to manage conflict and achieve international security. In this chapter, we turn to efforts to gain security and manage conflict through structures and institutions of cooperation. We begin by considering the challenges of cooperation faced by the players in world politics. We then turn to a discussion of diplomacy, international law, and international organization as cooperative approaches to peace, security, and cooperation. We conclude by considering the prospects and problems for states and non-state actors as they try to cooperate in their quest for mutual security.

....

Law of the Sea Convention: a treaty that first went into force in 1982 and then was revised in 1994; 167 states are parties to this treaty, as is the EU, which sets rules for the use and protection of the high seas and its resources.

7-1 COOPERATION AND ITS CHALLENGES

>> **7-1** **Identify the underlying challenges to cooperation in pursuit of security.**

At first glance, the benefits of cooperation seem obvious and compelling: greater peace, prosperity, and justice; and resources and expertise shared to solve difficult problems that cross borders. Yet in world politics, cooperation is often more difficult to attain than we might expect. Cooperation can benefit everyone, but actually establishing the institutions, norms, and rules for cooperation is difficult and tends to be incomplete and episodic.

Let's take another recent example. There's no question that violence and death are partly a result of the ready availability of conventional arms in the international system, whether used by states or by rebel groups, terrorists, and criminal networks. In 2013 the UN concluded an Arms Trade Treaty to create international rules to prevent conventional weapons from getting into the wrong hands. To date, more than 130 countries have signed the treaty (including the US in 2013), and 110 are officially parties to it. It went into effect on December 24, 2014. However, the US has not ratified the treaty, and Russia and China did not even sign it. Although major weapons manufacturers in the international system have a vested interest in ensuring that their sales to legitimate buyers are not constrained, each passing day without more regulation of such weapons means more deaths globally that might have been avoided. So cooperation is needed, but achieving it is hard.

Throughout this text, we have stressed three underlying challenges affecting world politics, and these challenges apply to cooperation in the pursuit of international security as well. First, the anarchic nature of world politics complicates cooperation. The absence of a central enforcer to prevent and punish wrongdoing creates incentives for the major political players—states—to take care of themselves and their own interests instead of cooperating. Second, the diversity of world politics also complicates cooperation. Even if anarchy could be managed, the fact that states and societies are so different—in size, regime type, economic capabilities, culture, interests, and many other factors—makes achieving harmony very hard. Add in the variety of non-state actors with their own identities, interests, and purposes, and this diversity just gets more difficult to manage. Third, the complexity of world politics also complicates cooperation. Over time more and more players—states and non-state actors—are engaged across more and more issues that are linked together and affect them. These linkages often provide opportunities for cooperation,

Indonesian military display arms confiscated from ex-Aceh rebels in 2019

Why is it so hard to control the possession of small arms like these?

CHAIDEER MAHYUDDIN/AFP via Getty Images

because a growing arena of transnational problems often requires players to work together, and the connections and interactions among players can enable them to give and take across several issues to arrive at mutual benefits. In effect, giving on one matter can be linked to getting on another. However, these complex links among actors and issues can also make finding and maintaining common ground on any given issue just that much harder.

Despite these challenges, states and other actors in world politics rely extensively on cooperative approaches to many problems and disagreements. Let's take up three key structures of cooperation by which states and other players in world politics seek international security: diplomacy, international law, and international organizations. As we do so, keep in mind the challenges that anarchy, diversity, and complexity pose for each area.

7-2 DIPLOMACY: NEGOTIATION IN WORLD POLITICS

>> **7-2 Explain the nature and forms of diplomacy.**

Perhaps the oldest structure of cooperation in world politics is diplomacy. The appeal of cooperation and conflict resolution through communication, bargaining, and negotiation is intuitive: To most people, talking is better than fighting. Let's begin by getting a sense of what diplomacy involves and then discuss some of its forms and uses.

7-2a The Nature and Role of Diplomacy

Have you ever had to work out a disagreement with a friend or an acquaintance? Maybe it took another person's intervention to help. In either case, you were engaged in **diplomacy**. In international relations, diplomacy is the art and practice of conducting negotiations between states and other actors in world politics. Sometimes the results are surprising.

Here's an example. In September 2019, South African mobs began vandalizing and looting stores owned by foreigners, most of them from other African states. Representatives of those other African states were quick to criticize the government of President Cyril Ramaphosa, accusing it of tolerating the violence and promoting xenophobia. Underlying these criticisms was the fact that South Africa had never fully embraced being a part of Africa, instead embracing its membership in the British Commonwealth. President Ramaphosa reacted with a "charm offensive." He sent diplomats to other African states to stress Pan-Africanism themes, with the message that the violence and xenophobia would no longer be tolerated and that South Africa desired to be an integral part of the African community. Putting action to words, at the same time South Africa ratified its membership in the African Continental Free Trade Agreement. These diplomatic steps were successful. The sharp criticism from other African states stopped just as South Africa was to take its turn as the chair

....

diplomacy: the art and practice of conducting negotiations between states and other actors in world politics.

Who Represents the United States Abroad?

The professional diplomats in the United States are generally foreign service officers found in the Department of State. FSOs, as they are known, are selected through a challenging process of examination (the Foreign Service Officer Exam), which consists of a written test, a personal narrative and interview for those who pass the written test, an intensive onsite oral examination involving a variety of problem-solving and applied activities, and a final review. Those who clear all these hurdles are then placed on a rank-ordered list and offered assignments as positions become available. It is no wonder that, like most professional diplomatic corps, the US Foreign Service is often considered elitist. After all, the demand to join is usually high, job openings are generally limited, and the selection process is very difficult. Even applicants who do well in each part of the process are not guaranteed a position.

FSOs serve abroad in embassies in the capital cities of foreign countries, in consulates in major cities of foreign countries, in other missions abroad, in IOs such as the United Nations, and in the United States as well. In their duties, they generally engage in five major activities:

1. They represent the US government overseas.

2. They present the views of foreigners to the US government.

3. They engage in diplomacy and negotiations on behalf of the United States.

4. They analyze and report on events abroad.

5. They provide policy advice to their superiors.

In recent years, FSOs have become increasingly diverse. In the past, most FSOs were white Protestant men who typically attended Ivy League schools. This pattern tended to make the Foreign Service an exclusive "old-boy network" in which family, background, education, and connections mattered a great deal. Over time, much has changed for the professional diplomatic corps of the United States and other countries. While it took lawsuits to accomplish progress, in the United States, women, minorities, and individuals who are not from the Northeast, not Protestant, and not upper- or upper-middle class have become an increasingly large part of the US Foreign Service. A significant step in this process occurred when Madeleine Albright was named the first woman to serve as US secretary of state in 1996 by President Bill Clinton. Secretary Albright was followed by Condoleezza Rice in George W. Bush's presidency and Hillary Clinton in Barack Obama's presidency. Nonetheless, the process of change has been slow, and the professional diplomatic corps of most states continues to be overrepresented by men.

This pattern extends to the top of the diplomatic pyramid as well. According to the Worldwide Guide to Women in Leadership, as of March 2017, only 28 of the roughly 200 foreign ministers in the world were women. How would international relations be different if more diplomats were women? ●

---

of the African Union in 2020. This example demonstrates the heart of diplomacy: the importance of communication and negotiation in pursuit of cooperation and conflict resolution.

This basic understanding of diplomacy also implies the existence of **diplomats**, individuals occupying positions in the foreign policy establishments of states or the management of other organizations who represent and negotiate on behalf of their country or employer. Such individuals may include the highest-ranking officials of a country (the head of state or of government) and foreign ministers, ambassadors, envoys, and other lower-ranking personnel (see "Spotlight On: Who Represents the United States Abroad?"). In the modern context, nongovernmental organizations and private individuals also engage in diplomacy.

One of the key foundations of the structure and institution of diplomacy in world politics is **diplomatic immunity**, which we discussed in Chapter 2. This practice, which has evolved since the time of the Greek city-states and is codified in the Vienna Conventions on Diplomatic Relations (1961) and Consular Relations (1963), ensures that the emissaries of states are protected as they perform their duties and conduct business with each other. It is really a very pragmatic idea based on reciprocity: If countries are to be able to sustain communication—even in times of violent conflict—and try to resolve disagreements, they must have confidence that their official representatives and negotiators will be able to engage in diplomacy safely.

....

diplomats: individuals occupying positions in the foreign policy establishments of states or the management of other organizations who represent and negotiate on behalf of their country or employer.

diplomatic immunity: the principle that accredited diplomats are exempt in almost all cases from prosecution under the laws of the state where they are assigned.

Indian leader Narendra Modi and Chinese leader Xi Xinping in recent talks

How do leaders work out their differences and come to agreement?

AP Photo/Manish Swarup, File

Yet embassies and embassy officials are increasingly the targets of state and non-state actors. For example, terrorist groups such as al-Qaeda and Hezbollah have specifically targeted US and other embassies and consulates for bombing in Lebanon (1983, 1984), Kenya (1998), Tanzania (1998), Pakistan (2002), Saudi Arabia (2004), Syria (2006), Greece (2007), Algeria (2007), Yemen (2008), and Libya (2012). Hezbollah also engaged in a decade-long campaign of kidnapping in Lebanon, often targeting embassy personnel. Iran seized US embassy personnel in late 1979 and held more than 50 people hostage for 444 days. If diplomats of states are targets of violence, what implications do you think this holds for the conduct and future of diplomacy—especially given that these attacks principally involve non-state actors?

7-2b The Art of Diplomacy

Let's now consider some general features and key characteristics of what many regard as the heart of diplomacy: *bargaining* (a term usually meaning more competitive and conflictual diplomacy) and *negotiation* (a term usually meaning more collaborative problem solving). Diplomacy generally involves negotiation over some issue of conflict in pursuit of common interests.

For diplomats on both sides of a dispute, the key to success is to find a solution to which both sides can agree. As Roger Fisher (1991) famously wrote decades ago, the other side should have something to say yes to—a benefit that appears desirable and enables them to avoid appearing as if they just gave in. In effect, diplomats try to fashion proposals that encourage

their counterparts to see that they have interests in and benefits from their adoption. The trick is finding how to do so.

We can imagine a hypothetical conflict between two states, as depicted in Figure 7-1. As the figure suggests, each state has its maximum demand, or ideal preference for an outcome, and diplomacy is involved in communicating those preferences. Each state also has its bottom line, or resistance point, which is the minimum it will accept at the outset of the diplomatic interaction. Part of diplomacy is trying to learn what that resistance point for the other side is, while protecting your own. Between the two resistance points is what we could call a **settlement gap**: the distance between the minimum demands of each side. How far apart the two sides are greatly affects the possibility of a successful diplomatic resolution to the conflict.

Finding ways to close that settlement gap and cooperate over common interests and resolve issues of conflict is the art of diplomacy. Obviously, persuasion might be involved, as might threats (see Chapter 6 and its discussion of compellence, or coercive diplomacy). Either or both sides might introduce a wide variety of "carrots" (rewards such as foreign aid) and "sticks" (punishments such as sanctions) to stress common interests and/or potential costs of failing to resolve the matter. Diplomats might also try to use a **linkage strategy** to connect other issues to the resolution of

....

settlement gap: the difference between the minimal preferences of two parties to a negotiation.

linkage strategy: in diplomacy, the strategy of connecting solutions on one issue to proposals on another to facilitate agreement.

FIGURE 7-1

The Structure of Negotiation

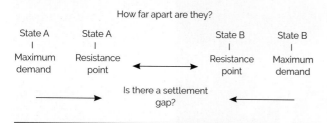

Source: Adapted from Paul Gordon Lauren, Gordon A. Craig, and Alexander George, *Force and Statecraft: Diplomatic Challenges of Our Time*, 4th ed. (New York, NY: Oxford University Press, 2007), 155.

the current one. For example, one state might agree to another state's preference on trade if the second state moves closer to the first on human rights. The parties to this conflict might even invite in a third party or parties to try to help them reach agreement.

7-2c The Forms of Diplomacy

Now that we have a basic sense of what diplomacy involves, let's consider some of the styles and types of diplomacy and how they have evolved over time. Modern structures and practices of diplomacy owe their shape and form to the development of the state system after the Treaties of Westphalia (1648) and, especially, since the early 19th century and the European Congress of Vienna (1814–1815).

Early diplomacy in the state system was an elite activity controlled by royalty, nobility, and other elites. By the early 20th century, diplomacy became the arena of professional diplomats. As time passed, however, the arena for diplomacy expanded considerably. This was partly a function of advances in communication and transportation technologies, which enabled state leaders to communicate directly with much greater ease. As modern transportation made the world shrink, meetings became more possible, and communications technologies (telephones, computers, and the like) allowed governments to link directly to each other and bypass their embassies. The expansion of global news networks, satellites, television, social media, and the Internet also make leaders much less dependent on their embassies and

professional diplomats for news and information about a foreign country.

As these technological changes took place, an interesting "back-to-the-future" kind of development occurred. Just as the early dominance of elites as the principal diplomats (e.g., royalty and nobility) gave way to more professional diplomatic corps by the mid-19th century, since then, there has been a return to the very high-level, personal diplomacy among leaders and their closest advisers and foreign policy personnel. State leaders can fly almost anywhere in the world in a day or two, so physically getting together for face-to-face **summit meetings** is much easier now than it was 100 years ago.

However, other forms of diplomacy have also thrived and expanded. Increasingly, **multilateral diplomacy** is common. As we discussed in Chapter 6, throughout the Cold War, the United States and Soviet Union engaged in bilateral diplomacy to work out cooperative arrangements to control their nuclear arms competition. However, most of the major arms control negotiations of the past two decades have involved a large number of countries in multilateral talks (see Chapter 6 for more on such treaties). Multilateral diplomacy has also been the norm in addressing a variety of other issues in world politics, many of which we address in other chapters. Complicated talks among hundreds of participants are the norm for issues related to trade and finance (see Chapter 8), international development (see Chapter 10), human rights (see Chapter 11), and the global environment (see Chapter 12). Globalization, the growth in the number and types of international actors, and the increasingly complicated and interconnected issue agenda all contribute to this shift, but it raises a question: In what ways does this development—the trend toward multilateral diplomacy—help and hinder successful diplomatic outcomes?

Sometimes parties to a conflict seek the help of others to resolve their disagreements. Perhaps the earliest notable example came in 1906 when US President Theodore Roosevelt won the Nobel Peace Prize for mediating the 1905 war between Russia and Japan. We can identify four main types of such **third-party diplomacy**: good offices, mediation, arbitration, and adjudication. Table 7-1 provides a simple introduction to each type. Let's think about these approaches to third-party diplomacy for a moment. First, notice that as we move from good offices to adjudication, the parties of the dispute relinquish more and more control over the outcome. What do you think that suggests about the kinds of disputes that are submitted for these types of diplomacy? Second, consider what makes a good third party in these situations. Should the third party be strictly neutral, or should the third-party participant have important interests at stake as well?

summit meetings: diplomatic meetings involving the top officials of their respective states (hence, "the summit").

multilateral diplomacy: diplomacy involving three or more states at a time; typically many states are involved.

third-party diplomacy: the engagement of an outside party in negotiations between the actual parties to a dispute to facilitate a resolution of the disagreement.

TABLE 7-1

Types of Third-Party Diplomacy

APPROACH	BEHAVIORS
Good offices	The least intrusive form of third-party involvement, in which the third party provides a place for the two sides to negotiate.
Mediation	The third party organizes the talks and proposes possible options to settle the dispute, but no settlement is forced on the participants by the third party.
Arbitration	The participants present information and views and agree in advance to accept an option developed by and determined by the third party to be in the best interest of all concerned.
Adjudication	In a court-like proceeding, the participants present their positions to the third party, who acts like a judge and decides which of the positions is "correct." The participants agree in advance to abide by the third party's decision.

Emma Watson speaks to the UN General Assembly
How can high-profile celebrities affect international relations?
Katz/Pacific Press/LightRocket via Getty Images

One significant change to diplomacy in the neo-Westphalian world has been the increasing role of non-state actors. This development includes the expanding role of international organizations such as the United Nations. However, it also includes a growing role for other non-state actors, including NGOs and private individuals. Commonly referred to as **track II diplomacy**, this type of diplomacy may involve private citizens (including celebrities, such as Angelina Jolie, Bono, and Emma Watson, or former leaders, such as Jimmy Carter or Tony Blair), NGOs, academic experts or specialists, and so on. Track II diplomacy offers ways to explore solutions to particular issues, conflicts, and disagreements without the burdens of formal state-to-state negotiations.

Many of these actors now often cooperate to handle issues through **conference diplomacy**. Large meetings of officials focusing on a restricted set of issues are nothing new, but the term has taken on special meaning in the neo-Westphalian era. Often under the sponsorship of international organizations such as the UN, large, issue-based conferences have been held to bring together representatives of states, international organizations, academia and **epistemic communities**, NGOs, individuals, and non-state national groups.

Major global conferences on land mines, women, population, human rights, the environment, and other issues have been held over the past several decades, some of which have now been regularized into annual

or periodic meetings. Examples include the series of conferences on global climate change that began with the 1992 Earth Summit in Rio de Janeiro and the World Conference on Women—the fourth of which was held in 1995 (see Table 7-2). Among other things, these multilateral conferences on women helped establish UN Women, a section of the United Nations focused on gender equality and the empowerment of women, which combined the UN Development Fund for Women (UNIFEM) and the Office of the Special Adviser on Gender Issues and Advancement of Women (OSAGI) and other efforts. By bringing together this mix of actors and stakeholders, conferences help create and sustain the regimes for specific issue areas and generate momentum toward solutions to multilateral problems.

7-3 INTERNATIONAL LAW: NORMS AND RULES WITHOUT CENTRAL AUTHORITY

>> 7-3 Describe the nature and functions of international law.

The second structure of cooperation that we want to consider is international law. According to Anne-Marie

track II diplomacy: the activities and involvement of private individuals, nongovernmental organizations such as civil society organizations, and religious and business leaders in dialogue and negotiation to facilitate conflict resolution.

conference diplomacy: large diplomatic meetings of many officials from states, international organizations, nongovernmental organizations, academia, and other non-state actors.

epistemic communities: networks of experts who bring their knowledge and expertise to the political arena to help policymakers understand problems, generate possible solutions, and evaluate policy success or failure.

Advocates for women's rights march

How might citizen groups affect international relations?

Salvatore Di Nolfi/Keystone via AP

TABLE 7-2

Conference Diplomacy and the World Conference on Women

CONFERENCE	LOCATION AND DATE	PARTICIPANTS	KEY RESULTS
First World Conference on Women	Mexico City, Mexico, June 1975	133 UN member states; about 4,000 NGO attendees and participants in parallel meeting	Establishment of a World Plan of Action and the UN Development Fund for Women
Second World Conference on Women	Copenhagen, Denmark, July 1980	145 UN member states; about 4,000 NGO attendees and participants in parallel meeting	Establishment of the Copenhagen Program for Action, stressing the need for attention to equal access to education, employment, and health care services; declared the UN Decade for Women
Third World Conference on Women	Nairobi, Kenya, July 1985	157 UN member states; 15,000 NGO representatives in parallel meeting	Adoption of the Nairobi Forward-Looking Strategies, stressing the eradication of violence against women and the promotion of peace and development
Fourth World Conference on Women	Beijing, China, September 1995	189 UN member states; 30,000 representatives from 2,500 NGOs in parallel meeting	Adoption of the Beijing Platform and the Beijing Declaration, identifying 12 areas of concern, including poverty, education, health care, violence, and inequality of economic and political opportunity
Fifth World Conference on Women	Originally targeted for 2015 but not completed	To be determined	To be determined

Slaughter (1995), **international law** "comprises all the law that regulates activity across and between territorial boundaries" (p. 516). Liberals and constructivists

have long stressed the development, application, and prospects of international law as a way to manage conflict and enhance security and trust among states. Realists, by contrast, tend to be very skeptical of the prospects—and even the desirability—of international law. Alternative theories such as Marxist explanations

international law: a body of rules that binds states and other agents in world politics in their relations with one another.

often see international law as a means that the rich and powerful use to structure the rules of the system for their own benefit. Understanding the role, promise, and problems of international law depends on understanding its nature, sources, and application.

7-3a The Nature of International Law

Beginning with the Dutch jurist Hugo Grotius—whose *On the Law of War and Peace* (1625) is widely regarded as the first book on international law (see the box "Spotlight On: The Just War Tradition and International Law")—international law was thought to hold great promise for the establishment of peace and justice in world politics. Yet one question we must take up right away is whether international law is really *law* at all. Some analysts, especially realists, like to place the term in quotation marks (i.e., "international law") to indicate that it is not really law as we understand the term. *Anarchy* does not mean chaos, but the anarchic nature of world politics means there are no central, authoritative institutions to make, enforce, and interpret laws that govern the members of the international system, unless the members themselves act. There is no international legislature to pass laws, and there is no international executive branch full of enforcement agencies to see that laws are obeyed. Furthermore, although a variety of courts have been established for the international system, none of them can compel compliance.

In short, international law is law in the absence of central authority, and that makes it different from domestic law. Liberal theorists acknowledge the impact of decentralization, but they stress the importance of international law for order and its influence on state behavior, often arguing that the vast majority of states choose to follow international norms and rules most of the time—just like most drivers slow down in school zones even when they can see that there are no police in sight. For realists, these characteristics make international law highly suspect and limited. In such a decentralized environment, they argue, adherence to norms and rules is driven by calculations of self-interest and capability, not legal obligation, so "international law" is really just a set of convenient practices that states have concluded serve their interests ... and that may be changed or ignored.

International law is also law in the absence of another factor that we commonly consider as part of law: shared values and principles. The great diversity in the perspectives, experiences, governments, characteristics, and cultures of the world's societies makes common values and principles hard to come by in world politics. A lot of international law has roots in European political thought, so it is not surprising that those from different cultures have occasionally questioned why such law should apply to them.

7-3b The Sources of International Law

So where does international law come from? Most scholars look to Article 38(1) of the modern-day World Court, or **International Court of Justice**, as the starting point on the sources of international law. According to this 1946 statute, international law comes from international conventions (treaties) agreed to by states, international custom, "general principles of law recognized by civilized nations," and judicial decisions and the writings of eminent jurists. Of these, the first two are understood as primary sources and the last two as secondary ones. Since 1946, the practices and decisions of international organizations such as the United Nations are also considered a fifth source of international law. Let's briefly review these sources and think carefully about how they influence the nature and application of international law—especially in terms of the consequences of anarchy, diversity, and complexity.

Treaties

The source of international law most comparable to legislation is treaties. A **treaty** is a formal, written agreement among states and is regarded as binding on the signatories. Indeed, a key principle of international law is *pacta sunt servanda*—or "the treaty must be served"—which holds that a formal agreement between states establishes legal obligations that should be upheld once made. Thousands and thousands of treaties and conventions exist, touching on practically every aspect of world politics, from ending wars (the Treaty of Versailles) to regulating fossil fuel emissions (the Paris Accords). However, states are not obligated to sign treaties, and the 1969 **Vienna Convention on the Law of Treaties** (yes, there is a treaty on treaties!) makes it clear that states that are forced to sign treaties are not obligated to uphold them. Thus, international anarchy and its corollaries—sovereignty and self-help—are seen in the voluntary nature of treaties, and the fact that only members of treaties and conventions are bound by them limits their scope. What are the implications for international law?

International Court of Justice: an international institution created in 1946 as part of the UN systems to apply international law to resolve conflicts brought voluntarily to it by states; also known as the *World Court*.

treaty: a formal, written agreement among states.

Vienna Convention on the Law of Treaties: a 1969 agreement among states defining the nature and obligations regarding treaties under international law.

The Just War Tradition and International Law

Hugo Grotius is often credited with being the father of international law, and one area to which he devoted a great deal of attention was the idea of rules for "just wars." Building on the philosophical and theological traditions and work of Augustine and Aquinas, Grotius set the just war tradition in international legal terms. Clearly tied to Western traditions and thought, including the moral arguments of philosophers and the Catholic Church, the development of international laws of war has long emphasized two questions: (a) *jus ad bellum*, or when the use of force is justified, and (b) *jus in bello*, or how wars should be fought once they have started.

The principles of *jus ad bellum*—which were and are the principal concern of international organizations such as the League of Nations and the United Nations in their efforts to keep the peace—emphasize such elements as just cause (*causa justa*, i.e., a case of aggression), competent authority (*auctoritas principis*, i.e., only duly constituted public authorities can decide to use force), right intention (*intentio recta*, i.e., the war must be waged for the purpose identified), last resort (i.e., other alternatives must be exhausted before the resort to war), and proportionality (i.e., the benefits expected from the war must equal or exceed the harm or evil to which it is a response). In recent years, the idea that the use of force should be authorized by the UN or another international organization to be legitimate has also gained significance.

The principles of *jus in bello*—which were the focus of efforts such as the Geneva and Hague Conventions (and treaties banning the use of chemical and biological weapons) to limit specific kinds of warfare and practices—stress the lawful ways in which combatants must behave during war. This aspect of the laws of war emphasizes such elements as distinguishing between combatants and noncombatants (i.e., force and violence should be directed only against combatants), proportionality/necessity (the level of force used should not be excessive and should be directed to the defeat of the military forces of the enemy, to limit unnecessary death and destruction), and fair treatment of enemy prisoners of war.

Hugo Grotius

Michiel van Mierevelt/Public domain/Wikimedia Commons

The development of the just war tradition in international law has also included attention to *jus post bellum*, or justice after war, which addresses post-conflict issues such as peace agreements and war crimes tribunals. Advocates such as philosopher Brian Orend argue that just war theory is incomplete without attention to what happens after wars end. ●

Recommended reading: Brian Orend, *War and International Justice* (Waterloo, ON, Canada: Wilfrid Laurier Press, 2001); and Michael Walzer, *Just and Unjust Wars* (New York: Basic Books, 1977).

Custom

Although treaties are probably the most significant source of international law in the contemporary context, historically most law derives from **custom**, which the World Court defined as "general practice [of states] accepted as law." Note that two things are present here: a general behavior *and* the idea that it is required (known as *opinio juris*). In effect, this source of international law indicates that law is what many states choose to do repeatedly over a period of time. For example, over time most states sharing a river as their boundary chose to mark their border at the midpoint of the river—or the midpoint of the deepest channel in the river where ships could navigate—as that location worked best for all

custom: the general practice of states accepted as law; a source of international law.

Myanmar's de facto leader, Aung Suu Kyi, testifying in 2019 at the International Court of Justice in a case filed by Gambia on the Rohingya genocide

What kinds of issues are most likely to come before the World Court?

International Court of Justice/ Handout/Anadolu Agency via Getty Images

concerned. This general practice eventually became the expected solution when future disputes over river boundaries arose. What are the consequences of a reliance on custom for the development and application of international law, especially given principles such as state sovereignty?

General Principles

The first auxiliary source of international law rests on the idea that evidence of a general practice among states (i.e., a custom) might be seen by identifying laws and practices that many states have adopted and enacted in their own societies. To the extent that many states have laws that look the same, such generally accepted and adopted laws suggest a custom and may form the basis for a treaty codifying the practices. For example, virtually all societies have national laws against assault, murder, or damaging the property of others, so international law recognizes these as general principles that should be respected internationally as well.

Court Decisions and Writings of Jurists

The second auxiliary source of international law points us to what other courts (both domestic and international) and legal experts (lawyers, judges, etc.) have identified as law in previous decisions and legal writing. For the most part, the court decisions involve those of international courts like the World Court or the European Court of Justice. However, in recent decades court decisions at the national or even local level have also been referenced. Indeed, the emerging principle of **universal jurisdiction**—most powerfully

and extensively developed in Europe—asserts that states themselves can prosecute violators of certain international laws even if the alleged violator is from another country.

A good example of this principle came in 1998, when former Chilean dictator Augusto Pinochet was indicted by a judge *in Spain* for human rights violations *in Chile* during his rule in the 1970s and 1980s. Pinochet was then arrested *in London* and was held for almost a year and a half as the British government engaged in legal proceedings and considered sending Pinochet to Spain for trial. Ultimately, the British government decided not to extradite Pinochet to Spain for trial (due to his poor health) and sent him home to Chile, where he was eventually indicted for human rights crimes in 2001. Pinochet died before legal proceedings could be completed, but this instance shows how a jurist's interpretation of international law can help shape it (we will discuss this idea more in Chapter 11).

Decisions of International Organizations

Although not mentioned in the World Court's statute, increasingly since 1946 the decisions of the most authoritative international organizations have also been considered sources of international law. For the most part, those decisions stem from the norms and

universal jurisdiction: the idea that states have a right and a duty to enforce international law when it comes to the most serious human rights abuses, such as genocide, crimes against humanity, torture, war crimes, extrajudicial killings, and forced disappearances, regardless of where these offenses may occur or whether or not the alleged violator is from another country.

principles embodied in the charters that establish such organizations, which member states sign when they join. In some ways, then, ensuing decisions—such as when the UN Security Council pronounces a judgment on state behavior or the World Trade Organization rules against a member state's trade practices—are more like interpretation and application of "treaty law," with the organization's charter as the treaty. However, such organizations also contribute to international law in at least three other ways. First, they interpret customary law and help shape what is regarded as custom and the legal obligations on states that stem from them. Second, they help develop norms and laws with their decisions and recommendations on what should be considered international law. Finally, there is considerable opportunity for international organizations to enter into poorly defined areas of international law to assert legal principles. Many of the more authoritative organizations—the UN Security Council again comes to mind—issue decisions that are partly applications and interpretations and partly assertions of principles.

Together, these sources provide the international community with the emerging and evolving norms and rules of international law. But how are these norms and rules enforced in a world without a central enforcer?

7-3c Compliance and Enforcement

Many observers quickly (and accurately) point out that most states uphold their obligations to most international laws most of the time and that such norms are important guides to and constraints on their behavior. Given that so much of international law emerges from custom and treaty, which states enter into voluntarily, this is not surprising. And to the extent that these norms and rules help states either manage or avoid disagreements and conflicts, international law is an important factor in cooperation. As liberals would assert, in an increasingly interdependent world in which states and other actors must interact regularly and extensively across many issues, international law contributes to orderly and predictable patterns that help guide behavior. Moreover, the principle of **reciprocity** leads most states to follow laws and conventions so that others will be more likely to do so as well. Indeed, it is easy to point to a whole host of matters—from mundane things like

international postal agreements and air traffic control to wealth- and prosperity-related issues involving trade, finance, and investment to international security matters involving border disputes, war, and violence—in which international norms, rules, and laws are central to successful (and peaceful) resolution of problems between states and societies. Too often, we take these things for granted, and, liberal theorists would say, the regular observance of international law in these matters is the norm for most states, most of the time.

However, realists might counter that it is not the "most of the time" that matters, but what happens when significant violations occur. As we have seen, most states do not attack other states most of the time. But what happens when one does? Most states may engage in fair trade practices most of the time. But what happens when a trade dispute does arise or a state is found to have violated a trade rule? And what about human rights issues? When violations of human rights standards occur in a given country, what enforcement occurs?

In general, the enforcement dilemma for international law follows closely on the challenges posed by anarchy, diversity, and complexity. Because central institutions are weak, the actors in world politics cannot rely on them for strong enforcement. That leaves three main avenues: national, horizontal, or vertical enforcement.

National Enforcement

States enforce some international law through their own national legal systems. In many such issues of **national enforcement**, national and local governments consider, and even integrate, international law into their rules and practices. Some states have integrated international law into their own national constitutions, either by revision or when they were initially drafted. For example, the Constitution of the United States declares that properly ratified treaties and conventions *are* the law of the land and therefore have the same status as any other law. And as we have seen, some states are aggressively advancing the principle of universal jurisdiction to use their national legal systems to apply key international legal principles.

Horizontal Enforcement

The most common approach is **horizontal enforcement**—those measures that states themselves can take to punish a state when it violates an international law. This enforcement approach is a direct function of the anarchic international system in which states are sovereign actors. States can protest diplomatically. They can threaten and enact a variety

---

reciprocity: in international law, the principle that a state follows international law so that others will do so in return.

national enforcement: states enforce some international law through their own national legal systems.

horizontal enforcement: those measures that states themselves can take when a state violates an international law and other states can attempt to punish the violator themselves.

The United States and the World Court

When are international institutions most likely and least likely to matter? Realists, liberals, constructivists, Marxists, feminists, and foreign policy theorists are all likely to have different answers to this question. Let's take a look at three examples of the World Court and cases involving the United States and consider what insights they offer on the role and influence of the World Court in practice. Remember, the US has regularly been a champion of the establishment of international courts and other organizations, but its relationship to them has been complex and highlights several key issues about the role and application of international law in world politics.

The United States and Iran, 1980

In the aftermath of the Iranian revolution, conflict between the United States and Iran escalated, and in late 1979, Iranian militants seized the US Embassy in Tehran, taking 66 Americans hostage. Although some were released, 52 Americans were held for 444 days by the Iranian government, which took control of the hostages from the militants soon after their capture. The United States protested and tried to gain the release of the Americans, including bringing the case to the World Court. In 1980, the World Court ruled that the hostage taking was a violation of international law and ordered the release of the hostages. Iran simply refused. The United States condemned Iran's decision and ratcheted up pressure, eventually attempting a military rescue mission that failed. The hostages were finally released in January 1981, on the same day that President Ronald Reagan took office, replacing Jimmy Carter.

The United States and Nicaragua, 1984

In the 1980s, the United States and Nicaragua were embroiled in a conflict stemming from the 1979 revolution in that country that overthrew longtime dictator and US ally Anastasio Somoza Debayle and replaced his regime with a leftist government led by the Sandinistas, a revolutionary movement that had spearheaded the rebellion against the Somoza regime. Concerned that a leftist regime with ties to Cuba and the Soviet Union would pose a threat to the Central American region, the United States soon took steps against the Sandinista regime, including organizing, equipping, and supporting the *Contras*, a counterrevolutionary movement composed largely of former Somoza supporters and disaffected Nicaraguan peasants, to fight against the new regime. In the course of this conflict, the United States engaged in the mining of Nicaraguan harbors to inflict damage on shipping. Nicaragua

charged the United States with violating international law in the harbor mining and what it characterized as aggression against Nicaragua and brought the complaint to the World Court.

The United States first argued that the World Court did not have jurisdiction and then argued that the United States was exercising its rights to self-defense. The World Court found in favor of Nicaragua and concluded that the United States had engaged in unlawful use of force in the mining and support for the Contras. It called on the United States to "cease and refrain" its unlawful use of force and to pay reparations to Nicaragua. The United States refused to comply, rejected the ruling, and promptly withdrew its acceptance of the World Court's compulsory jurisdiction. Subsequent efforts by Nicaragua to bring the World Court's judgment to the United Nations for support failed: The United States vetoed UN Security Council resolutions supporting Nicaragua several times in 1985 and 1986, and when the UN General Assembly voted 94 to 3 that the United States should comply with the court's ruling (only El Salvador and Israel joined the United States in opposing the resolution; on a subsequent resolution of the same nature, only Israel joined the United States), the United States ignored the resolution.

The United States and Iran, 1988

In 1988, the USS *Vincennes* shot down Iran Air Flight 655 in the Persian Gulf during the US naval operation to protect Kuwaiti oil transport and other shipping. All 290 people onboard were killed. Iran charged the United States with violations of international air traffic laws and took the case to the World Court. In 1989, the United States agreed to take part in the proceedings, in part to avoid appearing hypocritical at a time when it was arguing for broader international cooperation and reliance on international law and organizations for international conflict resolution. Seven years later, in 1996, the United States and Iran reached an agreement with the World Court's help to settle the dispute and end the case without the World Court's ruling. The United States agreed to pay $61.8 million to compensate the Iranian victims' families, but the settlement did not involve any admission or acceptance of legal guilt or responsibility.

Even more recent situations help illustrate the dilemmas underlying these cases. For example, the United States is a member (since ratification in 1990) of the international Convention Against Torture and Other Cruel, Inhuman or Degrading Treatment or Punishment. What do you

(Continued)

(Continued)

think would happen if the World Court concluded that the United States had violated international law through the aggressive interrogation procedures implemented in the post–September 11 war on terrorism? In 2018, in response to a World Court ruling against US applications of sanctions on Iran and a complaint brought to the World Court by the Palestinians protesting the move of the US embassy to Jerusalem, the Trump administration announced US withdrawal from two treaties—the 1955

Treaty of Amity (a US–Iranian agreement) and the compulsory settlement "optional protocol" to the 1961 Vienna Convention of Diplomatic Relations.

1. How might realists, liberals, constructivists, Marxists, feminists, and foreign policy theorists explain these cases and their outcomes?
2. What do these cases suggest about the enforcement of international law? ●

of economic sanctions (see Chapter 9 for a thorough discussion of this form of economic statecraft), such as boycotting or embargoing trade with the violator. They can even threaten or use force in a wide range of ways to punish the violator.

The problems with these horizontal mechanisms are pretty obvious and are a good reason why international law is not applied very evenly. If states themselves determine when a violation occurs, and what to do in response, that opens the door for highly selective application of law. Friends, allies, trading partners, and states with cultural ties might be protected by some states. For example, the United States proved reluctant to apply sanctions to South Africa in the 1970s and early 1980s in spite of the brutally repressive white minority apartheid regime that systematically violated the core human rights of the majority Black population, in part because of the perception of that country's strategic importance and economic ties (see the box "Theory in Action: The United States and the World Court").

Even the measures available to states in this horizontal approach are problematic. Diplomatic protests might be significant for small issues, but for major issues involving security, they are likely to be too weak. For example, diplomatic protests did not stop the Russian annexation of Crimea or further incursions into eastern Ukraine, and they did little to prevent the Assad regime in Syria from attacking its own people. As we detail in Chapter 9, economic sanctions are problematic; research suggests they rarely work, and they impose costs on the sanctioning state itself as well as on ordinary citizens in the target state. Using the military to enforce international law is costly, and most states do not have the capacity for doing so. That means the world depends on the most powerful countries for such actions, and those countries may have other interests at stake that lead them

to avoid military intervention in some instances that would appear to warrant it. Finally, to the extent that horizontal enforcement is likely to work, it is most effective when the measures are broadly enacted by a relatively large multilateral coalition. Given the great diversity of interests, linkages, and capabilities, assembling such a coalition is difficult to achieve.

Vertical Enforcement

There are international institutions that enforce international law from the top down. However, because of the anarchic character of the international system, few international institutions have the authority and/or capability to enforce international law against violators, which are often states. **Vertical enforcement** is thus rare, and, instead, most international institutions are limited to identifying and condemning violations and recommending or authorizing the member states of the organizations to take actions to enforce a rule or punish a violator. For example, members of the United Nations sign a charter to gain membership, and when they violate principles of the charter, their actions can be discussed in the UN General Assembly, which can call for actions by other members in response. The UN Security Council can also consider alleged violations and authorize punitive actions such as sanctions and even the application of military force. In both cases, however, member states themselves must agree to take up the measures and may choose not to do so. You can imagine how important the relative power and interests of individual states can be in these instances.

International courts also play a role, although generally not much like the courts with which we are familiar. The International Court of Justice, or World Court, which we discussed earlier, is a 15-judge panel located in The Hague, Netherlands, that hears cases on disputes between states (but only between states, and only states can bring cases). The judgments of the World Court are supposed to be binding. However, the World Court does not have **compulsory jurisdiction**; both parties to a dispute must voluntarily submit the

vertical enforcement: the enforcement of international law by international institutions.

compulsory jurisdiction: in international law, the condition in which parties to a dispute must submit the case to a court.

The Marshall Islands, International Law, and the World Court

In 2014, the Marshall Islands, a small state in the Pacific Ocean with a population around 50,000 (about the same size as Sheboygan, Wisconsin), sued nine other states in the World Court for violating the nonproliferation regime and Nonproliferation Treaty (NPT; see Chapter 6). This island state was the site of almost six dozen nuclear tests in the 12 years after World War II, the results of which caused long-term harm to its citizens and territory. According to the foreign minister of the Marshall Islands, "Our people have suffered the catastrophic and irreparable damage of these weapons, and we vow to fight so that no one else on earth will ever again experience these atrocities."

Nuclear test at the Bikini Atoll, Marshall Islands, 1954

What chance does tiny Marshall Islands have to win a case in the World Court against countries like the United States, the United Kingdom, France, Russia, China, India, Pakistan, Israel, and North Korea?

Courtesy of the US Department of Defense

According to the Marshall Islands, as signatories of the NPT, the United States, the United Kingdom, France, Russia, and China—the official nuclear weapons states of the treaty—were obligated to work toward nuclear disarmament by Article VI of the treaty. The Marshall Islands also brought the case against India, Pakistan, North Korea, and Israel for violating what the Marshall Islands characterized as customary international law against acquiring nuclear weapons. The court documents filed in the cases assert that "the long delay in fulfilling the obligations enshrined in article VI of the NPT constitutes a flagrant denial of human justice."

India, Pakistan, Israel, and North Korea are not signatories of the NPT. Moreover, only the UK, India, and Pakistan have accepted the compulsory jurisdiction of the World Court (Borger 2014; Keating 2014). The US, France, Russia, China, North Korea, and Israel did not respond to or acknowledge the case brought by the Marshall Islands. India, Pakistan, and the UK appeared before the court to answer to the complaint in April 2016. Eventually, the World Court ruled in the fall of 2016 that no legal dispute between the Marshall Islands and these three existed and dismissed the suit on procedural grounds, concluding that it did not have jurisdiction to rule on the matter (Lui 2016).

1. Why do you think the Marshall Islands would choose to go to the World Court to achieve its goals on this matter?

2. What do you think of the results?

3. What does this example suggest about the nature of international law and its enforcement? ●

case to the court before it can act. When the court does render a judgment, it relies on the members themselves to agree to implement it as well. From its establishment right after World War II until mid-2017, the World Court rendered decisions in less than 150 cases . . . in total. Think about that for a moment: It should tell you something about the court's role and the constraints it faces. For further consideration, see the box "Foreign Policy in Perspective: The Marshall Islands, International Law, and the World Court."

Most other international courts are limited by the same issues already highlighted. Regional organizations such as the Organization of American States (in the Western Hemisphere) and the African Union have courts whose operations are much like the World Court. The European Court of Justice, by contrast, which is the highest court of the European Union and interprets EU laws for all member states, is much more authoritative. Another example is the International Criminal Court (ICC), which we discuss in detail in Chapter 11. The ICC exists to try individuals (not states) accused of committing aggression, genocide, war crimes, and crimes against humanity. Specialized international courts also exist to help interpret and apply international law. Examples include the World Trade Organization Dispute Settlement Body; the International Tribunal on the Law of the Sea; and special tribunals established for conflicts in the former Yugoslavia, Rwanda, Cambodia, Lebanon, and Sierra Leone.

7-4 INTERNATIONAL ORGANIZATIONS: THE EUROPEAN UNION, THE UNITED NATIONS, AND MANY OTHERS

>> **7-4   Evaluate the nature and functions of international organizations.**

Our second structure of cooperation is international organizations (IOs). Let's consider the nature and role of IOs and reflect on why sovereign states—which tend to guard their sovereignty and independence so jealously—would establish international institutions in the first place. Then, we will review the types of IOs that exist, with some brief examples. We will conclude this section with a short evaluation of the United Nations and its role and functions in fostering cooperation.

7-4a Why Do International Organizations Exist?

Why would independent states in an anarchic world establish international institutions that constrain their independence and freedom? According to the *Yearbook of International Organizations*, there are well over 6,000 IOs (not including nongovernmental organizations), which include institutions like the United Nations, the World Trade Organization, and many other more specialized bodies like the International Labor Organization and the World Health Organization. This is a large number in a world that is supposedly dominated by just under 200 independent states. Understanding why they exist is contentious, and multiple perspectives and arguments have been offered. For analytical purposes, we can organize the arguments into two categories: power-based explanations and problem-based explanations.

Power-Based Explanations

One set of arguments stresses that IOs reflect state interests and, in particular, the interests of the most powerful states. For example, both realist and Marxist-based approaches to world politics like world systems theory argue that powerful states create IOs to support norms and practices that advance their interests and channel other states into behavior that the powerful prefer. Realists stress self-interested states, while Marxist-based approaches stress economic elites and the interests of powerful capitalist states, but the common core of the argument is that such states sponsor IOs to control and constrain the behavior of others. The example of the United States and the World Court nicely illustrates this dynamic: The United States supported the World Court when its interests were served in the case of the Iranian hostage crisis but ignored it in the Nicaraguan harbor mining and Iranian airliner cases when its interests were not served. Liberal approaches also offer power-based arguments—often contending that powerful states establish IOs to serve very broad interests in order and stability, while sacrificing narrower and more specific outcomes and bearing the costs of providing some "public goods" for the benefit of all (and themselves, of course; Bull 1977). Less powerful states also attempt to establish or steer IOs toward protecting and asserting their interests, relying on their ability to outnumber powerful states in voting procedures within existing IOs to redirect and create new IOs (Ikenberry 2000).

Problem-Based Explanations

Another perspective focuses on the common problems faced by states and other actors in world politics. These arguments—usually offered by liberal and constructivist theorists—emphasize the need and desire among states and others to cooperate to address problems together in order to expand benefits and reduce conflict. A good example of this argument is the one we discussed in Chapter 6 when we described theories of functionalism and neo-functionalism and the promotion of transnational cooperation on economic and social problems that grow to link societies together (Krasner 1985). In the context of this chapter, IOs are established to enable specific technical cooperation on economic and social issues that build linkages and shared interests among societies. The benefits from these linkages and the cooperation they promote often expand to more areas, leading to even greater cooperation and institutional connections

(Mitrany 1966). As we said in Chapter 6, a good example of this can be seen in the development of the European Union and the various institutions it now involves.

Another example of this explanation focuses on the presence of transnational problems that transcend state boundaries and cannot be addressed by the actions of any one state. The need to address such issues—like those of the environment, disease, and others—leads states to establish IOs to help coordinate their efforts more effectively and efficiently. Think about the role played by the World Health Organization during the 2020 COVID-19 global pandemic, for example. We might also include arguments that center on the need to cooperate to provide and sustain collective goods. In Chapter 12, we discuss the concept of "the tragedy of the commons," in which common resources (like the oceans) are susceptible to abuse or overuse, in which case IOs may help states share and preserve such resources or refrain from short-sighted exploitation in favor of longer-term calculations. In any of these cases, the bottom line is that states have reasons to cooperate and manage conflicts and that, once established, the IOs that are created take on lives of their own and influence and channel state behavior.

The Roles and Functions of International Organizations

There are strengths and weaknesses to both power-based and problem-based explanations by themselves. Together, however, these arguments suggest a range of roles and functions for IOs as structures and institutions for cooperation and conflict management. Thus, IOs

- Serve as instruments for states to advance their interests and influence other states to play the game of world politics according to the rules and interests of the powerful

- Serve as forums for states to communicate, negotiate, and advance their interests and may even provide support for bargaining and negotiation in third-party diplomacy

- Generate and disseminate information and technical expertise

- Regularize interactions and habits of behavior on issues and facilitate national and transnational linkages and networks that contribute even further to norms of procedure and behavior

- Coordinate and pool resources to address common problems

- Contribute to the generation of and institutionalization of norms and rules

- Reduce uncertainty, enhance communication and interactions, and reduce the incentives for cheating in world politics

- Constrain state behavior and expand avenues for punishment

In short, IOs perform many different roles and functions in the contemporary system.

7-4b Types of International Organizations

With as many as 6,000 IOs in the world today, we cannot identify and discuss them all. In this section, we categorize types of organizations and provide examples of each. In the remainder of the chapter, we discuss some of the most prominent examples of IOs, with particular attention devoted to two of the most important IOs in world politics: the European Union, the most powerful regional IO; and the United Nations, the most expansive global, multipurpose IO.

Type I: Scope and Membership

One good way to develop a sense of IOs is to categorize them according to scope (or the range of issues they address) and membership (or who is eligible to join them). For scope, a simple distinction we can make is between IOs that address multiple issues across the political, economic, and social spheres and those that address just a single issue. In terms of membership, we can simply distinguish between IOs that allow any state to join (global) and those that restrict membership on the basis of geographic region (regional). If we combine these two dimensions, we get the categories shown in Table 7-3. Let's take up each with some examples.

First, there are a wide variety of *global, single-issue* IOs that include members from all over the world but concentrate on a single issue. Examples of these include the International Monetary Fund, which emphasizes balance of payments and financial matters, and the World Trade Organization, which addresses the trade relations and trade practices among its members. Many other such IOs exist for issues related to the environment, global health, human rights, nuclear energy, and a great variety of other things.

Second, there are many *regional, single-issue IOs*. A common issue on which such IOs focus is economic cooperation, and APEC, or Asia-Pacific Economic Cooperation, is a good example of this type of IO. In fact, a large number of the regions and

TABLE 7-3

A Typology of International Organizations

MEMBERSHIP	SCOPE	
	SINGLE-ISSUE	MULTIPLE-ISSUE
Global	International Monetary Fund World Bank World Trade Organization	United Nations
Regional	Andean Common Market European Environment Agency Inter-American Institute for Cooperation on Agriculture Asia-Pacific Economic Cooperation	European Union Organization of American States African Union Association of Southeast Asian Nations

even subregions of the world (the Andean Common Market illustrates a subregional IO of this type) have some kind of economic organization to promote trade and economic integration. The example mentioned—the Andean Common Market—is a customs union for Bolivia, Ecuador, Colombia, and Peru. Just as for global IOs of this type, regional, single-issue IOs exist for the environment, global health, human rights, nuclear energy, and a great variety of other things.

Third, *regional, multiple-issue organizations* are also on the rise. Perhaps the best and most powerful example of these is the European Union (see Map 7-1 and our more detailed discussion in the next section). The EU unites 27 European countries in an economic, social, and political organization characterized by a common market and currency (for 19 of its members), with central political and economic institutions such as the European Parliament, the Council of the

European Union, the European Council, the European Commission, the European Court of Justice, and the European Central Bank. Other regional, multiple-issue IOs include the Association of Southeast Asian Nations (ASEAN) and the Economic Community of Western African States (ECOWAS). Like the EU, many of this type of IO began as regional, single-issue IOs (economic) and have expanded into other issue areas.

Fourth, the most obvious *global, multiple-issue IO* is the United Nations, which addresses virtually every issue that can be imagined in world politics in one way or another. We discuss the UN and its subsidiaries more thoroughly later in this chapter.

Type II: Decision Process

Another way to distinguish IOs is according to how they make their decisions. This not only highlights some important differences but also lends itself to some insights on the role, influence, and impact of different kinds of IOs. For the purpose of analysis, we can distinguish between three decision processes: majority rule, weighted voting, and unit veto, which has two subtypes.

Majority Rule Some IOs make their decisions on the basis of simple or modified **majority rule**, with the results depending purely on the numbers. A good example of this is the UN General Assembly, in which all member states have equal representation and each state has one vote. On any given issue, the majority rules (a two-thirds threshold is required for issues related to peace and security, new members, and the peacekeeping budget). Not surprisingly, this decision rule is generally favored by less powerful states such as those of the developing world, for the simple fact that they outnumber the powerful and wealthy. So, for example, in 1974, developing states (known as the Group of 77, or G-77 then) used the UN General Assembly to pass the Declaration on the Establishment of a New International Economic Order, designed to give greater control and advantage to developing states in economic relationships like trade, finance, aid, and investment. Not surprisingly, developed states opposed this resolution. IOs with majority voting rules are often used to establish new IOs or subsidiaries that reflect the interests of the majority as well.

Weighted Voting Other IOs adopt a **weighted voting** decision rule, in which member votes are weighted according to size, power, wealth, or the like. This provides greater control and influence to those countries that have a greater role or responsibility, bear greater burdens for providing resources, or just have more power. A good example is the **International Monetary Fund (IMF)**. All members of the IMF are

---

majority rule: in international organizations, a decision process that relies on voting with one vote per member, in which gaining a majority of the votes prevails.

weighted voting: in international organizations, a decision rule in which member votes are weighted according to some factor related to size, power, or wealth.

International Monetary Fund (IMF): one of the Bretton Woods organizations created in 1946 to help maintain a cooperative international financial system. The IMF helps countries facing balance-of-payments problems with short-term loans and also helps countries reschedule their debt.

MAP 7-1

The European Union

What benefits does membership in the EU provide to the countries of Europe?

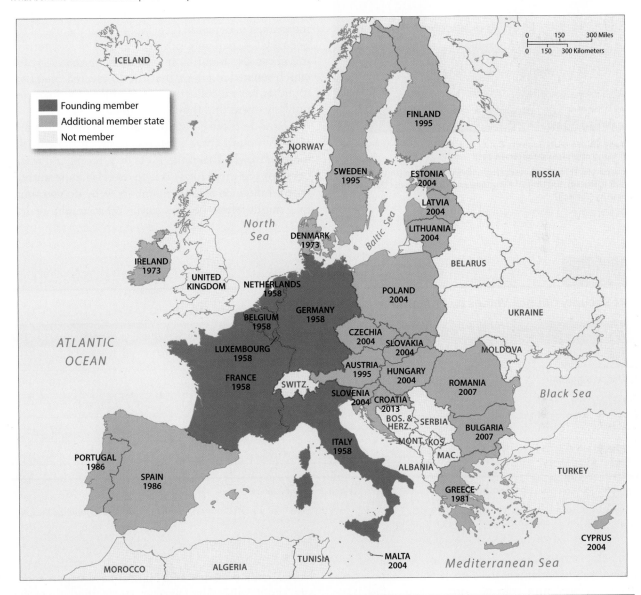

Source: European Union, "EU Member Countries in Brief," http://europa.eu/about-eu/countries/member-countries/index_en.htm.

represented but are assigned a share of the vote based on the size of their contribution—or quota—to the IMF's lending capital (which is, in turn, based on the size of the country's economy). France and the United Kingdom, for example, each have about 4.0% of the votes, Japan has about 6.2%, and Germany has about 5.3%. China has about 6.0%, but the United States has about 16.5% of the vote, the largest share. Contrast these percentages with, say, Sierra Leone, which has less than 0.1% of the vote, Chile, which has about 0.4%, or Brazil, which has about 2.2%. It is also worth noting that the IMF usually requires a 70% majority for aid

and financing decisions and an 85% majority for major decisions, such as those involving IMF decision-making processes, which means the United States can block the latter all on its own.

Unit Veto In IOs with a **unit veto** decision rule, some or all members can block decisions with their votes. As US President Abraham Lincoln is reported to have

unit veto: in international organizations, a decision rule in which some or all members can block decisions with their votes. In a pure unit veto decision rule, every member exercises a veto; in a modified unit veto, only some members have the veto power.

Russia vetoes a UN Security Council resolution condemning Syria for using chemical weapons in 2017

How do you think the possession of the veto by the United States, France, Russia, the United Kingdom, and China affects the UN Security Council?

Albin Lohr-Jones/Pacific Press/LightRocket via Getty Images

members—the United States, Russia, China, France, and the United Kingdom—are permanent. These **P5** (or Perm-5, as they are often known) are the main founders of the UN and the world's first official nuclear weapons states, and each possesses a veto so that if any one votes against a substantive Security Council measure, it is defeated (see Table 7-4 on the use of the Security Council veto power). Passage of substantive measures also requires at least nine affirmative votes, which means, in effect, that the 10 elected members together have a collective veto to block the P5 in the unlikely event that they are unified.

How do these categorizations help us understand IOs? Although there are exceptions, in general the more narrowly drawn the IO is (e.g., scope and membership), the more likely it is to exercise more authoritative influence over its members. Why do you think this might often be the case? What might realist,

---

TABLE 7-4

UN Security Council Vetoes by P5 Members, 1946–2019

COUNTRY	1946–1959	1960–1969	1970–1979	1980–1989	1990–2000	2001–2019
United States	0	0	21	42	5	14
United Kingdom	2	1	12	14	0	0
France	2	0	7	7	0	0
Russia	66	14	6	4	2	27
China*	0	0	1	0	2	14

Source: Data compiled from Security Council Veto List. http://research.un.org/en/docs/sc/quick.

*China's seat on the UN Security Council was held by Taiwan from 1949 to 1971 before the UN General Assembly voted to recognize the People's Republic of China (mainland) as the lawful representative of China.

---

once said, "Gentleman, the vote is 15–1 . . . the 1 prevails." A pure unit veto decision rule requires unanimity, so every member effectively exercises a veto. This was the case in the League of Nations, the forerunner to the United Nations. A modified unit veto assigns the veto power to some members of the IO. The best example of this decision rule is the UN Security Council, which is made up of 15 members. Ten of those members are elected by the UN General Assembly (with regional allocations for Africa, Latin America, Asia, Europe, Eastern Europe, and "other areas") for two-year terms, and each of these members has one vote in the UN Security Council. The other five

liberal, constructivist, and Marxist-based approaches say about this? Also, weaker states tend to prefer majoritarian IOs, while more powerful states tend to prefer IOs with weighted or unit veto systems. Finally, in general the most authoritative IOs in the world today—the ones whose decisions are the most binding on their members—tend to be less representative and less egalitarian in their decision schemes. The UN General Assembly, for example, is the most representative IO in the world and makes its decisions on majority voting, but its measures are very rarely binding. The UN Security Council, which includes less than 10% of the world's member states and is dominated by the P5, is among the most powerful and authoritative. Again, consider why you think this is the case and what realist, liberal, constructivist, and Marxist-based approaches might offer as explanations.

P5 (or Perm-5): the five permanent members of the UN Security Council—the United States, the United Kingdom, France, China, and Russia—each of which holds veto power.

FIGURE 7-2

The World Bank Group

Source: Reproduced with the permission of the Department of Finance, 2017 https://www.fin.gc.ca/bretwood/bretwd17-eng.asp.

7-4c Key International Organizations in World Politics

With these ways of distinguishing between IOs in mind, let's briefly summarize some of the major international organizations.

The International Monetary Fund (IMF) The IMF was established at the end of World War II as part of the Bretton Woods system of international financial organizations to improve cooperation and coordination of the world's economy. This 189-member global, single-issue organization has weighted voting and originally served two purposes: (a) as a source of emergency lending for countries with balance-of-payments crises, with loans drawn from the pooled resources of IMF member states, and (b) as an exchange rate regime in which member currencies were pegged within a small range of fluctuation to the value of the US dollar, which itself was fixed at the value of $35 per ounce of gold. To achieve the first purpose, the IMF granted short-term loans to aid countries with financial crises with conditions typically attached to guide liberal reforms in recipient states. The IMF's exchange rate regime ended in 1971 when the US unilaterally suspended the fixed exchange rate of the dollar, starting a floating exchange rate system that continues today. Since its existence, the IMF has also served as a kind of global economy watchdog, collecting and disseminating economic information about member states and the world economy to facilitate planning and coordination. IMF activity in this arena became more public beginning in the 1990s.

The World Bank Also part of the Bretton Woods system, the **World Bank** is actually a group of five institutions (see Figure 7-2) created to provide long-term developmental loans to members. The World Bank is also a global, single-issue institution with 189 members, and its voting power is weighted by member contributions, which are based on member states' economies. In 2020, the most powerful members (in terms of their voting weight) were the US (15.44%), Japan (7.76%), China (4.78%), Germany (4.08%), the UK (3.80%), France (3.80%), India (2.95%), Canada (2.85%), Saudi Arabia (2.69%), Russia (2.69%), and Italy (2.57%). The main emphasis of the World Bank's lending activities is poverty reduction and sustainable development.

The World Trade Organization (WTO) In 1995, the WTO replaced the General Agreement on Tariffs and Trade (GATT), which sought to promote free trade but lacked enforcement powers for its decisions. Unlike the IMF and the World Bank, the WTO operates in a consensus-oriented fashion, rather than a weighted voting system, with each of the current 164 (as of 2020) member states having an equal voice. However, states with the largest economies set the WTO's agenda.

Like its predecessor, the WTO promotes trade liberalization through **most-favored nation (MFN)**

World Bank: a Bretton Woods organization created in 1945 that provides loans and grants to countries for long-term development. The World Bank started by helping fund the reconstruction of Europe after World War II and later focused on helping countries in the developing world grow their economies.

most-favored nation (MFN): the trade status that members of the GATT gave to each other, ensuring that each received the best trade terms available. MFN could also be granted to nonmembers if a country chose to do so.

status (in the United States, MFN is now referred to as NTR, or normal trade relations). Each member is required to give all other members the lowest tariff rate available—this rate was considered the MFN rate. The key to the WTO is its enforcement powers over free-trade rules and practices. Basically, if one state blocks another state from selling its products, the two states can go to the Dispute Settlement Body—effectively a "trade court"—and the WTO will determine if a rule is being broken. If the trade barrier is illegal under WTO rules, then the plaintiff state is permitted to sanction the other state to regain the revenue lost by not being able to sell its goods and services.

Since its establishment in 1995, the WTO has heard more than 525 trade disputes. In 2017, for example, Qatar brought complaints against Saudi Arabia, Bahrain, and the United Arab Emirates on issues related to intellectual property rights and trade in goods and services; the US brought complaints against China (subsidies for aluminum production) and Canada (wine sales); Russia brought complaints against Ukraine (restrictions of trade and transit) and the European Union (trade measures targeted at Russian steel); Brazil brought complaints against Canada (aircraft sales); and Costa Rica brought complaints against Mexico (avocados). In short, the WTO has the ability to write rules, administer them, adjudicate disputes, and penalize those who break the rules—effectively enforcing the agreements GATT could only hope were accepted voluntarily.

However, since 2017, the US has blocked appointment of members of the WTO's dispute settlement body. In December 2019, it thus suspended its operations because it did not have sufficient members to perform its functions. As a consequence, one of the most authoritative international organizations was hamstrung, and the international governance of world trade was left without an independent adjudicator for the world trading system.

Examples of Regional Single-Issue Organizations In the last several decades of the 20th century, many regional organizations focused on particular issues were established. As noted, one area for the growth of such organizations is economic cooperation, with the Andean Common Market, which we discussed earlier, as an example. Another good example in the category of economic cooperation is the 21-member Asia-Pacific Economic Cooperation (APEC), established in 1989 to foster economic growth, strengthen the Asia-Pacific community, and reduce tariffs and other trade barriers across the Asia-Pacific region. There are many, many other regional organizations focused on different issues as well, far too many to summarize here. Two illustrations identified in Table 7-3 highlight this area,

however. The Inter-American Institute for Cooperation on Agriculture was originally established in 1942 to promote the development, coordination, and expansion of regional agricultural production and trade in the Western Hemisphere. In the last decades of the 20th century, it expanded to 33 states in the region and increasingly concentrated on sustainable agricultural development. The European Environment Agency serves as another example, but in a different way, because this agency was created within the European Union, a much larger, regional, multiple-issue organization. Established in 1990, the European Environment Agency began its activities in 1993–1994, providing information and coordinating the efforts of EU members to pursue environmental safety and environmentally sustainable economic development.

Examples of General Regional Organizations Our last category includes broad, regionally based organizations that address a wide scope of issues. Regionalism, typically defined by geographic proximity and interdependence among a specific group of states (as well as non-state actors), seeks to foster cooperation among such players for their mutual benefit. In the latter 20th and early 21st centuries, regional organizations became increasingly important in world politics. There are a variety of such IOs, with different degrees of development, scope, influence, and authority.

In the Middle East, regional organizations are the least developed, despite the unifying ties of language, ethnicity, and religion, and only two deserve serious mention. The League of Arab States was created in 1945 to promote and foster Arab unity, but its role has been very limited. Its main body is a council formed of the foreign ministers of its member states, which now includes 22 countries (although Syria has been suspended since 2011 because of its actions in its civil war). The Gulf Cooperation Council (GCC) was established in 1981 and includes the six Arab states of the Persian Gulf region: Bahrain, Kuwait, Qatar, Saudi Arabia, Oman, and the United Arab Emirates. The GCC was created to promote economic cooperation among its members but also as a response to the threat posed by Iran after the Shi'a Iranian revolution.

In Asia, in addition to APEC (discussed earlier), there is the Association of Southeast Asian Nations (ASEAN), which currently has 10 member states. Very decentralized and more informal than other regional organizations, ASEAN stresses consultation, coordination, and consensus-building, and it also hosts the ASEAN Regional Forum (ARF) to promote cooperative security in Asia, which now includes 28 members (including the EU, the United States, Russia, India, China, Canada, and others).

In Africa, the great diversity of the continent's peoples and states has worked against strong regional organizations. The African Union (AU) has 55 current members and has the goal of becoming as unified as the EU at some point. One interesting aspect of the AU is its Pan-African Parliament, mostly as a consultative body, to which each member sends five legislators (one of which must be a woman). The AU also created the Economic, Social and Cultural Council; the African Court of Justice; the African Central Bank; the African Monetary Fund; and the African Investment Bank. Africa is so large that it is not surprising to find that subregional organizations have also been established, including the Economic Community of West African States (ECOWAS) and the Southern African Development Community (SADC) as well.

The oldest regional IO in the Western Hemisphere is the Organization of American States (OAS), which now includes all 35 countries from North, Central, and South America and the Caribbean. Located in Washington, DC, the OAS includes a General Assembly, a Permanent Council, and an Inter-American Council for Integral Development (all of which are one state–one vote, majority institutions); a secretariat to handle day-to-day activities; an Inter-American Court of Human Rights; and an Inter-American Development Bank. The OAS also has a number of specialized agencies that address health, gender, and cultural matters, among other things. The role of the OAS has expanded since the end of the Cold War, moving from US-dominated efforts to resist communism to a greater variety of roles in conflict resolution, support for democracy and human rights, and other activities. The Western Hemisphere also has a number of subregional organizations, mostly geared toward economic cooperation. These include the United States–Mexico–Canada Agreement (the USMCA, formerly the North American Free Trade Agreement, or NAFTA), the Common Market of the South (MERCOSUR), the Andean Common Market (discussed earlier), the Central American Common Market (CACM), and the Caribbean Community (CARICOM).

7-4d The European Union: The Most Powerful Regional Organization

The European Union is the largest, most developed, and most authoritative multiple-issue regional organization in the world. No other regional organization even comes close. Why do you think Europe has had so much more success than other regions in building a regional organization? After all, this was the location of regular and bloody wars among its major states for hundreds of years.

Political science scholars Margaret Karns and Karen Mingst (2010) suggest that regionalism fundamentally requires deliberate policy choices by leaders but is also heavily influenced by other factors. The most important of these are basic power dynamics among the states of the region; common identities, based on such things as culture, religion, historical experiences, common ideology, and even common external threats; regime types, with similar governments more likely to be able cooperate; economic connections and interdependence; and perhaps even similar economic systems and levels of development. Let's keep these factors in mind as we consider the origins, development, structures, and roles of the European Union.

Origins and Foundations of the European Union After centuries of war, culminating in the devastation of World War II that left much of the continent of Europe in ruin, European leaders began to try to build regional institutions that would unite their countries in cooperative structures that would help them work together and avoid such costly wars in the future. Driven by the ideas of functionalism, developed by people like David Mitrany and Jean Monnet, who argued that relatively small, practical steps toward integration could "build peace in pieces," European leaders took steps to build the habits and practices of cooperation. Monnet, often regarded as "the father of Europe" for his contributions to European integration, helped develop the first serious step toward a united Europe, the 1950 Schuman Plan, named for French Foreign Minister Robert Schuman, to create the European Coal and Steel Community (ECSC). In 1951, the ECSC came into being with six original members, establishing a common market centered on the trade of French coal and German steel, thus uniting two central antagonists of World Wars I and II through trade and commerce. Its creators not only hoped to foster economic growth and cooperation; they were also driven by their views of the pacifying effects of trade to try to "make war not only unthinkable but materially impossible," as Schuman put it. In this way, what is now the European Union was born.

The Development of the European Union The European Union of today grew slowly from the ECSC, as its founders intended. In 1957, the Treaty of Rome established the European Economic Community (EEC), which began in 1958, for the six members of the ECSC to deepen economic integration and create a broader common market for goods and services beyond coal and steel. Fifteen years later, in 1973, the EEC expanded, with longtime holdout United Kingdom joining with Ireland and Denmark to become members of the community.

Further political development ensued. In the mid-1980s, Greece (1985), Spain, and Portugal (1986) joined the European Community, and the member states also pushed their integration forward with the Single European Act, which finished the creation of the common market and laid the foundations for the broadening and deepening of European integration after the Cold War's end.

What we know now as the European Union emerged in 1992 with the conclusion of the Maastricht Treaty, which not only strengthened European political and legal structures (broad areas of economic and social policy, labor, and citizenship) but also laid the groundwork for the single European currency—the euro—to be used by member states, replacing their own national currencies. The Maastricht Treaty also established the Common Foreign and Security Policy (CFSP), to foster more cooperation and coordination of members' foreign and defense policies. Austria, Finland, and Sweden joined the EU in 1995, bringing membership to 15.

The EU continued to broaden and deepen after Maastricht. The treaties of Amsterdam (1997), Nice (2003), and Lisbon (2007) all strengthened EU institutions and regional democratic practices. The EU also continued to expand, this time to the east to include members from Eastern Europe for the first time. In 2004, 10 new states—Cyprus, Czech Republic, Estonia, Hungary, Latvia, Lithuania, Malta, Poland, Slovak Republic, and Slovenia—joined the EU. Romania and Bulgaria followed in 2008, and Croatia joined in 2013. The EU now has 27 members spanning Western and Eastern Europe. (In 2020, one member—the United Kingdom—completed the process of leaving the EU initiated after a 2016 national referendum.) Furthermore, the euro was successfully introduced on January 1, 1999, replacing the national currencies of 19 of the EU members—the so-called Eurozone, consisting of Austria, Belgium, Cyprus, Estonia, Finland, France, Germany, Greece, Ireland, Italy, Latvia, Lithuania, Luxembourg, Malta, the Netherlands, Portugal, Slovakia, Slovenia, and Spain.

Structure and Operations Although the EU today has many agencies and sub-agencies that attend to a

....

European Commission (EC): the executive branch of the EU. The Commission is led by a president; it has budgetary powers; and it includes 27 members that oversee policy development in agriculture, trade, social policy, the environment, and other areas.

European Council: the EU body made up of the heads of government of the EU member states, who represent the interests of their member states within the EU.

Council of Ministers (CoM): the EU legislative body made up of sitting ministers of their national governments, who represent their member states and approve all EU legislation.

European Parliament (EP): the EU legislative body made up of directly elected representatives; it amends, approves, or rejects EU laws, together with the Council of Ministers.

broad array of matters (see Figure 7-3), the organization's structure revolves around five main institutions with executive, legislative, and judicial functions. The most powerful institution is the **European Commission (EC)**, which is basically the executive branch of the EU. The Commission is a supranational institution, meaning that it has powers above and beyond the member states. It has its own budgetary powers, which gives it substantial independence from member-state pressures, and its purpose is to represent the interests of the European Union as a whole, not any individual member states. The 27-member (one from each member-state) Commission is headed by a president (in 2020, Germany's Ursula von der Leyen) and oversees policy development in agriculture, trade, social policy, the environment, and other areas. Each office or portfolio in the Commission is led by an individual from a different EU member country, and the president of the Commission (not the member states themselves) appoints these individuals.

The **European Council** is made up of the heads of government of the EU member states, who come together collectively at EU Summits twice every six months (more frequently if needed) to represent the interests of their member states within the EU. As you might expect, these meeting are well publicized, and the European Council is perhaps the most visible of the EU institutions. In reality, though, it has little executive or legislative power over EU policy, mostly serving as an advisory and agenda-setting body.

The legislative institutions of the EU include the Council of Ministers and the European Parliament. The **Council of Ministers (CoM)**, more formally the Council of the European Union, is the more powerful of the two and can be seen as an "upper house," like the US Senate. Council membership varies depending on the issue at hand: When defense and security matters are on the agenda, member states send their defense ministers; when foreign affairs are at hand, foreign ministers attend; if the issue is economic, finance ministers show up. No matter who attends, when the CoM meets, its members represent their member states and are themselves members of their national governments. Any and all EU legislation must be approved by the CoM. Most of the time, the European Parliament must also approve legislation (see Figure 7-3), but in some instances the CoM has exclusive legislative authority and the parliament can serve only in an advisory function. Thus, the CoM is widely regarded as the more powerful of the two legislative institutions, though attempts to democratize the EU by extending the powers of the parliament have increasingly been made.

The **European Parliament (EP)** is the second of the two legislative institutions and is often seen as the "lower house," like the House of Representatives

FIGURE 7-3

Major Parts and Functions of the EU

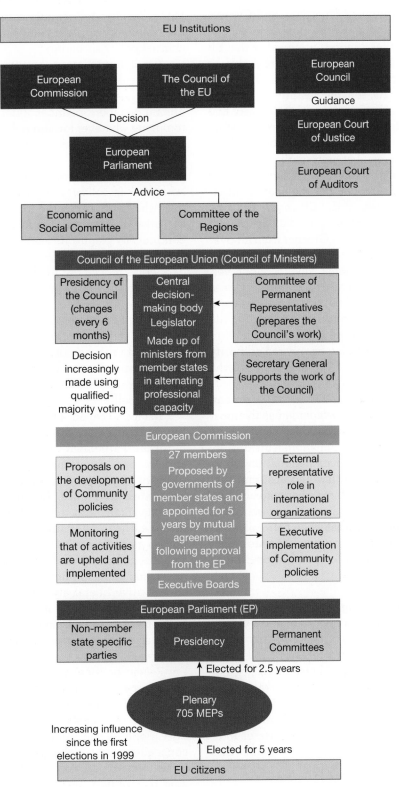

in the United States (see Figure 7-3). The 2007 Lisbon Treaty fixed EP seats at 751, but seats were reapportioned after the UK's exit in 2020. Now, 705 seats are allocated proportionally according to population. Germany has the most seats (96), and Cyprus, Malta, and Luxembourg have the minimum (6; see Figure 7-4). All of these representatives to the EP are directly elected, so the parliament is regarded as the most democratic of the EU institutions. No other regional IO—or any IO, for that matter—has such a body with real authority. Elections are held every five years (since 1979), and citizens in each member state directly elect their representatives, who serve only in the EP (not in their member-state parliaments) and are elected to serve the interests of European citizens and the EU as a whole, not the specific interests of their home states. In the EP, representatives sit with fellow members of their political parties (e.g., Conservative, Social Democrat, Greens) from all over Europe, not with other representatives from their home countries. The parliament amends, approves, or rejects EU laws, together with the CoM, in areas such as consumer protection, the single market, workers' rights, asylum and immigration, agriculture, the environment, and animal welfare, but not in foreign and defense policy. The EP also has shared authority over the EU budget (with the CoM) and oversees the European Commission.

The judicial branch of the EU is the **European Court of Justice (ECJ)**, widely regarded as the most powerful and successful international court of its kind. The ECJ is truly a supranational institution; its rulings take precedence over national law. It is charged with interpreting EU law and ensuring that it is applied equally across all member states. There is one judge for each member state. The power of the ECJ is illustrated by the fact that when national law is seen to be in violation of EU law, member states must change their national laws to come into compliance with EU law.

Contributions and Challenges The role of the EU in European politics is evolving constantly. As its founders hoped, the EU has broadened and deepened over the decades since World War II, and peace and cooperation among its members is a reality, not a dream. Even former enemies such as France and Germany now see themselves as partners in a zone of peace. Furthermore, member states have come to see their interests collectively, not just as those of individual states. European citizens still see themselves

as French, German, Italian, and so on, but they also have developed a common identity as Europeans. Today, the EU controls the monetary policy of most of its members, and no member state in the Eurozone has monetary policy autonomy. Politically, integration is not as deep, and member states still enjoy substantial policy autonomy.

Challenges remain, though. Although the EU has tried to enhance common foreign and defense policy and has had some success harmonizing policy among members, member states enjoy the full power to pursue whatever foreign policies they prefer. Thus, in the face of challenges such as terrorism, the Iraq War, Iranian nuclear proliferation, and responding to Russian assertiveness and intervention, the EU has struggled to follow a common approach. Disputes over whether to widen the EU even further, especially to Turkey or Ukraine, and relations with the US also continue to plague its members. Economically, the Great Recession of 2008–2010 and the 2009 European debt crisis rocked the EU and led to disenchantment in the public over the costs and outcomes of integration as the EU responded to severe budget deficits in Greece and other member states' financial bailouts to shore up and revive their economies. This led some economists to warn that the monetary union of the EU could not survive without fiscal integration, as a single currency without a single fiscal policy cannot sustain itself.

In fact, so-called "Eurosceptics" question the EU's future. In the May 2014 European elections to the European Parliament, many observers were shocked and worried about the significant gains made by right-wing, generally anti-EU parties in many member states. In France, for instance, the right-wing National Front won the election with almost 25% of the vote (the most of any party), and other right-wing parties gained seats in the UK, Denmark, and Austria. In subsequent national elections, right-wing parties also made gains in numerous EU states. Mainstream conservative, liberal, and centrist parties still hold the majority in the EP and most EU member states, but these results caused many EU supporters to worry about a possible change in public opinion and political power.

Recent political events in several countries have amplified these concerns. Clearly, the most consequential of these was the UK's "Brexit." Fueled by fears over the impact of the EU's migration and refugee policies and more general concerns over the consequences of globalization and EU integration, British voters outside major urban centers overpowered the support for the EU from Northern Ireland, Scotland, and the London urban area and cast their ballots to begin the lengthy and difficult process of exiting the EU.

....

European Court of Justice (ECJ): the EU's judicial branch whose rulings take precedence over even national law; it is charged with interpreting EU law and ensuring that it is applied equally across all member states.

FIGURE 7-4

European Parliament Seats per Country, January 2020

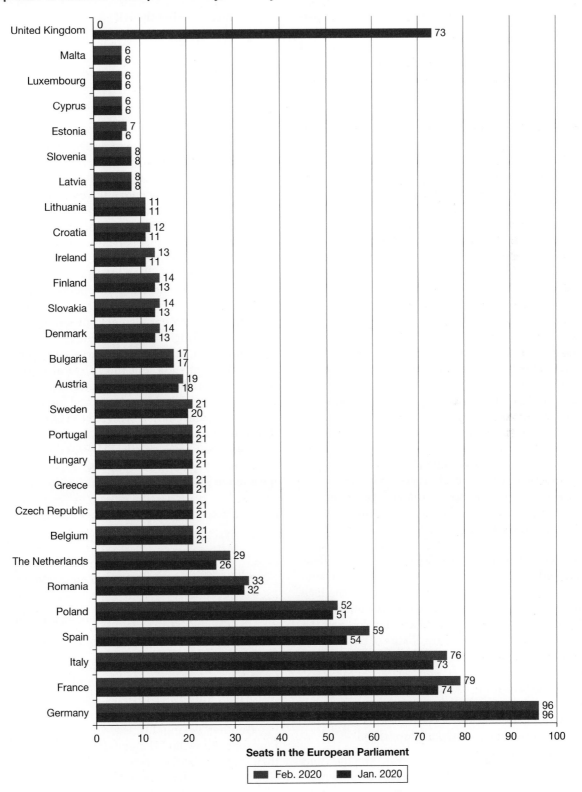

Source: © European Parliament https://www.europarl.europa.eu/news/en/press-room/20200130IPR71407/redistribution-of-seats-in-the-european-parliament-after-brexit.

Rising concerns about the prospect of other EU members leaving the EU grew in the aftermath of the UK vote, especially for the Netherlands, France, Italy, and Poland, where right-wing anti-EU parties showed considerable strength. Since 2015, a series of competitive elections across Europe demonstrated growing support for these nationalist parties, including record high successes in France, Germany, Austria, and others. Right-wing nationalist candidates lost in key elections for their country's leadership in France, Austria, and the Netherlands, and in Germany Angela Merkel won a fourth term, although the far-right was much more successful at the polls than expected.

However, elsewhere in the EU, the authoritarian turn accelerated, fueled by a combination of concerns about disenfranchisement, being on the losing side of globalization, and the disruption of familiar social orders caused by immigration and other factors. EU members Poland, Hungary, and Greece highlight the disturbing trend, and some observers also point to "democratic deficits" and the structures and policies of the EU itself as problematic for addressing this development. As Keleman (2020) noted,

> the EU has in recent years shown itself to be a hospitable environment for the emergence of increasingly autocratic member governments. . . . First, the EU's . . . ingrained reluctance to interfere in the domestic politics of its member states help shield national autocrats from EU intervention. Second, funding and investment from the EU helps sustain these regimes. Third, the free movement of persons in the EU facilitates the exit of dissatisfied citizens, which depletes the opposition and generates remittances, thereby helping these regimes endure. (p. 481)

As a consequence, the EU's future is now murkier than ever before. In 2017, the European Commission contemplated a range of potential futures in the face of the challenges facing the EU and its member states. Reflecting far greater uncertainty and division over the future, in its "White Paper on the Future of Europe," the European Commission (2017) outlined five futures:

- "Carrying on" by deepening single-market integration and foreign/defense cooperation, with national control over other matters; other areas would be nationally governed.

- "Nothing but the single market," emphasizing deepening certain key aspects of single-market integration without further integration and coordination on other political, social, security, or defense/foreign policy matters.

- "Those who want more do more," in which members would move to greater integration at different rates and levels, without needing approval of the EU-27 (leaders from all EU members but the UK).

- "Doing less more efficiently," in which the EU would focus on priorities in trade and core elements of the single market, security, migration, and the management of borders and defense, leaving other economic and social matters for local control.

- "Doing much more together," in which the EU would push for further integration and work in as many policy areas as possible, taking steps to share more power, resources, and decision making and expanding cooperation among members across all areas.

At the EU's Rome Summit in 2017, the EU-27 issued a statement calling attention to the contributions of the EU to the economic, political, and social well-being of its members and region. This important post-Brexit statement also acknowledged key challenges, including elevating issues such as migration, terrorism, and rule of law to a more prominent place on the agenda. But the EU-27 also expressed support for further integration, strengthening of the single market and the Eurozone, and foreign/defense cooperation and commitment to NATO, among other things to maintain the EU.

Two years later, at the EU Brussels Summit in 2019, the European Council (2019) approved a strategic agenda for 2019–2024, focusing on four priorities:

- Protecting citizens and freedoms

- Developing a strong and vibrant economic base

- Building a climate-neutral, green, fair, and social Europe

- Promoting European interests and values on the global stage

The first of these again stressed steps to control borders, illegal immigration and refugee flows, terrorism, and other threats like cyber-activities, disasters, and disease.

Another vexing EU issue is the future of the Eurozone. Allowing EU members using the euro to set their own fiscal policy means wealthier members (like Germany) may have to continue bailing out poorer members that pile up national debt (like Greece and possibly Italy, Spain, or Portugal). Switching to a single, centralized fiscal policy for all Eurozone members

Can Europe Unite?

Recently European states have faced a number of challenges that raise the question as to how united Europe is—or possibly can be. When many other factors are stripped away, the role of geography must be acknowledged as part of the drivers of intra-European tension.

FIGURE 7-5

COVID-19 GDP Forecast for European Union

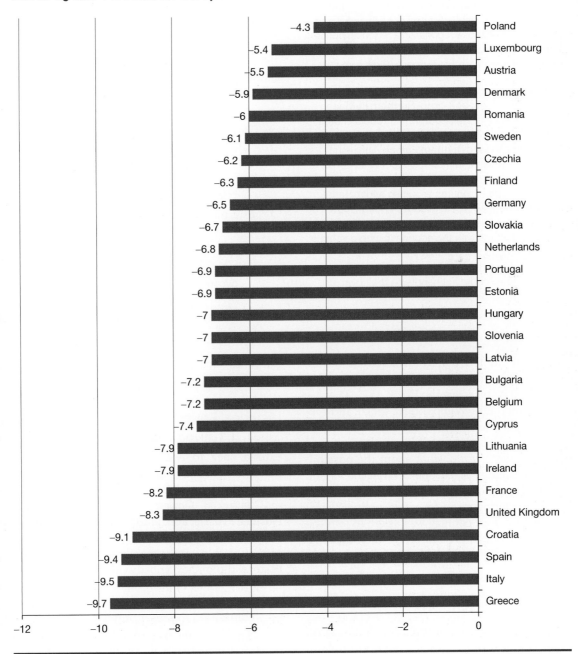

Source: Data from European Union, 2020.

(Continued)

(Continued)

Despite the historical trajectory of the European Union pulling Europeans together, geography may be pulling them apart. In addition to the unique position of the UK as an island state and the tensions that led to its Brexit, both east–west and north–south tensions exist. East–west tensions have flared recently over whether and how to accommodate the flood of migrants fleeing Middle East violence. To get to wealthier and more welcoming states like Germany or Sweden, migrants often pass through poorer states like Greece, Macedonia, and Hungary, and their passage through Eastern Europe put a financial and a cultural strain on those regimes. Macedonian police tried and failed to stop the migrants, as did a fence put up by Hungary for that purpose (Birnbaum 2015).

North–south tensions in Europe flared following the Great Recession of 2008–2010. Northern European states are wealthier than southern European states in part because, historically, it took less land and fewer people to feed northern Europe. The result was excess human and material capital that could spur economic development. Poorer-quality land in southern Europe meant more human and material capital was needed just to produce enough food. The result is that northern European states like Germany, France, and others with the economic wherewithal were called on to bail out states with fragile economies like Greece, Portugal, and Spain from the debt crises they could not handle on their own.

The COVID-19 pandemic in 2020 further revealed such tensions (see Figure 7-5). As Europe suffered from the spread of the disease, member states in the south like Italy and Spain, which suffered greater harm to their people and their economies, pushed for a more extensive EU-wide recovery program, while others from the north like Germany, the Netherlands, and Austria, which suffered less harm, were reluctant to support plans that would require them to foot the bill.

Finally, there's the unique case of the UK. As an island state, the British long held the rest of Europe at arms-length. They were part of Europe but not totally. The British were latecomers in joining the EU, refused to give up their own currency to join the Eurozone, and then became the first state to leave the EU.

1. Will the EU be able to handle the strains of European migration—particularly in Eastern Europe?

2. Can wealthier European states be counted on to bail out poorer ones?

3. Is the British departure from the EU surprising?

4. How might realists, liberals, constructivists, Marxists, and feminists explain these dynamics? ●

would solve that problem but, by further eroding state sovereignty, might create more Brexit situations in which frustrated states leave the EU.

What do you think? Will political, social, and economic challenges lead to further reversals for the EU? Given the changes in the distribution of power and leadership in today's world, what about the possibility of a "United States of Europe"? What forces and factors might lead to one outcome or the other? What would these scenarios mean for world politics? How would you vote if your country was asked to join the EU? Now, have a look at "The Revenge of Geography: Can Europe Unite?" and think about the questions it poses.

7-4e The United Nations

Let's conclude our discussion of IOs by focusing on the United Nations, which offers a good example of the nature, roles, influence, and challenges facing the structures and institutions of cooperation and conflict management. We'll consider its background,

purposes, structure, and roles in peace/security and other areas of world politics.

Historical Foundations of the United Nations

Although the UN was established in 1945, its roots extend back to two international institutions from the 19th and early 20th centuries. The first is the Concert of Europe (1815–1854), which we introduced in Chapter 6. Composed of Great Britain, Russia, Austria, Prussia, and, in 1818, France, the concert was a multilateral organization established in the Congress of Vienna to promote stability, cooperation, and multilateral diplomacy (mostly informal) and to help sustain the balance of power after the Napoleonic Wars. It did not include minor powers and was fundamentally committed to preserving the status quo.

The Crimean War of 1854 resulted in the collapse of the Concert of Europe, and the next historical precursor to the UN did not appear until the end of World War I (1914–1918). In the wake of that war's devastation, the Treaty of Versailles produced the

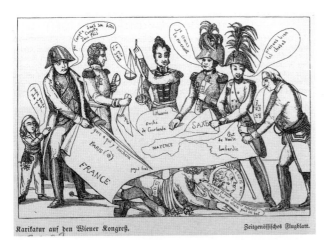

Members of the Concert of Europe argue over a map of Europe

How do you think the exclusion of minor powers affected the Concert of Europe? Could a different organization have stopped it?

Bettmann/Getty Images

The League of Nations meets to consider German rearmament in 1935

Why did the League of Nations fail to check aggression before World War II?

AP Photo/Staff/Putnam

League of Nations, an IO dedicated to collective security (see Chapter 6) and the resolution of disputes between states. The League of Nations began with 32 members (ironically, not the United States, which had been the prime instigator of the idea in the first place) and grew to include 57 members by 1938, on the eve of World War II. A General Assembly included all members, and a League Council consisted of great powers as permanent members, with a few smaller powers regularly rotating membership. As we discussed in Chapter 6, the central focus of the League of Nations was collective security, but it proved unable to meet the challenges of that task. Its members had difficulty defining aggression and enlisting the support of great powers to counter it when it did not directly involve them. Further, the League Council's requirement for unanimous decisions prevented it from responding to the aggression by Germany, Italy, and Japan that caused World War II.

Enter the United Nations

Thus, the **United Nations (UN)** did not emerge from scratch after World War II. Many of its features have their origins in the Concert of Europe and the League of Nations. World War II was still underway when diplomats from many countries, led by the United States and United Kingdom, began work on the new organization. Its name derives from US President Franklin D. Roosevelt's 1942 description of the 26 states cooperating to fight the Axis powers as the "united nations." Fifty-one countries joined and drafted the UN Charter in San Francisco in 1945 (see "Spotlight On: The Basic Purposes of the UN"). When the countries that would

be the P5 of the UN Security Council and a majority of the remaining signatories ratified the charter, the UN was born in October 1945. Shortly after that, the League of Nations officially disbanded.

Although the UN shared its predecessor's emphasis on peace and security, it was designed to be a broader IO from the start. The UN Charter identifies its main purposes as peace and security, the development of friendly relations and harmony among nations, and cooperation on international problems. It also embraces the sovereign equality of all states and restricts the UN from interfering in the domestic jurisdiction of its members.

The UN is a universal IO, with all states entitled to membership once they sign and ratify the UN Charter. From the original 51 members, the UN grew to its current membership of 193 countries, driven by the decolonization of Africa, Asia, and the Middle East during its first three decades and then the post–Cold War emergence of independent states primarily from the former Soviet Union and Eastern/Central Europe. Once they join, member states participate in an extensive IO, which has its headquarters in New York City and major offices in Geneva (Switzerland), Vienna (Austria), and Nairobi (Kenya). The UN also has regional commissions and specialized agencies located throughout the world.

....

League of Nations: an international institution created after World War I for collective security and the resolution of disputes between states.

United Nations (UN): an international institution established after World War II to promote peace and security, the development of friendly relations and harmony among nations, and cooperation on international problems.

The Basic Purposes of the UN

According to Chapter 1, Article 1 of the UN Charter, the new IO formed after World War II had four main purposes:

Article I

The Purposes of the United Nations are:

1. *To maintain international peace and security*, and to that end: to take effective collective measures for the prevention and removal of threats to the peace, and for the suppression of acts of aggression or other breaches of the peace, and to bring about by peaceful means, and in conformity with the principles of justice and international law, adjustment or settlement of international disputes or situations which might lead to a breach of the peace;

2. *To develop friendly relations among nations* based on respect for the principle of equal rights and self-determination of peoples, and to take other appropriate measures to strengthen universal peace;

3. *To achieve international co-operation in solving international problems of an economic, social, cultural, or humanitarian character*, and in promoting and encouraging respect for human rights and for fundamental freedoms for all without distinction as to race, sex, language, or religion; and

4. *To be a centre for harmonizing the actions of nations* in the attainment of these common ends.

Article II

The Organization and its Members, in pursuit of the Purposes stated in Article I, shall act in accordance with the following Principles.

1. The Organization is based on the principle of the *sovereign equality of all its Members.*

2. All Members, in order to ensure to all of them the rights and benefits resulting from membership, *shall fulfill in good faith the obligations* assumed by them in accordance with the present Charter.

3. *All Members shall settle their international disputes by peaceful means* in such a manner that international peace and security, and justice, are not endangered.

4. All Members shall *refrain in their international relations from the threat or use of force against the territorial integrity or political independence of any state*, or in any other manner inconsistent with the Purposes of the United Nations.

5. All Members shall *give the United Nations every assistance in any action it takes* in accordance with the present Charter, and shall refrain from giving assistance to any state against which the United Nations is taking preventive or enforcement action.

6. The *Organization shall ensure that states which are not Members of the United Nations act in accordance with these Principles* so far as may be necessary for the maintenance of international peace and security.

7. *Nothing contained in the present Charter shall authorize the United Nations to intervene in matters which are essentially within the domestic jurisdiction of any state* or shall require the Members to submit such matters to settlement under the present Charter; but this principle shall not prejudice the application of enforcement measures under Chapter VII.

It is interesting to see the broad scope envisioned for the United Nations. Please have a look at the full UN Charter at http://www.un.org/en/charter-united-nations/index.html. ●

The Structure of the United Nations

As Figure 7-6 shows, there are six principal organs of the UN, each of which has its distinctive nature and role to meet the UN's basic purposes. Let's briefly summarize each of them, although even a brief look at Figure 7-6 indicates that we will not be able to describe every piece and sub-piece.

The UN General Assembly (UNGA) As described earlier, the **UN General Assembly (UNGA)** is the plenary body of the UN, so all UN members have a seat in the assembly. It functions on a one state–one vote, majority-rule principle (with a two-thirds majority required for some issues), and it is the central

UN General Assembly (UNGA): the plenary body of the UN in which all UN members have a seat. Functioning on a majority-rule decision process, it is the central forum for discussion of global issues.

FIGURE 7-6

The Structure and Institutions of the United Nations

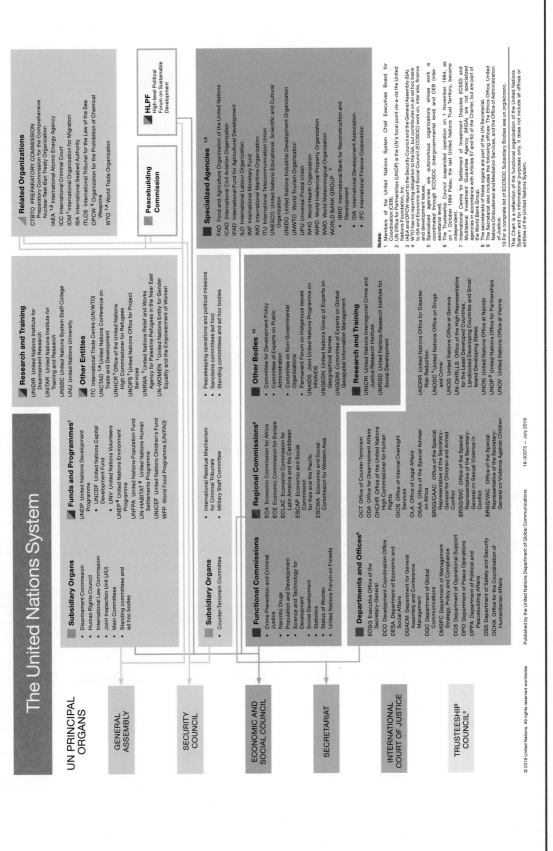

The United Nations System

UN PRINCIPAL ORGANS

GENERAL ASSEMBLY

Subsidiary Organs
- Disarmament Commission
- Human Rights Council
- International Law Commission
- Joint Inspection Unit (JIU)
- Main Committees
- Standing committees and ad hoc bodies

Funds and Programmes¹
- UNDP United Nations Development Programme
  - UNCDF United Nations Capital Development Fund
  - UNV United Nations Volunteers
- UNEP⁸ United Nations Environment Programme
- UNFPA United Nations Population Fund
- UN-HABITAT⁸ United Nations Human Settlements Programme
- UNICEF United Nations Children's Fund
- WFP World Food Programme (UN/FAO)

Research and Training
- UNIDIR United Nations Institute for Disarmament Research
- UNITAR United Nations Institute for Training and Research
- UNSSC United Nations System Staff College
- UNU United Nations University

Other Entities
- ITC International Trade Centre (UN/WTO)
- UNCTAD ¹,⁸ United Nations Conference on Trade and Development
- UNHCR ¹ Office of the United Nations High Commissioner for Refugees
- UNOPS ¹ United Nations Office for Project Services
- UNRWA ¹ United Nations Relief and Works Agency for Palestine Refugees in the Near East
- UN-WOMEN ¹ United Nations Entity for Gender Equality and the Empowerment of Women

Related Organizations
- CTBTO PREPARATORY COMMISSION Preparatory Commission for the Comprehensive Nuclear-Test-Ban Treaty Organization
- IAEA ¹,³ International Atomic Energy Agency
- ICC International Criminal Court.
- IOM ¹ International Organization for Migration
- ISA International Seabed Authority
- ITLOS International Tribunal for the Law of the Sea
- OPCW ³ Organization for the Prohibition of Chemical Weapons
- WTO ¹,⁴ World Trade Organization

HLPF
High-level Political Forum on Sustainable Development

SECURITY COUNCIL

Subsidiary Organs
- Counter-Terrorism Committee
- International Residual Mechanism for Criminal Tribunals
- Military Staff Committee
- Peacekeeping operations and political missions
- Sanctions committees (ad hoc)
- Standing committees and ad hoc bodies

Peacebuilding Commission

ECONOMIC AND SOCIAL COUNCIL

Functional Commissions
- Crime Prevention and Criminal Justice
- Narcotic Drugs
- Population and Development
- Science and Technology for Development
- Social Development
- Statistics
- Status of Women
- United Nations Forum on Forests

Regional Commissions⁹
- ECA Economic Commission for Africa
- ECE Economic Commission for Europe
- ECLAC Economic Commission for Latin America and the Caribbean
- ESCAP Economic and Social Commission for Asia and the Pacific
- ESCWA Economic and Social Commission for Western Asia

Other Bodies ¹⁰
- Committee for Development Policy
- Committee of Experts on Public Administration
- Committee on Non-Governmental Organizations
- Permanent Forum on Indigenous Issues
- UNAIDS Joint United Nations Programme on HIV/AIDS
- UNGEGN United Nations Group of Experts on Geographical Names
- UNGGIM Committee of Experts on Global Geospatial Information Management

Research and Training
- UNICRI United Nations Interregional Crime and Justice Research Institute
- UNRISD United Nations Research Institute for Social Development

Specialized Agencies ¹,⁵
- FAO Food and Agriculture Organization of the United Nations
- ICAO International Civil Aviation Organization
- IFAD International Fund for Agricultural Development
- ILO International Labour Organization
- IMF International Monetary Fund
- IMO International Maritime Organization
- ITU International Telecommunication Union
- UNESCO United Nations Educational, Scientific and Cultural Organization
- UNIDO United Nations Industrial Development Organization
- UNWTO World Tourism Organization
- UPU Universal Postal Union
- WHO World Health Organization
- WIPO World Intellectual Property Organization
- WMO World Meteorological Organization
- WORLD BANK GROUP ⁷
  - IBRD International Bank for Reconstruction and Development
  - IDA International Development Association
  - IFC International Finance Corporation

SECRETARIAT

Departments and Offices⁹
- EOSG Executive Office of the Secretary-General
- DCO Development Coordination Office
- DESA Department of Economic and Social Affairs
- DGACM Department for General Assembly and Conference Management
- DGC Department of Global Communications
- DMSPC Department of Management Strategy, Policy and Compliance
- DOS Department of Operational Support
- DPO Department of Peace Operations
- DPPA Department of Political and Peacebuilding Affairs
- DSS Department of Safety and Security
- OCHA Office for the Coordination of Humanitarian Affairs
- OCT Office of Counter-Terrorism
- ODA Office for Disarmament Affairs
- OHCHR Office of the United Nations High Commissioner for Human Rights
- OIOS Office of Internal Oversight Services
- OLA Office of Legal Affairs
- OSAA Office of the Special Adviser on Africa
- SRSG/CAAC Office of the Special Representative of the Secretary-General for Children and Armed Conflict
- SRSG/SVC Office of the Special Representative of the Secretary-General on Sexual Violence in Conflict
- SRSG/VAC Office of the Special Representative of the Secretary-General on Violence Against Children
- UNDRR United Nations Office for Disaster Risk Reduction
- UNODC United Nations Office on Drugs and Crime
- UNOG United Nations Office at Geneva
- UN-OHRLLS Office of the High Representative for the Least Developed Countries, Landlocked Developing Countries and Small Island Developing States
- UNON United Nations Office at Nairobi
- UNOP ⁹ United Nations Office for Partnerships
- UNOV United Nations Office at Vienna

INTERNATIONAL COURT OF JUSTICE

TRUSTEESHIP COUNCIL⁶

Notes:
1 Members of the United Nations System Chief Executives Board for Coordination (CEB).
2 UN Office for Partnerships (UNOP) is the UN's focal point vis-a-vis the United Nations Foundation, Inc.
3 IAEA and OPCW report to the Security Council and the General Assembly (GA).
4 WTO has no reporting obligation to the GA, but contributes on an ad hoc basis to GA and Economic and Social Council (ECOSOC) work on, inter alia, finance and development issues.
5 Specialized agencies are autonomous organizations whose work is coordinated through ECOSOC (intergovernmental level) and CEB (inter-secretariat level).
6 The Trusteeship Council suspended operation on 1 November 1994, as on 1 October 1994 Palau, the last United Nations Trust Territory, became independent.
7 International Centre for Settlement of Investment Disputes (ICSID) and Multilateral Investment Guarantee Agency (MIGA) are not specialized agencies in accordance with Articles 57 and 63 of the Charter, but are part of the World Bank Group.
8 The secretariats of these organs are part of the UN Secretariat.
9 The Secretariat also includes the following offices: The Ethics Office, United Nations Ombudsman and Mediation Services, and the Office of Administration of Justice.
10 For a complete list of ECOSOC Subsidiary Bodies see un.org/ecosoc.

This Chart is a reflection of the functional organization of the United Nations System and for informational purposes only. It does not include all offices or entities of the United Nations System.

© 2019 United Nations. All rights reserved worldwide   Published by the United Nations Department of Global Communications   19-00073 – July 2019

Source: From The United Nations System Chart © (2019) United Nations. Reprinted with the permission of the United Nations.

forum for discussion of global issues. As less-developed countries gained numerical dominance, the UNGA began to reflect the perspectives and priorities of those countries, as it offered the smallest countries in the world their most important diplomatic opportunities. The UNGA may debate any issue that arises under the UN Charter, and its work is achieved mostly through its wide range of committees that operate year-round. The UNGA meets formally each year in September, where it typically takes up 300 or so resolutions for discussion and voting and when member states make presentations and speeches.

The opening ceremony of the 2019 United Nations meetings
What do you think are the UN's primary contributions in world politics?
REUTERS/Lucas Jackson

The UN Security Council (UNSC) As described earlier, the **UN Security Council (UNSC)** is a 15-member council that carries the primary UN responsibilities for peace, security, and collective security operations. It can meet at any time it is deemed necessary and holds meetings each year in conjunction with the UNGA meetings as well. Operating via the P5 veto system discussed earlier, the UNSC is entitled to investigate any dispute it considers important for international peace and security, and UN members can bring issues to the UNSC as well. The Cold War largely froze the UNSC, with the United States and the Soviet Union taking turns blocking most of its potential operations. Since the Cold War ended, it has been more active, and it engages in a range of efforts, including resolutions condemning specific behavior, efforts to mediate conflicts before they erupt, authorizing sanctions against states deemed to violate the peace, dispatching peacekeeping forces and establishing cease-fires to provide opportunities for conflict resolution, and authorizing military action against aggressors (see Chapter 6 for more on the UN, collective security, and peacekeeping).

The Secretariat The **UN Secretariat** is basically the UN's bureaucracy—its major administrative arm. Employing almost 38,000 staff in New York and around the world, the Secretariat manages and administers the activities authorized by the UNGA and the UNSC. As suggested by the entries in Figure 7-6, the Secretariat covers a wide range of functions, from

peacekeeping operations and humanitarian issues to public information and facilities safety.

The Secretariat is directed by the **UN Secretary-General**, a very high-profile figure elected by the UNGA at the recommendation of the UNSC who serves a five-year term. There have been nine UN Secretaries-General since 1946. Each has brought a distinctive style and agenda, but all have been men (see Table 7-5 for the names and dates of these leaders). The UN Secretary-General enjoys some discretion in administering the UN budget and can

UN Security Council (UNSC): a 15-member council that carries the primary UN responsibilities for peace, security, and collective security operations.

UN Secretariat: the bureaucracy and administrative arm of the UN.

UN Secretary-General: the head of the UN Secretariat; the UN's administrative leader elected by the UNGA at the recommendation of the UNSC.

TABLE 7-5

UN Secretaries-General

UN SECRETARY-GENERAL	COUNTRY	YEARS IN OFFICE
Gladwyn Jebb	United Kingdom	1945–1946
Trygve Lie	Norway	1946–1952
Dag Hammarskjöld	Sweden	1953–1961
U Thant	Burma	1961–1971
Kurt Waldheim	Austria	1972–1981
Javier Perez de Cuellar	Peru	1982–1991
Boutros Boutros-Ghali	Egypt	1992–1996
Kofi Annan	Ghana	1997–2006
Ban Ki-moon	South Korea	2007–2016
António Guterres	Portugal	2017–present

Who Pays for All of This, Anyway?

The 2020 budget for the United Nations was about $3.1 billion for its core activities and all those of its special programs for development, social, educational, environmental, and humanitarian purposes around the world. In addition, the UN peacekeeping and security budget added $6.5 billion. This is clearly a broad global mandate to cover with less than $10 billion, and when one remembers that the entire US federal budget is about $5 *trillion* (or approximately 300 times the budget of the UN), the limits of the UN budget are even more obvious. Still, where does the UN funding come from?

The UN budget comes from two main sources. First, all member states are assessed dues, based on the relative size of their gross domestic product, which make up the core budget. These dues range from 0.001% of the budget to 22%. The top figure used to be 25% but was adjusted down at the insistence of the United States in 2000 (the United States is the only state paying the top rate). Currently, the top dues-providers are the United States at 22%, China at 12.005%, Japan at 8.564%, and Germany at 6.09%. Additional special assessments are also made for all UN peace and security operations based on a similar formula, but the five permanent members of the UN Security Council are also responsible for an additional surcharge (that veto power has its price). Thus, the US share of the security and peacekeeping assessment is 27.89% of the $6.5 billion in this category (China and Japan follow, with 15.22% and 8.56%, respectively). Second, for the specialized programs, voluntary contributions from member states provide the budget, which means that available funds may vary considerably for these programs.

According to the UN Charter, payment of dues is obligatory. In Chapter IV, the Charter states:

A Member of the United Nations which is in arrears in the payment of its financial contributions to the Organization shall have no vote in the General Assembly if the amount of its arrears equals or exceeds the amount of the contributions due from it for the preceding two full years. The General Assembly may, nevertheless, permit such a Member to vote if it is satisfied that the failure to pay is due to conditions beyond the control of the Member.

In 2019, the UN claimed that its members were about $2 billion in arrears. For 2020, five countries were in arrears (Central African Republic, Comoros, São Tomé and Príncipe, Somalia, and Venezuela). Central African Republic and Venezuela had their voting privileges suspended.

Historically, however, the most problematic country when it came to paying dues was the United States. Beginning in 1985 under the Reagan administration, the United States began deliberately withholding a portion of its dues, a practice continued for a decade by Congress in the US budgetary process. Eventually, the country's unpaid UN dues amounted to more than $1 billion. In the late 1990s, US Senators Jesse Helms (R-NC) and Joe Biden (D-CT) worked out a deal with the Clinton administration and the UN in a highly contentious debate that lasted several years before it produced an outcome. The resolution combined a US commitment to pay up most of its arrears in installments (the United States still contests a significant amount) in return for a reduction in the US assessment for the regular budget from 25% to 22%. The United States now pays its annual assessed dues in full. ●

---

call special sessions of the UNGA (see "Spotlight On: Who Pays for All of This, Anyway?"). The occupant of the position—currently António Guterres of Portugal—can also bring issues to the UNSC for consideration. According to the UN Charter, the UN Secretary-General must be impartial when serving in this role.

The Economic and Social Council (ECOSOC) The UN's goals involving problems of an economic, social, and cultural nature are primarily the responsibility of the **UN Economic and Social Council (ECOSOC)**, and it is by far the broadest and largest of the UN's organs. It has 54 members elected by the UNGA for three-year terms, and it meets one month of each year.

As Table 7-6 shows, ECOSOC at least nominally supervises a wide array of commissions, committees, and specialized agencies, the most well-known of which include the WTO and IMF (see Chapter 8), the Commission on Human Rights (see Chapter 11), the UN Children's Fund (UNICEF), the World Health Organization, the International Atomic Energy Agency, the UN Educational, Scientific and Cultural Organization (UNESCO), and a whole host of others on such things as the status of women, population, and refugees. Seventy percent of the human and financial resources of

....

UN Economic and Social Council (ECOSOC): the component of the UN that handles matters considered economic or social, broadly defined.

the UN fall under ECOSOC's purview. The UN website officially describes ECOSOC as

the central forum for discussing international economic and social issues, and for formulating policy recommendations addressed to Member States and the United Nations system. It is responsible for:

1. promoting higher standards of living, full employment, and economic and social progress;

2. identifying solutions to international economic, social and health problems;

3. facilitating international cultural and educational cooperation; and

4. encouraging universal respect for human rights and fundamental freedoms.

Although it is often highly controversial—the United States has regularly tussled with ECOSOC and its subsidiaries, including UNESCO (which the United States boycotted from 1984 to 2003 on the grounds that it was not only bloated and inefficient but also anti-American in its words and deeds; in 2011 the United States stopped funding UNESCO because it admitted Palestine as a member)—the sheer magnitude of the agencies, commissions, and programs under its auspices, resource constraints, and the substantial independence of a great many of its specialized agencies have all combined to reduce ECOSOC's influence, even while its component parts play increasingly important roles.

TABLE 7-6

The Specialized Agencies, Funds, and Programs of the United Nations

ECOSOC FUNCTIONAL COMMISSIONS	ECOSOC AD HOC BODIES
• Statistical Commission	• Ad Hoc Open-Ended Working Group on Informatics
• Commission on Population and Development	**Expert Bodies Composed of Governmental Experts**
• Commission for Social Development	• Committee of Experts on the Transport of Dangerous Goods and on the Globally Harmonized System of Classification and Labelling of Chemicals
• Commission on the Status of Women	• Intergovernmental Working Group of Experts on International Standards of Accounting and Reporting
• Commission on Narcotic Drugs	• United Nations Group of Experts on Geographical Names
• Commission on Crime Prevention and Criminal Justice	**Expert Bodies Composed of Members Serving in Their Personal Capacity**
• Commission on Science and Technology for Development	• Committee for Development Policy
• Commission on Sustainable Development	• Committee of Experts on Public Administration
• United Nations Forum on Forests	• Committee of Experts on International Cooperation in Tax Matters
ECOSOC Regional Commissions	• Committee on Economic, Social, and Cultural Rights
• Economic Commission for Africa (ECA)	• Permanent Forum on Indigenous Issues
• Economic and Social Commission for Asia and the Pacific (ESCAP)	**Other Related Bodies**
• Economic Commission for Europe (ECE)	• Committee for the United Nations Population Award
• Economic Commission for Latin America and the Caribbean (ECLAC)	• Executive Board of the International Research and Training Institute for the Advancement of Women
• Economic and Social Commission for Western Asia (ESCWA)	• International Narcotics Control Board
ECOSOC Standing Committees	• Program Coordinating Board of the Joint United Nations Program on HIV/AIDS
• Committee for Program and Coordination	
• Committee on Non-Governmental Organizations	
• Committee on Negotiations with Intergovernmental Agencies	

The Trusteeship Council Originally established to supervise territories emerging from colonial rule after World War II, the Trusteeship Council contributed to the process of decolonization in the first three decades of the UN. It discharged its last responsibility in 1994 with the independence of Palau and has suspended its operations.

The International Court of Justice (World Court) We discussed the World Court in the section on international law in this chapter. This organ is the principal judicial body of the UN. The UNGA and UNSC elect its 15 judges to nine-year terms, and they must come from different countries. Their decisions are rendered by majority vote.

Let's take up two last points before we move on. First, we want to emphasize the range and extent of the specialized agencies of the UN system and the contributions they make in many political, social, economic, cultural, and environmental issues (see Table 7-6). When you consider all the particular problems and issues that are addressed, the transnational cooperation and coordination, and the technical expertise and resources that are pooled in these agencies, it is easy to understand the arguments offered by functionalists (see Chapter 6) and others about how IOs can foster and extend linkages among states.

Second, it is in the various elements of ECOSOC, and in the UN Secretariat as well, that the thousands of nongovernmental organizations concerned with virtually every issue imaginable are linked into IOs. We will talk about this in detail in Chapter 13, on transnational networks. Let's just say for now that these networks are fostered in part through the structures and institutions of cooperation within the UN system.

The Contributions and Limits of the UN

So how has the UN contributed to cooperation and the management of conflict? First, we can safely say that the UN's effectiveness is hampered by the same three challenges that affect every other aspect of world politics. Anarchy means that the UN ultimately depends in large part on the willingness of its members—sovereign states—to support and participate in its activities. Remember, the UN is not the "world police" and does not have the ability to enforce international law, agreements, or even the outcome of its own votes. Diversity means that the UN is hampered in part by the array of perspectives and preferences held by the widely diverging member states, nations, and nongovernmental organizations with which it works. Complexity means that the tasks confronting the UN are not simple but instead are complicated and increasingly linked. Moreover, the forces of interdependence and globalization are adding new issues to the agenda daily, and the UN's resources are limited. At the same time, the widespread backlash against globalization and its perceived impact on national sovereignty has led many states—including the US—to question and challenge the role and activities of the UN.

Second, the UN has fallen well short of the hopes and expectations of its founders and early supporters in the area widely thought to be its primary purpose—collective security. As the quote from George H. W. Bush at the beginning of the chapter suggested, there is consensus that the Cold War contest between the United States and the Soviet Union locked up the UN Security Council and prohibited it from addressing many issues of peace and security from 1946 to 1989. However, former President Bush's comments that the UN was poised to fulfill its lofty goals in the post-Cold War world seem awfully optimistic with the advantage of hindsight. To be sure, the UN has authorized and engaged in a great many peace operations since the end of the Cold War. But as our discussion in Chapter 6 suggested, it has struggled to contribute to the prevention, containment, and resolution of post–Cold War conflicts—especially the civil wars and non-state conflicts of the past 30 years. These struggles suggest that the machinery forged in response to the experiences of the early 20th century to deal with conflicts *between* states faces many challenges in dealing with conflict and security issues today. Furthermore, political divisions among key UNSC members—growing differences between the United States, Russia, and China, in particular—have continued to constrain its role and actions. The UN has made many positive contributions to peace and security, but its overall record is mixed.

Third, the UN's most significant effect may well be in the arenas in which its roles and functions were originally deemed secondary (due to the pressing peace and security problems of the time). Indeed, when we consider the contributions of the UN to fighting disease, protecting the environment, caring for refugees, and promoting and protecting human rights, on the one hand, and the far-reaching impact of the UN's specialized economic agencies in building and facilitating economic interdependence and cooperation, on the other hand, it is hard to resist concluding that these more technical and functional areas are the arenas of the UN's greatest accomplishments. Fortunately, it is precisely to these areas that the next chapters now turn, so we will be better positioned to make such judgments in the concluding chapter.

CONCLUSION

Former US President George H. W. Bush was overly optimistic when he speculated that the end of the

Cold War and the successful international response to Iraq's invasion of Kuwait in 1990 heralded a new era in which collective security and the rule of law prevailed in international relations. As we have seen, the world faces problems that continue to exceed its capacity to resolve them peacefully and effectively. However, this chapter also indicates that cooperative approaches to those problems by states, international organizations, nongovernmental organizations, and individuals play a role in managing conflict and seeking security. Even the arena of international security is not solely about military power and the use of force. As you reflect on the ideas and information covered in Part II of the text, consider again the traditional arena of international security and the approaches that states and others have embraced in pursuit of security. Do you see an evolution or trend, or are the actors in world politics stuck in cycles in which problems and solutions are repeated endlessly? To what degree do you think military power and force will continue to take center stage in this arena? What changes do you think are most important for the future? ●

KEY CONCEPTS

7-1 Identify the underlying challenges to cooperation in pursuit of security.

First, the anarchic nature of world politics complicates cooperation. The absence of a central enforcer to prevent and punish wrongdoing creates incentives for the major political players—states—to take care of themselves and their own interests instead of cooperating. Second, the diversity of states and societies in size, regime type, economic capabilities, culture, interests, and many other factors makes achieving harmony very hard. Finally, the complexity of world politics also complicates cooperation. Over time more and more players—states and non-state actors—are engaged across more and more issues that are linked together and affect them.

7-2 Explain the nature and forms of diplomacy.

Diplomacy is the art and practice of conducting negotiations between states and other actors in world politics. It involves *bargaining* (a term usually meaning more competitive and conflictual diplomacy) and *negotiation* (a term usually meaning more collaborative problem solving). Diplomacy generally involves negotiation over some issue of conflict in pursuit of common interests. Diplomacy may be bilateral, multilateral, or third-party and may even involve non-state actors.

7-3 Describe the nature and functions of international law.

International law is law in the absence of central authority, and that makes it different from domestic law. International law is also law in the absence of shared values and principles due to the great diversity in the perspectives, experiences, governments, characteristics, and cultures of the world's societies. The sources of international law are international conventions (treaties) agreed to by states, international custom or general practices of states accepted as law, "general principles of law recognized by civilized nations," judicial decisions and the writings of eminent jurists, and the practices and decisions of international organizations such as the UN. Liberals and constructivists stress the development, application, and prospects of international law as a way to manage conflict and enhance security and trust among states. Realists tend to be very skeptical of the prospects of international law. Alternative theories often see international law as a means by the rich and powerful to structure the rules of the system for their own benefit. There are three main avenues of enforcement: national, horizontal, and vertical.

7-4 Evaluate the nature and functions of international organizations.

There are power-based and problem-based explanations for the creation and maintenance of international organizations. Among other functions, IOs serve as instruments of states to influence other states; as forums for states to communicate, negotiate, and advance their interests; and as influential actors contributing to problem solving, coordination, norm and rule creation, and enforcement. IOs may be universal or regional in membership and single-issue or multiple-issue in scope, and they employ a range of voting and decision processes. The European Union is the most developed and powerful regional organization in the world, and the UN is the broadest and most universal IO.

KEY TERMS

Law of the Sea Convention 182

diplomacy 183

diplomats 184

diplomatic immunity 184

settlement gap 185

linkage strategy 185

summit meetings 186

multilateral diplomacy 186

third-party diplomacy 186

track II diplomacy 187

conference diplomacy 187

epistemic communities 187

international law 188

International Court of Justice 189

treaty 189

Vienna Convention on the Law of Treaties 189

custom 190

universal jurisdiction 191

reciprocity 192

national enforcement 192

horizontal enforcement 192

vertical enforcement 194

compulsory jurisdiction 194

majority rule 198

weighted voting 198

International Monetary Fund (IMF) 198

unit veto 199

P5 (Perm-5) 200

World Bank 201

most-favored nation (MFN) 201

European Commission (EC) 204

European Council 204

Council of Ministers (CoM) 204

European Parliament (EP) 204

European Court of Justice (ECJ) 206

League of Nations 211

United Nations (UN) 211

UN General Assembly (UNGA) 212

UN Security Council (UNSC) 214

UN Secretariat 214

UN Secretary-General 214

UN Economic and Social Council (ECOSOC) 215

REVIEW QUESTIONS

1. How do anarchy, diversity, and complexity set the stage for understanding the contributions and challenges of structures and institutions of cooperation?

2. What is diplomacy, and how do states and other actors in world politics use it to manage conflict and build peace?

3. How is international law different from domestic law?

4. What are the sources and mechanisms of enforcement for international law, and what are their consequences for its role and impact in world politics?

5. Why do states form international organizations?

6. What are the central forms and types of international organizations, and how do they affect world politics?

7. What are the main pieces and contributions of the UN?

THINK ABOUT THIS

Reforming the UN Security Council

At the end of World War II, the United States, the United Kingdom, and the Soviet Union took the lead in establishing the UN Security Council as part of the new United Nations international organization. These three, along with France and China, established themselves as permanent members of the UNSC and provided themselves with the veto power in the council. More than seven decades later, and despite the dramatic changes that have occurred in the world, these five states continue to hold their privileged position in the UNSC. Many proposals for reform of the UNSC have been offered in recent years, with then–UN Secretary-General Kofi Annan calling for speedy action to expand the council's membership in 2005. Although many suggestions for reform have been made, the most attention has been directed to changing the number of permanent members (with the veto power). After all, why should the UN's most powerful organ reflect the conditions at the end of World War II? Proposals to add Brazil, Germany, India, and Japan (called the G4 in this context) to the ranks of the permanent members have been offered (Russia, France, and the UK have indicated their support for this proposal). Africa has also argued for a permanent member from among the states of its region, and the Islamic world has argued for the same for its members. Opposition exists to every proposal: For example, Mexico and Argentina oppose Brazil; South Korea and China oppose Japan; Italy and Spain, and much of the developing world, oppose Germany; Pakistan opposes India; and so on. Significant disagreement also exists over whether any new permanent members should have the veto power enjoyed by the existing P5. To achieve UN Security Council reform, at least two thirds of the members of the UN—and all the current permanent members of the UNSC—must agree. What do you think?

Is UNSC reform a good idea? What are the most important prospects and implications, good and bad, of doing so?

FOR MORE INFORMATION . . .

Cini, Michelle, and Nieves Perez-Solorzano Borragan, eds. (2016). *European Union Politics*, 5th ed. Oxford, UK: Oxford University Press.

Damrosch, Lori, and Sean Murphy. (2014). *International Law*, 6th ed. Eagan, MN: West Publishing Company.

Diehl, Paul F., and Brian Frederking. (2015). *The Politics of Global Governance: International Organizations in an Interdependent World,* 5th ed. Boulder, CO: Lynne Rienner.

Morrow, James D. (2014). *Order Within Anarchy: The Laws of War as an International Institution*. New York, NY: Cambridge University Press.

United Nations (official English language website): www.un.org/en

Weiss, Thomas G., David P. Forsythe, Roger A. Coate, and Kelly-Kate Pease. (2016). *The United Nations and Changing World Politics,* 8th ed. Boulder, CO: Westview Press.

PART III

Economic Security

CHAPTER 8
The Pursuit of Economic Security: Trade, Finance, and Integration

CHAPTER 9
Economic Statecraft: Sanctions, Aid, and Their Consequences

CHAPTER 10
International Development: Relations Between the Haves and Have-Nots

Donald Trump and Boris Johnson

Are economic nationalists like British Prime Minister Boris Johnson and US President Donald Trump the new normal?

8 The Pursuit of Economic Security

Trade, Finance, and Integration

Learning Objectives

After studying this chapter, you will be able to . . .

8-1 Trace the connections between money, power, and security.

8-2 Identify the different historical approaches and theories that drove the world economy.

8-3 Explain the rise of liberalism and free trade and its consequences, challenges, and alternatives.

8-4 Describe the nature and implications of liberalism and globalization for world politics.

Chapter Outline

8-1 Money, Power, and Security

8-2 The National Economy Era: Colonialism and Mercantilism

8-3 The International Economy Era: Free Trade, Liberalism, and Marxism

8-4 The Global Economy Era

The Global Economy and the Resurgence of Nationalist Economics

After World War II, the trajectory of international economics was dominated by the integration of national economies into larger entities. States sought their future economic security via membership in international organizations such as the World Trade Organization or regional free trade agreements like the European Union and North American Free Trade Agreement. Yet that trajectory has recently begun an abrupt U-turn.

In the summer of 2016, UK voters surprised the world and passed a national referendum endorsing the withdrawal from the EU, albeit by a narrow margin (51.9% to 48.1%). Some British voters expressed concerns over immigration, but many said they were upset by the degree to which the EU's executive branch in Brussels—the European Commission—could tell the British what to do. The infringement on British national sovereignty stung. Britain's exit, or Brexit, will have enormous economic implications. Prime Minister Theresa May was unable to work out a withdrawal agreement with the EU that her Parliament would accept, but her successor Boris Johnson did, and British withdrawal became effective on January 31, 2020. Yes, the British regained unfettered control of their economic and immigration policies, but now the British would have to renegotiate all their trade agreements with each of the 27 other members of the EU and almost certainly lose the preferential treatment the

EU provides its members. Only time will reveal the full impact of this vote.

In 2016, Donald Trump, then–Republican candidate for the US presidency, endorsed the idea of Brexit. One of his campaign themes was the premise that US trade agreements had been unfair to the United States, and he promised that, if elected, the US would renegotiate many of them. Shortly after taking office, he withdrew the US from the new Trans-Pacific Partnership (TPP) that had been negotiated by the Obama administration. The TPP was an agreement by 11 Pacific Rim states to reduce their trade barriers and to create a trade dispute settlement process for TPP members. Trump also targeted the historic North American Free Trade Agreement (NAFTA) with Mexico and Canada. After long negotiations, Trump announced a new United States–Mexico–Canada Agreement (USMCA), which he said fixed some of the flaws of NAFTA. Mexico ratified the agreement in late 2019, the US did so in early 2020, and Canada completed the ratification process in March of that same year. The new agreement went into effect in July 2020. The Trump administration also began a trade war with China in 2018 by raising tariffs on billions of dollars of Chinese imports into the US. China promptly retaliated by raising tariffs on billions of US goods entering China.

Supporters of the trade policy changes endorsed by the Trump administration said they provided more national control over the US economy and protected the jobs of American workers. Opponents said that they were protectionist measures, and similar measures in the past had led to economic stagnation and cycles of recession and, in one case, the Great Depression.

These examples raise interesting questions:

1. Has the era of international economic integration fundamentally ended?

2. Is increased national control over one's economy a good or bad thing? If so, who wins and who loses?

3. How has globalization contributed to these recent dynamics?

INTRODUCTION: MONEY IS POWER

The idea that "money is power" is as old as money itself, and as states seek greater security in the world, many argue that they must therefore seek money. Remember, one implication of Marxist thought is that wealth makes one more secure, and poverty makes one less secure and more vulnerable to others. But how does wealth make you secure? You could buy a more potent military to make you more secure, but in today's world, a modern military is a pricey tool of statecraft. Feeding, clothing, housing, and training troops has always had a cost, but the cost of the weapons troops employ has skyrocketed in recent decades, due largely to technological advances. The price of having enough modern weapons to make you feel secure starts in the billions and goes up from there. Rather than investing heavily in troops and weapons you hope you do not have to use, due to the resulting costs in blood and treasure, how else can you use money to provide the power to ensure your security? For that matter, does more wealth always mean more security? How has the globalized economy provided wealthy states with opportunities or constrained their options? How do poor states improve their economic situations? What do all these economic connections mean for the broader relationships among the players in international politics?

8-1 MONEY, POWER, AND SECURITY

>> **8-1   Trace the connections between money, power, and security.**

Depending on what measure you prefer, China is either the world's largest or second largest national economy. Its military has a very large ground force, but, outside of possibly India, China lacks a substantial threat on the ground. China's perceived threats come from potential enemies across the Pacific Ocean. China is rapidly building a more modern navy and air force. The fastest way to modernize its military would be to buy modern weapons from others who have already developed them, but that would make China vulnerable if those partners ever chose to withhold deliveries of weapons or necessary spare parts. So China is creating its own modern weapons industry, but that takes time, as well as money taken out of its domestic, manufacturing, export-driven economy. Clearly, wealth can equal power, but it's not a simple or straightforward equation.

8-1a Complex Linkages in International Relations

There's more to the connection between money and power than simply building a powerful military and then using the military to secure critical resources or accomplish political goals. In fact, the complex linkages between politics and economics touch every part of international relations. Wealth can not only be used to gain power; it can also alter anarchy. That's a big feat, considering that we discuss anarchy throughout this book as an enduring feature of international relations. However, liberal theorists always highlight examples like the European Coal and Steel Community (ECSC). The ECSC started as a six-state organization in 1950 to control and coordinate the production of steel in Europe. The French developed the concept in part to ensure that Germany did not build an aggressive military—a country needs steel for its military—and threaten European stability as it did in 1914 and 1939. Thus, the ECSC was an economic organization that coordinated steel production and helped create a type of security community for Europe. Its effect over the course of several decades was dramatic. This organization was the seed that grew into the European Union, which is now an integrated, 27-state economic union. Thus, the *political* desire to constrain Germany after World War II led to *economic* integration. In turn, this created new order in part of the international system, effectively reducing the anarchy between the EU member states. In this case, money did not mean power, but it has created more security for more than six decades. For the global system, such integration didn't happen overnight; it happened in stages over time. See the box "Spotlight On: Levels of Interdependence and Integration."

The logic linking economic integration and peace is quite intuitive. If two countries with significant political divisions, such as a historical rivalry, are economically integrated, they become dependent on one another. In time, their mutual dependency not only will reduce the conflict but also may lead to a

Levels of Interdependence and Integration

Historically, states have integrated slowly and through a rather regular process. Here we describe the different levels of integration that occurred through the past 200 years:

- *Level I (19th and 20th centuries).* States trade goods and some services with each other. Trading is somewhat limited early in this period because of the cost and limitations of transportation. In the 20th century, transportation improved so that more than high-cost goods could be shipped at a profit.

- *Level II (mid-20th century).* Businesses begin to locate production facilities in other states, thus creating multinational corporations. Trade between states increases with the ability to fly goods from one country to another and the development of standardized container ships that allow even bulk cargoes to be carried across oceans at a lower cost. Services such as banking, insurance, and investment begin to be traded across state borders.

- *Level III (late 20th century).* Businesses, governments, and individuals begin to invest and own businesses in other countries. For example, the American automobile manufacturer Chrysler (originally one of Detroit's "Big Three" automobile businesses) was purchased by a German firm, Daimler AG, and then by Italian automobile manufacturer FIAT.

Thus, what was once a huge American firm is now owned by an Italian firm. Individuals and groups of investors also regularly buy and hold stocks and other stakes in companies from other countries. For example, anyone with investments in mutual funds or a pension program typically has their wealth tied to the economic success of companies around the world, not just those in their own country.

- *Level IV (late 20th century).* Many European states integrate into a **Eurozone** to create a **supranational organization**. Not only did many European countries create a free-trade zone and customs union; they merged their currencies into one—the euro. As a result, these countries must coordinate how much debt their governments can accrue and how much currency can remain in circulation. Imagine the United States coordinating with Canada and Mexico on how much money the United States could print and spend. This level is the highest integration attained in the modern era. ●

....

Eurozone: the portion of the European Union that uses the euro currency rather than a national currency. These countries include Austria, Belgium, Cyprus, Estonia, Finland, France, Germany, Greece, Ireland, Italy, Latvia, Lithuania, Luxembourg, Malta, the Netherlands, Portugal, Slovakia, Slovenia, and Spain.

supranational organization: an institution, organization, or law that is over other states. For example, the EU is a supranational organization because it has authority over many European states.

---

true positive peace—not simply a lack of conflict but a sharing of societal norms and beliefs. The liberal peace-through-integration idea, also referred to as "peace by pieces" (see the discussion in Chapter 6 on security communities), should work both between countries and within countries. For example, if a hostile ethnic division exists within a country, conflict could be reduced by tying the two ethnic groups together so that they need each other for their survival.

Marxist or world systems theorists might cite another example in the loans granted by the World Bank, an international organization that funds development projects around the world. Although loans are generally given to countries in need, the World Bank often requires the recipient country to engage in free-market reforms, thereby compelling recipient states to do something they have previously resisted. Such mandated free-market reforms change local relationships, with some local economic actors benefiting

and others losing the advantages they previously enjoyed. More directly, World Bank loans have sometimes been used to coerce other states, as the United States did when it blocked loans to Chile between 1970 and 1973 in an attempt to coerce the Chilean president, Salvador Allende, to step down from power. In this example, *economic* power was used to seek a *political* goal. Similarly, donors may use **bilateral** foreign aid (loans from one state directly to another) to accomplish both economic and political goals. When donors like China require recipients of their foreign aid to purchase Chinese products and services, the donors are doing more than just benefiting their own economies and pleasing locally important constituencies; they are also denying the recipient of other choices in the international free market. Once again, money is power. Another golden rule can be inferred:

....

bilateral: a relationship between two states or parties.

A US Army soldier walks toward a burning oil well in Iraq's vast southern Rumaila oilfields

How many linkages does oil have with your country? How many does it have with you?

REUTERS/Yannis Behrakis

Those who have the gold get to make the rules! But can the rules prevent one's own workers from losing their jobs to cheaper foreign labor in a globalized labor market? Do well-meant rules always improve things? What about unforeseen consequences? NAFTA stimulated the Mexican industrial sector, but Mexican farmers lost market share to US farm products made cheaper by industrialized farming and subsidies. The bottom line is that finding the balance point to ensure economic security is a tricky matter.

8-1b Markets and Governments: A Sometimes Tense and Codependent Relationship

Both the tension and the symbiotic relationship between the government and the market are fundamental to the connections between politics and economics. Governments try to maintain control of their territorial borders—we noted in Chapter 2 that this is a necessary component of sovereignty—but borders hinder businesses in selling goods and services. When governments tell their businesses that they cannot sell products to certain countries, such announcements generally do not endear the government to those corporate entities. For example, Hughes Communications would love to sell more satellites and services to Chinese purchasers (and the Chinese would love to buy them), but US regulations on the export of high-tech items limit what Hughes can sell. Similarly, US agribusiness giant Archer Daniels Midland would like to sell more food on the world market, but, again, governmentally imposed sanctions limit such sales (as in the case of Cuba) or prevent them (as in the case of North Korea). These restrictions are based on the realist desire to pursue national interests above all else.

Governments also create and enforce property ownership laws, thereby protecting commercial investments and creating the law and order that businesses require. Governments can be the agents of businesses in prying open previously closed foreign markets, as the United States did in the 1990s when China sought US support for its entry into the World Trade Organization (WTO). Entrance into the WTO meant lower and fewer restrictions on trade with China. One result of that pressure is that China purchased more than 3 million General Motors vehicles in 2019, and Ford sales reached almost 1 million in 2016 before dropping in each of the next four years. Many of these are exported from the US, but most are now made in Chinese factories. Additionally, governments provide public goods—such as infrastructure and education—that businesses need. Smooth highways and educated workers make for more profitable business. The economy provides the government with the source of tax revenues needed to maintain power and security in the global system. Thus, overall, businesses and governments need each other, but at times their individual interests diverge, if not directly clash.

The connections between politics and money may be straightforward and ubiquitous, but the question of how states acquire wealth is not. The means by which a state could gain wealth and thus security have changed dramatically since the Treaties of Westphalia. Over time, states pursued wealth by colonialism and mercantilism, capitalism and liberalism, and Marxism. Although the dominant system today is a liberal (meaning "free") or capitalist market economy marked by relatively free or liberal trade, the wide acceptance of that system is only relatively recent, and the capitalist system has experienced serious difficulties over the past decade or so. To understand the pursuit of wealth and power and how the world economy has developed, let's consider different economic practices and policies that evolved through time. If we begin with the establishment of the Westphalian system in 1648, we can divide the development of the world economy into three major eras, each of which had some distinctive characteristics (see Figure 8-1).

8-2 THE NATIONAL ECONOMY ERA: COLONIALISM AND MERCANTILISM

>> **8-2 Identify the different historical approaches and theories that drove the world economy.**

The first major era of the world economy was the National Economy Era, which best describes the

FIGURE 8-1

The Development of the World Economy

 The National Economy Era, 1648–1815

 The International Economy Era, 1815–1975

 The Global Economy Era, 1975–present

late stages of the pre-Westphalian and early part of the Westphalian eras. During this phase of the world economy, most economic activity occurred within, rather than across, the borders of states. During this period, the pursuit of wealth and security had two most important features: mercantilism and colonialism. As states engaged in economic activity and competed with each other for wealth and power, most of them embraced an economic philosophy called **mercantilism**. Mercantilism promoted the idea that the government would work directly with business leaders to promote economic growth by subsidizing the businesses and forbidding the purchase of goods and services from other countries unless absolutely necessary (a practice called **protectionism**). Governments would also use their militaries to secure resources for businesses—a process nicely illustrated in the film *Master and Commander: The Far Side of the World* (2003). By helping domestic businesses make money and protecting them from foreign competition, the government could advance its national interest by making its economy stronger. With a stronger economy came a stronger military that could be used to gain more colonies.

As states engaged in these mercantilist strategies, they also competed for control of foreign territories to gain exclusive access to their resources. Even before the Westphalian era began, European powers such as Spain and Portugal sought out new territories for conquest and colonization as it became more difficult to take European territories away from societies better able to protect themselves. This process, **colonialism**, was the first modern way in which states could increase their wealth. Going back centuries, states would attack and pillage each other for economic gain, but colonialism was different. The imperial state would discover new territory; claim the land, inhabitants, and wealth for itself; and create a colonial government to rule the new land, such as in Spain's colonization of the Americas. As the cartoon suggests, the colonial government would extract raw materials, such as gold, silver, and agricultural products, and send them back to the **metropole**, or mother country. It was like adding another smaller economy to the existing state, rather than simply plundering the land for a one-time gain of wealth.

Mercantilism, colonialism, and the pursuit of wealth

Is it surprising that European countries sought colonies?

Sarin Images/GRANGER

Of course, once the Europeans advanced into the Americas, Asia, and Africa, serious competition for the new land began. These conflicts were imperialistic wars that aimed to gain and maintain the most valuable colonies around the globe. For example, the British and French fought over North American colonies, the British and Dutch fought over Indonesia and South Africa, the British and Portuguese fought over India, the British and Russians fought over

mercantilism: an economic policy that combines business and government. The government uses its power—including its military—to enhance private business, and private business provides revenues to the government to maintain and enhance its power.

protectionism: a policy of blocking or restricting the trade from other countries in order to "protect" domestic businesses from economic competition with foreign companies.

colonialism: the situation in which one country takes over another country and administers it with a local bureaucracy.

metropole: the "mother city" or center of an empire. The metropole of the British Empire (which included colonies on every continent except Antarctica) was London.

Why Did the Europeans Colonize Asia, Africa, and the Americas, Not the Other Way Around?

For centuries the international system has been dominated by states in Europe, and since 1945 a former European colony, the United States, has been a dominant power. This situation is just something that most of us accept as the way things are, but have you ever asked yourself why Europe has such a dominant role and not China, or Egypt, or Brazil, or some other country? For example, China was more advanced than Europe when Marco Polo visited it in the 1200s. So why didn't the Chinese colonize the world? Similarly, the Inca civilization was very advanced and powerful and yet was easily toppled by the Spanish—why?

In *Guns, Germs, and Steel*, Jared Diamond (1997) argues that Europe provided a hospitable physical environment to domesticate plants and livestock not found in other parts of the world. These plants and animals not only provided food but also were easily transplanted into other areas. Wheat is an excellent example of a food that developed in Europe but can be grown in many climates around the world. Relatively abundant food that could be transplanted to both North and South America provided the Europeans with the means to colonize, but *why* did they seek out other lands?

Although history is too complex to name a single cause, the rise of capitalism in Europe is one very powerful reason for Europe's dominance to this day. At its root, capitalism promotes the constant seeking of more wealth, and seeking more wealth means *expansion*. European merchants and governments continually sought to expand their reach and consequently colonized and conquered much of the world. In addition to the push of capitalism, Christianity also promoted the idea that the Europeans should go out and convert the world's population to their religion. Thus, religious impulses reinforced economic ones.

Compare Europe's push for exploration to the Chinese. Despite the fact that Chinese Admiral Zheng took seven voyages to explore much of Asia and the Indian Ocean between 1405 and 1430, the successors of the Chinese emperor he served turned inward. Satisfied with their wealth and culture, they sought to isolate themselves from the rest of the world. By 1500, it was illegal in China to build an oceangoing ship. It isn't surprising, then, that the Chinese didn't colonize the world.

It is now easier to answer the question: Why did the British and other European states end up controlling China? Because these countries developed oceangoing vessels that allowed them not only to explore but also to project their power and conquer countries they discovered. Without having a capitalist economy, China didn't have the same internal pressures to continually increase profits, nor did China have a religion that pushed it to create missions around the globe.

Thus, the capitalist search for more wealth and power led the Europeans to seek out and control the rest of the world, and their more robust plants and animals helped pave their way to controlling much of Africa, Asia, and the Americas.

1. Had the Chinese not isolated themselves, how would the world be different, or would it?

2. Is there something else about Europe that made it the powerhouse it was for so many years? ●

Sources: Jared Diamond, *Guns, Germs, and Steel: The Fates of Human Societies* (New York, NY: Norton, 1997); and Fareed Zakaria, *The Post-American World* (New York, NY: Norton, 2009).

Afghanistan, and so on. As a result of such conflicts, by the late 19th century, one could say that "the sun never sets on the British Empire" because it in fact did not. It was always daylight somewhere in the British Empire. As these examples demonstrate, the British were not the only European imperialists, but they were arguably the most successful imperialists in history. See "The Revenge of Geography: Why Did the Europeans Colonize Asia, Africa, and the Americas, Not the Other Way Around?"

The problem with mercantilism is that if all states follow this **beggar-thy-neighbor** philosophy and forbid most trade with other countries, then there would be almost no international trade. Consequently, states

beggar-thy-neighbor: an economic policy that stresses trade protectionism and causes other countries to bear the costs of efforts to secure prosperity at home.

would not be able to increase their wealth except through the acquisition of more colonies. As you can imagine, this led to a competitive and conflict-oriented world economy.

8-3 THE INTERNATIONAL ECONOMY ERA: FREE TRADE, LIBERALISM, AND MARXISM

>> 8-3 Explain the rise of liberalism and free trade and its consequences, challenges, and alternatives.

In the second era, trade between states grew and played an increasingly important role in world politics. Two factors more than any others arose in the latter part of the National Economy Era and led to the International Economy Era. In the late 18th century, economists Adam Smith and David Ricardo advanced powerful arguments for the idea of free trade rather than mercantilism as the optimal approach for the pursuit of wealth and power. In his path-breaking work, *The Wealth of Nations*, Adam Smith argued that efficient, competitive nations should specialize their economies to be more effective at creating wealth, focusing their activities on the product or products they produced better than other countries, and trading with other states for the rest. This idea became known as **absolute advantage**.

David Ricardo then added to Smith's ideas and argued that, through free trade, all countries—even inefficient ones—would develop and could become wealthy by focusing on producing the products they themselves made best—even if they did not produce these things better than any other country. This concept—the basis of modern trade theory—is known as **comparative advantage**. (See "Theory in Action: Should Countries Pursue Free Trade?" for a discussion of these ideas and the advantages of free trade.) What is important for us to understand here is how this idea emerged and influenced key leaders—especially in Britain—to engage in different approaches to economic security.

Smith's and Ricardo's ideas—and the policies to which they led—are referred to generally as *liberal economic policy*. It is very important to understand what we mean by *liberal*. It is not the US domestic political meaning, for example, to describe a "liberal Democrat," nor are we discussing the international relations theory called liberalism. Instead, liberal economic policy simply means economic policy that is driven by supply and demand in a free market rather than controlled or regulated by government.

The second factor is mostly technological—the rise of the **Industrial Revolution**. At about the same time that free trade was being advanced, a major transformation of economic activity also began. The Industrial Revolution shifted economic activity from hand production to processes involving increasingly advanced machines that enabled large-scale production on the farm, in businesses, and in factories. Manufactured products—first textiles and then other goods—became the core of economic growth in more and more countries as the Industrial Revolution proceeded in the 19th and 20th centuries.

The combination of these two factors—free trade and the Industrial Revolution—led to the International Economy Era. As we said, in this era, trade *between* countries became more important—you have to be able to get the raw materials needed for manufacturing and then be able to sell all those products somewhere! This era was not without its ups and downs, of course, and both mercantilism and colonialism also persisted as major practices. By the 1800s, the Industrial Revolution was well underway, and the competition for foreign trade and colonies was fierce. In the mid-1800s, Great Britain began to rise in economic and military power and gained the status of hegemon, or dominant world power. For the next seven decades, leaders in London pushed the world to engage in less protectionism and greater free trade, and the British took the lead in reducing barriers to trade to encourage others to do the same. During this period, the amount of trade worldwide increased significantly, and states increased their overall wealth substantially. During the early and middle 1800s, British leadership—and economic power—was central to the establishment of free trade and significant economic growth.

8-3a World (Trade) War

In the late 1800s, however, the British economy began to suffer relative to the other states, particularly compared to two rising powers: Germany and the United States. Both the Germans and the Americans raised tariffs, blocking trade to protect their infant industries. Because neither of these countries had the tremendous industrial capacity that the United Kingdom did, they were not as dependent on trade, and in the

---

absolute advantage: when a country is more efficient than another country at producing a single good.

comparative advantage: being more efficient at producing a good or service relative to another good or service. Even if one country has an absolute advantage over another in all products, both countries benefit by specializing in the products they each produce most efficiently (their comparative advantage) and trading for the others.

Industrial Revolution: the transition of many of the world's states from an agricultural economic system to one based on industry. During this period, factories replaced farms as the biggest producer in many countries.

Should Countries Pursue Free Trade?

Why should states engage in free trade? Wouldn't it be better for a country to sell products to other countries but not buy any foreign goods so that it could make money from other countries? With some exceptions, the answer is no. The majority of economists argue that free trade benefits all states that participate, even if the trading partners are not equal in their abilities.

An example will help (see Table 8-1). Imagine two states, Dragonstone and Winterfell. Dragonstone is particularly good at producing food—it takes its citizens only one hour to produce a pizza, but it takes Dragonstone two hours to produce a bicycle. Winterfell is better at bicycle production compared to pizza production. It takes that country three hours to produce a bicycle but six hours to produce a pizza. If the two countries divided an eight-hour day evenly between pizza and bicycles, Dragonstone would produce four pizzas and two bicycles. Winterfell would produce one and one-third bicycles but only two-thirds of a pizza. In total, eight units (four and two-thirds pizzas and three and one-third bicycles) would have been produced between the two countries.

If the two countries specialized in what they do best and then traded with each other, both countries would be better off. Dragonstone would produce eight pizzas in an eight-hour day, and Winterfell would produce two

and two-thirds bicycles. In total, that's ten and two-thirds units produced—more than before. Thus, by specializing and trading, the two countries both have more.

In the real world, this principle still applies. The United States is better at producing the designs for iPhones and iPads because of the technical skill and training of its workforce. China is better at assembling these products because its labor costs are significantly lower. Similarly, the United States is better at producing higher education—American colleges and universities are the best in the world. Saudi Arabia is best at producing oil. This does not mean that the United States does not produce some oil and Saudi Arabia has no higher education, but that the two countries specialize more in the areas where they have a comparative advantage.

So should countries always engage in trade? If you ask economists, they would likely say yes. There are many situations, however, in which a country might not want to trade specific products, or perhaps even most products. First, buying military weapons from others could put a country at risk if the state from which it buys its weapons becomes an enemy. If a state depends on another state for its weapons, it is also dependent on that state for its security. Smaller states do not have much choice, but for larger states, there is a long history of producing many of the state's weapons domestically to avoid such vulnerabilities.

TABLE 8-1

Benefit of Specialization

	NO SPECIALIZATION OR TRADE			
	HOURS TO PRODUCE		TOTAL PRODUCED IN AN 8-HOUR DAY (SPLITTING TIME EVENLY FOR BOTH PRODUCTS)	
	Pizza	Bicycle	Pizzas	Bicycles
Dragonstone	1	2	4	2
Winterfell	6	3	0.67	1.33
Total Combined Production = 4.67 pizzas + 3.33 bicycles = 8 units produced				
	WITH SPECIALIZATION AND TRADE			
	HOURS TO PRODUCE		TOTAL PRODUCED IN AN 8-HOUR DAY (SPECIALIZING IN ONE PRODUCT)	
	Pizza	Bicycle	Pizzas	Bicycles
Dragonstone	1	2	8	
Winterfell	6	3		2.67
Total Combined Production = 8 pizzas + 2.67 bicycles = 10.67 units produced				

Similarly, selling weapons to a potential enemy isn't a good policy because those weapons could be turned against you. The United States is the world's largest arms seller and has even sold weapons to some countries that later became its enemies. For example, the United States secretly armed the mujahideen in Afghanistan with Stinger surface-to-air missiles when they were fighting the Soviets in the 1980s. Some of the mujahideen later became members of the Taliban and al-Qaeda, and not all of those Stinger missiles have been accounted for!

Quality control is another issue that could lead a state to not purchase goods from other countries. There was a large recall of toys produced in China in 2007 because lead paint—dangerous to small children who might ingest it—was used. Similarly, environmental and labor concerns could influence people to purchase only domestically produced products. Some may purchase only locally produced vegetables and fruit because transporting those products from other countries tends to pollute heavily. As we discuss later in the chapter, some universities will not sell college apparel made in countries that do not have laws protecting the workers making all of the clothes with the university's logo.

Another reason not to engage in trade is to develop an industry within your own country. For example, allowing only domestically produced farm equipment to be sold in one's country gives local farm equipment producers more customers and thus profits. Those profits could be used to develop the industry. We go into a deeper discussion of this policy, called import substitution industrialization, in Chapter 10. Beyond that, some observers argue that certain industries are so vital for economic growth and competition (in today's world, microchips are a good example) or so strategic for security (perhaps steel, or some strategic metals) that a country should be engaged in their production if possible.

In each of these cases, an economist might tell you that specialization and trade are still better because they are more efficient (see Table 8-1). It is a compelling argument, but perhaps efficiency is not the only factor to consider in this situation.

1. What other goods or services might a country not want to trade freely?

2. Could you defend that argument before an economist? ●

---

case of the United States, its domestic economy was so large that it had plenty of customers at home. Although France was already established as an economic power, it followed suit and instituted a series of protectionist measures that restricted foreign trade. It did this in part to hurt the British and in part to protect its own economy from the trade restrictions in the United States and Germany. These actions hurt the British economy by reducing the flow of goods and services it could sell overseas. Because the United Kingdom is an island state, it was very dependent on trade with other countries (another revenge of geography). Thus, the restrictions in trade by the United States, France, and Germany were particularly problematic for the British.

As other states gained in power relative to the British, London was no longer able to persuade or compel them to engage in free trade. Markets began to close to foreign trade, and the competition to sell goods overseas and colonize the remaining areas left unclaimed by the imperial powers contributed to World War I. In particular, the United Kingdom and France already controlled many colonies, and the United States controlled large sections of Latin America (although these were not officially colonies). Germany, by contrast, had few colonies (chiefly in Africa), and these were not particularly valuable. The Treaty of Versailles that ended World War I placed a huge debt burden on Germany, forcing the fragile democracy to pay for costs of the war. This crushed

the German economy and sent it into a state of **hyperinflation**. When an economy suffers from hyperinflation, it simply means that its money loses its value at an extremely rapid rate. Instead of a typical rate of inflation, say 3% (the level targeted as healthy in the United States prior to 2007), hyperinflation can mean inflation rates in the hundreds or thousands of percent. For Germany, it meant that the cost of a loaf of bread could go up by 10 times in a single day! At the worst point in its economy, the German Bundesbank actually printed a currency note worth 100 trillion marks; postage stamps were valued at 50 billion marks. In today's terms, that would mean a stamp in the United States would cost about $63 billion. Just imagine what your latte would cost! It's almost impossible to even imagine such economic problems.

By the mid-1920s, the major countries in the world decided that the best way to help their weak economies was to close off trade with other countries and resume many of the beggar-thy-neighbor approaches to wealth that were characteristic of mercantilism. Instead of helping matters, these protectionist policies caused serious **trade wars** between the major world

....

hyperinflation: a situation in which a currency loses its value very quickly. Regular inflation occurs at relatively low levels (3–5% per year), but hyperinflation means a currency can lose most of its value in a year, a month, or even a day.

trade war: a situation in which many or all states engage in protectionism. The states try to block imports and promote exports, but because all countries do this, very little international trade occurs.

economies, and as a consequence the level of global trade plummeted. As trade plummeted, less money changed hands and thus less wealth was produced. This trade war contributed to the Great Depression in the United States and around the world. This economic disaster also had major political consequences. The severe economic depression provided a perfect environment for an extremist like Adolf Hitler to rise to power in Germany, and it pushed the Japanese military to attempt to secure and put under direct Japanese control additional resource-rich territories around the Pacific Rim. Although these events were not the only causes of World War II, they did contribute directly to it.

It is important to note that even though mercantilism was viewed as a contributing factor to World War II and roundly criticized by the leading economists in the world, it did not disappear after the war. Several states continue to practice modern-day forms of mercantilism, such as import substitution and export-led growth. In Chapter 10, we discuss these policies and the countries (e.g., Japan, South Korea, and Mexico) that either have practiced them or continue to practice them to this day.

8-3b Marxism

As the ideas of Smith and Ricardo were beginning to take hold, another economic approach was born. Though embracing the Industrial Revolution, this economic system did not seek to gain wealth as much as it sought equality among all people. As we discussed in Chapter 4, Karl Marx developed the theory of communism that asserted there were five epochs in the history of human society. The first was primitive communism, which was essentially the simple hunter-gatherer society found throughout the world before the rise of civilizations. Second was feudalism, the agricultural system of lords and serfs that reigned during the Middle Ages and into very early modern times in Europe and Asia. Next was capitalism, the system in which goods and services (labor) were sold. Marx predicted that capitalism would end with a revolution of the workers and the creation of a new government that would take over the economy and make it equal for all people. This stage, called socialism, would end when the government "withered" away and a new utopian, communist world would exist with no government, no inequality, and no poverty.

Marx expected the socialist revolution to start in Great Britain during the Industrial Revolution. Instead, it started in Russia in 1917 and led to the rise of the Union of Soviet Socialist Republics (better

....

centrally planned (or command) economy: an economy that is run by the government rather than private citizens. Examples include the Soviet Union and North Korea.

known as the Soviet Union). More socialist revolutions began, most notably in China, North Korea, Vietnam, Cambodia, and Cuba. The Soviet Union also created or sponsored socialist governments throughout Eastern Europe in countries such as Poland, East Germany, Czechoslovakia, Romania, Bulgaria, and Hungary.

In practice, though, these regimes became little more than autocracies seeking to control their people and the wealth of the country. Three of the world's four worst mass murderers were Marxist dictators. Joseph Stalin, the leader of the Soviet Union from the late 1920s to 1953, had approximately 38 million Soviet citizens murdered, nearly five times the number of people who died in the Nazi concentration camps during the Holocaust. The leader of China from 1949 to 1976, Mao Zedong, also presided over the deaths of millions of people, and Pol Pot, the dictator of Cambodia, had 20% of that country's population tortured and killed. Each of these three dictators all professed to follow some form of Marxism, though in reality they were no more than dictators. Marxist ideology and policy themselves do not endorse mass killing or the repression of people. In fact, it aims to liberate people from unjust working conditions and the misbelief in capitalism. The philosophy created by Marx, however, has been misused regularly throughout history.

8-3c Marxism Implemented

Aside from the autocratic nature of the regimes and some homicidal leaders, most Marxist countries attempted to modernize their economies and provide full employment for all of their citizens. In a Marxist system, the government controls the economy entirely or almost entirely. Thus, every business, factory, and firm is owned by the state, and every worker is employed by the state. The government determines what will be produced, how much it will cost, and when people are permitted to purchase goods. This is referred to as a **centrally planned (or command) economy**.

Although the Soviets and Chinese were able to make some strides toward modernizing and developing their economies, ultimately, central control of the economy failed. In the case of the Soviet Union, as long as it was relatively easy to do *more* of what the Soviet economy already had the ability to do—cultivate more land, cut more lumber, make more steel, and so on—the Soviet economy grew nicely. However, once the easy limits of such additional effort were reached and the Soviet economy had to become more innovative, its growth slowed. For example, the Soviets largely missed the electronics revolution brought on by the use of transistors and then semiconductors that led to the development of personal computers in the 1980s. By the mid-1980s, the Soviet economy stopped growing altogether and began to shrink. The result was a near economic collapse and a complete collapse of the government. In China's case, the government started moving away from the centrally planned economy in the late 1970s. Free-market reforms improved the economy and greatly increased the standard of living for many Chinese. To this day, there are few governments that profess a belief in Marxism as an economic policy—North Korea and Cuba being the only notable cases, and Cuba began some limited market reforms in the mid-1990s and expanded them recently. The rest of the world has embraced some form of capitalism, although as we discuss in later chapters, some of Marx's ideas are implemented in even the most capitalist countries to this day.

Many proponents of Marxism argue that Marxism failed not because the theory and its prescriptions were wrong but because the countries that adopted Marxism were not ready. They argue that unless a state has gone through capitalism, it cannot become socialist and then finally communist. None of the countries that embraced Marxism were truly capitalist before Marxism took hold, and many were simply advanced feudal societies. According to this perspective on Marxism, they were doomed to fail from the start, and Marx is still right: As capitalism develops and spreads, it will ultimately fail and give way to a socialist government. Do the consequences and challenges of globalization—including the Great Recession of 2008–2010, populist reactions such as Brexit, and even the rapid spread of the COVID-19 global pandemic and its harsh human and economic consequences—suggest that could happen?

8-3d From International to Global Economy Eras: The Liberal International Economic Order After World War II

As World War II drew to a close, American leaders reflected on what led to such a destructive conflict. The general sense of governmental leaders was that World War II was largely a consequence of the trade war and economic discrimination between nations. The trade war created greater discord between the states and drove their economies into severe crisis.

FIGURE 8-2

Worldwide Trade From 1870 to 2014

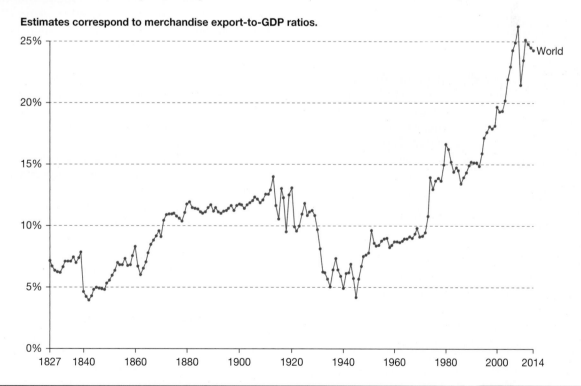

Estimates correspond to merchandise export-to-GDP ratios.

Source: Michel Fouquin & Jules Hugot. 2016. "Two Centuries of Bilateral Trade and Gravity Data: 1827–2014," CEPII Working Paper 2016-14, May 2016, CEPII; found via https://ourworldindata.org/international-trade.

Note: Shown is the sum of world exports and imports as a share of world GDP (%).

The economic discrimination took the form of competition for resources and territory—Germany wanted more and better territorial assets, and Japan wanted more resources, while the entrenched imperial powers had no interest in giving up any of their wealth. Leaders in the United States, and to a lesser extent in the United Kingdom and France, began to believe that if countries could agree to trade freely—and cooperate together to do so—then countries would become wealthier and there would be a greater chance for continuing peace after the war. Looking at Figure 8-2, you can see why US leaders believed trade was so important—the United States accounted for a large portion of world trade by the end of World War II.

A pedestrian using a mobile phone walks past a Walmart store in Beijing, China
Apart from the signs, could you tell this person wasn't in Europe or the United States?

Brent Lewin/Bloomberg via Getty Images

International Trade and International Peace

Why should liberalized trade make countries better off and promote peace? First, as we noted earlier, modern theories of free trade are based on Ricardo's idea of comparative advantage (more so than Smith's idea of absolute advantage). Ricardo showed that if countries specialize in making the products at which they are most efficient (compared to what else they produce), and then trade them with other countries, they would be able to make more money than if they tried to produce all the products they need. For example, the United States can get oil more cheaply from Saudi Arabia than produce all of it in America, while the Saudis can buy apples more cheaply from the United States rather than try to grow them in the desert. There are serious consequences to free trade (see the earlier box "Theory in Action: Should Countries Pursue Free Trade?"), but its overall economic benefits seem widely accepted by major trading powers.

The second advantage of international trade is that countries that trade with one another tend not to fight each other on the battlefield. The idea originated with Immanuel Kant, who suggested more than 200 years ago that commerce and war were not compatible. For example, if two countries exchange many goods and services, such as the United States and China, then war between the two would be bad for business. A war between the United States and China would end the exchange between the two countries. For the United States, that would mean the production of iPhones, iPads, and other consumer electronic devices would have to be moved. That is, the factories that produce these goods would have to be built elsewhere. Your smartphone, laptop, or TV would cost significantly more if the company that made it had to rebuild an entire factory. Similarly, the birthday gift for your nephew or niece could cost twice as much if it wasn't produced in China. At the same time, the Chinese would no longer receive the large payments for assembling the electronics, toys, and other goods that the United States purchases. Many of their factories would have to shut down, unemployment would skyrocket, and their economy would suffer. War would simply not be good for business. What would China do with all these unemployed workers—put them in the military? Could it afford to pay them?

There is another pacifying effect of trade that is less obvious. As two states trade with one another, they begin to learn about each other's cultures. Levi's blue jeans and the television show *Dallas* were popular in the Soviet Union in the final years of the Cold War. In 1989, Pepsi launched a commercial about how Soviet young adults were drinking Pepsi and acting just like Americans. Through this cultural exchange, Americans and Soviets realized they were not that different from each other. The sandwich franchise Subway is now the most common restaurant around the world, with over 42,000 shops in more than 110 countries. Most anyone from anywhere can get their favorite Subway sandwich whenever they want it! Think about what these things suggest. Essentially, it is harder to hate someone if they like the same clothes, entertainment, and food because they are not so strange and foreign; they are a lot like you. Thus, trade can help countries better understand each other, and with understanding comes a greater willingness to talk rather than fight.

New York Times columnist Thomas Friedman (1999) once argued that countries with McDonald's franchises never go to war with each other. Although this "Golden Arches" theory has been proven wrong—for example, NATO countries went to war with Serbia over Kosovo, Russia invaded the Republic of Georgia and Ukraine, and Israel invaded Lebanon—the issue was obviously more about the economic and cultural linkages represented by McDonald's than about the fast-food operation itself. The idea that commerce can lead to peace is a powerful one.

Building a Liberal International Economic Order

Given these reasons why trade might promote economic growth and help keep the peace, in 1944 the United States convened a meeting in Bretton Woods, New Hampshire, to help ensure that countries would not engage in another trade war like the one precipitating the Great Depression and World War II. The result was the establishment of what is often referred to as the **liberal international economic order (LIEO)**, which combined commitments to the ideas of free trade and free-market economics with the construction of international institutions to help countries coordinate and cooperate in their pursuit of economic security. Like the early decades of the International Economy Era, the LIEO also involved the leadership of a hegemon, with the United States drawing on its role as the most powerful country in the world to build the LIEO and help it operate.

Taking its name from the location of the talks, the meeting established what came to be known as the **Bretton Woods system**, which created the World Bank and the International Monetary Fund (IMF), international organizations that we introduced and described in Chapter 7. (Chapter 10 discusses how the Bretton Woods system promotes economic development as well as other development issues.) As noted in Chapter 7, the World Bank is an IO that seeks to help countries develop their economies. The organization provides loans to countries for development projects such as building port facilities, water systems, airports, or other infrastructure. Some of these loans have been very successful and others problematic and troubled. The successes are almost completely limited to smaller projects, such as building schools and clinics. The failures, unfortunately, tend to be big. For example, in the early 1980s, the World Bank loaned Brazil funds to develop iron ore mining. When the price of steel (iron infused with carbon through smelting) dropped, Brazil turned to cutting down its rain forests to make charcoal for the smelting so that it could pay back the loan. Thus, the World Bank contributed—unintentionally—to deforestation. In the 1990s, World Bank conditions placed on loans to Bolivia required the water supply to be privatized. As a result, a US-based transnational corporation—Bechtel—controlled the water supply (the government even made collecting rain water illegal) and

charged so much that citizens could not afford it. This led to resistance, uprising, and violence before Bolivia took back control from the company. The World Bank has also been criticized for contributing to the growing debt of developing countries and for serving as an agent of the wealthiest countries in the world by pushing capitalism, privatization, and access to developing world markets, resources, and cheap labor.

Because of failures and criticisms such as these, the World Bank's sole focus on growth for the first five decades gave way to more attention to sustainable development. The World Bank also now tries more to provide advice, collect data, and report on the economic development of the world in an attempt to help developing countries be part of the plan to grow their economies in responsible ways. The World Bank has also begun paying greater attention to the social and economic impact of its policies.

According to its website, the IMF, also described in Chapter 7, seeks "to foster global monetary cooperation, secure financial stability, facilitate international trade, promote high employment and sustainable economic growth, and reduce poverty around the world." Originally, the IMF had two functions. First, it was a source of emergency funds, mostly short-term loans and financing for countries facing balance-of-payments problems, so that its member states would work together to address these problems rather than act unilaterally and inflict harm on others (we discuss this function in Chapter 10).

Second, the IMF also sought to fix all currencies at one level and coordinate those levels so that there would be no floating or changing exchange rate. This policy also reduced beggar-thy-neighbor policies by requiring IMF members to work together to manage their currency values rather than acting alone in self-serving ways that could hurt other states. However, the IMF was too small and too underfunded to accomplish such a task. Instead, the United States took on this role, establishing the "US gold standard" because the United States fixed its currency value to gold (at $35 per ounce) and the other IMF members pegged their currency rates to the gold-backed US dollar (with small ranges for adjustment as coordinated and approved by the IMF). The US gold standard is often referred to as one of the four Bretton Woods institutions (see the next section for a discussion of the third), but by 1971, the United States could no longer support the system and was running out of gold to back the dollar. In 1971,

liberal international economic order (LIEO): the post–World War II international economic system built on commitments to free trade and free-market economies.

Bretton Woods system: a system named for the location of the 1944 conference in New Hampshire that established the family of international organizations created after World War II to maintain and promote the liberal international economic order; the two core institutions created were the International Monetary Fund and the World Bank.

President Nixon ended the US gold standard, thus allowing currencies to float in value in the marketplace of supply and demand, and although the emergency loan/financing function of the IMF continued, its fixed exchange rate function ended.

Although the IMF could not control currencies, it did take the lead in helping countries that were having difficulty with debt and balance of payments. This process is similar to an individual person facing bankruptcy and rescheduling their debt. At the country level, the IMF provides large loans and guarantees loans for commercial banks to provide the country the cash needed to continue paying its debts. Think of an infusion of cash that allows the country to pay the minimum required on its loans. These loans and guarantees do not come unconditionally. Instead, the IMF compels the troubled country to decrease its spending; this policy is referred to as an **austerity program**. The indebted country usually must cut back all non-essential spending—as defined by the IMF—such as assistance to the poor, public health spending, and public education. The programs "work" in that these countries regain the ability to continue making their payments, but there is a serious social cost. The state placed under the austerity program cuts spending so much that its citizens often get hurt—less food, medical care, and education. Are these the costs of fixing your economy?

The World Bank and the IMF are supported by dues paid by member states based on the wealth of the member state. Thus, the United States pays more to the two organizations than does Canada or South Korea. Control of the organizations is also based on how much the member states contribute; thus, the wealthiest nations, such as the United States, Japan, and Germany, have tremendous control over the organizations. Because of their large contributions, traditionally the IMF president is from Europe, and the World Bank president is from the United States. How do you think Marxists or other critical theorists view these organizations?

But What About Trade?

During the Bretton Woods conference, the diplomats also tried to create an organization that would govern international trade. Negotiations for the International Trade Organization failed, however, largely because of disagreements over how agriculture could be traded. Shortly after the failure to create a functioning trade organization, the **General Agreement on Tariffs and Trade (GATT)** was created with a more limited goal: to promote free trade in the world. The organization promoted trade liberalization through most-favored nation (MFN) status (in the United States, MFN is now referred to as NTR, or normal trade relations). Each GATT member was required to give all other members the lowest tariff rate available—this rate was considered the MFN rate. During the many rounds of negotiation, GATT encouraged states to reciprocate toward each other when making trade deals. Thus, if Canada offered Japan a lower tariff rate on imported sake, Japan should offer Canada a lower rate on its imports of maple syrup.

GATT had two big weaknesses. First, it could not enforce any of the agreements its members made. Cooperation was completely voluntary. If a member did not want to reciprocate or it wanted to cheat on a trade deal, there was nothing that GATT could do about it. Second, GATT covered only tariffs, but there are other barriers to or problems with trade. Countries can subsidize a business, using tax dollars to pay for the development of products. This is considered "unfair" because the private business is getting help from its government. Airbus, the multinational European airplane manufacturer that competes with US-based Boeing, benefited from significant government subsidies, about which the United States complained bitterly, but GATT could do nothing. The other type of trade issue is the **nontariff barrier**. These are simply arbitrary rules that make it difficult to impossible for one country to sell its products in another. For example, the Japanese claimed it was a safety requirement that all cars could hold a certain amount of air pressure when the windows were rolled up. American cars were "leaky" at the time, making it more difficult for them to be sold in Japan. Thus, the Japanese government was able to block trade with the United States without using a tariff, and, again, GATT was unable to do anything about it. Even with these limitations, GATT nudged major economies in the direction of freer trade for nearly 50 years.

8-4 THE GLOBAL ECONOMY ERA

>> 8-4   **Describe the nature and implications of liberalism and globalization for world politics.**

The establishment of the LIEO after World War II contributed to the development of the current era of

---

austerity program: a program of severely restricted government spending, often on welfare programs, imposed when the country must balance its accounts.

General Agreement on Tariffs and Trade (GATT): an organization of countries that agreed to work together to reduce trade barriers and promote free trade. Other members were considered "most-favored nations" and received preferential trade agreements. The GATT was replaced by the World Trade Organization in 1995.

nontariff barrier: a requirement that foreign goods or services must meet that is specifically designed to block or obstruct those goods or services from sale in that market.

the world economy—the Global Economy Era. The LIEO promoted and spread free trade and encouraged market economies that worked together, and it established international institutions to tie states together and help them cooperate. The LIEO also created the foundations for non-state actors such as multinational corporations and private financial institutions to operate more freely across borders and to extend their operations to more and more countries. Consequently, the LIEO basically fostered the forces of globalization that led to the Global Economy Era. Just as technology played a key role in the transition from the National Economy Era to the International Economy Era, it also was central to the transition from the International Economy Era to the Global Economy Era. In the latter case, the dramatic revolutions of technology in the past several decades—the computer era, the radical advance of information and communication technology, and the rapid development of faster and more efficient transportation—all played critical roles. Together, these factors constitute the core of the forces of globalization that shape the modern economy and the pursuit of economic security in it.

8-4a The Modern Economy

In the Global Economy Era, the world has gravitated toward **capitalism** as the dominant economic system. Even leaders from socialist parties—such as three consecutive presidents of Brazil (Luiz Inácio Lula da Silva, Dilma Rousseff, and Michel Temer)—promote liberal trade with other countries. Instead of closing their borders to other countries and enacting laws that allowed the government to take over the economy, as many Latin American leaders did in the past, Brazilian leaders such as the three just mentioned embraced policies to limit inflation, pay off loans to the IMF, and push for stable economic growth—policies that are very similar to those of developed capitalist states like the United States and Germany.

In the Global Economy Era, the share of virtually every country's economy made up of exports or imports has grown dramatically. France, Italy, Germany, and the UK all have well over half their economies determined by tráde, and the US figure is almost 30%, although many have seen their shares dip slightly over the past five years or so. Interestingly, in the early 1970s, the share of the US economy determined by trade was in the single digits. The economies of both China and Russia are about half international, and most developing countries have even higher proportions based on trade. This is a very good illustration of what the Global Economy Era means—talking about a "national" economy makes less and less sense when so much economic activity crosses borders, and

US entrepreneurs like Apple's Steve Jobs and Steve Wozniak produced the world's first personal computers in the 1970s

In what year did the Russians produce their first homegrown, mass-marketed personal computer? Is capitalism the best system for innovation?

Bettmann/Getty Images

a good share involves the activities of foreign companies in other states.

Global Trade, on Steroids

In 1995, GATT, the LIEO institution promoting free trade, was replaced by the more powerful and effective World Trade Organization (WTO). Like GATT, the WTO is essentially a trading club in which all member countries agree to keep their markets open to foreign trade from other members by limiting tariffs and other trade barriers. If one state blocks another state from selling its products, the two states can go to the Dispute Settlement Body—effectively a "trade court"—and the WTO will determine if a rule is being broken. If the trade barrier is illegal under WTO rules, then the plaintiff state is permitted to sanction the other state to regain the revenue lost by not being able to sell its goods and services. In short, the WTO has the ability to write rules, administer them, adjudicate disputes, and penalize those who break the rules—effectively enforcing the agreements GATT could only hope were accepted voluntarily.

Let's consider an example to illustrate this process. Even before the WTO was created, the EU placed a ban on hormone-fed beef—such beef could not be sold in Europe. The United States contested the ban, and in 1997, the WTO ruled in favor of the United States because there is no scientific evidence suggesting that hormone-fed beef has any health-related side effects. Preferring "traditional" to "new and improved," the EU would not lift its ban on the meat, so the United States placed tariffs, as authorized by the WTO, on certain EU products to recoup the money lost from not being able to sell beef in the EU. The dispute continues to this day.

As another example, President George W. Bush in 2002 initiated an 8–30% tariff on all steel imports—a huge increase from the previous 0–1% tariff. The EU and states like Japan and South Korea filed suit against the United States in the WTO's Dispute Settlement Body. The WTO found against the United States, but the Bush administration would not back down. The EU threatened to sanction the United States in accordance with the WTO ruling (just as the United States has sanctioned the EU over its hormone-fed beef ban), and the United States lifted the steel tariffs.

Another example involves US cars and SUVs sold in China. Following the 2008 US government bailout of American automobile companies, the Chinese government applied tariffs of 8–22% on US cars and SUVs. That meant that a Chevrolet Suburban could cost 22% more in China than in the United States. The Chinese government claimed that these tariffs were to compensate for the loans the US government gave to the auto companies. The US claimed the tariffs were a violation of WTO rules, essentially accusing China of cheating. After a year of deliberation, the WTO found in favor of the United States. Although China had already lifted the tariffs, the WTO said that it had violated WTO rules by imposing the tariffs with no evidence that Chinese auto producers or the Chinese people were hurt by Chrysler, Ford, and GM.

Although the case was settled easily, it does show how a trade war begins (see the Foreign Policy in Perspective box later in this chapter). The Chinese saw an opportunity to gain against US automobile producers, so they exploited it. These tariffs clearly hurt the US, especially economically beleaguered Detroit, Michigan. Without the WTO, might the US have retaliated with tariffs against Chinese products? Could that have led to more tariffs by China? Of course, neither happened because each country has willingly subjected itself to WTO rule, thereby limiting its sovereignty.

It is not just the trade of goods and services that tie the global economy together. The speed of communication makes things possible today that weren't even dreamed of a few decades ago. During the Iraqi invasion of Kuwait in 1989, as its capital city was evacuating, employees of the National Bank of Kuwait *faxed* bank records out of the country, which enabled the bank to continue functioning even after the invasion. It took hours and hours. At the time, this was considered a modern miracle. Now, however, we can transfer information almost instantaneously through the world's computer networks. The speed with which we can access and transfer financial information means that we are all a little closer together. When you travel to Scotland, for example, you can get off the airplane, walk over to an ATM, and withdraw money from your bank account denominated in pounds sterling. After just a few seconds, you are on your way to getting some delicious haggis. All of a sudden, the foreign country isn't so foreign, and you're not so far away from home.

Non-state Actors and the Pursuit of Wealth

Economic liberalism not only promotes free markets and free trade; it also creates an environment in which non-state actors of a wide variety matter, from international and nongovernmental organizations to multinational corporations to individual people. In the global economy, international organizations, such as the WTO and IMF, affect the behavior of and relations between states in many ways. Nongovernmental organizations (NGOs) are also increasingly active and can have dramatic effects as well (see our discussion of the neo-Westphalian era in Chapter 2 and our discussion of transnational advocacy networks in Chapter 13). Multinational corporations (MNCs) play a powerful role as well. According to the WTO, world foreign direct investment increased from $10.1 billion in 1970 to a high-water mark of $3.1 trillion in 2007. Following the Great Recession, it dropped to $1.2 trillion in 2018, but the overall trend is increasing over time. Moreover, the top 500 MNCs in the world controlled more than 70% of global trade by the start of the 21st century. As if that isn't impressive enough, the volume of money that crosses borders *each day* now exceeds $3 trillion, as businesses, banks, and investors move money around in pursuit of profit.

In the globalizing world, individuals matter, and sometimes they matter a lot. It is certainly easier to understand how an organization such as the IMF or the WTO, or a major MNC such as Samsung, can affect how nations pursue wealth, but do you think an individual can affect an entire country? On September 11, 2001, we witnessed a non-state actor—al-Qaeda—mobilize the world's most powerful military, but can a person or a small group affect a state's economy? Surprisingly, the answer is sometimes yes.

In 1992, George Soros contributed to the severe devaluation of the British currency, the pound sterling, so much that it was said he "broke" the Bank of England. Soros was a currency speculator, meaning that he and his company bought and sold other currencies for profit. In 1992, Soros's group purchased approximately 10 billion British pounds, and on September 16, it sold them—all of them, in one day. The selling of such a large number of pounds caused the weakened currency to **devalue**, or become worth less than just the day before, because suddenly the supply of pounds sterling on the market far outweighed the demand for them. Immediately after the devaluation, Soros bought up pounds because they were much cheaper. The process netted Soros a profit of $1.1 billion. Great Britain lost an estimated 3.3 billion pounds (almost $6 billion in today's market). Aside from the economic costs, the Conservative Party in Britain lost the elections following the crisis, leading to the rule of the Labor Party. Thus, one man was able to shake a large country's economy to the point that there were significant economic and political repercussions. We have not since seen one of the world's richest people (like Jeff Bezos, Bill Gates, or Warren Buffett of the United States or Carlos Slim Helú of Mexico) make a profit-based decision on a scale like Soros did, but in 2011 French and Swiss financial institutions were shaken when previously unknown individual employees made huge unauthorized investment bets that went bad.

The influence does not always have to be negative, however. Soros donated billions to charity over the years. An example of individuals making an even bigger impact is the Bill and Melinda Gates Foundation. The foundation is dedicated to promoting world health, and with its $47 billion endowment and health budget of over $1.3 billion, it spends more on promoting world health than the UN's World Health Organization! To put this in some perspective, it means that Bill and Melinda Gates, along with co-investor Warren Buffett, exceeded the amount of money being spent on global health by the UN.

These stories are not commonplace, of course, but they demonstrate how, in a liberal world economy, a few individuals can have an impact on politics, the economy, and the global quality of life. It is not just the big countries and organizations that matter.

Liberalism in Practice

Although most countries in the world are capitalist and engage in foreign trade, they are not entirely liberal. Instead, all three of the economic systems discussed play a role in most countries. For example, the

Bill and Melinda Gates play with a child in Mozambique

The Gates Foundation takes a practical approach to philanthropy by funding projects such as medical research in Africa that will yield big payoffs in the form of lower infant mortality. Should all grant programs seek to maximize the benefits, or is there some value to funding smaller-issue projects?

REUTERS/Juda Ngwenya

governments in Great Britain, France, and Germany created a joint initiative to build commercial airplanes. The governments each gave the contracts to build different components of the planes to different companies within each of the three states. In the end, the multinational company Airbus was born and now supplies about half of the world's commercial airliners. This policy was clearly not Marxist or liberal, as the governments created a company and gave the business to private industries. This was mercantilism or, as it is more commonly called now, *national industrial policy*.

Those governments also allow private capitalism to operate within limits, but they rely on socialist-themed programs such as substantial government benefits to citizens, including fully paid maternity leave and universal health care. These services, many of which are under serious pressure from the economic crisis in Europe, are paid for by higher levels of taxes than most US citizens would find acceptable. For its part, the United States also engages in at least two of these three economic approaches. Although largely capitalist and liberal in its basic economic approach, the United States has a long history of regulating private industry and providing social programs to ease the impact of capitalism on such things as the environment, poverty, and inequality; the welfare of children; and, in the case of the Affordable Care Act, health insurance and access to medical

devalue: a situation in which a currency, such as the US dollar, loses its value compared to other currencies. For example, the Chinese government sets the exchange rate between the US dollar and the Chinese yuan, and currently, the yuan is devalued; it is worth more than the Chinese will trade it for.

care. Indeed, all developed market economies engage in such practices to one degree or another and often impose significant regulations on private industry in the name of the greater good. At the same time, the US federal government can and does direct businesses not to sell certain products to certain parties currently being sanctioned for political reasons (i.e., a mercantilist approach). Thus, the three systems—mercantilism, capitalism, and Marxism—all contribute to how states function today, with capitalism having the largest impact of the three (see Table 8-2).

8-4b Globalization and the Global Economy

As we discussed in Chapter 2, globalization is the global spread of technology, money, products, culture, and opinions through foreign trade, investment, transportation, and cultural exchange. The term is somewhat loose and covers a broad range of economic phenomena, but through this process, countries become integrated into a common global network whereby they know more about each other but are also tied to each other through interdependencies. This definition clearly covers a vast array of issues, so it is worthwhile

to discuss a few examples. We focus mainly on trade, production, and information in this chapter and take up investment, especially foreign direct investment, in Chapter 10. In each of these examples, we try to show how globalization can challenge both the security of a state and the way anarchy functions.

iPhones, Hollywood, and Terrorists

The Apple iPhone is famous and almost ubiquitous on campuses around the United States. Many people know that Apple has its headquarters in California—Cupertino, to be exact. The conceptual development, technical design, and manufacturing process are all centered in and directed from the headquarters in California. The actual process is much more complex, though.

Apple uses manufacturers from all over the world to produce the hundreds of components for the iPhone. Many of them have headquarters in wealthy countries and subsidiaries around the world as well. For instance, the iPhone's accelerometer is manufactured by Bosch Sensortec, which is based in Germany, but that company has subsidiaries in China, South Korea, and Taiwan. Similarly, the glass screen on most iPhones comes from Corning, a US-based company

TABLE 8-2

Summary of Economic Approaches

	COLONIALISM/ MERCANTILISM	CAPITALISM	MARXISM
Core principles	The state works with private business to procure more wealth and aggressively targets other states to colonize or take their money.	The state and private business must be separate. The economy must be free to be efficient, and efficient economies mean more wealth for everyone.	The state must take over and administer the economy to create an equitable distribution of wealth.
Core critique	The approach tends to cause trade wars between powerful countries. The costs of colonization can be severe to weaker states.	Not all countries gain wealth at the same rate, so there are large inequalities. There are also huge fluctuations in the economy, such as during the Great Recession.	There are large inefficiencies in a state-run economy, and they usually fail.
Relation to security	The state and private business work together to make the state more secure by attaining more wealth.	Security is enhanced by economic connections and interdependencies between states.	Because the government controls the economy, it can use it at will to develop its military. Many Marxist countries had large militaries.
Relation to power	Money is power.	Although money can be used to develop power, wealth has other effects.	Money is considered the root of all political strife as well as power.
Relation to anarchy	The system is anarchic; the state uses the lack of central government to take control of other countries.	Anarchy can be overcome or reduced by complex interconnections between countries, such as in the EU.	Although anarchy exists only because non-Marxist states compete, considerable friction occurs between different Marxist regimes because of different interpretations of policy.

with factories in Australia, Brazil, Denmark, India, Malaysia, and elsewhere. US-based Qualcomm contributes baseband processors and LTE cellular chips but has them manufactured by factories in Asia. All told, hundreds of suppliers send their components to Apple's assembly partners—Foxconn (Hon Hai) in Shenzhen, China, and, more recently, Pegatron, outside Shanghai, China. Apple recently moved some of its assembly to India as well.

Thus, when you open your web browser and visit the Apple website to order an iPhone, you are gaining access to a server somewhere in the United States. Once you have ordered the iPhone, the order is ultimately transmitted to the facility in China, where the iPhone is assembled from components sourced from all over the world, then packaged and shipped. The shipping company, UPS, will likely move the package through Hong Kong, China, where it will clear customs to come into the United States. It will then probably travel through South Korea, Alaska, and finally the local UPS facility in your region. Your order will have traversed the Pacific Ocean for a product designed in the United States, made all over the globe, assembled in China, and shipped through South Korea, and all of this may take place within a matter of days.

What does this mean for world politics? The lucrative connections among so many companies and countries to design, manufacture, assemble, and sell products like the iPhone have important implications for anarchy and the relationships between countries. Think about all the cooperation that must happen for something like the iPhone production and sales process to occur. That multiple countries can be involved in such complex and profitable business deals means that the international system has order, even though it is decentralized. Companies like Apple do not connect people, firms, societies, and countries in pretty complex linkages that are an important part of globalization without a clear expectation that these relationships will be respected and protected—even without a global government. Do you think these linkages and dynamics have consequences for security? Might they reduce the prospects for conflict—especially military conflict—between the countries connected in their webs? Let's turn to another example that tells another story.

The reach of US media around the world and the effects those media have can be dramatic. American movies, typically produced in Hollywood, California (and often filmed in Canada), provide excitement and romance to viewers around the globe. They also create great offense to conservative cultures, particularly extremist religious groups. For example, Islamists find the wide reach of Hollywood extremely offensive. Terrorist organizations such as al-Qaeda and the Islamic State use the entertainment media that Hollywood creates as an example of the corrupt nature of Western civilization, particularly almost globally available US television shows such as *Modern Family* and *Revenge* and movies that include revealing love scenes, seminude actors, or families with LGBTQIA couples. These extremist groups view the content of this type of programming as an attempt to pollute and destroy their culture and to corrupt their young. They thus feel justified in attacking the United States and are able to recruit members because they claim to be defending what is morally right (at least in their eyes). To be sure, Hollywood did not create Islamist terrorists, but the cultural exchange of popular entertainment contributes to the hatred directed at the United States. In one of the many ironies of globalization, al-Qaeda and Islamic State terrorists use modern technology—such as cell phones, satellite phones, websites, e-mail, and popular encrypted messaging applications like Telegram, Signal, and WhatsApp—developed by the same countries they hate and attack. In this case, globalization may have partly caused a decrease in US security.

The Spread of Globalization

The means through which globalization spreads around the world is best understood through two processes: broadening and deepening. *Broadening* refers to new states becoming incorporated into the global economy. Today, nearly every country in the world is involved with the global economy in some significant way through trade and cultural exchange (see Table 8-3). In fact, states that are not globally integrated must actively choose to stay separate from the world. For example, Bhutan, the tiny state east of the Himalayas, did not allow television or the Internet until 1999. Another example is North Korea, which is such a closed, autocratic society that relatively little trade and exchange occurs with the rest of the world. Aside from countries such as Bhutan until 1999, or North Korea to this day, most of the world is integrated into the global economy to some extent.

The second process, *deepening*, refers to how much of a state is touched by globalization and to what extent. For example, in the early 2000s, only 4.5% of the population of India used the Internet (data from the World Development Indicators). By 2019, that proportion had exploded to nearly 40%. That is more than 500 million Internet users, the second highest number of Internet users in the world, behind only China. Since it opened itself to the Internet, Bhutan has modernized and integrated with the rest of the world. As it has, the share of Bhutan's population using the Internet grew from zero in 1999 to about 48% in 2017. That may not seem like much compared to the 87% of Americans who use the web every day, but it shows how quickly global information networks spread, a key element of globalization. Even more

Contrasting technology in India

Both of these pictures are from India, but they are clearly different. Can you think of a similar situation in your country?

Adeel Halim/Bloomberg via Getty Images

Prashanth Vishwanathan/Bloomberg via Getty Images

TABLE 8-3

Globalization Index for the Top and Bottom Three Countries, 1971, 1991, and 2019

YEAR	COUNTRY	RANKING
1971	Luxembourg	71.53
	Canada	70.83
	Belgium	68.41
	Rwanda	15.23
	Nepal	13.74
	Bangladesh	12.03
1991	Netherlands	83.94
	Switzerland	83.87
	Belgium	83.81
	Burundi	19.24
	Equatorial Guinea	19.02
	Laos	17.76
2019	Luxembourg	93.04
	United Kingdom	92.85
	Sweden	92.51
	Aruba	35.78
	Somalia	32.63
	Eritrea	29.88

Source: Adapted from Swiss Economic Institute, Zurich, KoF Index of Globalization,https://kof.ethz.ch/en/forecasts-and-indicators/indicators/kof-globalisation-index.html.

interesting is that most of the growing connections come through wireless connections to increasingly sophisticated smartphones like Apple's iPhone or Samsung's Galaxy.

The deepening of globalization, while quite advanced, continues to this day. Most locales are affected in some way by the global economy. There may be many small towns in countries like India that have never had an American visit them, but many people in these towns will have watched US television programs such as *Game of Thrones, Young Sheldon,* or *Dancing With the Stars.* Similarly, in 2018, 15 million people visited South Korea, but there had been more than 3 billion viewings of "Gangnam Style" on YouTube.

Further, because of globalization, we are all connected to and can be affected by events a world away. For example, in 2011, horrible floods in Thailand, where about 45% of the world's mobile computers are manufactured, meant the supply of hard drives plummeted and costs skyrocketed, which affected governments, businesses, and consumers alike. Any major increase in the price of oil quickly impacts the whole world, causing prices on all products to increase because oil is used in every product, at least for its transportation, if not also its production. A successful terrorist strike in another state on a port critical for shipping oil would mean that you will pay more to fill your car's gas tank or to buy products made of plastic. These and the many other connections between states and societies driven by globalization mean that everyone is more exposed to the effects of things that happen in other parts of the world.

Good examples of how the linkages of globalization serve as transmission belts connecting economies and societies can be seen in some of the economic crises of the past two decades. For example, around the turn of the 21st century, policies in the United States that allowed banks to give home loans more easily, often to people who might not be able to otherwise afford them (referred to as subprime loans), led to a real estate bubble that began to burst in 2006, leading to the Great Recession of 2008–2010, which crushed economies all over the world. People were unable to pay their mortgages, building stopped, banks lost immense sums of money, and people lost their jobs, feeding a super-charged cycle of decline. Banks and investment firms began to lose vast sums of money and, unsure of the worth of their assets, many basically stopped loaning money, leading to a credit crisis. Global stock markets plunged in value: The Dow Jones Industrial Average—the gold standard for how stock markets perform—reached a high in October 2007 of 14,164. A mere 17 months later, in March 2009, it had lost 54% of its value, closing at 6,547. Over the next decade, recovery from the Great Recession proceeded faster in some countries (e.g., the United States) than in others (e.g., in Europe), but most have faced new challenges from the economic crisis stemming from the 2020 global pandemic.

Another example comes from the case of Greece, whose economy grew at the fastest rate in the Eurozone between 2000 and 2007. This rapid growth attracted many foreign investors, which subsequently allowed the Greek government to engage in heavy spending that exceeded its tax revenues. Greece began to run up significant debts—much like individuals who spend more than they earn and run up huge credit card debts. To cover their bad policies, Greek government officials lied about their borrowing, downplaying the true size of their debt. Although the deception lasted for just a short time, it ended with a crisis for the Greeks that had dramatic effects for the rest of Europe as well. Because the collapse of the Greek economy would drag many other European states down with it, the EU led negotiations to provide Greece with billions in loans from the EU and the IMF in several packages between 2010 and 2016. In

Violent protest in Greece

Even in a normally tranquil country like Greece, an economic meltdown can reduce the country to violence. Could this happen in your country?

REUTERS/Alkis Konstantinidis

return for the bailout, the Greek government committed to making deep spending cuts and raising taxes—policies referred to as an austerity program (mentioned earlier in this chapter). Although the austerity program helped stabilize the economy of Greece, which remains in the Eurozone today, it angered Greeks because their benefits and pensions were being cut. Workers took to the streets in protest, and Greek support for the EU plummeted. In 2017, the Greeks had one of the lowest favorability ratings for the EU (about 30%) and the highest level of support (about 36%) for an exit like the one the UK chose in its 2016 referendum (Stokes, Wike, and Manevich 2017). Key factors included frustration over the way the EU and the global economy determined what the Greek government could and could not do.

Positive Effects of Globalization

We have thus far discussed how most of the world is connected in this integrated network we call globalization. Let's now consider the effects of this integration. Globalization has both positive and negative consequences. On the positive side, most economists agree, and the historical record shows, that countries engaging in more open trade experience better overall economic growth than those who do not. This does not mean that such growth is shared equally across all members of society or all sectors of the economy (it is not). In the aggregate, however, more open trade is associated with growth in GDP.

Additionally, the more a country is open to trade and thus globalization, the less likely there will be forced labor, particularly among women. Women also benefit from less economic discrimination when their country is more globalized. These benefits result from the presence of MNCs that tend not to discriminate against women or engage in forced labor. These corporations

A Bhutanese spiritual leader using a laptop

Bhutan did not allow the Internet to be connected until 1999; now it is beginning to touch all parts of Bhutanese society. Do you think such a small, poor country will benefit from the Internet?

ROB ELLIOTT/AFP/Getty Images

are often concerned with their public image in large, developed states and wish to avoid the bad press that some companies (such as Nike) have experienced in the past (see the next section, "Costs and Consequences of Globalization"). The presence of these international employers can push local employers to mimic the labor practices of their competitors. Many of these MNCs also pay their workers a salary that is competitive by local standards, although as we discuss in the next section, there are many complaints about how MNCs treat local workers. What is particularly important to realize about the jobs created by MNCs is that they would not otherwise exist if the company did not build or operate a manufacturing plant in the country. Cannondale Bicycle Corporation, for example, has almost all of its bikes made in Taiwan, although its headquarters are in Connecticut. As mentioned earlier, Apple assembles most of its products in China and has the components for those products manufactured all over the world. In both cases, Cannondale and Apple are creating jobs in the respective countries. Thus, those workers have more opportunities for employment, and employment provides money and, especially for women, greater independence.

Another benefit of open trade and connection to the global economy is peace, both inside countries and between states. First, greater trade openness makes genocides and ethnic cleansing less likely because if the country tends to trade with other countries, there are international businesspeople and journalists in the country. This attention from the outside world means that widespread, horrific violence like the kind that occurred in Rwanda in 1994 is less likely. In that case, there was very little trade with the outside world, and as the situation in Rwanda became violent, businesses and even states withdrew their personnel. Without the presence of international diplomats, businesspeople, and journalists, the world did not fully know that a genocide was beginning, one that would not end until approximately 800,000 people had been murdered. It is not clear that the international community would have responded if news cameras had been everywhere, but it is also not clear that the militias would have attacked defenseless adults and children in front of the cameras. Rwanda is an extreme case, but the lesson is that a foreign presence, including the media, tends to limit what a government might do to its people. Look at the pressures on Egypt's economy after the Arab Spring when tourists chose to go elsewhere.

One of the main reasons for US leadership in creating the IMF, World Bank, and GATT/WTO, as previously discussed, was to ensure more cooperation and trade between states in the hope that they would help limit interstate war. Remember the idea of the democratic peace—the concept that two democracies will not fight each other—as discussed in Chapters 3, 5, and 6.

Along with democracy, significant trade between two countries makes them much more peaceful toward each other. Thus, globalization, with all of the interstate trade and exchange that it entails, may make wars between states less likely. Consider the extremely close relationship between the United States and Canada. The two are among each other's largest trading partners, with more than $1.5 billion in merchandise crossing the border each day. Even when there are trade disputes, such as 2017 clashes over timber and dairy trade, the thought of a militarized dispute between the two states is ridiculous, in part because of the close trade relationship. (For a humorous treatment of that possibility, see the movie *Canadian Bacon* [1995].) Not only do Americans and Canadians buy and sell a great deal from each other; that relationship is indicative of the understanding the two societies have of each other. Think about this: Which is more foreign to you, Canada or Russia? Which do you see as potentially more threatening to US interests? Now, also consider the extensive economic links between China and the US: Do those links also reduce the possibility of war between the two states?

Finally, it is worth noting that exposure to other cultures is generally a good thing. From such simple pleasures as having access to international foods and foreign films, we can learn more about our fellow humans and come to appreciate their cultures and views. Although this benefit is not tangible and certainly not universally appreciated, a truly closed society does not have access to German beer, French wine, American movies, Swiss cheese, Canadian maple syrup, Vietnamese prawns, Japanese electronics, South African diamonds, and so on. Not only do global supply chains bring us many of the things we buy and often help reduce the costs of such items; the transportation linkages created also make it easier for us to travel to the rest of the world more quickly and easily than before, and often at a

Vacant streets in the Democratic Republic of the Congo
Civil violence in a country destroys not only people and buildings but also the desire to run a business. How might a country recover from such violence when this is what is left?

lower cost. And globalization may have saved your life or that of someone you love. In just the past 10 years, the winners of the Nobel Prizes in Medicine, Chemistry, and Physics came from more than a dozen different countries. Without open trade and globalization, we wouldn't have all those products, culture, or modern inventions that we take for granted.

Costs and Consequences of Globalization

We now turn to the drawbacks of globalization, and there are many to choose from. First, we discussed how an MNC's bringing jobs to a country can result in less economic discrimination and forced labor, but not all MNCs are so benevolent. For example, apparel companies have long been criticized for labor conditions in the overseas factories that manufacture their products. In 1989, a Nike contractor in Thailand was accused of paying its employees a "training wage," an amount far below the legal minimum wage. Following these reports, strikes and protests hit the Nike production facilities. Through negotiations, many of these issues were addressed, but problems still persist. Nike contracted with producers in Vietnam, where workers are not permitted to organize outside the official communist party. Although the workers are constrained by the government, they still initiated a strike in 2008 for higher wages, which at the time were only $59 per month. Try to find a major clothing retailer paying its foreign factory workers what most in the US would consider a fair living wage. You won't.

In addition to poor wages, many of these factories or sweatshops have long hours and poor working conditions. Because the factories are subject only to local laws, and many of these countries do not have labor protection laws, 16-hour days and child labor persist, and few physical protections exist. In the past 20 years, working conditions have improved considerably as world public opinion has turned against such inhumane practices. Companies have faced pressure to address poor working conditions in their own or their partners' factories, as happened to Apple in 2016 in the Pegatron factory noted earlier. Organizations such as the Worker Rights Consortium report on poor labor practices, attempting to bring them to the attention of the public and thereby put pressure on the companies. In 2010, for example, the University of Wisconsin ended its contract with Nike over workers' issues. In 2017, Georgetown, Rutgers, and Northeastern cut or threatened to cut their ties to Nike over these same issues. Nike eventually sidestepped some of these problems by agreeing to let Worker Rights Consortium inspectors visit their foreign plants. According to Human Rights Watch (2017), in 2017, a public coalition of activists and advocates pressed major corporations to embrace a "transparency pledge" to reveal where their clothing products were made. Of

A sweatshop in Southeast Asia
These unpleasant working conditions show some of the other costs involved in apparel making. When you spend your money on jeans, shirts, and hoodies, who profits?
iStock.com/Liuser

the 72 companies lobbied to take this step, 17 did so, including Adidas, Levi's, Nike, and Patagonia, but many others resisted or fell short of the standard. Although such actions do not usually critically wound an MNC's profits, they do put pressure on MNCs to reform so as to avoid future boycotts and lost profits. No corporation's management team likes to have a negative media spotlight shining on the company.

One way of ameliorating these low wages is an idea originated by US religious groups in the 1940s. The idea, called **fair trade**, is to pay the original producers of a product more. Initially it applied to handcrafts sold mostly in churches. Today fair trade is big business that has moved well beyond church sales. Most fair trade products, which include coffee, chocolate, handcrafts, and so on, are certified by the organization Fairtrade International. Products with the "fair trade" designation are typically sold at a slightly higher price, with the idea that the increased price, or at least a portion of it, will go to the original producer.

Although the idea is a good one, it is not clear how well it works. In some studies, less than 2% of the increased price actually went to the producer. Studies showed coffee farmers received only $0.18 more for a pound of coffee costing $5 more than a non–fair trade pound of coffee. One of the best studies of fair trade is *Brewing Justice* (2014), in which the author (Daniel Jaffee, an economist) shows that coffee farmers did tend to earn more for fair trade coffee and that those earnings helped increase the development of the farmer's community (because the farmer had more to spend and invest). However, the book also warns that fair trade is not the cure for the costs of globalization. It can help, but more needs to be done.

Another negative effect of globalization is that it can put tremendous pressure on states and ultimately weaken them. As noted earlier, the complex

---

fair trade: the concept that producers should be paid a fair price for their products.

connections and linkages of globalization and inter-dependencies *create* vulnerabilities and reduce the control that states have over what happens to them and what they do. For instance, the more countries open their economies to the global marketplace by engaging in foreign trade and investment, the more they expose themselves to considerable competition and influence from forces outside their control, both from state and from non-state actors. Although some people within the country will benefit from the foreign trade, others will be harmed, which can also generate political pressure and problems. Imagine a country that chooses to open up its markets because it has a very profitable mining industry; however, the country's agriculture production is small and not very efficient. When exposed to the global food market, the country's farmers would likely be unable to compete. If the country does not subsidize or protect the farmers in some manner, they will lose their livelihoods. Thus, there is pressure on the country both to join the global economy so that its mines can make profits and to compensate the farmers who lose their farms and ability to support themselves. Now think about how that dynamic might affect those engaged in manufacturing jobs when, as we illustrated with the Apple example, globalization makes it possible for companies to roam the world to find places or partners for their manufacturing. Such pressures have led to challenges to free trade; see "Foreign Policy in Perspective: Free Trade Under Threat?"

A real-world example of this negative outcome can be found in Mexico. Due to the **North American Free Trade Agreement (NAFTA)** of 1994 (which was replaced by the **United States–Mexico–Canada Agreement [USMCA]** in 2020), Mexico's previously largely closed economy was opened up to US and Canadian businesses. Although this was great for the Mexican workers employed assembling televisions and other electronic products in *maquiladoras* (export assembly plants typically near the US–Mexican border) or those manufacturing US-branded cars and trucks, it was catastrophic for many Mexican farmers and agricultural companies that suddenly had to compete with products from industry giants such as ConAgra and Archer Daniels Midland. When the same thing happened in Japan beginning in the 1960s, Japan's openness to trade with others meant

small Japanese rice farms suddenly had to compete with very efficient rice producers from Burma, the United States, and other states. Japan's strong economy at the time allowed the government to respond in two ways: first, with heavy subsidies to keep Japan's iconic rice farmers in business; and second, with a heavy media campaign to convince Japanese consumers that domestically produced Japanese rice was superior (in nutrition, taste, consistency, stickiness, etc.) to cheaper, imported rice.

The pressure that globalization exerts on states is made worse because governments want to attract investment from MNCs. To attract MNCs, the government must typically offer significant tax breaks, and these tax breaks must be competitive with other countries; otherwise, MNCs have less reason to invest in the country. The consequence of the tax breaks is that the government may attract MNCs, but it has less tax revenue to pay for the displaced farmers. Furthermore, MNC profits typically go back to their home state; they generally do not get reinvested in the host country that produced the wealth. Thus, the "multiplier effect" that economists stress from private direct investment is limited for the host society. In the end, the country may benefit from globalization, but the government may have less money to help out those citizens who are hurt by open trade policies.

Russia faces a slightly different problem due to globalization. When the Soviet Union controlled the economy, people had to buy domestic products—only those made within the Soviet Union and some other government-approved products. As the country opened its markets to foreign products, many Russians lost their jobs. Simply put, they worked at factories that produced products so poor in quality or performance that no one would buy them if they had a choice. Once European-, Japanese-, Chinese-, and US-made products were available, why buy inferior, Russian-made ones? Although some companies attempted to increase the quality of their goods, this process takes a long time. This problem is worse in Russia than in many other states because many Russian cities were built around a single, massive factory, with the factory being the primary employer and reason for the city to exist in the first place. In such ultimate company towns, when the factory closes, no other significant options for employment exist. In the face of such economic uncertainties, parents living in such areas are choosing to have fewer—or, in many cases, no—children. The result is that Russia's population is decreasing. To try to reverse this trend, Russia has created a program of cash incentives to parents for each child born and has created a new holiday for the purpose of procreation—in short, a day of conception! Globalization also has some non-democratic consequences, at least in states where governments

....

North American Free Trade Agreement (NAFTA): a free-trade agreement between Canada, Mexico, and the United States. The agreement greatly reduced all barriers to trade between the three countries and resulted in a significant increase in trade of goods and services between the three. NAFTA was replaced by the United States–Mexico–Canada Agreement (USMCA) in 2020.

United States–Mexico–Canada Agreement (USMCA): a 2020 free-trade agreement between Canada, Mexico, and the United States that succeeded the North American Free Trade Agreement.

Free Trade Under Threat?

Over the centuries, much of the world came to accept the fundamental idea that trade is good. Over time, world trade became freer and more extensive, as witnessed by the increasing number of free-trade agreements (FTAs) around the globe. For example, according to the US International Trade Commission's website, the US had free-trade agreements with 20 different states in 2017, and in 2015 trade with those states represented 47% of US total trade. Perhaps more important, the US had a trade surplus with those free-trade partners! Yet *domestic political pressures* in the US and elsewhere have put new stress on the premise that free trade brings important benefits.

In 2016, Donald Trump was elected president of the United States. Although historically most Republicans favored free trade and market-based capitalism, one part of President Trump's political base rejected free trade, as they saw themselves as its victims. Many of these voters found themselves poorly paid, underemployed, or unemployed, as their former jobs could now be done more cheaply by foreign workers (or even robots). This populist, or nativist, set of voters found their voice in Trump, who called for the North American Free Trade Agreement (NAFTA) to be renegotiated and questioned the assumptions behind free trade's appeal. Within his first two years in office, President Trump withdrew from the Trans-Pacific Partnership (TPP), threatened to withdraw from NAFTA (triggering its renegotiation as the USMCA), and started a major trade war with China.

Similar anti-trade pressures have been seen in Europe. Although there were multiple reasons for the UK's decision to leave the EU, some of them were economic. The UK Independence Party led by Nigel Farage argued that Britain needed to regain its sovereignty—both economic and political. This call resonated, particularly in smaller English towns that had not prospered as much as larger, more cosmopolitan cities. The resulting political pressure led to the surprising vote, albeit by a narrow margin, to leave the EU, which the UK eventually did in early 2020. Britain is not alone in seeing a rise in concerns over free trade. Public demonstrations in countries such as Germany and Belgium occurred in 2016, protesting the proposed Transatlantic Trade and Investment Partnership (TTIP, which included the US) and the EU–Canada Comprehensive Economic and Trade Agreement (CETA). Opponents feared that such agreements favored the interests of major corporations over those of small businesses or even the public, and the lack of transparency regarding the negotiations of these agreements just fed such fears (van der Wolf 2016). Italy's Five Star Movement, an opposition party led by Beppe Grillo, challenged Italy's participation in both the TTIP and CETA as infringements on Italian sovereignty. In 2018, the Five Star Movement gained the most votes of any party but was unable to create a coalition government under its control.

When the first or second largest economy in the world—the United States—and the first and third largest in Europe—Germany and Italy, respectively—witness a backlash against free trade, supporters of free trade have reason to be concerned. Free trade, like capitalism itself, produces losers as well as winners. It is not just the domestic politics of winners and losers that lead states to embrace or reject free trade or FTAs. First, states are concerned with their security. An FTA can provide important economic growth, strategic products, and a reduced likelihood of conflict with the other member or members of the FTA. Thus, signing an FTA can enhance a state's security. Similarly, if all of the other countries in a region are signing FTAs, then not signing one could threaten a state's security. In essence, it is not good to be the last state left out in the cold while all the neighboring countries have joined FTAs. The US might find that to be the case after withdrawing from the TPP.

But becoming vulnerable to the actions of others through increased trade may have security consequences as well. Ask Europeans if they feel more secure by being increasingly dependent on Russia for natural gas. Further, economics bleeds over into politics. For example, South Korea prefers to sign FTAs not only with other countries that have signed FTAs but also with fellow democracies (Drury, Krieckhaus, and Yamamoto 2014). South Korea, like other developed democracies, prefers signing FTAs with other democracies because democracies are more accountable and thus less likely to cheat on an agreement. For as much as the venerable Adam Smith and David Ricardo were right—free trade helps all participating economies grow—we must consider the domestic politics of the states, their security interests, and how trustworthy they consider each other. Thus, a realist, liberal, or Marxist perspective can't explain fully *why* states engage in trade and particularly FTAs. We must employ a foreign policy perspective to understand international trade.

1. What factors explain the shift of much of the developing world toward free-trade practices over the past several decades?

2. How might other domestic factors such as culture influence the trade relations between states?

3. How can a government overcome domestic objections to free trade?

4. Should states consider moral and ethical issues when choosing to trade with another state? ●

attempt to represent the public. This may seem counterintuitive, but consider the following logical sequence. Part of the globalization process involves states joining international organizations, particularly trade organizations such as the WTO. In many cases, such as the WTO, the states agree to the rules of the organization. For example, the WTO does not permit steel tariffs like the ones the United States initiated, nor does the organization allow a state to ban a good without proof that the good in question is dangerous. Thus, the EU ban on hormone-fed beef—enacted through a basically democratic process—was ruled illegal. In effect, by joining the WTO, countries give up a part of their sovereignty. Essentially, the rules of the WTO shape, constrain, and may even supersede the domestic laws of the member states. Banning hormone-fed beef, for example, is a domestic decision, albeit one with international consequences. The EU ban does not say that foreign beef cannot have been fed hormones; it says that any beef, domestic or foreign, cannot be sold in the EU if the cattle were fed hormones. Thus, globalization drives changes from Westphalian sovereignty to neo-Westphalian sovereignty, where states have limits on the ability to make decisions about what happens inside their borders. The EU wanted non-hormone-fed beef, but the WTO overruled its sovereignty by ruling that it could not ban such beef. Of course, the EU still bans hormone-fed beef, but it pays a penalty to do so—sort of like paying a penalty to exercise your sovereignty.

Another example of how the WTO can circumvent democratic rule concerns the gasoline shipped to the United States from Venezuelan refineries. In 1993, the US Environmental Protection Agency (EPA) ruled that all gasoline sold in the United States must meet certain standards for minimal contaminants. Venezuela challenged the rule in 1995, saying that it treated foreign refineries differently from domestic refineries, establishing higher baseline standards. The WTO agreed, stating that countries can establish environmental standards, but they must keep them the same for foreign and domestic companies. After an unsuccessful appeal, the EPA adjusted the Clean Air Act rules to eliminate the differing standards. Critics would say that the Clean Air Act—enacted by a democratically elected body (the US Congress)—was effectively changed by an international organization that has no accountability to the American public.

The hormone-fed beef and Clean Air Act are good examples of how governmental preferences for the domestic population (i.e., sovereignty) are no longer sacrosanct. To be sure, the United States and the states in the EU chose freely to join the WTO. The process to join was very democratic. However, by agreeing to the rules, all countries give up a bit of their right to rule themselves.

Yet another example of sovereignty slipping away concerns the EU. Although not directly part of globalization, the economic and political integration in Europe is connected to and facilitates greater globalization with the European states. Countries joining the EU transfer significant authority to the EU from their individual governments. For example, in many European states, such as Sweden and Germany, parents are restricted in what they may name their child. In Sweden's case, the child may not have a double surname (i.e., two last names). In Spain, however, having both parents' names is traditional. A case arose when a married couple—the wife was Spanish and the husband Swedish—had a child in Sweden. The Swedish government would not permit the parents to give their son a double surname. The parents appealed the decision, and the EU overruled Sweden. Thus, Swedish law was overturned by the supranational EU.

A much more controversial issue in the EU arises from the organization's rules about immigration, refugees, and labor migration. Because the EU requires its members to adhere to open standards for the movement of people—including labor workers—across borders of its members, countries in the EU have faced growing pressure from their own citizens who are concerned that such immigration may create a more competitive jobs environment and reduce opportunities, and maybe even depress wages and benefits. Such concerns were at the heart of the 2016 Brexit vote in the UK. They are also central to the US decision to abandon the TPP trade agreement, to replace NAFTA with the USMCA, and other anti-trade initiatives undertaken by the Trump administration.

Coupled with the impact of globalization on the movement of people in general, and the identity and cultural clashes that have occurred in many countries in Europe, the US, and elsewhere, such problems have fueled and been fueled by a populist backlash against globalization and trade. This backlash is reflected in developments such as the Brexit vote; the election of Donald Trump as US president; and the growing strength of nationalist parties in Europe, such as the National Front in France, the Party for Freedom in the Netherlands, Viktor Orban's Fidesz party in Hungary, and others around the region. Such movements tend to be anti-globalization, nationalist, and even anti-democratic.

Although we discuss stratification and inequality more thoroughly in Chapter 10, we should note that the positive effects of globalization on aggregate economic growth seem to come with significant increases in inequality, both between and within countries. Between countries, the gap between the wealthiest countries and the poorest countries has increased in the global economy. Within a given country, globalization has led to growing gaps between the wealthiest citizens and the rest of the people. In both cases, there are exceptions—poor countries and people who have risen in globalization—but the trend is the opposite.

Finally, what is particularly complicated about the backlashes against globalization is how they have changed over time. In the 1990s, the opposition to globalization was led by socialists and those representing the working poor. As jobs shifted in and out of countries more rapidly, the poorest elements were left unemployed and destitute. Fast-forward 20 years, and the opposition isn't focused on the poor but instead is concerned about the middle and lower classes in developed countries being left behind both economically and socially. It's not that the working poor are in better shape; it's just a different voice objecting to globalization. Time will tell if this backlash against the impacts of globalization continues or even grows.

Can States "Opt Out" of Globalization?

One might suggest that if the member states do not like the rules or decisions of the organizations to which they belong, they could simply leave the organizations. However, the costs of leaving the WTO, the EU, or most large international organizations are very high. If a country resigned its membership from the WTO, it would have to negotiate new trade arrangements with each of its trade partners. Thus, if the United States left because of the gasoline dispute with Venezuela, it would have to negotiate with well over 100 countries to strike a deal on what could be traded and what tariffs should be—on all traded goods and services, not just gasoline. In 2020, the UK began grappling with the realities of these problems as it left the EU: Not only was the withdrawal process difficult, with the EU disinclined to be accommodating, but the UK economy also slowed sharply across several dimensions after the vote. Indeed, Brexit—along with the consequences of the global pandemic—contributed to the 2020 economic recession in the UK. Brexit also reignited interest in independence from the UK for Scotland, whose citizens overwhelmingly prefer to stay in the European Union.

The UK experience further illustrates the problem that if a state decided to leave one or more organizations and withdraw itself even partially from the global economy, other states would likely not trust the departing state very much. Could one rely on a country that decided to pick up its marbles and not play, just because it didn't like a specific ruling? One would be rightfully concerned about whether a state that quit once might not do so again. Thus, one's reputation for trustworthiness or credibility is involved in such arrangements, and although intangible, these are meaningful factors that policymakers will consider.

Although some states might be able to bear the cost of leaving the global economy, for all it would be difficult, for most it would be crippling, and it could come with unanticipated consequences. For example, the US withdrew from the TPP. One of Washington's implicit goals in joining the TPP had been to limit China's domination of trade in the region, as China was intentionally not included in the organization. Since the US withdrew from the TPP, some Asian and Pacific states have strengthened their trade ties with China, as it remains the dominant trade partner of the region. In short, leaving the global economy or integrated trade relationships is not really an option that countries seriously entertain. They may resist the pressures of organization membership, as the EU did with hormone-fed beef, by simply paying the cost of sanctions. Alternatively, states may create education programs for workers displaced by globalization, and in some cases countries will choose not to join organizations. Other countries simply go along with globalization as best they can. Regardless of the tactic that a state follows, the world is becoming more and more globalized.

CONCLUSION

Think back to Figure 8-1, which showed the National, International, and Global Economy Eras. Those three eras capture much of the history of the world's economy over the centuries. These were big changes, but even within each era, there were constant shifts. In 1992, Francis Fukuyama wrote a book titled *The End of History and the Last Man*. His basic thesis was that democracy and capitalism had not only won the day but had become the final stage of human history. He suggested that there would be no new economic or political systems. Many would have probably agreed with him in 2008, before the start of the Great Recession. Capitalism seemed to be a juggernaut; it seemed unstoppable, inevitable. That is no longer so clear. Instead, governments had to intervene in the private market to keep it from collapsing—a policy more akin to mercantilism than capitalism—and many countries are facing anti-globalization, anti-capitalist, and anti-democratic movements in a backlash against some of the challenges of a global economy.

The Globalization Index has increased 55% over the past 40 years, so clearly the world economy is becoming more and more interconnected. Is capitalism slowly chugging forward, dealing with bumps and delays along the way? Are mercantilism and communism dead?

Perhaps Fukuyama was right, and our economic history is over. Perhaps, like Mark Twain, reports of globalization's death are greatly exaggerated.

Though the world has shifted to a global economy, it still seems possible that the future is not yet fully written. It seems reasonable to conclude that states will try anything to attain wealth, power, and security from their economies. If that is true, in which type of country would you be happiest? Why? Now that the world's economy is so much more global and inter-connected, how does that affect the role and practices of states as they try to gain economic security? Given the need for countries to secure resources and wealth to maintain their physical security, which economic system—mercantilism, capitalism, communism, or some combination—is best suited to create wealth and transfer it into security for people, especially in the current global economy? Which type of state will likely be the most peaceful? These are hard questions to answer, but they are the questions that will face the world in the coming years. ●

KEY CONCEPTS

8-1 Trace the connections between money, power, and security.

Wealth is an essential part of power and security in world politics, and there is more to the connection between money and power than building a military and using it to secure critical resources such as territory and oil. States have important interests in the pursuit of wealth and development, and politics and economics are connected. There is both tension and a symbiotic relationship between government and the market. Governments try to maintain control of their territorial borders, but businesses see borders as slowing down their ability to sell goods and services. However, governments also create and enforce property ownership laws, thereby protecting commercial investments and creating the law and order businesses require. Economic interactions can also affect the consequences of anarchy, as economic interactions and interdependence can not only reduce conflict but may lead to a true positive peace.

8-2 Identify the different historical approaches and theories that drove the world economy.

The world economy has evolved through three eras since the beginning of the state system: national to international to global. In the National Economy Era, most economic exchange occurred within the borders of states. States pursued mercantilism and colonialism to help domestic businesses make money, protect them from foreign competition, and gain wealth by controlling foreign territory. The Industrial Revolution and the rise of free trade began the International Economy Era. Technological advances and the development and expansion of the liberal international economic order led to the Global Economy Era.

8-3 Explain the rise of liberalism and free trade and its consequences, challenges, and alternatives.

The idea of free trade developed by Adam Smith and David Ricardo and the Industrial Revolution led to the International Economy Era. First the United Kingdom, and then others, began to believe that if countries could agree to trade freely, the countries would become wealthier and there would be a greater chance for continuing peace after war. British power in the 19th century and American power after World War II helped promote liberalized trade to make countries better off and promote peace. Marxism also arose in this era as a competing idea and system, especially in the 20th century. After World War II, the US led the development of the liberal international economic order (LIEO). The LIEO promoted and spread free trade and encouraged market economies that worked together, and it established international institutions to tie states together and help them cooperate. The LIEO also created the foundations for non-state actors such as multinational corporations (MNCs) and private financial institutions to operate more freely across borders and to extend their operations to more and more countries. Technological change—the computer era, advances in information and communication technology, and faster transportation—all played critical roles in the transition to and nature of the Global Economy Era, in which more and more economic transactions cross borders.

8-4 Describe the nature and implications of liberalism and globalization for world politics.

The modern economy is driven by the power of capitalism and the forces of globalization. These forces produce increasingly broad and deep economic connections among the states and societies of the world. Over time, capitalism has produced economic growth and great wealth, and free trade and the institutions supporting the LIEO have contributed to interdependence and peace among countries. These forces have empowered non-state actors and constrained the power of states but also contribute to inequality and injustice, and they have made the economies of individual states far more vulnerable to global economic forces. Globalization is the global spread of technology, money, products, culture, and opinions through foreign trade, investment, transportation, and cultural exchange. Through this process, countries become integrated into a common global network whereby they know more about each other but are also tied to each other through interdependencies. On the positive side, globalization contributes to economic growth and development. MNCs can bring jobs to a country that result in less economic discrimination and forced labor, particularly among women. There is also a greater likelihood of peace, both inside countries and between states. There are also drawbacks of globalization. The era of the global economy has seen increasing inequality within and between states. Not all MNCs are benevolent, and they can exploit labor and society for their own gain. Globalization can put tremendous pressure on states by exposing them to competition in the global marketplace, ultimately weakening them. Finally, globalization tends to be non-democratic because the process involves states joining international organizations, particularly trade organizations such as the WTO, and agreeing to certain rules that are not subject to the domestic political process.

KEY TERMS

Eurozone 225

supranational organization 225

bilateral 225

mercantilism 227

protectionism 227

colonialism 227

metropole 227

beggar-thy-neighbor 228

absolute advantage 229

comparative advantage 229

Industrial Revolution 229

hyperinflation 231

trade war 231

centrally planned (or command) economy 232

liberal international economic order (LIEO) 235

Bretton Woods system 235

austerity program 236

General Agreement on Tariffs and Trade (GATT) 236

nontariff barrier 236

devalue 239

fair trade 245

North American Free Trade Agreement (NAFTA) 246

United States–Mexico–Canada Agreement (USMCA) 246

REVIEW QUESTIONS

1. How have countries historically sought wealth?

2. How does the historical pursuit of money differ from the current pursuit?

3. Is communism dead, or do aspects of it influence states to this day?

4. Why has capitalism had such a big impact on the world, and will it continue to have a powerful impact in the future?

THINK ABOUT THIS

Is Globalization Good, Bad, or Ugly?

In the book *Has Globalization Gone Too Far?* well-known economist Dani Rodrik asks whether the wide and rapid spread of trade, technology, and culture that is globalization is costing people in developing countries too much. As developing countries compete for trade opportunities, they lower the conditions in which their citizens must work. Lower pay, fewer benefits, and longer hours all lead to greater human costs. To stay competitive, governments cannot easily raise taxes to alleviate these costs. So globalization can end up extracting large human costs from countries. It can also bring wealth and better human rights. Globalization is good, bad, and at times ugly. Consider this complicated issue: What are the major pros and cons of globalization? How might states make globalization sustainable or "good"? Are the human costs of globalization simply the cost of development and progress?

On balance, is globalization a positive force or a negative force in world politics?

FOR MORE INFORMATION . . .

Global Economics

Ravenhill, John, ed. (2017). *Global Political Economy*. Oxford, UK: Oxford University Press.

Globalization

Lechner, Frank and John Boli, eds. (2019). *The Globalization Reader*, 6th ed. Hoboken, NJ: Wiley-Blackwell.

Rodrik, Dani. (2011). *The Globalization Paradox: Democracy and the Future of the World Economy*. New York, NY: Norton.

Rodrik, Dani. (2017). *Straight Talk on Trade: Ideas for a Sane Economy*. Princeton, NJ: Princeton University Press.

Steger, Manfred. (2017). *Globalization: A Very Short Introduction*, 4th ed. Oxford, UK: Oxford University Press.

Stiglitz, Joseph. (2017). *Globalization and Its Discontents, Revisited: Anti-Globalization in the Age of Trump*. New York, NY: Norton.

Mercantilism

Rogowski, Ronald. (1990). *Commerce and Coalitions*. Princeton, NJ: Princeton University Press.

Saul Loeb/AFP/Getty Images

The UN Security Council votes to impose new sanctions on North Korea in 2017

How hard must it be to sanction a country that has limited connections with the rest of the world?

AP Photo/Mark Lennihan

9 Economic Statecraft

Sanctions, Aid, and Their Consequences

Learning Objectives

After studying this chapter, you will be able to…

9-1 Identify the many ways in which wealth can be used to influence other countries.

9-2 Trace the complex nature of economic sanctions, why they are used, and what consequences they have.

9-3 Identify the potential benefits and consequences of foreign aid.

Carrots and Sticks?

After taking office in 2017, the US Trump administration

- Tried to cut foreign aid by about 30% in each subsequent annual budget proposal

- Threatened recipients with the loss of foreign aid if they did not support US foreign policy agendas

- Proposed prioritizing bilateral aid but not multilateral aid through international organizations

- Cut foreign aid to Guatemala, Honduras, El Salvador, and Nicaragua

- Terminated foreign aid to the Palestinian Authority

- Imposed economic sanctions on Iran, North Korea, Venezuela, Cuba, Turkey, and Russia

- Increased military aid to Saudi Arabia and the United Arab Emirates for use in the Yemeni civil war

- Raised tariffs on imported steel and aluminum and started a trade war with China

Although only actions by the Trump administration are listed here, we could easily create similar lists for previous US presidents, as well as for other world leaders. These actions raise some interesting questions about how states use wealth as a form of power to influence and coerce other states:

1. What might the Trump administration have been trying to accomplish through the use of these economic tools of statecraft?

Chapter Outline

9-1 Economic Statecraft

9-2 Economic Sanctions

9-3 Foreign Aid

2. How do the players in world politics use foreign assistance and sanctions to get others to do what they want?

3. What consequences follow the use of these economic tools? When and how might they be most effective? Ineffective?

INTRODUCTION: USING WEALTH TO INFLUENCE OTHER COUNTRIES

As we discussed in Chapter 8, there are many reasons for states to seek wealth and even more ways for them to attain it. In addition to the military power and prestige that wealth brings to an individual state, it also endows the state with a tool that can be used to influence or coerce other states. Both the power and the potential to coerce can mean greater security. In fact, a famous political economist, Albert Hirschman, argued that countries should structure their trade to make other states dependent on them because that would increase their influence and security. In the simplest of terms, one state can *give* money to or *take away* money (and thus business opportunities) from other states. By attaching conditions or demands to the *giving* or *taking* of money, one state may influence another state and pursue economic security for itself. For example, the primary purpose of US antidrug aid is to reduce the flow of illegal drugs into the United States, subsequently lowering crime and making the country more secure. The process of giving and taking money for political purposes is called **economic statecraft**: the use of economic means (money) to secure political ends (or goals).

....

economic statecraft: the use of economic means to secure political ends.

9-1 ECONOMIC STATECRAFT

>> **9-1   Identify the many ways in which wealth can be used to influence other countries.**

What are we getting at when we say "giving or taking" money or economic opportunity? From a realist perspective, the concept is actually quite simple, although the ways in which states can give and take money are many. For example, Russia might give money in the form of grants or low-interest rate loans to Kazakhstan so that the Kazakh government treats ethnic Russians living there favorably. Russia might also expect that Kazakhstan will allow the Russian military to keep bases in the country in return for the grants and low-interest rate loans. Russia might also have offered aid to reward Kazakhstan for joining the Eurasian Economic Union. Thus, Russia provides funds and economic opportunity to Kazakhstan to increase Russia's influence, its own economic (and international) security, and the security of Russians living abroad. Another example is China, which has increased its foreign

aid budget by about 20% per year since 2005 in a bid to expand its engagement and influence in the world, especially in Africa, where China seeks access to a variety of natural resources and political capital among its many states (see Map 9-1).

Another less obvious example is for one country to give another a special trade deal. If a country like Japan normally charges a 10% **tariff** on beef, but it offers Australia a 5% tariff, then it has made it cheaper and easier for Australian ranchers to sell their beef to Japan. That is effectively the same as giving the Australians money. This trade deal could be offered in return for a similar deal for the Japanese—for example, a lower tariff on Japanese televisions and PlayStation game consoles sold in Australia.

Each of these examples is about "giving" money in return for some economic or political benefit. What about "taking" money or economic opportunity? A good example of taking wealth or money are the **economic sanctions** the US imposed on Venezuela, North Korea, Iran, Russia, and others described in the chapter opener. The Iran action is especially interesting because it comes after a multilateral agreement between Iran, the US, European states, and others in which Iran agreed to limit and/or eliminate its nuclear weapons programs, in return for relief from extensive sanctions imposed by the UN. After 2005, the UN, led

....

tariff: a tax on products imported into one country from other countries.

economic sanction: the cessation of some or all economic exchange between two countries.

MAP 9-1

Where the World Sends Its Aid, 2018

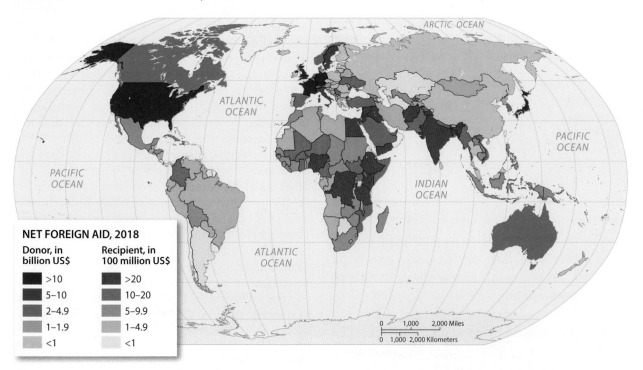

NET FOREIGN AID, 2018

Donor, in billion US$	Recipient, in 100 million US$
>10	>20
5–10	10–20
2–4.9	5–9.9
1–1.9	1–4.9
<1	<1

Iran, Nuclear Weapons, and Sanctions

Although there had been significant chatter about an Iranian nuclear program for years, the US formally accused Iran of trying to develop nuclear weapons in 2002. For the next four years, the US and EU led negotiations with Iran to end its nuclear program. After fits and starts, the UN Security Council passed sanctions against Iran in 2006 in an attempt to coerce Iran to comply. Another nine years passed with more sanctions and no real movement toward negotiations.

However, in 2015 the five permanent members of the Security Council, Germany, the European Union, and

Iran concluded the Joint Comprehensive Plan of Action or "Iran nuclear deal." According to this agreement, the sanctions were lifted (some immediately, and some in phases), and Iran agreed to end its nuclear weapons program and allow oversight and inspections. Just three years later, the Trump administration withdrew from the deal and reimposed US sanctions on Iran, despite regular certification by the International Atomic Energy Agency, the US Department of Defense, and US intelligence agencies that Iran is complying with its obligations under the deal. What happened to end the impasse and pave the way for the deal? Why did the US abandon it? ●

by European countries and the United States, had cut off trade with Iran because of its development of fissile material needed to make a nuclear weapon but agreed to lift those sanctions once Iran complied with a 2015 comprehensive agreement with the UN Security Council's five permanent members, plus Germany and the European Union (see "Spotlight On: Iran, Nuclear Weapons, and Sanctions"). Why would the US impose additional sanctions in 2017?

For a very long time, the United States also maintained comprehensive sanctions against Cuba. Soon after Fidel Castro took over Cuba in 1959, the US began sanctioning the Caribbean island with hopes that Castro would step down. As a communist, Castro was seen as a security threat to the United States, because Cuba is only 90 miles from the US coast and the island would provide an opportune base of operations for the Soviet Union in the Western Hemisphere. This threat later became real during the 1962 Cuban Missile Crisis when the Soviet Union placed medium- and intermediate-range nuclear missiles in Cuba. Though Castro originally had no intention of breaking ties with the United States, American leaders saw the situation as dangerous and attempted to coerce the new leader. First, the White House put a quota on sugar imports, but those sanctions rapidly grew into a complete embargo on all Cuban goods and services. For more than five decades, US citizens were prevented from buying Cuban products (including the famous Cuban cigars), directly traveling to Cuba, or selling the island-state almost anything. There was also a limit on how much money family members in the United States could send their relatives in Cuba. In the 1990s, in an attempt to coerce Castro even further, the United States threatened to sanction *other countries* doing business with Cuba. In 2016, the US relaxed a number of those sanctions in an effort to

improve US–Cuban relations and hasten Cuban liberalization, but the Trump administration reversed course the next year and reestablished stricter sanctions in 2017. Originally, the US government tried to topple the Castro regime through an economic embargo, and now it continues to try to use its vast economic power to coerce Cuba to allow democratic reform in the country.

Another example is the response to increasingly aggressive Russian actions. For instance, when Russian President Vladimir Putin moved his troops into the southern Ukrainian province of Crimea in 2014, US and EU leaders placed sanctions on Russian high-level officials and firms. The economic pressure was meant to stop the Russians from taking more provinces in Ukraine and to push them out of Crimea. So far, the sanctions have had little effect—Russia annexed Crimea and continues to support rebels in and put pressure on eastern Ukraine, where many of the people are Russian-speaking and of Russian ethnicity. Europeans were also hesitant to impose harsh sanctions on Russia because of Russian threats to cut off oil and gas supplies to Europe in response (see Map 9-2). However, in 2016–2017, after Russia aggressively interfered in elections in the US and other European countries, the US and the EU expanded sanctions against Russian leaders and organizations in response. These examples illustrate that "taking money" to coerce another country can be accomplished simply by cutting off an important resource and that countries can retaliate for being sanctioned in the first place.

Now that we understand that wealth by itself can be used to influence other states and increase security, we need to explore briefly the long history of economic statecraft in international relations. Then we will turn to the many different ways in which economics are used for political purposes.

Cuba is full of vintage cars because Cubans were unable to purchase new US cars after 1958

These cars are certainly an odd side effect of the sanctions against Cuba. What do you think will happen to them and the rest of Cuba once the sanctions are ended?

Andreas Jansen/Barcroft Media via Getty Images

MAP 9-2

The European Union's Reliance on Russian Natural Gas

Source: Data extracted in October 2020 from Eurostat (2020), "EU Imports of Energy Products—Recent Developments."

9-1a The Long History of Economic Statecraft: Money as a Carrot and a Stick

References to economic statecraft date back to approximately 500 BCE, when the famous Chinese general Sun Tzu spoke of defeating one's enemies without resorting to military conflict and how important the economy was to leaders and their armies. A few hundred years later in ancient Greece, both Plato and Aristotle feared the power economic statecraft could have on a state. Between 400 and 300 BCE, they argued that states should be as self-sufficient as possible. That is, states should be able to provide for themselves as much as possible without trading with other states. Trade with foreigners (even if those foreigners lived a few hundred miles away) was considered to be corrupting and would likely lead to weakness within the state. Both the great city-states of the period, Athens and Sparta, held as a badge of honor their limited trade with other states and their ability to function on their own.

In the late 1700s, Alexander Hamilton—first secretary of the US Treasury—strongly believed that the state's economy could and must be used as a form of influence, not just a way to build military power. His belief that commerce itself was a coercive foreign policy tool influenced George Washington during his presidency. From the time of its birth, the United States used economic statecraft as a crucial part of its foreign policy (Gilbert 1961).

Economic statecraft has a long history, both in the writings of intellectuals such as Plato and Hamilton and in the practice of international relations. One of the major reasons Japan decided in 1941 to bomb the US naval fleet at Pearl Harbor was an embargo that Australia, Great Britain, the Netherlands East Indies (the colony that later became Indonesia), and the United States placed on Japan. In an effort to keep the Japanese from expanding their empire in Asia and the Pacific, the four Western powers stopped selling the Japanese empire iron, steel, and oil. All three of these goods were critical to the Japanese plans for continued expansion. This move by the Western powers seriously threatened Japan's industrial strength and military power. Japanese officials believed that if they did not strike back at the United States and other countries promptly, they would be quickly weakened to the point that they would be unable to continue their expansion and the growth of their power and influence. Thus, economic pressure hastened Japanese aggression, their eventual attack on Pearl Harbor, and the US entrance into World War II.

The history of granting aid to other countries was more difficult to follow until the last five decades because states and international organizations did not carefully track aid. Further, most transfers of money were based on colonial ties and generally flowed from the colonies back to the imperial power. However, since World War II, aid has become an important part of international relations. In 1960, approximately $32 billion (in 2015 constant dollars) of development aid was given globally. By 2019, that number had risen to about $170 billion (in 2015 constant dollars). In that time, world population doubled, while aid more than quintupled. It is notable how much aid has grown and how important it has become. Some states rely on international assistance just to keep their people from starving, and, sadly, even with the dramatic increase in aid over the decades, poverty and malnourishment are still pervasive problems throughout the world.

Economic sanctions and foreign aid have been around for centuries and are becoming more and more a part of our lives. Many questions surround how these policies are used as well as whether or not they are effective. In the sections that follow, we explore these questions in depth.

9-2 ECONOMIC SANCTIONS

>> **9-2** **Trace the complex nature of economic sanctions, why they are used, and what consequences they have.**

An economic sanction is a policy that reduces the economic exchange between two states for a political goal. However, not all economic reductions or restrictions should be considered sanctions. States regularly bargain with each other over trade, but this bargaining does not constitute a sanction because it involves economic issues rather than political issues. For example, in 2017, the United States believed that Canada was flooding the US market with softwood lumber and threatened to impose a tariff on Canadian lumber that would have increased its price by about 20%. This may sound like a small disagreement, but many Canadian and American leaders feared a possible trade war that could spread to other products and sectors, with conflicts over dairy, steel, and aircraft already occurring. However, this is fundamentally different from sanctioning Iran to end its nuclear weapons program. Because these kinds of negotiations are so common, it is better for us not to think of them as sanctions. Instead, we need to focus on those economic means that are aimed at political ends.

9-2a The Types of Economic Sanctions

One state can impose an economic sanction on another state in four basic ways. These are often, but not always, combined into one set of sanctions. The most common type of sanction is a trade sanction that cuts the exchange of goods between the two countries. The second type is exemplified at the opening of the chapter—cutting foreign aid. Sanctions that cut aid to another country were used more during the Cold War and, although not uncommon, are used less today. Another common type is a financial sanction that freezes the movement of assets (e.g., money in bank accounts) for the sanctioned country. Finally, third-party sanctions actually threaten a third country that is doing business with the main target of the sanctions. This type of sanction is relatively new and far more complicated than the other forms of economic coercion. Let's explore each of these more carefully.

Import and Export Sanctions

Trade sanctions are the most common and easy to understand, whether they are import or export sanctions. In both types of sanctions, the sanctioning state (referred to as the sender) reduces or cuts off completely either (a) goods and services coming from the sanctioned country (referred to as the target)—these are import sanctions (boycotts)—or (b) goods and services being sold to the sanctioned country—export sanctions (embargoes). When we think of sanctions, **import and export sanctions** are most often what come to mind, and with good reason: 69% of all sanctions include import or export restrictions (Hufbauer, Schott, Elliott, and Oegg 2009).

Together, these types of sanctions can be referred to as trade sanctions, but such trade sanctions do have distinct differences. Import sanctions hurt businesses in the target country by not allowing them to sell their goods in the sender country—such as not letting Cuban sugar or cigars be sold in the United States. This can cause those businesses in the target country to go bankrupt or at least lose significant profits.

Sanctions affect the sender country as well. Import sanctions also often cause the prices of goods made by the target country to rise in the sender country. Because the supply of the good is limited due to the sanction, prices may go up. Thus, if Japan decides not to buy Burmese rice to punish the repressive former military government in Burma, Japanese consumers might have to pay more for rice, and Japanese rice farmers will earn more for their crops. There are also businesses in the sender country that imported and then sold the sanctioned goods. They lose business as well, as did the US sugar companies that imported raw cane sugar from Cuba, refined it, and then sold it on the US market. Some of those businesses were tied so closely to Cuban suppliers that they went bankrupt after import sanctions were imposed on Cuba (and the

CEO of one of those firms committed suicide). More recently, the US oil and gas industry opposed extending new sanctions against Venezuelan oil exports, arguing that such action would raise prices, reduce profits, and cost jobs in US refineries. The costs to both the sender and the target in the recent US–China trade war will take some years to accurately calculate.

Imagine if the United Kingdom decided to sanction all of the countries in the Persian Gulf for human rights violations by not buying any oil from them. The United Kingdom would have to rely on its oil from the North Sea, which could not match the production from Saudi Arabia and the other Gulf states. As a consequence, oil prices in the United Kingdom would skyrocket. This would hurt the British citizens who have to pay more for gasoline, but it would help oil firms like British Petroleum because BP could sell its products for higher prices than it could before the sanctions. Although this hypothetical example is extreme—no country would stop buying oil from the entire Persian Gulf region—it illustrates how the sanctions can have different effects in the sender country.

Export sanctions tend to cause prices to rise in the target country because there are fewer products being sold. This type of sanction can also cause serious production problems in the target. For example, the United States began restricting the sale of replacement truck parts to Chile in the early 1970s as part of a set of economic sanctions. The US government didn't like Salvador Allende, the new, democratically elected Chilean president, who was accused of ties to socialism and the Soviet Union. Without the truck parts, it became very difficult for Chile to keep its truck fleet on the road. Although the parts may not have had much monetary value, their importance to transporting goods within Chile was dramatic. Due to tactics such as this, the Chilean economy was destabilized, and Allende was later overthrown by his military.

Export sanctions do not typically cause prices to rise in the sender country because they restrict the sender's domestic businesses from selling to the target. For example, China might restrict the sale of rare metals to the EU if it did not like the EU policy toward the Chinese province of Tibet. This would not cause prices to rise in China, but it would make it more difficult for EU countries to manufacture certain electronics requiring those metals and thus cause the price of those products to increase in Europe. Russian natural gas export sanctions on countries like Ukraine would not cause natural gas prices in Russia to increase; they would just cause Russia's natural gas company Gazprom to lose some expected revenue.

Aid Sanctions

In addition to cutting off the trade with another country, the sanctioning state can also reduce or eliminate the

---

import and export sanctions: when one country scales back on or stops buying products from, or selling them to, another country.

monetary aid it gives, which is called an **aid sanction**. Of course, this assumes that the sender gives aid—whether it is military, development, or humanitarian—to the target country before the sanctions are initiated. For example, in 2017 the US threatened to suspend aid to Pakistan and actually withheld military aid to Egypt; these are great illustrations of this type of aid conditionality. The United States allocated and planned to provide these funds but took the actions to try to force the recipients to change their behavior.

Another good example is antidrug aid by the US. In this case, the US State Department must certify that the country receiving the aid is doing its part in battling the production and trafficking of illegal drugs. If it is determined that the country is failing to combat drugs, then the aid is cut off. This may seem like a simple transaction—stop paying the country when it fails to do its part—but it is very much a sanction. Think of it this way: The United States is sanctioning the target for allowing drugs to be produced or trafficked by reducing or ceasing to provide aid. The country is being punished for not following through on the policy the United States wants.

This process of certification extends beyond antidrug aid. In 1974, the US Congress passed the Jackson-Vanik Amendment that required the State Department to certify that all countries receiving any type of aid not engage in human rights violations. Originally, the amendment was aimed at the Soviet Union, which at the time did not allow Soviet Jews to emigrate to other countries, but it soon became a way for the United States to sanction other countries that violated human rights. This practice was not applied evenly—for many years countries that were allied with the United States were permitted to violate human rights, but the law required closer inspection of the aid-granting process.

A similar strategy was adopted in 1976, when the US Congress began requiring that all countries receiving aid not be involved in supporting terrorist groups. This list of terrorist supporters is relatively short, but the consequences of being on it are severe: The United States cannot provide aid or conduct trade with any listed country. Because the United States is the first or second largest economy in the world, this can be a severe penalty. Being denied access to US consumers is very costly for foreign providers of goods and services. As such, several countries on the list have worked to change their policies. A good example of this—ironically, given later events—is Libya. Realizing that he needed trade and support from the United States to boost his economy, former Libyan leader Muammar Gaddafi took steps to formally end his support of Islamic terrorists and normalize relations with the United States in 2006. Clearly, that more positive relationship with the United States ended once

Gaddafi ordered his troops to fire on the Libyan people during the civil war that led to his downfall in 2011.

Financial Sanctions

The third type of sanction is a **financial sanction**. The most common version of this kind of sanction involves the sanctioning country's freezing the bank accounts of the target country, its government officials, or other members of the elite hierarchy of the society. For example, when Iranian students stormed the US Embassy and took hostages in 1979, President Carter froze all of the Iranian bank accounts in the United States. Approximately $12 billion in money, gold, and other Iranian assets was held by US banks. Once the accounts were frozen, the Iranian government did not have access to any of the funds. This placed a serious burden on the Iranians, especially once the Iran-Iraq war started in 1980 and they needed the money to support their war effort. These were the funds that Iran initially got back in the Iran nuclear deal.

In 2011, the Arab League made headlines when its member countries imposed financial sanctions against Syria, such as freezing assets and cutting off transactions with the Syrian central bank, for the Assad regime's violent crackdown against Arab Spring dissenters. Western countries also froze the bank accounts of Syrian business leaders with close ties to Syrian President Bashar al-Assad as a way to put pressure on the regime.

The US and EU sanctions on a set of specific Russian leaders with close ties to President Vladimir Putin following the Russian intervention in Ukraine and democratic elections in the US, Europe, and elsewhere were hoped to have the same effect. By freezing the assets of these particular individuals—and only them—held in US and EU banks and limiting their use of those banks for international transactions, the United States and the European Union have made their lives less profitable. Such targeted sanctions focused on specific individuals and leaders are sometimes known as **smart sanctions** because they seek to punish those individuals actually responsible for a regime's behavior, rather than the state's population as a whole. In this case, the hope was that they would pressure Putin to stand down in Ukraine. All the countries on which the new US sanctions mentioned in the chapter opener were imposed faced asset freezing,

---

aid sanction: cutting off aid to a country in order to get it to change its behavior.

financial sanction: the freezing of a country's financial assets held in another country.

smart sanctions: sanctions that target specific individuals thought to be responsible for a regime's bad behavior rather than targeting a state's entire economy.

blocked access to banking and other financial transactions, and other financial sanctions.

Although this type of sanction was very effective in punishing the Iranians during the late 1970s, such sanctions have since become more difficult to impose because of the proliferation of offshore banks. As major banks took hold in places such as Bermuda, Antigua, Barbuda, the Cayman Islands, Cyprus, and elsewhere, governments and leaders began keeping their funds in more than one country. Thus, if Japan wanted to freeze the assets of China, it could freeze only China's money that was kept in Japanese banks. If funds were held in other countries, Japan would have to get the cooperation of each country and bank to freeze the funds. Given that those offshore banks are successful because they typically do not permit such political meddling, financial sanctions have become less effective with time.

One significant exception is worth noting. In 2007, the US Treasury requested that Banco Delta Asia in Macao freeze the assets of Kim Jong-il, the late North Korean dictator. Kim had been laundering money from the sale of drugs and illegal weapons through this and other banks in order to support his oppressive regime. Normally, such a request would be ignored. However, the United States told the banks that if they did not comply, it would be illegal for US banks and firms to do business with them. Although Banco Delta Asia did not comply, many other banks in Macao did stop doing business with North Korea because they valued business with the United States more than their business with North Korea. Further, Macao officials tightened money-laundering laws and enforcement.

Third-Party Sanctions

The most recent type of sanction gained notoriety in 1996, when the US Congress passed the Helms-Burton Act (also known as the Libertad Act). Senator Jesse Helms and Representative Dan Burton believed that the sanctions against Cuba were not working. Since 1960, the United States had severed all economic interactions with the Caribbean island-state, making the sanctions against Cuba some of the most comprehensive in the world. Yet after 36 years and eight US presidents, the leader of Cuba—Fidel Castro—was still in power. Helms and Burton proposed a new way to put pressure on Cuba. Because the United States did not have any economic interactions directly with Cuba, there was no direct way to apply more economic pressure. The United States simply could not trade less with Cuba because it did not trade with

Cuba at all. Instead, the Helms-Burton Act directed the United States to sanction other countries doing business with Cuba. For example, if a Canadian hotel corporation planned to invest in building a resort in Cuba, the United States could sanction Canada to stop the investment, limit the ability of that Canadian company to do business in the United States, or even arrest its CEO if that person happened to enter the United States.

This is considered a **third-party sanction** because a third country (Canada, in the preceding example) is the target of the sanctions. The new US sanctions imposed on North Korea in mid-2017 included comparable third-party sanctions, as have previous US efforts against that state. Such third-party sanctions are particularly important when the sanctioning state does not trade or invest in the target state. The United States did not sanction North Korea (because it has no economic relationship with the totalitarian state), but it did threaten sanctions on third parties—in this case, offshore banks in Southeast Asia—with such economic relationships.

Not surprisingly, third-party sanctions such as those in the Helms-Burton Act and the 2017 sanctions against North Korea drew considerable criticism from both within the United States and other countries. In the 1990s, Canada and Spain did considerable business with Cuba and objected; more recently, China raised concerns about third-party sanctions against North Korea, as it is North Korea's largest trade partner. This type of sanction can generate great pressure, however. In the Cuba example, greater pressure on Cuba occurred because fewer countries wanted to invest, for fear that they would be sanctioned by the United States. The downside to third-party sanctions is that the sanctioning country may end up sanctioning its own allies. For instance, the Helms-Burton sanction put significant stress on diplomatic ties between Canada and the US. States must therefore be careful when employing this kind of sanction.

9-2b Total Sanctions

The previously described types of sanctions are not mutually exclusive. Countries can deploy multiple types of sanctions, including total or comprehensive sanctions, or the cutoff of all economic connections to the target. Although such sanctions are not common, they do exist. The US sanctions against Cuba, North Korea, and Iran are good examples. During the height of the sanctions periods with these countries, there was some minor economic activity with the United States, but it is ultimately trivial compared to what it would be like if there had been no sanctions.

Two other examples are the sanctions against South Africa and Rhodesia (now called Zimbabwe)

third-party sanction: a sanction levied against a third-party state to keep that state from doing business with the primary target of the sanctions.

during the time of their apartheid regimes. In both cases, a white minority ruled the country, and when called on to open the political system to all citizens of the state, both refused. The UN mandated comprehensive sanctions against each country, and slowly almost all other countries began to follow the UN mandate. In Rhodesia, a long civil war broke out, which ultimately ended white minority rule. South Africa's transition away from apartheid was somewhat more peaceful. The tremendous pressure from around the world—including sanctions by most countries and divestment by huge multinational corporations—led the white minority regime in South Africa to negotiate an end to apartheid, which paved the way for the election of Nelson Mandela, South Africa's first Black president.

These total or comprehensive sanctions are not the norm, but they do occur and at a huge cost to the targeted country. Many policymakers and activists argue that military action might be more humane than a total embargo of a state. That may sound farfetched, but when you consider that sanctions—when applied severely—can cut a state's economy in half, you can see why sanctions are not necessarily considered the most humane option available for trying to coerce another state.

9-2c The Many Purposes of Sanctions

We have discussed thus far the different ways in which one state can sanction another, but what might the sanctioning country seek from the sanctions? The list of sanction goals is long and includes some rather specific and even obscure goals. For example, in 1978, China sanctioned Albania for making anti-Chinese comments. In this case, the sanctions were used simply as a way to signal to the Albanians and the world that China was upset about the critical comments. That may sound a little childish, but signaling other countries is an important part of international relations because it informs countries about each other's preferences. For most sanctions, however, their goals can be divided into five types.

First, one of the goals sought by a sanctioning country is to weaken the target state's military and economy. This goal harkens back to the writing by Sun Tzu and is often considered "economic warfare" because it is so closely tied to military conflict. The basic idea is that the sanctioning country wants to weaken the target before attacking (or being attacked). Thus, the sanctions have a distinct security objective and are often used as a prelude to war. While such sanctions were rather common in the first half of the 20th century, they have become uncommon because sanctioning other countries as a way to soften them

up before an invasion violates international norms of conflict resolution. Today, countries are expected to try to work out their differences before going to war, rather than slowly bleeding their opponent's military before attacking them. Obviously, things have changed over the past 100 years or so.

Second, sanctions are also commonly used to destabilize a government, often in hopes of changing the leadership, type of government, or its policies. The sanctions against Cuba fit this description, as do the US sanctions against the regimes in Nicaragua, Panama, North Korea, and others. These sanctions sent a signal to the world not only that the United States opposed the regimes in these countries but also that the US meant to make it difficult if not impossible for these regimes to function. By causing unemployment, inflation, and supply shortages, the sanctions were supposed to lead to disruptions in the economy and public life. Such efforts worked well in some places—Panama and Yugoslavia come to mind—but not in others (Cuba and North Korea, for example). Sometimes your neighbors just get tired of your actions. In 2017, Saudi Arabia, the United Arab Emirates, Bahrain, and Egypt cut off trade with Qatar, saying its policies promoted terrorism and destabilized the Middle East region. Instead of changing its behavior, however, Qatar found alternative suppliers from which to purchase food and other goods in a matter of weeks, and Qatar's oil and natural gas sales were largely unaffected. Like many sanctions, these did not have their intended effect.

Third, in another security-related purpose, states often use sanctions in an effort to limit the proliferation of nuclear weapons. Canada has taken the lead several times, starting in the 1970s by sanctioning India and Pakistan for proliferation and the EU (known as the European Community at the time) and Japan for a failure to maintain nuclear safeguards. Other states such as Australia and the United States have also used sanctions as a means to stop countries from developing nuclear weapons. The International Atomic Energy Agency (IAEA) can also have a profound effect on antiproliferation sanctions. The agency is authorized to determine if a country is proliferating or maintaining adequate nuclear safeguards. When the IAEA reports that a state like Iraq is developing nuclear weapons, it often triggers many countries to impose sanctions. The sanctions by the United States and the European Union against Iran are a prime example of these efforts. After 2005, the UN authorized sanctions against Iran because Iran rejected international inspections of its nuclear program. Leading the sanctioning effort, Europe and the United States cut off trade and investment with Iran, moving to lift the sanctions only after Iran agreed to limit and end its nuclear programs in the 2015 accords with the UN's Permanent 5, the EU, and Germany. Since 2018, the US has reimposed, or attempted to reimpose, many of these sanctions against Iran since withdrawing from the 2015 accords.

The final two goals have also become the most popular in recent decades. Since 1990, more than half of all sanctions were aimed at human security goals, such as promoting better human rights, democracy, or both. With the end of the Cold War, democracy, as a form of governance, developed into an international norm, and as discussed in Chapter 11, a minimal level of human rights has also largely become a norm of accepted behavior. Developed democratic states embraced the new norms and the idea that they should promote democracy and human rights. It was, so to speak, "time to put your money where your mouth was." If the democratic countries in the world believed in spreading democracy and human rights, then they needed to support it.

Guinea offers a prime example. A former French colony in West Africa, Guinea gained independence in 1958 and has since had a series of autocratic rulers. In an attempt at democratization, the country held elections in 2002, but there was widespread fraud by the then-dictator, President Lansana Conté. The EU sanctioned Guinea—one of the poorest countries in the world—by cutting off all aid. In 2004, the EU and Guinean leaders met to address the problems identified by the EU. At first the negotiations worked, and Conté allowed for some freedom of the press by licensing several private radio stations in 2006. The EU started sending aid to Guinea again, but within months, Conté's police began shooting protestors. A year later, President Conté declared martial law. The Guinean people continued to fight for democracy, and after the death of Conté and a subsequent military **coup d'état**, in November 2010 they elected a new leader.

Although this case is certainly not a successful example of sanctioning, it is typical. Sanctions aimed at promoting democracy usually fail. Sadly, most dictators do not care if the European Union, the United States, or some other democratic country cuts their aid or trade. The leaders are primarily interested in staying in power, so they ignore the sanctions and—as we discuss in detail in the next section—shift the harm caused by the sanctions onto the public. Even with the poor record of performance, however, economic sanctions have become one of the primary means by which countries try to compel and coerce autocratic leaders into democratic reforms.

Sanctions are also often used to promote human rights reforms. Sometimes, the sanctions are as simple as an attempt to bring a civil war to an end. In 2003, the UN imposed an **arms embargo** and a subsequent asset freeze on the Democratic Republic of the Congo because of the tribal fighting and civil war. In just five years, the violence killed an estimated 2.5 million people. Once again, the sanctions did not succeed in significantly limiting the fighting, but it was the international community's attempt to stop the violence and subsequent massive human rights violations.

Most human rights sanctions are more direct than the 2003 sanctions against the Congo. Usually, they are responses to poor treatment of people by a government rather than a civil war. The aid sanctions imposed by the US against Egypt in 2017 are an example of this objective, but there are many others. In 2014, the US, Sweden, Norway, Denmark, and the Netherlands reduced the level of aid to Uganda after the state passed a strict law against same-sex relationships. Arguing that the law was a violation of human rights, the sanctioning states sought to pressure Uganda to repeal the law. The sanctions were a failure, as Uganda did not reform its treatment of lesbian, gay, bisexual, transgender, queer, intersex, and asexual (**LGBTQIA**) individuals, but the US and other European countries continued to try to promote bisexual, transgender, queer, intersex, and asexual (LGBTQIA) rights on the African continent. In the case of Malawi, the pressure was rather effective. Although no sanctions were imposed, the US used the threat of reducing aid to the developing country if legal protections for members of the LGBTQIA community were not put in place. Although progress was slow, the impact on these human rights in Malawi has been significant (see the box "Theory in Action: Leverage, Sanctions, and LGBTQIA Rights").

9-2d The Failure of Economic Sanctions

As you may have noticed, sanctions do not often attain their goals. Estimates of economic sanction success assert that only between 5% and 33% of economic sanctions meet their goals even modestly. Most sanctions fail because the economic costs they impose on the target country are limited and usually lower than the cost of compliance. That is, the sanctions may cause the economy to lose 3% of its annual growth (the average for all sanctions)—to put that in relative terms, that's about 7 million jobs lost in the United States—but the cost to the leaders of the sanctioned country to comply with the sender's demands is often very high. We should not be surprised, for

....

coup d'état: literally translated as a "strike against the state"; when there is a forceful change in government that overthrows the current leadership.

arms embargo: not selling weapons to a country.

LGBTQIA: individuals identifying as lesbian, gay, bisexual, transgender, queer, intersex, or asexual.

Leverage, Sanctions, and LGBTQIA Rights

With the signing of the Universal Declaration of Human Rights in 1948, the promotion of human rights around the world officially became part of the foreign policy of all states that signed the declaration. Of course, what is "official" and what is policy are two different matters. Beginning with President Jimmy Carter in 1977, the US began to emphasize a country's human rights record more than it had before when making foreign policy. This emphasis waxed and waned until after the Cold War, at which point it became a key foreign policy component of most advanced democracies. In 2011, the US, and then the UK, made it clear that rights regarding sexual orientation must be promoted as human rights. But how does a country promote human rights in another country?

Anti-LGBTQIA activists march through the streets of the Ugandan capital, Kampala, on March 31, 2014, in support of the government's stance against same-sex relationships

When can external economic sanctions overcome widespread political attitudes?

ISAAC KASAMANI/AFP via Getty Images

One answer is economic sanctions, but laws governing sexuality are some of the most deeply rooted in a country's culture and, therefore, hard to change. Simply not selling some products to another country isn't going to compel it to change laws that are so grounded in values, culture, and even identity. In the case of Uganda in 2014, the US sanctioned the African state for passing a severe law against same-sex relationships. The Ugandan president and legislature did not bow to the pressure (the Ugandan constitutional court did rule the law invalid, but not because of the sanctions), and violence against LGBTQIA Ugandans and supporters of LGBTQIA rights increased dramatically. So, again, how do you pressure other countries to improve their human rights?

Malawi and Zambia provide helpful explanations. Malawi is very dependent on Western donors for aid. The country's economy is weak, and Malawi needs the development aid it receives to survive. The US and the UK have openly pressured Malawi with the threat of sanctions (cutting Malawi's aid) to reform their laws concerning LGBTQIA individuals. The result has been slow but steady improvements in the rights of LGBTQIA people. The US and the UK have significant leverage over Malawi because of its need for the development aid they supply. As a result, the US and the UK have been able to push Malawi into improving its human rights.

In Zambia, the story is different. The Zambian economy is much stronger and not very dependent on foreign aid. Zambia, like most developing countries, has very strict anti-LGBTQIA laws. US and UK diplomats quickly realized that direct, overt pressure on Zambia would fail and likely lead to more severe laws like the one in Uganda. Instead of the threat of sanctions, diplomats have attempted to privately express their frustration with Zambian anti-LGBTQIA laws. No public pronouncements are made, but the Zambian government knows the US and the UK would prefer improved human rights. Further, the two countries have also increased support for local nongovernmental organizations that promote LGBTQIA rights. Although there has not been much improvement in Zambian rights, enforcement of the laws has softened somewhat, and there have been no backlashes against LGBTQIA individuals like those that occurred in other countries.

Considering the previous discussion, think about these questions:

1. Many countries are not dependent on foreign aid, so how can they be pressured?

2. How would our different theories (i.e., realism, liberalism, constructivism, foreign policy analysis, Marxism, and feminism) view the use of sanctions?

3. Would each of the theories say that states should promote human rights?

4. What other ways could we achieve better human rights globally? ●

Are Sanctions on North Korea Finally Working?

In 2016 and 2017, North Korea dramatically increased its testing of short-range, intermediate-range, and long-range missiles. In 2017, the regime threatened the US territory of Guam with the possibility of a missile test launched in its direction, but instead it launched a missile over Japan, causing air raid sirens to go off over four Japanese provinces and scaring untold Japanese citizens. Experts calculated that the missile, if targeted differently, could have reached the middle of the United States, thus potentially imperiling Chicago, for example. The North Koreans followed that test with a news release that they had finally mastered the technique of miniaturizing a nuclear warhead to fit on a missile, and then they successfully tested a hydrogen bomb, one exponentially more destructive than any tested beforehand. The UN responded with new economic sanctions on North Korea, banning anyone from purchasing North Korean coal, iron, or seafood or from employing North Korean workers—thereby cutting North Korea's total foreign exports by one third (Taylor 2017).

North Korea continued its nuclear and missile programs. Why? Because it saw no alternative. Here's the deal: The number-one priority of the Kim family regime in North Korea is to stay in power. Staying in power depends on keeping North Korea's large military and its leaders happy. Keeping military leaders happy requires having the weapons to keep enemies at bay. The best weapons to do so are perceived to be nuclear weapons and the means to deliver them over large distances. Further, North Korean elites have seen how regimes without nuclear weapons have been subjected to heavy US pressures for major policy changes or even regime changes: Think of Iran's nuclear deal and the pressures on Syria's regime, not to mention the cases of Muammar Qaddafi in Libya or Saddam Hussein in Iraq. Even the "color revolutions" that challenged or replaced repressive regimes in Czechoslovakia, Georgia, Ukraine, Kyrgyzstan, Belarus, Moldova, and Tunisia were seen as externally directed efforts at regime change fueled by US assistance. Even Russian President Vladimir Putin called sanctions "useless" in changing North Korean behavior, saying the North Koreans would rather "eat grass" than give

up their nuclear program ("North Korea Nuclear Crisis" 2017).

US President Donald Trump called on China, North Korea's major trading partner, to do more to force a change in North Korea's behavior. However, until very recently, China has long resisted this course of action because of the possibility of hundreds of thousands—or possibly millions—of North Koreans flooding across the border into China to find a better quality of life if the North Korean regime were to collapse. Moreover, a nonnuclear North Korean regime could fall in the face of military pressure from South Korea, Japan, and the United States. The result could be US military forces right on China's border, a situation Chinese President Xi Jinping would like to avoid, even at the cost of a nuclear North Korea. Yet China has recently clamped down on trade with North Korea in keeping with the international sanctions authorized in 2017, with results beginning to show in the North Korean economy. As the *Wall Street Journal* reported, "The question now is whether economic pain will persuade North Korean leader Kim Jong Un to change his nuclear strategy" (Page, Jeong, and Talley 2018). Economic pain helped push Kim Jong-un to meet with President Trump in their 2018 and 2019 summit conferences. However, in early 2020, Kim announced he would not continue North Korea's self-imposed moratorium on testing and in March began a new round of missile tests. By late 2020, it was increasingly clear that North Korea was not changing course, and, if anything, its nuclear programs posed even greater threats (Bierman 2020). Hence, whether economic pressure will lead to progress on the Korean peninsula remains to be seen.

1. What else can be done with a regime so isolated from the rest of the international system as North Korea?

2. Are there military options to consider that don't risk the lives of the 10 million South Koreans who live in Seoul, just 40 miles from the North Korean border?

3. Is there any circumstance that would lead the Kim regime to give up nuclear weapons? ●

example, when North Korean leader Kim Jung-un ignores US and UN sanctions. Giving in to such sanctions might lead to his political downfall. The choice between trading with more states, on the one hand, and being the leader of North Korea, on the other, is not exactly a difficult one for a dictator (see "Foreign

Policy in Perspective: Are Sanctions on North Korea Finally Working?"). Similarly, the Chinese might have lost billions of dollars if the United States had fully sanctioned them after turning the Chinese army against their own protesters in Tiananmen Square, but Chinese leaders believed that giving in to demands for better human rights would be the beginning of the end of the Chinese Communist Party's rule of the People's Republic of China—again, not a difficult choice to make.

Another reason sanctions often fail is related directly to anarchy. First, sanctions impose costs on the target, but there is nothing that can make the target comply. Because there is no central authority in the international system, one state can sanction another, but there is no authority that can resolve the dispute conclusively. Thus, the target can ignore the sanctioning state's demands and pay the cost of the sanctions, as Qatar did. Second, other countries can trade with the sanctioned state—busting the sanctions, so to speak. This was the case in Qatar as well, as others like Iran stepped up to sell Qatar the food it previously imported from the sanctioning states. Because there is no central authority, there is nothing to keep other countries from busting the sanctions except fear of the sanctioning state. For example, the US could sanction North Korea, but so far there is nothing to keep the Chinese from trading with North Korea. In this way, anarchy profoundly weakens a country's ability to use its economy to influence other states.

Finally, some research indicates that sanctions may be most effective at the threat stage but are less effective when actually imposed. For example, K. Chad Clay (2018) concludes that threats to impose sanctions for human rights abuses may result in improvement, but the imposition of sanctions probably results in worsening human rights performance. Of course, the dilemma is clear: As Clay notes in his research, if threats to impose sanctions are never carried out, eventually the threats won't likely work, either!

If sanctions fail so often, then why do leaders continue to use them? Let's try to answer that question next.

The Paradox of Economic Sanctions: Why Do States Use Them if They Fail So Often?

For many years, scholars thought that sanctions were used not to influence the target but to help out domestic producers. For example, Germany might sanction the importation of Japanese cars to help out domestic car manufacturers like Volkswagen. However, more recent research shows that sanctions tend not to be used to protect domestic producers. Instead, most sanctions are initiated in reaction to something the target country did. For example, the apartheid regime in South Africa and poor human rights and ethnic cleansing by the Sudanese government in Darfur led to sanctions by the UN. Thus, most sanctions are used to influence the target country.

That still does not answer the question of why sanctions are used when they fail so often. We cannot assume that the leaders of countries that use sanctions are stupid and do not know that sanctions usually fail. We must instead assume that leaders fully understand that sanctions rarely work. So, again, why do they continue to use them?

In part, the answer lies in the message the sanctions send to the target country and to the rest of the world. Even though the sanctions themselves may not coerce the target state into changing its human rights, for example, it does send the message that the sanctioning countries disapprove. The United States and the UN both levied sanctions against Sudan because of the ethnic cleansing of non-Arab Muslims and others in Darfur. More than actually expecting the conflict in Darfur to end, the United States and the UN needed to send a message to the Sudanese government that it strongly disapproved of the treatment of its non-Arab inhabitants. According to the US, Sudan's human rights record gradually improved, and the 20-year-old sanctions program against Sudan was ended in October 2017. It is hard to determine if this signal was successful because of how long it took—an issue that plagues many sanction cases. Ultimately, sanctions are a way for the sender to show the target how much it disapproves of, disagrees with, or is angry about some actions the target country has taken, and *sometimes* that disapproval leads to change.

In addition to sending a message to the target country, sanctions also send a signal to other nations. The UN sanctions against Sudan showed the world that the UN would not ignore ethnic cleansing—that it would respond with economic measures. Thus, other political regimes that may be considering violating their people's human rights can look at the Sudan case and realize that if they do practice ethnic cleansing against a portion of their population, there will be consequences. However, it is hard to know if sanctions stop other countries from abusing human rights: We most easily observe cases in which a state abuses its people, not when it does not. For instance, sanctions did little to prevent Myanmar's persecution of its Rohingya Muslim minority, nor did they end repression against Turkic Muslims in China's Xinjiang province. Perhaps they will in the future.

Thus, sanctions are often used to send a message. Canada made it clear to the world, for example, that it strongly opposed nuclear proliferation because it sanctioned several countries for not taking enough care in the production of nuclear material used in bomb making. Sanctions can sometimes compel the target to change its policies, but more often they are a form of strong political communication between countries. At the very least, economic sanctions satisfy the sender's domestic political need to *do something* regarding the problem posed by the recipient state. Such domestic pressures often help explain the sender's actions.

Women and Economic Sanctions

Previously we discussed some of the negative and counterproductive consequences of sanctions. In addition to generally hurting the population and driving down human rights and democracy, feminist theorists point out that sanctions have a particularly negative effect on women (see Figure 9-1). Several case studies show how women suffer in countries that are targeted by sanctions.

The case of Iraq is particularly disturbing. Prior to 1990, Iraqi women enjoyed considerable freedoms and relative equality for a Middle Eastern country. Many worked outside the home because it was safe for them to travel and the state provided child care. That changed radically after the UN imposed sanctions: Women disproportionately lost their jobs and had to turn to the informal labor market, including sewing, cleaning, and too often prostitution (Al-Jawaheri 2008). One Iraqi physician, a woman, commented, "During the sanctions period, all of the ministries encouraged women to resign or retire early." Child care ended, leaving women to care for their children and making it increasingly difficult for them to work. "Domestic violence, as well as street violence targeting women, increased particularly during the embargo" (Al-Ali 2007). Marriage became entirely about financial security; a husband who could provide food and a home developed into a necessity as women tried to survive.

Iraq is an extreme case because the sanctions were so comprehensive and crushing. However, similar situations result even when less severe sanctions are used. When Myanmar's exports were banned, the textile businesses there were crushed. Women dominated this industry, and when it shrunk, they were left without jobs. Many turned to prostitution to feed their families.

FIGURE 9-1

Probability That Women's Economic Rights Will Be Violated

Notice how much more likely women are to suffer when sanctions (the solid line) are applied to a poor country.

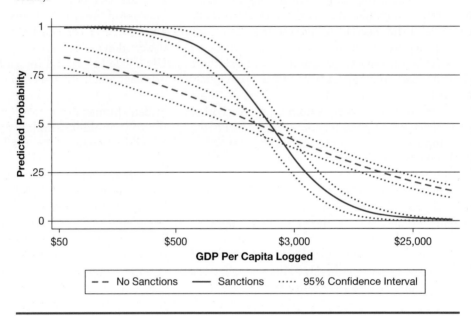

Source: A. Cooper Drury and Dursun Peksen, "Women and Economic Statecraft: The Negative Impact Economic Sanctions Visit on Women," *European Journal of International Relations*, 2014.

Unfortunately, a study shows that these examples are not uncommon (Drury and Peksen 2014). When a country is sanctioned, the women there face much greater economic discrimination as a result of taking pay cuts, being demoted, or losing their jobs altogether. They also face greater social discrimination. In poor countries, which tend not to have great respect for women in the first place, sanctions almost make it a certainty that they will lose basic rights, such as deciding whom to marry, where and when they can travel, and other basic reproductive rights.

Sanctions aren't the only form of economic statecraft that has negative impacts on women. International Monetary Fund loans that require states to privatize parts of their economy and cut public spending have serious negative consequences for the economic rights of women. These same policies can also lead to increased human trafficking for labor. Unfortunately, these findings raise more questions about the use of economic statecraft. Although bombing and armed invasion are more extreme than an economic sanction, it is important to realize that these economic tools are not without human costs as well. When a large country cuts off trade with another, it threatens the security of the target country. Women are often the most vulnerable group within a country because their rights are not as widely respected. However, women are not the only vulnerable group. There is also good reason to suspect that children suffer even more when their country is sanctioned. Clearly, sanctions can reduce both women's and children's situation to one of fear.

1. Is there some way to protect women when sanctioning another state?

2. If the EU and the United States want to stop Iran or North Korea from developing or deploying nuclear weapons, are the human costs associated with sanctions worth it?

3. If sanctions cause such problems and military action is an even more dangerous option for countries trying to coerce another state, what other options are available? ●

9-2e The Costly Consequences of Sanctions

Even though sanctions do not succeed very often and may be used just as a way to send a message, they still can have powerful effects on the targeted state. In the most extreme cases, such as Iraq between 1990 and 2003, the sanctions caused the economy to shrink by nearly half—a devastating effect. As noted earlier, on average a sanctioned country loses 3% of its annual economic growth. For example, if it is growing at a healthy rate of 3.5% before the sanctions, the sanctions will cause the growth rate to fall to 0.5%. While not necessarily devastating, that loss of 3% in growth is a serious recession in most countries, especially if it persists over several years. Thus, sanctions may not achieve their goals, but they do considerable damage to the sanctioned country's economy. Unfortunately, as TV ads often say, "that's not all!"

Even while they are appealing as statements and may inflict punishment, sanctions tend also to have a detrimental effect on human rights, the level of democracy, and respect for women in target countries (see "Spotlight On: Women and Economic Sanctions"). When a country is sanctioned, the leaders are being threatened by another country. They often react to the sanctions by tightening their hold on power, often by repressing their public to quash any possible dissent against their rule. In Iraq, for instance, during the decade-plus of sanctions in the 1990s that hurt the Iraqi economy, ordinary Iraqi civilians paid a far higher price than Saddam Hussein and the ruling elite. Estimates suggest that 250,000–500,000 children under the age of five may have died because of the sanctions.

In another example, in the mid-1980s, Manuel Noriega, the leader of Panama, became increasingly involved in drug smuggling and took a more hostile stance toward the United States. US President Ronald Reagan sanctioned Panama. Shortly after Reagan announced the sanctions, Noriega created paramilitary forces called "dignity battalions" to intimidate and repress his political opponents. Until the US-led invasion removed him in late 1989, Noriega became more and more autocratic and removed all democratic rights from Panama. The sanctions—meant to influence Panama's foreign policy toward the Soviets—actually led the country into autocracy.

Similarly, in 2019 new sanctions on Iran led to higher gasoline prices there, and large public demonstrations against the regime resulted. Security forces turned on the protesters, and 1,500 Iranians were killed in November 2019 alone. Thousands of other Iranians were arrested. The government became even more repressive.

Another example is the arms embargo on Bosnia in the early 1990s. The idea was to limit the number of weapons in the hands of the Bosnian Serbs and the Bosnian Muslims—the two sides embroiled in a civil conflict. Unfortunately, the embargo only made things worse. Neighboring Serbia supported the Serbs in Bosnia, so the Bosnian Serbs were well armed. This left the Bosnian Muslims underarmed and vulnerable. After the situation deteriorated significantly, the United States secretly encouraged Iran to give weapons to the Bosnian Muslims to even the fighting and, it was hoped, limit the bloodshed. Only after a NATO intervention and occupation did the ethnic cleansing end.

So what are leaders to do if they want to coerce or at least send a message to another state? This is just one of the unfortunate trade-offs that leaders must make when considering any kind of coercive action. Military intervention is certainly more drastic, but economic sanctions have significant costs as well.

9-3 FOREIGN AID

>> **9-3**   **Identify the potential benefits and consequences of foreign aid.**

We have discussed the ways in which one state can influence or coerce another by taking money from the other state and thereby causing economic pain. In addition to an economic "stick," countries can also use economic "carrots" to entice, coax, or simply pay off another state. Although most **foreign aid** does not officially impose conditions on the recipient state, it is often a politicized process. We turn next to the different kinds of aid and the conditions that lead countries to grant aid. We then address the effect of aid on the recipient country.

Foreign aid can be broken down into four different types: (a) development aid aimed at helping the recipient's economy, (b) military aid aimed at strengthening the recipient state's security, (c) democracy aid aimed at promoting democratic reforms, and (d) humanitarian aid aimed at providing immediate help in an emergency or disaster. Let's address each of these to examine what the aid is meant to do and the politics that surround it.

9-3a Development Aid

What we usually think about when we are thinking of aid is **development aid**—aid that is given to countries that are poor and struggling to develop their economies. It is also the most plentiful type of aid. According to the Development Assistance Committee of the **Organisation for Economic Co-operation and Development (OECD)**, $152.8 billion was given to states to help promote the growth of their economies in 2019. This amount, while large, does not fully capture how much assistance is given to other countries. Instead, it includes only official government aid given by the 37 countries in the OECD. It does not include aid given by non-OECD donors or private donations given by individuals, foundations, and organizations such as the Bill and Melinda Gates Foundation, Oxfam, and Lutheran World Relief. Why not include all countries and donors? Quite simply, it is too difficult to tally up how much is given by all the different countries and groups in the world.

....

foreign aid: aid given by one country (the donor) to another country (the recipient) for health, economic development, or poverty relief.

development aid: aid given to a country to help develop its economy.

Organisation for Economic Co-operation and Development (OECD): an organization of 37 member states that promotes liberal economic and political reforms.

Sustainable Development Goals: 17 goals to achieve by 2030 to continue and improve on the progress of the Millennium Development Goals.

That nearly $153 billion in aid can seem rather small. When you consider that the aid is given to help the more than 6 billion people in the developing world, the annual dollar amount is only about $25 per person. Thus, developing countries receive a large amount, but once you consider how many people live in those states, the amount isn't nearly as big. Compared to the extent of human needs, development aid is literally like a drop in the ocean (see the box "Spotlight On: US Development Aid in Perspective").

Determinants of Development Aid

Why give this aid? In the simplest of terms, aid should reduce poverty. As spelled out more specifically by the UN's Millennium Development Goals, aid should "eradicate extreme poverty and hunger." Under this program, states were to work together to cut in half the number of people living on less than $1 per day and the number of people suffering from hunger. Part of this goal was for wealthy states to donate 0.7% of their GDP as development aid. Therefore, aid should, first and foremost, help eliminate poverty. By 2015, many of these goals were largely met, and they were replaced by the **Sustainable Development Goals**—17 goals to end poverty, protect the planet, and improve the lives and prospects of everyone, everywhere. If such goals are met by 2030, the improved quality of life should indirectly reduce political instability in the target states. Countries whose citizens have an acceptable quality of life have less reason to revolt and are associated with less violence, instability, and insecurity.

Following these goals, poorer, less-developed countries are the only states that qualify and are officially given aid based on their need. Once a country's economy develops and rises out of poverty, and it no longer needs assistance, donor states could be expected to stop providing aid. However, the largest portions of aid do not always go to the poorest countries (see "The Revenge of Geography: Did the Berlin Wall Fall on Africa?"). In 2017, for example, Syria received the most development aid of any country in the world—over $10 billion. However, there are many states that are much poorer. Sierra Leone, Eritrea, and South Sudan all have a GDP per capita of less than $1,700; Syria has a GDP per capita of just slightly less than $3,000. Why does Syria get so much aid? The answer is the United States and other major donors are trying to meet the needs of a population in the midst of a civil war.

As this example illustrates, there is a lot more to the granting of aid than simply a desire to alleviate poverty. Political scientists and economists have studied the question of what leads countries to give aid. In addition to the level of poverty, four factors stand out as important in the allocation of development aid.

US Development Aid in Perspective

There is considerable criticism around the world about how much development aid the United States provides. Most non-Americans argue that the United States does not give enough. In fact, global public opinion almost uniformly criticizes the United States for the small portion of aid given relative to the size of its economy. Yet from 2017 to 2020, the Trump administration proposed slashing the US foreign aid budget by about 30% every year. So how much aid does the United States give? Although there is an answer to this question, it is not a simple one—like the rest of international relations, it is complex.

Before we look at the actual numbers of US aid, it is first worth considering what the average American thinks. Recently, when asked what portion of the US federal budget was devoted to international aid, the median American response was 26%. When asked how much should be spent, the median American response was 10%. In reality, about 1% of the budget goes to foreign aid, and only about 1.3% if military and security assistance are included. If you consider only discretionary spending (e.g., not interest payments on the debt or other mandated entitlement programs), then about 2.5% of the budget is spent on aid. Thus, depending on which number you use, the average American overestimates how much the United States spends on aid by 10 to 25 times!

So what are the "real" numbers? First, let's consider the total aid in dollars. In this measure, the United States does very well. It contributed $34.3 billion in 2018. That accounts for 24% of all aid according to the OECD. The next largest donors are Germany ($25 billion) and the United Kingdom ($19.4 billion). Thus, by this accounting, the United States gives approximately 37% more aid than Germany and 77% more than the UK. Why do people criticize the United States?

The second "real" number is what portion of a country's economy is devoted to aid (see Table 9-1). It is certainly easier for the United States to give more than a smaller, less wealthy state. Thus, it is important to consider how much aid is given compared to the size of the donor's economy. When considering the percentage of GDP (gross domestic product, or the total size of the domestic economy) given in aid, the United States does not stack up very well. In 2018, US aid totaled only 0.17% of its economy. The United Kingdom's aid, by contrast, totaled 0.7%, four times the level of US aid, and the United Kingdom doesn't do that well compared to other donors. The biggest aid donor, once the size of the economy is taken into account, is Sweden, which gave 1.04% of its economy in aid—more than seven times as much as the United States. Look at Table 9-1 to see how the OECD countries stack up. The United States does great in the first column but is well below average in the second column. When you consider those numbers, you can understand why there is so much global criticism. ●

TABLE 9-1

Top Aid Donors by Actual Amount and as a Percentage of GDP

	2018 OFFICIAL DEVELOPMENT AID	
	AMOUNT OF AID IN MILLIONS OF CURRENT US DOLLARS	AID AS A PERCENTAGE OF GDP
Sweden	5,840	1.04
Luxembourg	470	0.98
Norway	4,260	0.94
Denmark	2,580	0.72
United Kingdom	19,400	0.70
Germany	24,990	0.61
Switzerland	3,090	0.44
Belgium	2,290	0.43
France	12,150	0.43
Finland	980	0.36
Ireland	930	0.31
Iceland	80	0.31
New Zealand	560	0.28
Canada	4,650	0.28
Japan	14,170	0.28
Austria	1,180	0.26
Italy	5,010	0.24
Australia	3,120	0.23
Spain	2,870	0.20
Portugal	390	0.17
United States	34,260	0.17
Slovenia	80	0.16
Korea	2,350	0.15
Czech Republic	320	0.14
Hungary	320	0.14
Poland	760	0.14
Greece	280	0.13
Slovak Republic	130	0.13

Source: Data from OECD at http://www.oecd.org/dac/financing-sustainable-development/development-finance-data, Organisation for Economic Co-operation and Development, 2017.

Did the Berlin Wall Fall on Africa?

The fall of the Berlin Wall in November 1989 is heralded as a great moment in human history, and it should be. It marked an end to 50 years of totalitarian oppression in East Germany, and more broadly to the beginning of democratic rule throughout Eastern Europe. Given the thousands of people who were killed by the repressive, autocratic regimes in Eastern Europe, there is little surprise that the German people were jubilant on November 9.

There were, however, negative side effects following the positive and historical end to autocratic rule in many European states. Many Eastern European countries maintained aid programs throughout Africa during the Cold War. Once those autocratic governments fell and the new democratic governments had to deal with fixing their own crumbling economies, many of their aid programs in Africa ended. States such as Romania and East Germany could not afford to continue providing development funds, loans, and investment. Without the Soviet Union to purchase their products and help fund their economies, Eastern European countries struggled to keep their own economies from collapsing completely. In this situation, it was unrealistic to think that they could continue to invest in African countries (see Map 9-3).

MAP 9-3

Political Map of Africa

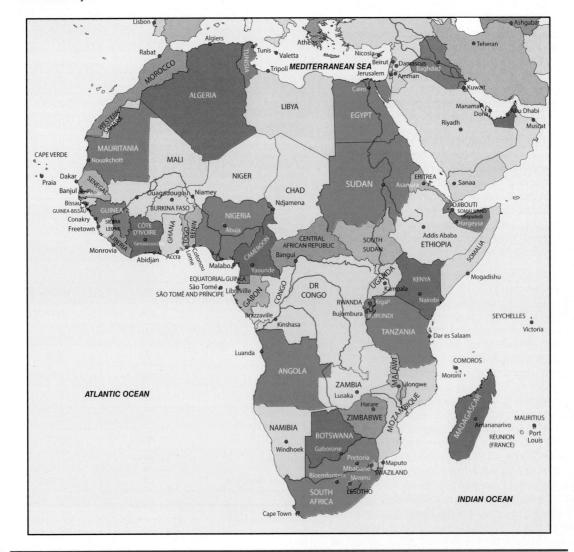

Additionally, West Germany began to redirect its aid to East Germany, whose economy was in shambles. After reunification, Germany had to continue to transfer funds to the former East Germany to rebuild its economy, factories, and power plants and to clean up serious environmental disasters left behind by the autocratic government. Germany, the largest economy in Europe, was not alone in its new interest in Eastern Europe. Other Western European states began to redirect their aid away from other countries, most of them on the African continent, toward Eastern Europe. It was more important for the states in Western Europe to help secure the economies of states in nearby Eastern Europe than those in Africa. If Romania, East Germany, or some other European state collapsed, it could directly threaten the security of Europe. The same might not be the case for Africa.

Private investment also shifted. Companies that might invest in countries on the African continent began to look east rather than south. Countries in Eastern Europe were not only closer and culturally more similar; they also had higher levels of education and a more stable, developed infrastructure. Ultimately, they were a safer and more profitable investment than many countries in Africa. As a result, less private investment was made in Africa.

Thus, the end of the Cold War meant freedom and development aid for millions of Eastern Europeans but less development aid and investment for millions in Africa. What could the leaders in Africa do? Sadly, there was no policy or diplomatic solution for the African leaders. This situation was a true revenge of geography—simply being in another part of the world meant there would be less help from wealthy countries for a full decade.

In another complex twist of fate, the lack of aid and investment from Europe in the 1990s made Africa one of the last regions open for new investment. Recently, China began investing significant resources into African countries in an attempt to gain access to and control of the petroleum, diamond, and other mineral resources there. Only time will tell if the Chinese investments will be a benefit for the region or another example of a powerful country extracting wealth from weaker countries.

1. This case illustrates how geography can severely influence politics. Could this situation have turned out differently, or did geography "determine" the outcome?

2. What could be done to get private investors more interested in Africa?

3. Was it morally "right" that less aid went to African countries? ●

First, as the Syria example illustrates, a security or strategic interest in the recipient country may lead the donor to give significantly more aid. Specifically, political scientists have shown that a military presence—troops—in a country makes it much more likely that aid will be given in large quantities. The recipient state has to be relatively poor—the United States does not give aid to Germany, even though American troops are stationed in Germany. However, if the country is poor and the donor state has troops stationed there, the level of aid will be higher.

Historically, the importance of a military/strategic interest was much greater during the Cold War. When the United States and NATO were confronted by the Soviet Union and the Warsaw Pact, the United States in particular gave copious amounts of money to virtually any developing country that swore to be anti-Soviet. The Soviets did the same thing by giving aid to states that professed a dislike of the United States and many Western states. In many cases, these small, poor states would play the two sides against each other in an attempt to gain more aid.

A good example is Cuba. Though communist, Cuba did not originally want to sever ties with the United States. Instead, the Cuban leader, Fidel Castro, hoped to trade with and get aid from both the United States and the Soviet Union. Shortly after the revolution, however, Washington began to break off all economic ties after Cuba began nationalizing private property. This led the Soviets to pour vast amounts of aid and investment into Cuba to support its economy. With the end of the Cold War, Cuba's economy went into a recession simply because the Soviet Union no longer existed, and Russia was not interested in providing so much aid. Similarly, neither Iraq nor Afghanistan received much US aid before 2001, but since then they have been recipients of among the highest amounts of aid.

Another good example comes from Egypt during the regime of Gamal Abdel Nasser (1952–1970). President Nasser needed development assistance to build a dam across the Nile River, and both the Soviets and the Americans promised aid packages. Realizing that it was being lured into a bidding war, the US government withdrew its aid offer, and Nasser was left with only the Soviet offer. As a result, the Egyptians found themselves locked into an increasingly close relationship with the Soviet Union, which Nasser's successor, President Anwar Sadat, chose to sever two years into his presidency.

A second factor affecting aid donations is the colonial history of the donor and the recipient. If the recipient country used to be a colony of the donor state, there is likely to be more aid given. The British give more to the states that they used to control as colonies. Similarly, more French aid flows to French-speaking countries (former colonies) than to English-speaking countries.

The last two factors that may lead a state to get more aid are (a) whether it is democratic and (b) if it trades openly with other countries. Free-trading democracies tend to get more aid than non-democratic states or those that limit the amount of trade with other countries (see North Korea). Most donor countries are democratic and have large international economies that engage in a lot of foreign trade. As donors, these democratic, free-trading countries prefer to give aid to similar countries. Thus, there is a bias toward those states that lean toward democracy and are willing to "do business" with the donors.

These effects often lead to criticisms of development aid. Some countries claim that countries such as France, Japan, and the United States give aid only with strings attached, namely that if you receive aid, you must then engage in free trade and perhaps democratic reforms. Although these claims are not illogical, development aid is officially "free" of such strings. In reality, the association between free-trading democracies and aid is more likely caused by the preferences of the donor states than explicit strings.

Toyota advertisement in Vietnam

Should the aid that Japan gives to countries like Vietnam be conditional on Toyota's right to sell cars there? Do you think that the person on the bike even notices or thinks about owning a Camry?

HOANG DINH NAM/AFP via Getty Images

Celebration as the Berlin Wall is torn down

Can you imagine cutting your city in half and becoming enemies with the other side overnight? Years later, how would you feel about these people, some of whom were your relatives and best friends?

AP Photo/Thomas Kienzle

However, trading relationships still matter. For example, Japan gives more development aid to states that import a lot of Japanese products than to those that do not. In short, some of that Japanese aid might be going toward the purchase of Sony personal computers, Toyota trucks, or Komatsu backhoes by the recipient regime.

Is Development Aid Effective?

Thus far, we have discussed how much aid is given worldwide and both the official and unofficial political reasons why countries tend to give development aid, but we haven't answered the question of whether the aid is effective. Does aid actually help the recipient country develop its economy and become less poor?

The answer is not particularly encouraging. Some scholars and policymakers claim that aid can effectively increase the wealth of an economy in some cases. One influential study showed that if the recipient country has good policies—namely, those that promote economic growth—then aid will make a positive difference in the economy (Burnside and Dollar 2000). According to the World Bank, aid in the amount of 2% of the recipient's GDP produces an additional 0.5% GDP growth *in countries with good governance and economic management*. Without good management, the same amount of aid *decreases* growth by 0.3%. This study was extremely influential because donor organizations such as the World Bank and the UN used it as a guide for their aid policies. Similarly, in 2002, President George W. Bush increased US foreign aid and specified that it should be given on the condition that the recipient governments follow good policies. At the same time, some policymakers suggested that aid should not be given to corrupt governments, regardless of their level of need, because they would likely misuse or waste the funds.

The position that aid "works" in countries whose governments have good policies is hotly contested, however. For example, as you can see from Figure 9-2, according to a study from the Organisation for Economic Co-operation and Development (OECD), there is no association between development aid and economic growth for the period 2000–2010, and a very similar disconnect has been found for a longer period going back to the early 1970s. The most common explanations are corrupt use of the aid and that the aid can compete with local farmers and business owners to drive them out of business.

Another reason aid might have little effect on economic growth could be the substitution effect. If a poor country has governmental leaders more interested in staying in power than in the people's welfare, then aid funds might be used to meet only the most pressing needs of the people, and any other revenue available to the state could be used to pay off political adversaries, reward political allies, and otherwise put money in the hands of the political elite rather than being used to promote more economic growth. Good examples of this can be found in the Palestinian Authority under the leadership of Yasser Arafat, Afghanistan under the leadership of Hamid Karzai, or Haiti under the leadership of Jean-Claude Duvalier. All these leaders relied on the presence of development aid to allow the kind of payoffs to political elites that kept them in power. In this way, the total amount of money invested in economic development did not significantly increase, despite the presence of development aid.

Recent studies show a more complex relationship between the type of regime in the recipient country and the effectiveness of the aid. In autocratic countries, aid has little effect on helping the economy develop unless the country enacts market-based reforms. This lack of effect by development aid may be the result of poor development projects, like a roadway example in Lesotho where new roads meant to help farmers bring their produce to market also let in more efficient foreign food producers as competitors. It could also be a function of the corruption in a country—the aid could be siphoned off and used for personal gain by leaders rather than development. If the spending of development aid by the recipient state is not monitored by the sender, corrupt leaders may simply put the money in their own pockets. Many states have begun developing strategies to bypass corrupt regimes and deliver the aid more directly to the people who need it. These strategies,

FIGURE 9-2

Foreign Aid per Capita (2000–2005) and Economic Growth (2005–2010) for 131 Developing Countries

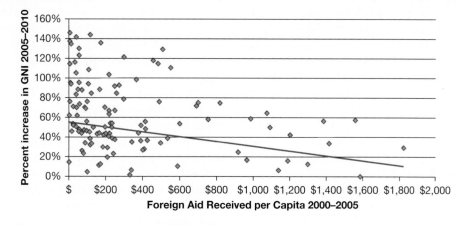

Source: Data from OECD Factbook 2011–2012, doi: 10.1787/factbook-2011-2012.

Mobutu Sese Seko's French villa

With most of the country he ruled—Zaire, now the Democratic Republic of the Congo—on the verge of starvation, President Mobutu lived in opulent wealth. How different is that from the French Revolution and Marie Antoinette's infamous line about cake? Why haven't humans learned about inequality?

FABRICE COFFRINI/AFP via Getty Images

while not perfect, have had beneficial impacts on the well-being of people in developing states, mostly by lowering the infant mortality rate. Still, scholars such as Breitwieser and Wick (2016) conclude that there are plenty of reasons to be pessimistic: When considering measures like school attendance, female life expectancy, HIV infection rates, and so on, development aid has no effect.

In democratic countries, however, the effects of aid are even less positive. Why? Some analysts argue that the reason lies in the fact that, in democracies, the close ties to the people lead governments to allocate more money toward public services and other expenditures rather than to market-based reforms that promote macroeconomic growth. These include not only services such as education and infrastructure—both of which tend to enhance economic growth—but also services that subsidize fuel and food. The latter certainly tend to help the poor working class, but they are not engines of economic growth. For example, both Venezuela and Iran use their oil wealth to subsidize the cost of fuel and food, and both their economies have suffered from sluggish growth. Venezuela is even worse off; under President Nicolás Maduro, its economy has been in crisis!

So when democracies receive aid, they often divert more funds to subsidies and other public projects to gain or maintain popularity with the people who elected them. Some of these expenditures may enhance growth, but many do not. Even if the aid is

targeted toward public works projects such as building a new road or airport, the democratic government can then spend more of its own funds on subsidies. Thus, the aid can often directly or indirectly subsidize public consumption of goods such as food and fuel. The end result is a negative effect of aid in democracies—less growth rather than more. The presence of such aid might even allow the recipient regime to postpone making necessary but hard choices about how it invests its scarce economic resources.

9-3b Military Aid

Another common type of foreign assistance is **military aid**. Often more controversial than development aid, military aid is given to allies in the form of funds to purchase military equipment or training; it can also be the simple gift of military equipment. Imagine Santa Claus delivering 1,000 Stinger surface-to-air missiles to the mujahideen to fight the Soviets in Afghanistan. In the case of the Stinger missiles that the United States gave to the mujahideen, the aid was actually covert. The United States hid the gift of the missiles—even the mujahideen didn't know for certain where they came from—so as not to challenge the Soviets overtly. Military aid is often more complicated because the donor state gives the money to be used to purchase weapons or training from the donor state. When given in this manner, the aid serves two functions. First, it supplies the recipient state with weapons. Second, it generates business for the arms producers in the donor country. For example, in 2014, Russia provided military aid to Iraq so that Iraq could purchase Su-25 attack jets made by Russia's United Aircraft Corporation. The Iraqi government got the jets it needed quickly, and the Russian corporation made more sales. Similarly, Russia has provided significant amounts of military aid in the form of heavy weapons to the Assad regime in Syria, even as Syria has engaged in violence—including the use of chemical weapons—against its own people.

Another less common use for military aid is money that is given to expand the number of troops in the recipient state. For example, the United States gave money to Colombia to expand and upgrade its military to better combat the drug producers and traffickers there. In this case, the aid was used for recruiting and training more troops. It is important to realize, however, that the outcome was the same regardless of the form the aid takes: a better-armed, more powerful ally.

military aid: aid given to a country that directly enhances its military capability.

Although many countries provide military aid, the United States is the biggest arms seller in the world and, consequently, the biggest provider of military aid. Aid is most often given to states for them to purchase US-made military equipment. The actual aid can come in the form of grants, low-interest loans, or other financial instruments. Of this type of military aid, Israel historically has been the largest recipient. According to the Congressional Research Service, the United States has provided Israel over $100 billion in military aid since 1948 and in 2016 signed an agreement to provide $38 billion for the 10 years from 2018 to 2028. Israel and Egypt together receive about 75% of all US military assistance. The aid certainly provides a high level of support for these two countries, but it also tends to keep relations between the United States and the other Middle Eastern states more tense, especially because so many of them are opposed to or even enemies of Israel.

The aid is not entirely one-sided in the Middle East. The United States has supported controversial sales of weapons to Saudi Arabia, Egypt, and Jordan, just to name a few examples. In the 1980s, the United States provided airborne warning and control aircraft (AWACs) and later sold the F-15S fighters to Saudi Arabia. In 2017, the US approved $110 billion of military sales to Saudi Arabia for the short term, with another $240 billion approved over the next 10 years. None of those US sales was well received by the Israeli government. However, Saudi Arabia is dependent on the United States for weapons. Without that military aid, the House of Saud, the ruling family of the country, could go the way of Egypt and Libya, except those taking over might easily be radical Islamists.

In the Egyptian case, the United States historically provided approximately $1.3 billion in military aid annually. The aid supported weapons purchases but also enhanced the professionalism of the military. The International Military Education and Training program (IMET) seeks to increase foreign militaries' cooperation with the United States and to promote democratic control of the military. This training was an important factor in the 2011 overthrow of Egypt's dictator, Hosni Mubarak. The army refused to shoot on unarmed civilians partly because there is a closer relationship between the army and the people and partly because the Egyptian military has a higher level of professionalism than many of its neighbors.

In the case of the Egyptian military's professionalism, US military aid ended up helping make

US-made M1A1 tanks owned by Kuwait

What are the consequences for the United States when foreigners see US military hardware on their streets? What are the consequences for the rest of the world?

AP Photo/Gustavo Ferrari

the transition from Mubarak's autocratic rule more peaceful. However, this view is a bit like wearing rose-colored glasses. It is true that the IMET increased the military's professionalism, but US military aid to Egypt and other Middle Eastern states such as Saudi Arabia almost certainly helped keep those authoritarian leaders in power for many years. Prior to Mubarak's overthrow, he was able to maintain his power largely because he had a military made powerful by US weapons and training. In 2017, the US suspended about $200 million in military aid to Egypt because of the new military-backed regime's poor human rights practices and its repression of NGOs. However, in 2018, the suspension was lifted, and these funds, along with over $1 billion more in military aid, were released to Egypt.

Another form of US military aid is peacekeeping operations outside of the UN. The goal of this type of aid is to increase the involvement of regional organizations such as the Organization of American States (OAS) and the African Union (AU) to deal with regional security problems such as those in Haiti and Sudan, respectively. The aid is also used to gather more multilateral support, such as the UN, for peacekeeping operations around the world. Either way, the donor gets help with an initiative that the donor favors.

It is important to note that military aid can often come back to hurt the donor country. The United States funded the mujahideen's fight against the Soviets in Afghanistan for years. Fighting as part of the mujahideen was Osama bin Laden. Similarly, the United States gave aid to Saddam Hussein in

Mujahideen with Stinger missile

Although they started out as US allies, the mujahideen became the Taliban and an enemy of the United States. What other countries are friendly with the United States now but could soon become opponents?

Robert Nickelsberg/Getty Images

the 1980s during his war with Iran. The US military also gave support to Ho Chi Minh's fight against the Japanese in Vietnam during World War II. In each of these cases and many others, what was once a convenient ally later became an enemy.

Determinants of Military Aid

Unfortunately, most academic studies of military aid concentrate on the United States, so we do not have a good understanding of the factors that other countries consider when giving military aid. In the United States, three components are critical to the decision. The first is the strategic value of the recipient country. During the Cold War, for example, the United States gave more military aid to those countries that were anti-communist and those that shared a border with a communist bloc state. The Cold War concern with Soviet expansion led the United States to provide vast quantities of aid to those "frontline" countries and to those pledging loyalty to the United States and Western Europe. A good example is South Korea, which received significant levels of aid because of its proximity to China and North Korea as well as its staunch anti-communist stand during the Cold War.

After the Cold War, strategic value was more loosely defined. Middle Eastern countries receive more aid, as do Latin American countries. The United States has provided billions of dollars, for example, to Colombia in an effort to combat the production and trafficking of cocaine. This type of security concern was less common during the Cold War but in the past two decades has become more common. Since 2001, countries such as the Philippines, Indonesia,

democracy aid: aid given to a country to enhance and consolidate its transition to democracy.

Pakistan, Iraq, and Afghanistan have seen their military aid increase as key states in the global war on terror.

The second factor influencing military aid is human rights. To some degree, the United States is less likely to provide military aid to countries violating human rights, especially after the end of the Cold War. There are many notable exceptions, especially during the Cold War. Many Latin American dictatorships—such as Honduras and Guatemala—received significant aid because they professed anti-communism and loyalty to the United States. In the Middle East, many countries benefiting from US military aid have poor human rights records (e.g., Egypt and Saudi Arabia). On average, however, countries violating human rights are less likely to receive aid, and this effect has apparently become more pronounced since the end of the Cold War.

Third, the regime type of the recipient countries matters—democratic countries are somewhat more likely to receive more aid. This democratic effect is also a more recent phenomenon starting in the 1990s, after the end of the Cold War. Once the United States was no longer concerned with the Soviet Union, it began to consider the value of democracy when providing military aid.

Finally, some states may provide military aid simply to generate income. Russia is a good example. Outside of oil and natural gas, military weapons are one of the few things Russia has to sell that others are willing to buy. Providing military aid can simply be a way to support your weapons manufacturers, not unlike "cash back" offers periodically provided by the auto industry.

9-3c Aid for Democracy

Another form of aid is targeted directly at promoting democracy. This support, **democracy aid**, is relatively new to the world, having really only started in the 1980s. Liberal theorists see this aid as a way to help a country become more democratic or to keep the country from slipping back into autocratic rule after a democratic transition. Like humanitarian aid, support for democracy is selectively targeted to specific countries.

Developed democratic countries have increasingly provided democracy assistance to try to spread democracy more widely throughout the international system. According to one study of the foreign policies of 40 developed countries between 1992 and 2002, there were substantial, although widely varying, commitments and efforts toward this end (Herman and Piccone 2002). Figure 9-3 shows the proportion of US foreign aid devoted to democracy assistance between 1975 and 2010—you can clearly see that such aid for

FIGURE 9-3

US Democracy Aid as a Proportion of Foreign Aid

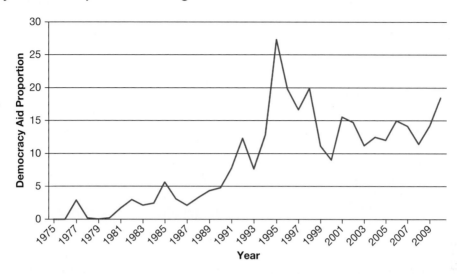

Source: Adapted from James M. Scott and Ralph G. Carter, "From Cold War to Arab Spring: Mapping the Effects of Paradigm Shifts on the Nature and Dynamics of U.S. Democracy Assistance to the Middle East and North Africa," *Democratization*, March 2014, doi: 10.1080/ 13510347.2013.877893.

democracy became a much higher priority after the end of the Cold War. For most developed democracies, democracy assistance reached 12–15% of foreign aid after 1995. Naturally, the kinds of aid vary widely across donors, but in general, democracy aid from the developed world shares a number of characteristics.

First, the assistance is typically directed to one or more of a common cluster of targets. Aid may be directed toward the establishment and functioning of elections and other constitutional arrangements to build the foundations of democratic rule (including monitoring elections to ensure fairness). Aid may also be directed toward helping build and empower the institutions of democratic government, including legislatures, independent judiciaries, and competent and accountable bureaucracies. Increasingly, democracy aid from the developed world has been directed to NGOs—or civil society actors such as women's rights, labor, and other public advocacy groups—to empower them to participate in democracy and hold governments accountable.

Second, democracy aid tends to come in smaller, more nimble packages. These packages are usually more carefully targeted to specific recipients and generally bypass the formal aid channels so that they actually reach the intended agents and purposes. For the United States, for instance, democracy aid generally constitutes only about 10–15% of US foreign aid (although some countries have received an even higher percentage), and the average aid package is considerably smaller than traditional developmental aid. This is not hard to imagine: The cost of a copying machine and a few computers to a women's rights group in Kenya is obviously *much* smaller than the cost of building and maintaining a dam in the same country. Yet such small packages may have payoffs far exceeding their size.

Small groups of protesters gather in central Cairo shouting anti-government slogans in Cairo, Egypt, September 21, 2019

Could aid from other countries help countries like Egypt democratize?

REUTERS/Mohamed Abd El Ghany

Finally, democracy assistance is most definitely a state *and* non-state phenomenon. An elaborate network of international organizations, official state aid agencies, quasi-state foundations, and private organizations from all over the globe collaborate to provide aid, advice, and support for democracy. As an example of this complicated network, the US Agency for International Development channels some of its efforts through the semi-private US National Endowment for Democracy, which, in turn, provides grants to civil society organizations in support of democratization in many countries.

The effectiveness of democracy assistance of these kinds is increasingly clear. Much research now concludes that democracy aid has positive consequences for democratization and democratic governance, even though general foreign aid does not (see Askarov and Doucouliagos 2013; Finkel, Perez-Linan, and Seligson 2007; Kalyvitis and Vlachaki 2010; Scott and Steele 2011). Figure 9-4 shows a simple relationship of this effect. Other studies have found that the combination of democracy aid and incentives generated by international organizations like the EU has been pretty effective in promoting and supporting democratization (Mansfield and Pevehouse 2006). Others, however, express concerns that such aid programs can be problematic because they too often

ignore the perspectives and unique characteristics of the recipients and instead force a one-size-fits-all template of democracy that reflects donor interpretations, concerns, and values. For example, Russian leaders have long accused Western groups like the National Endowment for Democracy as being havens for spies and provocateurs who want to overthrow the Russian regime. Other countries such as Mexico and China have also objected to the National Endowment for Democracy operating within their borders. However, given the embrace of democracy by the developed world, such aid is not likely to disappear, although from 2017 to 2020, the US Trump administration annually sought to scale back commitments of democracy aid for the first time since the end of the Cold War.

9-3d Humanitarian Aid

So far we have discussed development aid, military aid, and democracy aid. Each of these is quite different, although development and democracy aid are clearly both meant to directly improve the recipient state. The last form of aid we will consider is meant to be the most directly positive in its intention. In the most benign form of this type of aid, states can give money to other states to help them recover from disasters such as earthquakes, floods, and famines. This type of grant is considered **humanitarian aid**. It is specific to the event and meant to help the country overcome the trauma caused by the disaster.

humanitarian aid: aid given to a country to help mitigate the effects from a disaster or other humanitarian emergency.

FIGURE 9-4

Change in Democracy for Democracy Aid Recipients and Nonrecipients

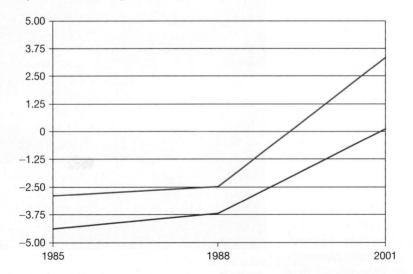

Source: James M. Scott, "Funding Freedom? The United States and US Democracy Aid in the Developing World, 1988–2001," Figure 2.3. From Dursun Peksen, ed., *Liberal Interventionism and Democracy Promotion.* Lanham, MD: Lexington Books, 2012.

A modern-day ghost town in Japan

A discarded bicycle in the exclusion zone around the Fukushima nuclear plant after the tsunami-caused meltdown in 2011. Do wealthy countries like Japan still need help after a disaster?

Jeremy Sutton-Hibbert/Getty Images

Humanitarian workers delivering supplies in Sudan

Can you imagine depending on supplies like these to stay alive? Do you think countries should donate more food, especially when so many people in wealthy countries are overweight?

REUTERS/Isaac Billy/UNMISS/Handout

In the face of the dramatic refugee crisis in and around Syria after 2011, more than half of Syria's population was forced to flee. The ensuing humanitarian crisis prompted billions in aid from donors. In 2019, the UN spent about $20 billion for humanitarian relief projects; globally, humanitarian aid reached about $30 billion. Although you might expect most of this going to address natural disasters in developing countries, not all humanitarian aid is directed there. The 2011 earthquake, tsunami, and subsequent nuclear power plant accident in Japan offers a poignant example. Even though Japan is one of the wealthiest countries in the world, countries from around the globe offered their assistance in dealing with the devastation. After Hurricane Harvey hit the US Gulf Coast in 2017, Mexico offered humanitarian assistance to Texas in the form of vehicles, boats, and food aid, and it was readily accepted.

This may seem like a silly point—of course one would give disaster aid only to a country that was struck with a disaster—but the bigger point is that unlike other forms of aid (development, military, and democracy), humanitarian assistance is a direct response to an emergency. As such, policymakers like to think that this type of aid is less politicized. In fact, people working in the disaster and humanitarian aid divisions of government (e.g., the Office of US Foreign Disaster Assistance) pride themselves in being apolitical (i.e., nonpolitical).

What disasters trigger the giving of humanitarian aid? For the US, the highest-ranking US official in the country struck by the disaster (usually the ambassador) must determine that the disaster is so big that the country requires assistance. That official must then contact the US State Department and request aid. Officials at the State Department then decide whether or not to send aid and how much is needed based in part on the ambassador's report.

The United States is by no means the only country that provides humanitarian assistance. However, all of the developed countries that do provide aid typically coordinate with each other to ensure that each disaster is responded to properly. In fact, this coordination is very thorough. Donors coordinate not only actual dollar amounts and types of aid (e.g., food, temporary shelters, and medical supplies) but also the transportation of those supplies. For example, the US military has the ability to transport huge quantities of goods via air in its C-130 Hercules and C-5 Galaxy transports. Countries such as Canada do not have that kind of transport capability, so the Canadians may provide the humanitarian supplies and the Americans could provide the transportation to get the aid where it is needed.

The success of humanitarian aid varies considerably. In the most successful cases, there are stories from relief workers that in a mere week after a catastrophic earthquake, the assistance was so successful that the previous homeless and starving people began to ask if there was anything better to eat besides the military Meals Ready-to-Eat (MREs). That's pretty successful. On the other hand, as Severine Autesserre points out in her book *Peaceland* (2014), humanitarian aid is less successful when aid workers fail to respond to what the local residents say they need or are more responsive to their donors than to the aid recipients.

Yet sometimes the affected country is so corrupt that a considerable amount of the aid is stolen. Humanitarian aid is also rendered ineffective when the emergency itself involves a civil conflict. To get humanitarian aid to the starving people of Somalia in the early 1990s, the United States—backed by the

UN—sent thousands of troops to protect the aid workers and the food that was being delivered to those in need. At first the effort was successful, but it then degraded into urban warfare, culminating in the two-day Battle of Mogadishu in which 19 Americans and 1,000–3,000 Somalis were killed. The case is portrayed in the movie *Blackhawk Down* and is hard to consider a humanitarian success.

Finally, it is worth asking whether humanitarian assistance is purely humanitarian or also political. For the most part, disasters themselves drive the aid process. That is, more severe events get more aid, usually. Politics does enter into the decision, however. If a hurricane had hit both Cuba and the Bahamas in 1985, only the Bahamas would have received US aid. Why? Because the Bahamas was a friend and Cuba was an opponent of the United States and would not have been provided humanitarian support. Depriving Cubans of humanitarian aid seems unlikely now, although the low level of US humanitarian aid sent to Puerto Rico (an American territory) following a 2019 earthquake certainly seems puzzling.

Other political issues have been shown to affect humanitarian aid. Scholars estimate that for each story in the *New York Times* (or other international and renowned media sources), an additional half-million dollars in aid is given. To put this in grim perspective, it means that just one *New York Times* story brings as much aid to a suffering country as 1,500 fatalities (Drury, Olson, and Van Belle 2005). Why are news stories so important? Because government officials use them to determine what is important to the public. One could interpret this to suggest that the government is being responsive to its citizens, but that would be cold comfort for disaster victims who don't get media coverage.

CONCLUSION

Wealth buys military power, prestige, and, as this chapter has demonstrated, the ability to use that wealth to influence other states. Whether the biblical assertion that "the love of money is the root of all evil" is true or not, it certainly seems to be the case that money is the root of all power and potential influence.

Economic statecraft is a far more complex form of power than military statecraft. The military can shield, threaten, and destroy, but economic power can be used to buy loyalties and give altruistically; it also can be taken away to weaken other states or simply to punish them. In the neo-Westphalian era, it seems that economic power rivals military power as a source of a state's relative standing in the international system. Perhaps economic power even exceeds military power at times.

It is often said that money is the most fungible form of power. We have shown here that money can be used for a huge variety of goals and in a huge variety of ways. It really seems that money can be used for anything, although as this chapter has also demonstrated, it does not always work: Sanctions fail, and development aid may hurt growth.

In Chapter 10, we focus specifically on the development of those countries without much wealth and their relationship with the developed, wealthy states. You will see that each of the chapters in this section on international economics fits together in one big system. The way states trade with one another, try to influence one another, and try to develop their economies are all tied together in the web of the world political economy. ●

KEY CONCEPTS

9-1 Identify the many ways in which wealth can be used to influence other countries.

The process of giving and taking money for political purposes is called economic statecraft: the use of economic means (money) to secure political ends (or goals). By attaching conditions or demands to the giving or taking of money, one state can influence another state and pursue security for itself. The ways in which states can give and take money are many, such as foreign aid of many kinds, a special trade deal, economic sanctions, or cutting off an important resource. References to economic statecraft date back to approximately 500 BCE. Over the centuries, many leaders, including Alexander Hamilton—the very first secretary of the US Treasury—strongly believed that the state's economy could and must be used as a form of

influence, not just as a way to build military power. In the post–World War II era, foreign aid has also become an important part of international relations and is now carefully tracked by states and international organizations.

9-2 Trace the complex nature of economic sanctions, why they are used, and what consequences they have.

An economic sanction is a policy that reduces the economic exchange between two states for a political goal. Trade sanctions cut the exchange of goods between the two countries, financial sanctions freeze the movement of assets (e.g., bank accounts) for the sanctioned country, aid sanctions restrict access to foreign assistance, and third-party sanctions threaten a third country doing business with the main target of the sanctions. Comprehensive sanctions cut off all economic connections to the target, which is rarely done but can exact a huge cost on the targeted country. Senders of sanctions may seek (a) to weaken the target state's military and economy; (b) to destabilize a government, often in hopes of changing the leadership or type of government; (c) to limit the proliferation of nuclear weapons; (d) to target human security goals, such as promoting better human rights, democracy, or both; or (e) to promote human rights reforms. Estimates indicate that only 5–33% of economic sanctions meet their goals. On average a sanctioned country loses 3% of its annual economic growth. However, most sanctions fail because the economic costs they impose on the target country are usually lower than the cost of compliance. Sanctions have a detrimental effect on human rights, level of democracy, and respect for women. Also, other countries can trade with the sanctioned state—busting the sanctions, so to speak.

9-3 **Identify the potential benefits and consequences of foreign aid.**

Foreign aid can be broken down into four different types: (a) development aid aimed at helping the recipient's economy, (b) military aid aimed at strengthening the recipient state's security, (c) democracy aid aimed at promoting democratic reforms, and (d) humanitarian aid aimed at providing immediate help in an emergency or disaster. Factors influencing the provision of development aid include recipient poverty, a donor's military or strategic interest in the recipient country, the colonial history of the donor and recipient, and recipient regime type and trade relations. Military aid is given to allies in the form of funds to purchase military equipment or training or as straight grants of military equipment. Democracy aid, which really only emerged in the 1980s, usually involves small, targeted packages of assistance designed to help a country become more democratic or to help keep the country from slipping back into autocratic rule after a democratic transition. Humanitarian aid is temporary assistance to recipients to help them recover from disasters such as earthquakes, floods, and famines.

KEY TERMS

economic statecraft 255

tariff 256

economic sanction 256

import and export sanctions 260

aid sanction 261

financial sanction 261

smart sanctions 261

third-party sanction 262

coup d'état 264

arms embargo 264

LGBTQIA 264

foreign aid 270

development aid 270

Organisation for Economic Co-operation and Development (OECD) 270

Sustainable Development Goals 270

military aid 276

democracy aid 278

humanitarian aid 280

REVIEW QUESTIONS

1. In what ways can one state influence another state without using its military?

2. Are sanctions successful, failures, counterproductive, or some combination of these?

3. Why is aid given, and what effects does it have?

THINK ABOUT THIS

Guns or Money?

Realists maintain that power defined in military terms is the most important instrument in international politics. However, world systems theorists and Marxist analysts would argue that wealth gives rich countries far more dominance in the international system—on a daily basis—than does military might alone. Some liberal, constructivist, and feminist theorists would also argue that economic statecraft is more

usable and likely to be more effective in the current world than is military force. Given what's going on in world politics and what you've learned up to this point, which position do you think is correct? Does might make right, or do those with the gold make the rules?

Under what conditions are the tools of economics likely to be most effective, and when are they likely to be least effective?

FOR MORE INFORMATION . . .

Aid

OECD, Aid Statistics: http://www.oecd.org/development/stats/idsonline.htm

Aid and Economic Growth

Jakupec, Viktor. (2018). *Development Aid—Populism and the End of the Neoliberal Agenda.* New York, NY: Springer.

Krieckhaus, Jonathan. (2006). *Dictating Development.* Pittsburgh, PA: University of Pittsburgh Press.

Democracy Promotion

Bridoux, Jeff, and Milja Kurki. (2014). *Democracy Promotion: A Critical Introduction.* London, UK: Routledge.

Wetzel, Anne, Jan Orbie, and Fabienne Bossuyt, eds. (2017). *Comparative Perspectives on the Substance of EU Democracy Promotion.* New York, NY: Routledge.

Economic Sanctions

Biersteker, Thomas J., Sue E. Eckert, and Marcos Tourinho, eds. (2016). *Targeted Sanctions: The Impacts and Effectiveness of United Nations Action.* New York, NY: Cambridge University Press.

Blackwill, Robert, and Jennifer Harris. (2017). *War by Other Means: Geoeconomics and Statecraft.* Cambridge, MA: Belknap Press/Harvard University Press.

Early, Bryan. (2015). *Busted Sanctions: Explaining Why Economic Sanctions Fail.* Redwood City, CA: Stanford University Press.

Humanitarian Aid/Interventions

Alexander, Jessica. (2013). *Chasing Chaos: My Decade In and Out of Humanitarian Aid.* New York, NY: Broadway Books.

Autesserre, Severine. (2014). *Peaceland: Conflict Resolution and the Everyday Politics of International Intervention.* New York, NY: Cambridge University Press.

The lives of the rich and the poor

What does the disparity between these two photos suggest about the problems between the wealthy and the poor? If the people in these photos traded places, could they even understand their new surroundings?

10 International Development

Relations Between the Haves and Have-Nots

Learning Objectives

After studying this chapter, you will be able to . . .

10-1 Describe the distribution of wealth around the globe.

10-2 Identify the reasons some countries have developed economies and some do not.

10-3 Compare the different strategies and policies countries have deployed to develop their economies.

10-4 Explain the role that international organizations play in development.

Chapter Outline

10-1 The Wealth Gap

10-2 Why Are Some Countries Rich and Others Poor?

10-3 Development Theories and Policies

10-4 International Organizations and Development

A Tale of Two Economies

In 1980, both Ecuador and South Korea were at similar levels of development. Both had a GDP per capita of slightly more than $5,500. South Koreans had a slightly longer life expectancy (2.8 years longer than Ecuadorans) and were a little more educated (1.9 years more than Ecuadorans). However, several factors seemed to be working against South Korea's prospects for development. Unlike Ecuador, it did not have significant oil reserves, so it could not draw income from that precious resource. Further, South Korea suffered the effects of a vicious war in the early 1950s.

Now, 40 years later, the similarities are gone . . . and it was not South Korea with its costly war and lack of oil that fell behind. Instead, South Korea is now a member of the Organisation for Economic Co-operation and Development with the other most developed countries in the world. Its average income per capita is almost $40,000, and less than 15% of its 52 million people live below the national poverty line. Ecuador, by contrast, has an average per-capita income of less than $12,000, and over 20% of its population lives below the national poverty line. What happened? Could two more years of education and a longer life allow you to increase your average income by more than three times in less than 40 years? Shouldn't oil help a country build its economy? It certainly seems like having something so valuable should help, but clearly it did not.

The best explanation for the difference lies in the policies that South Korea followed. Sometimes acting like a drill sergeant, its government promoted exporting manufactured goods to other countries. To be successful, this policy meant that you had to be involved directly in industry. Businesses that made goods that could be sold to countries in North America and Europe were valued above other companies, and the population sacrificed what could be considered basic luxuries such as televisions and cars so that the economy could grow rapidly.

Ecuador, alternatively, did not promote exports. Instead, it protected many of its own companies and subsidized necessities for its people. Further, the country did not industrialize the way that South Korea did. Instead, most of its income came from natural resources such as oil, seafood, cut flowers, and other agricultural goods, rather than from manufactured products.

Certainly other factors played a role. South Korea benefited from being an important military ally of the United States during the Cold War. Because of its proximity to the Soviet Union, North Korea, and China, South Koreans were given some preferential treatment when it came to their trade policies. As a result, they were able to sell more goods in the United States while purchasing less from their ally. Ecuador, though nominally an ally of the United States, was not as strategically important and thus tended not to receive the same preferential treatment as South Korea. South Korea also has a larger population than Ecuador. In the end, however, the stark fact remains that South Korea is now a wealthy state and Ecuador is not, even though they both started out poor.

This comparison raises some interesting questions:

1. How was South Korea able to become so wealthy?

2. What failures did Ecuador experience that caused its economy to stagnate?

3. Could other countries have helped Ecuador?

INTRODUCTION: THE DIFFERENCES BETWEEN THE RICH AND THE POOR

The tale of Ecuador and South Korea illustrates just how radically levels of development can differ among the countries of the world. Many scholars and policymakers categorize the differences between the rich and the poor as the North and the South, sometimes referred to as the north–south divide. This refers to the general tendency for wealthy countries to be in the Northern Hemisphere, while the poorer countries tend to be in the Southern Hemisphere. Of course, this dichotomy does not work perfectly. For example, Australia is a wealthy, developed country clearly in the south, and the Republic of Georgia is a poor, developing country in the north. A more accurate description of these two types of countries is as either a **developed country** or a **less-developed country (LDC)**. Like rich and poor, have and have-not, these terms provide a better and more accurate view of the world, so let's use those terms to understand the complexity of which countries are wealthy and which are not. As we will see, these international development matters involve very important international relations involving countries, international organizations, nongovernmental organizations, transnational corporations, and other players, including individuals.

10-1 THE WEALTH GAP

≫ 10-1 Describe the distribution of wealth around the globe.

Whether you call a country developed, rich, wealthy, or one of the "haves," the amount of money it has relative to the size of its population is critical to the survival

....

developed country: a wealthy country with an economy that tends to produce manufactured goods and services for export.

less-developed country (LDC): a country that is poor or has an economy that is less able to support its population. These countries typically export raw materials and agricultural products.

World Health Organization (WHO): the UN organization that deals with health issues around the world. It is responsible for the eradication of smallpox.

and well-being of its people. When we use the terms *rich* or *wealthy* in this chapter, we do not mean to imply that these countries and their populations are able to afford every possible luxury and take vacations in exotic locales. Instead, the terms *rich* or *developed* mean that a country's economy can clearly support more than the basic necessities of life. The terms *poor* or *less-developed* or *have-not*, by contrast, mean that the country's economy may not be strong enough for its population to get the minimum 2,600 calories a day, as recommended by the **World Health Organization**.

It is important to realize that a lack of development, or being a poor country in this sense, is the cause of far more deaths than all the international and civil wars discussed in Chapter 5 combined. We all know about the horrors of war—and wars are horrible—but many more people die each day because they cannot get enough food or clean drinking water. Just think: More people die from malnutrition and water- and food-borne parasites than from bullets and bombs. It is also often the case that hardships such as these are destabilizing within countries and can result in tension and conflict within and between countries as well, such as when they prompt migration across borders. Perhaps we should ask ourselves why the world spends more on weapons than on development, when the lack of development is a bigger killer and thus a bigger threat to human security for more people than any war has ever been. What do you think?

As we noted in Chapter 8, money means power, which in turn often means security. Wealthy states have more autonomy because they are more secure, thanks to their stronger economies. For example, Canada can disagree with China more easily than Bangladesh can because Canada is less vulnerable to economic coercion. Canada's citizens are also more secure because they have ample access to nutrition and medical services, unlike the people of Bangladesh. Development means not only that a country's people can meet the minimum daily caloric intake but also that the country has a stronger, more secure position in the international system. Do you think that is why countries spend so much on weapons—because they want more security? Could a strong, developed economy alone give a country security? That is, could a wealthy country still be secure without a military because it claimed neutrality? It would be a big risk to take; both Sweden and Switzerland are rich, neutral powers, but both still spend money on their militaries. Japan, by contrast, is wealthy and not neutral. Its defense spending has been rising slowly over the last few years, but it still spends only about 5% of its governmental budget on the military. Is it secure? If so, is its human security derived from its economy and its international security derived from its island status and its military alliance with the United States?

Clearly, the consequences of being born in a rich or a poor country are dramatic. For that reason, scholars and policymakers exert significant effort trying to figure out why countries are poor and how they can develop their economies. Also, the gap between rich and poor states exerts a powerful effect on the international relations between states in each group. We will address these issues in this chapter, but first let's turn back to exploring the differences between the haves and have-nots.

10-1a Our Understanding of the Rich and the Poor

As we have discussed throughout this book, complexity is a true theme in international relations, and its role in the distribution of wealth is no different. Not only is wealth distributed differently; people's perceptions of rich and poor countries also tend to differ radically. For instance, most Americans viewed Japan's economy in the 1980s as much stronger and more vibrant than that of the United States. Many Americans thought that the Japanese economy was bigger and that the Japanese **GDP per capita** (the nation's wealth divided by the population, or wealth per

person) was higher. As you can see from Figure 10-1, that perception was simply wrong. Today, many Americans tend to think that the Chinese economy is larger and more powerful than it really is, particularly when measured by GDP per capita. These misperceptions are unfortunately common.

It wasn't just the average American who thought that the Japanese were in the process of rising above the United States. In a famous book published in 1987, *The Rise and Fall of the Great Powers*, historian Paul Kennedy argued that powerful nations rise and fall largely based on their economies, and he predicted that Japan's time had come to take its place at the top of the world. Nothing illustrated his thesis better than the cover art for the book: a Japanese businessman climbing to the top of the world pedestal while the Uncle Sam character steps down. That prediction couldn't have been more wrong. Beginning in 1991, Japan entered a long recession from which it still hasn't fully recovered. Originally referred to as the "lost decade," it is now called the "lost decades" because it has been going on for nearly 30 years. As

GDP per capita: the measure of a country's development. It is the total size of a country's economy divided by the population.

FIGURE 10-1

GDP in Selected Countries, 1970–2018

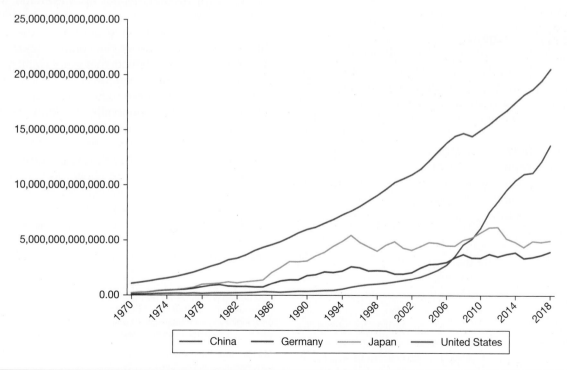

Source: World Bank World Development Indicators, 2018.

you can also see, in 2010 China's economy passed Japan's to become the second largest in the world and has even overtaken the US economy when considering the actual cost of goods in China.

Because of these complexities, we cannot easily answer the questions of why some countries are wealthy and some are poor, how those countries relate, and what the future looks like. Instead, we must first have a good picture of how wealth is distributed around the world. In the next two sections, we discuss the details of how wealth is distributed across countries and then within countries. Once we have an understanding of where the money and economic productivity are, we can turn to understanding how the money was made and what consequences that has for international relations.

10-1b The Countries That Have Wealth and the Countries That Don't

In 2019, the average GDP per capita in the world was $11,460 (measured in current US dollars), according to International Monetary Fund (IMF) estimated data. That number—while low—may not sound too horrible at first. Many college students live on not much more than that amount in the United States, but think about the fact that the *average* per-capita income in the world is over $1,000 *lower* than the 2019 US poverty line! However, that number does not give the best picture of the world. It is an average and does not show how much difference there is between the rich and the poor. That means about 3.9 billion people— over 50% of the world's population—lived well below the world's average GDP per capita. Compare that to the United States, where the GDP per capita was $65,111, the 7th highest in the world. Alternatively, the top two countries, Luxembourg and Switzerland, had GDPs per capita of $113,196 and $83,716, respectively; the lowest two countries, Burundi and South Sudan, had GDPs per capita of $309 and $275, respectively. In fact, the 10 poorest countries in the world in 2019 had a GDP per capita no higher than $513. To emphasize this point, this means that in the 10 poorest countries, the average person lived on less than $2.00 a day. That's less than the cost of a latte at Starbucks! For a striking contrast, take a look at Maps 10-1 and 10-2. They are very revealing. Map 10-1 depicts the countries of the world by their population, and Map 10-2 depicts them by their wealth, both in 2018. What does the contrast between these two maps suggest about economic security and world politics?

The UN uses another measure for extreme poverty: the percentage of people living on less than about $2 per day. As Map 10-3 shows, there are many countries where only a small fraction of the population lives on so little money. Unfortunately, there are

also many countries in which the majority of the population lives on less than $2 per day.

Thus, although it's overly simplistic, the world can be divided into these two groups: developed countries and developing countries. In the simplest of terms, these are the rich and the poor, the haves and have-nots of the world. To be sure, there is a middle ground—countries that are moderately developed, such that their economies can support the basic needs of the people plus a little more. Even so, it is striking how easily we can divide the countries of the world into two categories.

Let's compare what might be considered "middle class" around the world. To make this comparison across countries, we need to understand what a dollar will purchase in different countries. To do this, economists have developed a measure called **purchasing power parity (PPP)**, a tool that lets us compare the value of currencies across countries. PPP converts a currency to a common value so that it can be compared to other countries. For example, it is much cheaper to live in Mexico than it is in Norway (the state with one of the highest costs of living). Perhaps the simplest way to understand PPP is with the **Big Mac Index**, a measure created by the magazine *The Economist* to explain different costs of living and values of currency. The Big Mac Index surveys the cost of the famous hamburger around the world and compares it to the average cost of a Big Mac in the United States. For example, in 2018, a Big Mac cost (on average) $5.51 in the United States. In Russia, it cost $2.09 (in US dollars), but in Switzerland, it cost a whopping $6.57! Purchasing power parity works in much the same way, allowing us to adjust the currencies of countries so that we can compare them, based on a group of basic products that every country uses.

So, let's use PPP to see how many people in the world have enough money to fit into the middle-class category (or higher). Generally speaking, the minimum amount of money needed for an individual to be considered middle class in the United States is at least $40,000. Based on 2019 PPP, 27 countries fit into this category, and a total of about 435 million people in the world are on average *at least* middle class. That's only 6% of the world's population.

Now let's consider the poverty line as defined in the United States. In 2019, the poverty line was $12,490 for one person. Again, based on PPP, 93 countries fall

....

purchasing power parity (PPP): a measure that compares two currencies and adjusts them so that they can be compared in a meaningful way. PPP allows us to compare the purchasing power of the yen in Japan with the peso in Mexico, for example.

Big Mac Index: a measure created by *The Economist* magazine that compares the value of currencies by comparing the cost of a Big Mac hamburger in different countries. The United States is used as the baseline cost for the index.

MAP 10-1

The Countries of the World, Sized by Population

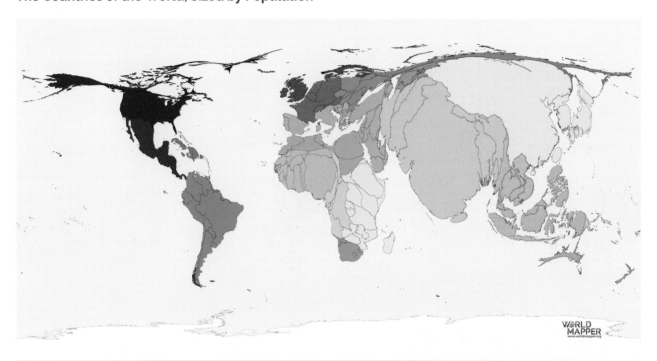

Source: Population Year 2018, World Mapper, https://worldmapper.org/maps/population-year-2018.

MAP 10-2

The Countries of the World, Sized by GDP per Capita

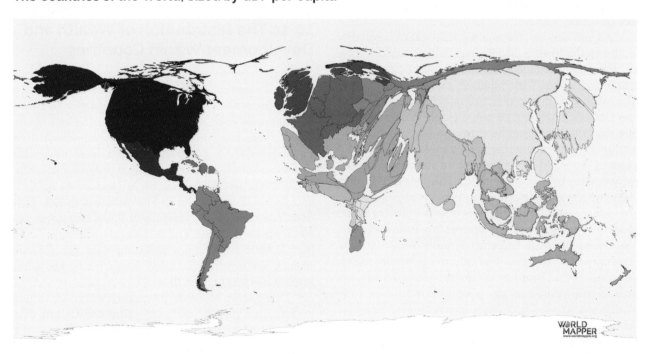

Source: GDP Wealth 2018, World Mapper, https://worldmapper.org/maps/gdp-2018.

MAP 10-3

Percentage of Population Living on $2 per Day or Less

Could you live on $2 per day? What's the absolute minimum that you could live on?

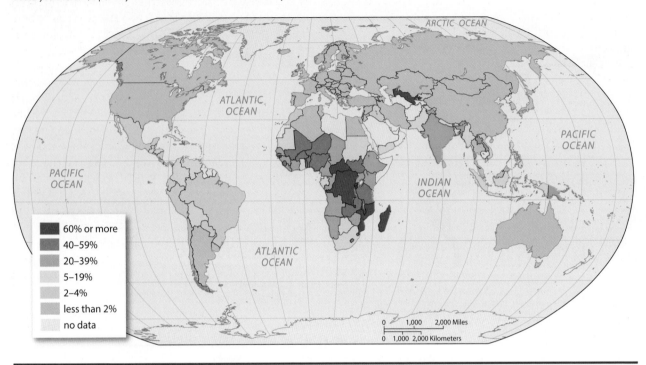

Legend:
- 60% or more
- 40–59%
- 20–39%
- 5–19%
- 2–4%
- less than 2%
- no data

Source: https://www.socialexplorer.com/blog/post/living-on-less-than-2-a-day-9229.

below the poverty line according to the US standards. That includes about 3.9 billion people—which is more than half of the world's population—who live below the US poverty line.

As you can see, there is a great deal of inequality in the world. Realize also that we defined middle class as being the absolute minimum in US standards, just $40,000 per year. That number includes only the top 11% of the world's population. Just think: If you lived in the United States and earned enough money to be in the top 11%, you would be earning well over $100,000 per year. This means that even people in the middle class of the world (by US minimum standards) are the very wealthy by global standards. The poor, by contrast, make up the vast majority of the world's population.

What does all this mean for how people live in the world? Working with the consulting firm DeLoitte, the Social Progress Imperative publishes an annual assessment of the social conditions in all countries. Its 2019 Social Progress Index report demonstrates that if the world had 100 people, 11 would be malnourished, 11 wouldn't have access to electricity, 41 wouldn't have access to clean fuels or cooking technology, 37 wouldn't have access to a piped clean water source, 27 would be without access to basic sanitation facilities, 52 would have no Internet access, and 68 wouldn't think where they live would be a good place

for LGBTQIA individuals. That's not a very pleasant world for many people.

10-1c The Distribution of Wealth and Development Within Countries

So far we have shown that there is tremendous diversity and unevenness in the distribution of wealth across countries. That's enough inequality to cause serious problems. However, that's not the end of the story. There is also a great deal of inequality *within* countries. When we discussed the level of wealth across countries, we were using averages. For example, in 2019, the GDP per capita in Canada was $43,602, and the GDP per capita in Pakistan was $5,190. That does not mean that everyone in those two countries each earned $43,602 and $5,190, respectively. Some people earned a lot more and some a lot less. For this reason, we must look inside countries to see what kind of inequality lives there.

One way to measure inequality within countries is through a statistic called the **Gini coefficient**. The World Bank's version of this measure ranges from 0 to 1,

Gini coefficient: a measure of the distribution of income in a country ranging from 0 to 1, where 0 means perfect equality and 1 means perfect inequality.

with 0 meaning that a country's income is shared equally by everyone. That zero score would mean, for example, that everyone in the United States would have earned $56,140 in 2019, even real-life billionaires like Bill Gates, Warren Buffett, and Jeff Bezos. A Gini score of 1 would mean that all of the wealth in a country is owned by one person. In reality, of course, there is no country that is perfectly equal or perfectly unequal. As you can see from the map of recent worldwide Gini coefficients (Map 10-4), there are considerable differences between countries. The most equal states tend to be in Europe, especially in Scandinavia, and the greatest inequalities appear in Africa and South America. Norway, for example, is consistently one of the most equal countries in the world. Norway's Gini coefficient of .259 reflects the impact of its extensive social welfare programs and progressive tax system. The most unequal country is South Africa, in which the Gini coefficient is .634. Just to give some comparison, the United States falls almost exactly in the middle of these countries at .490. That means that in 2019 the wealthiest 10% of the population had 70% of the country's income, leaving the rest of the wealth to the remaining 90%. The distribution of income in the United States doesn't sound very equal in those terms, does it?

Another way to look at inequality within states is to compare the average GDP per capita with the other two measures used to create the **Human Development Index (HDI)**. The HDI is a measure created by the UN to determine how developed a country is in terms of its people, and later in the chapter we'll talk about how important that is for an economy. The index combines the wealth, life expectancy, and education of the population. If the income in a country is reasonably distributed, then life expectancy and education level should be commensurate with income. What do we mean here? Well, in a wealthy, developed country like Canada, the GDP per capita in 2019 was $43,602, the life expectancy was 82 years, and, on average, adults had about 13 years of education. In Qatar, the GDP per capita was $110,489, but the life expectancy was 80 years, and, on average, adults had 9.7 years of education. You might say that isn't that big a difference, but when you consider that Qatar's GDP per capita is so high, those differences become striking.

Let's take a look at two other countries. In Nigeria, a poor state but one with oil, the GDP per capita was

....

Human Development Index (HDI): a measure of the level of human development in a country. It includes GDP per capita, life expectancy, and education levels.

MAP 10-4

Worldwide Gini Coefficients

Africa is the most unequal part of the world when it comes to Gini coefficients, followed by South America. What do you think this means?

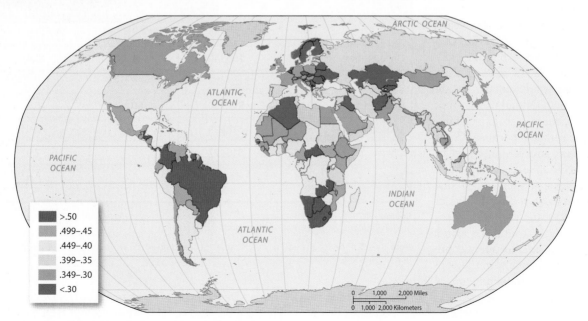

Legend:
- >.50
- .499–.45
- .449–.40
- .399–.35
- .349–.30
- <.30

Source: World Bank Group.

FIGURE 10-2

Adults 25 and Older With No Formal Education

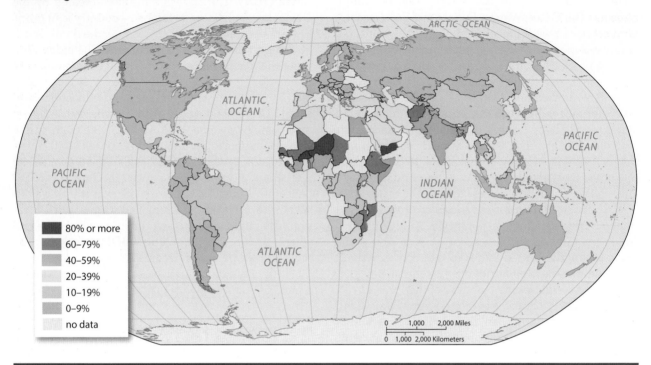

80% or more
60–79%
40–59%
20–39%
10–19%
0–9%
no data

Source: Pew Research Center, http://www.pewresearch.org/fact-tank/2017/01/11/about-one-fifth-of-adults-globally-have-no-formal-schooling.

$5,086, the life expectancy was 54 years, and the average length of education was less than 7 years. In Costa Rica, a developing country without oil, the GDP per capita was $14,790, the life expectancy was 80 years, and the length of education on average was 8.7 years. Note that Costa Rica's scores on life expectancy and education are better than Nigeria's and not that different from Qatar's. Why? Perhaps because Costa Rica has a much higher level of equality than either of the other two states. Think about this in another way: Take a look at Figure 10-2 and consider access to education around the world. As you can see, in many countries, more than 40% of the population goes without any formal education. Notice the parts of the world where that is the case and also notice where the proportion is below 10%. Then, take a look at Table 10-1—or the most recent

TABLE 10-1

2019 HDI, GDP per Capita, Life Expectancy, and Education

COUNTRY	HDI	GDP PER CAPITA (2011 PPP)	LIFE EXPECTANCY	MEAN YEARS OF EDUCATION
Canada	0.922	$43,602	82.3	13.3
United States	0.920	$56,140	78.9	13.4
Qatar	0.848	$110,489	80.1	9.7
Costa Rica	0.794	$14,790	80.1	8.7
Mexico	0.767	$17,628	75.0	8.6
China	0.758	$16,127	76.7	7.9
Nigeria	0.534	$5,086	54.3	6.5

Source: UN Development Programme, *2019 Human Development Index Ranking*, http://hdr.undp.org/en/content/2019-human-development-index-ranking.

Note: The GDP per capita figures in this table are based on 2011 PPP values and thus are different from those cited in the text.

Human Development Report from the UN Development Programme—and compare the different HDI indicators. You may find some more startling differences.

Unfortunately, it is much more difficult to get a good picture of how equal or unequal income is within countries than it is between countries. Gini coefficients are often missing or dated for many countries in the map. That is because calculating the measure is very difficult. To accurately measure equality, researchers must complete a sample of household surveys in each country. Although that would be easy—though expensive—in the United States, can you imagine completing a household survey in war-torn Afghanistan or Syria? Thus, our understanding of how equally wealth is distributed within countries is just an estimate. What we can conclude is that there is a great deal of difference between the rich and the poor in many countries, as well as between countries, and that those differences have important consequences for world politics.

10-2 WHY ARE SOME COUNTRIES RICH AND OTHERS POOR?

>> **10-2** **Identify the reasons some countries have developed economies and some do not.**

Now that we have explored the striking differences between the wealth and development of countries around the globe, we need to examine how they got that way and how some have been able to improve over the past several decades and others have not. There is not, of course, an easy answer to these questions.

Before we turn to the different policies that countries use to develop, we need to look at some of the **structural factors** that can either increase or decrease a country's level of development. These factors include natural resources and the colonial history of a country. We refer to these as structural because they cannot change, or at least it is difficult to conceive of how they would change. Thus, they are the structure or foundation with which a country must work as it develops.

10-2a Natural Resources

The first and probably most obvious factor to consider is the natural resources a country has. Just like the unequal distribution of income, the world's resources vary tremendously by country. For example, the United States is fortunate to have an abundance of land and good climate for agriculture, and it is rather rich with natural resources such as oil and coal. Looking at the history of the United States, much of its initial power came from these natural resources, especially its agriculture. The relative ease with which the United States

could grow food meant that it could expend less effort feeding its population and focus more on industrialization. Given all those natural resources, it would be hard for the United States not to become a powerful and wealthy state, a point Peter Ziehan makes in his book *The Accidental Super Power*.

Conversely, Afghanistan has few natural resources, a very inhospitable climate, and poor land for crops. The difficulty in growing food meant that Afghanis had to expend a huge effort just to feed themselves. Spending all of that time and effort on food production left little time for industrialization or the education that it requires. Given the lack of resources, how could it grow and develop into even a moderately developed state?

Although these two examples leave out a great deal of detail in how the different countries developed, the point is that the resources a country starts with will have a big effect on how wealthy the country becomes. But is it that simple? Do countries with resources always develop? To answer that question, we only need to look at a country such as Nigeria. The country has significant oil and natural gas reserves and is considered "oil rich" according to the CIA's *World Factbook*. Having resources as valuable as oil and natural gas should make one rich, right? When gasoline sells for around $3 per gallon in the United States, having a bunch of oil should mean you could develop your economy into a wealthy state. That's not always the case. Nigeria's GDP per capita, controlling for the cost of living with PPP, is only $5,086 and, in fact, has changed very little since 1970. In Iran, another country rich with oil, the most recent GDP per capita (2015) was $18,166 (using PPP), less than half of what Americans consider middle class.

Former Venezuelan Oil Minister Juan Pablo Pérez Alfonzo once called oil "the devil's excrement," and he didn't call it that because it's messy and dark (Useem 2003). Instead, he meant that although oil may seem like a great gift, it is really a curse—specifically, what economists refer to as the **resource curse** (Sachs and Warner 1995). As it turns out, having a wealth of natural resources that are nonrenewable (such as oil and minerals) does not make a country wealthy—it makes it poor. Why?

The reason for this peculiar relationship between resources and economic development is threefold. First, oil and other high-profit minerals tend to drive up the costs in an economy. Because oil is so valuable, companies are willing to pay workers more to extract the oil. This means that the cost of labor increases in

---

structural factors: historical and environmental factors that influence how a country can develop its economy.

resource curse: the curious negative effect for a country's economy when the country has a valuable resource, such as oil.

Afghanistan and the United States

Given these pictures, is it surprising that the United States is wealthy and Afghanistan is destitute?

DMITRY KOSTYUKOV/AFP via Getty Images

iStock.com/6381380

a country. That's fine if you work in the oil industry, but if you don't, you can't compete with other countries. For example, if oil workers earn $30 per day, then other jobs will have to pay a similar amount to attract workers. However, many companies cannot afford to pay their workers that much or even close to that amount. Thus, those companies fail, and without them, the country's only source of economic growth will be oil.

Second, oil and minerals are commodities, and their prices can shift radically over short periods of time. For example, the inflation-adjusted price (in 2020 dollars) of a barrel of crude oil in 1980 was $117.30, in 1990 it was $45.65, in 2000 it was $41.02, in 2010 it was $84.24, and it rose to over $100 in 2013 before falling to $39.42 in mid-2020. Such fluctuations make economic growth difficult, to say the least. In one decade, a country could be making large sums of money from exporting oil, and in the next, the price has been cut by almost two thirds! Because it is difficult to develop other industries when a country is oil or mineral rich, these fluctuations mean the entire economy goes up and down based on the world price for the natural resource. For example, in 2008, Russia had to slash its government spending because the Great Recession caused oil revenues to fall to about half of what had been expected. Price increases helped Russia over the next few years, but recent drops have again reduced its revenues. Because Russia is so dependent on oil for foreign exchange, such changes have major effects on the Russian economy and Russia's potential aggressiveness abroad.

The third cause of the resource curse is not economic—it's political. In many oil- and mineral-rich

countries, the governments tend to be very corrupt and inefficient. The wealth that these resources can produce is simply too tempting, and unfortunately, that temptation is too often not resisted. Often, leaders will extract wealth from the state to pay off their supporters—a tactic called **patronage politics**—while ignoring the needs of their people. In cases like Nigeria, the profits from oil have been squandered through extremely high levels of corruption and generally poor governance, and the Nigerian people have paid for it with poverty and frequently recurring civil conflict. Venezuela is possibly even worse off, with a collapsed economy, food and electricity shortages, refugee flight out of the country, and corrupt governance. In cases like Saudi Arabia and Kuwait, the gap between the rich and the poor is estimated to be huge. Many live in abject poverty, while a few enjoy opulent wealth that is hard to imagine. Oil did not bring these societies security; for most of their citizens, it brought *insecurity*.

The great income gap within these countries means that the elite in control of the resources—those in government—do not spend those resources on building the country's infrastructure and improving the common good. Instead of using the oil money to build schools and roads and to invest in manufacturing, the money is often used to build palaces. Unfortunately, palaces do not help a country develop its economy.

It's important to remember that resources don't just mean oil and minerals. At the beginning of this section, we mentioned the value of fertile land. The United States could not have risen up to the superpower that it has become without the abundance of its agriculture. Cheap food means that citizens and the government can spend more money investing in the economy, particularly investing in industrialization.

....

patronage politics: using state funds to pay off private or semiprivate political supporters.

Of course, the United States is just one case and perhaps not the best example because of its large size and the protection from the rest of the world that the Atlantic and Pacific Oceans provide. Geographer Jared Diamond (1997) shows that one reason European states were so successful in colonizing the world—and not the other way around—was that they were fortunate to develop domesticated plants and animals that could live in many regions in Europe. That allowed their civilizations to grow and develop into powerful states that then searched and conquered much of the less-developed world. Although food was not the sole source of their power, it did provide them with a strong base on which to develop. Similarly, modern Europe provides another example of the importance of agriculture. Compare the northern European states with southern European states. Northern Europe is wealthier and more developed. Why? Northern Europe had more fertile ground and thus needed less land to support its population and fewer farmers to produce the food. That meant more wealth and consequently greater industrialization, which led to more development. The same was not true for southern Europe. Farm productivity was lower, and more resources were needed just to produce enough food, so there was less wealth and less subsequent industrialization—both conditions that continue today. Agriculture may not be the powerful development engine that industry usually is, but without it, it's hard to have industry (see the box "The Revenge of Geography: Does Being in the South Make You Poor?").

As you can see, a country's natural resources can be an important factor in its development but not always in the way one would expect. Particularly valuable resources like oil, natural gas, and diamonds tend to make development more difficult, and basic resources such as food and building materials can be powerful engines of development. Natural resources aren't the only structural factor that influences whether a country is rich or poor, but those resources are tied to the next structural factor we'll discuss—a country's colonial history.

10-2b Colonial History

The original settlements by Europeans in Australia, Canada, New Zealand, and the United States created great benefits for both the colonial powers and their former colonies. These countries inherited from Europe two important factors that led to their economic success. First, John Locke's idea of property rights created an important rule of law that is required for successful capitalist growth. Second, the settlers brought with them a tradition of education—the only way a country can improve its workforce. Both of these traditions

were adopted by the governments in these emerging countries (originally colonies), and as a result, their levels of development came to equal or even rival those in Europe (Krieckhaus 2006). These original European—almost completely British—settlements or colonies fared relatively well, and some can now be considered among the best and most secure countries in the world in which to live. Of course, the true costs to the indigenous populations in these states were very high, but here we are considering only the development of the modern economy.

Unfortunately, elsewhere colonization by European powers did not have such a beneficial impact—quite the opposite, in fact. For example, countries colonized by European powers in the later 1800s tend to be poor, underdeveloped, and far less secure. Although some countries such as Japan and China were able to ward off the imperial powers and stay largely independent, many countries—especially those with valuable natural resources—fell prey to the European and American desire for profits and raw materials. Instead of bringing traditions of property rights and education, the imperial powers tended to force their colonies to produce raw materials for use back home in the metropole. Many of these states were new imperial powers in Europe—such as Belgium and Germany—and sought colonies for short-term gains to their own economy and to build a more powerful

The rich and the poor live in close proximity in Mumbai, India
Do you think these stark differences just across the street from each other make for a stable society?

Tim Graham/Getty Images

Does Being in the South Make You Poor?

Although the terms *north* and *south* may be inaccurate, they were created for a reason. Countries in the Northern Hemisphere tend to be more developed than those in the Southern Hemisphere. Again, that is a gross oversimplification and one that does not help us understand what is going on in the development of different countries. But is there something to being in the south?

It is not "south" that matters, but whether or not the country is in the tropics. Countries that are in the tropics tend to develop only to the level that the size of their economy can support. That may sound obvious, but economies in temperate climates tend to develop into wealthy states—regardless of their size. Look at the United Kingdom. It's relatively small, but it has a very large, developed economy. In the tropics, small states do not develop into large economies. Why?

Certainly, it's unpleasant to work outside when it's very hot. It can even be dangerous when the heat and humidity are high. Although some scholars argue that the growth of bureaucracy in the United States is connected to the development of air conditioning, that doesn't seem like enough to make a difference because humans adapt extremely well to their environment. Humans live in frozen tundras, swampy jungles, and arid deserts. What other animal can do that?

Scholars think that in temperate climates frost tends to kill off parasites and other organisms that compete for food grown in agriculture (Masters and McMillan 2001). This also includes the ability to store food once it has been harvested. Hot, wet conditions make storing grain very difficult. This is the main reason that spicy food often comes from countries that have a hotter climate—the spices were originally used to preserve the food and cover the taste of food that was beginning to go bad.

In temperate climates, agriculture was far more viable and thus made a better investment. It also produced more food that could be stored, which produced

more wealth that, in turn, allowed the countries to grow more rapidly. As we discussed earlier, agriculture helps create a foundation for a country to industrialize. When fewer people are needed to feed the population, that means more people are available to work in other industries. Tropical climates simply do not have that same foundation.

Is the story that simple? Does heat limit growth? Of course, the answer is no. There are many factors that influence economic development. Factors such as a country's regime type and whether or not it suffers from the resource curse are also critically important to development—more than its distance from the equator. However, it is important to realize that a factor as simple as the temperature can influence development. When countries face difficulties in growing and storing food, they must invent ways to overcome those difficulties. That means it is harder and more costly just to survive. Clearly, that means it is also more difficult to build up profits, invest them, and develop into a modernized, developed economy.

Finally, a few other factors seem important. Increased population density makes it hard to feed that same population; more of the land is consumed with housing and less with agriculture. A rapidly increasing population also stresses a society's resources, making it difficult to accumulate enough extra resources for increased domestic investment. Areas physically cut off from coasts or other trade routes face difficulties getting products to market or buying easily from others. Mountain ranges in particular make both travel and agriculture difficult.

1. What other factors could make hot weather impede economic growth?

2. What can countries in the tropics do to improve their economies?

3. If the climate is getting warmer, will that make it more difficult for all countries, or has technology made that irrelevant? ●

military, in contrast to the longer-term investments that the United Kingdom created with its colonies. Needless to say, extracting raw materials was not a recipe for growth and development.

This is where there is a connection to the resource curse. Powerful core countries like the United States, the United Kingdom, and France sought valuable

natural resources in periphery locations such as Saudi Arabia, Iran, and Nigeria. Although not always successful in attaining control and extraction of the oil, these powerful states often exacerbated the problem of bad governance common to these particularly resource-rich states. When trying to control the resources, the powerful countries found it useful to pay off the leaders of the resource-rich state or to provide them other benefits they desired. This policy would not help the people within the state, but it did make the leaders loyal to the powerful, pseudo-imperial country. It also tended to make these leaders dependent on the political and military support of the powerful country because much of their population saw the payoffs for what they were: corruption. The benefit of this policy—for the powerful country—was that even if the resource-rich state gained its independence, it was still tied closely to the powerful state, which could maintain control or at least influence over the resources—a process known as **neocolonialism**. As a result, the great powers often contributed to the corruption and bad governance of the country. This was certainly not always the case, however, because the temptation of easy money was often enough to lead to corruption and bad government policies without any outside help.

10-3 DEVELOPMENT THEORIES AND POLICIES

>> **10-3** **Compare the different strategies and policies countries have deployed to develop their economies.**

As the second half of the 20th century wore on, colonialism gasped out its last few breaths. That meant that most countries were independent and thus able to determine their own economic policies. To be sure, the great powers and former colonizers still had a great deal of influence in their former colonies or, in the case of the United States, its zone of influence. Still, countries around the world, both great and small, started developing theories and policies that would help the poor countries develop into modern, wealthy states. Of course, we already know the end of the story, because so many people in the world continue to live in poverty. A handful of these policies worked, but sadly, most failed completely or at least mostly failed to attain their goal of development. Let's turn now to the different ways in which countries pursued development.

10-3a Modernization

Beginning in the 1950s, economists and policymakers set out to duplicate the massive success of the European and US economies. Although there certainly were problems with the modern economies in these countries, overall they had generated tremendous wealth and lifted several of those states to great power status. Clearly, they had done something right, hadn't they? If poorer countries simply followed the path laid out by the developed countries, then they too should develop. From this logic was born **modernization theory**.

The theory is pretty simple. Countries simply need to follow the path that the already wealthy states followed, and they too will become rich. This process entailed transforming a country's traditional society and economy into a modern one. What exactly was "modern" in the 1950s? Basically, it meant embracing Western ideas about the functioning of a society and its economy. Specifically, an emphasis on individualism was important. Following the ideas of liberalism (see Chapter 8), if individuals follow their own desires, the country as a whole will prosper. That means that individuals succeeding in an economy should be rewarded with profits, and those who do not succeed should get no such reward or profit. Consequently, there will be some winners, who should subsequently continue to do well and contribute to the economy, and there will be some losers, who do not.

This may seem very logical or at least familiar to those of us raised in Western society—some businesses succeed and some fail—but it was a significant change from some traditional societies that emphasized the group (family, tribe, clan, etc.) over the individual. Imagine growing up in a society where everyone in a family works for the success of the family as a whole and then being told that you should work only for your own success. That would be quite a shock.

This emphasis on individual economic rewards was supposed to spur economic growth. Successful entrepreneurs would reinvest in the economy, building more and more wealth. In the end, the country as a whole would benefit, just as it had in Europe and the United States.

The other aspects of modernization theory argued that countries should industrialize as much as possible and move away from agricultural production. This meant that there should be emigration into the cities as the country urbanized. Clearly, this theory was developed well before the ideas of environmental responsibility and organic-anything had appeared. The more processed and urban a country was—the better.

There were significant problems with modernization theory, and perhaps the best way to explain them is with a metaphor. Imagine that you had the idea of starting a fast-food restaurant in 1940. You could serve burgers, fries, and soft drinks. Given that no

....

neocolonialism: the practice of maintaining control over smaller, developing countries by keeping strong, dependent links to their governments and/or dominating their economies. This allows a powerful state to control a smaller state without colonizing it.

modernization theory: a theory in the 1950s and 1960s that suggested all countries should be able to develop by following the practices of wealthy states in Europe and North America.

such restaurants existed at that time, you could easily begin to dominate the market. Just think: Yours could be the first restaurants to spread out along the new interstate highway system in the United States. The idea that people could enjoy the same food as they traveled across the country would be worth billions. We know this for a fact because McDonald's was founded in 1940 and is now a multibillion-dollar corporation.

Imagine trying to start a new fast-food restaurant now. You would have to compete with all of the current restaurants, from McDonald's to Taco Bell to Subway to Chick-fil-A and many more. It would be hard to think of a way to compete with these giants and actually make a profit, yet that is essentially what modernization theory suggested. Undeveloped countries should just do what the rich countries did, but when the rich countries developed, they didn't have any competition except for themselves. It's better to be the first computer company than the 24th, right? This doesn't mean that it couldn't be done. It simply means that it would be difficult and thus rather unlikely that countries would succeed. At a minimum, it meant that states wanting to modernize needed to develop strategies that worked in the current world environment, rather than one in which there were no modern super-powered economies.

Another problem with modernization theory is the idea that the path taken by Europe and the United States was an easy one. The Industrial Revolution may have been an exciting, dynamic period in history, but it was also plagued with horrible working conditions, little or no protection for workers, heavy pollution from coal, and so on. To think that the rest of the world should modernize in the same manner would mean that the global environment would suffer (as noted later in Chapter 12) and that the people in each of those developing countries would also suffer (see "Spotlight On: Climate, Climate Change, and Economic Development"). It certainly seems like there should be a better alternative, don't you think?

10-3b Dependency Theory

The first alternative to modernization theory was driven partly by theory and partly by a desire for social change. Scholars and policymakers focused on the critique that modernization theory would not work because the less-developed states would have to compete with the huge Western economies. They began to argue that it wasn't just the competition from the large economies that was stifling growth in developing countries. Instead, they argued that large corporations in Europe and the United States created a system of dependency when they invested in poorer countries, and that dependency made it so that the poor countries would never be able to grow, an idea that fit well with world systems theory.

First, let's explore the background on multinational corporations (MNCs). When Company A from one country invests enough money in Company B in another country to control Company B or it creates a new subsidiary company in another country, it is considered **foreign direct investment (FDI)**. Normally, any investments of 20% or more of a company's stock give control and are considered FDI. During the early 1900s, more and more corporations from wealthy countries invested heavily in the developing countries. For example, United Fruit Company (now Chiquita Brands International Sàrl, Swiss-owned but based in North Carolina) owned fruit plantations throughout Latin America and virtually controlled those exports. Similarly, International Telephone and Telegraph Corporation (based in New York) held a stake in Chilean copper mines and owned and controlled the telecom industry in Chile and elsewhere in South America. Once a company controls companies in other countries, it is considered an MNC. Current-day examples of MNCs are McDonald's, which has restaurants all around the world; Anheuser-Busch InBev, the Belgian brewing company that purchased Anheuser-Busch in 2009; and Unilever, which began as Lever Brothers in the 1890s by selling soap in Britain and now sells consumer goods in 180 countries.

Foreign direct investment can be a good thing because it indicates that there is value in the **host country**. However, these MNCs often tended to extract raw materials (bananas, copper, etc.) for use or consumption in their **home country** and keep the profits from the sale of those raw materials in the home country. This was particularly true through the 1970s.

An example should highlight how this worked and how it could be detrimental to the host country: United Fruit grew bananas in Guatemala and sold them in the United States and around the world. The profit from the bananas did not stay in Guatemala; it went to the United States, where United Fruit was headquartered. The workers on the banana plantations were paid, but rather poorly, and United Fruit had to build some infrastructure to ship the bananas (it owned the only railroad in Guatemala), but all of the profits from bananas grown in Guatemala left the country.

---

foreign direct investment (FDI): when a company in one country invests in a company in another country that leads the investor to have control over the new company.

host country: the country in which a multinational corporation owns other companies.

home country: the term used to describe where the headquarters of a multinational corporation is based.

Climate, Climate Change, and Economic Development

Weather has always affected the economy. Perhaps most dramatically was the 95 years of sporadic, long-lasting droughts in 820 CE that led to the collapse of the Mayan civilization. Less dramatic but more recent, the Dust Bowl drought in the US during the 1930s prompted thousands of farmers to flee their land in hopes of finding a way to earn a living elsewhere.

Droughts and floods are acute climate impacts on human development, but climate can also have other, more powerful and lasting effects. States in tropical climates have significantly lower levels of economic development because the climate creates serious challenges. First, agricultural production tends to be significantly lower in tropical climates compared to temperate zones. Tropical farmers face greater problems with soil erosion, access to irrigation, and pests. As a result, citizens have less food, which leads to the second problem—health. Lower nutrition levels in tropical countries mean people are less able to ward off illness. Further, warm climates are prone to difficult-to-control conditions such as malaria and parasitic infections. Even controlling for income,

health outcomes (e.g., infant mortality) are lower in tropical countries.

When we then consider the changing climate, things get more unpredictable. More countries will have issues with agriculture because shifting weather patterns will likely lead to more droughts or floods. As food becomes less secure, disease will likely increase, and a sick population is bad for the economy. Climate change itself may result in the broader diffusion of diseases to new, previously unaffected areas and, perhaps, even the return of some long-dormant diseases. Can the effects of problems like drought, floods, and diseases on development be addressed if the long-term climate change challenge is ignored? How can the world approach development in a sustainable way in light of these challenges? ●

Sources: Gallup, John Luke, Jeffrey D. Sachs, and Andrew D. Mellinger. "Geography and Economic Development." *International Regional Science Review* 22, no. 2 (1999), 179–232; and Sachs, Jeffrey D. *Tropical Underdevelopment* NBER Working Paper No. w8119. Washington, DC: National Bureau of Economic Research, 2001.

As a consequence of this process, Guatemala (or any developing country with MNCs) could not develop because it didn't have any capital to invest—all of the capital was owned by foreign corporations, and profits generated were taken out of the country. This realization was called dependency theory, and its proponents argued that because large MNCs kept the profits, the poor countries would always stay poor. Dependency theorists noted that even though the large MNCs paid local workers and built infrastructure such as roads and ports needed to export the raw materials, these benefits did not provide the developing country with much and certainly not enough to begin to develop an economy independent of the large corporation.

At the beginning of this section, we pointed out that dependency theory was part theory and part call for social change. Thus far, we have explained the theory part; what about social change? As you probably noticed, the theory rests on logic very similar to Marxism. Although Marxism emphasizes economic class above all else, the dependency theorists simply apply that logic to countries (rather than people). So instead of a focus on the capitalist owner extracting profits from the worker, the theory argues that rich states, such as Belgium, extract profits from the poor

states, such as the Congo. Thus, the social change aspect of dependency theory came from Marxist ideas.

Proponents of dependency theory argued that developing states needed to revolt against the corporations and take their property, whether that was a copper mine, a fruit plantation, or a factory. This process of taking foreign-owned property is called **expropriation**. One example of this is Cuba, where Fidel Castro, after overthrowing the Batista government, in 1960 confiscated all private property in Cuba (including plantations, resorts, etc.) in the name of the Cuban people. He then proceeded to redistribute the profits to the Cuban people with varying degrees of success. To this day, there are Cubans who fled Castro's revolution who claim they still own property in Cuba and will someday take it back.

Once the new socialist governments had taken the property from the corporations and nationalized it, they could begin developing their economy. With **nationalization**, the profits from those holdings would provide

....

expropriation: the taking—or nationalization—of property owned by a foreign company with or without compensation.

nationalization: when a government takes ownership of private property—land, a company, or an asset.

money for investment and allow the government to engage in socialist policies rather than capitalist policies. A good example is Egypt. In the 1950s, Egypt's new socialist government nationalized major enterprises with the stated intent of reinvesting this new capital in the Egyptian economy. By the time President Hosni Mubarak was overthrown in 2011, Mubarak himself was thought to be a billionaire, but the Egyptian economy was stagnant and most Egyptians were poor, living on less than $2,300 per year.

Thus, the end result was not often beneficial to the developing country. Of course, expropriation was met with great resistance by large corporations and their home countries. The home governments did not want their MNCs to lose their property in the host countries and their ability to make so much money. Even though expropriation was taking privately held property, states often saw it as a threat to their security because it threatened their economic well-being. As a consequence, they often funded covert activities against socialist movements and supported dictators who guaranteed that they would get to keep their property.

The socialist policies often did not work for the same reason Marxism tended to fail around the world. In theory, an economy that strives for equality makes sense, but in reality, it is often too inefficient to succeed. Cuba might be the most successful example because it is still truly socialist and has a rather high level of equality and human development compared with its level of wealth. Of course, at least some of Cuba's success can be attributed to the support it received from the Soviet Union for 30 years. When it received aid from Moscow, Cuba did well, but with the collapse of the Soviet Union and end of the Cold War, that aid dried up. Now its level of development is far behind that of many other Latin American countries. It is also beginning to allow private ownership, perhaps a sign that it is moving toward a non-socialist, semi-liberal economy.

In addition to the failure of many of the policies advocated by dependency theorists, later studies showed little evidence to support the idea of dependency. Most studies found that investments by MNCs—FDI—tended to benefit countries rather than hurt them. Although profits and raw materials were often extracted from countries, significant capital was left behind, along with a developing infrastructure to support the MNC. Thus, few people today espouse dependency theory, at least under that name.

Dependency theory did fail in practice, and FDI was shown to have a number of beneficial effects in the host countries, but the theory was not simply a flash in the pan or an unfortunate fad. Not all of the scholars working with dependency theory espoused radical social change. Instead, they pointed to the inequalities of the exchange common to the relationship between poor and rich countries (and their corporations). With time, many less-developed countries took a stronger stance toward the corporate investment and made sure that there were clear benefits for their people. There are certainly many cases of poor working conditions and poor treatment by large corporations in developing countries (see Chapter 8 for examples), but those conditions have improved greatly over the past decades—perhaps partly due to the work of dependency theorists.

10-3c World Systems Theory

The failure of dependency theory did not mark the end of socialist approaches to development. As described in Chapter 4, world systems theory, which developed concurrently with dependency theory, is a Marxist-inspired theory that argues the political-economic world is divided into different levels or zones of power (Wallerstein 1974, 1979). That power structure determines each individual state's ability to develop its economy; it also constrains its foreign policy, but we will focus on the economy here. Notice that world systems theory suggests there is a hierarchy of power in the world, but the world system is still based on a lack of a world governing authority. Wealthy states are able to develop their economies better than poor states because the system is anarchic.

According to world systems theory, the world is divided into three economic zones: the core, the semi-periphery, and the periphery (see Map 10-5). These zones divide up the world's production similar to a division of labor, with each zone producing specific types of products. There is a hierarchy to these zones and to the products they produce, so let's turn to that next.

The core states are the wealthy, capitalist countries. These include most European states, Australia, Canada, Japan, and the United States. These states tend to make first-generation products that provide the highest level of profits. First-generation products right now would include iPhones, iPads, and other technology-based products; financial instruments (stocks, bonds, etc.); pharmaceuticals; and advanced military weapons. All these products are cutting-edge technologies that have been developed in core states. Sometimes referred to as secondary goods because they require some processing or building, they all have value added by the labor that is used to make them. They also provide the biggest profit margins to the core states. Core states promote free trade of these goods, arguing that tariffs are bad for development.

The semi-periphery and the periphery are the middle and poor states, respectively. Peripheral states tend not to produce manufactures but instead export raw materials—sometimes called *primary goods*—to

MAP 10-5

The Countries of the Core, Semi-Periphery, and Periphery

What does the hierarchy between countries reflected in this map signify for the relationships between the people, groups, companies, and governments of these states?

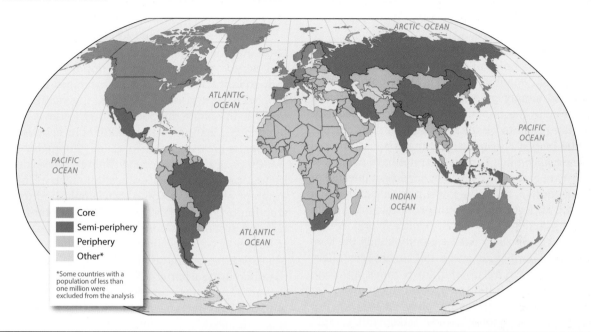

the core and, to a lesser extent, the semi-periphery. The core tends to place tariffs or other trade barriers on these products. The effect of this policy is to reduce the profits for the peripheral country and to protect workers in the core who might be engaged in producing raw materials such as food, lumber, and so on.

Examples of peripheral states include Honduras, Kenya, Iraq, and Vietnam. These states all produce raw materials or cheap labor that benefits the rest of the world but provides little profit to the producing state. According to world systems theory, the core and semi-periphery states exploit these periphery countries by extracting value from them. Put simply, the rich and middle states force the poor states to sell their products more cheaply, and thus the poor countries have an extremely difficult time developing their economies.

It is worth noting that many of the oil-producing states are often considered to be in the periphery. Although they make a high profit from the oil they sell, their economy is completely dependent on oil—they have nothing (or almost nothing) else. This puts them in a vulnerable position, and it means their economy is not very dynamic. It cannot grow without an increase in oil prices. Just think what would happen to states in the Middle East if more auto manufacturers copy Volvo and say they will make only electric

or hybrid electric cars at some point in the next few years, or if countries like France and the Netherlands follow through with their proposals to ban gasoline- and diesel-powered vehicles. Would the world still be concerned about Middle East peace? Would the region become like Africa—poor and relatively ignored by the rest of the world?

Semi-peripheral states act as the middle ground between the core and the periphery. They tend to make second-generation products that are profitable but not as much so as products made in the core. Examples of these products are automobiles and components for electronics. Just a decade ago, computers would have been on the list of first-generation products, and although many computers are still high-tech products, states such as China have begun producing and selling these on the world market. Computers are not as profitable as they once were. In 1990, an entry-level desktop computer was around $2,400; today it costs less than $400. Notice that many of these products are still made in the core. The important thing to realize is that things like automobiles are also made in the semi-periphery and are not the high-profit products they once were decades ago.

Examples of countries in the semi-periphery include China (although its economy continues to advance toward the core), India, Mexico, and Brazil.

Each of these countries sells both raw materials or cheap labor and manufactured goods. They make more profit from their production than the periphery states but do not generate the same per capita income as core states.

The relationship between these states is exploitive, according to world systems theory. The core exploits both the semi-periphery and the periphery by demanding lower prices for imports and selling its goods at higher prices. The semi-periphery does the same to the periphery, which in the end is at the bottom of the ladder and simply gets exploited. This exploitation and hierarchy is economic but also concerns security. Core states tend to be the most secure, their citizens have the longest life spans, and there is less internal and external conflict. Peripheral states have much less security, are more often involved in violent internal or external conflict, and have fewer human rights and a lower life expectancy. Remember, for example, from Chapter 5 that military conflict since World War II has almost exclusively been located outside the core states. Semi-peripheral states fall in between these two. States can move up and down zones, although movement tends to be upward and uncommon. For example, China was in the periphery in 1973 when it began to open up to foreign trade. Today, with its rapid economic growth and developments, such as taking over the ThinkPad laptop line from IBM (by Chinese-based Lenovo), it is solidly in the semi-periphery and is closing in on the core. The United States, Canada, and Australia were all originally periphery states but became core states 100–200 years ago.

World systems theory has much to offer in its explanation of the world economic structure, and it has generally eclipsed dependency theory. The description of what products the three zones produce, what profits they make, and how world systems theory affects their development is quite accurate. It also nicely describes the differing levels of security each zone enjoys because of the close connection between economic development and physical security.

The theory does, however, have limitations. First, it places so much emphasis on structure that there is no way to explain how different states can develop out of one zone and into a higher one. If everything is structural, for example, then why do some economic policies work and some fail? Why did South Korea outgrow Ecuador?

The second limitation is that the theory is only partly scientific; it is also based in the Marxist ideology that ultimately advocates social change. There is nothing wrong with social change or taking an ideological position on an issue such as development, but remember that part of the theory is ideology and only part of a social scientific approach to the world economy.

10-3d Import Substitution Industrialization

Another approach to development that was very popular throughout the developing world—especially Latin America—and inspired by dependency theory and world systems theory is **import substitution industrialization (ISI)**. Sometimes used in conjunction with expropriation policies, the main purpose of ISI is to enable the poor country to develop independently a manufacturing sector of its economy that will be the growth engine for its development.

ISI policy was supposed to help countries develop by first protecting their domestic industry. The government of the developing state would limit or even stop imports of manufactured goods with tariffs, quotas, and so on. This policy would force those goods to be produced domestically because they were either too expensive or unavailable for import. As domestic manufacturing firms started up, they could more easily succeed because they would not have to compete with the big companies in the wealthy countries. As these domestic companies got better at producing their products, they could begin to export them and compete on the world market. Once they had developed enough to compete with the wealthy states, the government could begin to allow imports again.

It sounds like a very good plan. Provide protection to new, infant industries so that they can become profitable, improve their products, and become truly competitive. However, these best-laid plans unfortunately failed to bring about development for the poor countries that adopted them.

The key to the ISI policy was first that the domestic producers would work to become more profitable and efficient. Only by doing that could they ever compete on the world market. Second, the government could only give protection for a short period, enough time for the domestic producer to become competitive. If the producer could not be effective on the world market, the government would have to let it fail. If the government did that, then the domestic producers would all work toward increasing their competitiveness.

For some countries at least, at first ISI worked well. The first products that were "substituted" for imports were nondurable items such as clothes. In all of these countries, there was a large domestic market for these items. Domestic producers were able to meet the continuous demand and grow their production capabilities.

ISI was working so well initially that countries began emphasizing industry over agriculture, a step

import substitution industrialization (ISI): a development policy that promotes cutting off international trade and substituting it with domestic production.

prescribed by ISI policy. Thus, more people began to work in industry and less food was being produced. Slowly, many countries that never imported food before had to start. This was not a problem originally because the industrialization helped pay for the food imports. So for a time, everything seemed to be working according to plan.

The next step in the process proved problematic, however. Domestic producers needed to produce more advanced durable goods such as cars and appliances. None of the countries attempting ISI had large enough populations to support a large domestic demand. Paraguay, for example, needs a steady supply of clothes, but it needs only so many refrigerators. Because there was less of a market for these durable goods, it was more difficult to make them profitable and therefore competitive with those from other countries.

Domestic producers quickly learned that they had a pretty sweet deal. Because the government limited imports from other countries, they could produce cheap products and charge relatively high prices, thus making huge profits. Instead of investing these high profits back into the manufacturing, thereby making it more efficient and competitive, they kept them. As a result, the people were left with high-priced, inferior products. So much for "durable" goods.

To ensure that the government would not pull the plug on their protection from foreign goods, the companies would often bribe government officials. Using their excess profits, they could pay off bureaucrats, legislators, and presidents. Once paid off, the government would continue the protection so that the companies could stay in business and keep making all that money.

To make matters worse for these countries, there was a global food shortage in the 1970s. Increasing demand from countries with growing populations combined with crop-destroying weather drove up food prices. Because these countries had emphasized industrialism more than agriculture and were importing food, they had to pay even more for the food just to survive. Consequently, the ISI policies intended to develop their economies ended up hurting them.

10-3e Export-Led Growth

Not all countries fell into this ISI trap, however. South Korea, Taiwan, Hong Kong, and Singapore all started ISI policies in the 1950s, but by 1960 they concluded that the policies weren't working and switched to the model that Japan used to rise from its post–World War II ruin. Instead of emphasizing the production of goods for domestic consumption—"substitutes" for imports—these countries began pushing their industries to produce goods for export.

This policy, called **export-led growth**, worked less by protecting domestic industry and more by promoting exports. To be sure, domestic industries were protected from foreign competition, as with the ISI policies, but generally they were protected only if they focused on developing exports. The governments of these countries gave tax breaks and other **subsidies** to domestic businesses that would create products for export. The governments also lifted minimum wage requirements and made sure that unions could not demand too much of their employers. This provided cheap labor, low taxes, and other valuable monetary incentives to export goods. As such, the producers in these countries became very good at competing on the world market.

Export-led growth was a fantastic success in these four countries. In fact, they were called the "Asian Tigers" because they were so successful and their economies had become so dynamic and competitive. Let's compare South Korea, which followed export-led growth, with Brazil, which followed ISI. As you can see from Table 10-2, South Korea started with a much lower GDP per capita. In the first decade of export-led growth, it grew more quickly than Brazil. In the following decades, it clearly sped ahead of Brazil. By 2010, it had a GDP per capita about twice as large, and South Korea's advantage grew even greater by 2018. Brazil's economy actually shrank a tiny bit in the most recent decade.

TABLE 10-2

GDP per Capita in South Korea and Brazil, in Constant 2010 Dollars

	SOUTH KOREA	BRAZIL
1960	944	3,417
1970	1,815	4,704
1980	3,700	8,350
1990	7,984	7,984
2000	15,105	8,803
2010	22,087	11,286
2018	26,762	11,026

Source: The World Bank, World Development Indicators, https://data.worldbank.org/products/wdi.

export-led growth: the idea that to develop a country's economy, the government should push for companies to focus on products that can be exported to other countries. The policy was most successful in Asian countries, such as South Korea and Singapore.

subsidies: funds given to companies by a government to help them grow.

Other Asian countries began to follow the Asian Tigers by adopting export-led growth policies. Indonesia, Malaysia, and Thailand did not have the same fantastic success as illustrated by South Korea but grew fivefold or more in the period between 1960 and 2018—significantly more than the ISI countries such as Brazil.

So why haven't all countries followed export-led growth? One reason is that as the world's economy has evolved to its current form—the global economy, as we described in Chapter 8—the ways of production have changed as well, and it is harder to compete in the global economy now than before. Globalization has also changed the way production occurs, so that companies are able to spread components and subsidiaries all over the world, and contract with others, in ways they didn't used to do. That has made it more challenging for countries to establish export-led sectors in the same way as before.

Another major component of the answer is that it's one thing to understand a policy and another to implement it. The successful Asian countries all had very strong, effective governments that were willing to place significant burdens on the population. The workers in these countries suffered low pay and few rights for many years. Consequently, the businesses could make even more profits and then reinvest them to become more efficient and successful. Many of the Latin American and African governments that adopted ISI policies were not nearly as strong or effective. They were more likely to take bribes and payoffs from industrial leaders. Many of them also tried to be populist in nature by providing more benefits to the public and thus did not squeeze their populations in the same way the Asian governments did. Although the earlier years of export-led growth were often difficult for the average citizen in these countries, their sacrifices helped create a developed, wealthier country for their children.

10-3f The Washington Consensus

By the late 1970s, global economic policy began to shift toward economic liberalism. Many of the attempts at socialism had failed to produce great gains in development, and the nationalist ISI policies had also led many countries into worse situations than they had previously experienced. From these failures,

policymakers began to embrace more **orthodox liberal** ideas. In particular, UK Prime Minister Margaret Thatcher and US President Ronald Reagan pushed the idea that economic growth would not come from government involvement in the economy but from a liberal economy and policy. This **neoliberal** approach was called the **Washington Consensus** because of the powerful push from the White House and from the Washington-based IMF and World Bank to adopt a package of economic and political reforms.

So what specifically did the Washington Consensus prescribe for the world's many economies? First, Thatcher, Reagan, and the other proponents pushed the idea that the best way for a country to develop was through democratic governance. In a democracy, those with a strong desire to succeed should be free to be more productive, which would be a driving force for development (see "Spotlight On: Democracy and Economic Growth"). Second, the market should be free as well. Countries should adopt policies that promote a market that is relatively unimpeded by government regulation and taxes. That free market should also be extended to international trade, where the country should not limit trade with other countries. Finally, the Washington Consensus pushed the idea that the private sector—not the government—was the best engine for economic growth and development. The socialist and ISI policies in the earlier decades relied heavily on government involvement in the economy; this policy, according to the consensus, must be rejected.

Whether through direct ownership of companies and resources or comprehensive interventions in the market, governments in developing countries had taken a very hands-on approach to economic growth. The Washington Consensus sought to change all of that and pushed its view through the policies of many of the large states (such as the United Kingdom and the United States) and through international organizations like the World Bank and the IMF.

Ronald Reagan and Margaret Thatcher
These two people had a tremendous impact on global economic policy that lasts to this day. Do you think they were right?

Jean-Louis Atlan/Sygma via Getty Images

....

orthodox liberal: an approach to economics that favors an extreme free-market approach in which government is very limited and most of a country is composed of private enterprise.

neoliberal: a return to liberal or free-market economics.

Washington Consensus: an orthodox liberal approach to development that took hold in the 1980s and was used to try to promote economic growth in poor countries. It had very limited success.

Democracy and Economic Growth

There seems to be a connection between democracy and economic growth. Most of the so-called rich countries in the world have democratic forms of government. That's a fact. These countries got rich by embracing free-market, capitalist ideas, which matched well with a limited government approach. By not overregulating the economy, individuals were free to innovate in creative ways, thus spurring economic growth.

In recent years, however, countries like China—with its form of state-managed capitalism—have enjoyed near double-digit economic growth rates, while the oldest democracies like the US and the UK have crept along with growth rates around 2–3%. A number of factors contribute to this outcome. First, with a state-managed economy, the government can direct resources to high-growth areas—but other areas or people get left behind. With democracies, growth rates tend to be slower but less volatile. Democracies, however, often consider how much of society's resources are passed back to the public in subsidies that are politically popular but economically

unwise, slowing economic growth and the production of new capital for investment. Additionally, democracies may be more prone to the kinds of populist or nativist leaders who encourage the protection of domestic industries at the expense of greater economic growth available through free trade and comparative advantage.

Indirect effects of regime type on economic growth should be considered here, too. Authoritarian regimes employing state-managed capitalism might be more prone to corruption and the diversion of societal resources into private pockets, given that the accountability of such officials may be limited. Over time, the economies of corrupt autocratic regimes tend to stagnate (Drury, Krieckhaus, and Lusztig 2006). Indirect effects of democracy often include a greater emphasis on public access to health care and education, as these policies are popular with the voters (Bueno de Mesquita, Smith, Siverson, and Morrow 2004; Lake and Baum 2001). Better educated and healthier citizens should be able to work both harder and smarter. So, on balance, is democracy good for economic growth or not? ●

The problem with the Washington Consensus was twofold. First, it was very much a top-down approach. That meant that policymakers in rich, core countries and in international organizations dictated to the poorer, periphery countries what economic policies they must follow. They were able to have this much power because many of the developing states needed loans to keep their economies from collapsing. The two big international organizations, the World Bank and the IMF, made loans conditional on the recipient government engaging in the liberal reforms named in the consensus. Thus, many of these developing countries had no choice but to adopt the liberal reforms. The problem with this top-down approach was that it was a "silver bullet" approach: One solution was to fit all problems. The liberal reforms required would cause massive economic and social change in many countries. Not only can such dramatic change be difficult to implement; it can also create such a shock that the society simply rejects it after a short period of time.

The second problem with the Washington Consensus was that it placed all of its emphasis on economic growth through efficiency and ignored the human costs of those efficiencies. Just as the export-led growth policies in the Asian Tigers tended to be hard on the population, so too were the liberal reforms

being advocated by the consensus. A free market creates many winners—businesses that thrive and produce wealth for their owners. Free markets also create many losers—failed businesses and fluctuating unemployment that leaves many without the ability to earn a living or make plans for the future.

Beginning in the late 1980s, policymakers began to respond to criticisms that the Washington Consensus ignored poverty in the name of economic efficiency. The consensus still promoted liberal markets and policies, but social welfare policies were viewed as the country's choice to provide a social safety net for its population. These reforms were institutionalized in 2002, at a UN conference on development in Monterrey, Mexico. The result was the **Monterrey Consensus**—a new policy that officially promoted the idea that liberal market reforms were the best way for countries to develop their economies but that growth must emphasize human security—it needed to promote human rights, gender equality, environmental protection, and poverty reduction. A major emphasis of the Monterrey Consensus was that it would take good governance to meet these latter

Monterrey Consensus: a 2002 framework for global development in which the developed and developing countries agree to take joint actions for poverty reduction, with emphasis on free trade, sustainable growth and development, and increased financial aid.

goals, something often lacking in many developing states.

The reforms that led to the Monterrey conference were driven by concerns and protests by the political left over the treatment of those hurt by liberalization. Activists and scholars questioned whether free-market reforms had gone too far, and the backlash successfully caused consensus to change. Recently, there has been another backlash against free markets, particularly liberal international trade, but this time it comes from the right side of the political spectrum, not the left side. Conservative populist movements such as Brexit in the UK, the US election of Donald Trump, and the German far-right party AfD (Alternative für Deutschland) all stress the need to back away from policies that promote free trade between countries because they hurt the average citizen. Instead, countries should develop policies that raise their countries and citizens above others.

Both the original objections of the political left to the Washington Consensus and the current right-leaning populist movements focus on the negative impact of liberalization on the middle and lower classes. The current populist movements have gained ground in developed countries; by contrast, the leftist movements were mostly in developing states. Further, the populist movements are distinctly nationalist; they promote their own national interests over (and often at the expense of) others. It is not clear if parties like the AfD or movements like Brexit will lead to another reform to economic policies or whether they will break down the Monterrey Consensus completely, rolling the world back to pre–Bretton Woods policies. What do you think? Are reforms needed? How will the world adapt to these changing demands?

About a decade ago, with China's rapid rise, a **Beijing Consensus** drew attention as an alternative development model. Not surprisingly, this alternative draws on the Chinese experience and economic model to stress pragmatism, innovation, and national determination of economic policies and priorities, far less emphasis on neoliberal policies, and a more neo-mercantilist approach (see Chapter 8) to development, with a greater role for the state. With China's rapid and continued economic success, and its growing role in providing foreign aid and investment in Asia, Africa, and Latin America, the appeal of this approach spread in the developing world and by 2020 was a significant challenger to Western models.

....

Beijing Consensus: an alternative development model based on China's economic approach, stressing national determination of economic policies and neo-mercantilist state involvement and direction of the economy.

Millennium Development Goals: eight goals chosen by the UN and over 20 international organizations in 2000 to dramatically improve the human condition by 2015.

10-3g The Millennium Development Goals and Beyond

In 2000, all the members of the UN and more than 20 international organizations working on international development agreed on a set of goals to guide international efforts to promote progress in developing countries. The **Millennium Development Goals** (MDG) that resulted included eight objectives to be pursued by 2015:

1. To eradicate extreme poverty and hunger

2. To achieve universal primary education

3. To promote gender equality and empower women

4. To reduce child mortality

5. To improve maternal health

6. To combat HIV/AIDS, malaria, and other diseases

7. To ensure environmental sustainability

8. To develop a global partnership for development

These ambitious goals led both to progress and to criticism. Although the goals had dates and targets and were relatively specific, critics argued that they were driven by donor—rather than recipient—purposes and decisions and that, in practice, they tended to focus on what donors could and should do rather than on progress in recipient countries. In addition, the MDG led to questions about their impact on environmental sustainability and their approach to women's issues in development (see "Theory in Action: Women in International Development").

Not surprisingly, the MDG had mixed results. The UN has characterized it as the most successful development program in history, and in some areas and for some countries, progress occurred. According to one summary (Galatsidas and Sheehy 2015; see also United Nations 2015a) of UN reports on the MDG:

- The number of people living on less than $1.25 per day was reduced from 1.9 billion in 1990 to 836 million in 2015, although the reduction in the proportion of people suffering from hunger fell just short of being reduced by half.

- Primary school enrollment figures rose from 83% in 2000 to 91% in 2015, short of the goal of universal enrollment.

- Gender parity in primary education was achieved in about two thirds of the developing countries.

Women in International Development

One of the issues long ignored by policymakers concerned with development was the status of women and the effect development had on them. Even though women make up approximately 50% of the world's population, they do not have equal status in most countries, and in undeveloped countries, their status and rights in society typically range from bad to abysmal.

According to all the theories of economic growth we have discussed, a growing, developing society should benefit men and women. In fact, there is nothing in ISI, socialism, export-led growth, the Washington Consensus, or the Monterrey Consensus that would suggest that men should benefit more from development than women. In fact, the empirical evidence is quite convincing: The more women are empowered economically, the faster the economy grows in those countries. If these theories and evidence are correct, then why aren't women doing better in developing countries?

Women tend to work in either unpaid jobs or in the informal sector of the economy. In poorer countries, women are almost completely responsible for the work of raising children and feeding the family. This work is unpaid, and thus women would not benefit from a growing economy unless the man of the house benefits from the economy. Further, development policies that follow the Washington Consensus or export-led growth tend to cut government spending, and the first items typically cut are social spending, which hurts women even if the economy benefits. For example, if the government spends less on supplying drinkable water, then it falls on women to walk farther to get the water.

When women work outside the home in poorer countries, it is often in jobs such as food service, cleaning, and prostitution. The value of these jobs does not rise at the same rate as jobs dominated by men in agricultural exports and especially industry. Women working as maids, cooks, and prostitutes are not part of a growing economy.

The irony here is that when women do well, so does the economy. When women are empowered, economies grow faster, and improving education for women and girls generally leads to higher economic growth as well. More opportunities for women in the economy and education also appear to lead to meaningful improvements in other things, including health and child mortality rates. For example, a 2013 IMF report, "Women, Work and the Economy," concluded that closing gender gaps in the labor market would "raise GDP in the United States by 5 percent, in Japan by 9 percent, in the United

Arab Emirates by 12 percent, and in Egypt by 34 percent" (Elborgh-Woytek, Newiak, Kochhar, Fabrizio, Kpodar, Wingender, et al. 2013: 4). In short, states that ignore the status of women actually hurt their own economies, and it is best for an economy if development policies pay special attention to making women part of the workforce.

Accomplishing this is not simple, though, and involves a great variety of efforts by states and international organizations. One particularly interesting means is through microcredit. Muhammad Yunus, a Bangladeshi economist, developed microcredit, in its modern form, as a way to alleviate rural poverty in his country. The idea behind microcredit is simple—give small, often short-term loans to poor entrepreneurs so that they can start their own business. Using his own money at first, Yunus quickly found that the recipients of microloans not only lifted themselves out of poverty; they also paid back the loans at a very high rate. What does this have to do with women? Approximately three quarters of all microloans today go to women, largely because they are more successful and more likely to repay the loans.

Overall, microcredit has been very successful, so much so that larger banks are getting involved in an effort to capitalize on the success of the loans. There are some pitfalls, however, to this increasingly popular form of development aid. Some studies show that larger loans to women are sometimes taken by their male relatives, thereby perpetuating the subservient role of women in these developing countries. Additionally, microcredit is based on capitalist values, which can maintain and extend inequality in developing countries. The loans help some but not all. As such, only a few are raised up out of poverty, while many others are left behind.

Even with these drawbacks, microcredit continues to be an effective way to enhance the lives and security of women as well as help their economy develop, as long as the purpose of the loan is considered carefully in each case and high-profit margins are not the primary motivation of the lender.

1. What other policies might be helpful in lifting women up to an equal status in developing countries?

2. Should development policies focus on women or simply wait until the country has developed to try to equalize their status?

3. As countries elect more women leaders, will more attention be paid to this important part of the economy? ●

- Although the child mortality rate continued to fall—reaching 43 deaths per 1,000 live births in 2015—that figure fell short of the target reduction of two thirds.

- Maternal mortality ratio was reduced by almost 50% but did not reach the MDG goal of a two-thirds reduction.

- Although progress was made in combating HIV/AIDS, slowing the rate of new infections, the goal of halting and beginning to reverse its spread was not achieved.

- The proportion of people without access to improved sources of water was more than halved over the period, with most progress achieved by 2010.

- Development assistance from rich nations to developing countries increased by about two thirds, although most donor countries continued to fall short of the target of providing 0.7% of their GDP in aid.

A report from the Brookings Institution found that between 21 and 30 million lives were saved by actions taken in pursuit of the MDG. Effects of the MDG program varied significantly by country and region, with important success stories coming from Africa and countries such as Brazil. The poorest countries in the world tended to see the greatest changes in trajectory for their development, although their gains were smaller in absolute terms because of the small size of their economies.

As the MDG program expired, the UN led an effort to establish a successor program to begin in January 2016. Focused on sustainable development, the 2030 Agenda for Sustainable Development consisted of 17 ambitious goals meant to build on progress from the MDG and continue efforts to end poverty, fight inequality, and tackle climate change. These Sustainable Development Goals include social, economic, and environmental targets stressing "everything from zero poverty, zero hunger, good health, quality education, gender equality, clean water and sanitation, and affordable clean energy, to decent work and economic growth, innovation, reduced inequalities, sustainable cities, responsible consumption, climate action, unpolluted oceans and land, and partnerships to achieve the goals" (United Nations 2015b). Unfortunately, progress has been slow. At the current pace, estimates show that the targets of the Sustainable Development Goals will not be met until 2073—not 2030!

10-4 INTERNATIONAL ORGANIZATIONS AND DEVELOPMENT

>> **10-4**   **Explain the role that international organizations play in development.**

So far we have discussed how countries can use policies to influence how they develop their economies and how other states—through MNCs—can affect a country's development. As we know from Chapter 8, other actors in the international system play a key role in the economies of both developed and developing states. Let's now turn to a discussion of these different organizations and how they affect the developing world. Although many organizations play a role in international development, we will discuss the four most important here.

10-4a The International Monetary Fund and the World Bank

The first two organizations to discuss are part of the Bretton Woods system and are sometimes called Bretton Woods organizations. As we explained in Chapter 8, the IMF's primary role now is to deal with balance-of-payments problems. This role makes the IMF the main international organization responsible for finance and debt. Balance-of-payments problems are created when a country cannot pay its external debt held by other countries or banks in other countries. This would be similar to when people cannot make the minimum payments on their credit cards and other loans. For an individual, bankruptcy is often an option, but defaulting on national debt is not so good for sovereign countries.

When a state cannot make payments on its debt, the IMF can step in and provide a short-term loan to help the country restructure its debt and budget. Referred to as structural adjustment loans, the loans are conditional on specific policies that the country must adopt, often including reducing its spending. From the perspective of the Washington Consensus, typical spending cuts involve social spending and food and fuel subsidies. That is, the IMF requires that the government cut back spending on public education, health services, and support for the poor (including food and fuel subsidies). As a result of these policies, the IMF is not terribly popular in developing countries when it has to step in to keep their government from going bankrupt. Imagine you are the leader of a small, developing country, and you are forced to make severe cuts to your budget—including

Debt Forgiveness

One of the defining characteristics of the modern world economy is the accumulation of debt by many states. Many states struggle with extremely high debt loads. Officially, this means the debt is in excess of 200% of the country's exports. To put that in the perspective of personal finance, it would mean that your debt is 200% greater than your income. Although some mortgages can exceed this amount, imagine having a monthly credit card bill debt that is two or three times as high as your monthly income! In many of the poorest countries of the world, this is the reality. In fact, in some, it is even worse: The interest on their accumulated debt alone exceeds their government revenues. Imagine if the *minimum* monthly payment on your credit card was greater than your monthly income! In poor countries, such a high debt load is considered unsustainable and perpetuates the extreme poverty in the country. A solution to this problem that has emerged in the past decade or two is debt relief.

Although debt relief has a long history dating back to **war reparations** in World War I, more recent policies aimed at alleviating the seemingly never-ending cycle of extreme poverty developed in the 1990s. Starting with religious organizations around the world as well as several NGOs, the movement was called Jubilee 2000, after the Catholic Church's celebration of the year 2000. This truly grassroots movement gathered activists from many different countries and walks of life and aimed to eliminate $90 billion in debt for the poorest countries in the world. This initiative eventually became known as the HIPCs initiative.

In 1998, large, peaceful protests were held in Birmingham, UK, during the G8 Summit. British Prime Minister Tony Blair took particular note and began pushing the issue of the HIPCs in the UK and with the other G8 countries. Around the same time, the World Bank and the IMF launched an initiative to provide aid to the HIPCs. The aid was aimed at reducing the debt load so that the countries could begin to develop and subsequently service the remaining debt. Table 10-3 shows the most current list of HIPCs funded by the World Bank and those under consideration. Note that most of the countries in the list are in Sub-Saharan Africa.

By 2016, over $126 billion in debt relief had been committed by the lenders participating in the initiative, with more than $50 billion delivered by that point. HIPC

TABLE 10-3

HIPC Debt Relief by the World Bank

FUNDED	
Afghanistan	Honduras
Benin	Liberia
Bolivia	Madagascar
Burkina Faso	Malawi
Burundi	Mali
Cameroon	Mauritania
Central African Republic	Mozambique
Chad	Nicaragua
Comoros	Niger
Côte d'Ivoire	Republic of the Congo
Democratic Republic of the Congo	Rwanda
Ethiopia	São Tomé Príncipe
The Gambia	Senegal
Ghana	Sierra Leone
Guinea	Tanzania
Guinea-Bissau	Togo
Guyana	Uganda
Haiti	Zambia
UNDER CONSIDERATION	
Eritrea	Sudan
Somalia	

Source: IMF, "Debt Relief Under the Heavily Indebted Poor Countries (HIPC) Initiative," April 2017, http://www.imf.org/en/About/Factsheets/Sheets/2016/08/01/16/11/Debt-Relief-Under-the-Heavily-Indebted-Poor-Countries-Initiative.

....

war reparations: payments from one country—usually the loser of a conflict—to compensate the victor's cost in money, lives, and property.

(Continued)

(Continued)

public debt fell from 100% of GDP for the approved recipients to less than 40%. IMF research indicated that average annual HIPC GDP growth increased from 1.9% for 1996–2005 to 2.6% for 2006–2001 (Marcelino and Hakobyan 2014). According to the IMF, the HIPC debt relief program enabled the 36 recipients to increase their poverty-reducing expenditure by over one and a half percentage points of GDP between 2001 and 2014. However, broader efforts to extend debt relief to more lenders and more countries have been limited, not surprisingly because that would mean many wealthy countries and commercial banks would lose a tremendous amount of money. However, the activists successfully brought the issue to the table and were able to influence the foreign policy of G8 countries and the largest international financial organizations in the world.

There are, of course, critics of debt relief, and not just from the banks that hold the debt. Some argue that the relief will not reach the poor and ultimately not lead to poverty reduction. These critics argue that money should be spent directly on the poor rather than the elites in government. Another criticism is that by waiving a country's debt, there is no reason for the HIPC not to take out more loans in the future and spend unwisely. Further, debt relief programs create an incentive for developing countries to manage their debt poorly because, if they do, they may be given debt relief. Many observers have concluded that debt relief works best in a limited range of circumstances, and especially when conditions are placed on the recipients ("Forgive and Remember" 2015). These criticisms are not without merit, but that still leaves the question of what to do with countries that cannot pay off their debt, ever.

1. Is debt relief a good idea, and should it be extended to more developing countries?

2. How might we best help both the indebted governments and the poor people in those countries?

3. Can you think of other movements like Jubilee 2000 that made a big impact in the way governments and organizations work? ●

---

those that affect the provision of basic services such as law enforcement, education, and other social services. How would you react? How do you think the public of such a country might react to reduced services that are so important to a society?

The success of the IMF is mixed. Some countries are able to pull out of their debt crisis and go on to build their economies. However, some countries cannot break the cycle of debt crises, and as a result, they and their people suffer. Often called HIPCs (highly indebted poor countries, pronounced HIP-sees), these states do not have a strong enough economy to pay back their loans, so they continue to cycle back and forth from spending cuts and new loans from either private banks or the IMF. Over the past decade, a movement has developed to provide debt forgiveness for these particular countries in order to break this cycle and give them a better chance toward progress (see the box "Foreign Policy in Perspective: Debt Forgiveness"). In 2005, this initiative offered 100% relief on most HIPC debt held by the IMF, the World Bank, and the African Development Fund, once a country was eligible. By 2015, 36 countries had received such relief, 30 of which were in Africa. In return for the relief, HIPCs were able and obligated to increase public investment in health, education, and other social services.

The other major component of the Bretton Woods system that is relevant here is the World Bank. The World Bank is actually a group of five organizations that provide loans to countries for the purpose of development projects. Originally called the **International Bank for Reconstruction and Development** because it was aimed at providing loans to Europe and Asia for reconstruction after World War II, the World Bank now aims at providing loans to poorer countries for economic development. These loans fund projects such as port facilities to increase the shipping capacity of a country, hydroelectric dams to provide electricity to cities in developing countries, and other big developmental projects.

Like the IMF, the World Bank has had varying levels of success in its development grants. Too often, the development projects do not match the needs of the country or simply try to bring a very undeveloped economy into the modern world economy without considering the possible negative side effects. In one perverse case, the World Bank helped Brazil develop steel smelting capacity. When the price of steel fell and that of coal (used in the process) rose, however, the Brazilians couldn't profitably produce steel and pay back the World Bank. So they began cutting down their rain forests to make charcoal for the smelting process. Thus, the World Bank indirectly contributed

....

International Bank for Reconstruction and Development: the original organization of the World Bank designed to promote reconstruction, especially in Europe after World War II.

to deforestation. Certainly not all of the bank's policies have gone awry, but because the World Bank focuses so strongly on liberal reforms, it historically has made some mistakes that hurt both the environment and people. However, like other international development funding agencies, the Millennium Development Goals and Sustainable Development Goals initiatives have moderated the lending practices of the World Bank since 2000.

Both the IMF and the World Bank get their funding from contributions paid by member states. The largest and wealthiest countries pay the most, but they also have the most control in the organizations. As we discussed in Chapter 7, both organizations have weighted voting, which means that the countries that contribute the greatest amount of loan capital to these institutions also have the most votes in the organizations. For years, if the United States opposed a loan, it had enough weighted votes by itself to stop the loan from going forward. Although that is less true now, it still means that several very wealthy states can veto loan proposals if they choose to do so. Finally, the IMF president has traditionally been from Europe and the World Bank president from the United States. Thus, the developed world maintains a great deal of influence in—if not control over—the organizations, a clear disadvantage to developing countries, according to Marxist and world systems theorists.

10-4b The World Trade Organization

We already discussed the World Trade Organization (WTO) in some detail in Chapters 7 and 8, but it is important to mention again here because of the role it plays in promoting free trade and the links between trade and development. Recall that the Asian Tigers were successful because they promoted exports, making their economies reliant on trade for development. Figure 10-3 shows how dependent some countries are on trade. As Figure 10-3 shows, the world's average for trade as a percentage of national economies is about 60%. Compared to that, notice how the United States is not particularly dependent (about 27%), even though it's the biggest trader in the world. Countries like Luxembourg, Ireland, and Hungary, however, are very dependent. Because the WTO is the main governing body for international trade, it can have a powerful effect on a country's development.

The voting structure in the WTO is one country–one vote, just like in the UN General Assembly and dramatically different from the World Bank or the IMF. However, the developed states still have control of the WTO's agenda. Thus, the issues that come up for discussion and vote are determined by the wealthiest countries. As a result, rich states maintain significant control over the policies that the WTO adopts.

10-4c The United Nations

The United Nations (UN) is probably the most well-known of the international organizations, though not necessarily because of its role in development. The UN has many functions and acts as an umbrella organization in many ways. It is not as involved directly with development and takes a backseat to many of these other organizations. Probably the most important role the UN plays in development is as a forum for all nations to discuss and build solutions to development issues. Because the UN represents all nations, it provides an open forum in which the poor countries can bring their issues to the table and discuss them with the wealthier states. That clearly is difficult if not impossible in the World Bank, the IMF, and even the WTO. Although these issues can also be addressed in the other organizations, the UN is more open to the developing states. That does limit its power, as developed states tend to put most of their efforts and funds into the IMF and the World Bank because they have

The World Bank, the International Monetary Fund, and the World Trade Organization

These three groups are very powerful actors in the world economy, but they don't answer to the people. Is this "democratic deficit" a problem? Can you imagine how you would react if one of their policies affected you and your country and you couldn't do anything about it?

FIGURE 10-3

Trade as a Percentage of GDP From Selected Countries for 2018

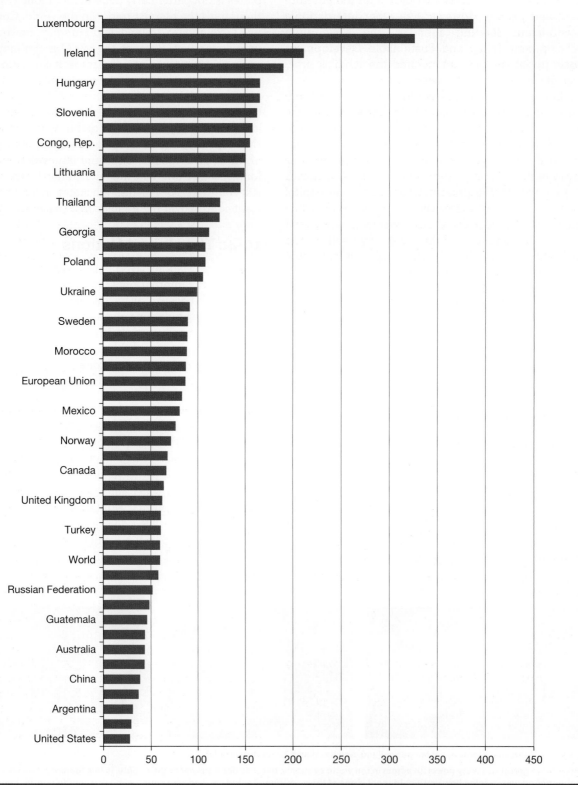

Source: Constructed by the authors from data from the World Bank, https://data.worldbank.org/indicator/NE.TRD.GNFS.ZS.

greater control of those organizations. However, the UN's broad mandate allows it to build a larger consensus. As we discussed earlier in this chapter, the best example of this was the negotiations that led to the Millennium Development Goals and Sustainable Development Goals.

The second area in which the UN influences development is indirect but extremely important: health. The World Health Organization (WHO), a specialized agency of the UN, is responsible for responding to world health problems. Perhaps no problem was more horrible and deadly than smallpox. The disease killed between 200 and 300 million people in the 20th century (Koplow 2003). By 1979, the WHO had exterminated the virus causing smallpox through a long campaign of vaccinations around the world. Significant improvements have been made in reducing the death tolls of HIV/AIDS as well. Although not always so successful, the WHO responds to epidemics and outbreaks such as the COVID-19 pandemic that spread rapidly across the world in 2020. The goal of such interventions is limiting the impact of outbreaks and their spread around the world or even within a country. Successes such as this reduce the strain diseases place on a country and thus its economy.

CONCLUSION

We said toward the beginning of this chapter that there was no single surefire way to develop an economy, and as you can see from the many failures and few successes, it's true. Even rich countries have trouble understanding how to put people to work in the short term. National economies are very complex layers of local, regional, national, and international interactions. Today's rich countries got rich through centuries of trial-and-error approaches, but the poor countries of today don't want to wait centuries to improve their people's lives and their own security. When it comes to improving human security, there is need for haste. Thus, many different means of improving the economies of poor countries have been tried, and many others surely will be tried in the years to come. ●

KEY CONCEPTS

10-1 Describe the distribution of wealth around the globe.

In 2019, the average GDP per capita in the world was $11,460. The 10 poorest countries had a GDP per capita below $600. In the US, the GDP per capita was $65,111, the 7th highest in the world. The top two countries, Luxembourg and Switzerland, each had a GDP per capita higher than $80,000, while the lowest two countries, Burundi and South Sudan, each had a GDP per capita below $400. By developed-world standards, about 435 million people in the world reach "middle class" status or higher, while the remaining 94% are poor. There is also a great deal of inequality within countries, which can be measured through the Gini coefficient. The most equal states tend to be in Europe, and the greatest inequalities appear in Africa and South America.

10-2 Identify the reasons some countries have developed economies and some do not.

Many factors affect the level of development in a country. Structural factors such as natural resources, climate and geography, and colonial history play a role. Factors such as human resources, leadership, and policy choices are also important, including the role of corruption and regime type and performance. Relations with and exploitation by foreign countries can also help or hinder development.

10-3 Compare the different strategies and policies countries have deployed to develop their economies.

Modernization theory contended that countries should follow the path of wealthy states and transform their traditional societies and economies into modern ones by embracing Western ideas, industrializing, and opening themselves to foreign investment and trade. Proponents of dependency theory argued that dominance and exploitation by wealthy states would keep poor countries poor unless they worked together and separated themselves from wealthy states. Import substitution industrialization promised to enable poor countries to develop the manufacturing sector in their economies by protecting their markets from foreign products and using government investment to develop domestic industries to produce those products instead. Export-led growth policy relies on government-industry partnerships to promote exports into the markets of wealthy countries. Neoliberal strategies stress the adoption of democratic governance, a free market, liberal trade and openness to foreign investment, and private-sector-led growth and development to achieve development.

10-4 Explain the role that international organizations play in development.

The IMF provides short-term loans to help countries deal with finance and debt issues associated with balance-of-payments problems (when a country cannot pay its external debt held by other countries or banks in other countries). Such loans are usually made conditional on specific policies that the country must adopt, often including reducing its spending. The World Bank is a group of five organizations that provide loans to countries for the purpose of long-term development projects. The WTO promotes free trade and the links between trade and development. Most broadly, the role the UN plays in development is as a forum for all nations to discuss and build consensus for solutions to development issues.

KEY TERMS

developed country 288

less-developed country (LDC) 288

World Health Organization (WHO) 288

GDP per capita 289

purchasing power parity (PPP) 290

Big Mac Index 290

Gini coefficient 292

Human Development Index (HDI) 293

structural factors 295

resource curse 295

patronage politics 296

neocolonialism 299

modernization theory 299

foreign direct investment (FDI) 300

host country 300

home country 300

expropriation 301

nationalization 301

import substitution industrialization (ISI) 304

export-led growth 305

subsidies 305

orthodox liberal 306

neoliberal 306

Washington Consensus 306

Monterrey Consensus 307

Beijing Consensus 308

Millennium Development Goals 308

war reparations 311

International Bank for Reconstruction and Development 312

REVIEW QUESTIONS

1. What are some key features of the gap between rich and poor states in world politics?

2. What structural factors lead a country to be rich or poor?

3. How unequal is the development in the world—both between countries and within countries?

4. What strategies do countries follow to develop their economies?

5. How do international organizations affect development?

THINK ABOUT THIS

Closing the Gap Between Rich and Poor

The gap between the haves and the have-nots in world politics is large and growing, and it affects almost every aspect of economic security, as well as important features of international and human security. However, achieving development—improving conditions and closing the gap between rich and poor—has been elusive for the players in world politics. Some observers, including economics professor William Easterly in his 2006 book *The White Man's Burden: Why the West's Efforts to Aid the Rest Have Done So Much Harm and So Little Good*, have argued that aid from the developed world has been ineffective at best and part of the problem at worst. Others, such as economist Jeffrey Sachs, whose work includes *The End of Poverty* (2005), argue that assistance from the developed world "is needed and can be highly successful." What do you think?

Is aid from the developed world the answer to poverty in the developing world?

The Big Mac Index

The Economist's Big Mac Index: https://www.economist.com/news/2020/01/15/the-big-mac-index

Colonies and Development

Acemoglu, Daron, and James A. Robinson. (2012). *Why Nations Fail: The Origins of Power, Prosperity, and Poverty*. New York, NY: Crown Business.

Banerjee, Abhijit V., and Esther Duflo. (2019). *Good Economics for Hard Times*. New York, NY: PublicAffairs.

Krieckhaus, Jonathan. (2006). *Dictating Development*. Pittsburgh, PA: University of Pittsburgh Press.

FOR MORE INFORMATION . . .

Milanovic, Branko. (2019). *Capitalism, Alone: The Future of the System That Rules the World*. Boston, MA: Belknap Press.

Microcredit and Muhammad Yunus

Grameen Bank: Banking for the Poor: https://www.grameen-bank.net

World Development Data

The World Bank's *World Development Indicators*: https://datacatalog.worldbank.org/dataset/world-development-indicators

PART IV

Human Security

CHAPTER 11
Human Rights: People, Human Security, and World Politics

CHAPTER 12
Managing the Global Commons: Whose Responsibility?

CHAPTER 13
Transnational Advocacy Networks: Changing the World?

Refugees awaiting their fate

Why doesn't the world do more to prevent such humanitarian crises?

Hristo Rusev/NurPhoto via Getty Images

11 Human Rights

People, Human Security, and World Politics

Learning Objectives

After studying this chapter, you will be able to . . .

11-1 Define human rights; the differences between individual, societal, and group rights; and how such rights have changed over time.

11-2 Describe the development of norms and codified rules regarding human rights.

11-3 Explain how states, international organizations, and nongovernmental organizations attempt to implement and enforce human rights standards.

Chapter Outline

11-1 The Evolution of Human Rights

11-2 The Human Rights Regime: From Norms to Rules

11-3 The Challenge of Implementation and Enforcement

Fleeing Civil War in Syria

The Arab Spring protests of 2011 sparked turmoil across the Middle East, but in Syria the turmoil quickly morphed into a civil war that raged for years. The Syrian government of President Bashar al-Assad was challenged by a variety of rebel groups, some motivated by Syrian nationalism and others by ethnic identity (such as the Kurds). On top of that, Islamic fundamentalists carved out a territory within both Syria and Iraq they called the Islamic State. Others states in the region got involved, with Iran (through its proxy force Hezbollah) and Russia supporting Assad but attacking the Islamic State, while Turkey, Saudi Arabia, and the United Arab Emirates provided military support to some rebel groups, as did the US indirectly. Pressed from all sides, the Syrian military launched chemical weapons attacks on its enemies, killing many noncombatants in the process, which prompted a series of joint US-UK-French airstrikes in 2018 on sites associated with Syria's illegal chemical weapons program. Trying to protect its longtime ally and client, additional Russian troops entered the civil war to help the Assad regime and to combat the Islamic State. The situation was chaotic, with many different factions pursuing different agendas. Russian forces came close to targeting US troops, Turkey shot down a Russian fighter jet, and such tense situations continue to threaten wider involvement in the war.

Of course, it was the Syrian civilians who got caught in the middle. Almost half a million Syrians have been killed, with about 50,000 of them children. When such violence flares, civilians flee if possible. Of the estimated pre-war population of 22 million, the UN estimates that more than half, at least 13.5 million, require humanitarian assistance. More than 11 million have been displaced from their homes, with over 6 million displaced internally and over 5 million fleeing abroad. Many can be found in neighboring countries like Lebanon, Jordan, Egypt, and Iraq, but the largest share—over 3 million—fled to Turkey. Over a million Syrian refugees made it to Europe seeking safety, only to find that they were unwelcome in numerous countries. Hungary vowed to keep them out with border fences and increased border guards. Greece tried to confine them to the island of Lesbos. Slovakia only wanted to accept Christian refugees. The UK and Poland didn't like being told by the EU how many refugees they were to accept. According to Human Rights Watch, most of this European resistance came from right-wing conservatives who just didn't like caring for refugees, particularly if they were Muslim. In the United States, the Obama administration accepted over 12,000 Syrian refugees in 2016. In 2018, under the Trump administration, the US accepted 62.

To reduce the number of refugees in Europe, the EU initiated a plan to reimburse Turkey for some of the financial burden of caring for the refugees. However, the Turkish government wanted more money and in 2019 began shipping over 900,000 Syrian refugees back into the regions of northern Syria that Turkish troops had retaken from Kurdish militias, despite the fact that both Syrian and Russian aircraft have attacked hospitals and refugee encampments there. (By the way, intentionally attacking civilian noncombatants is a war crime, specifically a "crime against humanity.")

While the Syrian refugee crisis is the single largest one in recent history, the worldwide numbers of people displaced from their homes—or refugees from their country—are staggering. According to the Office of the UN High Commissioner for Refugees, in 2018, 37,000 people were forced to flee their homes each day. At the end of 2019, nearly 80 million people had been forcibly displaced worldwide, with about one third of them forced to leave their own country. The vast majority of those refugees leaving their countries ended up in the countries relatively close by, which put a tremendous financial strain on those host governments. In 2019, the top five refugee-hosting countries were Turkey (with 3.6 million), Pakistan (with 1.4 million), Uganda (with 1.3 million), Germany (with 1.1 million), and Sudan (with 1.0 million). Talk about the Revenge of Geography! How long can these countries be expected to sustain the costs of such numbers?

1. Why are refugees often unwelcome in other countries?

2. Should the countries that just happen to be next door be forced to pay for these refugees?

3. What does all this tell us about human rights and human security?

INTRODUCTION: REDEFINING SOVEREIGNTY FROM PROTECTING BORDERS TO PROTECTING PEOPLE

The idea that the people have rights that deserve protection is not new. Ancient Greeks and Hebrews established a tradition of moral philosophy, and this emphasis on the rights of individuals was well reflected in later Christian thought and actions of the early current era. Due to the moral norms established in Europe by the Catholic Church and writers such as St. Augustine, it was possible in 1215 for King John of England to be forced by his noblemen to sign the

first-generation human rights (individual rights): rights that individuals have simply because they are human beings and that are not to be violated by governments.

Magna Carta, which specified a series of rights due to freemen. Most notably, the document included the idea that a person could not be imprisoned without cause sanctioned by law or the judgment of one's peers. Since that time, the rights people deserve—just because they are human beings—have evolved and grown in both number and type.

11-1 THE EVOLUTION OF HUMAN RIGHTS

>> **11-1** **Define human rights; the differences between individual, societal, and group rights; and how such rights have changed over time.**

Over time, three major types of human rights have evolved due to changing events and political circumstances. These include individual rights, societal rights, and group rights. Let's discuss each in turn.

11-1a Individual Rights

As indicated previously, human rights began as an insistence that monarchs could not do whatever they wished, whenever they wished. By the late 17th century, writers such as John Locke had extended the basic argument made by religious writers such as St. Thomas Aquinas—that people had some rights that could not be taken away by the government—to make the broader point that governments existed based only on the consent of the governed. By the late 18th century, many in Europe and North America had embraced the ideas that government should be limited to the powers granted to it by its citizens and that the citizens possessed natural rights. Such ideas shaped the justifications of both the American and French Revolutions and were incorporated into the US Declaration of Independence (1776), the French Declaration of the Rights of Man (1789), and the US Constitution's Bill of Rights (1791). Because they led the way, these individual rights are now referred to as **first-generation human rights (individual rights)**.

These first-generation individual rights emphasized political and civil rights. As such, they prescribed the rights to freedom of speech, freedom of assembly, freedom of religion, freedom of the press, the right to due process of law, and so on. They also often included the economic right to property, but what that actually meant varied by who was asked. For most people, it initially meant tangible things like real estate. Remember, however, that the Magna Carta specified the rights due to "freemen." Obviously, not all people were equal under the law. Some were not free, as slavery existed almost everywhere in the world. Slaves were considered property to be bought and sold

Police scuffle with protesters during a demonstration at El Prat airport, in the outskirts of Barcelona, Spain, in 2019

Should a government's treatment of its citizens be a concern for other countries?

AP Photo/Bernat Armangue

against their will, and those willing to be indentured servants could sell their services for an agreed-upon period of time. However, attitudes changed over time, particularly as Christianity expanded in the Western world and Christian culture precluded Christians from owning other Christians. Slavery began to be outlawed by various Western states and principalities across the 18th and 19th centuries.

Although now outlawed nearly everywhere, slavery continues to exist informally in many places, often in the form of indentured immigrants or servants or those held captive by the sex trade. Girls, boys, women, and men can be the victims, and regions such as Southeast Asia, Eastern Europe, Central America, and the Middle East are particularly notorious for human trafficking rings. Films such as *Taken* (2008), *The Whistleblower* (2010), and *Not My Life* (2011) and the documentaries *The Storm Makers* (2014) and *The Abolitionists* (2016) provide graphic depictions of this practice.

As the term *freemen* also suggests, political rights generally did not apply to women as much as to men, because men initially held most of the political rights in society. Still, the idea of women's rights is not new. The Quran articulated the idea that women had specific rights, medieval women had some rights to own property and participate in municipal government in parts of Europe, and feminists like Abigail Adams and Mary Wollstonecraft advocated for women's rights during the time of the American and French Revolutions. However, women generally did not achieve full political rights in most developed countries until the early 20th century. In many developing countries, they still lack equal rights in society

and under the law. We discuss this more later in the chapter.

11-1b Societal Rights

The emphasis on individual rights came under significant attack by intellectuals speaking on behalf of the working class in 19th-century Europe. Although the Industrial Revolution produced a large working class, capitalism practiced without any societal protections often transformed the working class into what would now be called the working poor. In Britain, Karl Marx wrote that these impoverished working classes should rise up in revolution against their oppressors; at the same time, democratic socialists embraced the desire for political change through nonviolent means to empower the working class—thus giving rise to the British Labour Party. These critics and reformers were united by the idea that "the people" deserved certain material and economic rights, not just individual civil and political rights. These so-called **second-generation human rights (societal rights)** included the rights to shelter, employment, education, and health care.

More attention was placed on these rights in the early to mid-20th century. The establishment of a communist regime in Russia in 1917 gave birth to the new Soviet Union, and it proclaimed itself to be a "worker's paradise." Everyone was guaranteed food, shelter, and employment. When the Great Depression of the 1930s

second-generation human rights (societal rights): material and economic rights that apply society-wide, such as the rights to education, employment, shelter, health care, and so on.

arrived, those guarantees made communism look pretty attractive compared to capitalism in other countries. The socialist initiatives seen in Europe became more widespread, and the US government also undertook large-scale public employment and social security programs to meet growing societal needs.

However, such societal or "material" human rights—whether guarantees of minimum levels of nutrition, shelter, health care, education, or employment—cost a significant amount of money. Such costs pose challenges, even for developed countries. In recent years the US and some European countries have been engaged in political struggles over the future of such programs in their respective countries. If the costs are challenging for wealthy countries, think how difficult it must be for extremely poor countries like Haiti, the Democratic Republic of the Congo, Nepal, or Zimbabwe to guarantee any minimal levels of societal human rights to their citizens. In most of these countries, expectations for basic second-generation human rights cannot be met or even dreamed about.

Furthermore, the Arab Spring of 2011–2012 shows what can happen when expected levels of societal human rights are not met for most people while elites seem to live very well. In both Tunisia and Egypt, there was widespread unemployment even among college graduates, yet the families of leaders such as Ben Ali of Tunisia, Mubarak of Egypt, and Gaddafi of Libya were amassing considerable personal wealth. Corruption by governmental elites may be harder for the public to accept when basic societal rights have not been met. As we noted in Chapter 5, revolutions often start over such societal disparities. Beyond the problem of meeting societal needs, some in society face additional challenges. We turn to group rights next.

11-1c Group Rights

The third major development in the evolution of human rights was sparked by the Holocaust in World War II. Persecution of unpopular minority groups within society was nothing new, but the genocide conducted against Jews, Roma (or Gypsy) peoples, and LGBTQIA individuals by the Nazi regime in Germany shocked many around the world once the truth was learned. Quickly the notion arose that regimes should not be free to persecute oppressed or unpopular groups simply because the actions happened within their national borders. Thus, **third-generation human rights (group rights)** sought to protect unpopular or minority groups from the oppression by the majority in society.

....

third-generation human rights (group rights): rights needed to protect unpopular or minority groups from the oppression of the majority.

Given the events of World War II, the initial concern was to protect those facing oppression based on race, ethnicity, or religion. That effort led to struggles for equal rights by a number of racial minority groups in the United States and many other countries. An important threshold was surpassed in the early 1990s, when arguably the most overtly racist regime, the Afrikaner regime in the Republic of South Africa, abolished apartheid, its official policy of apportioning political, economic, and civil rights based on one's skin color.

However, oppression based on ethnicity or religion is harder to eradicate. Such oppression continues in many states and involves many groups, as the opening illustration of the plight of Syrian refugees indicates. Ethnic struggles have beset Europe in recent years, whether among Serbs, Kosovars, Croats, and Bosnians in the former Yugoslavia; France's deportations of Roma peoples back to Romania and Bulgaria; or Russian-speaking and Ukrainian-speaking groups in Ukraine. Religious intolerance is also fairly widespread in the international system. Violence is often directed at minority religious or spiritual groups; depending on the location, they could be Christians, Muslims (Sunni or Shi'a), Baha'i, Hindus, Falun Gong, or others.

Other groups are the victims of discrimination and violence as well. In most societies in the world, women's rights are more limited and poorly protected than those of men. Bias is pervasive globally. In 2020, the UN Development Programme's new Gender Social Norms Index found that, globally, nearly 90% of men and women held some form of bias against women; about half thought men made better political leaders, over 40% thought men were better business executives and have a greater right to a job, and 28% thought a man could be justified for beating his wife (United Nations Development Programme 2020). In many parts of the world, women face restrictions that most reading this book would find appalling. They are often the subject of arranged marriages; in practice, they often have limited legal rights compared to men; in some cases, they cannot travel outside the home without a male relative accompanying them; restrictions are often placed on their ability to be in the company of men not part of their immediate family unit; and so on. These restrictions are based on religious interpretations, traditional customs, or both.

For example, Islam calls on its followers to dress modestly. However, for women, that can range from wearing scarves (called *hijabs*) that cover their hair in more liberal Islamic societies (such as Morocco or Kuwait) to *burkas* or *chadris* in more conservative societies (like Afghanistan) that cover their entire body head-to-toe and leave only a mesh through which to see. Violation of these rules can result in punishments up to and including public execution, which happened in Iran during the 1980s.

These clothing issues are not limited to the Middle East and Southwest Asia. A 2011 law in France banned the wearing of any scarves or veils that cover the face. Thus, Islamic women who wear the *niqab*—a veil covering the face below the eyes—or the burka can be fined, as can their husbands if their husbands mandated such attire. The official justification of the new law is public safety related; government-issued photo IDs mean nothing if the face cannot be seen. Belgium and the Netherlands also adopted bans on these religious face coverings, and other countries in Europe and elsewhere have done so as well.

Harm to women is also widespread. Sometimes it is culturally reinforced. In many traditional societies, women are often denied access to education, as schooling is seen as unnecessary to women's roles as wives, mothers, and homemakers. Where women are expected to move into the home of their husband, they may face abuse from their mothers-in-law. In some places, wives sometimes face such physical and emotional abuse from their husband's family that they commit suicide. In some societies, women who stray from socially accepted sexual roles face being murdered by their husbands, fathers, or brothers in what are called **honor-killings**, and the perpetrators are often not punished. Finally, an estimated 70 million girls and women from Africa and Southwest Asia have experienced **female genital mutilation** (sometimes referred to as *female circumcision*) as a societal ritual marking one's transition to womanhood. The UN has condemned this practice as a form of child abuse.

Women are also the targets of even more violent behavior. Women worldwide face being sold as indentured servants, workers in the sex trades, or sexual slaves by brokers or even their own family members, and violence is routinely used to keep them in line. In many places, unaccompanied women are targets for sexual predators. For example, in 2019, *ABC News* aired stories of former US Peace Corps volunteers who had been victims of rape and sexual assault and the lack of support they had received from the Peace Corps. Similarly, women in journalism now talk more openly about the number of times they have faced sexual assaults while reporting from other countries.

However, the worst violence against women may come during civil wars, insurgencies, or other instances of intrastate wars. In such circumstances, out-of-control troops rape and kill women because they can, as part of a deliberate strategy to punish or shame one's enemies, or as a means to bond conscripted soldiers to their unit or militia (Cohen 2016). For example, during the 1992–1995 civil war in Bosnia, Muslim women were captured, raped, and sent back to their homes, only to be ostracized or worse by their own families because of the rape. For a graphic, compelling story about these "rape camps," check out the 1998 movie *Savior*. Even when women and girls escape the immediate violence of civil war, they are not necessarily safe. Often, in refugee camps set up to provide care for people fleeing violence, women face similar abuse. For example, after 2011, numerous reports indicated that women and children in refugee camps set up to care for those fleeing civil war in Syria faced horrible abuse as men from neighboring states used the camps for sexual exploitation and sex trafficking.

Not surprisingly, in recent years, women have become the focus of considerable human rights activity in the global arena. The United Nations has historically included a focus on the needs of women, in terms of eliminating overt discrimination and identifying ways to empower women in their local societies. Likewise, the needs of children, particularly those in circumstances in which they are powerless to help themselves, have been an important and highly visible focus of the UN. Children face exploitation when they are denied access to education, are forced to work long hours for little or no pay, are conscripted into militias and are forced to kill or be killed, or are bought and sold like commodities. We will have more to say later in the chapter about UN efforts on behalf of the needs of women and children.

A third-generation human rights example that has not yet been as well addressed by the global community concerns the rights of LGBTQIA individuals. With the exception of Russia and a few Eastern European countries, more developed states tend to be more tolerant regarding one's sexual orientation, but in numerous places in Africa, Asia, and the Middle East, same-sex relationships are not just frowned on; they are illegal. In some Islamic societies, same-sex relationships are punishable by death. Even where this is not illegal, most societies still discriminate against same-sex couples having marriage rights or legal rights as families—such as rights to adopt children or to be considered "next-of-kin" during health crises. In fact, only 31 countries in 2020—a mere 16% of the total—legally recognized same-sex marriage; some other countries permit civil unions of some sort. If it seems that societies often become generally more

honor-killings: the murders of girls or women by their husbands, fathers, brothers, or other family members when they are thought to have violated socially acceptable sexually based roles. By killing the offender, the men in the family seek to restore the family's honor and are often not prosecuted for their crimes.

female genital mutilation: the cutting away of part of the external genitalia, based on the belief that, by reducing sexual pleasure, women will remain chaste until married and faithful to their husbands thereafter. Some societies also believe this is a religious requirement for women to behave modestly or that it may increase fertility.

liberal over time, we can expect more tensions between the LGBTQIA community and more conservative elements within those societies. One potential battleground for these rights may be in Latin America, where the Costa Rica–based Inter-American Court of Human Rights ruled in 2018 that gay marriage should be recognized in the region.

As you might guess, efforts to enumerate and enforce such group rights are controversial. In some developing countries, leaders argue that protecting minority group rights contradicts protecting the cultural values of the majority. Thus, they raise the issue of **cultural relativism**: Are third-generation rights really universal, or are they an expression of Western values that are imposed on non-Western societies? A number of Asian leaders, particularly those in Malaysia and Singapore, have raised this issue over time, arguing essentially that societal harmony and order are higher priorities in Asian culture than the rights of individuals or minority groups. Russian President Vladimir Putin, aided by the Russian Orthodox Church, contends that gay rights are contrary to Christian culture. What do you think? Are human rights universal, or do they vary from culture to culture?

It would be difficult to argue that the worst-case example of third-generation human rights is not a universal concern, and that is the problem of *genocide*—the killing of an entire group of people because of who they are. Although the Treaties of Westphalia included an expectation that sovereigns would respect the religious rights of their citizens, the Holocaust showed that unpopular minorities still faced the threat of extinction from their own governments. Thus, Raphael Lemkin, a Jewish legal expert who fled Poland after the Germans invaded in 1939, created a new word in his 1944 book *Axis Rule in Occupied Europe* by combining the Greek word *genos* (for "race" or "tribe") and the Latin word *cide* (for "killing"). After the war, Lemkin successfully pressed to get the term *genocide* accepted in international law, which it was in the 1948 Convention on Genocide

Argentinian President Cristina Fernandez (center) celebrates Argentina's becoming the first Latin American state to legalize same-sex marriage in 2010

Should majoritarian religious beliefs outweigh the civil rights of same-sex couples? What about other minority groups?

DANIEL GARCIA/AFP via Getty Images

(described later in the chapter). He spent the rest of his life pressing states to accept the Convention, thereby helping create the precedent that such horrific crimes could not be ignored simply because they were done by the state within its own borders.

The term may be of relatively recent origin, but genocide may be as old as humanity. A number of governmental or societal campaigns in the past century have been considered by many to be genocidal in nature, and unfortunately the list is long. Candidates for the genocide label from just the past 100 years are listed in Table 11-1. The total number of dead over the past 100 years from such genocidal campaigns has been estimated in excess of at least 100 million people. The complex interactions of national and tribal groups in just one area are illustrated in the box "Revenge of Geography: Turmoil in the African Great Lakes Region."

Both the recurrence of genocides and long-term conflicts such as the one between Hutus and Tutsis in Africa demonstrate that in the late 20th and early 21st centuries, unpopular groups inside a state were increasingly likely to be the targets of violence, either by other groups within the state or by the state itself. Based on this new security challenge, an international norm arose that stressed that states had "a responsibility to protect their own citizens from avoidable catastrophe, but that when they are unwilling or unable to do so, that responsibility must be borne by the broader community of states" (Chretien 2003). At first this **responsibility to protect (R2P)** was directed at threats of physical violence, based on the belief that all groups within a state had the right to

· ·

cultural relativism: the idea that human rights are not truly universal and that different cultures have different systems of rights. This term particularly comes into play when non-Western societies argue that international human rights standards have a Western bias and do not reflect non-Western values.

responsibility to protect (R2P): the norm that states have a responsibility to protect their citizens from avoidable harm, and if they cannot or will not do so, the international community has a responsibility to intervene.

TABLE 11-1

Genocidal Campaigns Over the Past Century

DATES	AGGRESSORS	VICTIMS	ESTIMATED DEATH TOLL
1915–1923	Ottoman Empire/Turkey	Armenians, Assyrians, Greeks	1.75 million or more
1919–1920	Soviet Union	Don Cossacks	300,000–500,000
1930–1932	Kuomintang Chinese regime	Tibetans	Thousands
1932–1933	Soviet Union	Ukrainians, Chechens	8 million
1937	Dominican Republic	Haitians	20,000–30,000
1939–1945	German Nazi regime	Jews, Slavs, Roma, people with mental illness, LGBTQIA individuals	8 million
1941–1945	Croatian Ustasha regime	Jews, Serbs, Roma	300,000–350,000
1947	India and Pakistan	Muslims (India) and Hindus and Sikhs (Pakistan)	500,000–1 million
1959	China	Tibetans	92,000
1963–2005	Indonesia	West Papuans	100,000 or more
1964	Zanzibar	Arabs	2,000–4,000
1966–1969	Nigeria	Ibos	600,000–1 million
1968–1979	Equatorial Guinea	Bubis	80,000
1968–1996	Guatemala	Maya	150,000 or more
1969–1979	Idi Amin regime in Uganda	Various tribal groups	300,000
1971	Pakistan	Bangladeshis	1.5 million or more
1972	Tutsi regime of Burundi	Hutus	80,000–210,000
1974–1999	Indonesia	East Timorese	100,000–150,000
1975–1979	Khmer Rouge regime in Cambodia	Various ethnic and professional minorities	1.7 million
1977–1979	Ethiopia	Ethiopian People's Revolutionary Party	150,000–500,000
1982	Maronite Christian regime in Lebanon	Palestinians	700–3,500
1988	Iraq	Kurds	3,200–5,000
1992–1995	Bosnian Serbs	Bosnian Muslims	97,000–200,000
1993	Hutu majority in Burundi	Tutsis	25,000
1994	Hutu majority in Rwanda	Tutsis	800,000
1998–2003	Both sides in Congo civil war	Twa (Pygmies)	Unknown
2003–present	Sudan	Darfuris	Est. 200,000–500,000
2016–present	Myanmar (Burma)	Rohingya	Est. 43,000

Sources: Laignee Baron, "More Than 43,000 Rohingya Parents May Be Missing. Experts Fear They Are Dead," *Time*, March 8, 2018, https://time.com/5187292/rohingya-crisis-missing-parents-refugees-bangladesh; "Genocide in the 20th Century," *The History Place*, http://www.historyplace.com/worldhistory/genocide/html; Human Rights Watch, http://www.hrwstf.org/wordpress/?page_id=4495; and R. J. Rummel, *Death by Government* (Piscataway, NJ: Transaction Publishers, 1997).

Turmoil in the African Great Lakes Region

Geography, politics, and clashing collective identities can combine to create a potent stew, and that has certainly been the case in the Great Lakes region of Africa. Including Uganda, Rwanda, Burundi, the western part of Tanzania, and the eastern portion of the Democratic Republic of the Congo, this area has been the site of considerable suffering.

The East African Rift Valley forms a string of rivers and lakes that provide the headwaters of the Nile and are considered by many to be the birthplace of humankind. Long before Europeans "discovered" the region in the 1860s, the mountains, valleys, rain forests, and abundant water supply drew many

Africans into relatively close proximity. When the British, Belgians, and Germans arrived as colonial rulers, they drew borders that made sense to them, with little regard for the natural borders of existing communities (see Map 11-1).

The colonial powers also sought to rule by co-opting local elites, and in line with the social Darwinist themes of the times, Europeans attributed characteristics to groups based on their physical appearance. Because the minority Tutsis often appeared to be taller and slimmer than the majority Hutus, the Belgians decided that the Tutsis were the superior of the two groups and allocated power on

MAP 11-1

Tribal Groups of the Great Lakes Region of Africa

Notice how historical tribal boundaries fail to conform to the political boundaries.

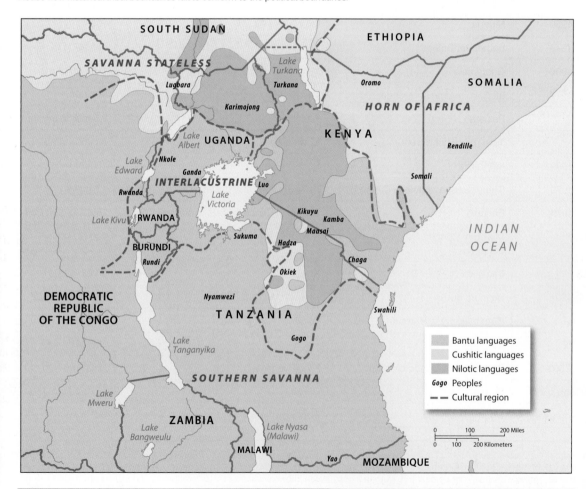

that basis. Given that Hutus made up around 85% of the population in the region, they were destined to be dissatisfied with this arrangement, and some Tutsis added insult to injury by mistreating Hutus. Three years before Belgium granted Rwanda its independence in 1962, local riots broke out there between Hutus and Tutsis. At least 20,000 Tutsis were killed, and many more fled to nearby Burundi, Uganda, and Tanzania. After independence, Rwandan Hutus used their numerical majority to control the government, and they often made Tutsis the scapegoats for their problems. Thus, over time, tensions between the two groups escalated. In the early 1990s, Tutsi exiles along with some moderate Hutus in Uganda formed the Rwandan Patriotic Front (the RPF) to overthrow the existing Hutu regime, and a campaign of violence between the Rwandan government and the RPF began.

The flashpoint came in April 1994 when someone shot down an airplane carrying the presidents of Rwanda and Burundi, both of whom were Hutus. Tutsis were immediately blamed, and Rwandans turned on the Tutsis. By the time the killing largely ended 100 days later, approximately 800,000 Tutsis and moderate Hutus—or about one of every 10 Rwandans—had died. The Tutsi-dominated RPF responded by driving the Rwandan government from power. With Tutsis back in charge in Rwanda, 2 million Hutus fled across the border into the eastern Congo.

Not surprisingly, the Hutus and Tutsis in eastern Congo soon formed militias for their own self-protection and went to war against each other. The Tutsi-led government in Rwanda invaded Congo twice to fight Hutu rebel forces there, and Tutsi forces from Uganda intervened in eastern Congo as well. The result of all this violence has been a death toll estimated at 5 million in the Democratic Republic of the Congo alone. A force of nearly 20,000 UN peacekeepers proved to be far too few to stop the violence, and at times some of the "peacekeepers" preyed on the local population, becoming killers and rapists as well. In a violent area where there is little rule of law or personal accountability and where women are often seen as a commodity rather than as individuals with rights, the inclusion of some "peacekeepers" from the nearby region itself may have been a very bad idea. It seems the region's inhabitants cannot escape these conflicts.

1. What could be done to dampen the violence in this region?

2. In this setting, is it possible to separate the two sides physically until their passions cool and mutual fears of each other subside?

3. Would non-African peacekeepers be a better choice, or would they just reinforce memories of imperialism in the region?

4. Would educational opportunities that integrate young Hutus and Tutsis be a long-term answer, or do society's lessons override what is learned in the classroom? ●

survive. In 2005, the UN General Assembly's World Summit formally embraced the responsibility to protect its citizens from such violence as a responsibility of each state. However, this notion evolved quickly into a broader norm that all groups within a society have a right to a reasonable, and sustainable, quality of life. Getting to this point, however, took a circuitous path. We turn to it next.

11-2 THE HUMAN RIGHTS REGIME: FROM NORMS TO RULES

>> **11-2** Describe the development of norms and codified rules regarding human rights.

After World War I, the overriding concern of the international community was the prevention of another "great war," so the new League of Nations sought to deter the outbreak of war through collective security, as noted in Chapter 6. Then, following the horrific events of World War II, an important concern of the new United Nations was to acknowledge and protect human rights. Two very important early actions by the UN were the passage of the Convention on Genocide and the Universal Declaration of Human Rights.

The 1948 Convention on the Prevention and Punishment of the Crime of Genocide, better known as the **Convention on Genocide**, was a treaty that both defined genocide and made it a crime, whether it occurred in peacetime or in wartime. Genocide was defined in Article 2 of the Convention as "acts committed with intent to destroy, in whole or in part, a national, ethnical, racial, or religious group," and those acts included killing or causing physical or

Convention on Genocide: a 1948 UN treaty that both defined genocide and made it a crime whether it occurred in peacetime or in wartime.

Rohingya refugees walk across paddy fields at dusk after crossing the border from Burma

Why does the international community respond to some refugee crises—like Syria—but not others, like the Rohingya people in Myanmar/Burma?

Dan Kitwood/Getty Images

mental harm to group members, putting the group in conditions that would destroy its members, preventing the group from having children, or taking away the group's children by force. As of December 2019, 152 states were parties to the treaty.

In a 48–0 General Assembly vote, the UN also approved the **Universal Declaration of Human Rights (UDHR)** in 1948. Based in part on the long-standing ideas of natural law and the more recent fears of fascism, the UDHR was a remarkable document for its time. It provided a comprehensive listing of natural rights people should be able to expect, and the list was long.

The UDHR declared that all people have equal rights, regardless of race, gender, religion, language, culture, birth status, national origin, or opinion. Everyone had the following rights:

- To life, liberty, and security, and not to be tortured or enslaved

- To be equal before the law with access to courts; to be protected from arbitrary arrest or detention; and to be presumed innocent until proven guilty

- To privacy and to protection of one's reputation

- To leave one's home country and to come back, as well as to seek asylum in other countries, and to have a nationality that can be changed if desired but not arbitrarily denied

- To marriage upon consent, and to divorce

- To own property

- To freedom of thought, religion, speech, opinion, and assembly

- To participate in governance through free elections and public service

- To social security and employment at a compensation sufficient for a life of dignity, health, and well-being, with special attention given to the needs of mothers and children, and with provisions for rest, leisure, and holidays from work with pay

- To a free education at least through elementary school, with parents being able to choose the type of education for their children

....

Universal Declaration of Human Rights (UDHR): a 1948 UN resolution, which provided a comprehensive listing of the rights of all people.

- To participate in the cultural, artistic, and scientific life of the community and have their intellectual property protected

- To an international social order in which all of these rights were possible

The UN's adoption of the UDHR set in motion an almost two-decade effort to flesh out its principles. Two landmark documents were adopted by the UN General Assembly in 1966 and came into force in 1976 that, in their own way, were products of the Cold War. The **International Covenant on Civil and Political Rights** was an agreement strongly supported by the United States and other Western states. It again enumerated the first-generation civil, political, and legal rights identified in the UDHR, coupled them with the idea that all peoples should have the right of self-determination, and set out procedures for the UN to monitor these rights. However, communist-governed states led by the Soviet Union wanted to emphasize second-generation collective rights, such as societal rights to adequate food, shelter, jobs, and so on. These collective rights became enumerated in the UN's **International Covenant on Economic, Social and Cultural Rights**. This treaty did the same thing for those types of rights, again specifying that all peoples should have the right of self-determination and setting out procedures for the UN to monitor these rights. In the eyes of the UN, these agreements along with the UDHR represent an International Bill of Human Rights.

The effort to transform such international norms into rules has continued over time through the creation of nine core UN human rights treaties, listed here with the years they entered into force:

- International Convention on the Elimination of All Forms of Racial Discrimination (1969)

- International Covenant on Civil and Political Rights (1976)

- International Covenant on Economic, Social and Cultural Rights (1976)

- Convention on the Elimination of All Forms of Discrimination against Women (1981)

- Convention against Torture and Other Cruel, Inhuman, or Degrading Treatment or Punishment (1987)

- Convention on the Rights of the Child (1990)

- International Convention on the Protection of the Rights of All Migrant Workers and Members of Their Families (2003)

- Convention on the Rights of Persons with Disabilities (2008)

- International Convention for the Protection of All Persons from Enforced Disappearance (2010)

You can see that the scope of human rights has expanded considerably over the past 350 years. While the UN General Assembly proclaimed a right to development in 1986, it has not yet been formalized as an international convention. To date, discussions about such an international convention on the right to development have revolved primarily around the legal and political difficulties that addressing this right would raise. Can you think of what some of those would be?

Although the UN has been very active in human rights matters, it has not been the only international organization dealing with such rights. Regional international organizations have acted in the human rights sphere as well. In 1953, the **European Convention on Human Rights** was created by the Council of Europe, and it listed a wide array of human rights, one of which is the abolishment of capital punishment. The European Convention is the strongest of the regional efforts on human rights, and it also created the **European Commission on Human Rights** to investigate allegations of human rights abuses and to monitor situations involving potential human rights violations. If it finds that human rights abuses may have occurred, it can refer them to the European Court of Human Rights, which we will discuss in more detail later.

In 1978, a somewhat similar **American Convention on Human Rights** went into effect. Created by the Organization of American States, the convention listed rights and created both an Inter-American Commission on Human Rights to investigate possible human rights violations and an Inter-American Court of Human Rights to issue rulings in such matters. One difference from the European version is that capital punishment was frowned on but not abolished.

....

International Covenant on Civil and Political Rights: a UN treaty effective in 1976 identifying the civil, political, and legal rights of all humans and establishing procedures for the UN to monitor these rights.

International Covenant on Economic, Social and Cultural Rights: a UN treaty effective in 1976 identifying the economic, social, and cultural rights of all humans and establishing procedures for the UN to monitor these rights.

European Convention on Human Rights: the Council of Europe treaty that went into force in 1953, which listed individual rights and created the European Commission on Human Rights and later the European Court of Human Rights.

European Commission on Human Rights: created by the European Convention on Human Rights, a very active body monitoring human rights situations in Europe. Individuals who believe their rights have been abused can appeal to the commission, which may, after investigation, refer the case to the European Court of Human Rights.

American Convention on Human Rights: the Organization of American States treaty that went into force in 1978. It created an Inter-American Commission on Human Rights and an Inter-American Court of Human Rights.

The United States and Human Rights

If asked, most US citizens would probably say that the United States has always been strongly associated with the promotion of human rights. Yet others in the international arena might see things differently. In fact, of the UN's nine core human rights treaties, the US has ratified only three. The political culture of the United States champions some human rights but not others, and the consideration of human rights issues gets complicated by the interaction with other political concerns in the US.

Like others, most Americans were shocked by the events of the Holocaust in World War II, so President Harry Truman signed the Genocide Convention and sent it to the US Senate in 1949. However, the Senate did not approve the treaty until 1986, 35 years after the treaty had gone into force in 1951. Some senators feared that the United States would be charged with genocide for its past and present policies toward Native Americans or African Americans. Others feared that approving the treaty would mean international law could override US state and federal laws. In essence, they feared a loss of Westphalian sovereignty. These sovereignty concerns were ultimately allayed by the strong support of President Ronald Reagan and legal reservations (or qualifying conditions) inserted by the Senate noting that the United States could exempt itself from any compulsory jurisdiction of the World Court in a genocide case and that nothing in the genocide convention overrode the US Constitution.

This concern over the loss of US sovereignty was nothing new. Some senators feared the UN Charter and the World Court could override the US Constitution. US approval of the UN Charter was gained only when a reservation was attached, noting that when it came to the jurisdiction of the World Court, the determination of what was a domestic matter—and thus beyond the court's jurisdiction—would be up to the United States.

The fear of international law overriding domestic law has surfaced at other times since then. The Covenant

on Civil and Political Rights went into force in 1976. The United States did not ratify it until 1992, and Senate approval came with multiple reservations and understandings, the most important of which was that it in no way contravened domestic US law. The United States has also not adopted an optional protocol to the covenant that abolished capital punishment. In 1989, the UN General Assembly passed the Convention on the Rights of the Child. The convention entered into force in 1990 and now has been ratified by all states except the United States and Somalia. US critics of the convention generally worry that it provides more legal protections to children than to their parents, and some fear it will override the laws of the 19 US states that allow the execution of 16- and 17-year-olds for capital crimes. In the 1990s, US President Bill Clinton's administration supported the creation of the International Criminal Court (ICC), which prosecutes individuals for **war crimes**, **crimes against humanity**, genocide, and aggression. Clinton's support was conditioned on the premise that the ICC's prosecutions would be subject to the approval of the UN Security Council—as one of the five permanent members, the United States had a veto with which to protect itself. However, that provision made it appear that prosecutions of British, Chinese, French, Russian, or US military personnel would be highly unlikely, so other states insisted it be deleted. Without the provision, some US critics, including President Clinton, feared that US military personnel might become the targets of capricious or politically motivated prosecutions. Other US critics had consistently opposed the court as an infringement on US sovereignty. Not only did the Senate refuse to approve the treaty creating the ICC; the US Congress passed a law authorizing the US government to go "rescue" any US military personnel from prosecution by the court.

More recently, the US has thus far refrained from joining the UN Convention on the Rights of Persons with Disabilities (181 members in 2020) and the Arms Trade Treaty (105 members in 2020). The former failed in the US Senate by six votes in 2012, and the latter, which focused on efforts to control sales of everything from small arms to battle tanks—which kill more people in the world than weapons of mass destruction—was initially derailed by US opposition during the George W. Bush administration. Conservative critics of the Arms Trade Treaty feared that it would override the US Constitution's Second Amendment, which allows citizens to keep and bear arms. Despite the active opposition of the National Rifle Association, Barack Obama's administration

....

war crimes: excessive brutality in war, in violation of international treaties or conventions.

crimes against humanity: acts of war against a civilian population; these can include the crimes of murder; enslavement; deportation or forcible transfer; imprisonment; torture; rape, sexual slavery, or any other form of enforced sexual violence; persecution on political, racial, national, ethnic, cultural, religious, gender, or other such grounds; enforced disappearance; apartheid; and other inhumane acts that create great suffering or serious mental or physical injury.

signed the treaty in 2013, but it has never been ratified.

It's very hard not to conclude that the US commitment to human rights took a hit during the Donald Trump administration. Seeking to fulfill campaign promises, the administration attempted to ban the entry of immigrants or refugees from several majority-Muslim states and was partially successful in doing so. It tried—mostly unsuccessfully—to construct a more extensive border wall with Mexico to keep migrants or asylum seekers out. In a further effort to deter migrants and asylum seekers from Central America, it separated thousands of children from their parents, which resulted in disturbing photos of kids in cages. Relatively few of those families were later being reunited, and some children died in US custody.

Beyond legal principles or political concerns, other international human rights issues appear to fail because they run counter to widely held US beliefs. Many US citizens feel that the responsibility for providing broadly defined human security falls on the shoulders of individuals, who should be free to succeed or fail based on their own merits. Many Americans are less comfortable with the idea of the government taking greater responsibility for ensuring a minimum standard of economic well-being, as well as minimum levels of health, food, environmental, and community security. Perhaps as a result of these cultural biases, the United States ranked only 26th in the 2019 Social Progress Index; Norway ranked first (Social Progress Imperative 2019). Contemporary debates about issues such as health care reform, immigration reform, the imposition of new environmental standards, and the like often illustrate these tensions over where to draw the dividing line between the public and private sectors.

1. Where do you think the government's responsibilities to promote human security end and yours begin?

2. When it comes to the international promotion and protection of human rights, should the United States lead, follow, or get out of the way? ●

In 1986, the **African Charter on Human and Peoples' Rights** came into force and was a product of the Organization of African States and its successor organization, the African Union. Like the other regional efforts, it created an African Commission on Human and Peoples' Rights and an African Court of Human and Peoples' Rights. The most interesting aspect of the African effort is the "peoples' rights" component. Not only did the charter list individual human rights; it also listed social responsibilities that people were to meet. These included duties to enhance family and community security and to recognize that individual rights existed in the context of collective and communal rights. Thus, these "African values" raise the issue of cultural relativism—to what extent values are universal or culturally defined.

By the late 20th century, human rights concerns began to coalesce around the broader idea of **human security**—an emphasis on the security of individuals and groups of people, not on the security of territory. People needed certain things to survive and needed more to live in dignity. For millennia, families, local communities, religious groups, and others we would now call **civil society groups** addressed human security at the local level, if it was addressed at all. In the neo-Westphalian era, however, the international community endorsed the right to human security.

First set out by the UN Development Programme in 1994, human security involved meeting a variety of needs if local governments and communities did not do so. These needs included economic security (meeting minimum needs to provide for oneself and family), food security (meeting minimum nutritional standards for all, particularly women and children), health security (assuring meaningful access to medical care sufficient to maintain reasonable health and avoid preventable diseases and deaths), environmental security (ensuring that the physical surroundings of peoples' lives did not harm them, and vice versa), personal security (ensuring minimum safety from violence or physical threats), community security (ensuring that social and communal groups were protected from violence or other threats), and political

....

African Charter on Human and Peoples' Rights: the treaty by the Organization for African Unity (later the African Union) that went into force in 1986 and listed individual rights and the responsibilities of individuals in a communal context. It also created the African Commission of Human and Peoples' Rights and the African Court of Human and Peoples' Rights.

human security: an emphasis on the security of people, not territory, first set out by the UN Development Program in 1994. It includes economic, food, health, environmental, personal, community, and political security for people.

civil society groups: NGOs that promote democracy and human rights on a global basis.

security (ensuring that people had meaningful opportunities to participate in a form of governance that they saw as legitimate). One can see how the human security principle blended easily with the "responsibility to protect" principle mentioned previously.

Moving such norms into rules meant most governments would have to take on far more tasks than ever before. The principle of human security thus quickly became mired in controversy. For some critics, the first question was whether it was even appropriate for governments to take on these responsibilities or whether they should be left in private hands—in short, the question of exactly where the private sector ended and the public sector began. If governments were the appropriate entities to guarantee human security, the second concern was how much would such programs cost and how would the needed funds be raised. Who pays for a reasonable quality of life for everyone? These questions have long bedeviled US foreign policymakers, as shown in the box "Foreign Policy in Perspective: The United States and Human Rights."

11-3 THE CHALLENGE OF IMPLEMENTATION AND ENFORCEMENT

>> 11-3 **Explain how states, international organizations, and nongovernmental organizations attempt to implement and enforce human rights standards.**

In an international system marked by anarchy, the problem is not just identifying which human rights matter most. The problem is also determining who will implement and enforce human rights standards. Without authoritative governing institutions, enforcement of any rules and norms—human rights included—is especially challenging. In general, the global political system relies on decentralized efforts that depend on the players themselves to implement and enforce human rights rules and norms. Not only does this ensure that diversity of values and perspectives complicates such efforts; it also means that capabilities and interests affect decisions to try to enforce the standards. In this context, actions to promote and enforce human rights rules and norms can come from many quarters. States, international organizations, and NGOs have all played such roles.

11-3a State-Based Initiatives

When they so desire, state governments or their people can contribute to progress in the human rights

restorative justice: a justice that seeks to repair the damage done to victims, to allow the victims a voice in the resolution of their grievances, and where possible to reintegrate both victims and the offenders into a more just society.

arena in several ways. They can engage in direct actions to implement or encourage human rights at home and abroad, they can provide incentives for others to do so or impose punishments for those who will not abide by global human rights norms, or they can enforce human rights standards through their own judicial systems via claims of universal jurisdiction.

Direct Actions

In most societies, the protection of human rights happens at the local level. Although local groups often find ways to protect the rights of members of their communities, sometimes state regimes get involved by modifying their own behavior to promote human rights within their borders. In recent years, 31 countries legalized same-sex marriage (see Table 11-2). In Latin America, Guatemala prosecuted numerous members of its security forces for their roles in human rights abuses in previous years, including the 2016 conviction of two former military officers on charges of crimes against humanity involving sexual violence against Mayan women. Their prosecution was the first-ever case involving violence against women from the country's four-decade-long internal conflict. Chile imprisoned over 100 former military, police, and civilians for their human rights crimes in the 1970s. The former president of Argentina, Cristina Fernández de Kirchner, was indicted on fraud and corruption charges. Two former Brazilian presidents—Michel Temer and Luiz Inacio Lula da Silva—were arrested for corruption in office. In Africa, Germany began negotiations with its former colony Namibia about compensation for its genocidal warfare against both the Herero and Nama tribes in 1904–1905. In the Middle East, Saudi Arabia gave women the right to drive, and Saudi women were elected for the first time to local municipal government positions. In Asia, President Park Geun-hye of South Korea was impeached, convicted, removed from office, and then arrested on criminal corruption charges. Japan's prime minister apologized and pledged millions of dollars to South Korean women forced to work as sex slaves in Japanese military brothels in World War II. And in perhaps the most innovative example, Bhutan made mandatory the consideration of four pillars of happiness (sustainable development, cultural preservation, conservation of the environment, and good governance) when passing new legislation. These examples represent direct actions taken by states to deal with their own human rights issues. If such direct actions are not taken to protect human rights by state authorities, then states may try other approaches.

One such approach is to conduct public campaigns to confront past human rights violations in the search for **restorative justice**. The basic idea of restorative justice can be found in its name: a justice that seeks to restore to victims what was lost through human rights abuses. It may not be possible to repair all the damage done to victims, but a series of steps can help promote societal healing:

- Publicly recognizing and acknowledging the hurt and damage done to victims

- Allowing the victims to publicly confront their abusers so that the abusers must hear what harm they've caused

- Encouraging the abusers to acknowledge their actions and to take responsibility for them (and under ideal circumstances to apologize for the harm they've caused)

- Allowing the victims a voice in the resolution of their grievances and then, where possible, reintegrating both victims and the offenders into a more just society.

For example, South Africa sponsored a Truth and Reconciliation Commission to deal with the injuries caused by apartheid; the victims were heard, and the perpetrators were offered amnesty if they fully and publicly confessed to their crimes. Brazil created a Truth Commission as well to identify the human rights abuses of past military regimes, with blanket amnesty for any former government or military officials accused of such wrongdoing. Australia's prime minister apologized for crimes against aboriginal peoples, including the kidnapping of children from their parents so that they could be raised in foster homes. Canada created a new province where native peoples could govern themselves—Nunavut, or "our land" in the Inuit language, and Canadian governmental meetings often start with acknowledging the indigenous First Nations of that region. South Korea acknowledged that fears of communist subversion drove some of its military units to massacre civilians in the confusing days shortly after the North Korean invasion in 1950. Cambodia allowed the radio and television broadcast of its trial of former Khmer Rouge officials for crimes against humanity, torture, and murder during the 1970s. In such ways, some regimes have tried to come to grips with the ghosts of their pasts.

Sometimes regimes that repeatedly fail to meet human rights standards will be successfully challenged by their own people. Such **populist revolutions** have become increasingly common in the late Westphalian and neo-Westphalian eras, and successful ones are typically directed against authoritarian regimes that do not allow sufficient freedom of speech, freedom of assembly, and elections seen as free and fair. A short list of successful popular revolts

TABLE 11-2

Jurisdictions Where Same-Sex Marriage Is Legal

COUNTRY	YEAR LEGALIZED
Netherlands	2000
Belgium	2003
Canada	2005
Spain	2005
South Africa	2006
Norway	2008
Sweden	2009
Argentina	2010
Iceland	2010
Portugal	2010
Denmark	2012
Brazil	2013
England/Wales	2013
France	2013
New Zealand	2013
Uruguay	2013
Luxembourg	2014
Scotland	2014
Finland	2015
Greenland	2015
Ireland	2015
United States	2015
Colombia	2016
Germany	2017
Malta	2017
Australia	2017
Austria	2019
Ecuador	2019
Northern Ireland	2019
Taiwan	2019
Costa Rica	2020

Source: Adapted from "Every Country Where Same-Sex Marriage Is Legal," *Stars Insider/MSN News*, June 26, 2020, https://www.msn.com/en-us/news/world/every-country-where-same-sex-marriage-is-legal/ss-BB15ZIDd#image=2.

populist revolutions: grassroots revolts typically against repressive governments, dominated by mass turnouts of the people.

against authoritarian rulers would include at least the following:

- The 1979 Iranian overthrow of the Shah's regime

- The 1986 Filipino overthrow of the Marcos regime

- The 1989 overthrow of the communist Husák regime in Czechoslovakia

- The 2003 overthrow of the Shevardnadze regime in Georgia

- The 2004 overthrow of the Yanukovych regime in Ukraine (which returned to power in 2010)

- The 2005 revolt against the Syrian military occupation of Lebanon

- The 2010 overthrow of the Ben Ali regime in Tunisia

- The 2011 overthrow of the Mubarak regime in Egypt

- The 2011 overthrow of the Gaddafi regime in Libya

- The 2014 overthrow of the Yanukovych regime in Ukraine

In such instances, the public's unwillingness to continue to tolerate abusive regimes reaches a critical mass and, given the right stimulus, topples regimes that previously appeared to be very stable.

Still, many human rights challenges remain. For example, China draws sustained criticism for its record. According to a 2020 Human Rights Watch report, the one-party state has constructed the largest high-tech surveillance system in history, going beyond extensive in-person surveillance to the widespread use of video cameras, facial-recognition software, mobile phone apps, and electronic checkpoints. The information collected is then subjected to big-data analysis techniques, with the goal of identifying citizens needing "re-education." The largest group of those being re-educated are about 1 million Muslims—primarily Uighurs, Kazakhs, and other Turkic peoples from western China—now detained in re-education camps and separated from their children, who are raised as orphans. The state has sought ways to limit Chinese access to the Internet, so that the regime's online critics cannot be heard. With the widespread monitoring of the public, a system of social credits for good behavior has been established, where individuals' access to societal privileges are

....

femicide: killing women and girls because of their gender.

earned or lost. Countries such as Turkey and Uganda still make criticism of the state or its leader a crime or grounds for involuntary commitment to a mental institution. Russian President Vladimir Putin and Belarusian President Alexander Lukashenko block critics from election ballots, and protesters seeking liberal democracy are attacked by security forces in Russia and Belarus. Extrajudicial killings of government critics in Venezuela totaled over 9,000 between 2018 and mid-2019. Civil wars in Syria and Yemen resulted in war crimes and crimes against humanity with the widespread killing of noncombatants.

Other examples may be less dramatic but are still quietly evident and very consequential. Women's rights to education, to employment outside the home, to the protection of law, and so on are still woefully inadequate in many parts of the world. The Inter-American Commission on Human Rights called out Brazil in 2019 for its rate of **femicide**—killing women and girls because of their gender. Despite a population of more than 200 million people, Brazil has less than 100 shelters for women who are victims of domestic abuse, with the result that four women were killed every day in 2019. Human trafficking—primarily of women and children—still occurs, along with modern-day slavery. According to a 2020 report by the US Conference of Catholic Bishops, over 40 million people are victims of slavery worldwide, with 25 million victims of labor or sex trafficking and 15 million victims of forced marriages. About 70% of those trafficked are women and girls. In 2019, the US National Human Trafficking Hotline reported over 48,000 cases of human trafficking, and the Trump administration proclaimed January 2020 as National Slavery and Human Trafficking Prevention Month. Estimates in 2019 by the US Department of Housing and Urban Development of the number of homeless people in the United States on a given night exceed half a million people. UNIDCF reports that nearly 50 million children are refugees from violence or poverty. In 2016, there were 26 countries where mothers could not pass on their citizenship to their children as fathers can, because women lost their independent identity upon marriage (Sengupta 2016). As discussed earlier, genocide and ethnic cleansing can still occur, as recent, ongoing violence against the Rohingya in Myanmar (Burma) shows. Examples like these lead many states to seek to change the behavior of others, and such state efforts fall into two broad categories: incentives and punishments.

Incentives

States concerned with promoting and protecting human rights in other countries often choose to reward those who improve their human rights record and work with other states and societies to facilitate improvements in human rights. A common method is through foreign assistance used as incentives.

Considerable activity has been generated in recent years in efforts to enhance democratization, by encouraging non-democratic states to embrace democratic reform or by helping regimes that have started down the democratic path to become even more democratic in practice. Such democratization efforts may be politically based. As such, they direct foreign aid to help fund and promote the work of civil society groups and political parties and to make free and fair elections the norm. A good example of the political approach is the work done by the US government directly (typically by the State Department) or by the NGOs that the government funds. These include groups such as the National Endowment for Democracy, the National Democratic Institute, and the International Republican Institute, which operate on a global basis. In Europe, both the European Union and its individual member states direct foreign assistance for similar purposes. In fact, many political parties in Europe have government-supported foundations that promote democracy abroad. Examples include the Konrad Adenauer Institute in Germany, the Jean-Jaurès Foundation in France, and the Westminster Foundation in the United Kingdom. As we described in Chapter 9, often smaller amounts of targeted democracy aid—such as support for free elections, aid to create or empower democratic institutions, and support for civil society organizations—produce more democratic reform and better human rights practices than do larger amounts of conventional foreign economic aid alone.

Still, more effort goes into foreign aid programs that are developmentally based than those that are politically based. These include efforts to improve the quality of life, improve delivery of basic community services, and promote the greater good. European states generally favor these approaches, as does the US Agency for International Development. Examples of such development programs include providing loan capital so that farmers and small business owners can borrow what they need to prosper; arranging logistical support so that local businesses can export their goods or services; helping build infrastructure such as roads, bridges, railroad lines, and airports; digging wells or building irrigation and water systems for local communities; constructing hospitals and medical clinics; building schools; and training needed professionals such as teachers, engineers, and medical personnel. The basic idea is that improvements in the overall quality of life directly address second-generation human rights and may also produce a citizenry that demands the right to play a greater role in their own governance (first-generation rights). States that lead the way in developmental assistance as a

percentage of their GDP include Norway, Sweden, Luxembourg, the Netherlands, Denmark, and the UK.

Sometimes external incentives are provided to acknowledge past wrongs. In 2011, the head of France's national railway company apologized to victims of the Holocaust for the railway's complicity in delivering thousands of European Jews to Nazi Germany for persecution, and in 2014, France created a $60 million fund to repay reparations to the living victims of the railway's Holocaust-related deportations. The incentive to make such an apology was the possibility of bidding on future contracts to build high-speed rail networks linking Orlando and Tampa, Florida, and San Francisco and Los Angeles, California. Members of Congress had France's national railway company in mind when they introduced a bill in the US House of Representatives in 2010 that required all bidders for such contracts to disclose any role they may have played in shipping Holocaust victims during World War II.

Punishments

States also take actions to punish those who abuse human rights. The mildest form of punishment involves public admonishments that embarrass a regime. For example, the United States routinely chastises China for its human rights record, which includes the repression of Tibetans and Uighurs in the western part of the country, the persecution of a variety of religious faiths and spiritual groups, the lack of political freedoms, and so on. China in turn publicly criticizes the United States for its problems with homelessness, the treatment of Native Americans and immigrants, and the treatment of detainees in the war on terror, as well as restrictions on personal freedoms due to the war on terror.

However, other penalties can carry more significance. As noted previously, most Western states enacted an array of economic sanctions against the white minority regime in the Republic of South Africa in response to its harsh apartheid policy that kept Black South Africans—the majority of the population—separate and denied them economic, political, civil, and even the most basic rights to physical integrity. Although these sanctions were applied unevenly and their impact is hard to measure precisely, they contributed to the pressure at home and from abroad that eventually helped end the repressive regime. However, these sanctions also generated serious hardships on the very people they were intended to help.

Belarus provides another interesting example. In 1994, Alexander Lukashenko was elected president of this former Soviet republic. After the election, he steadily increased his power, diminished the ability of others to oppose him politically, and changed the constitution to remove limits on presidential terms. Prior to the 2010 presidential election, the European Union offered Belarus investment opportunities and nearly $4 billion in economic aid in return for an election that could be certified as "free and fair." Shortly after winning an election widely derided as fraudulent, Lukashenko had 600 dissidents arrested, including seven of the nine other candidates who ran against him for the presidency. The United States and the EU countries imposed a variety of targeted sanctions against a total of 157 Belarusian officials, including Lukashenko and two of his adult sons. The identified individuals were banned from entering the United States or EU countries, any assets they had in the United States or EU were frozen, and additional US sanctions were imposed on a large Belarusian government-owned company. Perhaps not surprisingly, Lukashenko dismissed these actions as part of a Western plot to dethrone him and as unwarranted interference in the domestic affairs of Belarus. In 2020, Lukashenko kept potential rivals off the presidential ballot and presided over a reelection that was widely considered fraudulent.

The efforts to identify specific individuals who can be held accountable for their regime's human rights abuses and to find ways to target them are a relatively recent trend in international politics. As discussed in Chapter 9, smart sanctions seek to punish those individuals actually responsible for a regime's bad behavior—and who are in a position to initiate changes in such behavior—rather than punishing the state's population as a whole. In large part, smart sanctions are a response to the impacts of comprehensive sanctions on Iraq by the international community following the 1991 Persian Gulf War. To punish Saddam Hussein's regime for its invasion of Kuwait in 1990 and to push it to stop human rights abuses at home against Shi'a and Kurdish separatists, these sanctions basically banned most economic transactions with Iraq. Most products would not be sold to Iraq, and Iraqi oil would not be purchased by others.

The human consequences of these sanctions were counterproductive, if not horrific. Saddam Hussein's family became even wealthier, as family members profited from their control of the illegal smuggling of luxury goods into Iraq. The quality of life for Saddam Hussein and the top officials of his regime thus did not suffer, and the regime did not change its bad behavior. Those who suffered were the citizens of Iraq. By the late 1990s, children died at the rate of 4,000–5,000 per month due to a lack of medicine and medical supplies, poor nutrition, and poor sanitation. Families were disrupted as skilled professionals left the country, economic stresses resulted in more divorces and instances of domestic violence, and couples wishing to wed often could not afford to do so. Crime and prostitution flourished as well, and many young people came of age with a profound sense of victimization at the hands of the international community. After the regime was overthrown, outsiders were shocked at the deterioration in Iraq's basic infrastructure over the 12 years that the sanctions had been in force. The electric grid barely functioned, poor maintenance had taken its toll on the production and shipping of oil and natural gas, and basic sanitation and clean water systems were lacking in many areas of the country. In short, it was clear that heavy-handed sanctions could produce as much or more harm as the human rights abuses that justified the sanctions.

Thus, the idea behind smart sanctions was born. Led by Switzerland, Germany, and Sweden in the late 1990s, the European Commission and the UN began studying ways to target sanctions at those actually making the decisions that led to human rights violations. Good examples of smart sanctions include the US "Magnitsky Law," which was passed in late 2012 to target and punish Russian individuals involved in the murder of Sergei Magnitsky, a Russian lawyer beaten to death in a Russian prison for his involvement in a tax fraud investigation targeted at Russian state officials. The 18 Russians originally targeted were banned from entry to the US and from access to the banking system. The US law inspired both the UK and Canada to pass their own versions of a Magnitsky law in 2017; Estonia (2016), Lithuania (2017), and Latvia (2018) have done so as well. In 2019, the EU Parliament urged member states to enact similar laws, and Kosovo passed one in 2020.

Universal Jurisdiction

Another way states can enforce human rights standards is through claims of universal jurisdiction, which we introduced in Chapter 7. Long applied to crimes such as piracy on the high seas, universal jurisdiction regarding human rights holds that states have a right and a duty to enforce international law when it comes to the most serious human rights abuses—such as genocide, crimes against humanity, torture, war crimes, extrajudicial killings, and forced disappearances—*regardless of where these offenses may occur.* Australia, Austria, Belgium, Canada, Denmark, Finland, France, Germany, the Netherlands, Norway, Senegal, Spain, the United Kingdom, and the United States have all exercised some form of universal jurisdiction over these serious human rights violations in the post–World War II period, subjecting the accused to trials before regular or specialized courts. According to Amnesty International, more than 163 states have claimed universal jurisdiction over at least one of these crimes. Some other human rights treaties—such as the Convention on Genocide and the Convention against Torture—require the states approving the treaties to accept the principle of universal jurisdiction to ensure that the rights get enforced.

A good example of this behavior comes from Spain. Spanish courts issued arrest warrants for former Chilean General Augusto Pinochet for the civilian deaths and disappearances that occurred during his rule, for Osama bin Laden for his promotion of terrorist attacks, for former Guatemalan military strongmen Efrain Rios Montt and Oscar Humberto Mejia for their actions during the Guatemalan Civil War, and for an Argentine naval officer accused of genocide and terrorism during Argentina's military rule. Spanish courts also launched investigations regarding the torture of detainees at the US base at Guantánamo Bay, suspected crimes by the Colombian rebel group FARC (the Revolutionary Armed Forces of Colombia), genocide authorized by Chinese officials in Tibet, and alleged crimes against humanity authorized by Israeli officials in the Gaza Strip. Such actions send the important message that human rights violators may not escape prosecution elsewhere, and their ability to travel outside their home country may be compromised. However, states are not the only enforcers of human rights standards. International organizations are deeply involved in these enforcement efforts.

Perhaps the most significant development in universal jurisdiction is the creation of a permanent international court where individuals accused of genocide, war crimes, crimes against humanity, and aggression, rather than states, can be tried. That permanent court is the **International Criminal Court (ICC)**, located in The Hague, Netherlands. The treaty proposing the court was signed in Rome in 1998, and the court was officially established in 2002. By the end of 2019, 123 countries had ratified the treaty, and 42 others were not part of the agreement. In terms of world systems theory categories, these outliers include one significant core state (the US), semi-periphery states (like China, India, Indonesia, Iran, and Russia), and periphery states (like Belarus, Ethiopia, Mali, Myanmar, Pakistan, Saudi Arabia, South Sudan, Sudan, Somalia, Turkey, Ukraine, and Vietnam). Put another way, realists might counter that opposition comes from states unwilling to let others have power over them—like the US, China, Russia, India, Iran, and so on.

The cases that come to the ICC are truly horrific. They include individuals charged with the systematic targeting of noncombatants by armed groups and government officials; the kidnapping, rape, and sexual exploitation of women and men, girls and boys; the forcible conscription of child soldiers whose families are often threatened with death if they don't comply; efforts to kill entire communities of people;

and so on. According to the ICC website, by late 2020, the ICC had issued 35 arrest warrants, 17 people were in detention, 14 remained at large, and charges were dropped on three people due to their deaths. Due to the difficulty of obtaining evidence and witnesses, these prosecutions move slowly. So far, eight convictions and four acquittals have been obtained. More notably, as of late 2020, each trial involved defendants from Africa. Leading the way were Democratic Congo (nine defendants), followed by Kenya and Sudan (with seven defendants each). The most high-profile defendants were Omar al-Bashir, the former president/dictator of Sudan, and current Kenyan President Uhuru Kenyatta. In 2020, the Sudanese government began its own prosecution of Bashir, but the charges against Kenyatta were withdrawn by the ICC.

Can you imagine how this record of arrests and prosecutions looks to members of the African Union—the AU? Do genocide, war crimes, crimes against humanity, or aggression happen only in Africa? In 2013, the AU held a special summit meeting to discuss a mass withdrawal from the court over its apparent targeting of Africa and African leaders. In 2016, The Gambia and South Africa filed paperwork to begin a possible withdrawal process, and Burundi formally left the court in 2017. Not surprisingly, the ICC has been under pressure to investigate other conflicts around the world. Subsequent situations under investigation have involved Georgia and Myanmar/Bangladesh, in addition to other African countries. Preliminary investigations have begun in cases occurring in Afghanistan, Colombia, Iraq, Palestine, the Philippines, Ukraine, the UK, and Venezuela. Interestingly, the preliminary investigation in Afghanistan includes possible charges of crimes against humanity by the Taliban and Haqqani network, as well as war crimes involving torture by Afghan and US government forces. In retaliation, the US Trump administration refused to issue a visa to allow ICC Prosecutor Fatou Bensouda to enter the US in 2019. In 2020, an appellate panel gave ICC Prosecutor Bensouda the authorization to proceed with an investigation of US actions in Afghanistan.

Given the heavy emphasis on African prosecutions to date, do you think it is unfairly targeting weak states in Africa, or is this just a region where the worst human rights violations occur? Many of these cases involve the exploitation or abuse of women and children. Should this be a cause for feminists? Consider then world systems and realist theorists on this issue. Does the world not care about women and children, or do core countries just think they can

---

International Criminal Court (ICC): an international court in the Netherlands that tries individuals accused of war crimes, crimes against humanity, genocide, and aggression.

push around periphery and semi-periphery states? To paraphrase Thucydides, do the strong do what they will, and the weak suffer what they must? What do you think: Is the ICC overall a positive development for human rights and human security?

11-3b International Organization–Based Initiatives

Not only have international organizations set global standards for human rights; they have also set up enforcement mechanisms. Sometimes they use *soft power* to try to create and enforce human rights standards, and at other times they use the *hard-power* approaches available to them.

Soft Power

As noted in Chapter 3, soft power involves the ability to get others to share your values, to get others to do want what you want, to persuade, to embarrass, to cajole, to lead by example, and so on. International organizations have long done that in the arena of human rights. For example, one of the six original main organs of the United Nations was the Economic and Social Council, which has functional commissions that deal directly with our broader notion of human security in the arenas of sustainable economic development, social development, women's rights, population control, crime prevention, and the applications of science and technology for development. Getting others to share an increasingly global set of values is arguably more effective in addressing such human rights issues than is the ability to coerce others to do so. All 15 specialized agencies of the UN illustrated in Chapter 7 address some component of human security—from economic regulation to food and nutrition issues to travel to cultural preservation—and they do so via the process of shared norms and values, negotiated agreements and standards, and so on. All of these are usages of soft power.

Two particular human rights emphases of the UN have long been addressed through soft power means. One involves the needs of children, which became readily apparent after World War II. This need prompted the creation of the United Nations Children's Fund in 1946, better known as **UNICEF** from the agency's original name, United Nations International Children's Emergency Fund. It became a permanent part of the UN organization in 1953.

Since then it has proven to be one of the most popular UN entities, and it received the Nobel Peace Prize in 1965 for its good works. In 1981, UNICEF sponsored the Child Survival and Development Revolution, an intensive effort to promote children's health through four readily available means: monitoring rates of growth, preventing avoidable deaths through oral rehydration therapy for children with dysentery, promoting breastfeeding to give children the best chance of good health during infancy, and expanding the availability of immunization against routine childhood diseases. In 1989, the UN General Assembly adopted the Convention on the Rights of the Child and in 1990 held a World Summit for Children to set global goals for their protection. In 2002, a special session of the UN General Assembly was held to assess global progress toward these goals for children, and for the first time, children were seated as delegates at the UN. All of these diplomatic efforts emphasized the establishment of shared values and thus can be considered soft-power initiatives.

Another major UN soft-power emphasis has addressed the needs of women. Although a variety of women's rights were listed in the Universal Declaration of Human Rights, the global women's movement of the 1970s put increased emphasis on women's rights. A series of victories for feminist theorists began when the UN declared 1975 as the International Women's Year to highlight global women's issues. It declared 1976 to 1985 as the UN Decade for Women, and in 1979 the **Convention on the Elimination of All Forms of Discrimination Against Women (CEDAW)** was adopted by the General Assembly. Four UN World Conferences on Women have been held: in Mexico City in 1975, in Copenhagen in 1980, in Nairobi in 1985, and in Beijing in 1995. To maintain momentum of these conferences, official five-year reviews were mandated after the Beijing conference. In 2000, women's rights were included in the UN's Millennium Development Goals, and they are highlighted as well in the follow-up Sustainable Development Goals. Again, diplomatic efforts such as these are soft-power initiatives. They seek to develop shared values regarding women's rights around the world. To get an idea of one of the gravest challenges facing women in many societies, take a look at "Spotlight On: The Issue of Femicide."

Beyond seeking to empower women more generally in areas of economic and social development, the UN Security Council has also used soft-power approaches in addressing the impact of violence on women. In 2000, the Security Council urged member states to include more women's representation in the areas of conflict prevention, conflict management, and conflict resolution. The next year, an International Conference on Women and Conflict Management

---

UNICEF: the United Nations Children's Fund, created in 1946 and recipient of the Nobel Peace Prize in 1965.

Convention on the Elimination of All Forms of Discrimination Against Women (CEDAW): the treaty approved by the UN General Assembly in 1979 to define discrimination against women and outline an agenda by which states can eliminate it.

The Issue of Femicide

In 2018, the UN Office on Drugs and Crime (UNDOC) issued a report entitled *Global Study on Homicide 2018: Gender-Related Killing of Women and Girls*. The report's documentation of the statistics on femicide were shocking, and worse yet, femicide is generally considered to be underreported due to cultural and societal norms. Femicide happens in all countries, rich and poor. According to the best records available, in 2017, 58% of the victims—87,000 women and girls around the world—were killed by someone the victims knew well—family members (24%) or intimate partners (34%). The rate of such killings seems to be on the increase, as the comparable number killed worldwide in 2012 was 48,000—47% of all female homicide victims. The continent with the highest rate of these killings was Africa, with 3.1 per every 100,000 females in the population. The second-highest rate was in the Americas, with 1.6 per 100,000 females. Oceana was next at 1.3, then Asia at 0.9 and Europe at 0.7 per 100,000 females.

Why does this happen? The easy answer lies in **patriarchy**, a system of social structures and practices that put men in charge and women in subservient roles. For many feminist theorists, patriarchy is inextricably linked to gender-based oppression. According to the UNDOC study (2018), "men and boys who adhere to rigid views of gender roles and masculinity—for example, the belief that men need more sex than women or that men should dominate women, including sexually—are more likely to use violence against a partner, among other negative outcomes" (p. 30). The World Health Organization has also found that men are more likely to attack women if as children they witnessed domestic violence, see violence as a normalized form of expression, or have a sense of entitlement over women in general.

To get more specific, there are some patterns of global femicide. Honor-killings, which we mentioned earlier, have gone on for centuries and are often not prosecuted. Typical offenses in honor-killings are engaging in premarital sex, refusing to participate in an arranged marriage, marrying an unacceptable spouse, being unfaithful to a spouse, or being a rape victim. Such killings seem to be more prevalent in rural areas of Asia and the Middle East than in other regions. Another femicide pattern is dowry-related killings, where the wife is accused of not paying enough dowry when entering the marriage. These seem more prevalent in South Asian countries than elsewhere. Many instances of femicide occur in wartime, when women are killed with the intent to destroy the fabric of a community or society, as was seen in the killing of Yazidi women in Syria and Iraq by Islamic State fighters. Also, many victims of femicide are aboriginal or indigenous women, when their marginalized status seems to make their deaths less significant.

Femicide raises these questions:

1. What can international organizations and NGOs do to try to limit femicide?

2. Can donor states impact femicide rates by linking aid to reductions in femicide?

3. If patriarchy is the root cause, how long must women and girls wait for equal treatment? ●

patriarchy: a system of social structures and practices that put men in charge and women in subservient roles.

in Africa stressed that wars no longer sought just to defeat enemies; aggressors further relied on the use of rape, forced pregnancies, and sexual slavery to break down societies by inflicting pain and humiliation on their victims. In resolutions passed in 2008 and 2009, the Security Council called on all parties in conflicts to protect women and girls from gender-based violence. Because the targeting of women and girls for mass rapes and other forms of gender-based violence has become so pronounced, in 2010 UN Secretary-General Ban Ki-moon appointed his first Special Representative on Sexual Violence in Conflict, Sweden's Margot Wallstrom. Perhaps even more significant, given the challenges facing women in Africa, was the 2012 election of Nkosazana Dlamini-Zuma as the chairperson of the African Union Commission. Formerly the South African minister of home affairs, Dlamini-Zuma became the first woman to lead the AU. That same year, Fatou Bensouda of The Gambia began her term (2012–2021) as the prosecutor for the ICC.

The rest of the UN family of organizations has also been active in pressing for women's rights through soft-power means. In 1993, the UN General Assembly passed the Declaration on the Elimination of Violence against Women. Other such efforts followed, including the UN Secretary-General's 2008 global campaign "UNiTE to End Violence Against Women." The UN has also taken on an institutionalized form of violence—the practice of female genital mutilation. Not only is this practice very painful

Fatou Bensouda, Prosecutor of the International Criminal Court (ICC)

What does the selection of the first woman to head ICC prosecutions suggest about international enforcement of human rights?

Luiz Rampelotto/Pacific Press/LightRocket via Getty Images

and often dangerous to the millions of young women and girls who are cut each year; it also can cause later health problems like recurring infections and problems with childbirth. Due to the UN's efforts to educate local communities about the harm caused by this practice, thousands of African communities have pledged to end female genital mutilation, but the practice continues in 30 countries in Africa, the Middle East, and Asia. So far, over 200 million women and girls have suffered such cutting (World Health Organization 2017). Thus, it is not surprising that the UN designated February 6 as the International Day of Zero Tolerance for Female Genital Mutilation.

A significant change regarding protecting the rights of women was the 2010 creation of a new organization—the United Nations Entity for Gender Equality and the Empowerment of Women, or simply **UN Women,** as it is called. UN Women represents the merger of four components of the UN that worked for gender equality and the empowerment of women: the Division for the Advancement of Women (DAW), the International Research and Training Institute for the Advancement of Women (INSTRAW), the Office of the Special Adviser on Gender Issues and Advancement of Women (OSAGI), and the UN Development Fund for Women (UNIFEM).

....

UN Women: the UN organization working for gender equality, created in 2010 with the merger of the Division for the Advancement of Women (DAW), the International Research and Training Institute for the Advancement of Women (INSTRAW), the Office of the Special Adviser on Gender Issues and Advancement of Women (OSAGI), and the United Nations Development Fund for Women (UNIFEM).

UN Human Rights Council: the body created by the UN General Assembly in 2006 to replace the UN Human Rights Commission in making recommendations regarding human rights issues.

Initially led by former Chilean President Michelle Bachelet and now by former South African Deputy President Phumzile Mlambo-Ngcuka, UN Women works directly with member states to implement international agreements regarding gender equity and women's empowerment. This emphasis means working more closely to match country-specific programming to local needs than has been the case in the past, as well as getting multiple governments to work together for such purposes. UN Women also coordinates UN efforts so that the organization speaks with one voice on women's rights issues, and it also serves as a broker and clearinghouse for information and knowledge about women's issues.

Initially, the UN's Human Rights Commission was meant to be one of the leading international institutions dealing with human rights issues. It was instrumental in drafting the Universal Declaration of Human Rights and issuing recommendations regarding human rights issues—again, employing soft-power approaches by articulating a statement of shared values. However, because its members were elected by the UN Economic and Social Council in open session on the basis of geographic representation, rather than on the basis of their own human rights record, over time its membership and actions became more controversial. Not only were states with poor human rights records often elected as members; they could also be elected to leadership positions. The Human Rights Commission also made politicized decisions, taking a particularly hard line toward the human rights violations of certain states (like South Africa or Israel) while ignoring other human rights situations where the bulk of its members were located (such as Africa, the Middle East, and Asia). Based on these shortcomings, the UN replaced the Human Rights Commission with a new body in 2006, the **UN Human Rights Council**.

To improve on the Human Rights Commission, members of the Human Rights Council would be elected by secret ballot of the entire UN membership, and voters could take into consideration the candidate state's human rights record. States serve three-year terms, and membership is apportioned across regions: 13 for Africa, 13 for Asia, 6 for Eastern Europe, 8 for Latin America and the Caribbean, and 7 for the Western European and Others Group (which includes the US, Canada, Australia, and New Zealand).

Once elected, member states could be suspended from the Human Rights Council by a two-thirds vote of the General Assembly if their own human rights records merited such action. Because states were still elected to the Human Rights Council on the basis of regional geographic representation, the frequency of states with the worst human rights records being elected to the council decreased only slightly (Libya's membership was suspended in 2011). The council also frequently ignores important human rights problems in many countries, and it actually issued fewer resolutions critical of the human rights situations in specific states than did its predecessor the Human Rights Commission. However, Israel continued to be targeted at an increased rate (Cox 2010).

Obviously, not everyone embraces a new set of values just because others do so. Some resist the power of example or persuasion to change their human rights policies. In those cases, hard-power approaches may be needed to punish bad behavior or reward good behavior. Let's talk about those next.

Hard Power

The spread of shared values, persuasion, the power of example, and other forms of soft power are not the only ways for international organizations to promote human rights. As we referenced in Chapter 3, hard power—the ability to coerce or reward—can be employed at times as well, even by international organizations, though the opportunity and ability for them to do so faces important constraints. Humanitarian interventions are one example of the use of such hard power. In just the post–Cold War era, the Economic Community of West African States (ECOWAS) intervened to stop civil wars in Liberia and Sierra Leone; the UN authorized humanitarian interventions to stop violence and protect civilians in Bosnia, Somalia, Rwanda, Haiti, Sierra Leone, East Timor, and Macedonia; and NATO intervened in Kosovo.

If and when peace can be largely established, international organizations will often authorize and provide armed peacekeepers to ensure the safety of civilians in areas of potential conflict. As of early

Nkosazana Dlamini-Zuma, the first woman chairperson of the African Union Commission

What does the election of the first woman to head the African Union suggest about the evolution of African attitudes and actions toward women?

Siyanda Mayeza/Foto24/Gallo Images/Getty Images

2020, UN peacekeepers could be found in Africa (in the Central African Republic, Democratic Republic of the Congo, South Sudan, Sudan, Mali, and Western Sahara), in South Asia (along the India–Pakistan border), in the Middle East (in Lebanon, the Golan Heights, and Israel/Palestine), and in Europe (in Cyprus and Kosovo). The AU contributes peacekeeping troops to UN peacekeeping missions in Africa and operates its own mission in Somalia. That AU Somalia operation began in 2007 and has been extended multiple times. In 2020, the mission was extended until 2021 in anticipation of Somalia's planned elections. NATO has peacekeeping troops stationed in Afghanistan and Kosovo, and it has assisted with the AU mission in Somalia. NATO also operates a training mission in Iraq and protects the airspaces of NATO countries close to Russia. In the past, the Organization of American States has engaged in peacekeeping missions in the Dominican Republic, Panama, and Haiti, and it has intervened to settle maritime conflicts between Colombia and Venezuela and between Trinidad and Venezuela. In sea operations, NATO conducts an anti-terrorism operation in the Mediterranean Sea, and the European Union has multinational naval fleets patrolling the waters off the Somalia coast to protect against piracy.

Hard-power approaches involve other punishments as well. For example, when the Syrian military turned on its citizens in 2011, the Arab League voted to suspend Syria's membership and impose sanctions, and the UN's Human Rights Council authorized an Independent International Commission of Inquiry to undertake an investigation that concluded that the Syrian regime was engaged in crimes against humanity. The UN Human Rights Council voted 37–4 to condemn the Syrian regime for the violence and transmit the report to the UN Secretary-General and other UN institutions (including the UN Security Council) for further consideration and action. Stymied by Chinese and Russian opposition in the UN Security Council, continued violence in Syria, including a number of massacres, led the United States and the EU to impose economic sanctions on Syrian elites to try to bring hard power to bear on those responsible for the violence against civilians. In 2017 and 2018, after evidence of Syrian use of chemical weapons in attacks against its own citizens, the US attempted to halt the attacks on civilians by coupling threats of further steps with a targeted bombing attack on the Syrian site believed responsible for the staging of the chemical weapons attacks.

The case of Libyan human rights and the UN also took an interesting turn in 2011. Colonel Muammar Gaddafi's regime turned the military and security forces loose against civilians protesting the authoritarian regime's rule, and the UN Security Council responded in multiple ways to what morphed into a civil war in Libya. First, it imposed smart sanctions against the regime. Gaddafi, his four sons and a daughter, and 10 other top intelligence and defense officials of the regime were banned from international travel, and their foreign financial assets were frozen. An arms embargo against the regime was also imposed, and mercenaries were banned from international travel to or from Libya. Second, the Security Council referred the Libyan use of deadly force against civilians to the ICC (discussed previously) for investigation of possible war crimes. These actions came one day after the United States imposed a freeze on Libyan governmental assets in the United States as well as on the assets of top Libyan leaders. The Human Rights Council voted to recommend to the UN General Assembly that Libya's membership on the council be suspended. Third, the Security Council authorized the imposition of a no-fly zone against Libyan military aircraft and called on members to protect the Libyan people. With that UN Security Council authorization in hand, NATO members began attacking Libyan military airfields, command-and-control centers and networks, and governmental troops and compounds. Clearly, the UN and NATO had moved from soft to hard power.

Another form of hard power involves trials and the threat of imprisonment for individuals who commit human rights abuses. Besides the ICC discussed earlier, international organizations have pursued these judicial efforts through the creation of temporary tribunals as well as through regularly established courts.

Due to the presence of ethnic cleansing, indiscriminate attacks on civilians, and the use of rape as a weapon, the UN created a special tribunal for the conflicts within the former state of Yugoslavia in the mid-1990s. As of 2020, this special court in the Netherlands had indicted 161 individuals, including heads of state, heads of government, senior military and police commanders, interior ministry officials, and lower-level security and political officials. Ninety were convicted and sentenced for their crimes, 19 were acquitted, and 13 more were referred to the newly independent countries of the former Yugoslavia for trial. The genocide in Rwanda also prompted the creation of another such special tribunal. As of 2020, this special court in Tanzania had convicted 62 individuals and acquitted 14.

Another set of trials is a hybrid of national and international efforts. These include a tribunal with both Cambodian and international judges to investigate and punish the crimes committed against the Cambodian people by the Cambodian Khmer Rouge government of the late 1970s. Another hybrid court was the Special Court for Sierra Leone, which was a joint effort by the government of Sierra Leone and the UN. This tribunal completed its work in 2013 convicting nine people to prison terms ranging from 15 to 52 years, including the high-profile case of former Liberian President Charles Taylor, who was convicted of war crimes and crimes against humanity, including the murder and rape of civilians, hacking off the hands of civilians, the use of slave labor in diamond mines, and reports of cannibalism. Taylor was sentenced to 50 years in prison in 2012.

Beyond the ICC and special tribunals such as these, there are other regional human rights courts, the most active of which is the **European Court of Human Rights (ECHR)**. Initially created in 1959 by the Council of Europe, the court's current operation is based on the European Convention of Human Rights, which went into force in 1953. Unlike many other international courts that are based in The Hague, Netherlands, the ECHR is located in Strasbourg, France. It has judges from all Council of Europe members, and it hears a wide variety of human rights cases. Examples include clarifying criminal rights, protecting marginalized groups, protecting professional and personal rights, providing for social welfare, and protecting the environment. Tens of thousands of cases are referred to the court each year, and since 1959, it has issued over 22,000 judgments. Three states stand out as most frequently sued over human rights violations. Over 22% of the judgments went against Russia, almost 13% went against Turkey, and 12% went against Ukraine. The most typical judgments rendered are instructions to change the offending policies or actions and, as needed, to pay monetary damages to the person or persons victimized.

11-3c NGO-Based Initiatives

Nongovernmental organizations (NGOs) also get heavily involved in the implementation and enforcement of human rights standards using both soft-power and at times hard-power approaches, as this arena is an important focus of the emerging **international civil society**—an international system based on norms promoting democracy and human rights. Many human rights NGOs exist and work toward the improvement of human rights conditions around the world. Consisting of organizations such as Amnesty International, Human Rights Watch, the International Red Cross, and hundreds of other organizations, small and large, local and international, such groups engage in a variety of activities to help strengthen human rights practices. First,

....

European Court of Human Rights (ECHR): a court created in 1959 by the Council of Europe; one of the most active courts involved in human rights cases.

international civil society: an international system based on the norms of democracy and human rights. This emerging system is marked by civil society organizations, NGOs that promote these values on a global basis.

Women's rights activists protest against gender violence in Colombia in November 2019

How can protest demonstrations stop human rights abuses?

AUL ARBOLEDA/AFP via Getty Images

they monitor and publicize human rights violations through both regular and special reporting. Amnesty International, for example, publishes an annual review of human rights practices around the world and periodic special reports on critical problems as they arise. Second, these groups engage in "shaming" violators of human rights standards through reporting and other publicity to try to persuade violators to end abuses. Third, they recommend courses of action to try to bring pressure on the violators of human rights through avenues such as those we have discussed. Finally, these groups try to support and empower local groups and victims of human rights abuses. As a result, their actions are important but not always appreciated by more powerful actors. Some targeted regimes accuse such human rights groups of being agents of their rival states (seeking to weaken the target regime) or view them as an infringement on their domestic sovereignty.

There are literally hundreds of such groups, and some of the more notable ones are listed in Table 11-3. A good example of such groups is Human Rights Watch (www.hrw.org). It began during the Cold War as Helsinki Watch in 1978, which was formed from a coalition of NGOs dedicated to monitoring the human rights practices of the Soviet Union in Eastern Europe.

Helsinki Watch embraced the concept of "naming and shaming," both in the press and in direct contacts, regimes that abused human rights—particularly civil and political rights. It found that even very repressive regimes would change their behavior to get such a media spotlight off of them and directed elsewhere.

The success of Helsinki Watch led to the creation of Americas Watch in 1981, which had among its initial concerns war crimes and the abuse of civilians in the various civil wars sweeping Central America at the time. Asia Watch (1985), Africa Watch (1988), and Middle East Watch (1989) quickly followed, and in 1988 Human Rights Watch was chosen as the umbrella name for all these NGOs.

The new Human Rights Watch quickly responded to the challenges of the times, focusing on helping bring those accused of genocide and ethnic cleansing to justice. It soon added the challenges of terrorism and of counterterrorism campaigns and began to focus on the continuing problems of endangered groups such as women and children, LGBTQIA individuals, and victims of human trafficking. It lent its support to the creation of the ICC and the passage of the treaty banning land mines (the 1997 Mine Ban Treaty). Human Rights Watch also now deals with long-term problems like homelessness and poor access to education. Whereas many national governments push these issues as well, NGOs such as Human Rights Watch can do so with a single-mindedness of purpose, without other cross-cutting national interests entering the policy equation. In short, these NGOs try to make headway on a wide variety of fronts to advance human security. (See "Theory in Action: Protecting Human Rights.")

Human Rights Watch is certainly not alone in advancing human security. A number of NGOs have been instrumental in advancing the causes of human rights, especially when one focuses on particular

TABLE 11-3

Selected Human Rights NGOs, Their Missions, and Links to Their Websites

NGO	MISSION	LINK
Human Rights Watch	Conduct research and advocacy on all areas of human rights under the Universal Declaration of Human Rights	www.hrw.org
Amnesty International	Protect prisoners of conscience and promote all areas of human rights under the Universal Declaration of Human Rights	www.amnesty.org
Bill and Melinda Gates Foundation	Reduce inequities around the world so that all lives have an equal value	www.gatesfoundation.org
CARE International	Address the underlying causes of poverty and provide disaster assistance	www.care-international.org
Carter Center	Alleviate suffering, resolve conflicts, and promote democracy	www.cartercenter.org
Committee to Protect Journalists	Promote freedom of the press through the protection of journalists from reprisals	www.cpj.org
Doctors Without Borders	Provide emergency medical aid in areas of conflict, epidemics, or natural disasters	www.doctorswithoutborders.org
Freedom House	Promote democracy, free markets, and the rule of law	www.freedomhouse.org
International Committee of the Red Cross	Protect victims of war and violence, provide humanitarian relief in emergencies, and support the rule of law	www.icrc.org

human rights issues. A good example was provided in South Africa by the struggle to end apartheid, which was considered a crime against humanity.

After a steady upswing in the number and severity of strikes and demonstrations against apartheid inside South Africa in the 1970s, the regime relaxed some of its restrictions on political and economic activity, and as a result of this opening, local Black civil society organizations—such as trade unions and other societal groups—began to operate. By the mid-1980s, external NGOs and national governments funneled large sums of money directly into the hands of these internal, anti-apartheid groups to support their activities. Moreover, these external NGOs put pressures on their own governments to distance themselves from South Africa, which was increasingly depicted as a racist regime. A significant development came when stockholders began to pressure foreign corporations to break their economic ties with South Africa. Fearing stockholder revolts, those corporations began to sell off their South African operations or assets and to take their money out of the country. Due to these external and internal pressures in which NGOs played a prominent role, the South African government abandoned apartheid. Since the end of apartheid, anti-apartheid NGOs inside South Africa have continued to monitor the actions of the government and of other, more conservative groups to ensure that elements of apartheid do not reappear.

A Red Cross ambulance becomes a target in war-torn Lebanon
When first responders are targets, is anyone safe?
REUTERS/Ali Hashisho

Protecting Human Rights:
NGOs and Humanitarian Intervention

When a gross violation of human rights occurs within a country, the related norms of responsible sovereignty and the "responsibility to protect" pose a dilemma for other states, international organizations, and other actors in world politics: whether and how to intervene in the humanitarian crisis. Since the early 1990s, the UN and other states—especially the US and its allies—have undertaken many military interventions to try to address such situations, particularly when the state in which the humanitarian crisis occurs is not able or not willing to take its own actions to protect its people. Since 1990, however, there have been hundreds of humanitarian crises around the world but relatively few military interventions to address them. Why does international military intervention occur for some humanitarian crises and not for others?

Obviously, things like the scale of the crisis and extent of human abuses are definitely part of the explanation, as are factors related to the importance of the country in world politics and legal and political arguments about sovereignty. One popular explanation also focuses on the role of media attention, posing a so-called CNN effect, in which crises receiving more media exposure and coverage are more likely to have international military interventions in response.

However, careful empirical analysis of the evidence over the past two to three decades suggests that the impact of the media on humanitarian military intervention is unclear and overstated. Addressing this problem, one recent analysis took a related but different approach, highlighting the potential role of international human rights NGOs such as Human Rights Watch and Amnesty International. According to political science scholars Amanda Murdie and Dursun Peksen (2014), an

"Amnesty International effect" exists that helps explain why international military intervention occurs in some situations but not others.

Murdie and Peksen argue that human rights NGOs play an important role because they inject vital and credible information—often with compelling and vivid examples—about human rights abuses into the discussion. Because they are highly regarded and trusted sources of such information, their role has consequences for states and international organizations. Human rights NGOs thus mobilize opinion and advocate for action to address humanitarian crises, "shaming" states and international organizations into action. When these authors examined the 16 years after the end of the Cold War in 1989, they found that humanitarian crises in which human rights NGOs engaged in advocacy and shaming were more likely to have international military interventions to address them, even when other relevant factors were accounted for. Consider what this means for human rights and world politics.

1. What does the role of human rights NGOs in international military interventions into humanitarian crises tell us about the role and impact of non-state actors in the human security arena—or about their impact on the notion of state sovereignty?

2. What are the broad implications for the tension between Westphalian sovereignty on the one hand and responsible sovereignty and the "responsibility to protect" norms on the other?

3. How would realist, constructivist, or liberal theorists react to this argument? ●

Another good example comes from meeting the needs of women. Besides UN Women, a number of other NGOs address women's needs. For example, the International Association for Maternal and Neonatal Health seeks to reduce the mortality rates for mothers and newborns in developing countries. Pathfinder International seeks to provide a number of programs to promote women's reproductive health, broadly defined. Besides maternal and neonatal care, these needs include family planning services, HIV- and AIDS-related programs, community-based health care programs, and so on. The Coalition Against Trafficking in Women has regional offices in Africa, Asia, Europe, and Latin America and the Caribbean. Women for Women International seeks to meet the many needs of women who are war survivors. The Central Asia Institute seeks to provide education primarily for girls in remote areas of Pakistan, Afghanistan, and Tajikistan. Many such organizations now exist to promote the rights of women and to respond to their needs.

The examples could go on and on, but the point is clear. Many NGOs exist to promote human rights in the international community. They raise funds, raise awareness, step in to provide services that national governments cannot or will not provide, and monitor the actions of national governments. They are vital players in the promotion of global human rights and human security, just as are states and international organizations.

CONCLUSION: THE EVOLVING HUMAN RIGHTS REGIME

Human rights have come a long way from limiting what governments can do and promoting the idea that humans possess some natural rights simply by existing; they have evolved into a set of norms, rules, and international agreements regarding the responsibility to protect the people—both entire societies and endangered groups—from preventable harm. These norms, rules, and agreements are monitored and enforced by states, international organizations, and NGOs alike, and the combination of all three makes it difficult for egregious violators of human rights to continue their actions without some international repercussions. In the neo-Westphalian international system, the idea that states can do whatever they want within their own borders is an outdated idea. The powerful norm of sovereignty has increasingly been challenged by the new norms involving human rights, leading to the rise of the responsible sovereignty principle. Non-state actors have played a central role in this change.

A look at past cases reveals a mixed picture. In some instances, the people of a state—often with the help of NGOs and international organizations—can reverse a pattern of human rights abuses themselves or even overthrow an abusive regime. In other cases, the victims of human rights abuses are relatively powerless to act on their own in the face of brutality, and soft- or hard-power interventions by state actors or other international organizations become necessary to protect human rights. Do you think human rights are becoming sufficiently recognized at the international level so that abusive behavior by regimes can be changed by the spotlight of negative publicity, or will outside interventions still be necessary in the future to curb the behavior of abusive regimes that are willing to use any means to stay in power? ●

KEY CONCEPTS

11-1 Define human rights; the differences between individual, societal, and group rights; and how such rights have changed over time.

The concept of human rights means that people are entitled to certain freedoms and opportunities and that governments must respect and protect those rights. First-generation rights emphasized the political and civil rights and freedoms of individuals. Obviously, not all people were equal under the law, as slavery existed almost everywhere in the world. Second-generation human rights stressed societal rights and opportunities such as the rights to shelter, employment, education, and health care. Third-generation human rights stressed group rights and sought to protect unpopular or minority groups from the oppression of the majority in society. Concerns include protections against oppression based on race, ethnicity, religion, gender, and sexual orientation. The development of human rights norms since the 18th century has challenged the traditional notions of sovereignty and fostered attention to human security and the development of a new international norm stressing that states have "a responsibility to protect their own citizens from avoidable catastrophe, but that when they are unwilling or unable to do so, that responsibility must be borne by the broader community of states."

11-2 Describe the development of norms and codified rules regarding human rights.

Right after World War II, human rights norms received significant attention from the new United Nations, which passed the Convention on Genocide and the Universal Declaration of Human Rights. About two decades later, the International Covenant on Civil and Political Rights and the International Covenant on Economic, Social and Cultural Rights were completed. These treaties further developed the norms and ideas of the earlier documents. Since the 1960s, the effort to transform such international norms into rules has continued through the development of nine core UN human rights treaties, many of which sought to develop and apply the norms to particular groups. Since World War II, regional organizations in Europe, the Americas, and Africa have also developed conventions and commissions to support and protect human rights. The European Convention and its supporting commission and court are the strongest of the regional efforts on human rights. By the late 20th century, human rights concerns began to coalesce around the broader idea of human security—an emphasis on the security of individuals and groups of people, not on the security of territory—and the "responsibility to protect" norm.

11-3 Explain how states, international organizations, and nongovernmental organizations attempt to implement and enforce human rights standards.

State governments can contribute to progress in the human rights arena by engaging in direct actions to implement human rights at home and abroad, providing incentives for others to do so or imposing punishments for those who will not abide by global human rights norms, or enforcing human rights standards through their own judicial systems via claims of universal jurisdiction. International organizations have set global standards for human rights and both soft- and hard-power enforcement mechanisms. Nongovernmental organizations also get heavily involved in the implementation and enforcement of human rights standards using both soft-power and at times hard-power approaches, as this arena is an important focus of the emerging international civil society.

KEY TERMS

first-generation human rights (individual rights) 322

second-generation human rights (societal rights) 323

third-generation human rights (group rights) 324

honor-killings 325

female genital mutilation 325

cultural relativism 326

responsibility to protect (R2P) 326

Convention on Genocide 329

Universal Declaration of Human Rights (UDHR) 330

International Covenant on Civil and Political Rights 331

International Covenant on Economic, Social and Cultural Rights 331

European Convention on Human Rights 331

European Commission on Human Rights 331

American Convention on Human Rights 331

war crimes 332

crimes against humanity 332

African Charter on Human and Peoples' Rights 333

human security 333

civil society groups 333

restorative justice 334

populist revolutions 335

femicide 336

International Criminal Court (ICC) 339

UNICEF 340

Convention on the Elimination of All Forms of Discrimination Against Women (CEDAW) 340

patriarchy 341

UN Women 342

UN Human Rights Council 342

European Court of Human Rights (ECHR) 344

international civil society 344

REVIEW QUESTIONS

1. What are human rights, and what are the three major types (or generations) of human rights?

2. How did human rights evolve into a system of international norms, and what are the major international human rights agreements?

3. What different types of things can states do to promote and protect human rights?

4. What different types of things can international organizations do to promote and protect human rights?

5. What different types of things can nongovernmental organizations do to promote and protect human rights?

6. How do the major international relations theories apply to the protection and promotion of human rights?

THINK ABOUT THIS

Are Human Rights Universal?

According to scholars such as Thomas Risse and Kathryn Sikkink, there are some elemental rights of the person that are truly universal. Certainly the UN's Universal Declaration of Human Rights is predicated on the premise that we all share a common set of rights. However, that declaration was written and passed in 1948 when the UN had only 58 members, the vast majority of which were from Europe and the Americas. Because the Americas had been colonized by European powers, this overlap in what these actors saw as universal human rights is not particularly surprising, as all these states reflected a Western/European heritage.

Now the UN has 193 members, with the vast majority of the new members coming from Asia and Africa. We noted earlier that some Asian and African leaders prioritized collective rights over individual ones. So what do you think?

Are human rights universal, or are they culturally based?

FOR MORE INFORMATION . . .

Basic Rights

Donnelly, Jack. (2013). *Universal Human Rights in Theory and Practice*, 3rd ed. New York, NY: Cornell University Press.

Hannum, Hurst. (2019). *Rescuing Human Rights: A Radically Moderate Approach*. New York, NY: Cambridge University Press.

Zwingel, Susanne. (2019). *Translating International Women's Rights: The CEDAW Convention in Context*. New York, NY: Palgrave Macmillan.

Enforcement

Hafner-Burton, Emilie M. (2013). *Making Human Rights a Reality*. Princeton, NJ: Princeton University Press.

International Human Rights

Alston, Philip, and Ryan Goodman. (2012). *International Human Rights—The Successor to International Human Rights in Context: Law, Politics, Morals,* 3rd ed. New York, NY: Oxford University Press.

Donnelly, Jack, and Donald J. Whelan. (2018). *International Human Rights*, 5th ed. New York, NY: Routledge.

International Organization Efforts

Greenhill, Brian. (2015). *Transmitting Rights: International Organizations and the Diffusion of Human Rights Practices*. New York, NY: Oxford University Press.

Heupel, Monika, and Michael Zurn, eds. (2017). *Protecting the Individual from International Authority: Human Rights in International Organizations*. Cambridge, UK: Cambridge University Press.

UN Efforts

United Nations, Human Rights: https://www.un.org/en/sections/what-we-do/protect-human-rights/index.html

The United States and Human Rights

Apodaca, Clair. (2019). *Human Rights and U.S. Foreign Policy: Prevarications and Evasions*. New York, NY: Routledge.

US Department of State, Bureau of Democracy, Human Rights, and Labor: https://www.state.gov/bureaus-offices/under-secretary-for-civilian-security-democracy-and-human-rights/bureau-of-democracy-human-rights-and-labor

Hristo Rusev/NurPhoto via Getty Images

Trash floating above a reef in the Pacific Ocean

What can be done about a huge plastic trash heap that imperils marine life but isn't in any country's territorial waters?

NOAA

12

Managing the Global Commons

Whose Responsibility?

Learning Objectives

After studying this chapter, you will be able to . . .

12-1 Identify the "tragedy of the commons," collective goods, and the environmental challenges facing humankind.

12-2 Describe the evolving environmental regime and the challenges of sustainable development.

12-3 Explain the concept of sustainable development and steps toward that goal.

12-4 Recognize emerging arenas of global competition and cooperation.

Chapter Outline

12-1 The "Tragedy of the Commons" Illustrated in the Environment

12-2 The Evolving Environmental Regime and the Challenges of Sustainable Development

12-3 The Challenges of Fostering Sustainable Development

12-4 Emerging Arenas of Competition and Cooperation

The Great Pacific Garbage Patch

All kinds of trash can be found in the world's oceans, particularly plastic, which takes an average of 450 years to decompose. In 1988, the US National Oceanic and Atmospheric Administration (NOAA) published a report identifying the presence of an enormous floating garbage patch in the Pacific Ocean, drawing on several years of work by numerous researchers. Formed over many years by the North Pacific Gyre, a vortex in the ocean whose swirl pulls in debris and waste (primarily plastics) from around the Pacific, the Great Pacific Garbage Patch has grown steadily since its discovery. According to a 2011 report by the US Environmental Protection Agency (EPA), the source of this floating garbage dump is "improper waste disposal or management of trash and manufacturing products, including plastics (e.g., littering, illegal dumping). . . . Debris is generated on land at marinas, ports, rivers, harbors, docks, and storm drains. Debris is generated at sea from fishing vessels, stationary platforms and cargo ships" (US Environmental Protection Agency 2011).

There are multiple floating patches of plastic garbage in the world's oceans, but the Great Pacific Garbage Patch is the largest. According to a 2018 study, it covers over 600,000 square miles (Lebreton et al. 2018). That's more than twice the size of Texas, or about the same size of Alaska. Moreover, the patch is growing larger every year.

We do not yet know how much damage these floating trash piles do to marine life, how (given their size) they may change surface ocean currents, or what other harm they might cause. A number of studies have been undertaken by countries such as Australia, NGOs, and international organizations, but action to control, reduce, or eliminate these patches has been limited. These huge patches of waste float freely in the ocean beyond the territorial control of any state. Thus, because the oceans are in the global commons, they are open for use by all but are no one's specific responsibility to clean up. As a consequence, these floating garbage patches potentially affect everyone, but no one takes responsibility for the problem.

1. Who should take the lead to address the floating garbage problem: countries with Pacific coasts or all states regardless of location?

2. Who should pay the cost of such clean-up efforts?

3. What challenges might arise in efforts to clean up the problem?

INTRODUCTION: MANAGING THE GLOBAL COMMONS AND THE CONSEQUENCES OF HUMAN ACTIONS

When an environmental disaster occurs within a state, Westphalian sovereignty suggests that the state involved is ultimately responsible for what happens within its borders. Its leaders may ask for international assistance, but the responsibility to ensure economic and human security is theirs. However, who is responsible when radiation from Japan's 2011 Fukushima nuclear meltdown pollutes the Pacific Ocean or blows toward North America on the winds of the jet stream? Who is responsible for taking care of what is beyond the borders of any particular state or common to all humankind, such as air, sea, and space?

12-1 THE "TRAGEDY OF THE COMMONS" ILLUSTRATED IN THE ENVIRONMENT

>> 12-1 Identify the "tragedy of the commons," collective goods, and the environmental challenges facing humankind.

In Westphalian sovereignty, *no one is responsible for the global commons (the oceans, the atmosphere, etc.)*, and thus our planet's health could be imperiled. This problem is the **tragedy of the commons**. According to Garrett Hardin, who coined the phrase in 1968, the tragedy of the commons occurs when a resource is shared and no one actor owns it—like air or water. The "tragedy" is that no one takes responsibility for its protection. Individual actors rationally seek their own individual gain, and the common resource is depleted or degraded as a consequence of their individual use and misuse. These public or **collective goods**—things that benefit everyone, whether or not one pays for their cost or maintenance—are not the responsibility of any one state actor, and thus their care typically falls through the cracks of Westphalian sovereignty. Consider the floating garbage patch in this light. Where does the neo-Westphalian "responsibility to protect" enter this picture?

Environmental issues provide good illustrations of the collective goods problem. Some of these issues cascade into others to produce even more collective goods problems.

12-1a Pollution

Pollution of our air, ground, and water provides clear examples of the collective goods problem. Every day we create tremendous amounts of waste—much of which is toxic or at least not easily biodegradable—that

the planet has to cleanse. Our automobiles, factories, power plants, and machines generate enormous amounts of pollution in many forms, and postconsumer waste literally piles up all around the globe. Although the smoke from a fireplace or a barbecue pit may smell great, when entire societies cook their food and heat their homes with wood-burning fires or rely on slash-and-burn agriculture, tremendous amounts of carbon dioxide (CO_2) and particulates are released into the air.

However, when coal is burned to fuel stoves, provide heat, power industry, or generate electricity, CO_2 and particulates are not the only things released. According to the Union of Concerned Scientists (2012), here is what is released by a typical coal-fired power plant each year (note that this does not include the pollution caused by mining the coal):

- 3.7 million tons of CO_2, equivalent to cutting down 161 million trees
- 10,200 tons of nitrogen oxide, which causes ozone and smog
- 10,000 tons of sulfur dioxide that causes acid rain
- 720 tons of carbon monoxide, a deadly gas
- 500 tons of particulates that get trapped in lungs and contribute to respiratory illness
- 220 tons of hydrocarbons that contribute to ozone and smog formation
- 225 pounds of arsenic, a toxic chemical
- 170 pounds of mercury, a toxic chemical
- 114 pounds of lead, a toxic chemical
- 4 pounds of cadmium, along with other toxic heavy metal compounds

These compounds imperil our human security not only because they get into the air we breathe but also because they fall to the earth and poison the ground and groundwater, run off into the oceans, and eventually find their way into the food that we eat. In children, the effects of such pollutants include lung, bladder, kidney, and liver cancers, birth defects, mental disability, and learning disorders, and these pollutants can produce convulsions, comas, and ultimately death. Respiratory diseases are more likely for all who breathe these compounds. Recent research shows that pollution is responsible for 9 million deaths worldwide every year (*The Lancet* 2017; Scutti 2017). That's one of every six deaths worldwide, more than the population of New York City, mostly in lower-middle-income and middle-income countries where the effects of industrialization are the worst. (See Map 12-1.)

---

tragedy of the commons: the idea that no one state is held responsible for things held in common—so-called collective goods—like the air and water, so their protection often goes unaddressed.

collective goods: things that benefit all concerned—whether or not they participate in their protection and maintenance—and are not owned by any one state actor.

MAP 12-1

Pollution Deaths in 2015

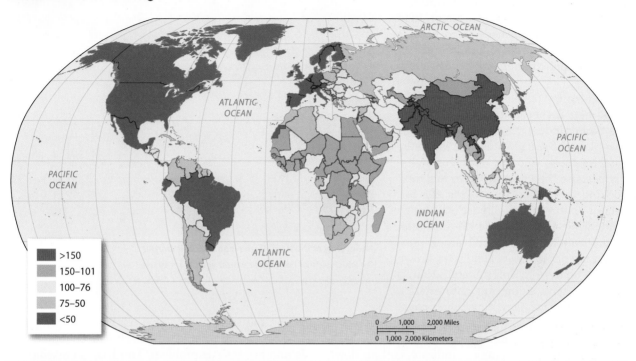

Legend:
- >150
- 150–101
- 100–76
- 75–50
- <50

Source: Data from Susan Scutti, "Pollution Linked to 9 Million Deaths Worldwide in 2015, Study Says," *CNN*, http://www.cnn.com/2017/10/19/health/pollution-1-in-6-deaths-study/index.html.

There are obvious economic effects as well. For years, the US steel industry relied on coal power to fuel its plants in the Midwest. Due to prevailing winds for much of the year, the emissions from these plants drifted north to Canada, where they fell back to earth in the form of acid rain. The acid rain killed off huge tracts of forest, thereby both hurting the timber industry (an important component of the Canadian economy) and reducing the number of trees that could be absorbing such toxic wastes from the atmosphere. No wonder the Canadians were mad at the United States—their economic security was being harmed.

At least these actions were relatively inadvertent, in the sense that relying on coal for industrial use began long before most people understood the negative consequences of what was released in the emissions. For years, however, the Soviet Union secretly disposed of some of its nuclear waste by dumping it in the Sea of Japan. The Soviets knew this radioactive waste was toxic, but they got rid of it the fastest, easiest way they could. Are you surprised Japan's relationship with Russia deteriorated when these revelations made the news? Although the health damage done to the Japanese as a result of this dumping of nuclear waste is unknown, the Japanese had reason to be concerned.

They had previously experienced major episodes of health-related disasters due to the effects of pollution. Previous Japanese victims of cadmium poisoning (from industrial wastes discharged into the sea) suffered from degenerative kidney disease, brittle bones, and extremely painful back and joint disabilities. Japanese who consumed mercury-poisoned fish had excessive degeneration of their central nervous systems. So, it's not hard to understand why although much of the Sea of Japan is legally considered international waters, the Japanese did not appreciate this threat to their health and livelihood.

Finally, as the opening to this chapter indicates, nuclear waste is not the only thing that gets tossed into the ocean. All kinds of trash can be found in the world's oceans, particularly plastic, which does not biodegrade quickly at all. The sad fact is that as part of the global commons, the oceans—like many other victims of pollution—potentially affect everyone, but they are no one's specific responsibility to clean up.

12-1b Deforestation

As mentioned previously, pollution can kill off forests; just ask the Canadians. However, the bigger threat to forests is the intentional cutting down of trees. According to the UN Framework Convention on Climate Change (UNFCC), the causes of **deforestation**—the destruction of forests faster than they can be replenished—are economic and include subsistence farming (48% of deforestation), commercial agriculture (32%), and logging or harvesting trees for economic purposes (14%) and fuel wood (5%; Forner et al. 2006). Although the timber industry may plant new trees to replace those harvested, that is not the case for those who cut down trees simply because they need wood to fuel their cooking or heating fires. Thus, the forests of Haiti are now almost completely gone, while the forests of the next-door Dominican Republic are still largely present, as the photo shows. Haiti is the brown country on the left. Unfortunately, Haiti is not alone, and significant deforestation has occurred in many developing countries. As we will see, such deforestation endangers both human and economic security.

Aerial view of the Haiti–Dominican Republic border
On which side of the border would you prefer to live?
NASA/Goddard Space Flight Center Scientific Visualization Studio

As the UNFCC numbers indicate, cutting down trees for firewood for cooking and heating may be a serious problem, but the more critical issue is cutting down trees to clear land for alternative usage like raising cattle or growing crops, which are more profitable for the landowners. The Brazilian rain forest provides a good example. Thousands of square miles of Brazilian rain forest are cut down each year, and the numbers are rising. The rate of deforestation in Brazil had declined in the early 2000s but began increasing again after 2013 during the Michel Temer and Jair Bolsonaro administrations. Moreover, as trees burn or decompose, they release their previously stored carbon dioxide. Reports estimate that up to 20% of the Amazon rain forest now actually emits more carbon dioxide than it stores (Gatehouse 2020).

So what difference does this make? First, trees are among the most productive generators of oxygen. Like other plants, trees "breathe in" CO_2, convert it to food, use it and store it, and then breathe out oxygen. As the oxygen mixes with hydrogen in the atmosphere, water forms and rain occurs. So fewer rain forests mean less oxygen and less rain. Second, trees reduce the most prominent of **greenhouse gases**—CO_2—by using it as food and storing it. As we will

see in the section on global climate change, greenhouse gases contribute to such climate change, which is another serious problem. Third, by increasing the number of cattle being raised, landowners contribute to the generation of methane gas, a natural gas produced in part by bovine manure. Although CO_2 gets a lot of attention as the leading greenhouse gas, methane is the second leading greenhouse gas. So deforestation in the Brazilian Amazon reduces the ability of the planet to clean its air of pollutants, reduces the amount of oxygen and water available to support life, and adds to the amount of greenhouse gases in the atmosphere.

On a global basis, the news regarding deforestation is bad but may be improving slowly. A UN report suggests that although deforestation remains a critical problem, especially in the developing world, the rate has slowed by as much as 50% in the past decade or so (UN Food and Agriculture Organization 2015). In 2005, 39 million acres were lost annually to deforestation. That's an area of almost 61,000 square miles, thus larger than the states of New York, New Jersey, and Connecticut combined. In the next decade and a half, the world could lose forest acreage twice the size of Texas. According to the World Wildlife Federation's website (https://www.worldwildlife.org/threats/deforestation-and-forest-degradation), we are losing up to 30 soccer fields of forest every minute. So we are still diminishing the planet's ability to produce oxygen, generate water, and absorb CO_2.

Beyond the impact on air quality, deforestation also carries other negative effects. Removing the forests also means removing most of the plant and

....

deforestation: the destruction of forests at a rate faster than they can be replaced or replenished.

greenhouse gases: those gases that trap the sun's heat and hold it close to the earth's surface; they include carbon dioxide, methane, nitrous oxide, and water vapor.

animal species that live in forests. We return to this issue in the section on biodiversity challenges, but one intriguing potential consequence is the impact this could have on future pharmaceutical drugs. As you probably learned, moldy bread led to the discovery of penicillin; it turns out that most pharmaceutical drugs come from organic compounds found in nature. Thus, as unknown chemical compounds and bacteria are destroyed through deforestation, that loss might involve chemical combinations that could form the basis for life-saving drugs of the future.

Another major negative impact of deforestation is an increased risk of floods and mudslides. Forests help mitigate the force of rain hitting the ground, and the tree roots help hold the soil together, thereby preventing soil erosion. Rain hits the upper canopy of leaves, filters through the leaves and branches, and then drops to the ground, there to be absorbed into the soil. Without the leaf canopy to filter the rain and the tree roots to hold the soil, rain hits the ground harder and a larger portion of that water runs off before it can soak in, thereby creating more flooding and mudslides nearby. Overall, fewer trees mean less rain; less rain means harder ground and more run-off when rain does fall, as well as more heat reflected back into the atmosphere at other times; and more heat means the creation of larger deserts, to which we turn next.

12-1c Desertification

Desertification is another threat to economic and human security. The term literally means the ongoing creation and expansion of deserts. More and more land each year is lost to desertification. The process is fairly straightforward and is linked to deforestation. As trees are cut down, less rain is generated. With less rainfall (and often aided by overgrazing of livestock), groundcovers become sparser, and the ground becomes harder. Thus, when rain does fall, it soaks in less and runs off faster, leaving the soil drier and reflecting more heat back into the air. At some point, there is insufficient moisture in the ground to support plant life, and new desert areas are formed, or existing deserts grow.

China provides a good illustration. More than a quarter of China is desert, and that desert is growing by about 1,300 square miles each year—or about the size of Rhode Island. As many as 400 million Chinese have lost the productive use of their land due to desertification, often having to move to cities for work, thereby putting even more stress on urban resources. As more and more water is drained from the soil, underground aquifers also dry up. As a result, the city of Shanghai has sunk about six feet in the past 20 years. According to the Chinese government,

a total of 660,000 square miles overall have been lost to desertification—an area more than twice the size of Texas, or about the size of Alaska. Fortunately, the rate of desertification has slowed in recent years through aggressive governmental actions to reclaim the land. Although the Chinese believe about one third of this lost land can be reclaimed from the desert, they estimate it will take *300 years* to do so (Associated Press 2011).

The problem of desertification is not just a Chinese problem; it is a global one. The UN estimates that by 2025, two thirds of the **arable land**—land suitable for agricultural cultivation—in Africa will be lost to desertification; similarly, one third of the arable land in Asia and one fifth of South America's arable land will be lost. As more of the earth's surface becomes desert, more heat from the sun is reflected into the atmosphere, which contributes in part to global climate change, to which we now turn.

12-1d Global Climate Change

Many of the problems discussed previously contribute to the broader phenomenon known as **global climate change**, which also threatens economic and human security. To be sure, the earth has undergone warming and cooling cycles over time. There have been ice ages before, and most of that ice melted for reasons we don't fully understand.

However, controversies about the realities and causes of climate change are political issues, not scientific ones. Countless scientific studies show both the empirical trend—increased temperatures—and the underlying causes—human-made pollution—of global climate change. The weight of evidence from the scientific community is absolutely clear. We have known since the 19th century that the earth's atmosphere traps the sun's heat and that the major contributors—the greenhouse gases—include CO_2, methane, nitrous oxide, and water vapor. What we have witnessed in recent years is a relatively rapid increase in the average temperatures on the planet, as shown in Figure 12-1.

As Figure 12-1 shows, the earth seems to have experienced significant warming patterns over time, and the increasingly steep trajectory of the line in the graph shows that the rate of change is accelerating quite significantly. According to the US government,

....

desertification: the creation of new, or enlargement of existing, deserts.

arable land: land capable of sustaining agriculture.

global climate change: marked changes in the warming and cooling of the planet's temperatures, thought to be accelerated by human activity such as industrialization and fossil fuel emissions, which produce greenhouse gases.

FIGURE 12-1

Global Annual Mean Surface Air Temperature Change Estimates Based on Land and Ocean Data

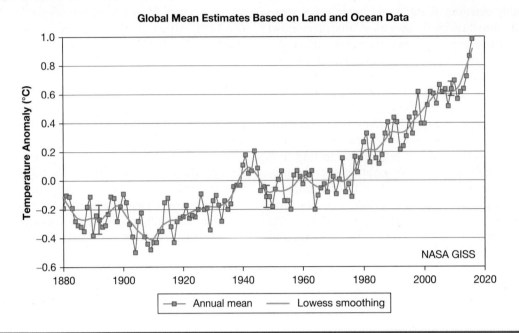

Source: Data from National Aeronautics and Space Administration, Goddard Institute for Space Studies, https://data.giss.nasa.gov/gistemp/graphs.

the hottest years in history have all come in the 21st century, and 2010–2019 was the hottest decade ever recorded (National Oceanic and Atmospheric Administration 2020).

In recent years, scientists have theorized that human activity—particularly the burning of fossil fuels (such as driving your car), which release greenhouse gases, and the use of aerosols—has made the current cycle more extreme. This is the conclusion of the thousands of scientists from 195 countries who form the **Intergovernmental Panel on Climate Change (IPCC)**, a scientific body created by the UN Environment Programme and the World Meteorological Organization. According to the IPCC, the scientific evidence is conclusive; human activity has contributed to making the current cycle of climate change more extreme than it would be otherwise. Indeed, in its most recent report, the IPCC confidently concluded that climate change is underway and a consequence of human activity (Intergovernmental Panel on Climate Change 2014). Moreover, a study of more than 12,000 peer-reviewed scientific papers on the subject of climate change published from 1991 to 2011 found that the overwhelming majority (97% of

those who reached a conclusion) were convinced by the evidence of human-caused climate change (Doyle 2013). Virtually every major national science academy around the world agrees, and not one dissents. According to the IPCC, we have only until 2030 to make drastic changes in our actions and lifestyles to avoid catastrophic global consequences (Miller and Croft 2018). Some of the past and future changes due to global climate change can be seen in Figure 12-2.

Although overall average global temperatures are increasing, as shown in Map 12-2, as parts of the planet warm up, other parts cool down. Much of the heating is found in the Northern Hemisphere, where more of the planet's population lives, and more of the cooling is happening in the Southern Hemisphere over water. Hence, the preferred scientific term for this phenomenon is *global climate change* rather than simply *global warming*. Increasing heat and drought have reduced the rates of carbon dioxide absorption by the rain forests in the Amazonian and Congo basins. More visible changes can be seen as a result of this average warming of the planet's land and water surfaces. Polar ice caps are melting at an unprecedented rate, threatening species such as polar bears and some seals with a loss of habitat and spawning massive new icebergs that break off from polar ice caps and threaten some shipping lanes (see Figure 12-3). In 2017, an iceberg the size of Delaware and weighing a trillion tons

Intergovernmental Panel on Climate Change (IPCC): a scientific body with 195 member states, created by the UN Environment Programme and the World Meteorological Organization in 1988.

FIGURE 12-2

Past and Future Changes in the Ocean and Cryosphere

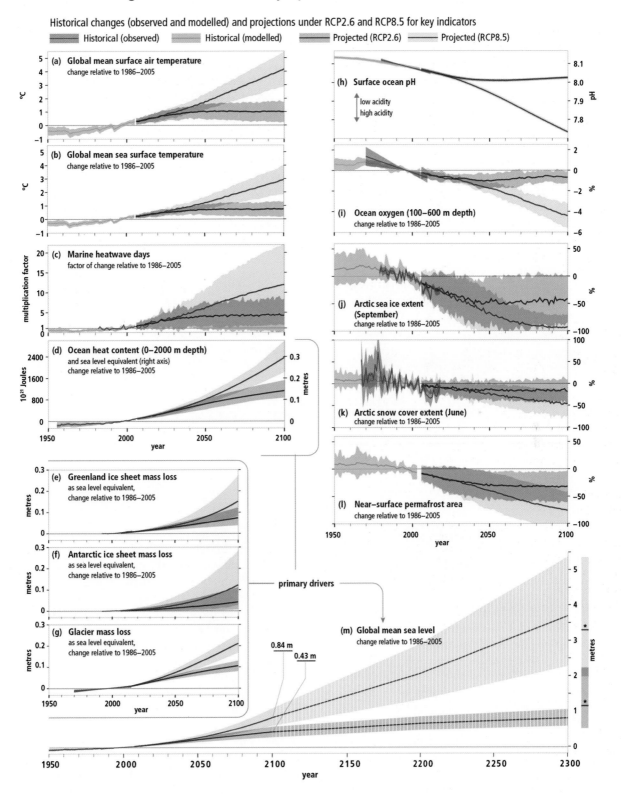

Historical changes (observed and modelled) and projections under RCP2.6 and RCP8.5 for key indicators

Historical (observed)   Historical (modelled)   Projected (RCP2.6)   Projected (RCP8.5)

Source: Figure SPM.1 from IPCC, 2019: Summary for Policymakers. In: *IPCC Special Report on the Ocean and Cryosphere in a Changing Climate* [H.-O. Pörtner, D.C. Roberts, V. Masson-Delmotte, P. Zhai, M. Tignor, E. Poloczanska, K. Mintenbeck, A. Alegría, M. Nicolai, A. Okem, J. Petzold, B. Rama, N.M. Weyer (eds.)]. In press. (https://www.ipcc.ch/srocc).

MAP 12-2

Increases in Annual Temperatures for a Recent Five-Year Period, Relative to 1951–1980

Who is most affected by global climate change?

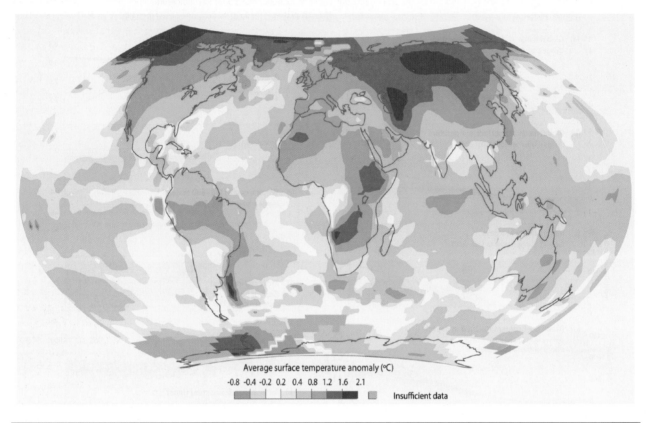

Average surface temperature anomaly (°C)

-0.8 -0.4 -0.2 0.2 0.4 0.8 1.2 1.6 2.1

Insufficient data

Sources: NASA's Scientific Visualization Studio (2018), https://climate.nasa.gov/news/2671/long-term-warming-trend-continued-in-2017-nasa-noaa/.

broke off from the Antarctic shelf. Mountain glaciers are melting at an increasing rate as well, with some nearly disappearing from view. For example, the ice on Tanzania's Mount Kilimanjaro has decreased by 86% since 1912 and by 26% since just 2000.

The result of freshwater ice melt is a rise in global sea levels. Estimates suggest that sea levels could rise from two to six feet over the 21st century. If so, 13 of the world's 15 largest cities—cities such as New York City, London, and Tokyo—would face serious flooding problems. In the United States alone, 40 million people living in coastal cities would be affected by rising sea levels. Particularly hard-hit would be the densely populated northeastern portion of the United States, where Massachusetts already loses 65 acres a year to the ocean. Sea levels have already risen a foot over the past 100 years, and those living in flat coastal plains rely on old, deteriorating seawalls to protect them from the ocean. Low-lying countries like the Netherlands and Bangladesh could face even more devastating consequences, and entire islands or island nations—such as the Maldives in the Indian Ocean—could be entirely under water by the end of this century.

If that isn't bad enough, releasing this much cold freshwater into the warming salt waters of the world's oceans could have another impact: Ocean currents could change. Although surface ocean currents can be directed by winds, deep ocean currents are products of differences in temperatures and salinity levels in water. Do you ever wonder why northern Europe has a relatively temperate climate despite being about as far north as Alaska? The answer is the Gulf Stream, which circles through the warm waters of the Gulf of Mexico and then carries that warmth across the Atlantic Ocean toward Europe. If melting ice caps caused salinity and temperature levels to change enough that the Gulf Stream changed directions, Europe might enter a deep freeze. Movies such as *The Day After Tomorrow* (2004) and *Interstellar* (2014) may sensationalize the phenomenon and time

FIGURE 12-3

NOAA GFDL CM2.1 Model Simulation

This image from the National Oceanic and Atmospheric Administration illustrates the shrinking Arctic ice cap. What might be the consequences of no ice cap in the Arctic?

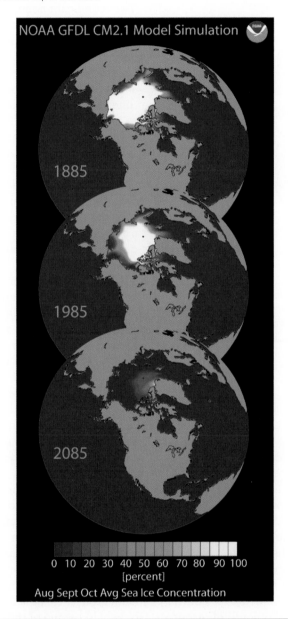

NOAA GFDL CM2.1 Model Simulation

1885

1985

2085

0 10 20 30 40 50 60 70 80 90 100
[percent]
Aug Sept Oct Avg Sea Ice Concentration

Source: NOAA Geophysical Fluid Dynamics Laboratory.

frame, but cataclysmic changes are not out of the question.

Whether or not ocean currents change directions, the waters of the earth's oceans are warming overall, and meteorologists agree that warmer waters produce more storms that are sufficiently intense to rise to the level of being "named" (and perhaps more frequent ones as well, but there is less scientific agreement on that). In recent years, there have been more named storms than normal. More tropical depressions are intensifying to become named tropical storms, and more of these named tropical storms continue to strengthen until they become hurricanes (also called cyclones and typhoons). Finally, more of the hurricanes that develop become even more powerful ones, routinely reaching Category 3 or 4 status in recent years. The result is considerable destruction and often many deaths, as Hurricane Katrina in the United States and Hurricane Ike in Cuba demonstrated in 2005 and 2008. In September 2017, *three* hurricanes developed almost simultaneously, wreaking havoc on Caribbean countries and the US, and that was *after* Hurricane Harvey hit Texas and Louisiana. There is also scientific speculation—but not definitive proof yet—that global warming patterns increase the amount of moisture in the atmosphere, which can lead to more intense and frequent tornadoes (and maybe other extreme weather, too).

12-1e Biodiversity Challenges

Human activity is not just harming the planet; it also reduces the diversity of species found here. As forests are diminished, the many species that live in those forests are often killed off as well. Plant and animal life is thus threatened. As noted in the section on deforestation, many pharmaceutical drugs are derived from chemical compounds found in nature. We have no idea how many undiscovered forms of life exist within the tropical rain forests of the world, but as they are destroyed, we may be killing off potential cures for deadly or other dread diseases in the process. The 1992 movie *Medicine Man* illustrated this dynamic well. In the film, developers cut roads through the Amazon rain forest in order to exploit the area's natural resources. In the process of destroying the trees, they unknowingly destroy the habitat that gives shelter to a species of insects that had developed a natural cure for cancer. Although the film was fictional entertainment, the premise on which it was based is frighteningly real. We could be missing out on unknown medical or other benefits by wiping out entire species of living things that exist only in unique microclimates or microenvironments. We could be killing the goose that laid the golden egg and not even know it.

Two other aspects of protecting species deserve mention. First, we know that different species affect each other in different ways. An easy-to-understand example is the fact that we depend on bees to pollinate many food crops. If the bee population died off, it would imperil overall food production. However, we should be wise enough to know that we don't understand all of these connections. So wiping out species could come back to haunt humans in ways we cannot foresee at this time. Second, there is an ethical

FIGURE 12-4

Primary Threats to Living Planet Index Populations

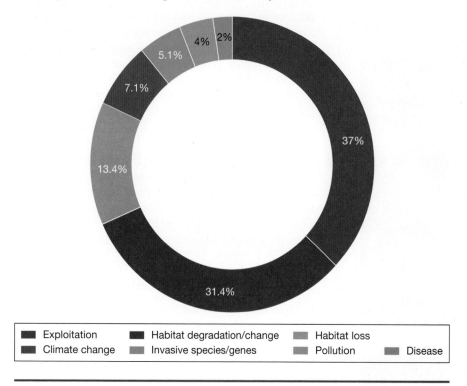

Exploitation
Climate change
Habitat degradation/change
Invasive species/genes
Habitat loss
Pollution
Disease

Source: *Living Planet Report*, 2014 http://assets.worldwildlife.org/publications/723/files/original/WWF-LPR2014-low_res.pdf?1413912230&_ga=1.249068103.1519708733.1473375366.

select these GMOs due to their economic appeal, other varieties of the species are necessarily reduced. The planet's food and fiber stocks become monocultural.

Two significant concerns arise. First, GMO seeds cost more and have to be purchased annually. Second, what if a disease or bug develops in nature that can attack that one major crop species? There are not as many alternative varieties of such plants that might offer other opportunities for food production. Should such diversity be lost in cereal grains that feed large parts of the world—like rice, corn, or wheat—the effects on the global food supply could be devastating.

Simply put, the more diversity there is among plant and animal life, the less threatened those species are by disease. The current rate of species extinction is 1,000 times higher than the rate of extinction found in the fossil record, and the projected rate of species extinction in the future is expected to be 10 times higher than the present rate. Like the other environmental issues discussed previously, biodiversity challenges also threaten economic and human security.

argument to be made here. What gives humans the right to eradicate other species? We may assume we are superior to other species, but how accurate is that assumption? We are only beginning to understand how intelligent sea mammals such as whales and dolphins are, that some trees and plants can communicate with others of their species in ways we cannot see, and so on. There is more to other species than many humans realize, and killing them off—even accidentally—may be a more profound act than most of us comprehend (see Figure 12-4). If we are superior, shouldn't we realize these complexities and know better than to wipe out entire species?

Again, at least these consequences are largely accidental. What is not accidental is the creation of plant seeds whose prominence in the agricultural markets reduces the diversity found among species. These are generally referred to as **genetically modified organisms (GMOs)**: organisms whose genetic makeup is intentionally altered to produce some advantageous result, like increased crop yields or greater resistance to insects or droughts. As more and more farmers

Whether considering pollution, deforestation, desertification, global climate change, or reductions in the earth's biodiversity, our current practices damage where we live and often destroy the habitats of other species. Not only is our economic and human security endangered; international security could be as well—to the extent that future conflicts may be waged over control of food supplies, clean water, and other vital resources. Gold could be one of those resources. Illegal gold mining is a global problem. In countries such as Peru, Colombia, Ecuador, Brazil, and Bolivia, illegal gold mining results in both deforestation and mercury poisoning (mercury is used to help separate the gold from other minerals) of both the workers and of the Amazon Basin. Peru resorted to sending in the army to shut down such illegal mining operations, but with profits of $1,000 per ounce, the miners reappeared as soon as the troops left. In Africa, mercury poisoning is increasingly commonplace in Ghana, where local gold miners

genetically modified organisms (GMOs): those organisms whose genetic makeup is intentionally altered to produce some advantage.

have operated—often illegally—for decades. A quick Google search indicates similar illegal gold-mining operations with similar dangerous consequences for the environment and miners' health in places such as the Democratic Republic of the Congo, Mongolia, Nigeria, South Africa, and Venezuela. Thus, humans have learned how to wring more and more economic benefit from the earth and its resources. The irony is that our actions are creating long-term threats to the quality of life for humanity and perhaps its future existence as well. Yet steps can be taken to produce more beneficial changes, and we turn to those next.

12-2 THE EVOLVING ENVIRONMENTAL REGIME AND THE CHALLENGES OF SUSTAINABLE DEVELOPMENT

>> 12-2 **Describe the evolving environmental regime and the challenges of sustainable development.**

Many different types of actors are expending considerable effort to arrest and change the damaging actions noted previously. Given the impact of anarchy on phenomena that occur in the global commons, states, international organizations, and NGOs all become involved in the effort to protect the earth's environment.

12-2a State Actions

States have tried any number of steps to address the environmental challenges they face, obviously with varying levels of success. Yet try as they might, individual state actions can do only so much. Environmental problems are global in scope, and not all states are able or willing to engage in significant efforts to do what they can to clean up their part of the environment. Existing state efforts can be seen primarily in battling pollution, deforestation, desertification, and global climate change within their borders.

Pollution

Unlike some environmental challenges, pollution can often be seen and is thus not easily ignored. Affluent states may have the advantage here, possessing the resources to devote to cleaning up obvious pollution problems. European countries have done quite well in this regard. Due to its concentration of heavy industries, Germany can still have some regional pollution problems at times, but most European states have experienced considerable success in cleaning up air pollution. Take a look at how clean the air is in the photo of Athens, a very large and congested urban area in Greece—one of the poorer countries of Europe.

When it comes to clean air, the other end of the spectrum may be China, which has some of the dirtiest and deadliest air in the world, as shown in the day-time photo of Tiananmen Square in Beijing. Here the Chinese set up a large TV screen so that they could see the sunrise or sunset.

The Chinese have tried to clean the air (particularly before the Beijing Olympic Games in 2008) by closing dirty factories, making auto emissions standards more stringent, and reducing the use of coal for heating homes. They have also begun prosecuting officials responsible for egregious pollution incidents. Yet when environmental concerns conflict with the commitment to rapid industrialization and

A sunny day in Athens, capital of Greece, one of the poorer countries in Europe

How can relatively poor Western states still have clean air?

Ann Johansson/Corbis via Getty Images

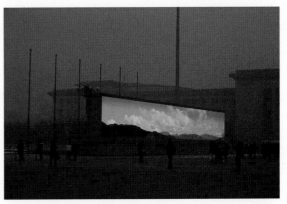

An LED screen shows blue sky in Tiananmen Square during dangerous levels of pollution

What happens to Chinese health when the government has to project a picture to show clean air?

Feng Li/Getty Images

economic expansion, economic security in China is still typically prioritized over environmental or human security.

Some pollution cannot be seen. Japan has been unable to fully stop the leakage of radioactive water into the Pacific Ocean from the Fukushima nuclear reactor complex damaged by a tsunami in 2011. In late 2016, French firms completed their two-decade-long work to design and erect a 32,000-ton steel arch to cover the entire Chernobyl nuclear reactor complex in Ukraine to stop the leakage of radiation from the 1986 explosion and fire there. The European Bank for Reconstruction and Development, Western countries, Russia, and Ukraine shared the costs of the project—which totaled more than $2 billion. Even after the arched building was put in place, costly work continued to remove and store the radioactive debris it covers.

Deforestation

Many countries have engaged in significant efforts to increase tree planting to slow down the deforestation trend. The US Agency for International Development contributed millions of dollars over time to such efforts in Africa, Asia, and Latin America. Some countries, such as Costa Rica, prohibited logging in certain forestlands in return for forgiveness of portions of their foreign debt. Kenya sponsored the planting of 25 million trees in Africa. Norway has sent over a billion dollars to countries such as Brazil, Indonesia, and Liberia to fight deforestation, and in 2020 Norway announced a commitment to only purchase products from deforestation-free supply chains. Still, there are bumps in the road. In 2014, Brazil refused to endorse a 2014 UN anti-deforestation initiative because it was left out of the consultation process. Brazil's deforestation

The French-built steel arch over the former Chernobyl nuclear reactor complex

Will building caps over nuclear disaster sites like this one in Chernobyl, Ukraine, protect us?

Stringer/Sputnik via AP

rate subsequently increased, and Norway responded by cutting its funding of Brazil's anti-deforestation efforts by two thirds (down to $35 million from a previous average of $110 million per year). Norway cited Brazil's apparent lack of commitment to the effort as the reason for the funding cut.

Nonetheless, the Sustainable Development Goals in the UN's 2030 Agenda for Sustainable Development established in 2015 include numerous mentions of deforestation, with Sustainable Development Goal 15 explicitly targeting progress in combating he problem. In pursuit of this goal, to "protect, restore and promote sustainable use of terrestrial ecosystems, sustainably manage forests, combat desertification, and halt and reverse land degradation and halt biodiversity loss," the UN's working group established a number of specific targets. In the most important goal for deforestation, SDG 15 stated: "By 2020, promote the implementation of sustainable management of all types of forests, halt deforestation, restore degraded forests and substantially increase afforestation and reforestation globally" (UN Food and Agriculture Organization 2017). As part of this effort, the relevant UN agencies seek to work closely with partner countries to bring more and more forest under management plans designed to conserve and protect them. For other aspects of this initiative, see "Spotlight On: Sustainable Development Goals."

Despite such efforts, the commercial appeal of cutting down forests—to clear land for agriculture, for livestock, for mining, or simply for the income the timber industry provides—can be overwhelming, and global rates of deforestation are increasing. Even in countries held up as success stories like Costa Rica, the damage has already been done. Only about half of Costa Rica's original rain forest remains, and only about half of the remainder is federally protected. For many, the tangible benefits of income in hand far outweigh the less obvious or often intangible aspects of cleaner air, less soil erosion, or the protection of forest species. What do you think is more important, development (often out of poverty) for the people of a country or the protection of the environment? In most cases, the allure of private goods outweighs that of collective goods.

Desertification

Halting the spread of the earth's deserts is a challenging task, as ways have to be found to retain the little moisture available in those regions so that new plantings can survive and barren ground can be covered. The UN targeted desertification in its 2030 Agenda for Sustainable Development as well, establishing several goals and targets for progress, but countries have to commit to the effort to fight desertification caused by human activities such as unsustainable

Sustainable Development Goals

The issue of deforestation is only one of the issues the UN confronted in the 2030 Agenda for Sustainable Development. After a lengthy discussion of the interconnections among issues of human security, the UN set forth 17 goals to essentially replace the Millennium Development Goals. These Sustainable Development Goals are as follows:

1. End poverty in all its forms everywhere

2. End hunger, achieve food security and improved nutrition and promote sustainable agriculture

3. Ensure healthy lives and promote well-being for all at all ages

4. Ensure inclusive and equitable quality education and promote lifelong learning opportunities for all

5. Achieve gender equality and empower all women and girls

6. Ensure availability and sustainable management of water and sanitation for all

7. Ensure access to affordable, reliable, sustainable and modern energy for all

8. Promote sustained, inclusive and sustainable economic growth, full and productive employment and decent work for all

9. Build resilient infrastructure, promote inclusive and sustainable industrialization and foster innovation

10. Reduce inequality within and among countries

11. Make cities and human settlements inclusive, safe, resilient and sustainable

12. Ensure sustainable consumption and production patterns

13. Take urgent action to combat climate change and its impacts

14. Conserve and sustainably use the oceans, seas and marine resources for sustainable development

15. Protect, restore and promote sustainable use of terrestrial ecosystems, sustainably manage forests, combat desertification, and halt and reverse land degradation and halt biodiversity loss

16. Promote peaceful and inclusive societies for sustainable development, provide access to justice for all and build effective, accountable and inclusive institutions at all levels

17. Strengthen the means of implementation and revitalize the global partnership for sustainable development

Should these goals be reached by 2030, the world will be a better place to live, but it looks increasingly likely that the world will fall short. ●

Source: United Nations, *Sustainable Development Goals: 17 Goals to Transform the World*, http://www.un.org/sustainabledevelopment/sustainable-development-goals.

farming, mining, and overgrazing and clear-cutting of land, as well as by climate change.

One example of country-level efforts is found in China, which has faced a considerable challenge in this regard. In 1978, the Chinese began a project to create a "Great Green Wall" of forested lands 2,700 miles long to contain the spread of the desert. The project was expected to take 73 years to complete. So far, the program has had only mixed success, as trees were planted in areas with insufficient rainfall to support robust tree life, and not all the trees were drought-resistant varieties. About a quarter of the trees planted so far have died, and the rest have not reached their normal growth due to the lack of available water. According to critics, planting drought-resistant shrubs and grasses might have worked better. However, China continued to press on in other ways, becoming the first country in 2002 to establish a law on prevention and control of desertification and adding other programs to fight desertification and deforestation. In 2017, the World Future Council and the UN Convention to Combat Desertification recognized China's combined efforts and progress by presenting it the Silver Award, one of several Future Policy Awards, bestowed on those states making the most progress. (Just so you know, the winner of the Gold Award was the Tigray region of Ethiopia, for its remarkable progress in restoring groundwater and preventing soil erosion.)

India also implemented a multimodal effort to combat desertification: Irrigation projects replenish local water supplies, rooftop systems catch and store rainwater, and wells channel rainfall runoff back into underground aquifers to augment the available groundwater supply. Drought-resistant vegetation barriers have helped retain the soil and prevent water runoff. Drought-resistant tree species also help and have been used to reduce the spread of sand dunes. Keeping livestock off the endangered lands has also been a key to helping the land recover from desertification.

Similar multimodal efforts have shown some success in reclaiming land from the Sahara Desert in Burkina Faso. There, small barriers are built and large depressions dug, both of which slow down rainfall runoff so that it has time to soak into the ground. Hedges or trees are planted around the depressions to help serve as windbreaks. Then the bare ground is covered with straw during the dry season to help retain the moisture. These techniques, relatively easily done at the local level, have shown some promise.

Global Climate Change

Although cynics might argue that global climate change is beyond the ability of any one state to influence, some are trying through various means, such as raising taxes on petroleum use, capturing carbon dioxide and methane gas, reducing dependence on coal, and mandating higher miles per gallon requirements for vehicles. Increasing reliance on renewable energy sources (like solar, wind, tidal, and hydroelectric) is a major initiative in many countries; the 2018 leaders in those efforts are listed in Table 12-1.

Overall, the Climate Change Performance Index creates an annual index score for each country based on its greenhouse gas emissions, energy use, renewable energy sources, and climate policy commitments. In its 2020 country ranking, no countries placed in the very-high-performance category, but 14 were ranked in the high-performance category. With index scores ranging from 75.77 to 60.60, those countries were, in descending order: Sweden, Denmark, Morocco, United Kingdom, Lithuania, India, Finland, Chile, Norway, Luxembourg, Malta, Latvia, Switzerland, and Ukraine. For comparison, 14 countries placed in the very-low-performance category, with index scores ranging from 40.76 to 18.80. Those were, in descending order: Turkey, Bulgaria, Poland, Japan, Russia, Malaysia, Kazakhstan, Canada, Australia, Iran, South Korea, Chinese Taipei, Saudi Arabia, and the US. To be fair, most African countries and many Latin American countries were not included in the rankings due to lack of data.

A broader measure is the biennial report of Yale University's Environmental Performance Index, which measures progress by states on ecosystem vitality (with indicators for agriculture, air effects on the ecosystem, biodiversity and habitat, climate change, fisheries, forestry, and water effects on the ecosystem) and environmental health (air pollution effects on humans, environmental burden of disease, and water effects on humans). Not surprisingly, those countries near the bottom of the rankings are among the poorest in the world. In 2018, the bottom 10 countries of the 180 ranked are developing states: in descending order, Central African Republic, Niger, Lesotho, Haiti, Madagascar, Nepal, India, Democratic Republic of the Congo, Bangladesh, and Burundi. By contrast, the top 10 countries (and 17 of the top 20) are in Europe. The ranking, in descending order, is Switzerland, France, Denmark, Malta, Sweden, United Kingdom, Luxembourg, Austria, Ireland, and Finland. The United States comes in 27th in the rankings, just ahead of Slovakia, but behind Cyprus, Canada, and Portugal. Wealth helps provide the resources needed to address environmental challenges, but it also takes political will—and that does not always require great affluence.

Still, there is only so much individual states can do within their own borders to address the greater environmental threats found in the global commons. For these threats, multilateral efforts are required, and like anything else, the questions of "who pays" and "how much" quickly arise. Oftentimes, actions must begin at the grassroots level and work up from there. We turn to such multilateral initiatives next.

TABLE 12-1

Top 10 Countries in Renewable Energy Production in 2018

RANK	COUNTRY	TOTAL RENEWABLE ENERGY (GWH)
1	China	1,398,207
2	United States	572,409
3	Brazil	426,638
4	Canada	418,679
5	India	195,242
6	Germany	193,735
7	Russia	170,077
8	Japan	169,660
9	Norway	140,240
10	Italy	109,962

Source: WorldAtlas.com, "Renewable Energy by Country," https://www.worldatlas.com/articles/top-15-countries-using-renewable-energy.html.

12-2b Public and Nongovernmental Organization Actions

Steps by ordinary citizens (better known as grassroots action) and NGOs help stimulate awareness

Which Non-state Actors Matter Most in the Environmental Arena?

Proponents of liberalism and neoliberalism should love environmental policy, as it seems like a natural match to demonstrate the influence of non-state actors. After all, environmental awareness arose at the grassroots level. The modern environmental movement gained traction beginning in the 1960s and 1970s. The World Wildlife Federation formed in 1961, Rachel Carson's *Silent Spring* was published the next year, and Paul Ehrlich's *The Population Bomb* came along in 1968. Earth Day as an annual event began in 1970, and over the next decade, groups like Greenpeace, the Natural Resources Defense Council, the Club of Rome, and the Ocean Conservancy were founded, and many others followed. Beginning in 1989, the Climate Action Network organized many NGOs to push for a global, comprehensive treaty to protect the environment with binding commitments on the signatories, and Al Gore's *An Inconvenient Truth* generated significant public attention to the issue.

But individuals and NGOs were not the only types of non-state actors interested in environmental issues. Businesses quickly realized they had a very large stake in any changes in environmental policy, so they got involved. After the 1992 Earth Summit, concerned businesses began to organize and to direct their focus at UN attempts to have a global, environmental treaty featuring binding commitments on its signatories. The World Business Council for Sustainable Development (WBCSD) was formed in 1995. Composed of the CEOs of over 200 corporations, the WBCSD is headquartered in Geneva, Switzerland. The organization became involved in the negotiations following the 1992 Earth Summit, and with its fossil fuel industry members actively involved, it prevented the binding targets for fossil fuel emissions in the 1997 Kyoto Protocol from being more aggressive than they were.

Constructivists note the importance of how issues are framed. The social construction of a narrative in

which an issue is placed can be crucial. In developed countries, business organizations like the WBCSD were quite successful in framing environmental issue solving in market terms. Market-based mechanisms seemed to offer a way for state actors to avoid having to make difficult societal and budgetary choices, and smart business leaders saw the opportunity to direct environmental policy debates in directions that had fewer negative effects on their bottom lines. Businesses could be "green" and profitable, too.

So which types of non-state actors have more influence with the UN as it addresses environmental issues? As Weiss et al. (2017) conclude, over time environmental NGOs like civil society organizations (CSOs) and state actors from the global south began to lose influence within the UN to transnational corporations (TNCs), business organizations, and state actors from the global north:

> The shift in UN architecture and agency, with increased TNC and reduced CSO influence, has led UN documents away from effective regulation and control, reducing prospects for their implementation at the national level, as well as conditions for reducing emissions and increasing environmental justice. (p. 1032)

Are the Marxist analysts right? Do those who have the gold get to make the rules?

1. Is non-state actor involvement in environmental policymaking a necessary ingredient for success or progress?

2. If so, which types of non-state actors do you want speaking for your interests?

3. Which type of theory do you feel is most useful here? ●

---

of environmental challenges facing the planet (see "Theory in Action: Which Non-state Actors Matter Most in the Environmental Arena?" for more on the role of non-state actors). These recognitions of the dangers resulting from certain human activities are nothing new. By the 19th century, urban reformers were beginning to call for water sanitation systems, proper waste disposal, and in the United States the Sierra Club was formed to protect wilderness areas from being spoiled by extensive human development.

In the early 20th century, wars and depression generally overshadowed efforts by reformers to protect coasts from pollution and people from the dangers of leaded gasoline. However, by the 1950s, deadly smog epidemics had helped promote more research into air quality, and the 1962 publication of *Silent Spring* by Rachel Carson helped launch the modern environmental movement. The fact that Cleveland's Cuyahoga River was so heavily polluted that it caught fire in 1969 further dramatized the problem. Also that year, SCOPE—the Scientific Committee on Problems of the Environment—was formed as an international NGO to coordinate science-based knowledge of environmental issues. The following year, at the prompting of US Senator Gaylord Nelson and aided by the organizational resources of Common Cause, the first Earth Day was held on April 22, 1970.

Over time, many NGOs took on the task of educating the public about the need to conserve resources and protect the environment. For example, Friends of the Earth International started in 1969, and it now links a network of 73 national environmental groups, with a total membership of over 2 million people. Based in Amsterdam, Netherlands, it focuses on promoting environmentally sustainable practices around the globe. Founded in 1974, Worldwatch Institute was created to be a totally independent research network promoting sustainable development and has partner organizations in 24 countries. Networks composed of NGOs like these pool resources, create human networks, publish research, create programs at the grassroots level, and promote actions by states and international organizations (see Chapter 13 for more on such transnational advocacy networks). For example, the Earth Day Network sponsors the Green Cities and Local Governments Campaign. Because over half the world's population now lives in urban areas, the campaign focuses on improvements in energy use, building construction, and transportation systems to reduce the **carbon footprint** of our urban areas.

However, for some people and organizations, such efforts are not enough. Some activists want to get out there and save the planet themselves. A few put themselves in harm's way to stop actions that they oppose. During the Cold War, for example, Greenpeace tried to stop French nuclear weapons tests in the Pacific by sailing its ship—the *Rainbow Warrior*—into the area of the nuclear tests. The crew was literally daring France to conduct the tests, knowing that people surely would die in the process. The tactic worked, but needless to say, it irritated the French government considerably. In 1985, the French dispatched a covert operations team that sunk the *Rainbow Warrior* in a New Zealand harbor, but one of the ship's crew was killed and two French operatives were captured before they could leave the country. The UN Secretary-General arbitrated the resulting dispute between New Zealand and France, and a deal was struck. The French were

required to acknowledge that they had broken international law, to formally apologize, to compensate the victim's family and Greenpeace, and to compensate New Zealand. In return, the two French operatives were ordered to serve three-year prison terms at a French naval base in the Pacific, but the French allowed them to return to France after less than two years. A new *Rainbow Warrior II* now sails the seas on behalf of Greenpeace's mission to promote sustainable use of the planet's resources. Yet for some people, Greenpeace hasn't done nearly enough, as discussed in the box "Spotlight On: Sea Shepherd."

12-2c International Organization Actions

Given the global nature of environmental challenges, coordinating the actions of states and NGOs is essential. International organizations can perform such tasks, as well as actively address the many environmental challenges found in the global commons. The United Nations has been at the forefront in this regard. The UN's environmental efforts are too numerous to discuss in their entirety, but we can examine what the UN has done through focusing on one important policy issue—the problems associated with global climate change—as well as other environmental priorities.

The UN and Global Climate Change

As we suggested earlier, global climate change is a problem that the international community has taken seriously for decades. The magnitude of the problem and its global scope—whether located within the territorial boundaries of sovereign states or in the global commons—make it the focus of concerted efforts at international cooperation. In 1972, the UN Conference on the Human Environment met in Stockholm, Sweden, and among its recommendations was the establishment of a new UN entity for the environment. That entity was the **UN Environment Programme (UNEP)**, which made addressing global climate change one of its priorities. By the mid-1980s, there was a growing awareness of the apparent impacts of global climate change, and in 1988, the previously mentioned Intergovernmental Panel on Climate Change was formed. This group of hundreds of scientists was aided by hundreds of economists, diplomats, and other public officials in its efforts to document the impacts of global climate change, determine its causes, and seek strategies to offset its effects. A series of environmental conferences resulted in the drafting of the **UN Framework Convention on Climate Change (FCCC)**, which was approved at the UN's Earth Summit in Rio de Janeiro, Brazil, in 1992. The convention recommended that fossil fuel emissions

----

carbon footprint: the amount of carbon dioxide we generate through our daily activities.

UN Environment Programme (UNEP): the UN agency dedicated to environmental protection, created in 1972.

UN Framework Convention on Climate Change (FCCC): a 1992 treaty calling for the reduction of fossil fuel emissions to 1990 levels by 2000.

Sea Shepherd

Canadian Paul Watson, one of the original cofounders of Greenpeace, left that organization to form what is now the Sea Shepherd organization in 1977 because he felt Greenpeace had become too timid. He wanted sea mammals aggressively protected, and state actors weren't doing enough to help. In the past, Sea Shepherd members physically placed themselves between baby Arctic seals and the hunters trying to kill them for their pelts. Given that the seal hunters used clubs, getting between them and their "harvests" was at times a risky proposition.

More famously, members also tried to sabotage whaling ships at sea and even placed themselves between whaling ships and the whales being hunted for their meat and oil. Members attacked the whaling ships and their crews with water cannons and stink bombs; sometimes they tried to foul the propellers or rudders of whaling ships with chains and ropes. In 2010 a larger Japanese whaling ship collided with the Sea Shepherd's *Ady Gil*, a speedboat valued by the group at $2 million, destroying the smaller boat. Both sides blamed the other for the incident. Just a month later, the Sea Shepherd ship *Bob Barker* collided with the Japanese whaler *Yushin Maru 3* in the waters of Antarctica. Both ships reported only minor damage from the collision. All told, the Sea Shepherds claimed in 2017 they had saved 6,000 whales from death (Watson 2017).

The group's activities have been captured on the reality television program *Whale Wars*, which aired on the cable network Animal Planet from 2008 to 2015. With the resulting publicity, celebrities such as Bridget Bardot, Darryl Hannah, Mick Jagger, Martin Sheen, and Sean Penn endorsed Sea Shepherd's activities, and Bob Barker, the former host of TV's *The Price Is Right*, donated the $5 million needed to buy the ship renamed after him in 2009.

A Sea Shepherd vessel challenges a Japanese whaling vessel in 2008

Is violent confrontation necessary to stop the extermination of some species? Would such violence be justified?

REUTERS/Institute of Cetacean Research/Handout via Reuters

However, mainstream environmental groups routinely criticized Sea Shepherd's aggressive tactics, noting that by attacking others, Sea Shepherd is committing crimes against people or property. In the case of the baby seals, these hunts are sanctioned by Canadian law during specified periods in the year and are thus fully legal. Sea Shepherd members counter with the argument that the Canadian laws are morally wrong and that provisions of international whaling treaties that allow the limited "harvesting" of whales for scientific purposes are intentionally exploited by countries like Japan simply to get whale meat, which the Japanese consider a luxury. In short, in an anarchic international system, if states won't protect animals at risk, members of the Sea Shepherds will. They will do so by enforcing international norms when no one else seems willing to do so.

What do you think? Are Sea Shepherds environmental heroes or criminals? Is it appropriate for NGOs to go beyond monitoring international activity to enforcing international norms and laws through direct, and at times destructive, action? If so, how far should they be willing to go? ●

be reduced to 1990 levels by the year 2000, and it created a **Global Environmental Facility** to collect and distribute the resources needed to enact such reductions on a worldwide basis. Although many environmentalists had pressed for making such fossil fuel emissions reductions mandatory rather than merely voluntary, the United States refused to support mandatory restrictions. As the world's largest fossil fuel

emitter at that time, the United States had leverage. Without some form of US participation in the FCCC, the convention would have little meaning.

The effort to convert voluntary reductions in fossil fuel emissions to mandatory ones began almost

Global Environmental Facility: the UN entity created by the UN Framework Convention on Climate Change to collect and distribute the financial resources needed to combat global climate change.

immediately after the Rio Summit, and it was led (not surprisingly) by the leaders of small island states who feared rising seawaters. In 1997, the **Kyoto Protocol** to the FCCC mandated that 37 developed states and the European Community (the predecessor to the EU) reduce their fossil fuel emissions by an average of 5% from the levels recorded in 1990, but developing countries were encouraged but not mandated to make reductions. Developing country delegates argued that their countries deserved the same right to industrialize by using whatever cheap fuel source was available, just like the developed countries had done in the past. As you can imagine, this did not go over well with the US, which refused to participate. The hard choices implicit in the reductions meant the protocol did not get enough ratifications to go into effect until 2004.

Other efforts continued to seek multilateral compliance with reduction targets for fossil fuel emissions that would include the US and other major emitter states. The only way to get the participation of such major emitters was to make the targets less ambitious and voluntary rather than mandatory. For example, in 2015, 196 countries met in France and concluded the Paris Agreement. In this agreement, which featured important discussions between China and the US (the top two emitters, respectively) on its features and their support, member countries committed to

a. Holding the increase in the global average temperature to well below 2°C above pre-industrial levels and to pursue efforts to limit the temperature increase to 1.5°C above pre-industrial levels, recognizing that this would significantly reduce the risks and impacts of climate change

b. Increasing the ability to adapt to the adverse impacts of climate change and foster climate resilience and low greenhouse gas emissions development, in a manner that does not threaten food production

c. Making finance flows consistent with a pathway toward low greenhouse gas emissions and climate-resilient development

To do so, the agreement specified that member countries set ambitious "nationally determined contributions" that represented progress, but each country was free to chart its own course. In this sense, it was voluntary. In 2016, the US and China jointly announced their support for the Paris Agreement, and 173 other countries and the EU all signed the

agreement on the first day possible—Earth Day (April 22, 2016). Since then, all countries have signed or, in the case of Syria and Nicaragua, announced their intention to sign, the agreement. However, in 2017, US President Donald Trump announced that the US was withdrawing from the accord, citing concerns about economic growth, US jobs, and the costs of global climate change assistance. The US withdrawal was completed in late 2020. Thus, the US is the lone holdout on an otherwise global accord. See the box "Foreign Policy in Perspective: A Lonely 'Leader'?" for more on the US and climate change.

The UN and Other Global Priorities

For all the talk about it, global climate change is only one of UNEP's priority areas. Beyond global climate change, UNEP's five other priority areas deal with disasters and conflicts, ecosystem management, environmental governance, harmful substances, and resource efficiency.

Disasters and conflicts present a variety of challenges. In recent years, UNEP sought to reduce the impact of ozone-depleting chemicals and to protect wetlands for migratory birds in war-torn Afghanistan, fought the dumping of toxic waste in Côte d'Ivoire, and improved access to drinking water in fast-growing Kinshasa, capital of the Democratic Republic of the Congo. Hurricane relief continued in Haiti, and in Nigeria, UNEP focused on cleaning up the chronic oil spills in the Ogoniland region of the Niger Delta. In Sudan, UNEP projects included fostering sustainable development and women's empowerment in conflict areas, as well as holding back desert growth and restoring agriculture in Northern Darfur. Famine relief was required in South Sudan. Further, the destruction caused by wars releases toxic substances into the environment, damages the ecosystem, and typically leads to the breakdown of local infrastructures that deal with environmental issues. UNEP has been called in to deal with the environmental consequences of wars in or near Afghanistan, Albania, the Democratic Republic of the Congo, Iraq, Lebanon, Liberia, Macedonia, the occupied territories of Palestine, Rwanda, Serbia, Sudan, and South Sudan.

Ecosystem management is another priority for UNEP. Preserving fragile or endangered ecosystems first requires a focus on developing the tools to manage ecosystems. These tools include building the scientific knowledge base required to understand how the material environment and living organisms interact and then learning how best to share such knowledge with relevant officials and other stakeholders in the area. Then these methods need to be put into use in locales where such tools are underdeveloped or missing. To date, UNEP has undertaken ecosystem management initiatives involving the broader

Kyoto Protocol: an addendum to the UN Framework Convention on Climate Change, which was negotiated in 1997 and entered into force in 2005; it imposed mandatory reductions in fossil fuel emissions for 37 developed countries and the European Community.

A Lonely "Leader"? The US and Climate Change

In 2015, 195 countries unanimously established the Paris Agreement, an accord that united developed and developing countries to commitments to undertake "ambitious" national efforts to combat climate change, with multilateral support in the form of global climate change funds from the developed world. Less than two years later, every country in the world—along with the European Union, which added its own commitment—had joined the agreement or announced its plans to do so in the very immediate future (Nicaragua had initial objections that the Paris Agreement was not demanding enough; Syria announced its intention to join in November 2017). Every country except one, that is.

The sole holdout is the United States. In June 2017, US President Donald Trump announced his intention to withdraw from the Paris Agreement, a process that would, at the earliest, begin in November 2019 and be completed in November 2020 because of the agreement's requirements. In doing so, the new administration ignored the influential role of the US in forging the agreement during the Obama administration in 2015, as well as the fact that every other country in the world supports the accord.

In addition to withdrawing from the Paris Agreement, by 2019 the Trump administration scrapped a clean power plan to cut fossil fuel emissions, loosened regulations on air pollution, rescinded or loosened rules about methane releases, reduced prior fuel economy targets for vehicles, narrowed the definition of what waters the US could regulate, took actions to make it harder to protect endangered species, made it easier to engage in commercial logging on federal lands, reduced the size of two national monuments (like national parks but created by executive order), reduced criminal enforcement of environmental laws

to a 30-year low, and removed climate change from the list of official national security threats.

Why would the US withdraw from the Paris Agreement and take these other steps to weaken environmental protection? According to Trump, the Paris Agreement undermined the US economy and hurt its ability to grow, compete, and expand jobs. He also claimed that the agreement encroached on US sovereignty and demanded costly US assistance to the developing world, draining funds needed at home while giving those countries advantages over the US in the competitive global economy.

Yet, *every* other country in the world supports the agreement. The US announcement was met with criticism by US allies and other countries, and it faced intense political opposition at home as well. We all benefit from clean air and a reduction in greenhouse gases. Yet whose responsibility is it to reduce emissions and clean up the air? Is it those with the most money or those who contribute the most to the problem? Again, the "tragedy of the commons" suggests that when something benefits everyone yet isn't anyone's particular responsibility—like clean air—fixing problems can get complicated. Poor countries generally want rich countries to provide the funding to improve their air quality as well, while rich countries often think poor countries should clean up their own pollution.

1. Why would the US change its position on the Paris Agreement?

2. What concerns and dynamics does the US decision represent?

3. How does the tragedy of the commons relate to this issue? ●

---

regions of Africa's Congo River Basin and Central Asia's Himalayan mountain range, as well as more specific programs in Kenya, Mali, and Uganda. These efforts also include projects to combat marine litter and the problem of microplastics, promote sustainable livestock production, and create online learning programs for ecosystems protection.

UNEP's environmental governance goals include helping create and support international decision-making processes dealing with environmental governance matters; promoting the implementation of such agreed-upon norms and goals;

helping environmental governing institutions at the regional, subregional, and national levels; and promoting sustainable development at the national level. In Africa and Europe, UNEP has supported ministerial conferences focusing on environmental issues. In Asia, it has focused its efforts on the problem of brown haze in the atmosphere and worked with the World Health Organization to address health issues in East and Southeast Asia. In West Asia, UNEP is helping collect the information needed to create geographic information system (GIS) databases for use in dealing with current and future environmental challenges in the Arab world. In North America, UNEP works with television's Discovery Network as an official partner of its Planet Green channel, building knowledge networks among the viewers. Efforts to combat the effects of harmful substances are another priority for UNEP. There is a convention on the shipment and disposal of hazardous wastes and a policy framework for dealing with hazardous chemicals. UNEP has studied the issue of persistent organic pollutants like polychlorinated biphenyls (or PCBs) and others, and there is a convention on controlling these substances, which are toxic and often carcinogenic. UNEP has also worked to reduce the pollution caused by toxic, heavy metals such as cadmium, lead, and mercury, as well as commonplace pesticides.

The final priority area for UNEP is resource efficiency, which in many ways is another term for **sustainable development**. The idea is to find ways to promote economic growth that do not degrade the environment or deplete nonrenewable resources, and that is a major challenge for the global community. Sustainable development is arguably the 21st century's greatest environmental challenge, so let's devote some special attention to it.

12-3 THE CHALLENGE OF FOSTERING SUSTAINABLE DEVELOPMENT

>> **12-3** Explain the concept of sustainable development and steps toward that goal.

Sustainable development sounds great, doesn't it? Who could object to it? Yet however wonderful it sounds, achieving sustainable development will be a challenge for the international system and its actors. See the box "The Revenge of Geography: What's Up With Mountain Societies?" for a discussion of the relationship of some geographic and environmental features to conflict and problem solving.

As we have seen in other instances, anarchy, diversity, and complexity complicate problem solving, and with sustainable development, there are many moving parts all in motion at once. Promoting sustainable development requires multimodal attacks on many simultaneous fronts by all possible international actors. States, international organizations, and NGOs have all been active. Individual states increasingly embrace environmental policies to address these issues, and people and NGOs have worked together across borders to raise awareness and generate

solutions. The UN's Sustainable Development Goals, which include efforts to improve water use, food supply, pollution, and energy, are a good example of coordinated efforts of the actors. International organizations and NGOs have begun to work on these issues. Other programs, such as the UN Environment Programme and the UN Framework Convention on Climate Change, are also important examples. Looking again at the 17 goals listed in the 2030 Agenda for Sustainable Development helps us understand the diversity and complexity issues faced by the UN in its efforts. Those goals can be divided into three broad approaches. Let's go through them.

12-3a Poverty Reduction

Goal 1 calls for ending poverty in all its forms, which should end hunger, achieve food security, and improve nutrition levels. These are parts of Goal 2. With poverty reduction, states and societies should thus be more able to address healthy lives and promote well-being for all at all ages (Goal 3). With more available money, increased education funding and access should be possible, thus seeking to ensure inclusive and equitable quality education and promote lifelong learning opportunities for all (Goal 4). With increased education and a desire to utilize all the human resources in society, progress might be made on achieving gender equality and empowerment of all women and girls (Goal 5). For example, this was the logic Saudi Arabia used when in 2018 it allowed women to obtain driver's licenses. The argument was that allowing women this greater freedom would help Saudi Arabia enhance its economic growth by getting more educated workers into the workforce.

How might all this work? China provides one example. According to a 2016 Chinese government report (People's Republic of China, State Council 2016), from 2011 to 2015, almost 110 million rural Chinese were lifted out of poverty. This was done using a variety of methods, such as funding improvements in agriculture and animal husbandry; matching national investment to local manufacturing needs; subsidizing rural medical care; resettling rural residents to areas with more job opportunities; improving rural education through increased funding and subsidizing the pay of teachers willing to relocate to rural areas; and promoting women's empowerment through increased access to job training, education, and increased funding for preventive medical care. Thus, reducing poverty may require a multifaceted approach.

12-3b Sustainable Economic Development

Obviously, poverty reduction requires sustainable economic development to fund it; although trees are

---

sustainable development: promoting economic growth without degrading the environment or depleting its nonrenewable resources.

What's Up With Mountain Societies?

Does geography play a role in conflict? The answer is easy: Of course it does. For example, any study of intrastate conflict—civil war—requires controlling for mountains because the insurgents can hide in them. Sure, we could talk about conflicts over territory or valuable resources—such as food, water, oil, and so on. A good case can be made that World War II began as both Germany and Japan had a need for more resources or "living room" than their territories provided.

But what about altitude? Do mountainous terrains somehow produce more violence? Judith Matloff, makes that case in her 2017 book *No Friends but the Mountains: Dispatches From the World's Violent Highlands*. At one point her son asked her why so many of the conflicts she had covered were in mountainous locations. She was struck by the pattern she saw. What makes high-altitude locations more prone to violence?

One factor is that mountains create natural boundaries, which often become state borders. So conflicts arise when these borders are challenged. Take the mountainous region where Pakistan, India, and China meet. The Indians and Pakistanis have fought two wars over control of Kashmir (India is up 2–0). In 1962, China and India fought over control of the mountainous Aksai Chin region of Kashmir, and China won. Another good example is found in the mountainous southern Caucasus region where Europe and Southwest Asia meet. Russia has been fighting to control that region for well over a century.

Beyond borders, there's another factor at play here—difficulty of governmental control. Just like mountains can create a physical barrier for a state border, they can also create a barrier to central governmental control of the region. The locals may create their own rules, norms, and customs and may not appreciate the government's efforts to impose control from outside. Think about what used to be called the North-West Frontier Province of Pakistan, now called Khyber Pakhtunkhwa. This territory helped form the border between India and Afghanistan during British colonial rule. Now it lies on the Pakistani side of the border with Afghanistan, but the Pakistani government finds it extraordinarily difficult to control. The result is that it became a safe harbor for terror groups operating in Afghanistan and elsewhere. Similarly, the mountainous Chiapas region of southern Mexico has often been ignored by the far-away government in Mexico City. Is it any wonder that it created the breeding grounds for Zapatista rebels or narcotraffickers?

Just another day on the road in Pakistan's Khyber Pakhtunkhwa region

Can you see why this area would be hard for the government in Islamabad to control?

Metin Aktas/Anadolu Agency/Getty Images

There's another factor—cultural isolation. Mountains create valleys where people tend to live, but the mountains keep the valleys separated. As a result, there's less interaction between locals and nonlocals. The resulting parochialism often generates a deep suspicion of outsiders or anyone seen as the "other." Conflicts between tribal or ethnic groups plague Afghanistan; ethnic conflicts have roiled both Bosnia and Kosovo. The Basques in Spain share this pattern, as do the Kurds in both Iraq and Syria. In fact, a 1993 book about the Kurds by John Bulloch and Harvey Morris shared a title with Matloff's book—*No Friends but the Mountains: The Tragic History of the Kurds*. All of these examples share mountainous terrain.

So how do we explain Switzerland's long history as a country whose neutrality has been recognized for centuries? It's mountainous, and it routinely gets listed as having the best quality of life in the world. It turns out that Switzerland is the exception that proves the rule. Its mountains provide a very difficult barrier for any outside attacker to overcome. As for the lack of intrastate violence, remember that Switzerland's government is based on a loose confederation of cantons, each of which has a significant degree of local control. So the Swiss managed to break the pattern.

1. What other conflicts can be associated with mountainous terrain?

2. What happens when environmental catastrophes happen in remote mountain areas? How do governments cope? ●

great for the environment, money still does not grow on them. Goal 8 calls for the promotion of sustained, inclusive, and sustainable economic growth, full and productive employment, and decent work for all. Meeting this goal would require a resilient infrastructure with inclusive and sustainable industrialization, which fosters innovation (Goal 9). The accomplishment of these goals by many countries should result in reduced inequality both within and among countries (Goal 10). That should make Goal 11 more attainable, making cities and human settlements inclusive, safe, resilient, and sustainable. To the extent that such progress is made, the result could be more peaceful and inclusive societies with increased access to justice for all and institutions that are effective, accountable, and inclusive (Goal 16). Yet all these efforts would benefit from improved global implementation efforts and a revitalized global partnership for sustainable development (Goal 17).

All countries would benefit from sustainable economic development, but some seem more likely candidates to make progress than others. In world systems theory terms, semi-periphery countries have considerable potential for progress in this area. Countries such as China, India, Mexico, and others have increased their economic means and may be able to invest in the kinds of institutions and infrastructure to make significant progress in a reasonably short period of time. We've already discussed China's efforts to promote sustainable development, so let's talk about India and Mexico. India is investing to rapidly expand roads to all villages; it is investing in basic agriculture infrastructure and job creation programs in rural areas, increasing access to mobile phones, and electronically disbursing support payments for the poor; for those facing food insecurity, it has issued food ration cards to the senior female head of each household (not the male); and it is investing in rural education, housing, and energy projects. Finally, India's National Health Policy is taking on the challenge of universalizing primary medical care for all. For its part, Mexico has focused on the development of modern manufacturing technologies to move beyond just assembling components into electronic goods. The result is major new automobile factories in Mexico that elevate local wage scales. Mexico is now among the top 10 auto manufacturers in the world supplying nearly 20% of the US auto market, with plants by BMW, Daimler (Mercedes Benz), Chrysler, Ford, General Motors, Honda, Kia, Mazda, Nissan, Toyota, and Volkswagen. NAFTA sure helped Mexico's auto industry.

12-3c Resource Preservation

Sustainable economic development hinges on the preservation of crucial resources. Agricultural practices will need to be adapted to make them sustainable over the long term (Goal 2). Farmers and livestock herders may have to change long-standing ways of doing things. People will need enough freshwater supplies to meet consumption and sanitation needs (Goal 6). Energy supplies will require careful innovation, to produce enough energy to meet our needs without harming the environment or enhancing climate change (Goals 7 and 13). At the same time, both land and water ecosystems need protection, for their own sakes and for the sake of humankind (Goals 14 and 15). In short, all these resource conservation and enhancement efforts will probably be required to ensure sustainable consumption and production patterns (Goal 12).

As noted earlier, there are many moving parts to the challenge of sustainable economic development. It will take investments of money, time, education, and awareness raising to get buy-in from all concerned stakeholders. The degree to which that will occur in an international system marked by sovereign states of highly varying wealth remains to be seen.

12-4 EMERGING ARENAS OF COMPETITION AND COOPERATION

>> 12-4 Recognize emerging arenas of global competition and cooperation.

The combination of rapid technological advances and heightened connections due to globalization has increased the size of what we first thought of as the global commons. On the one hand, new spaces are emerging as opportunities for competition or cooperation, while on the other, new pressures arise from the increased connectivity of humans and societies. This combination affects international relations in the 21st century in new and/or heightened ways. Let's talk about some of these new arenas.

12-4a Maritime Developments

For decades, the Chinese government claimed the South China Sea as its territorial waters. It's called the South China Sea for a reason, right? In 1947, the then-Chinese government issued a map with an Eleven-Dash Line that included most of the South China Sea. In 1952, the new Communist regime in Beijing "gave back" the Gulf of Tonkin to Vietnam, making it a Nine-Dash Line demarking China's claim to the waters and their resources.

For years, other countries—Vietnam, the Philippines, Taiwan, Malaysia, and Brunei—also maintained their own claims to these waters. In the

1990s, the various countries escalated their naval patrols in the area, which at times began to fire shots at one another. In the early 2000s, they tried to drive off competitors' ships exploring for undersea oil and natural gas. To solidify their claim, beginning around 2013, the Chinese began dredging sand from the seabed and dumping it onto reefs in the area. Soon these outcroppings of coral began to look like islands. The Philippines brought a claim against China to the Permanent Court of Arbitration at The Hague, which in 2016 ruled against China. China ignored the ruling and continued to build islands.

What's at stake here? First, international law under the UN Conference on the Law of the Sea gives states a 12-mile territorial sea off their coasts. These waters, and everything in and under them, belong to the coastal state. Beyond that, coastal states have first right to exploit the sea and seabed for economic value out to a total of 200 miles off their coasts. Thus, with overlapping national claims to parts of the South China Sea, things get complicated. Moreover, no one outside China seems to agree that China's claims go beyond the normal 200-mile limit. Second, significant resources are at stake. In addition to the commercial fishing rights involved, there's thought to be considerable oil and natural gas reserves under these waters. Third, whoever controls these waters may control international shipping through them. According to the Council on Foreign Relations (2020), over $3 trillion in trade and 40% of the world's shipments of liquefied natural gas pass through these waters annually.

Given the stakes involved, more than just the coastal competitors have become involved. The US, the UK, and Australia have sent their ships through these seas and their aircraft through its airspace in what are dubbed "freedom-of-navigation" operations, and Japan has sold naval vessels to Vietnam and the Philippines so that they can more capably defend their territorial claims. Chinese ships and aircraft normally shadow these others and at times have come dangerously close. The Chinese have responded with increased naval patrols through these waters, fortified by some of their new islands. For example, Fiery Cross Reef/Yongshu has an airstrip long enough for combat jets and bombers, missile batteries, radars, and troops barracks. Given all these military forces operating in close quarters, any mistakes could turn deadly.

While the competition is not yet as advanced, the Arctic Ocean is a similar new area of maritime competition. Global climate change has resulted in so much shrinking of the Arctic ice cap that much of the Arctic Ocean is now navigable. For months each year, ships can now transit between the Atlantic and Pacific Oceans via the Arctic, often shaving weeks off their previous travel times. Where ships can navigate, fishing and oil and gas exploration can occur. Russia

The Fiery Cross Reef located in the South China Sea
Does building new islands give you legitimacy to exploit additional maritime resources?
DigitalGlobe via Getty Images

and Canada have the longest coastlines on the Arctic, but Norway, Denmark, Finland, Iceland, and the US have Arctic coastlines as well. All want in on the sizable commercial and national security benefits of this recently accessible area.

Russia staked its claim in 2007 by planting a Russian flag on the Arctic seabed at the North Pole. Since then, it has built numerous new naval and air bases on the coast and enlarged others. To fully control these waters, icebreakers are needed, and there's an "arms race" of sorts with them as well. The three largest fleets of icebreakers (Russia, Finland, and Canada) total 63 icebreakers, with 22 more in some stage of construction or planning.

Pardon the pun, but things are heating up in the Arctic. In 2018, the first container ship successfully made the passage from the Pacific to the Baltic, shaving over a week off its normal travel time. Now numerous container ship companies are negotiating transit rates with Russia. To keep its foot in the door, NATO has conducted naval exercises in the Arctic, and Russia has stepped up its Arctic military exercises as well. As these Arctic Ocean and South China examples show, new initiatives and technologies are opening up new areas of the global commons for competition and cooperation.

12-4b Cyberspace as a New Arena (and Outer Space as a Revisited One)

In the 1980s and early 1990s, limited governmental and private sector computer networks were developed creating a cyberspace of interconnected digital technologies, but the Internet as we know it today dates to the creation of the World Wide Web and its browsers in the mid- to late 1990s. Since then, almost every place in the world has become connected via the Internet, and computers and smartphones connect us easily to it. We now rely on the Internet for business, pleasure, information, and personal and professional communication.

For all the benefits of knowing almost anything and communicating instantaneously, this new virtual space comes with dangers as well. As we discussed in Chapter 5, cyberwarfare is the attempt by one state or nation to cause disruption, discord, damage, death, or destruction by using computers and other digital devices to carry out digital attacks on the computer systems of another. Hacking and hackers are at the core of cyberwarfare, but the concept refers to the actions of states/nations, or directed by states/nations, rather than those in which individual hackers or criminal groups might engage. However, non-state actors such as terrorist groups may also engage in cyberwarfare. This could range from online bullying to planting malicious information online to trying to take down a country's electric grid or banking systems.

Cyberattacks are increasingly common. For example, in 2014, North Korea hacked the network of Sony Pictures Corporation after it released *The Interview*, a movie making fun of North Korean leaders. In 2017, it hacked the network of Bangladesh's Central Bank, making off with a reported $81 million before it was stopped. Other commercial cyberattacks followed, often ransomware attacks where a corporation's computer network was effectively shut down or critical information stolen and held until a ransom was paid. In 2016 and 2017, Russia's Internet Research Agency launched large-scale initiatives to influence first US and then French presidential elections. Deceptive websites and social media platforms were used to sow social discord and discredit candidates thought to be anti-Kremlin. Indications are that similar Russian cyberattacks began well in advance of the 2020 US presidential election.

There are many reasons why cyberwarfare is troubling. First, it takes relatively little investment compared to physical forms of warfare. Second, the more economically developed countries are, the more they rely on computer networks for virtually everything—utilities, transportation, banking and finance, commercial activity, and logistics of all kinds. Their vulnerabilities expand exponentially. Third, there's very little international law governing cyberspace. There is a Convention on Cybercrime that was drafted in 2001 by the Council of Europe along with Canada, Japan, the Philippines, South Africa, and the United States. By 2019, 64 countries had ratified it. The convention seeks to promote and harmonize national laws involving cybercrime and promote international cooperation in policing cyberspace. Yet other questions loom. Perhaps the most significant is this: Are cyberattacks legally considered acts of war?

There's one more thing on cyberspace's horizon. People on the frontiers of the digital world are now talking about the coming technological singularity of connecting the cyber and physical worlds. In the words of a former technical director of mission analytics at the US National Security Agency:

> Cyber Physical Systems are creating "open systems" able to dynamically reconfigure, reorganize and operate in closed loops with often full computational and communication capability. Machine Learning can be fully integrated within a CPS network and this will soon be followed by partial, and eventually full, Artificial Intelligence—often without the ability of humans to observe the ongoing processes of the system. (Trevino 2019: 3)

Whether this coming singularity of the virtual and physical worlds benefits or terrorizes humankind is yet to be known, but the international system cannot regulate cyberspace as it is currently configured. What will happen in the future?

Finally, concerns about cyberspace return our attention back to outer space. While exploitation of outer space used to be the preserve of just a few states, now many countries are launching their own satellites, to improve their communication and Internet access, weather forecasting, and intelligence collection. Private companies are now active as well, with companies such as US-based SpaceX and UK-based OneWeb launching dozens and dozens of small satellites to expand global access to broadband services. This increased connectivity could promote greater worldwide cooperation.

However, outer space was once an arena of conflict, with the US Strategic Defense Initiative (aka "Star Wars") as the archetype of what could lie ahead. It envisioned weaponizing space as a defensive shield against the Soviet Union, but defensive systems would destabilize mutual deterrence or could be reconfigured as offensive systems. Either of these possibilities was scary, but the dissolution of the Soviet Union essentially ended the program. However, in 2019, the US created a new component to its military establishment. The purpose of "Space Command"—which would have a Space Force—is to ensure "space superiority." That sounds like a move that will be contested by others with the ability to do so. Stay tuned.

12-4c Human Migration

As we have noted throughout this book, human security is everyone's goal—to be safe, to be able to take care of ourselves and our families, and to have a positive future in sight. Wherever human security is threatened, people will always try to leave, and globalization makes such human migrations take on a new scale. In the 21st century, millions have tried to escape danger or just seek better opportunities, and their numbers are stressing their new host countries.

In recent years, three waves of migrants poured out of the Middle East and North Africa. The first wave was in response to civil violence and state repression brought on by the 2011–2012 Arab Spring and represented the largest mass migration since World War II. By 2015, about 16.7 million people had fled their countries, and 33 million more were still in their country but internally displaced from their homes (Kingsley 2015). While most refugees are housed in neighboring countries, conservative estimates are that over half a million made it to Europe. The second wave of migrants fled North and West Africa due to climate change. Increasing heat and decreasing rainfall meant people could no longer provide for their families through farming and livestock production. Unfortunately, separating the numbers of these migrants from others is very difficult, but it appears thousands went to Europe. Third, by 2018, nearly 7 million refugees had fled Syria due to its civil war (Todd 2019).

Waves of refugees from violence and deprivation were found in the Americas as well. Violence and crime in Central America drove roughly 250,000 refugees each year to the US from 2016 to 2019 (Leutert and Spalding 2019), causing the US to sharply restrict border crossings. Economic collapse in Venezuela also created a flood of migrants to neighboring countries. By 2019, approximately 4.5 million Venezuelans had fled the country seeking someplace where they could feed their families (UN Migration 2020).

The challenge for the international system, of course, is answering the question of who is responsible for taking care of these staggering numbers of refugees and migrants. Are they everyone's problem or just the problem of the host state? How would realism, liberalism, constructivism, Marxism, feminism, and foreign policy analysis answer such a question?

12-4d Pandemic Diseases

Pandemics—epidemics that spread over a wide area—are not new. In the Middle Ages, the plague may have killed as much as half the population of Europe. From 1918 to 1920, influenza A H1N1—then called the Spanish flu—killed an estimated 50 million people worldwide (proportionally, that's the equivalent of more than 215 million people today). There were no flu vaccines at that time, and the pandemic would have been worse if it was as easy to travel internationally then as it is now.

Despite a variety of flu vaccines now, globalization and the porous nature of state borders in the neo-Westphalian era continue to multiply the possibilities of epidemics going global to become pandemics. Influenza A H1N1—also called swine flu—reappeared in 2009, killing approximately 300,000 people in its first year alone. About half of those killed were in Africa and Southeast Asia (Dawood et al. 2012). An Ebola virus pandemic began in West Africa in 2014 and in two years killed over 10,000 people, with most of the deaths occurring in Africa (Centers for Disease Control and Prevention 2020).

Most recently, in late 2019, a virulent new coronavirus (SARS-CoV-2, often referred to by the disease it causes, COVID-19) began spreading from China to Europe and on to other locations. Like other coronaviruses before it—such as SARS and MERS—it causes cold and flu-like symptoms and targets respiratory systems. Unlike the conventional seasonal flu, however, COVID-19 has a sharply higher death rate. Modern international travel served as key transmission belts for the spread of the highly contagious and harmful disease (see Map 12-3). By the fall of 2020, the virus had swept across globe, infecting more than 25 million people in 188 countries and resulting in almost 1 million deaths. Countries struggled to respond, with some, such as New Zealand, Taiwan, and South Korea, more successful than others, such as the US and Brazil, where the virus continued to spread at an alarming rate. Unfortunately, although the global and transnational nature of the pandemic and its public health consequences clearly demonstrate the need for international cooperation (e.g., Brown and Susskind 2020), little effective effort between states to do so occurred, despite a G20 virtual summit in April 2020 that resulted in pledges by member states to develop health measures, expand medical supplies and research, and increase spending to sustain and boost the global economy. In fact, in September, the US announced that it would not even cooperate with the World Health Organization and the rest of the world to develop and distribute a vaccine. Why do you think global efforts fell short of the cooperation that might have mitigated the problems of the pandemic more effectively? Does this crisis illustrate the tragedy of the commons or something different?

CONCLUSION: MANAGING THE GLOBAL COMMONS

As human activity damages our environment and increases our vulnerability to threats outside state control, the challenges of coping with systemic stresses become everyone's problem—but these involve complex issues. For example, the tradeoff between

MAP 12-3

Air Routes of the World

Think about how many hours separate events in one place from the people in another from this perspective. What does this image suggest about the "transmission belts" that connect the world?

Source: Courtesy of Dr. Dirk Brockmann.

economic growth and protecting the environment is a difficult one for many to accept. Environmentalists are beset by the **time horizon problem**—the fact that the worst effects of the problem have not yet been seen, but to avoid them, one needs to act by spending money or making sacrifices now. Getting people to

....

time horizon problem: the fact that the worst effects of environmental problems have not yet been seen, but to avoid them, one needs to act (and spend money or make sacrifices) now.

sacrifice now for a problem they don't yet see, have not yet experienced, or may never experience personally (though their children probably will) is a tough sell.

The expansion of the global commons—in physical terms as well as virtual ones—confronts an international system still marked by anarchy. Addressing narrowly defined national interests may satisfy realist theorists but may not solve the larger problems. Fostering international cooperation regarding shared problems may become the greatest challenge of the 21st century. ●

KEY CONCEPTS

12-1 Identify the "tragedy of the commons," collective goods, and the environmental challenges facing humankind.

The "tragedy of the commons" refers to the idea that when a resource is shared and no one actor owns it—like air or water—then no one takes responsibility for its protection. So-called public or collective goods—things that benefit everyone, whether or not one pays for their cost or maintenance—are not the responsibility of any one state actor, and thus their care typically falls through the cracks of Westphalian sovereignty. Transnational problems such as pollution, deforestation, desertification, global climate

change, and biodiversity challenges are some key problems of the commons.

12-2 Describe the evolving environmental regime and the challenges of sustainable development.

In the anarchic system of world politics, states, international organizations, and nongovernmental organizations are all involved in the effort to address transnational problems and protect the earth's environment. States have tried many approaches, but there is only so much that individual states can do to solve problems that affect the global commons, and some states are more willing to address them than others. Non-state actors have been especially important to transnational challenges, and their actions often begin at the grassroots level and work up. International organizations can set agendas as well, and they help support and coordinate the actions of states and nongovernmental organizations as well as take direct actions to preserve the global commons themselves. Integral to this is finding ways to promote sustainable economic development that does not harm the environment. Within states, short-term economic security seems to outweigh broader conceptions of human security. Consequently, international organizations such as the United Nations often have to become the lead actors in promoting multilateral cooperation.

12-3 Explain the concept of sustainable development and steps toward that goal.

There are many moving parts to the challenge of sustainable economic development. It will take investments of money, time, education, and awareness raising to get buy-in from all concerned stakeholders. The degree to which that will occur in an international system marked by sovereign states of highly varying wealth remains to be seen. The 2030 Agenda for Sustainable Development helps us understand the diversity and complexity issues faced in these efforts. Sustainable development goals can be divided into three broad approaches: poverty reduction, sustainable economic development, and resource preservation. Promoting sustainable development requires multimodal attacks on many fronts by all possible international actors. States, international organizations, and NGOs have all been active. Individual states increasingly embrace environmental policies to address these issues, and people and NGOs have worked

together across borders to raise awareness and generate sustainable development, the goal of which is to promote economic growth without degrading the environment or depleting its nonrenewable resources. The UN's Sustainable Development Goals, which include efforts to improve water use, food supply, pollution, and energy, are a good example of coordinated efforts of international organizations. Other programs, such as the UN Environment Programme and the UN Framework Convention on Climate Change, are also important examples.

12-4 Recognize emerging arenas of global competition and cooperation.

New arenas for competition and cooperation can be seen in the early 21st century. The desire to control the resources of the South China Sea has driven China to build artificial islands and claim national sovereignty over sea areas claimed by other states or thought to be in the global commons. Climate change has opened up the Arctic Ocean for greater resource exploitation and commercial transit. Now Russia, Canada, and others are competing to control these spaces. The virtual world of cyberspace—and outer space—expands at lightning speed, opening up new ways to connect with others as well as to benefit or harm them. The greater connectivity between societies brought on by globalization has produced millions of refugees and migrants when their human security has been threatened by civil wars, societal violence, or inhospitable climate changes. Increased societal connectivity also leads to continuing pandemics, as epidemics in one country or region can often go global, requiring extreme responses.

KEY TERMS

tragedy of the commons 354

collective goods 354

deforestation 356

greenhouse gases 356

desertification 357

arable land 357

global climate change 357

Intergovernmental Panel on Climate Change (IPCC) 358

genetically modified organisms (GMOs) 362

carbon footprint 368

UN Environment Programme (UNEP) 368

UN Framework Convention on Climate Change (FCCC) 368

Global Environmental Facility 369

Kyoto Protocol 370

sustainable development 372

time horizon problem 378

REVIEW QUESTIONS

1. What is the "tragedy of the commons"?

2. What do terms such as *pollution, deforestation, desertification, global climate change,* and *biodiversity challenges* mean?

3. How have states, international organizations, and nongovernmental organizations dealt with environmental problems?

4. What is sustainable development, and why is it a desirable goal?

5. What new arenas have emerged for global competition and cooperation?

THINK ABOUT THIS

Rapid Urbanization and Environmental Sustainability

According to a 2013 UN report, by 2050, 70% of the world's population will live in urban areas, but 80% of that global urban population will be located in developing countries (UN Department of Economic and Social Affairs 2013). Recent statistics bear out these trends. According to 2018 data from Statista, the top 10 countries with the largest urban populations were as follows: China (837 million), India (461 million), United States (269 million), Brazil (183 million), Indonesia (148 million), Japan (117 million), Russia (107 million), Mexico (105 million), Nigeria (99 million), and Pakistan (74 million). Think about the different types of environmental challenges created by this continuing urban population growth, including those highlighted by the recent and devastating spread of the COVID-19 virus.

Given these challenges, who should bear the "responsibility to protect" the environmental sustainability for those living in these developing world urban areas, and how might that be done?

FOR MORE INFORMATION . . .

Books

Dutton, Peter, Robert S. Ross, and Oystein Tunsjo, eds. (2012). *Twenty-First Century Seapower: Cooperation and Conflict at Sea.* New York, NY: Routledge.

Goldsmith, Connie. (2019). *Pandemic: How Climate, the Environment, and Superbugs Increase the Risk.* Minneapolis, MN: Twenty-First Century Books.

Gore, Al. (2006). *An Inconvenient Truth: The Planetary Emergency of Global Warming and What We Can Do About It.* Emmaus, PA: Rodale Books.

Kremling, Janine, and Amanda M. Sharp Parker. (2017). *Cyberspace, Cybersecurity, and Cybercrime.* Thousand Oaks, CA: Sage.

O'Neill, Kate. (2017). *The Environment and International Relations,* 2nd ed. New York, NY: Cambridge University Press.

Sen, Amartya. (1999). *Development as Freedom.* New York, NY: Anchor Books.

Movies

The Cove (2009)
The Day After Tomorrow (2004)
Erin Brockovich (2000)
An Inconvenient Truth (2006)
Interstellar (2014)
Medicine Man (1992)

Websites

Alternative Energy: http://www.altenergy.org
Carbon Footprint Calculator: http://www.carbonfootprint.com/calculator.aspx
National Geographic, Environment: https://www.nationalgeographic.com/environment

Videos

Mark. Bittman, "What's Wrong With What We Eat." *TED Talks:* http://www.ted.com/talks/lang/eng/mark_bittman_on_what_s_wrong_with_what_we_eat.html

Pollan. Michael. "A Plant's-Eye View." *TED Talks:* http://www.ted.com/talks/michael_pollan_gives_a_plant_s_eye_view.html

The Salton Sea, An Example of Environmental Degradation in the United States: The Accidental Sea: http://www.youtube.com/watch?v=otIU6Py4K_A

NOAA

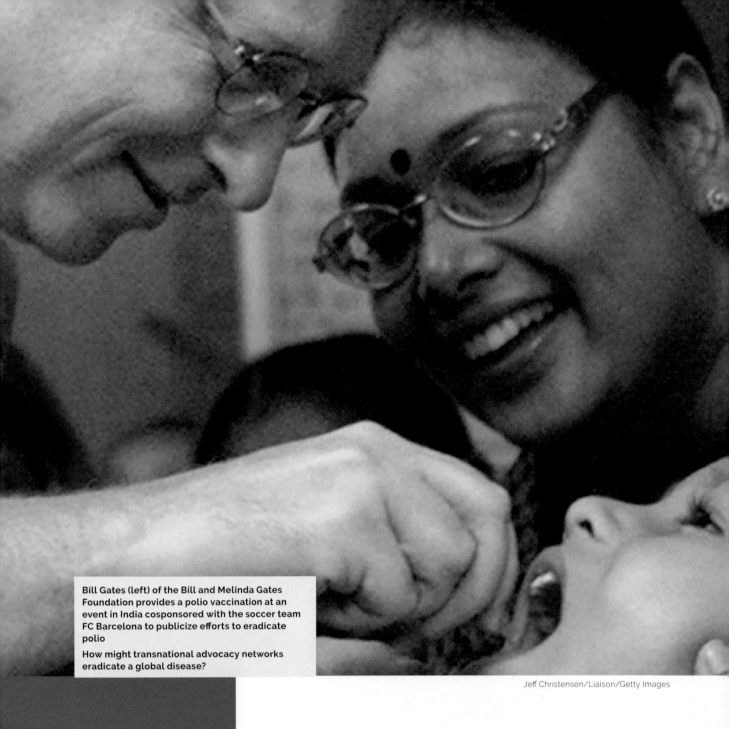

Bill Gates (left) of the Bill and Melinda Gates Foundation provides a polio vaccination at an event in India cosponsored with the soccer team FC Barcelona to publicize efforts to eradicate polio

How might transnational advocacy networks eradicate a global disease?

Jeff Christensen/Liaison/Getty Images

13 Transnational Advocacy Networks

Changing the World?

Learning Objectives

After studying this chapter, you will be able to . . .

13-1 Explain the concept of transnational advocacy networks (TANs) and how they differ from other international actors.

13-2 Identify how TANs affect human security.

13-3 Describe the two major types of TANs and the kinds of actions in which they engage.

Chapter Outline

13-1 What Are Transnational Advocacy Networks?

13-2 How Do Transnational Advocacy Networks Affect Human Security?

13-3 The Diverse World of Transnational Advocacy Networks

Why Do People Still Get Polio?

Poliomyelitis, more commonly known as polio, is a highly contagious viral infection that attacks the central nervous system and causes paralysis that can range from mild to acute. *There is no cure.* In the 1950s, it was common to see worst-case polio victims totally enclosed from their necks down in metal cylinders called "iron lungs" that assisted their breathing. However, the introduction of newly developed vaccines in the 1960s immunized the body so that the virus could not survive. Without human hosts for the virus, it died out.

Or did it? Although the virus virtually disappeared from wealthy and developed nations that could afford mass inoculation campaigns relying on an injectable vaccine made from a dead poliovirus strain, it never died out in other places. By 2019, only Afghanistan and Pakistan suffered from the traditional form of the wild virus. However, many developing countries rely on a cheaper, oral vaccine based on a weakened but live version of the virus. Over time, that milder live version of the virus spreads through communities and strengthens naturally. In 2019, new polio outbreaks were reported in China, Myanmar, Pakistan, the Philippines, and several African countries. Although the case numbers are relatively low, they are rising (Beaubien 2019).

Because polio never fully disappeared, in 2010 the Global Polio Eradication Initiative (GPEI) was started. This initiative is a network of international organizations (IOs), nongovernmental organizations (NGOs), state actors, and private individuals that promotes efforts to combat polio and coordinates actions for the greatest impact. For the 2013–2020 period, nearly $7 billion was pledged by states and NGOs for this purpose. In 2016 alone, $972 million was allocated or disbursed to combat polio. The largest share for 2016 (57%) came from NGOs and philanthropies like the Bill and Melinda Gates Foundation ($292 million) and Rotary International ($106 million). Abu Dhabi's Crown Prince Mohammed bin Zayed al Nahyan contributed $30 million by himself. States contributed the other 43%, with the largest donors being the US ($121 million), the UK ($54 million), and Norway ($32 million; Global Polio Eradication Initiative 2016). In 2020, GPEI's efforts were concentrated in the three remaining countries—Afghanistan, Nigeria, and Pakistan—where the disease is endemic (Global Polio Eradication Initiative 2020).

GPEI's efforts to eradicate polio and to prevent its return are certainly in the interest of the greater good. This highly contagious disease can be spread easily by an infected person boarding an airplane, and within 12–24 hours that person could arrive anywhere in the world and could have infected all the plane's passengers (if they haven't been immunized). Yet the need for such a network of international actors is troubling, and it raises important questions:

1. Why wasn't the polio problem addressed sooner in developing countries?

2. What do you make of the fact that the second largest share of GPEI's funding comes from the private sector?

3. What other global problems might best be handled by such international networks of actors?

INTRODUCTION: A NEW FORM OF INTERNATIONAL ACTOR?

As we noted in Chapter 2, NGOs have been around for a long time. The Catholic Church has long been an influential NGO—in the pre-Westphalian era, it often had great influence over otherwise independent rulers. Beginning in the early 19th century, civil society organizations, as a type of NGO, were at the heart of the antislavery and women's suffrage movements. In the modern neo-Westphalian system, however, NGOs increasingly work together to achieve common aims, and they often work with other types of actors such as states, IOs, individuals, and social movements. In many ways, these networks represent a major change in world politics, moving away from the old state-centric system emphasized by realists. Some even argue that these persistent networks constitute a new international actor whose essence is cooperation to address global problems. Our focus in this chapter is on these transnational advocacy networks—what they are, what they do, how they affect human security, and what impact they may have in the future.

13-1 WHAT ARE TRANSNATIONAL ADVOCACY NETWORKS?

>> 13-1 **Explain the concept of transnational advocacy networks (TANs) and how they differ from other international actors.**

When we talk about **transnational advocacy networks (TANs)**, the operative word is *networks*. In Chapter 2, we discussed states, IOs, NGOs, and even individuals as types of actors in international politics. TANs are formed when these types of actors come together transnationally in coalitions to form broader recurring networks. Thus, TANs are networks defined by reciprocal, voluntary actions across national borders by domestic and international nongovernmental actors, social movements, multinational or transnational corporations and businesses, individuals, IOs, and states.

....

transnational advocacy networks (TANs): networks defined by reciprocal, voluntary actions across national borders that (a) must include non-state actors (such as individuals acting alone, social movements, transnational or multinational corporations, or nongovernmental organizations), (b) may include states or international organizations as well, and (c) represent a recurring, cooperative partnership with (d) differentiated roles among the component parts.

Zionism: the movement to create a Jewish homeland in Palestine.

Although some scholars specifically exclude governments from membership in TANs, we take a broader view. We share the idea that any definition of TANs *must* include non-state actors such as NGOs, social movements, or individuals because a network comprised solely of governmental actors would be an IO, an international regime, or perhaps some form of alliance structure. Thus, the presence of nongovernmental actors is the key to identifying TANs. That said, other national and international governmental actors may often act as network members when they contribute to the network by providing it with funding and other forms of sponsorship or by actively promoting its goals, as shown in the chapter-opening vignette (Keck and Sikkink 1998; Slaughter 2004). So our working definition of a TAN is a multinational network that (a) must include non-state actors (such as individuals acting alone, social movements, multinational or transnational corporations, or NGOs), (b) may include states or IOs as well, and (c) is a recurring, cooperative partnership with (d) differentiated roles among the component parts. The idea of different actors with differentiated roles is what distinguishes TANs from multinational NGOs like Amnesty International that have affiliated chapters doing similar things in many countries.

Skeptics might argue that TANs are nothing more than groups of NGOs, but the persistent issue networks they create and operate are a product of the neo-Westphalian world and globalization. Certainly, early versions of such networks played roles in world politics; they probably arose as soon as people began to cross national borders regularly. For instance, during the era of the Crusades, such a network linked European governments, the Roman Catholic Church, wealthy (and pious) individuals, and the Poor Fellow-Soldiers of Christ and of the Temple of Solomon—better known as the Knights Templar. The values these actors shared included securing Jerusalem and the surrounding area as bastions of Christianity and safeguarding the ability of Christian pilgrims to travel to and from the Holy Land safely. Later this network evolved into one of the first international banking systems, as the Knights Templar created a monetary transfer process that freed travelers from having to carry large amounts of cash and from which the Knights Templar profited handsomely.

Additional examples include **Zionism** and the Zionist Organization (now called the World Zionist Organization), created to promote the movement of Jews to Palestine in the early and middle 20th century, and Islamic Relief Worldwide, created in the United Kingdom in 1984 to address problems such as sustainable livelihoods, health and nutrition, water and sanitation, education, orphans and child welfare, and emergency relief and disaster preparedness in Islamic countries.

What we see in these historical examples are earlier versions of TANs—transnational networks dedicated to addressing problems that cross borders. As these examples show, such networks arise and are maintained on the basis of shared values and differentiated roles. Network members advocate and act on shared ideas, positions, or goals, and they make choices to protect, defend, and advance those shared notions. The component parts that make up TANs are unique actors in their own right, but when they join into such networks to pursue shared goals in a cooperative enterprise, they create a new entity entirely.

Although TANs might not exactly be new, the accelerating globalization of the past 50 years or so has greatly facilitated their creation and operation. As noted in Chapter 2, globalization refers to the increasing integration of global society through economic, technological, political, and cultural means. If you are passionate about a subject, you could potentially create a TAN by searching the Internet by topic area or keyword to find other people or organizations that share your values, creating a Facebook page and encouraging others to sign up, or creating a blog or website regarding the subject at hand. Then those identified as sharing your values could be linked, either online or perhaps in person, and the network would be formed. For much of the world, email and social media outlets can be the communications link between network members, and for those areas with limited computer availability, cell phones (and particularly smartphones) can serve this role. What TAN might you want to create? Would it contribute to human security?

13-2 HOW DO TRANSNATIONAL ADVOCACY NETWORKS AFFECT HUMAN SECURITY?

>> **13-2 Identify how TANs affect human security.**

Transnational advocacy networks are innovators. They seek to create or change norms—or unwritten standards of acceptable and unacceptable behavior—which help reduce the consequences of anarchy in the international system that realists tend to emphasize. If successful, their efforts in this regard tend to follow a **norms life cycle** (Finnemore and Sikkink 1998). The first phase of the cycle involves *creating new norms*. The individuals who are passionately committed to the issue, often called **policy entrepreneurs**, do

everything they can to get others to share their vision and commitment. They seek to define or frame the issue in ways designed to persuade others to accept that the values or goals they are pressing are legitimate ones for the public arena. For example, these goals could include the idea that it is unacceptable to ignore the victims of conflicts or that access to adequate nutrition or health care is a human right. The second phase is a *norms cascade*, in which the number of people sharing these values increases until there are enough people pressing the issue that it reaches the agendas of governments, which are held accountable for their actions or inactions on the matter. Examples could include rich countries now routinely budgeting money each year to meet the needs of refugees or being held accountable for their environmental records. Finally, the third phase is *norm internalization*, in which so many international actors share the norm that following it becomes virtually automatic. In such instances, the only time the issue becomes contentious is when the norm is not followed. A good example would be the international shock and outrage directed at the United States for its treatment of detainees in the war on terror that followed the September 11, 2001, attacks on New York City's World Trade Center and the Pentagon, as this behavior violated long-standing Geneva Conventions regarding the treatment of prisoners of war.

In their efforts to create and enforce norms, TANs play at least three important roles in international politics. They popularize ideas, influence states, and encourage and enable cooperation. Let's discuss each of these important roles. Keep in mind that what is most important here is not memorizing the names of actual TANs. Instead, our focus should be on what these examples illustrate in terms of how TANs affect world politics.

13-2a Popularizing Ideas

As we noted in Chapter 3, constructivists argue that reality is socially constructed on the basis of shared ideas. People agree on how things are and then act on that basis. The power of TANs to influence human security comes from this starting point. What does security mean in society? For much of human history, security meant protection from violent harm, and states developed military forces to meet this need. However, in the modern period, other aspects of security have arisen as concerns.

....

norms life cycle: the idea that TANs are successful when they can create new norms, create a norms cascade forcing governments to act on those norms, and get norms internalized to the point that following them becomes routine and largely unquestioned.

policy entrepreneurs: individuals committed to innovative policy change and who voluntarily work to achieve such changes.

What about the consequences of wars? As more and more wars are internal (or intrastate), the fighting takes place in the midst of civilian populations. What do many civilians do in such a situation? As the Syrian civil war illustrates so well, they leave. The problem is that these refugees have pressing needs; in the short term they require water, food, shelter, and medical care, and in the long term they require assistance to go back home to resume their lives or to set up new homes and lives elsewhere. Who calls attention to their needs?

One such group is the Toronto-based Refugee Research Network. Its office is at York University, and its management committee is made up of individuals based in Canada, Colombia, India, Iran, and the United Kingdom. As its website shows (http://refugeeresearch.net), this TAN—like many others—is actually a network of networks. It brings together the Global Refugee Policy Network (centered at Oxford University) to study the problems refugees face and what can be done about them; the Emerging Scholars and Practitioners on Migration Issues Network, which ensures that research continues into the future and that the results of these migration studies get publicized through its journal *Refugee Review* and other social media outlets; the Asia Pacific Forced Migration Connection, which is another network of networks focusing on issues such as refugee law, human trafficking, and the migration of labor; and the Latin American Network for Forced Migration, which is based in Colombia and fosters the sharing of knowledge of forced migration in the region. Through this TAN, policy specialists, scholars, concerned public officials, and like-minded individuals join in the effort to combat one of the most pressing international public policy issues in the early Neo-Westphalian era.

While intrastate wars create refugees, another consequence of wars is the weapons left behind that can still injure or kill. Landmines and cluster munitions are good examples. These cheap and effective weapons are easy to deploy. Unfortunately, very few combatants make the effort to remove them after a conflict. The result is that they cause injury and deaths for local civilians for years after a conflict has ended. Just imagine knowing that you couldn't walk across a field on your way to school because it might be filled with mines. The International Campaign to Ban Landmines is a global network of more than 1,400 different groups active in over 100 countries that brought media attention to these pressing issues. This TAN was formed in 1992 by American aid worker Jody Williams and groups such as Handicap International, Human Rights Watch, Medico International, the Mines Advisory Group, Physicians for Human Rights, and the Vietnam Veterans of America Foundation. When Princess Diana of Wales championed the effort, media attention to this cause increased dramatically, and winning the Nobel Peace Prize in 1997 further bolstered the group's efforts to popularize the need to deal with the problem of landmines and cluster munitions. Following her death, Diana's son Prince Harry continued her work with this effort.

TANs popularize other aspects of human security as well. As noted in Chapter 12, over a billion people are chronically malnourished. One network seeking to publicize that issue, as well as addressing it more directly, is the Global FoodBanking Network (https://www.foodbanking.org). This TAN was created in 2006 by national food bank associations in Argentina, Brazil, Canada, Mexico, and the United States. It has now helped create or link 792 food bank organizations in 32 countries (Global FoodBanking Network 2016). Beyond linking food bank organizations, it promotes global leadership strategies from leaders across 60 countries, shares knowledge and best practices, and provides technical assistance to all involved. Important funding and support for the network come from religious and humanitarian NGOs, foundations

Prince Harry meeting victims of landmines in Mozambique
How has the personal involvement of royals affected this effort?
The HALO Trust/Getty Images

Do TANs Reflect Their Home Cultures?

It's ironic that advocacy networks expressly designed to transcend national borders have become objects of criticism by those who see them as missionaries of a foreign culture. In essence, some see TANs as instruments of a form of cultural imperialism that has clear geographic roots.

The most common expression of this idea begins with the fact that many TANs are headquartered in developed countries, overwhelmingly in North America and Europe. Thus, the norms they popularize are basically *Western* norms. For example, TANs emphasizing the spread of democracy focus on the presidential or parliamentary forms of democracy practiced in Europe and North America. Critics would say that the result is an overemphasis on a particular *form* of democracy—with a resulting obsession by Westerners with elections and civil society organizations—and a lack of appreciation for non-Western modes of public input. Is relying on a council of elders to make important decisions a legitimate form of representation more in line with local customs in a place like Afghanistan? When Afghanistan's president wants to reach out to the Afghan people, he hosts a *loya jirga*—a grand council of elders. Local assemblies of elders, called simply *jirgas*, often deal with community concerns in both Afghanistan and parts of Pakistan as well. Is this also representation?

Women's rights organizations provide another example. Is the idea that women and men should have the same rights a universal value, or just a Western perspective? For example, most people in North America and Europe would consider gender equality rights a universal value, as does the UN's Universal Declaration of Human Rights. However, some women in non-Western societies might disagree, and certainly it seems some of the men do. To take a more extreme example discussed in Chapter 11, a set of surgical practices performed in some traditional societies may be thought of there as "female circumcision," which has an almost clinical connotation. Yet in most Western societies, these practices are increasingly called "female genital mutilation," which sounds awful. Do you think this is a case of Western TANs imposing their cultural values on traditional societies, or is it a violation of values that should be considered universal?

Here's a different type of example. Many groups and individuals affiliated with jihadist networks have expressed the desire to create a "new Caliphate." That is, they want to impose Islamic rule over as much of the world as possible, thereby merging the secular and religious sectors. Is this another instance of groups and individuals from one region or culture using transnational networks to impose their values on others? What do you think?

1. Are TANs reflections of the geography from which they are based?

2. Can TANs ever escape the cultures of the regions from which they arose?

3. Are there universal values that override regional or cultural ones? If so, who decides which ones are universal? ●

---

associated with large agribusinesses (e.g., General Mills and Kellogg), and corporate actors such as Cargill Incorporated, Bank of America, and Walmart.

For such TANs, an interesting question is whether their values and norms are universal or reflective of just a certain region or culture. This issue is discussed in the box "The Revenge of Geography: Do TANs Reflect Their Home Cultures?"

In almost all cases, the ultimate target of TAN activity is states. As noted in Chapter 2, although states are not the only significant international actors in the neo-Westphalian international system, in many ways states remain the most powerful actors in the system. TANs seek to influence their behavior, and we turn to that next.

13-2b Influencing States

The essential goal of most TANs is to get sovereign states to act on the values embraced by the TAN. Like many of the NGOs that often compose them, a common way most TANs do this is through the practice of "naming and shaming." As a child, you may have been told "sticks and stones may break my bones, but words can never hurt me." That's true, if you have a very thick skin and a healthy dose of self-esteem. Still, no one likes to be publicly called out for bad behavior—that includes the leaders, elites, and people of a state. For states, their reputations are prized possessions, and states will often change behavior that others find objectionable to get the international spotlight off them and shifted elsewhere.

At times this happens in a way called the **boomerang model**, as shown in Figure 13-1. If NGOs within a state are unsuccessful in changing the state's actions that they oppose (which is quite often the case in authoritarian states), they can use TANs to mobilize individual opinion leaders, NGOs, other states, and IOs, which can then pressure the state from outside. State regimes that might be unwilling to change as a result of domestic pressures will often change their behavior when it becomes clear that their behavior has hurt them internationally.

One very good example of the boomerang model in operation is the anti-apartheid network that helped bring an end to the discriminatory white-minority regime in South Africa about 25 years ago. Through most of the latter half of the 20th century, neither violent nor nonviolent protest directed at the Republic of South Africa from within could force the white Afrikaner regime to end its policy of apartheid—the assigning of legal and societal rights based on skin color. However, literally hundreds of groups in Europe, Australia, the United States, and elsewhere, along with thousands of individuals who formed an anti-apartheid social movement, were able to create a network coordinating their actions with states and other IOs to bring pressure on the Afrikaner regime.

This naming-and-shaming campaign had important effects. As noted in Chapter 9, corporations also felt the pressures of this movement. Their shareholders demanded that the corporations stop doing business as usual with the Afrikaner regime, and South Africa found itself a pariah state in international politics. Most others in the international system felt South Africa's policies were morally wrong, and almost no one wanted to cooperate with a state with such policies—particularly one that had been called out for its actions. Consequently, businesses and money fled the country. The anti-apartheid TAN increased the outside pressures on the regime until the costs—moral, political, and economic—were more than the regime was willing to pay. So South Africa changed the apartheid policy that had been in force since 1948, allowing full multiracial elections in 1994.

A different example of the boomerang model came in 2014 as states reacted to the kidnapping of hundreds of Nigerian schoolgirls, illustrated in the box "Foreign Policy in Perspective: The Case of the Nigerian Schoolgirls."

boomerang model: a model in which internal groups repressed by their own states turn to TANs to put pressure on other states; those states then put pressure on the repressive state from the outside. In short, repression against internal groups can boomerang back and cause new external pressure on the repressive state.

FIGURE 13-1

The Boomerang Model of TAN Activity

How vital are TANs to citizens facing authoritarian regimes?

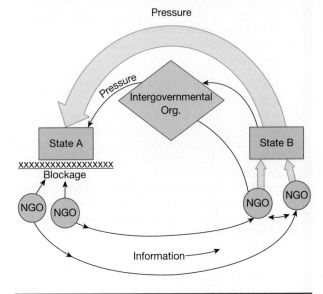

Source: Based on Keck, M., & Sikkink, K. (1998) *Activists beyond Borders: Advocacy Networks in International Politics.* Cornell University Press.

A different example of a TAN influencing a state involves a criminal network. The Russian Mafia fits our definition of a TAN because it is a network marked by reciprocal, voluntary actions across national borders by domestic and international nongovernmental actors and individuals who fulfill differentiated roles in pursuit of shared values. The values these TAN members advocate are acquiring wealth, via illegal as well as legal means. Crimes such as narcotrafficking, human trafficking, computer fraud, prostitution, arms trading, and kidnapping are among its areas of focus, and it has often encroached into legitimate businesses such as banks and financial institutions. Its leading members include Solntsevskaya Bratva (reputedly linked to the Russian intelligence agency FSB and arguably the single most successful criminal organization in the world, with an estimated annual revenue of over $8 billion); Bratski Krug (also known as the Family of Eleven with leadership based in Yekaterinburg); Tambovskaya Prestupnaya Grupirovka, which is based in St. Petersburg; and the Chechen Mafia from the Caucasus region (Porter 2015).

The Case of the Nigerian Schoolgirls

Boko Haram, an Islamist militant group operating in northern Nigeria, received seed money from Osama bin Laden in 2002 to help it create an Islamic state ruled by Sharia law in northern Nigeria, where most of Nigeria's 50% Muslim population live. Due to this and its links to al-Qaeda in the Islamic Maghreb, Boko Haram was designated by the US Department of State as a foreign terrorist organization in November 2013.

Inside Nigeria, the group remained a deadly, but largely local, threat. However, the global notoriety of Boko Haram shot off the charts in April 2014 when it kidnapped 276 largely Christian Nigerian schoolgirls. A total of 57 of them escaped from the trucks carrying them, but the others were forced to convert to Islam and were threatened to be sold (to places such as Chad and Cameroon) unless hundreds of Boko Haram militants jailed in Nigeria, Niger, and Cameroon were released. When the Nigerian government failed to launch an operation to find the kidnapped girls, the girls' mothers—and other Nigerian mothers—began a social movement: "Bring Back Our Girls!" With the help of Twitter, the movement went global at #BringBackOurGirls, with both Pope Francis and US First Lady Michelle Obama responding to the call.

US, British, and French offers to send military advisers to assist the Nigerian government in locating the girls were initially rebuffed. Yet after two weeks of international shaming in the mainstream press and social media and by both Nigerian and global civil society organizations, the Nigerian government accepted the external offers of assistance to help find them. Nearly a month after the girls' abduction, Nigerian President and Commander in Chief Goodluck Jonathan declared that a military offensive would be undertaken to return the girls and evict Boko Haram from northern Nigeria.

That military offensive never occurred, as Nigerian military leaders apparently don't think they have the capability to defeat Boko Haram on its "own" turf. Instead, negotiations were undertaken, and by 2019, 107 girls had been released or found, but 112 were still missing. Moreover, in February 2018, Boko Haram abducted another 110 schoolgirls. What do you think about this episode?

Parisians make a public push on behalf of kidnapped Nigerian girls

How can a network like #BringBackOurGirls force a state to act?

Nicolas Kovarik/Pacific Press/LightRocket via Getty Images

1. How would the Nigerian government have responded without the pressure from this quickly formed, transnational network of individual activists, groups, and state actors?

2. Does the mean the boomerang model did or didn't work? ●

Sources: Stephanie Busari and David McKenzie, "Into Danger's Arms: Chaos as Schoolgirls Flee Boko Haram," *CNN*, March 5, 2018, https://www.cnn.com/2018/03/01/africa/dapchi-nigeria-boko-haram-intl/index.html; Paul Cruickshank and Tim Lister, "Boko Haram Has Kidnapped Before—Successfully," *CNN*, May 12, 2014, http://www.cnn.com/2014/05/12/world/boko-haram-previous-abductions/index.html; Eli Lake, "Boko Haram's Bin Laden Connection," *The Daily Beast*, May 11, 2014, http://news.yahoo.com/boko-harams-bin-laden-connection-041508136—politics.html; Fidelis Mbah, "Nigeria's Chibok Schoolgirls: Five Years On, 112 Still Missing," *Aljazeera*, April 14, 2019, https://www.aljazeera.com/news/2019/04/nigeria-chibok-school-girls-years-112-missing-190413192517739.html; Hannah Strange, "Bring Back Our Girls? The Nigerian Government Is Focusing More on Its PR Strategy and Silencing Criticism," *The Telegraph*, July 2, 2014, http://www.telegraph.co.uk/women/womens-life/10940077/Bring-back-our-girls-The-Nigerian-government-is-focusing-more-on-its-PR-strategy-and-silencing-criticism.html; US Department of State, "Background Briefing on Designation of Boko Haram and Ansaru as Foreign Terrorist Organizations and as Specially Designated Global Terrorists," November 13, 2013, http://www.state.gov/r/pa/prs/ps/2013/11/217532.htm; Vivienne Walt, "Nigerians Critical of Government's Slow Kidnappings Response," *Time*, May 11, 2014, http://time.com/95558/nigeria-kidnappings-government; and Morgan Winsor, "Boko Haram Releases 21 Chibok Schoolgirls in Nigeria 2 Years Later," *ABC News*, October 13, 2016, http://abcnews.go.com/International/boko-haram-releases-21-chibok-schoolgirls-nigeria/story?id=42772745.

An example of this TAN's ability to influence states came in 1999. When NATO launched a bombing campaign against Yugoslavia for its repression of the residents of its Kosovo region, a number of the properties being bombed were owned or controlled by individuals or organizations associated with the Russian Mafia. Several members of the Russian State Duma (the lower body of Russia's national legislature) introduced a prominent Yugoslavian businessman, Dragomir Karic, to a visiting delegation of members of the US House of Representatives at a meeting in Vienna. According to the congressional leader of the trip, Karic had been previously identified to him by the US intelligence community as the leading representative of the Russian Mafia in Yugoslavia. Karic told the members of the congressional delegation that NATO was destroying his property and, if they could tell him what the government of Yugoslavia had to agree to in order for the bombing to stop, he could get Yugoslavian President Slobodan Milosevic to accept those terms. When asked how he could be sure Milosevic would agree, Karic replied that he "owned" Milosevic. Despite the fact that Milosevic had previously said he would never allow NATO peacekeepers in Kosovo, such peacekeepers were a crucial component of the agreed-upon terms. When Karic faxed those terms to Milosevic, Milosevic reversed his previous position (perhaps mindful of the fact that telling the Russian Mafia "no" was often extraordinarily bad for one's health). One week later, former Russian Prime Minister Viktor Chernomyrdin formally proposed those terms to NATO and Yugoslavia, both NATO and President Milosevic accepted them, the Kosovo War ended, and this TAN's membership had to be pleased that their assets in Yugoslavia were no longer being bombed.

13-2c Encouraging and Enabling Cooperation

The Russian Mafia illustration may be an extreme case, but the fact remains that TANs routinely facilitate international cooperation. A more typical example is provided by the International Red Cross and Red Crescent Movement. Consisting of nearly 100 million individual members, the International Committee of the Red Cross, the International Federation of Red Cross and Red Crescent Societies, and 192 national Red Cross or Red Crescent societies, the movement is the world's largest humanitarian network, with 165,000 local branches, over 450,000 staff members, and over 10 million volunteers. Its four major areas of emphasis include promoting humanitarian values, responding to disasters, helping others prepare for disasters, and providing health and community care where needed. In early 2020, the network pressed for additional global support for Greece to care for Syrian refugees trying to enter from Turkey, pursued global efforts to get aid to developing countries in their response to the COVID-19 outbreak (including getting an exemption from UN sanctions to provide such aid to North Korea), sent humanitarian aid to the Philippines after a significant volcano eruption, and sent money to help Mongolian herders deal with an extreme winter (International Federation of Red Cross and Red Crescent Societies 2020).

Another way TANs promote and encourage international cooperation is by endorsing international agreements. When widely respected TANs endorse a new treaty or agreement, that endorsement may help sway the minds of undecided legislators who must cast a vote on the agreement or provide the political cover for those who have already decided to cast what they feel could be a controversial vote for the agreement. For example, the International Criminal Court (or ICC) provides a service many in the international system see as absolutely necessary: holding individuals to account for crimes against humanity, war crimes, genocide, or aggression when their home states will not prosecute them for such crimes. Yet when facing a vote to ratify the Rome Statute that created the ICC, some legislators worried about the political costs involved. Their critics charged that those legislators were supporting a supranational organization that threatened their state's sovereignty. However, the Coalition for the International Criminal Court helped legislators who supported the ICC. This TAN—composed of 2,500 civil society organizations in over 150 different countries—provided expert opinions showing how the ICC's principle of complementarity allowed national courts to retain their full sovereignty over such cases—thus preventing the ICC from ever hearing the cases—if those national courts were willing to prosecute the cases themselves. Thus, the coalition provided political cover and protection for those who wanted to approve membership in the ICC by giving them arguments that countered the "protect our sovereignty at all costs" challenge.

TANs also monitor the actions of states to ensure effective cooperation with established norms. A network of human rights organizations regularly reports on the human rights records of states with member organizations like Freedom House, which releases an annual listing of freedom scores for each country, and Human Rights Watch, which also issues country reports each year. A group called UN Watch does the same thing for the UN. Similar networks exist to ensure compliance with environmental agreements and norms. One such network is the Millennium Ecosystem Assessment. This network of networks was created in 2001 at the recommendation of UN Secretary-General Kofi Annan to assess how human activity was affecting ecosystems and how those ecosystems worked to enhance human security. The Millennium Ecosystem Assessment relied on the work of over 1,300 experts worldwide and was governed by a diverse board of directors. The board included representatives from IOs such as the UN, the World Health Organization, the World Bank, the Caribbean Development Bank, and the Global Environmental Facility; NGOs such as the Consultative Group on International Agricultural Research, the United Nations Foundation, the International Council for Science, the World Conservation Union, and others; and individuals from the business, scientific, development, and educational sectors in the Americas, Europe, Africa, and Asia. Its final assessment documenting the environmental challenges facing a wide array of ecosystems was released in 2005 (Millennium Ecosystem Assessment 2005).

As we suggested, however, not all TANs are alike. Let's take a look at different types of TANs and what they do.

13-3 THE DIVERSE WORLD OF TRANSNATIONAL ADVOCACY NETWORKS

>> **13-3** **Describe the two major types of TANs and the kinds of actions in which they engage.**

As noted at the beginning of the chapter, transnational advocacy networks *must* include nongovernmental actors—usually NGOs but at times social movements, individuals, businesses, or some combination thereof. They may *also* include governments and governmental bodies such as IOs. When you think about it, this range of membership means TANs can be quite diverse in their interests and actions. We categorize TANs by their basic orientation—self-oriented or other-oriented—and then introduce some specific examples and their actions. Understanding the types of TANs being illustrated is more important than trying to remember the specific example used in each case.

13-3a Self-Oriented TANs and What They Do

While the early research on TANs focused on those advocating for the greater good, there's no reason TANs can't arise with members motivated by self-interest. These can be thought of as **self-oriented TANs** because they exist *primarily* to pursue private goods. You could say these are actors rationally pursuing

their own self-interests. Although many such self-oriented TANs exist, three types that come immediately to mind include business TANs, organized crime TANs, and terrorist TANs. We'll consider each of these in turn.

Business TANs

One example could be a network that includes businesses and the people and groups that benefit from their activity. Here we are talking about something more than just multinational corporations, which as institutional actors are networks of corporations tied together through common ownership and responsive to common management. Business TANs exist when individuals and groups join with business entities to create a network that cooperatively exists over time and across national boundaries. A good illustration is what happens when a business from abroad comes into a new country. For example, when Toyota chose to build a truck assembly plant in San Antonio, Texas, a TAN called Team Toyota was created that included Toyota Motor Corporation and a new entity called Toyota Motor Manufacturing, Texas, Inc. It also included groups in Texas that wanted to bring the business there. Those included the Economic Development and Tourism division of the Office of the Governor of Texas, the Texas Workforce Commission, the Greater San Antonio Chamber of Commerce, and the City of San Antonio. Even though the plant's subsequent manufacturing employees would be nonunion

Former Texas Governor Rick Perry welcomes Toyota Motor Corporation President Fujio Cho to San Antonio, the site of a new Toyota Tundra factory

Are Tundra pickups American or Japanese vehicles? Do you care?

AP Photo/Eric Gay

self-oriented TANs: TANs that advocate values that primarily benefit the network members.

employees, a variety of labor unions were included in the TAN, as union contractors got the opportunity to bid for construction contracts for the plant.

The result of this TAN was the development of a pickup truck assembly plant that directly or indirectly generated almost 7,000 new jobs (Martinez 2017). Other members of the TAN included those other businesses in Japan and Mexico that manufactured the component parts for trucks assembled in San Antonio. All these TAN members shared an interest in seeing Tundra and Tacoma pickups rolling out of the San Antonio plant because they all benefited in some way. As long as the TAN members helped each other, they all were winners. Similar beneficial results could be expected when new networks helped lead to new auto assembly plants by Nissan (in Smyrna, Tennessee), BMW (in Spartanburg, South Carolina), Mercedes (in Vance, Alabama), and Kia (in West Point, Georgia).

However, not all self-oriented TANs produce such win-win scenarios. Some pursue their own private interests at the expense of others; a good example would be transnational organized crime groups.

Organized Crime TANs

Many organized crime networks fit our definition of TANs, at least to the degree that they involve networks of people and groups engaged in ongoing *transnational* activity with defined roles. In some instances, participants in these criminal networks may even include government officials, either as

....

INTERPOL: the International Criminal Police Organization created in 1923 and based in Lyon, France.

Members of the Russian Mafia undergo extensive tattooing

Once a member, can one later choose to leave a criminal TAN like the Russian mafia?

REUTERS/Eduard Korniyenko

active participants or as more passive participants who simply choose to look the other way.

There are many prominent transnational criminal networks. A common pattern for their international networking with other groups begins with narcotics trafficking—getting the drugs from areas of cultivation to processing facilities, and then to final shipments to markets. Once involved in such international networks, other markets are seen, such as human trafficking for the sex trade or for slave labor. As their activities and revenues increase, network members need to hide their profits from law enforcement and taxing agencies, which leads them into global money laundering networks, as shown in the box "Spotlight On: How Do Criminal TANs Develop?" As these cooperative activities increase and become routine, the members of such networks may engage in reciprocal services—such as murder-for-hire schemes. Examples of such global criminal TANs include the Russian Mafia; the Italian American Mafia; Italy's *Camorra* network; Japan's *Yakuza*; China's *Fuk Ching* and Triad networks; the *Heiji* network based in Taiwan; Thailand-based networks with names such as *Jao Pho* and *Red Wa*; and Mexican-based *Los Zetas*, Jalisco New Generation, and Sinaloa cartels. Some criminal TANs have been alleged to promote what has been called a modern-day form of cannibalism. See the box "Spotlight On: Trafficking in Human Organs."

As globalization made it easier to travel, communicate, and transfer funds on a worldwide basis, transnational organized crime increased. As a result, the UN General Assembly passed the UN Convention against Transnational Organized Crime in 2000; it went into force in 2003. The convention seeks to promote awareness on the part of signatories of the transnational aspects of organized crime, encourage the passage of new national laws against such crimes, and facilitate cooperation in the arrest and extradition of such criminals. It also has specific protocols that emphasize efforts to stop trafficking in people, smuggling of migrants, and illegal manufacturing or trafficking of firearms. As of 2020, 190 states had signed and 147 had ratified the convention. There is also a UN Convention against Illicit Traffic in Narcotic Drugs and Psychotropic Substances, passed by the UN General Assembly, which entered into force in 1990. It has 191 signatories, and 87 states have ratified it. This treaty expanded a previous one from 1961 that dealt only with narcotic drugs. In these ways, the UN has sought to promote international cooperation in opposing the actions of criminal TANs.

However, transnational criminal networks predate the creation of the UN, and since 1923 the International Criminal Police Organization, better known as **INTERPOL**, has been promoting international

How Do Criminal TANs Develop?

The pattern by which a criminal network TAN develops is somewhat different from that seen when groups dedicated to the greater good get started. Let's focus on one such criminal network as an example—Mexico's Flores cartel.

The cartel, operated by Raul Flores Hernandez, operated for decades in the shadows of the more visible Sinaloa, Jalisco New Generation, and *Los Zetas* cartels, but its operations were outlined in 2017 when the US Treasury Department named Flores and his drug cartel as "Significant Foreign Narcotics Traffickers" under the Foreign Narcotics Kingpin Designation Act. Raul Flores began his criminal network activities in the 1980s as part of the Sinaloa cartel. Despite forming his own organization operating in Mexico City, Jalisco, and Guadalajara, he managed to avoid becoming the target of either of the two biggest rival cartels in Mexico—the Sinaloa and Jalisco New Generation organizations. His good personal relationship with Joaquín "El Chapo" Guzmán and the other leaders of the Sinaloa cartel protected him from them. The leaders of the Jalisco New Generation cartel left him alone because he provided them with occasional intelligence about the Sinaloa cartel and helped launder their drug profits.

The Treasury Department's press statement showed how Flores operated. Most of the 21 Mexican nationals who were named as providing support for the cartel were family members or trusted friends of Flores, but the key to the growth of the network was the other people and entities named in the Treasury statement. Forty-two business entities were named as fronts for Flores's money

laundering efforts; these included a Mexican soccer club, a casino, a sports rehabilitation center, a music production company, and numerous bars, restaurants, and tourist businesses. Two prominent Mexicans were named as agents of the cartel. The Treasury Department said both Mexican soccer star Rafael Márquez Álvarez and singer Julio César Álvarez Montelongo, also known as Julión Álvarez, held assets on the cartel's behalf and acted as Flores's front men with others. Rafa Márquez is a former captain of Mexico's national soccer team, has represented the country in four World Cup competitions, and played in Europe for the Barcelona and Monaco club teams. Julión Álvarez is a popular *norteño* music artist, a style that often features songs about drug traffickers and their exploits. All 21 Mexican nationals named in the Treasury announcement are barred from entering the United States or engaging in any business activities with US entities, and any assets they have in the United States are frozen. All the individuals named face potential prison terms and large fines if arrested and convicted, and the Mexican government—working with the US Drug Enforcement Agency, the Department of Homeland Security, and the Customs and Border Protection Agency—has seized known assets of the Flores cartel as part of its war on narcotrafficking. ●

Sources: Chivis Martinez, "Soccer Star Rafael Marquez Named in Largest Mexican Cartel Kingpin Designation," *Borderland Beat*, August 9, 2017, http://www.borderlandbeat.com/2017/08/soccer-star-rafael-marquez-named-in.html; and Christopher Woody, "The US Sanctioned a 'Smooth as Butter' Cartel Operator and a Mexican Soccer Star Allegedly Working With Him," *Business Insider*, August 9, 2017, http://www.businessinsider.com/us-sanctions-raul-flores-hernandez-and-rafael-marquez-2017-8.

cooperation in pursuing criminals across national borders. Based in Lyon, France, INTERPOL has 194 member countries, and it seeks to enforce national criminal laws and enforce the spirit of the Universal Declaration of Human Rights (see Chapter 11). At the present time, INTERPOL is placing particular focus on combating criminal networks operating in developing countries, emphasizing human trafficking networks and cybercrime.

What's really frightening is the possibility that transnational organized crime networks might get involved with another type of self-oriented TAN— terrorist networks. We turn to these next.

Terrorist TANs

As we discussed at some length in Chapter 5, terrorism involves indiscriminate violence aimed

at noncombatants to influence a wider audience. Terrorist groups have been around since ancient times, but they were usually active just within their own home political territory. Transnational terrorist networks did not become a notable factor in international politics until the rise of loosely associated anarchist networks in the late 19th and early 20th centuries. Because terrorists may form networks to use violence to impose their values on others, they fit our definition of self-oriented TANs.

But what values are they trying to impose? In Chapter 5, we differentiated terrorists into four groups. The first is criminal terrorists, which we just discussed. The second is nihilist terrorists who simply want to destroy the existing order without an agenda of replacement. The anarchists previously mentioned would fit this definition. So too would Germany's Red

Trafficking in Human Organs

Human organ *donation* is a long-established practice, but there are not enough donors to meet the global need. In just the US, according to the American Transplant Foundation, about 120 new names are added to the transplant waiting list each day, while approximately 20 people die each day while waiting for a transplant. Not surprisingly then, some with enough money who cannot get a transplant through legal channels will turn to the black market of illegal organ sales, and criminal organizations have sprung up to meet this need. According to a Council of Europe study, during the 1999 Kosovo War, some members of the Kosovo Liberation Army executed Serbian prisoners and then sold their transplantable organs on the black market. Hashim Thaçi was the political leader of the Kosovo Liberation Army at the time, and he is now the president of Kosovo. According to the Council of Europe study, he also heads the Drenica Group, an organized crime network involved in the sale of human organs. Others alleged to be part of the ring include doctors in Kosovo, Albania, Turkey, and Israel who harvested the organs from poor people who were willing to sell them for as much as $20,000—money that some of them claimed they never received. These organs were then transplanted into wealthy recipients from Canada, Germany, Israel, and Poland who were willing to pay up to $200,000 for the transplants. Talk about a profit margin! Seven individuals associated with this group have been criminally charged to date. Further, this network may be linked with another one based in South Africa that enticed poor Brazilians and Romanians to sell their kidneys, which were then sold to wealthy Israelis.

Yet these are not the only such criminal networks engaging in these practices. The sale of healthy kidneys may be most pronounced in India. Beginning in the 1980s, many from the Middle East traveled to India to purchase kidneys from living donors. The practice was outlawed in India in 1994, but it continues on the black market, often controlled by crime rings that began as drug traffickers. According to many news reports, China has also been a source of black-market human organs, harvesting healthy organs from executed prisoners for sale in China, Taiwan, and elsewhere. One study claims imprisoned members of the Falun Gong—a spiritual movement outlawed in China—have been specifically targeted as unwilling organ donors by the Chinese government. According to that study, over 40,000 transplants occurred in China between

Victims of human organ trafficking display their scars
Can the international community take effective action to end this practice?
AP Photo/K.M. Chaudary

2000 and 2005 in which the source of the transplanted organ cannot be identified. Another study suggests that 10% of all kidney transplants are done on a "commercial" basis, and an untold number of the donors are forced by criminal rings to give up a kidney.

In most countries, the sale of human organs is illegal, and it is considered unethical by the World Health Organization. Yet criminal rings seeking profits exist to meet the needs of what has been come to be called "transplant tourism." Should this practice be decriminalized? Is "informed consent" to donate organs really possible when the donors are very poor? What do you think about this? ●

Sources: Dan Bilefsky, "Seven Charged in International Organ-Trafficking Ring Based in Kosovo," *The New York Times*, November 16, 2010, A4; Doreen Carvajal and Marlise Simons, "Report Names Kosovo Leader as Crime Boss," *The New York Times*, December 16, 2010, A19; Asif Efrat, "Organ Traffickers Lock Up People to Harvest Their Kidneys: Here Are the Politics Behind the Organ Trade," *Monkey Cage/The Washington Post*, December 7, 2016, https://www.washingtonpost.com/news/monkey-cage/wp/2016/12/07/organ-traffickers-lock-up-people-to-harvest-their-kidneys-here-are-the-politics-behind-the-organ-trade; Gregory M. Lamb, "China Faces Suspicions About Organ Harvesting," *The Christian Science Monitor*, August 3, 2006, http://www.csmonitor.com/2006/0803/p16s01-lire.html; and Nancy Scheper-Hughes, "The Global Traffic in Human Organs," *Current Anthropology* 41 (2000), 191–224.

Army Faction (also known as the Baader-Meinhof Gang). This 1970s network included German Marxists trying to bring down what they saw as a fascist-leaning German state and other groups from the Middle East and elsewhere.

The third type of terrorist group is nationalist terrorists. A variety of Palestinian groups would fit this definition, to the extent that they cooperated as networks. Although many in the Arab world considered them freedom fighters, an umbrella group such as the

Palestine Liberation Organization (PLO) sought to create an independent Palestinian state through the use of indiscriminate violence against noncombatants. The PLO included many different groups located in different countries, the largest of which ultimately was Fatah—the group led by Yasser Arafat.

The fourth type of terrorist group is revolutionary terrorists, those seeking to overthrow the social and political order and replace it with something more to their liking. Examples would include some revolutionary Marxist organizations during the Cold War and, more recently, the better-known examples of revolutionary terrorist networks such as Hezbollah, al-Qaeda, and the Islamic State, who seek to overthrow the existing secular order and replace it with a regional or global Islamic regime.

Although Hezbollah is based in Lebanon, it qualifies as a terrorist network because it has cells in Africa, Europe, and both North and South America; it relies heavily on the material support it receives from Iran and Syria; it has provided support to Hamas in the Gaza Strip; and it has conducted operations in Lebanon, Israel, Syria, Argentina, and Egypt. Its goal is to create Islamic regimes in Lebanon and Palestine and potentially elsewhere in the Arab world. So it fits here. However, the two best contemporary examples of revolutionary terrorist self-oriented TANs would be al-Qaeda and ISIS, and we devote an entire box to them: "Spotlight On: Al-Qaeda and ISIS."

Regardless of the type of terrorist network involved, the international community has sought to confront it. In the 1970s and 1980s, the key concern was coordinating police efforts to protect airliners from being hijacked. By the 1990s, the focus had turned to confronting violent attacks by more revolutionary terrorist groups. After 9/11, state actors like the United States, the United Kingdom, Canada, and others went to war with the Taliban regime in Afghanistan over its support of al-Qaeda, aided by the local anti-Taliban Northern Alliance—a group made up of several minority ethnic groups in Afghanistan, including Tajiks, Hazaras, Uzbeks, and Turkmen. Once that war was largely over, an International Security Assistance Force authorized by the UN Security Council took responsibility for Afghanistan, and then NATO forces took control of the effort to occupy and rebuild a stable, relatively peaceful, and, it was hoped, democratic Afghanistan. NATO forces were scheduled to leave Afghanistan by the end of 2014, but US forces stayed on to help train Afghan troops. In 2020, US and Taliban negotiators agreed to a truce in the fighting there, which, if it held, could lead to US troops leaving Afghanistan. As they say, only time will tell whether this US and NATO effort to help the Afghans is successful.

In 2006, the UN General Assembly passed a Global Counter-Terrorism Strategy to address the root causes of terrorism, promote international cooperation in dealing with terrorist threats, build the capacity of both states and the UN to combat terrorism, and ensure that the global fight against terrorism did not violate standards of the rule of law or human rights. By stressing that terrorism represented criminal acts *regardless of its motivation*, the UN was trying to get beyond the political debate that previously deadlocked the institution over the notion that "one person's terrorist is another's freedom fighter." Such definitional dilemmas caused the UN to be largely hamstrung in dealing with terrorism before the events of 9/11.

However, as we noted earlier, self-oriented TANs were not the first ones studied by scholars. Many TANs advocate values that are primarily oriented at helping others and promoting the greater good. Let's change our focus and take a look at them.

13-3b Other-Oriented TANs and What They Do

When we talk about **other-oriented TANs**, it is hard to escape our emphasis on broader aspects of human security, as that theme seems to connect such groups who generally seek to promote collective goods. There are many possible examples of such networks. Let's talk about networks focusing on personal, economic, health, and environmental security.

Personal Security–Oriented TANs

These TANs emphasize the needs of people to be safe from physical harm. At one extreme is the threat of nuclear war. Although there is the Nuclear Nonproliferation Regime, which we discussed in Chapters 2 and 6, it is composed solely of state actors and IOs. However, a number of NGOs form a transnational network to assist in this effort to prevent the use of nuclear weapons. One such actor is the US-based Nuclear Threat Initiative. In 2008, it created the World Institute for Nuclear Security in Vienna, Austria, which joins together NGO and national officials from Australia, Finland, Norway, the United Kingdom, and the United States, along with representatives of the International Atomic Energy Agency, in a cooperative effort to strengthen the protection of existing nuclear materials from theft or misuse.

A well-known example of a human security–oriented network is the International Campaign to Ban Landmines, mentioned earlier in this chapter. Less well-known examples would be other human rights–related networks that seek to protect people's right to personal security. One such network is the

other-oriented TANs: TANs that advocate a set of values that primarily benefit others besides themselves.

Al-Qaeda and ISIS: Global Jihadist Networks

In 1988, a 31-year-old Saudi named Osama bin Laden created what would become a major Islamic terrorist network dedicated to conducting **jihad**—or a holy war—against Western nonbelievers. That network has now outlived him, as he was killed by US Special Forces in 2011 at his hideout in Abbottabad, Pakistan.

To begin, bin Laden was the 17th of 52 (or possibly 54) children of Muhammad bin Laden (who had more than 20 wives over his lifetime). Muhammad bin Laden was a Yemeni who worked his way up to become the wealthiest construction contractor in Saudi Arabia. Shortly after the Soviet Union invaded Afghanistan in 1979, young Osama bin Laden left Saudi Arabia to go fight on behalf of his Muslim brethren there. With a college degree, construction expertise, and a personal inheritance of approximately $250 million, he was able to help support the Afghan mujahideen in its armed resistance to Soviet rule. As the fighting was winding down in 1988, bin Laden created an organization called *al-Qaeda*, Arabic for "The Base." If Islamic forces could defeat a superpower such as the Soviet Union, bin Laden thought anything might be possible if Allah willed it, including purging Islamic areas of Western corruption and reinvigorating Islam everywhere.

Like other TANs, al-Qaeda advocated its own values (using violence to expel nonbelievers from the Islamic world and expand Islamic rule around the globe) and sought to influence the actions of states to achieve those goals. To do so, al-Qaeda established camps in Afghanistan where volunteers were trained in the use of weapons and explosives and screened for their skills, potential to move freely in Western societies, and willingness to become martyrs as needed. Attacks attributed to al-Qaeda have varied widely and spanned the globe. Among many other attacks, in 1996 the Khobar Towers apartment complex in Saudi Arabia was bombed, killing 19 US troops and injuring 400. In 1998, US embassies in Kenya and Tanzania were bombed, killing 12 Americans and over 200 others—mostly Kenyan Muslims. In 2001, nearly 3,000 were killed in the 9/11 attacks on the World Trade Center and the Pentagon. Since then, dozens if not hundreds have been killed in the Middle East, Europe, and Asia by al-Qaeda and its many affiliate groups.

Before bin Laden's death, an affiliate group known as al-Qaeda in Iraq was formed by Abu Musab al-Zarqawi. This group tried to start a sectarian war between Sunni and Shi'a Muslims in Iraq, and bin Laden repudiated the group for its indiscriminate killings of other Muslims. After

Osama bin Laden (left) and Ayman al Zawahiri (right)
Who would have predicted the impact that these two men would have on world politics?
REUTERS/Hamid Mir/Editor/Ausaf Newspaper for Daily Dawn

al-Zarqawi was killed in a 2006 US airstrike, his group later evolved into ISIS—the Islamic State in Iraq and Syria. ISIS initially carved out a territorial base in northern and western Iraq and then expanded into northern and eastern Syria. Abu Bakr al-Baghdadi emerged as the group's new leader, and its early successes drew others to its fold. Hundreds of Muslims from other countries found their way to ISIS-controlled territory, where they were trained to fight. Many stayed there, but dozens—maybe hundreds—were sent back to their home countries so that they could launch attacks there.

In recent years, ISIS-affiliated groups have been found in Afghanistan, Chad, Egypt, Libya, Nigeria, Pakistan, the Persian Gulf states, Russia's Dagestan province, Tunisia, and Yemen. Similarly, al-Qaeda-affiliated groups have emerged in many of these same countries as well as others. Some groups, like Boko Haram in Nigeria, switch their allegiance from one group to the other. It's literally hard to tell the players without a scorecard.

One thing seems perfectly clear, however. These networks have staying power. Al-Qaeda survived the killing of Osama bin Laden, with Ayman al Zawahiri stepping up to take control. As noted earlier, al-Qaeda in Iraq survived the killing of Abu Musab al-Zarqawi by morphing into ISIS under the leadership of Abu Bakr al-Baghdadi, who was later killed by US forces. The territorial space ISIS controlled in Iraq and Syria has been reduced to virtually nothing, but ISIS operatives are still around. Trying to eradicate these terrorist TANs is a little like playing whack-a-mole. What would it take to make such networks disappear? What steps could be taken to minimize their appeal? Is violent conflict inescapable? ●

....

jihad: "holy war" or "holy struggle" in Arabic. To some Muslims, it means the daily struggle within oneself to overcome evil; to others, it means conducting war against non-Muslims.

Universal Human Rights Network (Unirights), which emphasizes the resolution of internal conflicts, demobilization of armed groups, reintegration of insurgents into society, civilian peacekeeping, and other human rights issues related to protection from violence. Its partner organizations include NGOs concerned with better peacekeeping; the needs of displaced people; and promoting democracy, civil society, and the rule of law internationally.

Finally, another example of networks seeking to ensure personal security are those dealing with human trafficking, a crime that often imperils women and children as sex slaves and men, women, and children as involuntary workers. The Global Emancipation Network is a US-headquartered network that uses big-data mining technologies provided by an array of high-tech partner organizations to collect evidence of human trafficking on the dark web as well as the rest of the Internet. It maintains a dataset of research on human trafficking and coordinates its evidence with law enforcement agencies and governments. It also provides links so that commercial businesses can ensure that their operations—hotels, banks, driving services, and so on—are not used by human traffickers. In 2020, the International Anti-Human Trafficking Network was established in the UK to do similar work and to influence the British government's human trafficking policies. La Strada International is another European-based network headquartered in the Netherlands. Its NGO affiliates work in most European countries to frame awareness of the problem in human rights terms, monitor trafficking networks, shape policies and best practices to aid the victims and reintegrate them into society, prosecute the criminals involved in these actions, and support research.

Once people's security from physical harm has been addressed, they need to provide a living for themselves and their families. That brings up economic security–oriented TANs.

Economic Security–Oriented TANs

In the 21st century, those seeking to ensure the economic security of others generally begin with an emphasis on some form of sustainable economic development, as we mentioned in Chapter 12. The foundations of sustainable economic development involve food and energy security.

It's no surprise that having sufficient food supplies is a huge challenge in many poor countries, and having food supplies that are sustainable is a further challenge. A regional network is French-based Afrique Verte International (Green Africa International) that, with the assistance of Swiss-based Fondation Assistance Internationale, creates both temporary and ongoing networks to deal with food issues in West Africa. It has over 200 affiliate groups in Burkina Faso, Mali, Niger, and Guinea, and 99% of its members are women. For example, in a study of market prices for the primary cereal grains these states consume and produce for export (rice, corn, millet, and sorghum), Afrique Verte International worked with various governmental agencies and NGOs in France, Burkina Faso, Mali, and Niger. By focusing on the best practices that work for farmers, Afrique Verte International provides guidance and assistance for many beyond just these countries.

A TAN with much broader scope is CGIAR (Consultative Group on International Agricultural Research), which bills itself as the world's largest global agricultural innovation network. Based in France, it links 15 agricultural research centers around the world with over 3,000 nongovernmental and governmental partner organizations operating in 70 countries. It promotes sustainable food availability with programs such as climate resilience farming and other innovations in all areas of agricultural management, knowledge, and technologies. CGIAR has trained over 1 million new agricultural specialists, and every program it operates has a focus on gender—due to the role of women in global food production—as well as on the UN's Sustainable Development Goals.

Beyond ensuring that people have enough to eat, another foundational step for sustainable development is getting people sustainable sources of energy. Nearly one third of the people on the planet—2.4 billion—rely on traditional biofuels like wood, straw, and dried dung to cook their food and heat their homes. Not only are these inefficient heat sources; the smoke and emissions they produce—often in homes without chimneys or other ventilation—are dangerous when inhaled and contribute to greenhouse gases. The International Network for Sustainable Energy (INFORSE) is a Danish-based network of 140 NGOs working in 60 different countries in Europe, Africa, North and South America, and Asia. It has regional coordinators in Argentina, Brazil, Denmark, India, Japan, Senegal, Slovakia, South Africa, and Uganda. Created at the Earth Summit in Rio de Janeiro in 1992, it has observer status at the UN's Economic and Social Council and has participated in the environmental conferences that followed the 1992 Earth Summit. Another Denmark-based network is more oriented to problem solving at the local level. The Global Network on Energy for Sustainable Development seeks to help countries develop energy sources that are cleaner, more efficient, and sustainable over the long term. Working with partner organizations and networks in Kenya, Senegal, South Africa, Argentina, Brazil, Thailand, China, India, Mexico, and the Mediterranean region, the network has success in

Solar panels provide power to a woman cooking in Benin

How far does the reach of TANs such as the Global Network on Energy for Sustainable Development extend?

DELPHINE BOUSQUET/AFP via Getty Images

promoting such initiatives as small-scale biogas operations, solar cookers, solar water heaters, and both rural and urban electrification.

Sustainable energy is not just the concern of developing countries and their Danish partners. As noted in Chapter 12, many developed countries are also seeking to find ways to exploit renewable and sustainable energy sources. The solar-powered photovoltaic (or solar PV) electric industry has a European-based advocacy network. Its members include the European Photovoltaic Industry Association headquartered in Belgium, national solar PV associations in Europe, private and governmental electric companies in Europe, and the European Commission. The network's goal is a very pragmatic one—enabling solar-powered electricity to be incorporated into national and regional electricity grids in Europe, particularly in times of peak demand.

With food and energy needs met, the foundations of economic security have been addressed. Once economic and physical security are assured, we often then begin to address our health security. Here, too, the transnational advocacy networks are involved in health-related areas—the topic of the next section.

Health Security–Oriented TANs

There are many ways to improve one's health security. Let's start at birth, because networks exist that seek to ensure the health of mothers and their newborns. Two that differ in their approaches are the International Planned Parenthood Foundation and Human Life International.

The International Planned Parenthood Foundation is a TAN that provides a variety of health-related services to women. Headquartered in London, it has 132 affiliated organizations and is active in 164 different countries. The services provided include help with family planning decisions, reproductive health, HIV-related care, maternal and childcare, and contraception and abortion-related services. By contrast, US-based Human Life International seeks to ensure maternal and child health while outlawing abortion-related services wherever possible. Affiliated with the Catholic Church, it links antiabortion groups and activists outside the church, raises awareness of the need to stop abortion and artificial means of contraception, and provides maternal and health care services in 100 countries. Not surprisingly, members of these two TANs typically see each other as rivals.

Beyond "beginning of life" questions, other TANs seek to promote better health for diseases that are difficult to treat. A good example is HIV/AIDS. Lots of attention is placed on Sub-Saharan Africa in this regard, as there are more cases of HIV/AIDS there than anywhere else (see Map 13-1). In 2019, almost 21 million people from East and Southern African were living with HIV/AIDS—that's about 7% of the population ages 15–49. Table 13-1 shows those African states meeting or exceeding the 5% figure in 2018, the latest year for which comprehensive data are available. The good news is that the percentage of adults living with HIV/AIDS is slowly going down, while the percentages of both adults and children on antiretroviral treatment are rising rapidly. Part of this success is due to TANs dedicated to treating these patients. Examples of such networks include the Network of African People Living with HIV/AIDS, the Eastern African National Networks of AIDS Service Organisations, the Canada-Africa Prevention Trials Network, and the African-European HIV Vaccine Development Network.

However, we'd be wrong to conclude that such networks only target HIV/AIDS in Africa. Let's consider some of the other less obvious examples, too. One such network links AIDS clinics and medical care providers in Mexico City with counterparts in the international foundation sector, national and international governmental entities, and NGOs. Another such network is TREAT Asia (Therapeutics Research, Education, and AIDS Training in Asia). This network seeks to provide health care to the almost 5 million people living with HIV/AIDS in the Asia/Pacific region. It connects the research of amFAR (the Foundation for AIDS Research) and corporate funding sources with participating medical clinics and research centers throughout Asia.

Some TANs deal with health concerns that involve underserved communities. A good example is the Global Health Council. Its membership is made up of over 400 entities, including universities, hospitals, NGOs, private corporations, and think tanks. Its board of directors draws individuals from major pharmaceutical companies and a host of other

MAP 13-1

HIV Prevalence Throughout the World, 2019

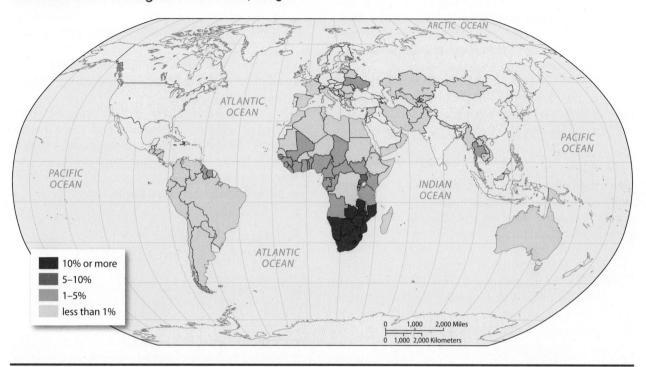

Legend:
- 10% or more
- 5–10%
- 1–5%
- less than 1%

Source: Benjamin D. Hennig, University of Sheffield, www.viewsoftheworld.net.

TABLE 13-1

Sub-Saharan States With 5% or More of Adults With HIV/AIDS, 2018

COUNTRY	PEOPLE LIVING WITH HIV/AIDS	ADULT (15–49) PREVALENCE %	ADULTS ON ANTIRETROVIRAL TREATMENT %	CHILDREN ON ANTIRETROVIRAL TREATMENT %	AIDS DEATHS
Botswana	370,000	20.3	85	38	4,800
Lesotho	340,000	23.6	60	70	6,100
Malawi	1,000,000	9.2	79	61	13,000
South Africa	7,700,000	20.4	62	63	71,000
Swaziland (Eswatini)	210,000	27.4	86	75	3,500
Uganda	1,400,000	5.7	73	66	23,000
Zambia	1,200,000	11.3	78	79	17,000
Zimbabwe	1,300,000	12.7	89	76	22,000

Sources: AVERT.org; UNAIDS data, 2018.

NGOs. It brings medical care to women and children and to those facing HIV/AIDS, malaria, and tuberculosis; it also promotes the development of health care systems more broadly. It and its members conduct programs and projects in over 150 countries in North America, the Caribbean, South America, Africa, the Middle East, the Caucasus region of Eurasia, South Asia, and Southeast Asia.

Finally, such TANs are created as they are needed to deal with new global health challenges. Following the development of a successful vaccine for COVID-19, the pandemic will almost certainly generate a new TAN comprised of the World Health Organization, major pharmaceutical companies, regional or national health care networks, medical societies, humanitarian NGOs, and states.

As mentioned previously, the activities of some of these health security TANs intersect with environmental issues. There are environmental security-oriented TANs, too, so let's take a quick look at them.

Environmental Security–Oriented TANs

Like the other TANs, environmental security-oriented TANs seek to popularize ideas, influence states by helping set their agendas and subsequent actions, and enable cooperation. An example of one such network that links environmental and health security is the Swiss-based International Society of Doctors for the Environment. This TAN links doctors whose focus is on environmentally caused health problems—such as the linkage of pollution to disease and early death. It educates doctors, the public, corporations, and governments on such issues and links up with a variety of other international networks to do so. Another example of such an environmental security TAN is the one put together by the Transnational Institute. It links a number of resource-based networks in Africa, Europe, and the Western Hemisphere to ensure that local people have access to and control over clean water supplies and to protect environmental resources such as water supplies and forests from ownership by corporations. Much of the network's activities lie in the areas of grassroots organizing and seeking to set national government agendas.

Both of these environmental security TANs are global in scope, but there are regional ones as well. Climate Action Network Europe (CAN-Europe) is pretty much what the name suggests. It focuses on climate change, emissions, and sustainable energy issues in Europe. This network links together over 120 member organizations in more than 25 European states. Among its major priorities is the careful monitoring of the EU's Emissions Trading System—a carbon trading mechanism designed to use market forces to reduce Europe's carbon footprint. Although CAN-Europe is a regional TAN, it also is a component of a global one. The broader Climate Action Network has similar regional networks in North America, Latin America, Asia, and Africa.

13-3c Evaluating TANs

Other-oriented TANs seek to make the world a better place for all; that's why they are often associated with the phrase "the greater good." In an increasingly globalized world system, both self-oriented and other-oriented transnational advocacy networks play important roles and can have surprisingly significant consequences for international politics. Whether or not you think these are positive roles and impacts probably depends on your theoretical orientation and perhaps even the network under consideration, as pointed out in "Theory in Action: Evaluating TANs in the International System."

As you can see, TANs can be evaluated from a variety of different viewpoints, and these evaluations vary dramatically. Regardless of how they're evaluated, TANs are an increasingly prevalent phenomenon in international politics and seem likely to become even more prevalent in the 21st century.

CONCLUSION: TRANSNATIONAL ADVOCACY NETWORKS AND THE GLOBAL FUTURE

Transnational advocacy networks are far more than just NGOs or NGOs plus their friends. When these transnational networks form, they become distinctly different entities that have an effect that is greater than the sum of their parts. TANs are not just an increasingly prevalent phenomenon in the neo-Westphalian system; they are increasingly significant actors in their own right. As the examples in this chapter show, TANs can change the structure of the playing field of international politics by introducing new issues and opening up that playing field to newer or weaker players; redefining the rules of the game of international politics to make it less state-centric by allowing non-state actors increasingly visible or important roles in world politics; threatening the security of even the largest states; and allying with other international actors—states, IOs, NGOs, social movements, and individuals—to create new issue alliances and foster counter-alliances among those actors that do not share their values.

How they do these things varies, of course, and the variance seems to depend on the type of TAN involved. Self-oriented TANs such as economic, criminal, or terrorist groups usually engage in direct actions to achieve their goals. Such actions may involve working with states, around states, or against states. Other-oriented TANs seeking to improve the greater good often rely on more indirect means, such as using their control of information to redefine issues and get them on governmental agendas, relying on symbolic politics to persuade other actors that their behaviors need to change (such as linking what they

Evaluating TANs in the International System

Like numerous other examples we've used in this book, evaluating TANs typically depends on your theoretical orientation. Realists and neorealists argue that in an international system marked by anarchy, states are the most important actors, and nothing matters to them as much as the ability to protect their national interests through military means. From that perspective, TANs are relatively unimportant, as they are too weak to force states to change their behavior if states choose to hold firm. Realists would see TANs as important only to the extent that they can be used to help reach a state's goals. Otherwise, they are unimportant or perhaps even a nuisance. Take Russian elections, for example. NGOs such as the National Endowment for Democracy, the National Democratic Institute, the International Republican Institute, and the International Foundation for Electoral Systems worked for years to promote democratic values, viable and functioning political parties and other civil society organizations, and respect for free and fair elections in Russia. Because promoting democracy in Russia has been a goal of all post–Cold War US administrations, the United States thinks this democracy promotion network is doing good work. However, because the network's activities hamper the Russian government's ability to do what it wants in the ways that it prefers and its statements and activities at times embarrass Russian officials, you can be sure that the Russian government thinks it is more than a nuisance; it thinks that members of the network are actually Western—if not US—covert agents seeking the overthrow of the Russian regime.

Liberals and neoliberals see states, IOs, NGOs, and a host of subnational actors as part of a very complex and diverse international system, and TANs fit right into that mix. More to the point, TANs promote and enable cooperation among the various component actors in the system, thereby serving the needs of those who might otherwise be left out or marginalized. With the exception of criminal or terrorist TANs, liberals and neoliberals would typically view TANs as forces for good in the international system. Thus, TANs promoting the rights of women and children, enhanced global health, environmental protection, democratic values, and so on are seen as the leading edge of a new, more cooperative international system, one that is becoming an international civil society.

Because they emphasize the social construction of reality and the importance of identity politics, constructivists see TANs as important facilitators in the evolving narrative that defines international politics. For example, if enough TANs say apartheid is wrong (i.e., it is not a matter of internal sovereignty for South Africa but instead is an affront to global human rights norms), then this new reality says apartheid is wrong and steps must be taken to abolish it. Further, TANs can help groups develop and express their collective identities (for example, seeing fundamentalist Muslims as victims of Western oppression or workers in San Antonio seeing themselves as part of a larger Toyota-based family). Thus, constructivists would see TANs as an essential component of an international system based more on shared ideas than on physical realities.

More critical theorists would offer a different view, depending on their theoretical orientation and the nature of the TAN involved. In his work, Karl Marx emphasized the need for the international working class to revolt against the bosses and owners. Thus, Marxists might well see revolutionary TANs as a way to work outside the state system to achieve a more just world. Certainly, early anarchist TANs did so.

World system theorists would probably interpret TAN importance by the type of TAN as well. Other-oriented TANs often rely on either network members from the core region of the international system or core states for funding. Thus, world system theorists might see core-dominated TANs as agents of core interests. In other words, they might see TANs as a disguised means for core states and elite classes to manipulate poor states located on the periphery of the international system in directions the core wants them to go. By contrast, world system theorists might see at least some self-oriented TANs as agents of change in the core-defined international system. They might not approve of the methods of terrorist TANs, for example, but they might appreciate how the actions of terrorist TANs can get a new set of concerns included on national or global agendas. Arise, oppressed minorities!

Finally, feminist theorists probably share world system theorists' appreciation of TANs as a means by which new issues can get on the global agenda. Through TAN activities, women's rights, women's needs, women's concerns, and women's roles in national and international affairs have been the focus of new attention over the past 40-plus years in ways that would have seemed unprecedented in earlier periods of the international system. So what do you think?

1. How important are TANs in international affairs?

2. Do they do things states won't do?

3. Do they merely represent the efforts of the weak to challenge more powerful state interests?

4. Are they a vehicle for states to accomplish their purposes through other means? ●

do to some unpleasant or negative symbol), working with state actors to accomplish their goals, and serving as monitoring agencies to hold governments publicly accountable for their actions.

Given these trends, TANs are forcing a space for themselves on the main stage of international politics in the 21st century. For good or ill, they address global needs or desires that either are underemphasized or go unmet. They don't rival states in power, but highly successful TANs can create and change parameters of acceptable behavior regarding specific issues that leaders of states and IOs increasingly choose not to violate. ●

KEY CONCEPTS

13-1 Explain the concept of transnational advocacy networks (TANs) and how they differ from other international actors.

Transnational advocacy networks, or TANs, are recurring networks that (a) must include non-state actors (such as individuals acting alone, social movements, or NGOs); (b) may include states, IOs, or TNCs as well; and (c) are recurring, cooperative partnerships with (d) differentiated roles among the component parts. Network members advocate and act on shared ideas, positions, or goals, and they make choices—rational or otherwise—to protect, defend, and advance those shared notions. When the unique actors that make up TANs establish such networks to pursue shared goals in a cooperative enterprise, they create a new entity. The accelerating globalization of the past 50 years or so has greatly facilitated the creation and operation of TANs, which can mitigate the effects of anarchy in world politics.

13-2 Identify how TANs affect human security.

Constructivists argue that reality is socially constructed on the basis of shared ideas. People agree on how things are and then act on that basis. The power of TANs to influence human security comes from this starting point: identifying problems, developing norms, and organizing and/or motivating action. For example, what does security mean in society? TANs expand the meaning and scope of security from traditional concerns about war and national security to include more emphasis on economic and human security. The essential goal of most TANs is to get sovereign states to act on the values embraced by the TAN. To achieve this,

TANs engage in strategies such as "naming and shaming," in which TANs monitor the actions of states to ensure effective cooperation with established norms; mobilizing individual opinion leaders, NGOs, other states, and IOs to take action; and engaging in direct action to deliver services and solve problems. For example, TANs routinely facilitate international cooperation by helping supply humanitarian relief and medical supplies.

13-3 Describe the two major types of TANs and the kinds of actions in which they engage.

There are two major categories of TANs, distinguished by their basic orientation—self-oriented or other-oriented. Self-oriented TANs advocate values and outcomes that benefit themselves and their members, rather than general benefits that extend to non–network members. Examples of self-oriented TANs include business TANs, organized crime TANs, and terrorist TANs. Examples of other-oriented TANs include human security–oriented TANs that emphasize the needs of people to be safe from physical harm; economic security–oriented TANs that address food and energy security issues to alleviate poverty and promote sustainable economic development; health security–oriented TANs that address issues such as disease control or the health of women and children; and environmental security–oriented TANs that seek to protect the environment and foster sustainable development practices. In an increasingly globalized world system, both self-oriented and other-oriented transnational advocacy networks play important roles and can have surprisingly significant consequences for international politics.

KEY TERMS

transnational advocacy networks (TANs) 384

Zionism 384

norms life cycle 385

policy entrepreneurs 385

boomerang model 388

self-oriented TANs 391

INTERPOL 392

other-oriented TANs 395

jihad 396

1. What are transnational advocacy networks (TANs)?

2. How do TANs differ from other international actors already studied?

3. How do TANs influence human security, broadly defined?

4. What are the two major types of TANs, and how do they differ?

5. What do such TANs do?

6. How might the importance of TANs be evaluated?

TANs, States, and the Future of World Politics

As the international system becomes more globalized, TANs increasingly connect a wide array of actors around their shared interests. Scholars representing the "English School" of international relations theory (people like Hedley Bull, Barry Buzan, Martin Wight, Robert H. Jackson, and others) have long talked about an emerging "global society," a real community with norms and shared values. Could TANs be the glue that helps hold together such a society?

Do you think TANs will replace states as the most significant actors in a more "human-friendly" international system at some point, or will states remain preeminent, with TANs seeking to influence state behavior whenever possible?

Andia, Tatiana, and Nitsan Chorev. (2017). "Making Knowledge Legitimate: Transnational Advocacy Networks' Campaigns Against Tobacco, Infant Formula and Pharmaceuticals." *Global Networks* 17, 255–280.

Keck, Margaret E., and Kathryn Sikkink. (1998). *Activists Beyond Borders*. Ithaca, NY: Cornell University Press.

Morselli, Carlo. (2009). *Inside Criminal Networks*. New York, NY: Springer.

Polak, Josine, and Ester Versluis. (2016). "The Virtues of Interdependence and Informality: An Analysis of the Role of Transnational Networks in the Implementation of EU Directives." In S. Drake and M. Smith, eds., *New Directions in the Effective Enforcement of EU Law and Policy*. Cheltenham, UK: Edward Elgar Publishing.

Sageman, Marc. (2008). *Leaderless Jihad: Terror Networks in the Twenty-First Century.* Philadelphia: University of Pennsylvania Press.

Slaughter, Anne-Marie. (2004). *A New World Order*. Princeton, NJ: Princeton University Press.

Smith, Jackie. (2004). "Exploring Connections Between Global Integration and Political Mobilization." *Journal of World-Systems Research* 10, 255–285.

Jeff Christensen/Liaison/Getty Images

PART V

Looking Ahead

CHAPTER 14
Security, Prosperity, and Quality of Life in the
Balance: Future Directions and Challenges

IR in the balance
How will anarchy, diversity, and complexity affect the search for security in the years to come?

iStock.com/chaofann

14

Security, Prosperity, and Quality of Life in the Balance

Future Directions and Challenges

Learning Objectives

After studying this chapter, you will be able to . . .

14-1   Identify the ways anarchy, diversity, and complexity shape world politics.

14-2   Describe the continuity and change in the meaning and role of security in world politics.

14-3   Explain the trends and emerging areas of concern for future world politics.

14-4   Assess the different ways in which theory, geography, and foreign policy perspectives will change and shape the future of the world.

Chapter Outline

14-1   Anarchy, Diversity, and Complexity in World Politics

14-2   Seeking Security

14-3   The Road Ahead

14-4   Theory in Action, Geography, and Foreign Policy in Perspective

How Big a Problem Is North Korea?

If there was ever a "rogue regime" in international politics, the Democratic People's Republic of Korea (North Korea) fits the definition. Long described as the "hermit kingdom," North Korea has been largely cut off from much of the rest of the international system for decades—in part due to its official ideology of *juche*, or self-reliance, and in part due to the international community's distrust of it. In recent years, North Korea has developed and launched one- and two-stage missiles, firing missiles across Japan's airspace and giving North Korea the capability to reach targets as far away as parts of Alaska. In 2017, North Korea tested a three-stage, intercontinental missile that experts said would have the capability to reach Chicago, Illinois, and tested a hydrogen bomb, a thermonuclear weapon that uses atomic explosions as triggers to an even more destructive blast. The test shook the ground so heavily that it set off air raid sirens across the border in China. At the same time, North Korea has been steadily working to reduce the size of its nuclear warheads, and in 2017 a North Korean government statement claimed it had miniaturized a nuclear warhead small enough to be carried on a missile. Is it any wonder that the rest of the international system is concerned about the threat posed by North Korea?

As these developments occurred, the international community reacted in multiple ways. In 2017, the UN Security Council voted 15–0 to impose economic sanctions on the regime. Although those sanctions did not target Korean leader Kim Jong-un personally, they did target businesses and individuals held responsible for the rocket testing. More to the point, they banned the purchase of North Korea's primary exports—coal, iron, iron ore, lead, and seafood. The sanctions also largely cut off North Korea's access to international bank loans. The results, according to the US ambassador to the UN, should cut North Korea's revenues by one third and represented the toughest-yet international punishments for a regime that refuses to follow international laws and norms (Roth 2017).

Yet North Korea's actions seem prudent from its perspective. The 1950–1953 Korean War never officially ended because no peace treaty exists. US troops never left South Korea, and each year North Korea watched as South Korea got wealthier and wealthier. Not surprisingly, then, each year as South Korea and the US conducted military exercises, usually designed to stop a North Korean attack, the North Korean military reacted to these exercises as if they were a prelude to an invasion of the north. Finally, after the US invaded Iraq in 2003 and forcibly changed the regime there, North Korean leaders could not ignore that the US had listed North Korea along with Iraq and Iran as part of an "Axis of Evil." Was North Korea to be next on the invasion list? From this perspective, a defensive arms build-up seemed warranted. The missiles and nuclear warheads could keep the US (and perhaps South Korea) at bay. However, internal pressures could be leading North Korea to build up its nuclear arsenal for offensive purposes. The North Korean military is arguably the only institution in the country that could force a regime change at Kim's expense. Keeping the military happy might be an internal reason to continue building missiles and warheads in spite of international pressures to cease and desist. This series of actions and reactions raises interesting questions:

1. How does the North Korea example illustrate the security dilemma?

2. What alternatives might be open to the concerned players: both Koreas, China, Japan, the United States, and the UN?

3. Should we expect summit meetings between Kim Jong-un and other leaders to lead to denuclearization on the Korean peninsula?

INTRODUCTION: INTERPRETING HOW THE WORLD WORKS

Throughout the last 13 chapters, we discussed the problems, patterns, and complexities of international relations. We emphasized how the search for security—broadly defined in terms of international, economic, and human dimensions—influences how states and non-state actors behave in the international system. To bring our survey of world politics to a close, rather than simply reviewing what we have already covered, let's step back and ask ourselves the fundamental question: *How does the world work?*

In the opening chapter, we suggested that making sense of world politics was often a daunting task, in part because of the many actors and the seemingly endless stream of events and activities—sometimes appearing to have no rhyme nor reason to them—that constitute international relations. Now, after working together through the preceding chapters of this text, we saw many examples of the range of these issues and events. We looked at problems from conflict to cooperation and from traditional security issues to quality-of-life concerns to identify the patterns and forces at work in the world and to try to understand their causes, connections, and consequences. We saw how states, nations, international organizations, nongovernmental organizations, transnational corporations, individuals, and transnational advocacy networks contributed to the dynamics of world politics. We also worked together to organize and interpret these issues by looking at them through various theoretical lenses, and by thinking about them in the context of the challenges that anarchy, diversity, and complexity present.

So we are in a better position now to address this question: How does the world work? Throughout the text, we discussed how different theoretical lenses take up this question of the underlying factors or forces driving world politics. These different theoretical perspectives give us useful tools to draw our own conclusions and offer our own explanations of international relations. We certainly don't (and shouldn't) need to restrict ourselves to how realists, liberals, constructivists, foreign policy theorists, Marxists, feminists, or other theoretical approaches think the world works. Those perspectives are important and helpful, but we already covered that. Instead, each of us should look at the many parts of world politics, consider and draw from the different explanations these lenses offer us, and ask ourselves how these puzzle pieces fit together into a coherent picture of international relations.

By now, it should be clear that there are a lot of moving pieces in international relations and that it is hard to keep track of all of the facts. Remember what we suggested in Chapter 13, when we said it is more important to remember the types of TANs and the concepts than recalling specific examples? That same rule applies here when trying to figure out how the world works. Instead of starting to think about the role and behavior of specific states and organizations, first ask yourself what constitutes the basic nature and behavior of humans. Are humans cooperative or conflictual? What leads them to violence, and what leads them to peace? Now ask yourself the same questions about the nature and behavior of large collections of people into nations and states. Does that change anything? Are people more conflict-prone or cooperative when they share a collective identity? Do states behave the way they do in world politics because of the nature of the individuals who compose them, because of their attributes and identities, or because of the nature of the international system in which they exist? Could the answer be "all of the above"?

The international system is—as our themes highlight—anarchic (decentralized, without an authoritative central government, but not chaotic), diverse (with actors of many types, perspectives, interests, and values), and complex (with many issues, problems, actors, abilities, and goals all increasingly linked together). Remember, however: At the core, the building blocks of all of this "stuff" are humans. War is the result of choices made by human beings, terrorism is an act in which humans engage, trade is a human activity, TANs are forged by human beings to address matters of global scale, and so on. Keep that in mind as you pull together all of the different moving parts into your own view of the world. Whatever your answer to the question—"How does the world work?"—it must be based on the relationships among people.

Now, to help us answer the question "How does the world work?" we first return to the anarchy, diversity, and complexity themes we have highlighted throughout these pages. Then we consider the concept of security, reflecting not only on its centrality to world politics but also the way its meaning and nature have changed over time. Once we have done that, we can feel more confident about offering some final thoughts about future challenges and dilemmas.

14-1 ANARCHY, DIVERSITY, AND COMPLEXITY IN WORLD POLITICS

>> 14-1 **Identify the ways anarchy, diversity, and complexity shape world politics.**

At the beginning of our exploration, we argued that three fundamental challenges—anarchy, diversity, and complexity—condition the behavior, interactions, and processes of world politics (see Figure 14-1). We saw the consequences of each of these challenges throughout the text: The anarchic structure of the international system—its lack of authoritative, central governing institutions—is a foundational element for understanding and managing conflict and war, and it conditions global economic interactions, the pursuit of wealth, the prospects for an effective regime that protects human rights, and cooperation beyond national borders. The diversity of actors, identities, values, and cultures is a critical issue for human rights and human security, while also greatly affecting conflict and economic relations. The complexity of the global political system makes global economic interactions and coordination challenging and makes the pursuit of international security and human security difficult.

Based on what we considered in the preceding chapters, at least four main observations might be made that can provide some insights as we consider how the world works.

14-1a These Challenges Are Pervasive

By now it is clear that virtually everything that happens in world politics is shaped in one way or another by one or more of these challenges. It is often said of domestic politics that "everything affects everything," and that seems just as true for international relations. Anarchy pushes international actors to try to achieve their goals through their own efforts—what we've referred to as *self-help*. Some actors—often, but not exclusively, IOs, NGOs, and TANs—reduce the anarchy in the system by forging connections over

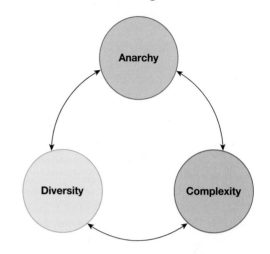

FIGURE 14-1

The Fundamental Challenges of World Politics

and across state boundaries. Their efforts help integrate actors and their activities, and they develop and change the system's norms to make both cooperation and following international norms more routine. However, their effectiveness is influenced by the diversity of the other actors involved: states (whether rich or poor, strong or weak, large or small), nations, IOs, NGOs, TANs, and influential individuals. The wide range of differences among these actors, from types of governments, cultures, levels of wealth and development, priorities and purposes, and many more, all affect many things: the problems that arise, which ones different actors elect to focus on, how they are defined and interpreted, and the ways in which the players interact over them. All of these actors have their own interests to pursue, and their interests often diverge or conflict with each other.

Then the complexity of the issues comes into play. States often address the security dilemma by purchasing more arms, thereby creating potential arms races at the regional or global level. The money spent on arms then reduces the amount of money available for investment to meet other security needs such as economic development, assuring a reasonable quality of life, protecting human rights and the environment, and so on. In fact, overspending in any of these areas can reduce a society's ability to meet other important needs. So finding the balance point—which provides a sustainable economy and a sustainable quality of life while protecting one's physical security from threats of harm—is a huge challenge for virtually all international actors.

Or, to take another example from the current context, shifts in global power and influence among states—particularly the new challenges to US leadership in world politics posed by the rise of China, the assertiveness of Russia, and changes in the US political and economic contexts—lead to a variety of efforts by the US and other state and non-state actors to adjust and respond. In the case of the US, some of these recent efforts—such as backing away from international agreements on climate change, going it alone on efforts to develop a vaccine against the coronavirus behind the global pandemic of 2020, pushing Iran to control nuclear proliferation, reducing support for free-trade and other multilateral agreements in North America and the Pacific regions, and increasing emphasis on military might—have resulted in reactions and new challenges from both friends and rivals that complicate US world leadership even further. As both of these examples, and many others throughout the preceding chapters, show, issues are connected, and it is rare that one can be treated in isolation. It is also increasingly challenging for the actors of world politics to determine which actions to take to address problems because of these linkages among them.

Think of the opening vignette in this chapter. What should the global community do about North Korea? No one wants a war in East Asia, certainly not the Koreans, the Chinese, the Japanese, or the Americans. Yet North Korea's efforts to protect itself are seen as threats to the peace and security of others. What can they do but punish North Korea and try to deter its use of military force? At the same time, can North Korea assume the good intentions of other countries and not see their actions, particularly actions meant to punish, as threatening? How can a conflict spiral be averted?

Anarchy contributes to these challenges, as there is no overarching authority to compel all concerned to play nice with each other. Diversity is clearly involved as well. North Korea is small and economically weak but militarily strong. South Korea has a modern, developed economy, but many of its citizens don't take the North Korean threat seriously. The US is the only state in the international system with true superpower capabilities, but Japan and China both have considerable military and economic power to bring to this conflict if necessary, and China does not want any actions that increase the rate of North Korean illegal immigration into China. China is already worried about North Korean refugees entering the country illegally. As for complexity, North Korea wants to feel safe, South Korea seems to want to be secure and left alone, and China wants no nuclear weapons on the Korean peninsula, but that horse has already left the barn. China also wants the advantages of being North Korea's economic safety valve but not the disadvantages of being responsible for North Korea's actions. Both Japan and the US want to feel safe from a North Korean threat that seems more likely as time goes on. So anarchy, diversity, and complexity significantly complicate this situation. Does anyone have a solution to this dilemma?

The pervasiveness of these three challenges across all the issue areas of world politics is obvious in another way as well. Keep in mind how often anarchy, diversity, and complexity were issues in the previous chapters. As you look at international relations now and into the future, which issues will be most affected by anarchy? What issues will be most challenged by the diversity found in world politics or the complexities involved? Which will be most challenged by all three?

14-1b These Challenges Are Changing

Anarchy, diversity, and complexity are persistent issues, but that does not mean that the challenges they pose are the same today as they were in the 19th century (or earlier). Each of the preceding chapters reveals important changes in the nature and effects of these challenges. As constructivists might say: "Anarchy is what international actors make of it." Following the creation of the Westphalian international system in 1648, state sovereignty reigned supreme within a country's borders. Only in the 20th century did meaningful cracks appear in that idea. Now in the neo-Westphalian system, national leaders cannot mistreat their own citizens within their own borders and expect members of the international system to stand idly by. The concerns of the international community over Syria's violent crackdown on its own people since 2011—and especially its alleged use of chemical weapons and chlorine gas several times in the past—illustrate the heightened attention such states now receive. In some cases, the international reaction will be in the form of soft power—from public denunciations and criticism to economic sanctions. In some cases (such as Kosovo in 1999, Libya in 2011, and Syria in 2017), members of the international system will respond with force—hard power—to try to protect a country's population from a regime that has abandoned its "responsibility to protect" its own.

Even as these challenges change, they are still affected by anarchy and the diversity and complexity involved. For example, when the Libyan government essentially went to war against its own people in 2011, NATO responded with air strikes to protect Libyans opposed to the regime. Although Libya exports oil and thus could potentially retaliate by withholding sales and deliveries of oil, the only NATO member heavily reliant on Libyan oil was Italy, and Italy was bearing the economic and political costs of dealing with the flood of Libyan refugees trying to escape the

An armed Ukrainian separatist guarding the crash site of Malaysian Airlines Flight 17, shot down over eastern Ukraine on July 17, 2014

What challenges for the US, Europe, and the UN does Russian support for Ukrainian separatists pose?

AP Images/Evgeniy Maloletka, File

fighting by reaching the closest European state—in this case, Italy. So NATO felt free to use force. At the same time, the Russian government has waged war against Chechen separatists in the southern part of the country since the 1990s, labeling virtually all who seek independence for Chechnya as "Islamic terrorists." The human rights abuses in Chechnya are at least as bad as, if not worse than, those in Libya, but NATO has not reacted to Russia's anti-Chechen campaigns. When Russia forcefully annexed Crimea in 2014, thus taking a slice out of Ukraine, and supported separatists in other areas in the eastern regions of that country, it raised much furor that resulted in some economic sanctions but little other coercive response from either the European Union or the United States. Even when the Russian-backed separatists shot down a Malaysian airliner, killing almost 300 civilians in July 2014, there was no strong coercive reaction against Moscow.

Russia provides 30–40% of Europe's imports of natural gas. Without that gas, many European countries would have less heat in the winter and less electricity year-round. Because Russia has proven willing in the past to cut off the flow of natural gas to Europeans, no hard power responses to these situations seem likely to come from Europe. So despite the many challenges noted earlier facing Russia, at least in the short run, Russia can push back against EU or NATO pressures (and that's not even considering Russia's military and nuclear arsenal). Yet with Russia's increasing interference in the domestic politics of countries near its borders, across Europe, and in North America, especially the United States, some

Western countries have adopted increasingly firm responses to counter the Russian challenges.

Furthermore, in today's world, a much more complex array of international institutions, transnational networks, and economic and social linkages between societies make the decentralized (anarchic) system of world politics very different from that of several centuries ago—or even just a half-century ago. As we have seen, globalization and interdependence, the spread of democracy, the development of international regimes for integration and coordination, and even the consequences of nuclear arms have altered the meaning and the effects of anarchy and the self-help it tends to produce. These institutions and connections do not centralize the international system like a strong national government might, but they do reduce the fragmentation and decentralization considerably. For example, the growing economic connections between countries fostered by globalization links people and states and their economic activities and welfare in ways never before seen or even imagined. That increased connectivity has both positive and negative effects. For most countries in the world, these connections increase the effects of—and their vulnerability to—things that happen in other parts of the world. The diffusion of democracy has changed the ways governments interact with each other and the ways they relate to their own people. However, those closer connections are not welcomed by all, and many places are struggling with public discontent due to concerns about losses of national identity and state sovereignty.

The complexities and diversities continue. The world's insatiable need for more and more energy resources has generated conflict, as well as efforts to find ways to cooperate to meet those needs and address their many consequences. As states try to ensure their energy needs, they affect others. They damage the environment with their mining and drilling operations, and energy use affects our water, air, and even our global climate. Nuclear accidents like the one in Japan in 2011 give pause to those who thought nuclear power would be their ticket to energy sustainability and independence. Farmers grow more corn and sugar cane for ethanol production, but that diminishes the amount of food available in regional markets. With less food available, prices increase in the face of greater demand. As poor people scrounge for even the minimum daily calories (around 1,200—the average American gets more than twice that amount), the burdens fall most heavily on women and children. Thus, these complex linkages just go on and on.

We could continue, but again, our intent is not to restate things we already considered in the preceding chapters. The idea is to prompt you to take up this thread. What do you think are the most important ways anarchy, diversity, and complexity have evolved over time? Is the world less anarchic than it was 100 years ago? What about 1,000 years ago? What about just 10 years ago? Does *anarchy* mean something different in the present context, when compared to other historical periods? What about diversity? Is it a greater challenge, leading to conflict and tension among different groups? Is there more of it, or are we simply more aware of each other's differences and different points of view, in part because of the effects of globalization? It's hard to imagine that the world isn't more complex now, but in what ways is that complexity important for the functioning of world politics, and how does that affect your life?

14-1c These Challenges Are Connected

Throughout the text, we have seen that these challenges do not operate in isolation. In fact, they are interrelated, and their combination creates its own effects. For example, anarchy and diversity interact. Diverse actors (whether states, IOs, NGOs, TANs, or people) have widely varying needs. International anarchy means states are essentially on their own to protect their interests. This situation can easily lead to distrust and self-regarding actions. Actors do what they feel they must to protect themselves, which reinforces the anarchy of the system. In such a setting, any advances in national/international security, economic security, or human security are at best partial and incomplete. One actor's benefits may often come at another actor's expense. Think about our discussions of conflict and cooperation in Part II, economic

interactions in Part III, and transnational issues such as human rights and the global commons in Part IV. What kinds of factors, developments, and issues can help reduce distrust and uncooperative behavior? Let's consider some current issues as examples, such as global terrorism, the challenges posed by North Korea or Iran and their nuclear programs, global efforts to address climate change, and so on. How do anarchy and diversity combine to make these problems even more significant, and what can be done to address these problems in light of these challenges?

Consider the connections between diversity and anarchy in the other direction as well. Human rights offer a good example. Although there is a Universal Declaration of Human Rights and many international treaties and conventions on specific rights, different countries (not unlike people) have different opinions or interpretations of those human rights. During the Cold War, the Soviet Union pointed out that the capitalist countries in the West always had at least some unemployment. To the Soviets, that was a violation of the human right to work. In China, labor unions are forbidden because the Chinese Communist Party claims to represent all workers. Many people in the United States would consider that a violation of a basic right shared by all people—the right to associate with others freely. Activities and opportunities that some take for granted as ordinary or acceptable in one culture can be considered inappropriate, highly offensive, or even worse by another. Speaking about more serious issues, consider the difficulties and disagreements over the International Criminal Court (ICC), which clearly involved the combination of diversity and anarchy. Is there international law for all individuals, or is it just for states—or just for *some* states?

So what do all those examples have to do with anarchy? You already know the answer. In anarchy, there is no authority to resolve these differences. How states manage the diversity between them is determined in part by the fact that there is no central lawmaking body to create the rules and no enforcement mechanism for a World Court decision saying one country is right and the other wrong when they come into conflict. They must use diplomacy or force to work out these differences.

Diversity and complexity also interact. Diverse actors have very different needs and preferences. Thus, complex issues become difficult to resolve, as actors perceive and react to different facets of those issues. The global economy provides a good example. For example, China's emphasis on export-led growth dramatically enriched China but did so at the expense of Chinese workers, whose low pay left them very poor but allowed Chinese exports to undercut their competitors' prices. Rather than improve the lives of millions of their citizens, the Chinese government chose to invest their profits in the safest possible place—the US economy. As Chinese capital flowed into the US treasury, the federal government could borrow and spend more money. The flow of Chinese capital was one of the factors that led US banks to try to make more loans (to generate income to pay interest on Chinese and other accounts). This dynamic contributed in part to the speculative housing bubble of the early 21st century, one of the key causes of the global Great Recession of 2008–2010, and the hardships it has generated for people everywhere.

Or consider how the forces of globalization have contributed to real challenges for the politics, policies, and interactions of states. As we saw in previous chapters, globalization has enabled terrorist challenges to individual states and the broader international community. The economic forces that are a major part of globalization have produced not only progress and economic growth but also backlashes against global economic integration, free trade, and immigration. Around the world, national groups often feel the loss of control that the interdependence of globalization brings, and at other times they may resent that globalization leads to external norms being extended to them. Europeans rejecting Syrians fleeing violence, Britons rejecting the EU, and Americans rejecting trade agreements with longtime allies are all examples.

But it is not only developed countries that express frustration. For example, Aung San Suu Kyi symbolized the quest for democracy during the many years of her house arrest in Myanmar (Burma). After receiving the Nobel Peace Prize for her work, she was released from house arrest and transitioned into Burmese politics. In recent years, the Burmese military cracked down on the Rohingya, a persecuted largely Muslim minority group in Myanmar. Rohingya villages were burned in what seemed an ethnic cleansing operation, driving refugees into nearby Bangladesh and Malaysia. Yet the former Nobel Peace Prize recipient, now the state counsellor (effectively the prime minister of Myanmar), defended the government's actions at the World Court and rejected the idea that the ICC had any jurisdiction over the issue. International criticism of her response has been sharp—Canada even rescinded her honorary Canadian citizenship!

Complexity and anarchy also interact. Even when international actors agree, coordinating action on issues and devising effective responses are difficult in an anarchic system. For example, almost everyone seems to be in favor of cleaning up the environment for the good of all. However, rich countries expect poor countries to change their behavior by polluting less, and many poor countries expect the costs of their antipollution efforts to be paid for by rich countries. Some developing countries also expect to be allowed to pollute freely until their material needs are largely met and they have the increased wealth to take on antipollution efforts themselves. Because there is no actor that can compel some to "give in" to the other side, there's been no agreement bridging this fundamental gap between rich and poor states, much like there are no clear rules or authoritative institutions to compel cooperation in other areas of the global commons.

Enough prompts from us. Think back on the preceding chapters: How do you think the interrelationships among anarchy, diversity, and complexity affect international security, economic security, and human security? Are any of these factors more important, or do they affect one type of security more than the others?

14-1d These Challenges Are Not Insurmountable

The forces of anarchy, diversity, and complexity present persistent challenges for world politics and often stymie even the best efforts to address problems constructively, while generating their own problems as well. However, we have seen in the preceding chapters that the players of world politics have been able to overcome them in many instances.

Anarchy exists, but IOs *are* built, problems *are* addressed through them, and progress *is* made because of them. The UN and a host of related organizations foster cooperation in many different arenas: economic (the International Monetary Fund, the World Bank and its regional development banks, the World Trade Organization, etc.), humanitarian (the World Health Organization, UNICEF, the Food and Agriculture Organization, the UN University, the UN Commissioner for Human Rights, etc.), and legal (the World Court, the ICC, special tribunals for regional conflicts, etc.), just to name a few. Transnational advocacy networks connect NGOs to other players, including states, IOs, TNCs, and individuals, to address transnational problems. Yet what factors mitigate such cooperation and progress? Has more progress been made in addressing economic and human security than national/international security? If so, why do you think this would be the case? Since the early 1960s, the members of the international system have sought to limit the spread of nuclear weapons through a series of landmark treaties and, at least according to the principles of the Nonproliferation Treaty, to reduce existing arsenals as well. Given recent developments with North Korea and Iran, how has that worked out? How far does trust go? Can the spread of nuclear weapons really be prevented, and could nuclear weapons ever be eliminated entirely?

As we saw in Chapter 13, diversity can divide, but consensus can be built. Key roles are played by not just states, IOs, or NGOs but also by transnational advocacy networks linking all these actors together. Such TANs increasingly serve a key function of linking all those who care about solving a problem and maintaining a communications link between those actors for coordinated action. The actions by such TANs may be to monitor nuclear proliferation, link medical care to the chronically underserved communities around the globe, promote education (particularly of women), help save refugees from the ravages of intrastate wars, and foster more sustainable and environmentally friendly energy development and use. Sadly, other TANs can work to impose one set of values on others. These include terrorist or criminal networks that can bedevil the efforts of states, IOs, and NGOs to combat them.

Complexity makes effective action hard but not impossible. In fact, the increasingly complex linkages among issues can provide opportunities as well as challenges, as we have seen. States can bargain across many of these linked issues, giving and taking across them in ways that help create some gains for each, when focusing on just one issue might have resulted in an impasse. The involvement of non-state actors such as IOs and NGOs may complicate the playing field, but it may also introduce new forums for cooperation and new ways of solving problems collectively. Think about the examples found throughout the text: When does the complex arena of actors produce the most progress?

Again, there are not many issues more complex than trusting rivals who possess nuclear weapons. Think of all those movies about the American West in which two rivals squared off against each other on a dusty street—trust was not the first thing on their minds; shooting straight and fast was. Yet arms control treaties have created a sophisticated set of rules and norms that regulate the biggest nuclear weapons powers in the system. The exceptions (such as India, Israel, North Korea, or Pakistan) have relatively few weapons and should not blind us to the larger fact that most nuclear weapons are governed by strong international norms (so long as Russia, China, and the US continue to abide by those norms). Another example is the global effort to control the spread of HIV infection. The virus and its consequences involve a complicated mix of standards of medical care, sexual practices, cultural and societal norms, the role of women in society, human trafficking, and so on. Yet the UN and other leading state actors united behind the Millennium Development Goals and its successor projects and have made a major dent in this global health scourge. The growth rates of HIV infection and AIDS have declined steadily each year since 2011, and we can hope that, like smallpox, HIV/AIDS may be eliminated in the future. Unfortunately, the recent global pandemic, which had already claimed almost 1 million lives by the end of 2020, has not spurred a comparable level of global cooperation. Indeed, as of yet, the international response to the coronavirus COVID-19 has not been coherent or coordinated. To the contrary, among other things, a "vaccine nationalism"—the effort by states to get a vaccine for their populations before others—has emerged in the US, China, Russia, and elsewhere.

Again, our most important concern at this point is not to advance what we think, and not to summarize what has been covered, but to encourage you to consider what *you* think now that you have worked through the material in the text. What actions and conditions do you think are most likely to allow the players of world politics to overcome the challenges posed by anarchy, diversity, and complexity? How do theoretical lenses like realism, liberalism, constructivism, Marxism, world systems theory, or feminism help us sort through such questions? What do these lenses tell us is likely, or at least possible?

14-2 SEEKING SECURITY

>> **14-2 Describe the continuity and change in the meaning and role of security in world politics.**

We have centered our exploration of world politics on the idea that the search for international, economic, and human security is a central motivating force in the international arena. As we indicated in the opening chapter and throughout the ensuing pages, however, we think *security* is a broad term that encompasses much more than simply military issues. One way to interpret the material presented in the book is to understand that a central aspect of world politics involves its players grappling with multiple dilemmas in the search for security.

Figure 14-2 shows the three dimensions of security that make up our conception of the matter. These dilemmas include efforts to be secure in the traditional sense of political and territorial independence, which is linked to concerns about military power, conflict, and war. But they also involve efforts to be secure economically—to experience economic growth and development, to gain or maintain access to resources and markets, and to achieve good and improving standards of living for the societies and communities that the actors serve and represent. Furthermore, we argued that these dilemmas also involve a host of concerns—some old and some new—about the ability of individuals to live well and safely in their communities and environments. These human security issues have grown increasingly important as the world has grown smaller through the forces of globalization and interdependence. Attention to matters of human rights, the environment, disease and health, nutrition, and a great variety of others is of much greater importance today than at the beginning of the Westphalian system over 350 years ago.

We should also note that these dimensions of security are not separate from each other, either, and they probably never have been, so unlike the figure we started with in Chapter 1, Figure 14-2 shows their intersections and connections. As we saw, concerns about economic wealth and development have led to issues of traditional military security in a great many instances, from World War II to later conflicts in the Middle East involving oil. Economic and human security issues are also directly linked. Without adequate levels of wealth, a country cannot provide for the basic needs of its population. After World War II, South Korea worked hard to ensure economic prosperity for its future citizens, and it was successful. Elites within the Nigerian government, conversely, could not resist the temptation to steal the vast profits of oil production from the people. Partly because of the corruption, Nigerians have poor education and health services and, as a result, have low life expectancy. Their lack of economic security led to a lack of human security, namely early death.

It is also increasingly clear that human security concerns about human rights, environmental degradation, diseases such as COVID-19, and the like have connections to the traditional security issues as well. Consider that many of the military actions of the past two decades—wars in the former Yugoslavia,

military actions in Libya, the Russian intervention in Ukraine, violence between Israeli Defense Forces and Palestinians in Gaza, and the military actions by the US and others in the Middle East against the Islamic State, for example—have human rights at their core. In the 1990s, the US Central Intelligence Agency even devoted intelligence gathering and analysis resources to tracking and studying environmental degradation in Africa as a means to help predict and prevent the eruption of violent conflict there. As former US CIA director Michael Morell (2020) recently argued, COVID-19's economic and financial harm, effects on instability (especially in conflict zones), and implications for global leadership make its consequences for current and future international, economic, and human security profound.

As we think about the quest for security in this light, we can offer a few observations synthesized from across the preceding chapters. These observations reflect both the centrality and the evolving aspects of security and are just a few that might be considered.

14-2a Traditional Military Security Concerns Continue but Are Evolving

We saw throughout the text that concerns for survival and safety, linked to power and military security, are persistent problems in world politics. The challenges posed by North Korea are one very good illustration of this. However, the nature of those problems seems to have evolved considerably over time, from the increasingly destructive wars between states for power and territorial control that marked the Westphalian era through World War II to the civil wars, identity-based conflicts, and asymmetric conflicts of the neo-Westphalian period. We saw what were once the most warlike and conflict-prone members of the international system—great powers—basically end violent conflict with each other. In their place, sadly, civil conflict—mostly outside the developed world—has become the most common type of war. For example, intrastate wars in Syria and Yemen have resulted in the deaths of hundreds of thousands, with large numbers of other states getting involved—like Russia, Iran, Lebanon's Hezbollah, Turkey, the US, France, Saudi Arabia, and the United Arab Emirates. Nearby, the rollback of Islamic State–controlled territory in Iraq and Syria promises to unleash a three-way sectarian war between Iraqi Kurds, Shi'a Muslims, and Sunni Muslims. The conflict between Israel and Palestinian forces continues as low-level, but seemingly constant, violence plagues Israeli and Palestinian communities.

Although millions may not die in each of these conflicts like they did in World War II, these wars are still very bloody and so common that their collective

The Pursuit of Security in Three Arenas

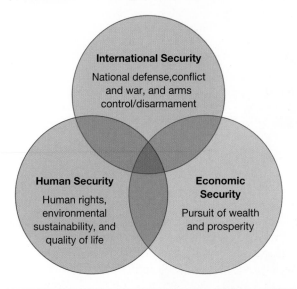

death tolls more than compensate for their smaller individual scope. At the same time, transnational terror networks have posed additional challenges for security. As we discussed in Chapters 6 and 13, such challenges to international security are not easily met through traditional security policies. The members of the international system will continue to face the consequences generated by this form of conflict, as well as those caused by applying traditional security measures (such as the application of military force) to problems that don't necessarily match up.

Can the world put an end to these conflicts? They are often fought with simple conventional weapons, so it isn't just a matter of regulating nuclear weapons or missiles. The bigger, wealthier countries might choose to intervene to stop these conflicts, but such interventions are not easy and often are "no-win" situations. Will international actors remain largely uninvolved in such conflicts until they are directly targeted? Can the UN, the Arab League, the African Union, NATO, or some other IO or alliance structure step up to protect the victims of violence, or is the neo-Westphalian period going to be marked by increased tribalism and identity wars?

14-2b Economic Security Concerns Gain Importance and Are Shaped by Globalization and Interdependence

We saw the evolution of economic security from an era of national economies at the beginning of the Westphalian system to an era in which an international economy with increasing trade and other economic transactions connected states, and finally to the development of the current global economy, which has made it increasingly difficult to separate and identify national economies at all. For example, does it even make sense to talk about "American" cars anymore? Ford autos are made in Mexico and Europe, and GM products are made in Canada and China. For that matter, about three of every four Japanese autos sold in the US are made in the US; BMWs, Kias, and Mercedes and others are made in US factories as well. The pursuit of economic security has been transformed from the dominant mercantilist practices of the 17th and 18th centuries to those conditioned by interdependence, globalization, and the deepening network of international institutions affecting economic activities and interactions.

During the 20th century, an ideological competition between capitalism and communism raged, sometimes violently. In 1989, one scholar went so far as to argue that history had ended. By that, Francis Fukuyama meant that democracy and capitalism had won the day and were the ultimate forms of government and economy that humans would ever produce. There would be no more communisms or fascisms. It seemed hard to refute his argument at the time, but since then, we have seen reversals of democracy in many parts of the world. In 2008, the world saw a near economic collapse, largely because of unconstrained or underregulated capitalism. Since then, we have seen backlashes against the forces and effects of the global economy in both developing and developed countries alike, including substantially weakened support for the core global free-trade regime that has dominated

Syrian Kurds demonstrate against Turkish threats near the Turkish border in October 2019

What challenges do the civil war and violence in Syria pose?

DELIL SOULEIMAN/AFP via Getty Images

the world economy since World War II, as Fukuyama (2017) later acknowledged. What does this mean for the search for a better economic system? Poverty is rampant—remember that most of the world's population live below the US poverty line—and inequality between the haves and have-nots of the world, both within and between countries, is worsening. Is our globalized system a good one? Is it the best one we can manage? How will the players of world politics contend with the emerging problem agenda of the present, which includes inequality, uneven economic growth, energy security, food security, water security, and security from intrastate conflict?

14-2c Human Security Issues Are Increasingly Central and Connected to Both Economic and Military Security

The arena of world politics—and those issues that are now considered as international or transnational concerns—has broadened considerably. For example, 100 or so years ago, a few diplomats may have discussed concerns for public health briefly, but such concerns were very low on any agenda—if they appeared at all. Instead, world leaders concerned themselves with military security and using their militaries to secure colonial possessions. Now, public health concerns are regularly on the agenda because they could affect everyone on the planet. In 2020, the COVID-19 coronavirus spread rapidly from China and, due to global air and cruise ship travel, quickly spiraled into a global pandemic within three months. Countries began restricting travel both inside and outside their borders to contain the virus, but these travel restrictions came too late. The global economy plunged steeply in the face of the shocks caused by the disease and efforts to control it, leading both the World Bank and the International Monetary Fund to warn of the steepest global economic downturn since the Great Depression.

Colonies are no longer acceptable, and military force is no longer considered a legitimate way to secure wealth, but the competition for profits has only increased as more countries strive to pull themselves out of poverty. States no longer struggle to secure their colonies with occupation and physical force, but now they must secure their economies from foreign competition, the outsourcing of jobs, capital flight, and many other dynamics of a global economy because maintaining jobs for their people is essential. This, of course, means increased attention to the skills and education of the workforce and many other issues that relate to economic competition, but it has also meant heightened concerns about immigration, jobs, and inequality.

One interesting window into this transformation of security and the international issue agenda can be seen simply by taking a brief look at the kinds of international or global conferences that have occurred over the past century or so. From conferences dominated by great powers trying to place limits on the initiation and practices of warfare (e.g., the Geneva Conventions), control arms races (e.g., the Washington Naval Conference), and respond to the aggression of one state against another in the first three decades of the 20th century, the last two decades have seen major international and global conferences on global climate change, women's rights, population and debt, development, and coping with economic crises. These conferences have also involved a broad array of states, IOs, NGOs, epistemic communities, and individuals, sometimes acting independently and often linked in transnational networks.

14-2d All Security Issues Have Heightened Effects on Women and Children

The transformations of security, and especially the increasing importance of human security, mean that the roles of women and children, and the effects of world politics on them, have become increasingly central to international relations. There is no issue or dimension of world politics that does not include these concerns in some way, as the many discussions throughout the last 13 chapters showed.

Think about how pervasive these issues are. In conflict, for example, the effects of war and violence on women are stark. Women continue to be horribly underrepresented in the highest levels of government, international organizations, management levels of corporations, and so on. Their absence may have a significant effect on the nature of decisions that these players make. If more women were leaders, would they choose violence less often? Violence directed specifically at women and children—including rape, sexual slavery, and murder—has been an instrument of warfare for as long as people have been fighting. Specific instruments of military security and warfare, such as the use of landmines and cluster munitions, have had devastating effects on the women and children of the societies in which their use is common. What percentage of the millions of refugees who flee violence and economic hardship each year do you think are women? And as we saw, the struggle for subsistence and prosperity around the world disproportionately affects women and children.

There is simply no society in the world in which women enjoy the same freedoms, rights, protections, and opportunities as men, and virtually every society struggles with these issues, inequities, and inequalities in one way or another. The security issues facing women and children are an important focus of the current neo-Westphalian era, as some states and many IOs and NGOs increasingly turn their attention to these issues.

Think of the preceding points as you consider the search for security in world politics, its dynamics, and its implications. What trends and developments do you think are most important? How have these trends and developments contributed to both continuity and change in the nature of world politics? How have they affected the focus on and salience of different issues in world politics? And going back to the three challenges we have emphasized, how do anarchy, diversity, and complexity affect the search for security across these three dimensions?

14-3 THE ROAD AHEAD

>> **14-3** **Explain the trends and emerging areas of concern for future world politics.**

Given the centrality of security—as we broadly defined it—the persistent challenges posed by anarchy, diversity, and complexity, and the elements of continuity and change we have discussed to this point, let's consider some future directions and challenges likely to be important as the patterns of world politics continue to unfold.

14-3a From State-Centric to Multi-centric System

Let's begin with a basic change that will affect many aspects of international relations: Future world politics are likely to be shaped by a set of major players different from those dominating most of the period since the Treaties of Westphalia. Since Westphalia, states have been the primary and dominant players, and the realist theoretical lens continues to afford them pride of place. However, as we saw, especially over the past half-century, non-state actors have become more important to international relations.

There are consequences for the future of world politics, many of which we have introduced and discussed in the preceding chapters. Traditional international security is likely to prove a very different issue as non-state national groups such as Palestinians, Chechens, and Kurds, as well as terrorist organizations and other militant non-state actors, continue to rely on the use of force. Traditional mechanisms of securing oneself are not as obviously applicable in an environment in which such players are active. Just to take one example, it is much easier to deter a state like the old Soviet Union, or maybe even contemporary Iran, from attacking with weapons of mass destruction than to deter them from promoting insurgency campaigns or engaging in cyberwarfare, and it's often easier to deter states than to deter non-state nations or terrorist groups. In what other ways is a multi-centric world of state and non-state actors likely to shape and affect international security?

Economic security has been and will continue to be shaped by this new array of players as well. Multinational corporations have crossed state lines so much that many of them have subsidiaries all around the world. McDonald's doesn't export burgers to France, because it has its own corporation and restaurants in France. For decades, international organizations worked to promote trade and economic stability, but with the creation of the WTO, the world created an organization that could enforce trade agreements. No longer are states sovereign in the way they were under the Westphalian system. Now, they must abide by rules created by international organizations or suffer consequences. In what other ways is a multi-centric world of state and non-state actors likely to shape and affect economic security?

Human security is no different. As we have seen, transnational advocacy networks are active and important across an increasing array of issues that affect the physical safety, economic well-being, and quality of life of individuals around the world. That is likely to continue in the future, with significant consequences for world politics. On the negative side, terrorist organizations have made the most powerful states the world has ever seen feel insecure. To take a relatively minor and simple example, the now-standard practice of having to pass through airport security screenings in even the smallest airports in the United States and elsewhere is annoying. However, it is because of terrorist threats and actions that we must all walk through security—often in our socks—or in some cases be electronically strip-searched. In what other ways is a multi-centric world of state and non-state actors likely to shape and affect human security?

14-3b Emerging Challenges and Dilemmas

As we have illustrated throughout the text, multiple factors combine to create new issues that create challenges and dilemmas for humankind. The physical security of more people is arguably threatened more now by intrastate conflict, terrorism, and pandemics than by more traditional national/international security threats. Globalization causes more societies to come in contact with each other, complicating physical and economic security as we all compete for the means of prosperity, while increasing the effects of basic identity concerns. Cooperation in sustainable development may be the path out of this particular economic dilemma, but promoting such development typically requires additional monetary or human resources. Finally, the planet's population is continually growing, creating additional competition for needed resources and services—like food, water, petroleum, other energy sources, education, health care, and so on. As noted, this squeeze on humankind hits women and children hardest. The failure to meet all these human security needs can in turn imperil economic development and create the foundations for new conflict.

New competition arises in new common spaces, and creative means of cooperation may be needed to resolve it. States compete—and clash—in cyberspace and in maritime spaces not previously contested, and then there's outer space. Where once core states like the US and Russia dominated "the race for space," now space vehicles are launched by semi-peripheral states (such as China and India) and even private corporations (like SpaceX and, possibly in the future, Virgin Galactic).

Thus, emerging trends suggest less frequent great wars, more frequent small or intrastate conflicts, more terrorism and cyberwarfare, and more competition for wealth and the things that contribute to its growth, with potential scarcity and relative deprivation conflicts emerging as a result. And these trends suggest that the locations and participants in the organized violence that has so often characterized international relations have shifted from the so-called great powers competing with each other to the less-developed world.

That's the bad news. The good news is that, even with the contemporary pressures and threats arrayed against it, an international architecture is in place to promote global cooperation and problem solving. That architecture includes thousands of IOs, NGOs, TANs, international conferences on shared problems, and the norms that all these actors and efforts create. So at the end of this course, how do you see it? Is our global glass half empty, or half full?

14-4 THEORY IN ACTION, GEOGRAPHY, AND FOREIGN POLICY IN PERSPECTIVE

>> 14-4 **Assess the different ways in which theory, geography, and foreign policy perspectives will change and shape the future of the world.**

We devoted considerable time in the text to discussing the connections noted in the "Theory in Action," "Revenge of Geography," and "Foreign Policy in Perspective" boxes. In each chapter, we introduced some questions and scenarios and showed how these different concepts had big implications for our understanding of international relations. Let's return to these issues one last time to try to integrate what we have learned so far and to think about what these issues mean for the future. We are, of course, speculating about the future—no one has a crystal ball—and you may very well have different ideas than we do. That is good, however, because it means that you have thought about the world in which we live and have a new and more complete understanding of it. Let's begin by considering these three concepts.

14-4a Theory in Action

Throughout the book, we gave examples of how theory informs the practice of international relations. We discussed many issues: cooperation dilemmas, intervention and human rights, conflict and its causes, how the democratic peace prompted the United States to increase its promotion of democracy, how countries should—or perhaps should not—engage in free trade, the role of NGOs on key problems, and others. The questions that we must now consider are (a) what will the theories we have discussed prescribe for the coming years and decades, and (b) which theories will lead to the best policies?

To answer this question, we must again think about how the world works. The different theoretical approaches told very different stories. Realism sees the world as very competitive and conflict-ridden. It clearly would suggest policies that promote the strength of the state and neglect the ideas of cooperation with other countries, equality, and environmental sustainability. Could realist policies create a world in which strong states are safe, but weak states are poor and lack human security, and the global environment is significantly degraded? Liberal policies might promote cooperation and development while paying less attention to national security. Could that lead to a world where trade flourishes, countries develop, and the environment is protected until a large-scale war breaks out because state security concerns were neglected? Constructivists stress the powerful role of ideas, norms, and identities in shaping what people and states want: Are the central ideas and norms of world politics changing for the better or the worse?

Marxist and world systems theory could suggest revolts by poorer states or simply more attention paid to development and equality. In the case of conflict between the rich and the poor, violence could erupt into a large scale with the deaths of millions. If economic development were the only focus, what would happen to the environment? Feminist theory is too diverse to suggest a single policy, but to be sure, greater attention would be paid to equalizing the treatment of women. Given the great diversity of cultures in the world—and their corresponding political and social institutions and practices—what consequences might that incur?

We purposely paint an extreme picture here. We must consider not only *how* we think the world of international relations works but also what consequences the answer to that "how" question will cause. If you think Marx was right about the world being driven by economic class, what does that mean for the future? What policies do you think would make the world a better place? Are those policies feasible? Consider all of the "Theory in Action" boxes—what have you learned, and what do you conclude, from them?

14-4b Revenge of Geography

Thomas Friedman argued that "the world is flat" in a book with that title. He simply meant that the world is becoming smaller, more interconnected, and more interdependent. Throughout this book, we showed how geographic factors can still have a powerful impact on politics. Perhaps the most gruesome examples were the Great Lakes region in Africa that helped spawn the terrible genocide in Rwanda along with several civil conflicts. But we also considered how geography affects security, interests, and wealth/development, as well as how a country's neighbors, or lack thereof, could increase or decrease its power.

Considering how the geographic setting can affect international relations, how will the increasingly "small" or "flat" world affect the future? There are more people, fewer resources, and a changing environment. The world will be a radically different place in 2050 than it was in 1950. What revenge will geography take next?

Perhaps it is best to think about specific changes in our environment, broadly speaking. For example, there was a theory called "peak oil" that suggests humans had tapped all of the big oil reserves and that our supply is going to begin dwindling, perhaps rather rapidly. By 2020, new technologies such as hydraulic fracturing have made "peak oil" seemingly a moot point, with a global oil glut, prices declining sharply, and numerous automobile companies around the world switching to greater production of hybrid or totally electric vehicles. We can expect differing effects on oil-exporting countries. Iran and Nigeria may be hurt more quickly than Russia or Saudi Arabia and the Emirates, but all may eventually be hurt. What consequences will such pain have on those countries, their regions, or the world?

Similarly, what effect might global climate change have? Whether the world heats up, cools down, or simply fluctuates more, agriculture will be affected dramatically. Wealthy countries like the United States and the EU states will likely be able to develop means to continue effective food production, but less-developed states may not. Any changes to the climate can result in temporary or even permanent loss of crops, which could result in famine. Sadly, famine often results in civil conflict and displaced people. These may be apocalyptic predictions, but they are worth considering. More important, consider what geographic changes will affect the future of international relations.

14-4c Foreign Policy in Perspective

Finally, we should consider the foreign policy behavior of both state and non-state actors who occupy the game board of world politics. As we discussed throughout the preceding chapters, key states such as the United States play a major role in the world. The United States, for example, has one of the biggest economies, the most powerful military, and what has long been a very attractive culture that has spread around the world in the form of entertainment, restaurant chains, and fashion. However, the US is certainly not the only state in the world, and its relative advantages are under increasing pressure from challenges arising from rivals, competitors, and even current friends. Other states such as Russia and China, and groups of states such as the European Union, also have their own interests and ideas. And, of course, the US will not remain the sole superpower forever. How will these power transitions play out?

What about the other players and their policies? What do middle-sized, developed, and very small states want in the world? What motivates them, and how do those things differ from the things that shape the concerns and behavior of major powers? And what about those non-state actors pursuing their agendas? In what ways are they changing the nature of world politics and shaping or influencing the behavior of major states such as the US, China, Russia, Japan, the members of the European Union, and others?

Most states face significant challenges in the global economy, for example, with debt mounting, the economic shocks and continued uncertainty of the global pandemic growing, volatility on the rise, growth slowing, and inequality increasing. For the US, the near-term economic outlook is unclear as the country struggles to recover from the effects of the coronavirus and its financial debt is high, to say the least. A significant portion of that debt is held by other countries, and one in particular—China—is a rising power. What will that mean for the future? Will China—with its dramatic economic expansion over the past three decades or so—play a more powerful and assertive role? Will China be able to tell the United States what to do in the coming decades?

The US economy is not the only one suffering from a steep downturn, though. For example, Europe is in a tenuous position. Issues ranging from the effects of the pandemic to the British withdrawal from the European Union and the rise of populist forces and political parties in many countries across the region illustrate areas of growing pressure. In mid-2020, the European Commission forecasted an even more severe recession and a longer struggle to recover than originally expected, which would have major repercussions worldwide. The weakness of the European economy makes wielding the tools of economic statecraft in situations such as Ukraine and elsewhere increasingly difficult. Economically, the effects of struggling economies in Europe and elsewhere ripple throughout the world. In international security terms, such economic weakness in Europe and around the world threatens stability, and history shows that military conflict is often preceded by economic problems.

With constraints and challenges such as these and many others facing the major players in world politics, what courses of action might they take to address the current and emerging problems of world politics? What courses should they take? Think about the different theories we discussed and how they explain to us how the world works. Which one of those perspectives makes the most sense to you as you think about how states and others act to achieve their goals? What do you think that suggests about the nature and role of the most powerful players in the system in general?

CONCLUSION

We began this chapter with a description of the challenges posed by North Korea to its neighbors and the United States. We also began this chapter with a suggestion that before we think of all the different facts discussed in this book, we ask ourselves what constitutes the basic nature of humans. Are we cooperative or conflictual? How do we connect these two—human nature and the dilemma created by North Korea's flouting of international norms and increasing security challenges?

The answer lies in the fact that the dispute with North Korea is a dispute among people—human beings. Kim Jong-un may seem very different from you—and he may be—but he is human, just as are his advisers. Thus, examples like this one remind us that international politics involves people and affects people. Understanding the basic nature of humans will help us understand how those people will behave. If you see people generally as cautious cooperators, then you would expect that the dispute over North Korea's nuclear challenge would end in some form of compromise, possibly with North Korean adherence to international norms about nuclear weapons in return for substantial concessions from the other involved actors. If you tend to think that humans are less cooperative and more self-interested, then you might expect that the United States, Japan, and perhaps South Korea would push North Korea to the brink of war, expecting North Korea to give in rather than face potential annihilation.

What would Kim Jong-un do, then? If you think wealth is the biggest factor in human behavior, then this issue, like many others, should be solvable through some form of payoffs to North Korean elites.

So maybe the North Korean situation is more understandable, albeit still dangerous. It is similar to most other disputes that people must address through cooperative diplomacy, violent conflict, or some in-between option. That is why it is so important to have a view of the world and an explanation for the question "how does the world work?" Because once you have an answer to that question, you can understand any aspect of international relations. ●

| KEY CONCEPTS |

14-1 Identify the ways anarchy, diversity, and complexity shape world politics.

The anarchic structure of the international system—its lack of authoritative, central governing institutions—is a foundational element for understanding and managing conflict and war, and it conditions global economic interactions, the pursuit of wealth, the prospects for an effective regime that protects human rights, and environmental cooperation. The diversity of actors, identity, values, and culture is a critical issue for human rights and human security, while also greatly affecting conflict and economic relations. The complexity of the global political system makes global economic interactions and coordination challenging and makes the pursuit of international security and human security difficult. Anarchy pushes international actors to try to achieve their goals through their own efforts. Some actors reduce the anarchy in the system by forging connections over and across state boundaries, integrating actors and their activities, and changing the system's norms to make both cooperation and following international norms more routine. However, their effectiveness is influenced by the diversity of the other actors involved. The wide range of differences among these actors—from types of governments, cultures, levels of wealth and development, priorities and purposes, and so on—affects the problems that arise, which ones different actors elect to focus on, how they are defined and interpreted, and in what ways the players interact regarding them. Then the complexity of the issues comes into play. These challenges are interrelated, and their combination creates its own effects, both challenges and opportunities.

14-2 Describe the continuity and change in the meaning and role of security in world politics.

A central aspect of world politics involves its players grappling with multiple dilemmas in the search for security. These dilemmas include efforts to be secure in the traditional sense of political and territorial independence, which is linked to the concerns about military power, conflict, and war. They also involve efforts to be secure economically—to experience economic growth and development, to gain or maintain access to resources and markets, and to achieve good and improving standards of living for the societies and communities that the actors serve and represent. Furthermore, these dilemmas also involve a host of concerns about the ability of individuals to live well and safely in their communities and environments, human security issues that have grown in importance in the neo-Westphalian world. These dimensions of security are not separate from each other but are linked in complex ways. The nature of these problems has evolved since the pre-Westphalian era. War has shifted from the increasingly destructive wars between states for power and territorial control that marked the Westphalian era through World War II to the civil wars, identity-based conflicts, and asymmetric conflicts of the neo-Westphalian period. Economic security issues have changed dramatically with the emergence of the global economy. Human security issues such as human rights, quality-of-life concerns, the environment, and the roles of women and children have risen in salience.

14-3 Explain the trends and emerging areas of concern for future world politics.

Non-state actors have become more important to international relations, which affects the nature of traditional security concerns. Economic security has been and will continue to be shaped by this new array of players as well. Multinational corporations have crossed state lines so much that many of them have subsidiaries all around the world. Transnational advocacy networks are active and important across an increasing array of issues, and that is likely to continue in the future, with important consequences for world politics. On the negative side, terrorist organizations have made the most powerful states the world has ever seen feel insecure. The physical security of more people is arguably threatened more now by intrastate conflict and terrorism than by more traditional national/international security threats. Globalization causes more societies to come in contact with each other, complicating physical and economic security as we all compete for the means of prosperity, while increasing the effect of basic identity concerns. Cooperation in sustainable development may be the path out of this particular economic dilemma, but promoting such development typically requires additional monetary or human resources. Finally, the planet's population is continually growing, creating additional competition for needed resources and services—like food, water, petroleum, other energy sources, education, and health care. Emerging trends suggest less frequent great wars, more frequent small or intrastate conflicts, more terrorism, and more competition for wealth and the resources that contribute to its growth. Such challenges are now confronted by an international architecture to promote global cooperation and problem solving composed of thousands of IOs, NGOs, TANs, international conferences on shared problems, and the norms that all these actors and efforts create.

14-4 Assess the different ways in which theory, geography, and foreign policy perspectives will change and shape the future of the world.

The playing field of international relations constantly changes and develops. Some changes are incremental (like the rise of China's economy), while others are startling (like the end of the Cold War or global pandemics). Most changes fall in between such extremes, but all of these developments need to be understood before actions in response are taken. Our theories help us understand and make sense of these changes. We can think of theories as tools, and some are better in certain circumstances than others. Realism may better explain conflict situations, while liberalism may help us understand the challenges to cooperation and how they can be overcome. Questions involving group identities and socially reinforced "truth" narratives can be addressed by constructivism. When people's quality of life matters, some answers might be provided by feminism or Marxist-based approaches. Anytime one country's actions become the key to better understanding, various approaches to foreign policy analysis can come into play. However, one factor in international relations remains relatively constant. Geography continues to advantage some people and disadvantage others. How different international actors cope with these changes helps determine our futures.

REVIEW QUESTIONS

1. What are the central challenges posed by anarchy, diversity, and complexity for the pursuit of security in international relations?

2. What does it mean to be secure in international relations?

3. What key trends and challenges are likely to shape the future of world politics?

The Challenge of Cooperation Revisited

Return now to the very basic puzzle we posed at the beginning of the book. In our first chapter, before we had the benefit of the information, insights, and interpretations from Chapters 2 through 13, we noted that despite all of the apparent benefits, cooperation is often difficult to achieve in world politics. This time, as you think about this puzzle, draw on your worldview, your understanding of how the world works. Realize that all of the theoretical lenses we covered can help you understand how humans—like you and your friends—interact and how states and non-state actors interact. We have seen many instances of productive cooperation in the world, and the intervening pages have also shown that conflict, war, poverty, and a lack of respect for humankind continue to be pervasive problems. There is little doubt that countries would benefit from agreement and collaboration to control the costly acquisition or dangerous spread of weapons, but they frequently do not do so. Mutually beneficial collaboration to promote economic growth and development is less common than we might expect given the benefits it provides. The establishment of institutions, norms, and rules to shape behavior on human rights and environmental sustainability in mutually beneficial and predictable ways is incomplete and episodic. Transnational advocacy networks are increasingly active across many issues in world politics, facilitating the emergence of norms and patterns of cooperation, but they are challenged by the anarchic structure and diversity of interests of the world. So now that we have completed our trek through the landscape of world politics, and you have thought systematically about the pursuit of all forms of security amid the challenges of anarchy, diversity, and complexity, let's ask once again:

Why is international cooperation so hard, and what factors and conditions inhibit and promote it?

Acemoglu, Daron, and James A. Robinson. (2012). *Why Nations Fail: The Origins of Power, Prosperity, and Poverty.* New York, NY: Crown Business/Random House.

Autesserre, Séverine. (2014). *Peaceland: Conflict Resolution and the Everyday Politics of International Intervention.* New York, NY: Cambridge University Press.

Cooley, Alexander, and Daniel Nexon. (2020), *Exit from Hegemony: The Unraveling of the American Global Order.* New York, NY: Oxford University Press.

DeNardis, Laura. (2020). *The Internet in Everything: Freedom and Security in a World with No Off Switch.* New Haven, CT: Yale University Press.

Drezner, Daniel. (2014). *Theories of International Politics and Zombies,* rev. ed. Princeton, NJ: Princeton University Press.

Forrester, Katrina. (2019). *In the Shadow of Justice: Postwar Liberalism and the Remaking of Political Philosophy.* Princeton, NJ: Princeton University Press.

Hester, Helen. (2018). *Exofeminism.* Medford, MA: Polity Press.

Jørgensen, Knud Erik. (2018). *International Relations Theory: A New Introduction,* 2nd ed. Berlin, Germany: Springer.

Kaplan, Robert D. (2013). *The Revenge of Geography: What the Map Tells Us About Coming Conflicts and the Battle Against Fate.* New York, NY: Random House.

Khanna, Parag. (2016). *Connectography: Mapping the Future of Global Civilization.* New York, NY: Random House.

Leichenko, Robin, and Karen O'Brien. (2019). *Climate and Society: Transforming the Future.* Medford, MA: Polity Press.

Milbank, John, and Adrian Pabst. (2016). *The Politics of Virtue: Post-Liberalism and the Human Future.* London: Rowman & Littlefield International.

Reveron, Derek, and Kathleen Mahoney-Norris. (2011). *Human Security in a Borderless World.* Boulder, CO: Westview.

APPENDIX OF WORLD MAPS

North America

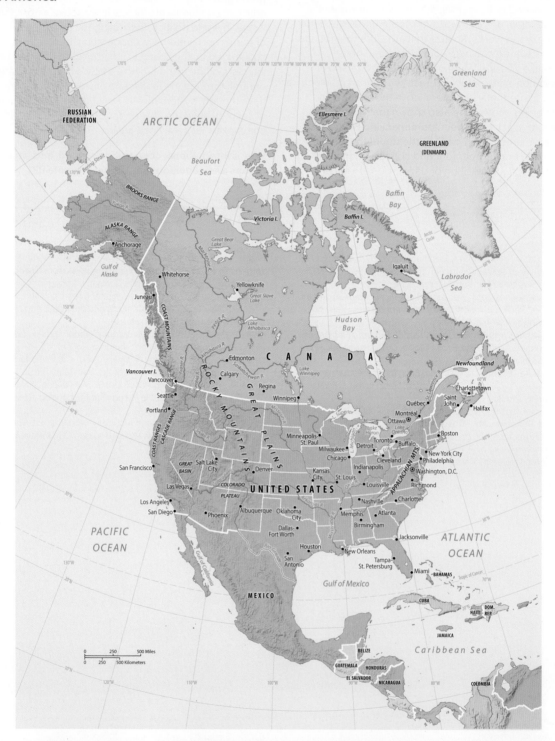

MAP A-2

South America

MAP A-3

Europe

MAP A-4

The Middle East

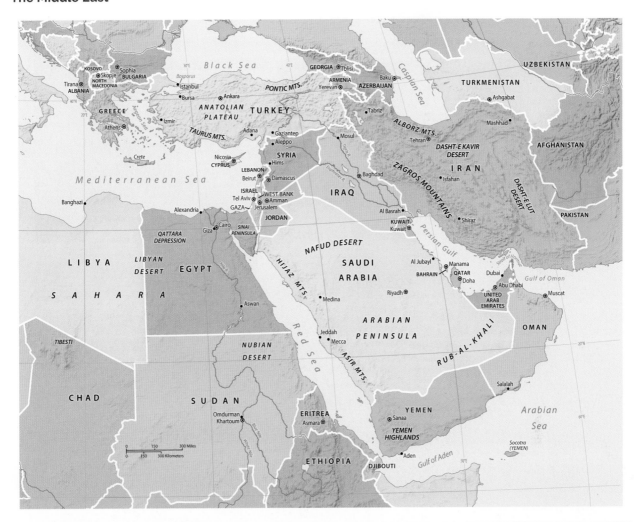

MAP A-5

Africa

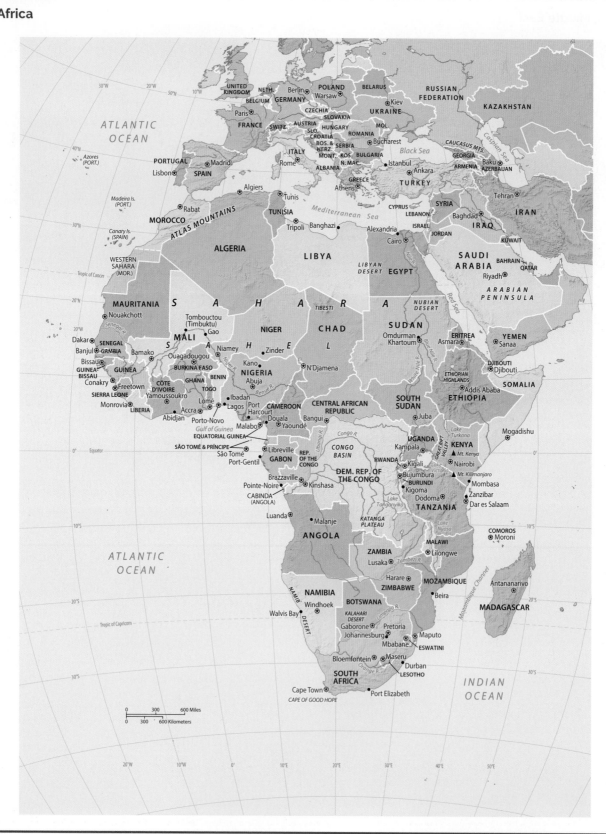

MAP A-6

South Asia

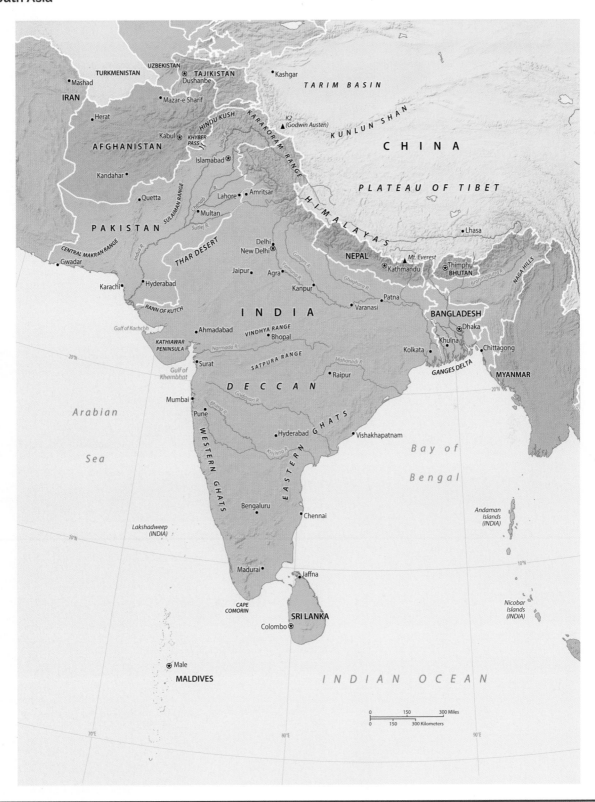

MAP A-7

East and Southeast Asia

MAP A-8

Russian Federation and Central Asia

MAP A-9

Australia and Oceania

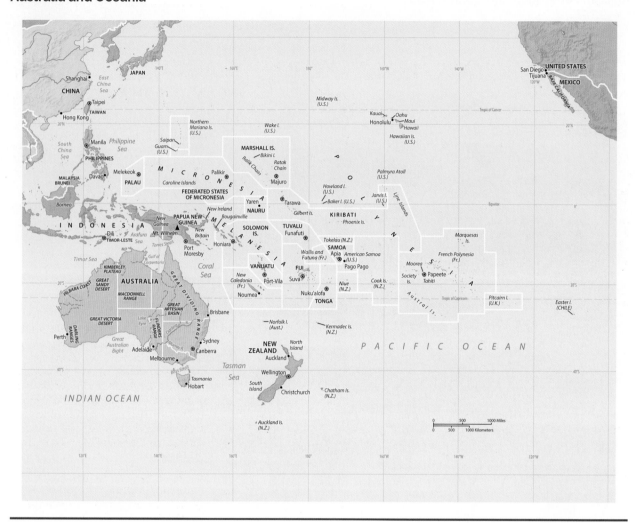

GLOSSARY

absolute advantage: when a country is more efficient than another country at producing a single good.

absolute gains: the total effect of a decision or situation on an actor.

advisory group: the set of individuals from whom leaders seek decision-making assistance.

African Charter on Human and Peoples' Rights: the treaty by the Organization for African Unity (later the African Union) that went into force in 1986 and listed individual rights and the responsibilities of individuals in a communal context. It also created the African Commission of Human and Peoples' Rights and the African Court of Human and Peoples' Rights.

agent-centered approach: understanding and explaining international relations by focusing on the individuals and groups who make decisions within the state.

aid sanction: cutting off aid to a country in order to get it to change its behavior.

alliance: a formal commitment between states to cooperate for specific purposes, such as mutual defense.

al-Qaeda: translated as "the base," this is a fundamentalist Islamic transnational terrorist organization, responsible for many attacks on Western countries and moderate Islamic countries; most infamously, it organized, funded, and perpetrated the September 11, 2001, attacks in the United States.

American Convention on Human Rights: the Organization of American States treaty that went into force in 1978. It created an Inter-American Commission on Human Rights and an Inter-American Court of Human Rights.

arable land: land capable of sustaining agriculture.

arms control: regulation of the amount, type, positioning, or use of weapons.

arms embargo: not selling weapons to a country.

arms race: peacetime competition in armaments by two or more states driven by conflict interests, fear, and suspicion.

asymmetric war: armed conflict between two or more groups of very different military size or power.

austerity program: a program of severely restricted government spending, often on welfare programs, imposed when the country must balance its accounts.

balance-of-power politics: patterns of shifting alliances, force, and counterforce among states as they seek power, counter the efforts of rivals, and confront security threats.

balancing: in alliances, forming coalitions to counter the rising power and threat of a state.

bandwagoning: in alliances, siding with a rising power to gain benefits.

Baruch Plan: a nuclear disarmament proposal authored by US statesman Bernard Baruch after World War II to place nuclear weapons and energy activities under the control and authority of the United Nations.

beggar-thy-neighbor: an economic policy that stresses trade protectionism and causes other countries to bear the costs of efforts to secure prosperity at home.

Beijing Consensus: an alternative development model based on China's economic approach, stressing national determination of economic policies and neo-mercantilist state involvement and direction of the economy.

Big Mac Index: a measure created by *The Economist* magazine that compares the value of currencies by comparing the cost of a Big Mac hamburger in different countries. The United States is used as the baseline cost for the index.

bilateral: a relationship between two states or parties.

bipolar: a distribution of power in the international system in which there are two great powers.

boomerang model: a model in which internal groups repressed by their own states turn to TANs to put pressure on other states; those states then put pressure on the repressive state from the outside. In short, repression against internal groups can boomerang back and cause new external pressure on the repressive state.

bounded rationality: the idea that leaders want to make rational or logical decisions but are limited by their lack of knowledge or other human factors.

Bretton Woods system: a system named for the location of the 1944 conference in New Hampshire that established the family of international organizations created after World War II to maintain and promote the liberal international economic order; the two core institutions created were the International Monetary Fund and the World Bank.

brinkmanship: the strategy of escalating conflicts or crises to nuclear threats in order to force the other side to back down.

capitalism: an economic system of complete or near complete free markets in which market forces determine what is purchased and what is sold. There are variations of capitalism, but the emphasis is on limited government involvement in and regulation of the economy.

capitalist class or bourgeoisie: the owners of businesses, factories, and the like, who profit from the work of laborers but do not work themselves.

carbon footprint: the amount of carbon dioxide we generate through our daily activities.

centrally planned (or command) economy: an economy that is run by the government rather than private citizens. Examples include the Soviet Union and North Korea.

civil society groups: NGOs that promote democracy and human rights on a global basis.

civil war: armed conflict between competing factions within a country or between a government and a competing group within that country over control of territory and/or the government.

coercive diplomacy: a strategy that combines threats and the selective use of force with negotiation in a bargaining strategy to persuade an adversary to comply with one's demand.

Cold War: a period of intense rivalry and competition from 1947–1989 between the United States and its allies on the one hand and the Soviet Union and its allies on the other.

collective action problem: a condition in which the uncoordinated actions of individuals lead to less than optimal outcomes because, although many individuals would benefit from cooperative action(s), few incentives lead any particular individuals to assume the costs of such action(s).

collective goods: things that benefit all concerned—whether or not they participate in their protection and maintenance—and are not owned by any one state actor.

collective security: an approach to security and conflict in which states join together into an organization, ban the use of force by its members, and commit themselves to joining together to respond to any attack by one member on any other member.

colonialism: the situation in which one country takes over another country and administers it with a local bureaucracy.

colonies: territories that are legally owned and controlled by another country, typically called the imperial power.

commitment problem: countries have a hard time committing to cooperative courses of action that assure their partners that they will keep their end of the deal for mutual benefit and forgo the possibility of their own short-term gains.

communism: the anticapitalist economic philosophy created by Karl Marx that promoted centralized control of a country and its economy for the equal redistribution of resources to the country's citizens.

comparative advantage: being more efficient at producing a good or service relative to another good or service. Even if one country has an absolute advantage over another in all products, both countries benefit by specializing in the products they each produce most efficiently (their comparative advantage) and trading for the others.

compellence: the use of military force to stop a foe from doing something it was already doing or to force it to start doing something it was not yet doing.

compulsory jurisdiction: in international law, the condition in which parties to a dispute must submit the case to a court.

Concert of Europe: a 19th-century multilateral organization composed of Great Britain, Russia, Austria, Prussia, and France to promote stability, cooperation, and multilateral diplomacy.

conference diplomacy: large diplomatic meetings of many officials from states, international organizations, nongovernmental organizations, academia, and other non-state actors.

consociational democracy: a form of government that guarantees representation to the different ethnic or religious groups within the country.

constructivism: a major theoretical approach to international relations emphasizing the importance of ideas, collective identities, and the social construction of reality.

constructivism (and ethnicity): an explanation of ethnic conflict that emphasizes the social construction of identity and the ways in which social interactions define ethnicity for groups of people.

conventional war: armed conflict between two or more states in which military forces of each side are used against each other and in which weapons of mass destruction, such as nuclear, biological, or chemical weapons, are not used.

Convention on Genocide: a 1948 UN treaty that both defined genocide and made it a crime whether it occurred in peacetime or in wartime.

Convention on the Elimination of All Forms of Discrimination Against Women (CEDAW): the treaty approved by the UN General Assembly in 1979 to define discrimination against women and outline an agenda by which states can eliminate it.

core: the economic zone composed of wealthy countries producing high-end products.

Council of Ministers (CoM): the EU legislative body made up of sitting ministers of their national governments, who represent their member states and approve all EU legislation.

coup d'état: literally translated as a "strike against the state"; when there is a forceful change in government that overthrows the current leadership.

crimes against humanity: acts of war against a civilian population; these can include the crimes of murder; enslavement; deportation or forcible transfer; imprisonment; torture; rape, sexual slavery, or any other form of enforced sexual violence; persecution on political, racial, national, ethnic, cultural, religious, gender, or other such grounds; enforced disappearance; apartheid; and other inhumane acts that create great suffering or serious mental or physical injury.

cultural exchange: programs involving the exchange of citizens—students, teachers, scientists, artists, and others—between countries to foster cultural understanding and cooperation.

cultural relativism: the idea that human rights are not truly universal and that different cultures have different systems of rights. This term particularly comes into play when non-Western societies argue that international human rights standards have a Western bias and do not reflect non-Western values.

custom: the general practice of states accepted as law; a source of international law.

cyberwarfare: the attempt by one state or nation to cause disruption, discord, damage, death, or destruction by using computers and other digital devices to carry out digital attacks on the computer systems of another.

cyclical theories of war: conflict based on the rise and relative decline of leading powers in the international system in which stability occurs as the victors in major wars assert themselves, and war occurs as a function of the subsequent and inevitable rise of challengers to those dominant powers.

defense: deploying and using military force to fight off an attack.

deforestation: the destruction of forests at a rate faster than they can be replaced or replenished.

democracy: a form of governance in which the people have a meaningful choice in selecting their rulers.

democracy aid: aid given to a country to enhance and consolidate its transition to democracy.

democracy promotion: a cluster of activities, ranging from diplomacy to aid to intervention, designed to foster and support democratization in other countries.

democratic peace: a state-level theory of war stating that institutional and normative characteristics of democratic regimes lead them to peaceful relations with each other.

dependency theory: a theory of development that argues that the dominance and exploitation of poor countries by rich countries prevents progress and development in the poor countries and makes them dependent on the wealthy countries.

desertification: the creation of new, or enlargement of existing, deserts.

deterrence: persuading a potential adversary to refrain from attacking through the threat of costly retaliation.

devalue: a situation in which a currency, such as the US dollar, loses its value compared to other currencies. For example, the Chinese government sets the exchange rate between the US dollar and the Chinese yuan, and currently, the yuan is devalued; it is worth more than the Chinese will trade it for.

developed country: a wealthy country with an economy that tends to produce manufactured goods and services for export.

development aid: aid given to a country to help develop its economy.

difference feminists: proponents of the feminist perspective who argue men and women are fundamentally different in their abilities, particularly in their approach to conflict.

diplomacy: the art and practice of conducting negotiations between states and other actors in world politics.

diplomatic immunity: the principle that accredited diplomats are exempt in almost all cases from prosecution under the laws of the state where they are assigned.

diplomats: individuals occupying positions in the foreign policy establishments of states or the management of other organizations who represent and negotiate on behalf of their country or employer.

direct deterrence: the use of retaliatory threats to discourage attacks against the state making the deterrent threat.

disarmament: the elimination of arsenals or classes or types of weapons.

distribution of power: a characteristic of the international system emphasized by realists based on the number of great or major powers and how power is distributed among them in a given period of time.

diversionary theory: the idea that states suffering from poor economic conditions or internal strife are more likely to resort to force outside their borders in efforts to divert attention from those internal problems or to rally the public behind their leadership.

economic sanction: the cessation of some or all economic exchange between two countries.

economic statecraft: the use of economic means to secure political ends.

embassies: properties that house the permanent diplomatic missions of other countries, typically located in the capital city of a state.

empirical theory: a theory based on real-world observations and explanations.

epistemic communities: networks of experts who bring their knowledge and expertise to the political arena to help policymakers understand problems, generate possible solutions, and evaluate policy success or failure.

ethnic cleansing: a form of violence in which an ethnic group purges or "cleans" a territory of its rival ethnic groups, by forced expulsion, violence, or death.

ethnic geography: the spatial and ecological aspects of ethnicity (e.g., where groups live in relation to one another), which affect the culture, politics, and social practices of states, nations, groups, and individuals.

European Commission (EC): the executive branch of the EU. The Commission is led by a president; it has budgetary powers; and it includes 27 members that oversees policy development in agriculture, trade, social policy, the environment, and many other areas.

European Commission on Human Rights: created by the European Convention on Human Rights, a very active body monitoring human rights situations in Europe. Individuals who believe their rights have been abused can appeal to the commission, which may, after investigation, refer the case to the European Court of Human Rights.

European Convention on Human Rights: the Council of Europe treaty that went into force in 1953, which listed individual rights and created the European Commission on Human Rights and later the European Court of Human Rights.

European Council: the EU body made up of the heads of government of the EU member states, who represent the interests of their member states within the EU.

European Court of Human Rights (ECHR): a court created in 1959 by the Council of Europe; one of the most active courts involved in human rights cases.

European Court of Justice (ECJ): the EU's judicial branch whose rulings take precedence over even national law; it is charged with interpreting EU law and ensuring that it is applied equally across all member states.

European Parliament (EP): the EU legislative body made up of directly elected representatives; it amends, approves, or rejects EU laws, together with the Council of Ministers.

European Union: a regional supranational organization with 27 member states.

Eurozone: the portion of the European Union that uses the euro currency rather than a national currency. These countries include Austria, Belgium, Cyprus, Estonia, Finland, France, Germany, Greece, Ireland, Italy, Latvia, Lithuania, Luxembourg, Malta, the Netherlands, Portugal, Slovakia, Slovenia, and Spain.

export-led growth: the idea that to develop a country's economy, the government should push for companies to focus on products that can be exported to other countries. The policy was most successful in Asian countries, such as South Korea and Singapore.

expropriation: the taking—or nationalization—of property owned by a foreign company with or without compensation.

extended deterrence: retaliatory threats to discourage attacks against allies and friends of the state making the deterrent threat.

external balancing: countering the power of a rival by forming coalitions with other states.

extra-systemic or extra-state war: armed conflict between a state and a non-state entity, such as colonial wars and wars with non-state national or terrorist groups.

extraterritoriality: the principle that one is exempt from prosecution of the laws of the state, typically applied in the case of an embassy.

fair trade: the concept that producers should be paid a fair price for their products.

fascism: a political ideology that glorifies the state over the individuals it comprises and that relies on nationalism and violence to bond the citizenry to the state.

female genital mutilation: the cutting away of part of the external genitalia, based on the belief that, by reducing sexual pleasure, women will remain chaste until married and faithful to their husbands thereafter. Some societies also believe this is a religious requirement for women to behave modestly or that it may increase fertility.

femicide: killing women and girls because of their gender.

feminist international relations theory: a feminist approach to understanding international relations that focuses on the role of women and gender and how historically the world has been dominated by men.

feudalism: a socio-economic-political system in which rulers granted land to the local aristocracy in return for their loyalty and support, and others worked the land in return for food, shelter, and protection from the local aristocracy.

financial sanction: the freezing of a country's financial assets held in another country.

first-generation human rights (individual rights): rights that individuals have simply because they are human beings and that are not to be violated by governments.

foreign aid: aid given by one country (the donor) to another country (the recipient) for health, economic development, or poverty relief.

foreign direct investment (FDI): when a company in one country invests in a company in another country that leads the investor to have control over the new company.

foreign policy analysis: a theoretical approach that focuses on the process and outcomes of foreign policy decisions made by the people and groups who determine a state's actions in international relations.

frustration-aggression theory: the idea that people resort to violence under conditions of persistent denial of expected treatment, for example, fairness and equality.

functionalism and neo-functionalism: technical cooperation on economic and social issues that build linkages and shared interests among societies and expand to more areas, leading to even greater cooperation and institutional connections.

fungible: the ability to use one type of power for multiple purposes.

GDP per capita: the measure of a country's development. It is the total size of a country's economy divided by the population.

General Agreement on Tariffs and Trade (GATT): an organization of countries that agreed to work together to reduce trade barriers and promote free trade. Other members were considered "most-favored nations" and received preferential trade agreements. The GATT was replaced by the World Trade Organization in 1995.

general deterrence: threats to retaliate in a context of underlying politico-military competition, but when there is no active military conflict generating the need to respond.

genetically modified organisms (GMOs): those organisms whose genetic makeup is intentionally altered to produce some advantage.

genocide: the deliberate killing of a religious, ethnic, or racial group.

Gini coefficient: a measure of the distribution of income in a country ranging from 0 to 1, where 0 means perfect equality and 1 means perfect inequality.

global climate change: marked changes in the warming and cooling of the planet's temperatures, thought to be accelerated by human activity such as industrialization and fossil fuel emissions, which produce greenhouse gases.

Global Environmental Facility: the UN entity created by the UN Framework Convention on Climate Change to collect and distribute the financial resources needed to combat global climate change.

globalization: the increasing integration of global society through the spread of technology, foreign trade, transportation, cultural exchange, political institutions, and social connections.

greenhouse gases: those gases that trap the sun's heat and hold it close to the earth's surface; they include carbon dioxide, methane, nitrous oxide, and water vapor.

groupthink: characteristics of some decision groups that result in a shared viewpoint or preference that leads the group to ignore relevant information and exclude dissenters from that viewpoint in order to protect it.

hard power: power based on coercive means, such as military force.

hegemon: a country that is an undisputed leader within its region or the world. After World War II, the United States was considered the world hegemon.

hegemonic stability theory: a theory holding that the international system is most stable when one state (the hegemon) dominates.

hegemony: domination of the international system by one country.

home country: the term used to describe where the headquarters of a multinational corporation is based.

honor-killings: the murders of girls or women by their husbands, fathers, brothers, or other family members when they are thought to have violated socially acceptable sexually based roles. By killing the offender, the men in the family seek to restore the family's honor and are typically not prosecuted for their crimes.

horizontal enforcement: those measures that states themselves can take when a state violates an international law and other states can attempt to punish the violator themselves.

host country: the country in which a multinational corporation owns other companies.

Human Development Index (HDI): a measure of the level of human development in a country. It includes GDP per capita, life expectancy, and education levels.

humanitarian aid: aid given to a country to help mitigate the effects from a disaster or other humanitarian emergency.

humanitarian interventions: military or nonmilitary interventions into a state by outside groups for the purpose of protecting endangered people and meeting the needs of the state's residents.

human nature: innate characteristics of human beings, said by some to be a cause of war.

human security: an emphasis on the security of people, not territory, first set out by the UN Development Program in 1994. It includes economic, food, health, environmental, personal, community, and political security for people.

hyperinflation: a situation in which a currency loses its value very quickly. Regular inflation occurs at relatively low levels (3–5% per year), but hyperinflation means a currency can lose most of its value in a year, a month, or even a day.

ideational: emphasizing the centrality of ideas and norms in shaping behavior and interactions.

immediate deterrence: the threat to retaliate against attackers who are believed to be actively considering specific military operations against the target.

imperialism: control and exploitation by one state of the economy, culture, and/or territory of others, usually called colonies.

import and export sanctions: when one country scales back on or stops buying products from, or selling them to, another country.

import substitution industrialization (ISI): a development policy that promotes cutting off international trade and substituting it with domestic production.

improvised explosive device (IED): a homemade bomb, often placed on roadsides and other sites, fashioned from an explosive device and a detonator, and usually triggered by remote device or "booby trap" mechanism.

individual level: locating the causes of behavior and outcomes in the nature and characteristics of people.

Industrial Revolution: the transition of many of the world's states from an agricultural economic system to one based on industry. During this period, factories replaced farms as the biggest producer in many countries.

institutions: structures, patterns, and mechanisms for establishing norms, rules, order, and cooperation in world politics.

instrumentalism: an explanation of ethnic conflict that stresses the role of leaders who emphasize and exacerbate ethnic differences (and commonalities) as a means to their own ends.

interdependence: mutual connections and reliance between international actors.

Intergovernmental Panel on Climate Change (IPCC): a scientific body with 195 member states, created by the UN Environment Programme and the World Meteorological Organization in 1988.

internal balancing: countering the power of a rival by increasing one's own power and military might.

International Bank for Reconstruction and Development: the original organization of the World Bank designed to promote reconstruction, especially in Europe after World War II.

international civil society: an international system based on the norms of democracy and human rights. This emerging system is marked by civil society organizations, NGOs that promote these values on a global basis.

International Court of Justice: an international institution created in 1946 as part of the UN systems to apply international law to resolve conflicts brought voluntarily to it by states; also known as the *World Court*.

International Covenant on Civil and Political Rights: a UN treaty effective in 1976 identifying the civil, political, and legal rights of all humans and establishing procedures for the UN to monitor these rights.

International Covenant on Economic, Social and Cultural Rights: a UN treaty effective in 1976 identifying the economic, social, and cultural rights of all humans and establishing procedures for the UN to monitor these rights.

International Criminal Court (ICC): an international court in the Netherlands that tries individuals accused of war crimes, crimes against humanity, genocide, and aggression.

international law: a body of rules that binds states and other agents in world politics in their relations with one another.

International Monetary Fund (IMF): one of the Bretton Woods organizations created in 1946 to help maintain a cooperative international financial system. The IMF helps countries facing balance-of-payments problems with short-term loans and also helps countries reschedule their debt.

international norms: unwritten rules or expectations of acceptable behavior.

international organizations (IOs): international organizations whose membership is restricted to states.

international system: the constellation of international actors and the relationships between them.

INTERPOL: the International Criminal Police Organization created in 1923 and based in Lyon, France.

interstate war: armed conflict between two or more states.

irredentist claims (or irredentism): claims to territory in another state based on historical control or the presence of people with common ethnic identity.

jihad: "holy war" or "holy struggle" in Arabic. To some Muslims, it means the daily struggle within oneself to overcome evil; to others, it means conducting war against non-Muslims.

Kyoto Protocol: an addendum to the UN Framework Convention on Climate Change, which was negotiated in 1997 and entered into force in 2005; it imposed mandatory reductions in fossil fuel emissions for 37 developed countries and the European Community.

Law of the Sea Convention: a treaty that first went into force in 1982 and then was revised in 1994; 167 states are parties to this treaty, as is the EU, which sets rules for the use and protection of the high seas and its resources.

League of Nations: an international institution created after World War I for collective security and the resolution of disputes between states.

less-developed country (LDC): a country that is poor or has an economy that is less able to support its population. These countries typically export raw materials and agricultural products.

levels of analysis: different perspectives from which international relations may be examined.

LGBTQIA: individuals identifying as lesbian, gay, bisexual, transgender, queer, intersex, or asexual.

liberal feminists: proponents of the feminist perspective who argue men and women can approach issues such as conflict the same way but that it is important to have equal representation of the two genders.

liberal international economic order (LIEO): the post–World War II international economic system built on commitments to free trade and free-market economies.

liberalism: a major theoretical approach to international relations emphasizing the role of individuals, norms, and institutions to explain patterns of cooperation and conflict in world politics.

linkage strategy: in diplomacy, the strategy of connecting solutions on one issue to proposals on another to facilitate agreement.

majority rule: in international organizations, a decision process that relies on voting with one vote per member, in which gaining a majority of the votes prevails.

Marxism: an argument developed by Marx and Engels that asserted all politics was determined by social class and that the world would progress through historical economic epochs.

mercantilism: an economic policy that combines business and government. The government uses its power—including its military—to enhance private business, and private business provides revenues to the government to maintain and enhance its power.

metropole: the "mother city" or center of an empire. The metropole of the British Empire (which included colonies on every continent except Antarctica) was London.

military aid: aid given to a country that directly enhances its military capability.

Millennium Development Goals: eight goals chosen by the UN and over 20 international organizations in 2000 to dramatically improve the human condition by 2015.

modernization theory: a theory in the 1950s and 1960s that suggested all countries should be able to develop by following the practices of wealthy states in Europe and North America.

Monterrey Consensus: a 2002 framework for global development in which the developed and developing countries agree to take joint actions for poverty reduction, with emphasis on free trade, sustainable growth and development, and increased financial aid.

most-favored nation (MFN): the trade status that members of the GATT gave to each other, ensuring that each received the best trade terms available. MFN could also be granted to nonmembers if a country chose to do so.

mujahideen: those who fight to liberate Muslims or traditionally Muslim lands from control by nonbelievers; the insurgency resisting the Soviet invasion of Afghanistan is the most widely known example.

multilateral diplomacy: diplomacy involving three or more states at a time; typically many states are involved.

multinational corporations (MNCs): companies that have subsidiaries (other companies) in multiple countries; also known as *transnational corporations (TNCs).*

multipolar: a distribution of power in the international system in which there are more than two great powers.

mutually assured destruction (MAD): the ability of both sides to field a secure, second-strike capability of sufficient size to destroy a significant portion of the other side's society.

nation: an identifiable group of people who share a collective identity typically formed around bonds based on factors such as shared language, culture, and the like.

national attributes: features of states or nations such as regime type, type of economy, culture, geography, resources, and the like.

national enforcement: states enforce some international law through their own national legal systems.

nationalism: the emotional connection of the mass public to their state.

nationalization: when a government takes ownership of private property—land, a company, or an asset.

national missile defense: the capability to protect a country from nuclear attack by shooting down incoming missiles.

nation-state: a state in which nearly all of the population are members of the same nation.

negative peace: a lack of conflict between two countries or groups.

neocolonialism: the practice of maintaining control over smaller, developing countries by keeping strong, dependent links to their governments and/or dominating their economies. This allows a powerful state to control a smaller state without colonizing it.

neoliberal: a return to liberal or free-market economics.

neo-Westphalian sovereignty: *see* responsible sovereignty.

nongovernmental organizations (NGOs): organizations whose membership is not restricted solely to states.

non-state actors: international actors that are not states; they may include international organizations, nongovernmental organizations, multinational corporations, and individuals.

nontariff barrier: a requirement that foreign goods or services must meet that is specifically designed to block or obstruct those goods or services from sale in that market.

normative theory: a theory based on prescription and advocacy of preferred outcomes.

norms: commonly held standards of acceptable and unacceptable behavior.

norms life cycle: the idea that TANs are successful when they can create new norms, create a norms cascade forcing governments to act on those norms, and get norms internalized to the point that following them becomes routine and largely unquestioned.

North American Free Trade Agreement (NAFTA): a free-trade agreement between Canada, Mexico, and the United States. The agreement greatly reduced all barriers to trade between the three countries and resulted in a significant increase in trade of goods and services between the three. NAFTA was replaced by the United States–Mexico–Canada Agreement (USMCA) in 2020.

North Atlantic Treaty Organization (NATO): a military alliance structure created following the outbreak of the Korean War in 1950 and led by the United States.

Nuclear Nonproliferation Regime: a formal treaty and its related rules set by the International Atomic Energy Agency regulating how states may develop, maintain, and use nuclear power and nuclear materials.

Nuclear Nonproliferation Treaty: a treaty prohibiting those with nuclear weapons from providing them to others and those without nuclear weapons from seeking them.

operational code analysis: the idea that leaders have a tendency to (a) prefer either conflict or cooperation and (b) believe they are either very effective or limited in their ability to control others.

Organisation for Economic Co-operation and Development (OECD): an organization of 37 member states that promotes liberal economic and political reforms.

organizational/bureaucratic politics model: a model in which foreign policy decisions are the products of large bureaucratic organizations doing what they know to do or see as in their organizational interest.

orthodox liberal: an approach to economics that favors an extreme free-market approach in which government is very limited and most of a country is composed of private enterprise.

other-oriented TANs: TANs that advocate a set of values that primarily benefit others besides themselves.

parsimony: the principle that simple explanations are preferable to complex explanations when other things are equal.

patriarchy: a system of social structures and practices that put men in charge and women in subservient roles.

patronage politics: using state funds to pay off private or semiprivate political supporters.

peacekeeping: the provision of third-party forces from the UN or other regional organizations to help keep peace by providing a buffer between parties in conflict, often along a border or an agreed-upon cease-fire line to monitor and maintain the peace.

periphery: the economic zone composed of poor countries that primarily export raw materials.

personality traits: varying characteristics of individuals, some of which may lead to more aggressive behavior and preferences.

P5 (or Perm-5): the five permanent members of the UN Security Council—the United States, the United Kingdom, France, China, and Russia—each of which holds veto power.

policy entrepreneurs: individuals committed to innovative policy change and who voluntarily work to achieve such changes.

political sovereignty: the principle that a state has authority and independence to rule without interference within its own borders.

polythink: characteristics of some decision groups that result in so many options and preferences being introduced that agreement on any one becomes unlikely, if not impossible.

populist revolutions: grassroots revolts typically against repressive governments, dominated by mass turnouts of the people.

positive peace: a situation between two countries that is not simply a lack of conflict but rather a mutual affinity for each other.

positive-sum: a condition in which all parties to an issue can benefit or "win."

power: the ability to get what you want.

power transition theory: a systemic theory holding that wars are most likely when changes in power distributions occur.

preemption: the use of military force to strike first when an attack is imminent to blunt the effectiveness of the impending attack.

prevention: the use of military force to strike first when an attack is inevitable to take advantage of a more favorable balance of forces, rather than wait for an adversary to gain the advantage from which to strike.

primordialism: an explanation of ethnic conflict that stresses the fundamental bonds of kinship and identity that establish ethnic differences that divide people and often generate ancient ethnic hatreds.

prisoner's dilemma: a situation in which two prisoners must decide whether to collaborate with each other or not.

proletariat: the working class that sold its labor for less than its value to the capitalists.

proportional representation: a democratic system in which parties or factions get approximately the same percentage of legislative seats as votes they received in the most recent election.

prospect theory: the idea that humans are rational but their rationality is situationally biased; that is, they are more risk averse when things work in their favor and more risk taking when things aren't going well.

protection: in alliances, an arrangement by a small state to gain help from a larger state.

protectionism: a policy of blocking or restricting the trade from other countries in order to "protect" domestic businesses from economic competition with foreign companies.

psychological needs: essential emotional and psychological requirements of humans, said to be hierarchical by theorists such as Maslow.

purchasing power parity (PPP): a measure that compares two currencies and adjusts them so that they can be compared in a meaningful way. PPP allows us to compare the purchasing power of the yen in Japan with the peso in Mexico, for example.

rational actor model: a model in which, as unitary actors, all states make decisions according to a rational process in which goals are ranked, options identified and evaluated, and selections made to maximize benefits according to the goals of the actor.

realism: a major theoretical approach to international relations emphasizing the competitive, conflict-ridden pursuit of power and security among states in world politics.

reciprocity: in international law, the principle that a state follows international law so that others will do so in return.

regime change: the change of a country's government or type of government.

relative deprivation: the discrepancy between what people have and what they think they deserve based on what others have.

relative gains: the comparative effect of a decision or situation on an actor relative to those of another actor.

resource curse: the curious negative effect for a country's economy when the country has a valuable resource, such as oil.

responsibility to protect (R2P): the norm that states have a responsibility to protect their citizens from avoidable harm, and if they cannot or will not do so, the international community has a responsibility to intervene.

responsible sovereignty: the idea of sovereignty as a state's responsibility to protect its citizens.

restorative justice: a justice that seeks to repair the damage done to victims, to allow the victims a voice in the resolution of their grievances, and where possible to reintegrate both victims and the offenders into a more just society.

revolution in military affairs: the transformation of weapons, military organizations, and operational concepts for military force that leverages the information and communications revolutions of the latter 20th and early 21st centuries.

second-generation human rights (societal rights): material and economic rights that apply society-wide, such as the rights to education, employment, shelter, health care, and so on.

security: survival and safety, typically referring to the military, intelligence, and law enforcement arenas but also including economic and human dimensions.

security community: a group of states bound by shared identities and interests and complex interactions among which security threats are virtually nonexistent.

security dilemma: the steps that states take to make themselves secure often result in threats to other states, whose reactions to those threats make the first state less secure; thus, what a state does to gain security can often make it less secure.

selectorate: those in a state who provide the power base for a leader.

self-help: the idea that individual actors are responsible for making themselves secure and protecting their own interests.

self-oriented TANs: TANs that advocate values that primarily benefit the network members.

semi-periphery: the economic zone composed of middle-income countries that produce secondary products.

settlement gap: the difference between the minimal preferences of two parties to a negotiation.

Six-Day War: the 1967 war between Israel, Egypt, Jordan, and Syria. Israel won the war and took control of the occupied territories (the Gaza Strip, West Bank, and Golan Heights).

smart sanctions: sanctions that target specific individuals thought to be responsible for a regime's bad behavior rather than targeting a state's entire economy.

social construction: creation of a concept by the interactions and ideas within a society.

socialism: an economic-political system in which the government controls the economy and redistributes wealth to create economic equality in the country.

soft power: power based on attraction and persuasion rather than coercion.

sovereignty: having supreme authority over people and territory.

sovereign wealth funds: investment funds owned by states.

stag hunt: a situation in which hunters must decide whether to collaborate with each other or act on their own.

state: a political-legal unit that (a) has an identifiable population, (b) is located within defined borders recognized by others, and (c) has a government with sovereignty.

state of nature: a hypothetical condition before the advent of government.

state or national level: locating the causes of behavior and outcome in the nature and characteristics of states and nations.

state-sponsored terrorism: terrorism that includes covert and overt repression of and violence against civilian populations and more extreme acts such as genocide, supported or perpetrated by the state.

stratification: unequal distribution of power, influence, and/or other resources.

structural factors: historical and environmental factors that influence how a country can develop its economy.

subnational actors: international actors typically seen as subparts of a state, such as individuals or local governmental entities.

subsidies: funds given to companies by a government to help them grow.

substate actors: groups within a state, such as political parties, insurgents, or ethnic groups.

summit meetings: diplomatic meetings involving the top officials of their respective states (hence, "the summit").

supranational organization: an institution, organization, or law that is over other states. For example, the EU is a supranational organization because it has authority over many European states.

supranational regimes: international organizations or sets of rules that can bind states even against their will.

sustainable development: promoting economic growth without degrading the environment or depleting its nonrenewable resources.

Sustainable Development Goals: 17 goals to achieve by 2030 to continue and improve on the progress of the Millennium Development Goals.

systemic or international level: locating the causes of behavior and outcomes in the nature and characteristics of the international system.

tariff: a tax on products imported into one country from other countries.

territorial integrity: the principle that other actors should not violate the territory or boundaries of a state.

terrorism: indiscriminate violence aimed at noncombatants to influence a wider audience.

theater missile defense: the capability to protect a specific or limited geographic area from nuclear attack by shooting down incoming missiles.

theories: tools for explaining cause-and-effect relationships among often complex phenomena.

third-generation human rights (group rights): rights needed to protect unpopular or minority groups from the oppression of the majority.

third-party diplomacy: the engagement of an outside party in negotiations between the actual parties to a dispute to facilitate a resolution of the disagreement.

third-party sanction: a sanction levied against a third-party state to keep that state from doing business with the primary target of the sanctions.

Thirty Years' War: a series of wars (1618–1648) that created many modern European states.

time horizon problem: the fact that the worst effects of environmental problems have not yet been seen, but to avoid them, one needs to act (and spend money or make sacrifices) now.

track II diplomacy: the activities and involvement of private individuals, nongovernmental organizations such as civil society organizations, and religious and business leaders in dialogue and negotiation to facilitate conflict resolution.

trade war: a situation in which many or all states engage in protectionism. The states try to block imports and promote exports, but because all countries do this, very little international trade occurs.

tragedy of the commons: the idea that no one state is held responsible for things held in common—so-called collective goods—like the air and water, so their protection often goes unaddressed.

transnational advocacy networks (TANs): networks defined by reciprocal, voluntary actions across national borders that (a) must include non-state actors (such as individuals acting alone, social movements, transnational or multinational corporations, or nongovernmental organizations), (b) may include states or international organizations as well, and (c) represent a recurring, cooperative partnership with (d) differentiated roles among the component parts.

Treaties of Westphalia: two treaties in 1648 that ended the Thirty Years' War and created the modern international system.

treaty: a formal, written agreement among states.

Treaty of Versailles: the treaty in 1919 that ended World War I, imposed heavy penalties on Germany, and created the League of Nations.

tripolar: a distribution of power in the international system in which there are three great powers.

unconventional war: armed conflict in which civilian and nonmilitary targets are emphasized, forces used include nontraditional forces outside organized militaries, and a wide array of weaponry, including weapons of mass destruction, may be employed.

UN Economic and Social Council (ECOSOC): the component of the UN that handles matters considered economic or social, broadly defined.

UN Environment Programme (UNEP): the UN agency dedicated to environmental protection, created in 1972.

UN Framework Convention on Climate Change (FCCC): a 1992 treaty calling for the reduction of fossil fuel emissions to 1990 levels by 2000.

UN General Assembly (UNGA): the plenary body of the UN in which all UN members have a seat. Functioning on a majority-rule decision process, it is the central forum for discussion of global issues.

UN Human Rights Council: the body created by the UN General Assembly in 2006 to replace the UN Human Rights Commission in making recommendations regarding human rights issues.

UNICEF: the United Nations Children's Fund, created in 1946 and recipient of the Nobel Peace Prize in 1965.

unipolar: a distribution of power in the international system in which there is one great power.

unitary actor: the simplified conception of a state as a single entity or actor.

United Nations (UN): an international institution established after World War II to promote peace and security, the development of friendly relations and harmony among nations, and cooperation on international problems.

United States–Mexico–Canada Agreement (USMCA): a 2020 free-trade agreement between Canada, Mexico, and the United States that succeeded the North American Free Trade Agreement.

unit veto: in international organizations, a decision rule in which some or all members can block decisions with their votes. In a pure unit veto decision rule, every member exercises a veto; in a modified unit veto, only some members have the veto power.

Universal Declaration of Human Rights (UDHR): a 1948 UN resolution, which provided a comprehensive listing of the rights of all people.

universal jurisdiction: the idea that states have a right and a duty to enforce international law when it comes to the most serious human rights abuses, such as genocide, crimes against humanity, torture, war crimes, extrajudicial killings, and forced disappearances, regardless of where these offenses may occur or whether or not the alleged violator is from another country.

UN Secretariat: the bureaucracy and administrative arm of the UN.

UN Secretary-General: the head of the UN Secretariat; the UN's administrative leader elected by the UNGA at the recommendation of the UNSC.

UN Security Council (UNSC): a 15-member council that carries the primary UN responsibilities for peace, security, and collective security operations.

UN Women: the UN organization working for gender equality, created in 2010 with the merger of the Division for the Advancement of Women (DAW), the International Research and Training Institute for the Advancement of Women (INSTRAW), the Office of the Special Adviser on Gender Issues and Advancement of Women (OSAGI), and the United Nations Development Fund for Women (UNIFEM).

vertical enforcement: the enforcement of international law by international institutions.

Vienna Convention on the Law of Treaties: a 1969 agreement among states defining the nature and obligations regarding treaties under international law.

war: organized, violent (i.e., military) conflict between two or more parties.

war crimes: excessive brutality in war, in violation of international treaties or conventions.

war reparations: payments from one country—usually the loser of a conflict—to compensate the victor's cost in money, lives, and property.

Warsaw Pact: the military alliance created by the Soviet Union as a response to the 1955 addition of West Germany into NATO.

war weariness: the idea that states that have most recently experienced a significant, costly war are more peaceful in the aftermath because of the impact of those costs and experiences.

Washington Consensus: an orthodox liberal approach to development that took hold in the 1980s and was used to try to promote economic growth in poor countries. It had very limited success.

weapons of mass destruction: nuclear, chemical, and biological weapons.

weighted voting: in international organizations, a decision rule in which member votes are weighted according to some factor related to size, power, or wealth.

Westphalian sovereignty: the idea that within a state's borders there is no higher authority than the government of the state itself.

winning coalition: the half of the voters whose support you must have to win an election.

World Bank: a Bretton Woods organization created in 1945 that provides loans and grants to countries for long-term development. The World Bank started by helping fund the reconstruction of Europe after World War II and later focused on helping countries in the developing world grow their economies.

World Economic Forum: a forum held in Switzerland every year that brings together wealthy individuals, corporate leaders, industry leaders, and heads of government to coordinate economic policies and initiatives.

World Health Organization (WHO): the UN organization that deals with health issues around the world. It is responsible for the eradication of smallpox.

world politics: political, economic, and social activities and interactions among states and a wide variety of non-state actors, such as international organizations, non-state national and ethnic groups, transnational corporations, nongovernmental organizations, and individuals.

world systems theory: a Marxist-based theory that explains international politics as the rich core states exploiting the semi-periphery and the periphery states, the semi-periphery states exploiting the periphery states, and the periphery states being exploited by both.

World Trade Organization (WTO): a supranational organization established in 1995 that promotes free trade between member countries; it sets the rules for international trade, administers them, and authorizes penalties for states that violate them.

zero-sum: a condition in which one party's benefit or gains require comparable losses by another party.

Zionism: the movement to create a Jewish homeland in Palestine.

REFERENCES

CHAPTER 1

Beer, Francis. (1974). *How Much War in History: Definitions, Estimates, Extrapolations, and Trends*. Beverly Hills, CA: Sage.

Buzan, Barry. (1991). *People, States and Fear: An Agenda for International Security Studies in the Post–Cold War World*. Boulder, CO: Lynne Rienner.

Levy, Jack S. (1983). *War in the Modern Great Power System, 1495–1975*. Lexington: University of Kentucky Press.

Nye, Joseph. (2005). *Soft Power: The Means to Success in World Politics*. New York, NY: Public Affairs Books.

Pettersson, Therese, and Magnus Öberg. (2020). "Organized Violence, 1989–2019." *Journal of Peace Research* 57 (4), 597–613.

CHAPTER 2

Dazkowski, Don. (2017). "The Expansion of American Fast Food Franchises." *The Balance*, June 19 (https://www.thebalance.com/how-american-fast-food-franchises-expanded-abroad-1350955).

Deng, Francis. (1995). "Frontiers of Sovereignty: A Framework of Protection, Assistance, and Development for the Internally Displaced." *Leiden Journal of International Law* 8, 249–286.

Diamond, Jared. (1999). *Guns, Germs, and Steel: The Fates of Human Societies*. New York, NY: Norton.

Gibbs, Walter. (2010). "Oil Company Near Settling Over Contract in Kurdistan." *New York Times*, January 25 (www.nytimes.com/2010/01/26/world/middleeast/26galbraith.html).

Global Policy Forum. (n.d.). "Globalization" (https://www.globalpolicy.org/globalization.html).

International Telecommunications Union. (2020). "ITC Facts and Figures" (https://itu.foleon.com/itu/measuring-digital-development/offline-population).

Jackson, Josh. (2019). "The 10 Highest-Grossing Movies of 2019." *Paste Magazine*, September 12 (https://www.pastemagazine.com/movies/highest-grossing-movies/the-highest-grossing-movies-of-2019/#10-how-to-train-your-dragon-the-hidden-world).

Jones, Bruce, Carlos Pascual, and Stephen John Stedman. (2009). *Power and Responsibility: Building International Order in an Era of International Threats*. Washington, DC: Brookings Institution Press.

Kramer, Samuel Noah. (1988). *History Begins at Sumer: Thirty-Nine Firsts in Recorded History*, 3rd ed. Philadelphia: University of Pennsylvania Press.

Steger, Manfred B. (2008). *The Rise of the Global Imaginary: Political Ideologies From the French Revolution to the Global War on Terror*. New York, NY: Oxford University Press.

"Timeline: Saddam's Violent Road to Execution." (2006). *NPR*, December 29 (http://www.npr.org/templates/story/story.php?storyId=4961744).

Trager, Robert F. (2010). "Diplomatic Calculus in Anarchy: How Communications Matters." *American Political Science Review* 104, 347–368.

Verpoorten, Marijke. (2005). "The Death Toll of the Rwandan Genocide." *Population-E* 60, 331–368.

Withnall, Adam. (2016). "Amnesty International Reveals the 10 Worst Attacks on Human Rights Across the World Last Year." *The Independent*, February 24 (http://www.independent.co.uk/news/world/politics/amnesty-international-reveals-the-10-worst-attacks-on-human-rights-across-the-world-last-year-a6892911.html).

Wong, Edward. (2006). "Iraq Charges Saddam With Genocide." *New York Times*, April 4 (http://www.nytimes.com/2006/04/04/world/africa/iraq-charges-saddam-with-genocide.html).

CHAPTER 3

Chretien, Jean-Pierre. (2003). *The Great Lakes of Africa: Two Thousand Years of History*. Cambridge, MA: MIT Press.

Doyle, Michael. (1986). "Liberalism and World Politics." *American Political Science Review* 80, 1151–1169.

Fearon, James, and Alexander Wendt. (2005). "Rationalism v. Constructivism: A Skeptical View." In Walter Carlsnaes, Thomas Risse, and Beth Simmons, eds., *Handbook of International Relations* (pp. 52–72). London, UK: SAGE.

Herman, Robert G., and Theodore J. Piccone, eds. (2002). *Defending Democracy: A Global Survey of Foreign Policy Trends, 1992–2002*. Washington, DC: Democracy Coalition Project (http://www.demcoalition.org/html/global_survey.html).

Howell, William G., and Jon C. Pevehouse. (2007). *While Dangers Gather: Congressional Checks on Presidential War Powers*. Princeton, NJ: Princeton University Press.

Keohane, Robert, and Joseph Nye. (2011). *Power and Interdependence*, 4th ed. New York, NY: Longman.

Mearsheimer, John. (2001). *The Tragedy of Great Power Politics*. New York, NY: Norton.

Morgenthau, Hans J. (2005). *Politics Among Nations: The Struggle for Power and Peace*, 7th ed. New York, NY: McGraw-Hill.

Mueller, John. (1989). *Retreat From Doomsday: The Obsolescence of Major War*. New York, NY: Basic Books.

Neyfakh, Leon. (2014). "Putin's Long Game? Meet the Eurasian Union." *Boston Globe*, March 9.

Nye, Joseph. (2005). *Soft Power: The Means to Success in World Politics*. New York, NY: Public Affairs Press.

Putin, Vladimir. (2011). "A New Integration Project for Eurasia: The Future in the Making." *Izvestia*, October 3 (http://www.russianmission.eu/en/news/article-prime-minister-vladimir-putin-new-integration-project-eurasia-future-making-izvestia-3-).

Russett, Bruce, and Jon Oneal. (2001). *Triangulating Peace: Democracy, Interdependence, and International Organization*. New York, NY: Norton.

Wendt, Alexander. (1992). "Anarchy Is What States Make of It: The Social Construction of Power Politics." *International Organization* 46, 391–425.

CHAPTER 4

Allison, Graham. (1971). *Essence of Decision: Explaining the Cuban Missile Crisis*. Boston, MA: Little, Brown.

Allison, Graham, and Philip Zelikow. (1999). *Essence of Decision: Explaining the Cuban Missile Crisis*, 2nd ed. New York, NY: Longman.

Badie, Dina. (2010). "Groupthink, Iraq, and the War on Terror: Explaining US Policy Shift Toward Iraq." *Foreign Policy Analysis* 6 (4), 277–296.

Bueno de Mesquita, Bruce, Alastair Smith, Randolph M. Siverson, and James D. Morrow. (2003). *The Logic of Political Survival*. Cambridge, MA: MIT Press.

Dahlerup, Drude. (1988). "From a Small to a Large Minority: Women in Scandinavian Politics." *Scandinavian Political Studies* 11 (4), 275–299.

Dion, Michelle L., Jane Lawrence Sumner, and Sara McLaughlin Mitchell. (2018). "Gendered Citation Patterns across Political Science and Social Science Methodology Fields." *Political Analysis* 26 (3), 312–327.

Dolan, Chris J., and David B. Cohen. (2006). "The War About the War: Iraq and the Politics of National Security Advising in the G.W. Bush Administration's First Term." *Politics & Policy* 34 (1), 30–64.

Duelfer, Charles A., and Stephen Benedict Dyson. (2011). "Chronic Misperception and International Conflict: The U.S.–Iraq Experience." *International Security* 36 (1), 73–100.

Hatemi, Peter, and Rose McDermott. (2012). "A Neurobiological Approach to Foreign Policy Analysis: Identifying Individual Differences in Political Violence." *Foreign Policy Analysis* 8 (2), 111–129.

Hudson, Valerie, Bonnie Ballif-Spanvill, Mary Caprioli, and Chad Emmett. (2014). *Sex and World Peace*, rev. ed. New York, NY: Columbia University Press.

Hudson, Valerie M., Bonnie Ballif-Spanvill, Mary Caprioli, and Chad F. Emmett. (2017). "The Heart of the Matter: The Security of Women, the Security of States." *Military Review* 97 (3) (http://www.armyupress.army.mil/Journals/Military-Review/English-Edition-Archives/May-June-2017/Hudson-Heart-of-the-Matter).

Immelman, A. (2017). "The Leadership Style of U.S. President Donald J. Trump." *Working Paper No. 1.2*. Collegeville and St. Joseph, MN: St. John's University and the College of St. Benedict, Unit for the Study of Personality in Politics (doi:10.13140/RG.2.2.32000.64001).

Kaarbo, Juliet, and Ryan K. Beasley. (2008). "Taking It to the Extreme: The Effect of Coalition Cabinets on Foreign Policy." *Foreign Policy Analysis* 4 (1), 67–81.

Kanter, Rosabeth Moss. (1977). "Some Effects of Proportions on Group Life: Skewed Sex Ratios and Responses to Token Women." *American Journal of Sociology* 82 (1), 965–990.

Marsh, Kevin. (2014). "Obama's Surge: A Bureaucratic Politics Analysis of the Decision to Order a Troop Surge in the Afghanistan War." *Foreign Policy Analysis* 10, 265–288.

Marx, Karl, and Freidrich Engels. (1848). *The Communist Manifesto*. Unpublished manuscript at Project Gutenberg (http://www.gutenberg.org/ebooks/61).

McAdams, Dan. (2016). "The Mind of Donald Trump." *The Atlantic*, June (https://www.theatlantic.com/magazine/archive/2016/06/the-mind-of-donald-trump/480771).

McGlen, Nancy E., and Meredith Reid Sarkees. (1993). *Women in Foreign Policy: The Insiders*. New York, NY: Routledge.

McGlen, Nancy E., and Meredith Reid Sarkees. (1995). *The Status of Women in Foreign Policy*. New York, NY: Foreign Policy Association.

McGlen, Nancy E., and Meredith Reid Sarkees. (2006). "*Foreign Policy Decision-Makers: The Impact of Albright and Rice.*" Paper presented at the annual meeting of the International Studies Association, San Diego, March 22.

Mintz, Alex, and Carly Wayne. (2016). *The Polythink Syndrome: U.S. Foreign Policy Decisions on 9/11, Afghanistan, Iraq, Iran, Syria, and ISIS*. Redwood City, CA: Stanford University Press.

Mitchell, David, and Tansa George Massoud. (2009). "Anatomy of Failure: Bush's Decision-Making Process and the Iraq War." *Foreign Policy Analysis* 5 (3), 265–286.

Nai, Alessandro, Ferran Martinez i Coma, and Jürgen Maier. (2019). "Donald Trump, Populism, and the Age of Extremes: Comparing the Personality Traits and Campaigning Styles of Trump and Other Leaders Worldwide." *Presidential Studies Quarterly*, January 22 (https://doi.org/10.1111/psq.12511).

Phillips, Anne. (1995). *The Politics of Presence*. Oxford, UK: Clarendon Press.

Sherman, Ryne. (2015). "The Personality of Donald Trump." *Psychology Today*, September 17 (https://www.psychologytoday.com/us/blog/the-situation-lab/201509/the-personality-donald-trump).

Tickner, J. Ann. (1992). *Gender in International Relations*, rev. ed. New York, NY: Columbia University Press.

"The Truly Inspiring Story of the Chinese Rubbish Collector Who Saved and Raised THIRTY Babies Abandoned at the Roadside." (2012). *Daily Mail*, July 30 (http://www.dailymail.co.uk/news/article-2181017/Lou-Xiaoying-Story-Chinese-woman-saved-30-abandoned-babies-dumped-street-trash.html).

Wittenberg-Cox, Avivah. (2020). "What Do Countries With the Best Coronavirus Responses Have in Common? Women Leaders." *Forbes*, April 13 (https://www.forbes.com/sites/avivahwittenbergcox/2020/04/13/what-do-countries-with-the-best-coronavirus-reponses-have-in-common-women-leaders/#3f96d5c43dec).

CHAPTER 5

Allison, Graham, (2017a). *Destined for War: Can America and China Escape Thucydides's Trap?* New York, NY: Houghton Mifflin Harcourt.

Allison, Graham. (2017b). "The Thucydides Trap." *Foreign Policy*, June 9 (http://foreignpolicy.com/2017/06/09/the-thucydides-trap).

Allison, Graham T., Jr., and Robert P. Beschel, Jr. (1992). "Can the United States Promote Democracy?" *Political Science Quarterly* 107 (1), 81–98.

Angell, Norman. (1910). *The Great Illusion*. New York, NY: Putnam.

Ardrey, Robert. (1966). *The Territorial Imperative*. New York, NY: Atheneum.

Badie, Dina. (2010). "Groupthink, Iraq, and the War on Terror: Explaining US Policy Shift Toward Iraq." *Foreign Policy Analysis* 6 (4), 277–296.

Bremer, Stuart. (1980). "National Capabilities and War Proneness." In J. David Singer, ed., *The Correlates of War II: Testing Some Realpolitik Models*. New York, NY: Free Press.

Bueno de Mesquita, Bruce, and Randolph M. Siverson. (1995). "War and the Survival of Political Leaders: A Comparative Study of Regime Types and Political Accountability." *American Political Science Review* 89 (4), 841–855.

Bueno de Mesquita, Bruce, Randolph M. Siverson, and Gary Woller. (1992). "War and the Fate of Regimes: A Comparative Analysis." *American Political Science Review* 86 (3), 638–646.

Burrows, Mathew J., and Peter Engelke. (2020). "US Global Leadership at Risk: Shaping the Post-COVID World Together." *Atlantic Council Strategy Paper Series*, July 7 (https://www.atlanticcouncil.org/content-series/shaping-post-covid-world-together/us-global-leadership-at-risk).

Campbell, Kurt M., and Rush Doshi. (2020). "The Coronavirus Could Reshape Global Order: China Is Maneuvering for International Leadership as the United States Falters." *Foreign Affairs*, March 18 (https://www.foreignaffairs

.com/articles/china/2020-03-18/coronavirus-could-reshape-global-order).

Cashman, Greg. (1993). *What Causes War? An Introduction to Theories of International Conflict*. Lanham, MD: Lexington Books.

Choucri, Nazli, and Robert North. (1975). *Nations in Conflict: National Growth and International Violence*. San Francisco, CA: Freeman.

Cohen, Dara Kay. (2013). "Explaining Rape During Civil War: Cross-National Evidence (1980–2009)." *American Political Science Review* 107 (3), 461–477.

Combs, Cindy. (2010). *Terrorism in the 21st Century*, 6th ed. Englewood Cliffs, NJ: Prentice Hall.

Debs, Alexandre, and H. E. Goemans. (2010). "Regime Type, the Fate of Leaders, and War." *American Political Science Review* 104 (3), 430–445.

Freeman, Michael. (1998). "Theories of Ethnicity, Tribalism, and Nationalism." In Kenneth Christie, ed., *Ethnic Conflict, Tribal Politics: A Global Perspective*. Surrey, UK: Curzon Press.

Friedman, George. (2017a). "5 Maps That Explain China's Strategy." *Business Insider*, November 10 (http://www.businessinsider.com/5-maps-that-explain-chinas-strategy-2016-1).

Friedman, George. (2017b). "10 Maps That Explain Russia's Strategy." *Business Insider*, July 23 (http://www.businessinsider.com/10-maps-that-explain-russia-strategy-2017-7/#russia-is-almost-landlocked-1).

Gartzke, Eric. (2007). "The Capitalist Peace." *American Journal of Political Science* 51, 166–191.

Gilpin, Robert. (1991). *War and Change in World Politics*. Cambridge, UK: Cambridge University Press.

Goemans, H. E. (2000). "Fighting for Survival: The Fate of Leaders and the Duration of War." *Journal of Conflict Resolution* 44 (5), 555–579.

Goldstein, Joshua. (1988). *Long Cycles: Prosperity and War in the Modern Era*. New Haven, CT: Yale University Press.

Greenberg, Andy. (2019). *Sandworm: A New Era of Cyberwar and the Hunt for the Kremlin's Most Dangerous Hackers*. New York, NY: Doubleday.

Gurr, Ted Robert. (1970). *Why Men Rebel*. Princeton, NJ: Princeton University Press.

Hennigan, W. J., and John Walcott. (2019). "ISIS Fighters Are Gaining Strength After Trump's Syria Pullout, U.S. Spies Say." *Time*, November 19 (https://time.com/5732842/isis-gaining-strength-trump-syria-pullout).

Herman, Robert G., and Theodore J. Piccone. (2002). *Defending Democracy: A Global Survey of Foreign Policy Trends 1992–2002*. Washington, DC: Democracy Coalition Project.

Hobson, John A. (1965). *Imperialism: A Study*. Ann Arbor: University of Michigan Press.

Hoffman, Bruce. (1999). *Inside Terrorism*. New York, NY: Columbia University Press.

Holsti, K. J. (1991). *Peace and War: Armed Conflict and International Order, 1648–1989*. Cambridge, UK: Cambridge University Press.

Homer-Dixon, Thomas. (1999). *Environment, Scarcity, and Violence*. Princeton, NJ: Princeton University Press.

Ikenberry, G. John. (2000). *After Victory: Institutions, Strategic Restraint, and the Rebuilding of Order After Major Wars*. Princeton, NJ: Princeton University Press.

Ikenberry, G. John. (2002). "Introduction." In G. John Ikenberry, ed., *America Unrivalled: The Future of the Balance of Power*. Ithaca, NY: Cornell University Press.

Ikenberry, G. John. (2011). "The Future of the Liberal World Order: Internationalism After America." *Foreign Affairs*, May/June (http://www.foreignaffairs.com/articles/67730/g-john-ikenberry/the-future-of-the-lieral-world-order).

Ikenberry, G. John. (2012). *Liberal Leviathan: The Origins, Crisis, and Transformation of the American World Order*, reprint ed. Princeton, NJ: Princeton University Press.

Janis, Irving. (1972). *Victims of Groupthink: A Psychological Study of Foreign Policy Decisions and Fiascos*. New York, NY: Houghton Mifflin.

Jesse, Neal, and Kristen P. Williams. (2010). *Ethnic Conflict: A Systematic Approach to Cases of Conflict*. Washington, DC: CQ Press.

Kalb, Marvin, and Deborah Kalb. (2011). *Haunting Legacy: Vietnam and the Presidency from Ford to Obama*. Washington, DC: Brookings Institution Press.

Kaplan, Robert D. (1994). *Balkan Ghosts: A Journey Through History*. New York, NY: Vintage Books.

Keegan, John. (2011). *A History of Warfare*. New York, NY: Random House.

Lake, David A., and Donald Rothchild. (1998). *The International Spread of Ethnic Conflict: Fear, Diffusion, and Escalation*. Princeton, NJ: Princeton University Press.

Laqueur, Walter. (2001). *A History of Terrorism*. New York, NY: Routledge Press.

Lenin, Vladimir. (1939). *Imperialism: The Highest Stage of Capitalism*. New York, NY: International Publishers.

Levy, Jack S. (1983). *War in the Modern Great Power System, 1495–1975*. Lexington: University of Kentucky Press.

Lorenz, Konrad. (1966). *On Aggression*. New York, NY: Bantam Books.

Mansfield, Edward, and Brian Pollins, eds. (2003). *Economic Interdependence and International Conflict: New Perspectives on an Enduring Debate*. Ann Arbor: University of Michigan Press.

McGuinness, Damien. (2017). "How a Cyber Attack Transformed Estonia." *BBC News*, April 27 (http://www.bbc.com/news/39655415).

Mearsheimer, John J. (2001). *The Tragedy of Great Power Politics*. New York, NY: Norton.

Modelski, George. (1978). "The Long Cycle of Global Politics and the Nation-State." *Comparative Studies in Society and History* 20 (2), 214–235.

Mueller, John. (1989). *Retreat From Doomsday: The Obsolescence of Major War*. New York, NY: Basic Books.

Mueller, John. (2005). "The Iraq Syndrome." *Foreign Affairs* 84 (6), 44–54.

Organski, A. F. K. (1968). *World Politics*. New York, NY: Knopf.

Organski, A. F. K., and Jacek Kugler. (1980). *The War Ledger*. Chicago, IL: University of Chicago Press.

Reiter, Dan. (2003). "Exploring the Bargaining Model of War." *Perspectives on Politics* 1 (1), 27–43.

Russett, Bruce, and Jon Oneal. (2001). *Triangulating Peace: Democracy, Interdependence, and International Organizations*. New York, NY: Norton.

Scott, James M., and Jerel A. Rosati. (2021). *The Politics of United States Foreign Policy*, 7th ed. Washington, DC: CQ Press.

Sederberg, Peter C. (1989). *Terrorist Myths: Illusion, Rhetoric, and Reality*. Englewood Cliffs, NJ: Prentice Hall.

Shinkman, Paul D. (2019). "Study: U.S. No Longer Dominant Power in the Pacific." *US News and World Report*, August 20 (https://www.usnews.com/news/world-report/articles/2019-08-20/us-no-longer-dominant-power-in-the-pacific-study).

Sjoberg, Laura. (2013). *Gendering Global Conflict: Toward a Feminist Theory of War*. New York, NY: Columbia University Press.

Small, Melvin, and J. David Singer. (1970). "Patterns in International Warfare, 1816–1965." *Annals of the American Academy of Political and Social Science* 391, 145–155.

Stewart, Frances, and Valpy FitzGerald, eds. (2001). *War and Underdevelopment: Vol. 1. The Economic and Social Consequences of Conflict*. Oxford, UK: Oxford University Press.

Terriff, Terry, Aaron Karp, and Regina Karp, eds. (2008). *Global Insurgency and the Future of Armed Conflict: Debating Fourth-Generation Warfare*. New York, NY: Routledge.

Thompson, William R. (1988). *On Global War: Historical-Structural Approaches to World Politics*. Columbia: University of South Carolina Press.

Tickner, J. Ann. (1992). *Gender in International Relations: Feminist Perspectives on Achieving Global Security*. New York, NY: Columbia University Press.

US Computer Emergency Readiness Team (US-CERT). (2017). "Alert (TA17-318A): HIDDEN COBRA–North Korean Remote Administration Tool: FALLCHILL," November 14 (https://www.us-cert .gov/ncas/alerts/TA17-318A).

US Department of Defense. (2011). *Dictionary of Military and Associated Terms (as Amended Through April 2010)*. Collingdale, PA: Diane Publishing.

Vasquez, John A., and Marie T. Henehan. (2010). *Territory, War, and Peace*. New York, NY: Routledge.

Wallerstein, Immanuel. (1974). *The Modern World System*. New York, NY: Academic Press.

Wallerstein, Immanuel. (2004). *World Systems Analysis: An Introduction*. Durham, NC: Duke University Press.

Warrick, Joby. (2016). *Black Flags: The Rise of ISIS*. New York, NY: Anchor Books/ Penguin Random House.

WorldVision. (2020). "Syrian Refugee Crisis: Facts, FAQs, and How to Help" (https:// www.worldvision.org/refugees-news-stories/syrian-refugee-crisis-facts).

Yourish, Karen, Derek Watkins, Tom Giratikanon, and Jasmine C. Lee. (2016). "How Many People Have Been Killed in ISIS Attacks Around the World." *New York Times*, July 16 (https://www .nytimes.com/interactive/2016/03/25/ world/map-isis-attacks-around-the-world.html).

Zetter, Kim. (2014). *Countdown to Zero Day: Stuxnet and the Launch of the World's First Digital Weapon*. New York, NY: Crown.

CHAPTER 6

Adler, Emanuel, and Michael Barnett. (1988). *Security Communities*. Cambridge, UK: Cambridge University Press.

Art, Robert J. (1980). "To What Ends Military Power?" *International Security* 4 (4), 3–35.

Art, Robert J. (1999). "The Fungibility of Force." In Robert J. Art and Kenneth N. Waltz, eds., *The Use of Force: Military Power and International Politics*, 5th ed. New York, NY: Rowman and Littlefield.

Brodie, Bernard. (2008). "The Absolute Weapon." In Thomas Mahken and Joseph A. Maiolo, eds., *Strategic Studies: A Reader*. New York, NY: Routledge.

Claude, Inis L. (1988). *Power and International Relations*. New York, NY: Random House.

Davenport, Kelsey. (2020). "Iran Abandons Uranium Limits." *Arms Control Today*, January/February (https://www .armscontrol.org/act/2020-01/news/ iran-abandons-uranium-limits).

Galdi, Theodor W. (1995). *Revolution in Military Affairs? Competing Concepts, Organizational Responses, Outstanding Issues* (CRS Report 95-1170 F). Washington, DC: US Government Printing Office.

Gartzke, Eric. (2007). "The Capitalist Peace." *American Journal of Political Science* 51, 166–191.

Gordon, Michael R. (2014). "Russia Displays a New Military Prowess in Ukraine's East." *New York Times*, April 21 (https:// www.nytimes.com/2014/04/22/ world/europe/new-prowess-for-russians.html).

Gordon, Michael R. (2017). "Russia Has Deployed Missile Barred by Treaty, U.S. General Tells Congress." *New York Times*, March 8 (https://www.nytimes .com/2017/03/08/us/politics/russia-inf-missile-treaty.html).

Jones, Daniel M., Stuart A. Bremer, and J. David Singer. (1996). "Militarized Interstate Disputes, 1816–1992: Rationale, Coding Rules, and Empirical Patterns." *Conflict Management and Peace Science* 15, 163–213.

Kant, Immanuel. (1996). "Toward Perpetual Peace." In Mary Gregor, ed., *The Cambridge Edition of the Works of Immanuel Kant: Practical Philosophy*. Cambridge, UK: Cambridge University Press.

Lamb, Christopher. (1988). *How to Think About Arms Control, Disarmament, and Defense*. Englewood Cliffs, NJ: Prentice Hall.

Mitrany, David. (1966). *A Working Peace System*. Chicago, IL: Quadrangle Books.

Morgenthau, Hans J. (1973). *Politics Among Nations*, 5th ed. New York, NY: Alfred A. Knopf.

Office of the Secretary of Defense. (2019). "Annual Report to Congress: Military and Security Developments Involving the People's Republic of China 2019" (https://media.defense.gov/2019/ May/02/2002127082/-1/-1/1/2019_ CHINA_MILITARY_POWER_REPORT .pdf).

Schelling, Thomas C. (1966). *Arms and Influence*. New Haven, CT: Yale University Press.

Shinkman, Paul D. (2019). "Study: U.S. No Longer Dominant Power in the Pacific." *US News and World Report*, August 20 (https://www.usnews.com/news/ world-report/articles/2019-08-20/ us-no-longer-dominant-power-in-the-pacific-study).

Walt, Stephen. (1987). *The Origins of Alliances*. Ithaca, NY: Cornell University Press.

Waltz, Kenneth. (1979). *Theory of International Politics*. New York, NY: McGraw-Hill.

Ward, Alex. (2020). "What Iran Stockpiling Uranium for a Nuclear Bomb Is Really About." *Vox*, March 5 (https://www.vox .com/2020/3/4/21164499/iran-nuclear-bomb-weapon-iaea-uranium).

Wright, Quincy. (1942). *A Study of War*. Chicago, IL: University of Chicago Press.

CHAPTER 7

Birnbaum, Michael. (2015). "Refugees Race Into Hungary as Border Fence Nears Completion." *Washington Post*, August 25 (https://www.washingtonpost.com/ world/europe/refugees-race-into-hungary-as-border-fence-nears-completion/2015/08/25/91f6e9c8-4aac-11e5-9f53-d1e3ddfd0cda_story .html).

Borger, Julian. (2014). "Marshall Islands Sues Nine Nuclear Powers Over Failure to Disarm." *The Guardian*, April 24 (https:// www.theguardian.com/world/2014/ apr/24/marshall-islands-sues-nine-nuclear-powers-failure-disarm).

Bull, Hedley. (1977). *The Anarchical Society*. New York, NY: Columbia University Press.

European Commission. (2017, March 1). *"White Paper on the Future of Europe: Reflections and Scenarios on for the EU27 by 2025."* Brussels, Belgium: European Commission (https:// ec.europa.eu/commission/sites/beta-political/files/white_paper_on_the_ future_of_europe_en.pdf).

European Council. (2019). "A New Strategic Agenda for the EU 2019–2024" (https:// www.consilium.europa.eu/en/eu-strategic-agenda-2019-2024).

Fisher, Roger. (1991). *Getting to Yes: Negotiating Agreement Without Giving In*, rev. ed. New York, NY: Penguin.

Ikenberry, G. John. (2000). *After Victory: Institutions, Strategic Restraint, and the Rebuilding of Order After Major Wars*. Princeton, NJ: Princeton University Press.

Karns, Margaret P., and Karen A. Mingst. (2010). *International Organizations: The Politics and Processes of Global Governance*, 2nd ed. Boulder, CO: Lynne Rienner.

Keating, Joshua. (2014). "Why the Marshall Islands Is Suing the World's Nuclear Powers." *Slate*, April 25 (http://www.slate.com/blogs/the_world_/2014/04/25/the_marshall_islands_is_suing_the_world_s_nuclear_powers_for_violating_international.html).

Kelemen, R. Daniel. (2020). "The European Union's Authoritarian Equilibrium." *Journal of European Public Policy* 27 (3), 481–499 (doi:10.1080/13501763.2020.1712455).

Krasner, Stephen. (1985). *Structural Conflict: The Third World Against Global Liberalism*. Berkeley, CA: University of California Press.

Lui, Kevin. (2016). "The Marshall Islands Cannot Sue Nuclear Powers for Proliferation, U.N. Court Rules." *Time*, October 5 (http://time.com/4520797/marshall-islands-lawsuit-nuclear-proliferation-icj).

Mitrany, David. (1966). *A Working Peace System*. Chicago, IL: Quadrangle Books.

Slaughter, Anne-Marie. (1995). "International Law in a World of Liberal States." *European Journal of International Law* 53, 503–538.

CHAPTER 8

Diamond, Jared. (1997). *Guns, Germs, and Steel: The Fates of Human Societies* New York, NY: Norton.

Drury, A. Cooper, Jonathan Krieckhaus, and Chika Yamamoto. (2014). "How Democracy Facilitates South Korean Interest in Free Trade Agreements." *Korea Observer* 45 (1), 39–60.

Friedman, Thomas L. (1999). *The Lexus and the Olive Tree*. New York, NY: Farrar, Straus and Giroux.

Fukuyama, Francis. (1992). *The End of History and the Last Man*. New York, NY: Free Press.

Human Rights Watch. (2017). "More Brands Should Reveal Where Their Clothes Are Made: 17 Align With Transparency Pledge; Others Should Catch Up" (https://www.hrw.org/news/2017/04/20/more-brands-should-reveal-where-their-clothes-are-made).

Jaffee, Daniel. (2014). *Brewing Justice: Fair Trade Coffee, Sustainability, and Survival*, updated ed. Oakland: University of California Press.

Stokes, Bruce, Richard Wike, and Dorothy Manevich. (2017). "Post-Brexit, Europeans More Favorable Toward EU." *Pew Research Center Global Attitudes and Trends*, June 15 (http://www.pewglobal.org/2017/06/15/post-brexit-europeans-more-favorable-toward-eu).

van der Wolf, Marthe. (2016). "Anti-Free Trade Movement Makes US-Europe Deal Unlikely." *Voice of America*, September 29 (https://www.voanews.com/a/anti-free-trade-movement-has-made-us-europe-trade-deal-unlikely/3529997.html).

CHAPTER 9

Al-Ali, Nadje Sadiq. (2007). *Iraqi Women: Untold Stories From 1948 to the Present*. London, UK: Zed Books.

Al-Jawaheri, Yasmin Husain. (2008). *Women in Iraq: The Gender Impact of International Sanctions*. London, UK: IB Tauris.

Askarov, Z., and Hristos Doucouliagos (2013). "Does Aid Improve Democracy and Governance? A Meta-Regression Analysis." *Public Choice* 157, 601–628.

Autesserre, Severine. (2014). *Peaceland: Conflict Resolution and the Everyday Politics of International Intervention*. New York, NY: Cambridge University Press.

Bierman, Noah. (2020). "North Korea Was Trump's Chief Foreign Policy Boast, but Things Got Worse on His Watch." *Los Angeles Times*, August 24 (https://www.latimes.com/politics/story/2020-08-24/north-korea-trump-foreign-policy).

Breitwieser, Anja, and Katharina Wick. (2016). "What We Miss by Missing Data: Aid Effectiveness Revisited." *World Development* 78, 554–571.

Burnside, Craig, and David Dollar. (2000). "Aid, Policies, and Growth." *American Economic Review* 90 (4), 847–868.

Clay, K. Chad. (2018). "Threat by Example: Economic Sanctions and Global Respect for Human Rights." *Journal of Global Security Studies* 3 (2), 133–149 (https://doi.org/10.1093/jogss/ogy006).

Drury, A. Cooper, Richard S. Olson, and Douglas A. Van Belle. (2005). "The Politics of Humanitarian Aid." *Journal of Politics* 67, 454–473.

Drury, A. Cooper, and Dursun Peksen. (2014). "Women and Economic Statecraft: The Negative Impact Economic Sanctions

Visit on Women." *European Journal of International Relations* 20 (2), 463–490.

Finkel, Steven E., Anibal Perez-Linan, and Mitchell A. Seligson. (2007). "The Effects of U.S. Foreign Assistance on Democracy-Building, 1990–2003." *World Politics* 59, 404–439.

Gilbert, Felix. (1961). *To the Farewell Address*. Princeton, NJ: Princeton University Press.

Herman, Robert G., and Theodore J. Piccone, eds. (2002). *Defending Democracy: A Global Survey of Foreign Policy Trends, 1992–2002*. Washington, DC: Democracy Coalition Project.

Hufbauer, Gary C., Jeffrey J. Schott, Kimberly Ann Elliott, and Barbara Oegg. (2009). *Economic Sanctions Reconsidered*, 3rd ed. Washington, DC: Peterson Institute for International Economics.

Kalyvitis, S., and I. Vlachaki. (2010). "Democratic Aid and the Democratization of Recipients." *Contemporary Economic Policy* 28, 188–218.

Mansfield, Edward, and Jon C. Pevehouse. (2006). "Democratization and International Organizations." *International Organization* 60, 137–167.

"North Korea Nuclear Crisis: Putin Calls Sanctions Useless." (2017). *BBC*, September 5 (http://www.bbc.com/news/world-asia-41158281).

Page, Jeremy, Andrew Jeong, and Ian Talley. (2018). "China, Finally, Clamps Down on North Korea Trade—And the Impact Is Stinging." *Wall Street Journal*, March 2 (https://www.wsj.com/articles/north-korea-finally-feels-the-sting-of-international-sanctions-1519923280).

Scott, James M., and Carie A. Steele. (2011). "Sponsoring Democracy: The United States and Democracy Aid to the Developing World, 1988–2001." *International Studies Quarterly* 55, 47–73.

Taylor, Adam. (2017). "What the New Sanctions on North Korea Mean." *Washington Post*, August 7 (https://www.washingtonpost.com/news/worldviews/wp/2017/08/07/what-the-new-u-n-sanctions-on-north-korea-mean/?utm_term=.0750298e6d8f).

CHAPTER 10

Bueno de Mesquita, Bruce, Alistair Smith, Randolph M. Siverson, and James D. Morrow. (2004). *The Logic of Political Survival*. Cambridge, MA: MIT Press.

Diamond, Jared. (1997). *Guns, Germs, and Steel*. New York, NY: Norton.

Drury, A. Cooper, Jonathan Krieckhaus, and Michael Lusztig. (2006). "Corruption,

Democracy, and Economic Growth." *International Political Science Review* 27, 121–136.

Elborgh-Woytek, Katrin, Monique Newiak, Kalpana Kochhar, Stefania Fabrizio, Kangni Kpodar, Philippe Wingender, Benedict Clements, and Gerd Schwartz. (2013). "Women, Work, and the Economy: Macroeconomic Gains From Gender Equity." *IMF Staff Discussion Note*, September (http://www.imf.org/external/pubs/ft/sdn/2013/sdn1310.pdf).

"Forgive and Remember." (2015). *Economist*, June 20 (https://www.economist.com/news/finance-and-economics/21654645-debt-relief-boosts-growth-only-when-it-comes-conditions-forgive-and).

Galatsidas, Achilleas, and Finbarr Sheehy. (2015). "What Have the Millennium Development Goals Achieved?" *The Guardian*, July 6 (https://www.theguardian.com/global-development/datablog/2015/jul/06/what-millennium-development-goals-achieved-mdgs).

Koplow, David A. (2003). *Smallpox: The Fight to Eradicate a Global Scourge*. Berkeley: University of California Press.

Krieckhaus, Jonathan. (2006). *Dictating Development*. Pittsburgh, PA: University of Pittsburgh Press.

Lake, David, and Matthew Baum. (2001). "The Invisible Hand of Democracy." *Comparative Political Studies* 34, 578–621.

Marcelino, Sandra R., and Ivetta Hakobyan. (2014, December). "Does Lower Debt Buy Higher Economic Growth? The Impact of Debt Relief Initiatives on Growth." *IMF Working Paper WP/14/230* (http://www.imf.org/external/pubs/ft/wp/2014/wp14230.pdf).

Masters, William, and Margaret McMillan. (2001). "Climate and Scale in Economic Growth." *Journal of Economic Growth* 6, 167–186.

Sachs, Jeffrey, and Andrew Warner. (1995, December). "Natural Resource Abundance and Economic Growth." *NBER Working Paper 5398*. Cambridge, MA: National Bureau of Economic Research.

United Nations. (2015a). *The Millennium Development Goals Report*. New York, NY: United Nations (http://www.un.org/millenniumgoals/2015_MDG_Report/pdf/MDG%202015%20rev%20(July%201).pdf).

United Nations. (2015b). *Sustainable Development Goals: 17 Goals to Transform Our World* (http://www.un.org/sustainabledevelopment/blog/2015/12/sustainable-development-goals-kick-off-with-start-of-new-year).

Useem, Jerry. (2003). "The Devil's Excrement." *Fortune*, February 3.

Wallerstein, Immanuel. (1974). *The Modern World System*. New York, NY: Academic Press.

Wallerstein, Immanuel. (1979). *The Capitalist World Economy*. New York, NY: Cambridge University Press.

CHAPTER 11

Chretien, Jean-Pierre. (2003). *The Great Lakes of Africa: Two Thousand Years of History* (translated by Scott Straus). Cambridge, MA: Zone Books/MIT Press.

Cohen, Dara Kay. (2016). *Rape During Civil War*. Ithaca, NY: Cornell University Press.

Cox, Eric. (2010). "State Interests and the Creation and Functioning of the United Nations Human Rights Council." *Journal of International Law and International Relations* 6, 87–119.

Murdie, Amanda, and Dursun Peksen. (2014). "The Impact of Human Rights INGO Shaming on Humanitarian Interventions." *Journal of Politics* 76 (1), 215–228.

Sengupta, Somini. (2016). "Citizenship Stops Here With Mother." *New York Times*, August 4, A8.

Social Progress Imperative. (2019). *2019 Social Progress Index*. Washington, DC: Author (https://www.socialprogress.org/?tab=2&code=NOR&compare=USA).

United Nations Development Programme. (2020). "Almost 90% of Men/Women Globally Are Biased Against Women," March 5 (https://www.undp.org/content/undp/en/home/news-centre/news/2020/Gender_Social_Norms_Index_2020.html).

United Nations Office on Drugs and Crime (UNDOC). (2018). *Global Study on Homicide 2018: Gender-Related Killing of Women and Girls*. Vienna, Austria: Author.

World Health Organization. (2017, February). "Fact Sheet: Female Genital Mutilation" (http://www.who.int/mediacentre/factsheets/fs241/en).

CHAPTER 12

Associated Press. (2011). "China Says Desertification Process Has Slowed." *Times of India*, January 4 (http://cmsenvis.cmsindia.org/newsletter/enews/NewsDetails.asp?id=33631).

Brown, Gordon, and Daniel Susskind. (2020). "International Cooperation During the COVID-19 Pandemic." *Oxford Review of Economic Policy* graa025 (https://doi.org/10.1093/oxrep/graa025).

Bulloch, John, and Harvey Morris. (1993). *No Friends but the Mountains: The Tragic History of the Kurds*. New York, NY: Oxford University Press.

Centers for Disease Control and Prevention. (2020). "Case Counts." *Ebola: Ebola Virus Disease*, February 19 (https://www.cdc.gov/vhf/ebola/history/2014-2016-outbreak/case-counts.html).

Council on Foreign Relations. (2020). "Territorial Disputes in the South China Sea." *Global Conflict Tracker*, March 6 (https://www.cfr.org/interactive/global-conflict-tracker/conflict/territorial-disputes-south-china-sea).

Dawood, Fatimah S., A. Danielle Iuliano, Carrie Reed, Martin I. Meltzer, David K. Shay, Po-Yung Cheng, et al. (2012). "Estimated Global Mortality Associated With the First 12 Months of 2009 Pandemic Influenza A H1N1 Virus Circulation: A Modelling Study." *The Lancet* 12 (9): 687–695 (https://www.thelancet.com/journals/laninf/article/PIIS1473-3099(12)70121-4/fulltext).

Doyle, Alister. (2013). "Scientists Say United on Global Warming, at Odds With Public View." *Reuters*, May 15 (http://www.reuters.com/article/us-climate-scientists/scientists-say-united-on-global-warming-at-odds-with-public-view-idUSBRE94F00020130516).

Forner, Claudio, Jürgen Blaser, Frank Jotzo, and Carmenza Robledo. (2006). "Keeping the Forest for the Climate's Sake: Avoiding Deforestation in Developing Countries Under the UNFCCC." *Climate Policy* 6 (3).

Gatehouse, Gabriel. (2020). "Deforested Parts of Amazon 'Emitting More CO_2 Than They Absorb.'" *BBC*, February 11 (https://www.bbc.com/news/science-environment-51464694).

Intergovernmental Panel on Climate Change. (2014). *Global Climate Change 2014: Synthesis Report* (https://ipcc.ch/report/ar5/syr).

Kingsley, Patrick. (2015). "Arab Spring Prompts Biggest Migrant Wave Since Second World War." *The Guardian*, January 3 (https://www.theguardian.com/world/commentisfree/2015/jan/03/arab-spring-migrant-wave-instability-war).

The Lancet. (2017, October 19). "The Lancet Commission on Pollution and Health" (http://www.thelancet.com/commissions/pollution-and-health).

Lebreton, L., B. Slat, F. Ferrari, B. Sainte-Rose, J. Aitken, R. Marthouse, et al. (2018). "Evidence That the Great Pacific Garbage Patch Is Rapidly Accumulating Plastic." *Scientific Reports* 8 (4666) (https://doi.org/10.1038/s41598-018-22939-w).

Leutert, Stephanie, and Sarah Spalding. (2019). "How Many Central Americans Are Traveling North?" *Lawfare*, March 14 (https://www.lawfareblog.com/how-many-central-americans-are-traveling-north).

Matloff, Judith. (2017). *No Friends but the Mountains: Dispatches From the World's Violent Highlands*. New York, NY: Basic Books.

Miller, Brandon, and Jay Croft. (2018). "Planet Has Only Until 2030 to Stem Catastrophic Climate Change, Experts Warn." *CNN*, October 8 (https://edition.cnn.com/2018/10/07/world/climate-crhange-new-ipcc-report-wxc/index.html).

National Oceanic and Atmospheric Administration. (2020). "2019 Was 2nd Hottest Year on Record for Earth Say NOAA, NASA." January 15 (https://www.noaa.gov/news/2019-was-2nd-hottest-year-on-record-for-earth-say-noaa-nasa).

People's Republic of China, State Council. (2016, October 17). "China's Progress in Poverty Reduction and Human Rights" (http://english.gov.cn/policies/latest_releases/2016/10/17/content_281475468533275.htm).

Scutti, Susan. (2017). "Pollution Linked to 9 Million Deaths Worldwide in 2015, Study Says." *CNN*, October 20 (http://www.cnn.com/2017/10/19/health/pollution-1-in-6-deaths-study/index.html).

Todd, Zoe. (2019). "By the Numbers: Syrian Refugees Around the World." *Frontline/PBS*, November 19 (https://www.pbs.org/wgbh/frontline/article/numbers-syrian-refugees-around-world).

Trevino, Marty. (2019). "Cyber Physical Systems: The Coming Singularity." *Prism: The Journal of Complex Operations* 8 (3), 3–13.

UN Department of Economic and Social Affairs. (2013). *Sustainable Development Challenges: World Economic and Social Survey 2013* (http://www.un.org/en/development/desa/publications/world-economic-and-social-survey-2013-sustainable-development-challenges.html).

UN Food and Agriculture Organization. (2015). *Global Forest Resources Assessment 2015* (http://www.fao.org/resources/infographics/infographics-details/en/c/325836).

UN Food and Agriculture Organization. (2017). *Keeping an Eye on SDG 15* (http://www.fao.org/3/a-i7334e.pdf).

Union of Concerned Scientists. (2012). "Environmental Impacts of Coal Power: Air Pollution" (http://www.ucsusa.org/clean-energy/coal-and-other-fossil-fuels/coal-air-pollution#.WePNHoWcFPY).

UN Migration. (2020). "Venezuelan Refugee and Migrant Crisis" (https://www.iom.int/venezuela-refugee-and-migrant-crisis).

US Environmental Protection Agency. (2011, November). "Marine Debris in the North Pacific" (https://nepis.epa.gov/Exe/ZyPDF.cgi/P100CYAN.PDF?Dockey=P100CYAN.PDF).

Watson, Paul. (2017). "The Whale Wars Continue." *Sea Shepherd Society*, August 28 (http://www.seashepherd.org/news-and-commentary/commentary/the-whale-wars-continue.html).

Weiss, Joseph S., Zhu Dajian, Maria Amélia Enríquez, Peter H. May, Elimar Pinheiro do Nascimento, Walter A. Pengue, and Stanislav Shmelev. (2017). "UN Environmental Policy: Non-state Actors, Trends, and the Regulatory Role of the State." *Journal of Political Ecology* 24, 1013–1037.

CHAPTER 13

Beaubien, Jason. (2019). "Polio Is Making a Comeback." *NPR*, November 15 (https://www.npr.org/sections/goatsandsoda/2019/11/15/779865471/polio-vaccine-may-be-preventing-the-end-of-polio).

Finnemore, Martha, and Kathryn Sikkink. (1998). "International Norm Dynamics and Political Change." *International Organization* 52, 887–917.

Global FoodBanking Network. (2016). *Annual Report 2016* (https://www.foodbanking.org/2016annualreport).

Global Polio Eradication Initiative. (2016). *Annual Report 2016* (http://polioeradication.org/wp-content/uploads/2017/08/AR2016_EN.pdf).

Global Polio Eradication Initiative. (2020). "Endemic Countries" (http://polioeradication.org/where-we-work/polio-endemic-countries).

International Federation of Red Cross and Red Crescent Societies. (2020). "Press Releases" (https://media.ifrc.org/ifrc/news/press-releases).

Keck, Margaret E., and Kathryn Sikkink. (1998). *Activists Beyond Borders: Advocacy Networks in International Politics*. Ithaca, NY: Cornell University Press.

Martinez, Weston. (2017). "New Toyota-Mazda Plant a Good Fit for Texas." *Fort Worth Star-Telegram*, August 29 (http://www.star-telegram.com/opinion/opn-columns-blogs/other-voices/article170070677.html).

Millennium Ecosystem Assessment. (2005). *Ecosystems and Human Well-Being: Synthesis*. Washington, DC: Island Press (https://www.millenniumassessment.org/documents/document.356.aspx.pdf).

Porter, Tom. (2015). "Gangs of Russia: Ruthless Mafia Networks Extending Their Influence." *International Business Times*, April 15 (www.ibt.co.uk/gangs-russia-ruthless-mafia-networks-extending-their-influence-1495644).

Slaughter, Anne-Marie. (2004). *A New World Order*. Princeton, NJ: Princeton University Press.

CHAPTER 14

Fukuyama, Francis. (1989). "The End of History." *The National Interest* 16, 3–18.

Fukuyama, Francis. (2017). "Francis Fukuyama on Why Liberal Democracy Is in Trouble." *Morning Edition, NPR*, April 4 (http://www.npr.org/2017/04/04/522554630/francis-fukuyama-on-why-liberal-democracy-is-in-trouble).

Morell, Michael. (2020). "Analysis: The National Security Implications of COVID-19." *CBS News*, May 8, 2020 (https://www.cbsnews.com/news/coronavirus-national-security-implications-analysis).

Roth, Richard. (2017). "UN Security Council Imposes New Sanctions on North Korea." *CNN*, August 6 (http://www.cnn.com/2017/08/05/asia/north-korea-un-sanctions/index.html).

INDEX

Figures are indicated by "*f*," tables by "*t*," and maps by "*m*".

ABM. *See* Anti-Ballistic Missile Treaty (ABM)
Absolute advantage, 229
Absolute gains, 60
The Accidental Super Power (Ziehan), 295
Acid rain, 355
ADA. *See* UN Atomic Development Authority (ADA)
Adams, Abigail, 323
Advisory group, 88–89
Affordable Care Act, 239
Afghanistan, 35, 68, 135, 275, 278, 339, 343, 370, 373, 383, 387, 395
  al-Qaeda in, 396
  conflict and war in, 32
  ethnic geography and conflict in, 32
  mujahideen and US, 276
  natural resources and development, 295
  NGOs in, 347
  Soviet invasion of, 116
  terrorist attacks in, 123
  tribal areas, 32*m*
  US involvement in, 70, 83
  women and, 106
Africa, 31, 334, 339, 341, 371, 428*m*
  Berlin Wall and, 272–273
  colonialism, 228
  development aid policies, 272–273
  HIV/AIDS in, 398, 399*m*, 399*t*
  and human rights, 333
  Hutus and Tutsis, 326, 328–329
  mercury poisoning, 362
  political map, 272*m*
  regional IOs in, 202–203
  state borders of, 31, 34*m*
  UN peacekeeping missions in, 343
African Charter on Human and Peoples' Rights, 333
African Commission on Human and Peoples' Rights, 333
African Continental Free Trade Agreement, 183
African Court of Human and Peoples' Rights, 333
African-European HIV Vaccine Development Network, 398
African Union (AU), 22, 195–196, 203, 277, 333, 339, 341, 343
Africa Watch, 345
Afrique Verte International (Green Africa International), 397
Aga Khan, 10
Agent-centered approach, 84
Agriculture, 297–298, 374, 420
Ahmadinejad, Mahmoud, 24
Aid sanctions, 255, 260–261
AIPAC. *See* American Israel Public Affairs Committee (AIPAC)
Airbus, 236, 239
Air pollution, 354

al-Assad, Bashar, 21, 117, 261, 321
Alawites, 21
al-Baghdadi, Abu Bakr, 39, 120, 396
Albania, 263
al-Bashir, Omar, 339
Albright, Madeleine, 102, 184
Allende, Salvador, 225, 260
Alliances, 157–159
Allison, Graham, 87–88, 113
Allison, Graham T., Jr., 136
al Nahyan, Mohammed bin Zayed, 383
al-Qaeda, 23, 39, 66, 83, 118, 120, 184, 238, 241, 395–396
Alternative für Deutschland (AfD), 308
al-Zarqawi, Abu Musab, 120, 396
Amazon rain forest, 356, 361
American Convention on Human Rights, 331
American Israel Public Affairs Committee (AIPAC), 89
American Revolution, 31
American Transplant Foundation, 394
Americas Watch, 345
Amnesty International, 22, 42, 66, 90, 338, 344–345, 346*t*, 347, 384
Amsterdam, 368
The Anarchical Society (Bull), 65
Anarchy, 189
  causes of war and, 131
  challenges of world politics, 8, 10, 409–414
  constructivist perspective, 70–71
  cooperation for international security and, 182
  economic sanctions and, 267
  feminist perspective, 101
  horizontal enforcement as, 192
  international law and, 189
  of international system, 8, 23–24
  liberal perspective, 64–65
  realist perspective, 57
  self-help, 23–24
  types of, 70–71
  UN and, 217
Andean Common Market, 198, 202
Angell, Norman, 65
Angola, 35, 93
Anheuser-Busch, 300
Annan, Kofi, 390
Annihilation, 31
Anti-Assad rebel groups, 21
Anti-Ballistic Missile Treaty (ABM), 162
Antidrug aid, 261
Antigua, 262
Apartheid, 194, 262–263, 267, 324, 335, 337, 346, 388, 401
APEC. *See* Asia-Pacific Economic Cooperation (APEC)
Apple iPhone, 240–241
Aquinas, Thomas, 322

Arab League, 261
Arable land, 357
Arab Spring, 21, 181, 244, 261, 324, 377
Arafat, Yasser, 275, 395
Árbenz, Jacobo, 96
Archer Daniels Midland, 226, 246
Arctic Ocean, 375
Ardern, Jacinda, 103
ARF. *See* ASEAN Regional Forum (ARF)
Argentina, 104, 339
Aristotle, 259
Armas, Carlos Castillo, 96
Armed conflict
  evolution and trends, 121–129
  nature of, 114–121
  terrorism, 118–121
  war. *See* War
Armed forces, 150–157
Armenia, 30, 72
Arms control, 7, 165–169
Arms embargo, 264, 269
Arms races, 157, 161–162
Arms Trade Treaty, 182
Art, Robert J., 60, 165
Article 1 of the UN Charter, 212
Article 2 of the Convention on Genocide, 329
Article 2 of the UN Charter, 27, 44, 212
ASEAN. *See* Association of Southeast Asian Nations (ASEAN)
ASEAN Regional Forum (ARF), 202
Asian Tigers, 305–307, 313
Asia-Pacific Economic Cooperation (APEC), 197, 202
Asia Pacific Forced Migration Connection, 386
Asia Watch, 345
Assad regime, 21–22, 85, 194, 261, 276
Assange, Julian, 27
Association of Southeast Asian Nations (ASEAN), 202
Asymmetric war, 117–118. *See also* Terrorism
Athens and Sparta conflict, 56, 359
Atomic Development Authority (ADA), 169
AU. *See* African Union (AU)
Aung San Suu Kyi, 413
Austerity program, 236, 243
Australia, 97, 256, 263, 288, 338, 375, 432*m*
  as core state, 302
  crimes against aboriginal peoples, 335
Austria, 204, 206, 208, 210, 338
Austria-Hungary, 31–32, 132, 155
Autesserre, Severine, 281
Authoritative government, 8
Autocracy, 90–91
Axis Rule in Occupied Europe (Lemkin), 326

Bachelet, Michelle, 342
Badie, Dina, 89
Bahrain, 202, 263

Balanced multipolar systems, 132
Balance-of-power politics, 63, 159–160, 170
Balancing alliance, 158
Balkans, 30
Ballif-Spanvill, Bonnie, 106
Bandwagoning, 158
Bangladesh, 97, 360
Bank for International Settlements, 36
Ban Ki-moon, 341
Barbuda, 262
Bardot, Bridget, 369
Bargaining, 185
    theories of war, 135
Barker, Bob, 369
Barnett, Michael, 72
Baruch Plan, 169
Battle of Mogadishu, 90, 282
Bayer, 23
Beasley, Ryan, 89
Bechtel, 235
Beggar-thy-neighbor policy, 228, 235
Beijing Consensus, 308
Belarus, 266, 337–338
Belgium, 75, 127, 204, 301, 325, 338
Bensouda, Fatou, 339, 341
Berlin, 35
Berlin Airlift, 35
Berlin Wall, 272–273
Bermuda, 262
Beschel, Robert P., Jr., 136
Bezos, Jeff, 293
Bhutan, 241, 334
Bhutto, Benazir, 104
Biden, Joe, 215
Big Mac Index, 290
Bilateral arms control agreement, 166
Bilateral diplomacy, 186
Bilateral foreign aid, 225
Bill and Melinda Gates Foundation,
    239, 346t, 383
Bin Laden, Osama, 39, 339, 389, 396
Biodiversity challenges, 361–363
Bipolar system, 63, 131–132
Blair, Tony, 311
Boeing, 236
Boko Haram, 389, 396
Bolivia, 198, 235, 362
Bolsonaro, Jair, 356
Bono, 10, 23, 38
Boomerang model, 388
Borlaug, Norman, 38
Bosnia, 43–44, 124, 172, 269, 325
Bounded rationality, 86
Bourgeoisie, 92
Bratski Krug, 388
Brazil
    anti-deforestation efforts, 364
    COVID-19, 377
    deforestation in, 356
    GDP per capita, 305
    illegal gold mining, 362
    IMF voting weight, 199
    as semi-peripheral state, 97, 303–304
    trade disputes, 202
    Truth Commission, 335
    World Bank loans, 235, 312
Breitwieser, Anja, 276
Bretton Woods system, 201, 235, 310, 312
Brewing Justice (Jaffee), 245
Brexit, 45, 95, 206, 210, 223, 248–249, 308

Brinkmanship, 161
Britain. See United Kingdom (UK)
British East India Company, 36
British Empire, 228
British Petroleum (BP), 23
Broadening and globalization, 241
Brodie, Bernard, 153, 160
Brunei, 374
Brussels Summit, 208
Bueno de Mesquita, Bruce, 90
Buffett, Warren, 10, 239, 293
Bulgaria, 93, 204, 232
Bull, Hedley, 65
Bulloch, John, 373
Bureaucratic organizations, 87
Bureaucratic politics model, 87–88
Burke, Tarana, 102
Burma, 121, 246, 260
Burton, Dan, 262
Burundi, 290, 328–329, 339
Bush, George H. W., 55, 104, 181, 217
Bush, George W., 9, 55, 65, 83, 89, 136–137,
    184, 238, 275, 332
Business TANs, 391–392

Cambodia, 232, 335, 344
Cameron, David, 95
Canada, 35, 53, 73, 158, 201–202, 236, 244,
    259, 262–263, 267, 281, 293, 294t, 302,
    335, 338, 355, 375, 395
Canada-Africa Prevention Trials
    Network, 398
Canadian laws, 369
CAN-Europe. See Climate Action Network
    Europe (CAN-Europe)
Cannondale Bicycle Corporation, 244
Capitalism, 237, 240t
    definition, 92
    in Europe, 228
    Marxism and, 232–233
    state-level explanations of war, 134
Capitalist class, 92
Caprioli, Mary, 106
Carbon dioxide (CO2) emission, 354, 356
Carbon footprint, 368
CARE International, 346t
Carr, E. H., 57, 64
Carson, Rachel, 367
Carter, Jimmy, 55, 86, 88, 91, 193, 261, 265
Carter Center, 346t
Cashman, Greg, 137
Castro, Fidel, 35, 93, 257, 262, 273, 301
Catholic Church, 36, 384
Catholics in Northern Ireland, 73–74
Causal relationships, 53
Cayman Islands, 262
CEDAW. See Convention on the Elimination
    of All Forms of Discrimination Against
    Women (CEDAW)
Central Asia Institute, 347
Centrally planned economy, 232
CETA. See EU–Canada Comprehensive
    Economic and Trade Agreement
    (CETA)
CFSP. See Common Foreign and Security
    Policy (CFSP)
CGIAR. See Consultative Group on
    International Agricultural Research
    (CGIAR)
Chamberlain, Neville, 166

Chávez, Hugo, 85
Chechen Mafia, 388
Chechnya, 411
Chemical weapons, 8, 21, 169, 190
Chemical Weapons Convention, 169
Chernobyl nuclear reactor plant, 364
Chernomyrdin, Viktor, 390
Child mortality, 310
Children's security issues, 417–418
Child Survival and Development
    Revolution, 340
Chile, 97, 191, 199, 226, 260, 334
China, 12, 23, 163, 280
    Albania and, 263
    anti-desertification efforts, 365
    Beijing Consensus, 308
    black-market human organs, 394
    claim to South China Sea, 374–375
    COVID-19, 133, 377, 417
    cyberwarfare, 128
    defense spending, 151f
    desertification, 357
    economic collapse, 232–233
    economic statecraft, 256
    economy, 420
    export-led growth, 412
    flow of capital, 413
    free trading, 230–231
    GDP per capita, 289f, 294t
    gender inequality in, 106
    geographic location of, 61, 140, 155
    Great Green Wall project, 365
    human rights and, 336
    IMF voting weight, 199
    India and, border conflict, 373
    international trade economy, 237
    Internet and, 41
    Marshall Islands case and, 195
    military, 29
    military spending, 152, 157, 175
    money, power and security linkage, 224
    naval power, 175
    North Korean refugees, 410
    nuclear weapons, 155, 157, 163
    in P5, 69, 170, 200
    Paris Agreement, support for, 370
    polio outbreak in, 383
    pollution problems, 363–364
    poverty in, 372
    security, 155, 175
    as semi-peripheral state, 97, 303–304
    size of military forces, 152
    socialist revolution, 232
    specialization and trading, 230–231
    state-managed capitalism, 307
    sustainable economic development, 374
    Thucydides trap, 113
    trade disputes, 202, 238
    trade war, 234, 238, 260
    UN budget, 215
    and US, 113, 266, 337
    World Bank voting weight, 201
    WTO and, 226
Chinese Communist Party, 35, 93, 412
Chiquita Brands International Sàrl, 96
Civil society, 42–43
    development programs, 38
    groups, 333
Civil society organizations (CSOs), 43, 280,
    337, 346, 367, 384

Civil war, 21, 43, 93, 116–117, 118*t*, 124, 126, 137–141
Classical realism, 58
Clay, K. Chad, 267
Clean Air Act, 248
Climate Action Network, 367
Climate Action Network Europe (CAN-Europe), 400
Climate change. *See* Global climate change
Climate Change Performance Index, 366
Clinton, Bill, 55, 65, 184, 332
Clinton, Hillary, 72, 102, 184
Clooney, George, 38
Club of Rome, 367
CNN effect, 347
Coalition Against Trafficking in Women, 347
Coalition for the International Criminal Court, 390
Coalition governments, 89
Coercive diplomacy, 165
Cohen, David, 89
Cold War, 14, 29, 31, 35, 44, 75, 93, 97
    bilateral diplomacy in, 186
    deterrence after, 163–164
    development aid and, 272–273
    Europe and NATO after, 68
    nuclear arms race, 157, 162
    UNSC and, 172, 214, 217
    US military aid during, 278
Collective action problem, 14
Collective goods, 354
Collective security, 66, 170–173
Colombia, 198, 276, 278, 343, 362
Colonialism, 226–229, 240*t*
    African national borders and, 31
    civil war and, 138
    development aid and, 274
    European imperialism and, 31
    explaining differences in economic development, 297–299
    Marxist theory and, 93–94
    neocolonialism, 299
Colonies, 94
CoM. *See* Council of Ministers (CoM)
Combs, Cindy, 121
Command economy, 232
Commercial liberalism, 65
Commitment problem, 15
Committee to Protect Journalists, 346*t*
Common Foreign and Security Policy (CFSP), 204
Communication
    arms control agreement for, 168
    technology, 41, 186
Communism, 33, 232
Comparative advantage, 229, 234
Compellence, 164–165
Complexity of world politics, 9–10, 409–414
    cooperation for international security and, 182
    UN and, 217
Comprehensive Nuclear Test-Ban Treaty, 169
Comprehensive sanctions, 262–263
Compulsory jurisdiction, 194
ConAgra, 246
Concert of Europe, 171, 210
Conference diplomacy, 187, 188*t*
Conflict and war, 7, 8, 10
    active state-based, 115*m*
    in Afghanistan, 32

armed conflict, nature of, 114–121
    causes of war, 121–129
    civil war, 137–141
    consequences of, 141–142
    constructivist perspective. *See* Constructivism
    in developing world, 124–126
    factors leading to, 130–131
    geography and territory, 130
    individual-level explanations, 136–137
    international conflict, 113–114
    just war tradition and international law, 190
    liberal perspective. *See* Liberalism
    Marxist theory and, 92–93
    military conflicts, 127*f*
    movies about, 123
    nature of war, 121–129
    power and, 63
    realist perspective. *See* Realism
    refugees from, 321–322
    state-level explanations, 134–136
    in Syria, 21–22
    system-level explanations, 131–134
    terrorism, 118–121
    Thucydides trap, 113, 132
Conflict and war, managing, 147
    alliances, 157–159
    arms control, 165–169
    balance-of-power politics, 159–160
    collective security, 170–173
    disarmament, 165–166, 169–170
    liberal approaches, 165–176
    military expenditures, 150–152
    military technology, 153, 155–157
    military weapons and resources, 150–157
    realist approaches, 149–165
    security communities, 173, 175–176
    and seeking security, 147–148
    size of military forces, 152–153
    using force, 160–165
Conservative populist movements, 308
Consociational democracy, 75
Constitution of the United States, 192
Constructivism, 69
    of actors, 71–73
    causes of war and, 131
    central dynamics of international relations, 74–77
    definition, 12, 69, 141
    feminist perspective, 101
    international law and, 188
    interpretivist, 71
    IOs and, 196
    nature of international system, 70–71
    positivist, 71
    postmodern, 71
    of power resources, 73–74
    realism, liberalism *vs.*, 77*t*
    variants of, 71
    See also Liberalism; Realism
Constructivists, 367, 385, 401, 410, 419
Consular Relations, 184
Consultative Group on International Agricultural Research (CGIAR), 397
Conté, Lansana, 264
Convention against Torture, 339
Conventional war, 116
Convention on Cybercrime, 376
Convention on Genocide, 326, 329, 332, 339

Convention on the Elimination of All Forms of Discrimination Against Women (CEDAW), 340
Convention on the Rights of Persons with Disabilities, 332
Convention on the Rights of the Child, 332, 340
Cooperation for peace/security, 182
    achieving, 182
    challenges, 182–183
    dilemmas of international relations, 12–15
    diplomacy, 183–187
    international law, 187–196
    IOs, 196–217
Core states, 94, 97, 98*f*, 302–304
Coronavirus. *See* COVID-19
Correlates of War, 117
Corruption, 324
Costa Rica, 150, 158, 202, 294, 364
Council of Ministers (CoM), 204
Council of the European Union, 204
Council on Foreign Relations, 375
Coup d'état, 264
Covariance, 53
COVID-19, 5, 7, 103, 133, 181, 197, 209*f*, 377, 378*m*, 400, 414–415, 417
Crimea, 52, 70, 72, 84–85, 157, 194, 257
Crimean War, 210
Crimes against humanity, 332
Criminal terrorists, 121, 393
Croatia, 204
CSOs. *See* Civil society organizations (CSOs)
Cuba, 30, 35, 87, 89, 91, 164, 232, 257, 260, 262–263, 273, 282, 301–302, 361
Cuban American National Foundation, 89
Cuban Missile Crisis, 35, 87, 91, 155, 164, 168, 257
Cultural exchange, 176
Cultural relativism, 326
Currency devaluation, 239
Currency exchange rate system, 201
Custom, 190–191
Cyber Command, 129
Cyberspace, 375–376
Cyberwarfare, 127–129, 376
Cyclical theories of war, 132–133
Cyprus, 204, 206, 262
Czechoslovakia, 93, 232, 266
Czech Republic, 204

Da'esh, 21. *See also* ISIS (Islamic State in Iraq and Syria)
Dalai Lama, 23, 38
Darfur, 172
Debt forgiveness, 311–312
Declaration on the Elimination of Violence against Women, 341
Declaration on the Establishment of a New International Economic Order, 198
Deepening and globalization, 241–242
Defensive force, 162
Defensive realism, 58
Deforestation, 355–357, 361, 364
Democracy, 31, 90–91
    aid, 278–280
    consociational, 75
    development aid and, 274
    economic growth and, 307
    economic sanctions and, 264
    promotion, 55, 176

Democratic peace, 51, 55, 65, 136, 244
Democratic Republic of the Congo (DRC), 42, 264, 324, 329, 363, 370
Democratization efforts, 337
Deng, Francis, 43–44
Denmark, 203, 206, 264, 338
Dependency theory, 94, 96, 301–302
Description use of theory, 54
Desertification, 357
    state actions, 364–366
Deterrence, 160–164
Devaluation, currency, 239
Developed country, 288
Developing world
    Environmental Performance Index, 366
    war in, 124–126
Development aid, 270
    definition, 270
    determinants of, 270, 273–274
    economic growth and, 275
    effectiveness, 274–276
    US, 271
    See also Foreign aid
Development theories and policies, 299
    Beijing Consensus, 308
    dependency theory, 301–302
    export-led growth, 305–306
    expropriation, 301–302
    ISI, 304–305
    Marxist theory, 301–302
    MDG, 308, 310
    modernization, 299–300
    Monterrey Consensus, 307–308
    Washington Consensus, 306–307
    WST, 302–304
Diamond, Jared, 228, 297
Difference feminists, 103
Dion, Michelle L., 100
Diplomacy, 60, 183
    art of, 185–186
    bilateral, 186
    coercive, 165
    conference, 187, 188t
    definition, 183
    diplomats, 30, 184
    in foreign embassies, 27–30
    forms of, 186–187
    linkage strategy, 185–186
    multilateral, 186
    nature of, 183–185
    negotiation, 185, 186f
    role of, 183–185
    third-party, 186, 187t
    track II, 187
Diplomatic immunity, 28, 30, 184
Diplomats, 30, 184
Direct deterrence, 160–161
Disarmament, 7, 165–166, 169–170
Discovery Network, 372
Discursive power, 73
Distribution of wealth, 288–295
Distributions of power, 63, 131–132
Diversionary theory, 90, 134
Diversity, 10
    cooperation for international security
        and, 182
    in international system, 8–9, 409–414
    UN and, 217
Division for the Advancement of Women
    (DAW), 342

Dlamini-Zuma, Nkosazana, 341
Doctors Without Borders, 346t
Dolan, Chris, 89
Dominican Republic, 356
Dragonstone, 230
Duelfer, Charles, 89
Dulles, Allen, 96
Dulles, John Foster, 96
Durkheim, Émile, 69
Dutch East India Company, 36
Duvalier, Jean-Claude, 275
Dyson, Stephen, 89

Earth Day, 367–368, 370
Earth Day Network, 368
Earth Summit, 187, 367, 397
East Asia, 430m
Eastern African National Networks of AIDS
    Service Organisations, 398
Ebola virus pandemic, 377
EC. See European Commission (EC)
ECHR. See European Court of Human
    Rights (ECHR)
ECJ. See European Court of Justice (ECJ)
Economic and Social Council (ECOSOC),
    215–216
Economic clout, 37
Economic Community of West African
    States (ECOWAS), 203, 343
Economic cooperation, 197
Economic crises, 5, 243
Economic development programs, 38
Economic disaster, 232
Economic growth
    democracy and, 307
    development aid and, 275
Economic inequality, 288–289
    colonial history, 297–299
    distribution of wealth across countries,
        290–292
    distribution of wealth within countries,
        292–295
    Gini coefficients, 292–293
    HDI, 293–294
    natural resources and, 295–297
    north–south divide, 288, 298
    rich and poor countries, 288–289
Economic liberalism, 65
Economic sanctions, 194, 259, 337–338
    aid sanctions, 260–261
    consequences of, 269
    definition, 256, 259
    failure of, 264, 266–267
    financial, 261–262
    import and export, 260
    and LGBTQIA rights, 265
    North Korea and, 62, 266
    paradox of, 267
    purposes of, 263–264
    third-party, 262
    total/comprehensive, 262–263
    trade, 259–260
    types of, 259–262
    women and, 268–269
Economics and war, 130
Economic security, 7
    market and government
        relationship, 226
    money, power and security linkage,
        224–226, 255

resurgence of nationalist economics,
    223–224
trends and emerging concerns, 418
and world politics, 416–417
Economic security–oriented TANs, 397–398
Economic statecraft, 256–258
    definition, 255
    economic sanctions, 259–269
    foreign aid, 259, 270–282
    history of, 259
Economic warfare, 263
Economy era
    Global Economy Era, 236–249
    International Economy Era, 229–236
    National Economy Era, 226–229
ECOSOC. See UN Economic and Social
    Council (ECOSOC)
Ecosystem management, 370–371
ECOWAS. See Economic Community of
    West African States (ECOWAS)
ECSC. See European Coal and Steel
    Community (ECSC)
Ecuador, 27, 198, 287, 362
Ecuadorian Embassy, 27
Educational programs, 38, 176
Education level, HDI, 293–294
EEC. See European Economic
    Community (EEC)
Egypt, 21, 244, 261, 263–264, 273, 277,
    302, 324
Ehrlich, Paul, 367
Eisenhower, Dwight, 45, 87
El Salvador, 35
Embassies, 27–28, 185
Emerging Scholars and Practitioners on
    Migration Issues Network, 386
Emissions Trading System, 400
Emmett, Chad, 106
Emotional decision makers, 86
Empirical theory, 53
The End of History and the Last Man
    (Fukuyama), 249
Energy companies, 37
Engels, Friedrich, 91
Environmental issues
    biodiversity challenges, 361–363
    collective goods, 354
    deforestation, 355–357
    desertification, 357
    global climate change, 357–361
    Great Pacific Garbage Patch, 353
    nuclear waste disposal, 355
    pollution, 354–355
    protective interventions. See
        Environmental protection
    tragedy of the commons, 354
Environmental Performance Index, 366
Environmental protection, 363
    anti-deforestation efforts, 364
    grassroots and NGO actions, 366–368
    IO actions, 368–372
    non-state actors in, 367
    SDG, 364–365
    state actions, 363–366
    2030 Agenda for Sustainable
        Development, 364–365
Environmental Protection Agency (EPA), 353
Environmental protection programs, 38
Environmental security–oriented TANs, 400
EP. See European Parliament (EP)

EPA. *See* Environmental Protection Agency (EPA)
Epistemic communities, 187
Estonia, 204, 338
Ethnic cleansing, 43, 244, 336, 344–345
Ethnic conflict, 138
Ethnic geography, 32, 138
Ethology, 136
EU. *See* European Union (EU)
EU-27, 208
EU–Canada Comprehensive Economic and Trade Agreement (CETA), 247
Eurasian Economic Union, 72, 256
Eurocentric international system, 25
Europe, 236, 426m
    borders in, 154m
    capitalism in, 228
    after Cold War, 68
    Concert of Europe, 171
    immigrants, 40–41
    international system and, 25
    Russia and, 139–140
    Russia cyberwarfare in, 129
    after Treaty of Westphali, 26m
European Bank for Reconstruction and Development, 364
European-based regional system, 31
European Coal and Steel Community (ECSC), 176, 203, 224
European Commission (EC), 204, 208, 223, 338, 421
European Commission on Human Rights, 331
European Convention on Human Rights, 331, 344
European Council, 204, 208
European Court of Human Rights (ECHR), 344
European Court of Justice (ECJ), 191, 196, 206
European Economic Community (EEC), 203
European Environment Agency, 202
European imperialism, 31
European Parliament (EP), 204, 206, 207f
European Photovoltaic Industry Association, 398
European Union (EU), 22, 45, 198, 199m, 203, 248, 337–338, 343, 411, 420
    Brexit, 45, 95, 206, 210, 223, 248–249, 308
    Brussels Summit, 208
    contributions and challenges, 206, 208, 210
    COVID-19, 209–210
    development of, 176, 197, 203–204
    economic sanctions, 261, 263–264
    European debt crisis and, 206
    Eurozone, 204, 208, 210, 225
    Greek financial crisis and, 243
    Guinea and, 264
    hormone-fed beef ban, 238, 248
    Iran and, 263–264
    origins and foundations of, 203
    in P5+1, 69, 170
    Rome Summit, 208
    Russian natural gas and, 258m
    structure and operations, 204–206
    trade disputes, 202
    UK withdrawal from, 223, 247, 249, 421
Eurosceptics, 206
Eurozone, 204, 208, 210, 225

Explanation use of theory, 54
Export-led growth policies, 305–306
Export sanctions, 260
Expropriation, 301–302
Extended deterrence, 161
External balancing, 159
Extra-systemic/extra-state war, 116
Extraterritoriality, 27

Fair trade, 245
Fairtrade International, 245
Falkland Islands, 104
Falun Gong, 394
Farage, Nigel, 247
FARC (Revolutionary Armed Forces of Colombia), 339
Fascism, 33
FCCC. *See* UN Framework Convention on Climate Change (UNFCC)
FDI. *See* Foreign direct investment (FDI)
Fearon, James, 71
Female circumcision, 325
Female genital mutilation, 325, 341–342, 387
Femicide, 336, 341
Feminism, 12, 100–107, 108t, 134, 137.
    See also Women
Feminist international relations theory, 84
Feminist theory, 419–420
Feudalism, 25, 91–92, 232
Financial sanction, 260–262. *See also* Economic sanctions
Finland, 204, 338
Finnemore, Martha, 72
First-generation individual rights, 322–323
First-generation products, 302
Fisher, Roger, 185
Five Star Movement, 247
Fondation Assistance Internationale, 397
Foreign aid, 270
    aid sanctions, 255, 260–261
    bilateral, 225
    definition, 270
    democracy aid, 278–280
    development aid, 270, 273–276
    economic statecraft and, 259
    humanitarian aid, 280–282
    military aid, 276–278
    political goals and, 225
    programs, 337
    Trump administration policies, 255
    US development aid, 271
Foreign direct investment (FDI), 300, 302
Foreign policy, 420–421
    agents in, 85
    analysis, 12, 84–91, 108t
    Brexit, 45, 95
    China's pursuit of security, 175
    debt forgiveness, 311–312
    definition, 84
    dependency theory, 94, 96
    economic sanctions on North Korea, 266
    free trade, 247
    group explanations of, 87–89
    individual explanations, 85–87
    interest groups and, 89–90
    Marshall Islands, international law and World Court, 195
    Nigerian schoolgirls, 389
    organizational/bureaucratic politics model of, 87–88

prospect theory, 86–87
public opinion and, 90
regime explanations of, 90–91
Russia and its neighbors, 72
security, seeking ways of, 9
societal explanations of, 89–90
US and climate change, 371
US and human rights, 332–333
US military power, 29
US potential conflicts, 133
Foreign Service Officer Exam, 184
Foreign service officers (FSOs), 184
Formal anarchy, 8, 23
Fossil fuel emissions, 368–370
France, 97, 127, 155, 158, 163, 206, 298, 303, 337–338, 368, 370, 418
    alliance between Russia and, 158
    in Concert of Europe, 210
    consequences of World War II, 141–142
    ECSC, 224
    in Eurozone, 204
    foreign trading restrictions, 231
    IMF voting weight, 199
    international trade economy, 237
    ISIS attack in, 118
    Marshall Islands case and, 195
    military force, use of, 51
    Muslim women and, 325
    nuclear weapons, 73–74, 155, 163
    in P5, 69, 170, 200
    right-wing anti-EU parties in, 206, 208
    Russia interference in presidential election, 129
    size of military forces, 152
    World Bank voting weight, 201
Francis, Pope, 10
Frederiksen, Mette, 103
Freedom House, 346t, 390
Freedom Support Act, 55
Free markets, 307
Freemen, 322–323
Free Syrian Army, 21
Free trade, 229, 247
    countries pursuing, 230–231
    GATT, 201–202, 236–237
    WTO and, 313, 314f
Free-trade agreements (FTAs), 247.
    See also North American Free Trade Agreement (NAFTA)
French Revolution, 31
Freud, Sigmund, 136
Friedman, George, 139–140
Friedman, Thomas, 55, 234, 420
Friends of the Earth International, 368
Frustration-aggression theory, 137
FSOs. *See* Foreign service officers (FSOs)
FTAs. *See* Free-trade agreements (FTAs)
Fukuyama, Francis, 249, 416–417
Fulbright educational exchange program, 176
Functionalism, 176, 196, 203
Fungible power, 60

G-77 (Group of 77), 198
Gaddafi, Muammar, 8, 117, 261, 266, 343–344
Gaddis, John Lewis, 163
Gambia, 339
Gandhi, Indira, 104
Gartzke, Erik, 65
Gates, Bill, 10, 23, 239, 293

Gates, Robert, 158
GATT. *See* General Agreement on Tariffs and Trade (GATT)
GCC. *See* Gulf Cooperation Council (GCC)
GDP per capita, 289–290
    countries of world, 291*m*
    HDI, 293–294
    natural resources and, 295
    South Korea *vs.* Brazil, 305
    trade *vs.*, 314*f*
Gender Social Norms Index, 324
General Agreement on Tariffs and Trade (GATT), 201–202, 236–237
General deterrence, 161
General Motors, 23
General wars, 116, 119
Genetically modified organisms (GMOs), 362
Geneva Conventions, 168, 190
Genocide, 141, 244, 326, 336, 345
    Convention on Genocide, 326, 329
    genocidal campaigns, 327*t*
    Marxist theory and, 93
    Rwanda, 43, 75, 93, 244, 344
Geographic arms control agreements, 168
Geographic information system (GIS), 371
Geography, 5, 7, 420
    Afghanistan, 32
    Asia/Africa/Americas colonization by Europeans, 228
    Berlin Wall, 272–273
    climate and economic development, 298
    conflict, 130, 139
    and EU, 209–210
    Hutus and Tutsis, 328–329
    mountain societies, 373
    and power, 61
    security and, 154–155
    TANs, 387
    wealth zones and peace, 99–100
    of world, 6
Georgia, 72, 107, 124, 147, 235, 266, 339
Gere, Richard, 38
Germany, 97, 100, 132, 155, 208, 236, 322, 324, 338, 363
    COVID-19, 210
    development aid policies, 272–273
    EP seats, 206
    in Eurozone, 204
    fascism in, 33
    foreign trading restrictions, 229, 231
    hyperinflation in, 231
    IMF voting weight, 199
    international trade economy, 237
    Marxist theory and, 92–93
    in P5+1, 69, 170
    Red Army Faction, 393–394
    size of military forces, 152
    UN budget, 215
    universal jurisdiction, 338
    withdrawal from Hague conference, 169
    World Bank voting weight, 201
    World War II and, 35, 92, 142
Geun-hye, Park, 334
Ghana, 362
Gini coefficients, 292–293
Global climate change, 357–361, 420
    change in global surface temperature, 357, 358*f*
    economic development and, 301

greenhouse gases, 356–357
    human activities and, 358
    hurricanes, 361
    increases in annual temperatures, 358, 360*m*
    melting glaciers, 358, 360
    ocean currents, 360–361
    past and future changes, 358, 359*f*
    state actions, 366
    UN and, 368–370
Global competition and cooperation, 374
    cyberspace, 375–376
    human migration, 376–377
    maritime developments, 374–375
    pandemic diseases, 377
Global Economy Era, 236–237
    globalization and global economy, 240–249
    liberalism in practice, 239–240
    modern economy, 237–240
    non-state actors, 238–239
Global Emancipation Network, 397
Global Environmental Facility, 369
GlobalFirepower.com, 62
Global FoodBanking Network, 386
Global Health Council, 398
Global IOs, 197
Globalization, 12, 40–41, 306, 385, 411, 413, 418
    broadening and, 241
    costs and consequences of, 245–249
    deepening and, 241–242
    impact on women, 106
    index, 242*t*, 249
    media, 241–242
    mobile production, sales process and, 241
    populist backlash against, 248–249
    positive effects of, 243–245
    spread of, 241–243
    states and, 245–246
    states "opting out" of, 249
    technology and, 40–41, 240–242
    trade openness and, 244
    wages and, 245
Global jihadist networks, 396
Global Network on Energy for Sustainable Development, 397
Global Policy Forum, 41
Global Polio Eradication Initiative (GPEI), 383
Global Refugee Policy Network, 386
Global Study on Homicide 2018: Gender-Related Killing of Women and Girls, 341
GMOs. *See* Genetically modified organisms (GMOs)
"Golden Arches" theory, 54–55, 234–235
Gold mining, illegal, 362–363
Gorbachev, Mikhail, 14, 35, 103
Gore, Al, 367
Governmental units, 23
Government and market relationship, 226
Great Depression, 232, 323–324
Great Pacific Garbage Patch, 353
Great Recession, 5, 42, 206, 210, 233, 238, 243, 413
Greece, 208, 210
    civil war, 35
    as EEC member, 203–204

in Eurozone, 204
    financial crisis, 243
    IMF and, 42
Greenhouse gases, 356–357
Greenpeace, 22, 66, 367–368
Grenada, 150, 158
Grillo, Beppe, 247
Grotius, Hugo, 63, 189–190
Group explanations of foreign policy, 87–89
Group rights, 324–329
Groupthink, 89, 137
Guatemala, 94, 96, 278, 300–301, 334
Guinea, 264
Gulf Cooperation Council (GCC), 202
Gulf Stream, 360
Gulf War, 116, 130, 141, 153, 172, 181
Guns, Germs, and Steel (Diamond), 228
Gurr, Ted Robert, 137
Guterres, António, 215

Hacking, 376
Hague conference, 169
Hague Conventions, 168, 190
Haiti, 275, 277, 324, 343, 356, 370
Hamas, 121
Hamilton, Alexander, 259
Hannah, Darryl, 369
Hardin, Garrett, 354
Hard power, 67, 343–344
Harmful substances, 372
Hatemi, Peter, 87
HDI. *See* Human Development Index (HDI)
Health security–oriented TANs, 398–400
Hegemonic stability theory, 132
Hegemons, 132–133
Hegemony, 78
Helms, Jesse, 215, 262
Helms-Burton Act, 262
Helsinki Watch, 345
Henehan, Marie, 130
Hepburn, Audrey, 38
Herzegovina, 43
Hezbollah, 21, 24, 121, 164, 185, 395
HIDDEN COBRA, 128
HIPC debt relief program, 311–312
Hirschman, Albert, 255
A History of Warfare (Keegan), 114
Hitler, Adolf, 33, 92, 232
HIV/AIDS, 398, 399*m*, 399*t*, 414
Hobbes, Thomas, 56–58, 62, 101, 136
Hobbesian anarchy, 70
Ho Chi Minh, 93
Hoffman, Bruce, 119
Hoffman, Stanley, 68
Holocaust, 326, 332, 337
Holsti, K. J., 130
Holy Roman Empire, 25
Home country, 300
Honduras, 278, 303
Hong Kong, 305
Honor-killings, 325, 341
Horizontal enforcement, 192, 194
Host country, 300
"Hot Line" agreement, 168
Hudson, Valerie, 106
Hughes Communications, 226
Human Development Index (HDI), 293–294
Humanitarian aid, 280–282
Humanitarian crises, 347
Humanitarian interventions, 43–44

Humanitarian relief programs, 38
Human Life International, 398
Human migrations, 376–377
Human nature, 136
Human organ donation, 394
Human rights, 348, 412
    collective rights, 331
    economic sanctions and, 264–265, 267
    empowerment and protection
        programs, 38
    group rights, 324–329
    human security and, 7–8, 333–334
    individual rights, 322–323
    international norms and rules, 329–324
    LGBTQIA rights, 325–326
    military aid and, 278
    protection of, 326, 329, 334, 347
    restorative justice, 334–335
    societal rights, 323–324
    UN and, 329–331, 340–343
    US and, 332–333
    violations, 334, 338, 345
    women and, 323–324, 336, 340, 387
    worst attacks on, 42
Human Rights Commission, 342
Human rights, evolution of, 322
    first-generation individual rights,
        322–323
    second-generation societal rights,
        323–324
    third-generation group rights, 324–329
Human rights, implementation and
        enforcement issues, 334
    hard power, 343–344
    incentives, 336–337
    IOs and, 340–344
    local level direct actions, 334–336
    NGO-based initiatives, 344–348
    punishments, 337–338
    soft power, 340–343
    special courts and tribunals, 344
    state-based initiatives, 334–338
    universal jurisdiction, 338–340
Human Rights Watch, 245, 321, 344–345,
        346t, 347, 390
Human security, 7, 333–334, 340
    TANs and, 385–391
    trends and emerging concerns, 418
    and world politics, 417
Human sympathy and war, 130
Human trafficking, 336, 392, 397
Hungary, 93, 158, 204, 208, 210, 232, 321
Hurricanes, 361
Hussein, Saddam, 9, 266, 269, 338
Hutus, 75, 326, 328–329
Hyperinflation, 231

IAEA. See International Atomic Energy
        Agency (IAEA)
ICC. See International Criminal
        Court (ICC)
Ideational aspect of power, 73
Ideational liberalism, 65
Identity politics, 39–40
Ideology and war, 130
IEDs. See Improvised explosive
        devices (IEDs)
Illegal gold mining, 362–363
IMF. See International Monetary
        Fund (IMF)

Immediate deterrence, 161
Immigrants, 39–41, 323, 333, 337.
        See also Refugees
Imperialism, 31, 227
Imperialism: The Highest Stage of Capitalism
        (Lenin), 93
Import sanctions, 260
Import substitution industrialization (ISI),
        304–305
Improvised explosive devices (IEDs),
        117–118
An Inconvenient Truth (Gore), 367
Independent International Commission of
        Inquiry, 343
India, 155, 263
    anti-desertification efforts, 365–366
    and China, border conflict, 373
    Marshall Islands case and, 195
    National Health Policy, 374
    nuclear weapons, 155, 163, 169
    Pakistan and, 24, 130
    security dilemma in, 24
    as semi-peripheral state, 97, 303–304
    size of military forces, 152
    social media globalization, 241–242
    sustainable economic development, 374
    terrorist attack in, 121, 123, 127
    World Bank voting weight, 201
Indian Ocean, 360
Indiscriminate violence, 119
Individual(s)
    causes of war and, 134, 136–137
    explanations of foreign policy, 85–87
    level of analysis, 10–11
    rights, 322–323
    as subnational actors, 23
    and world politics, 4–5
Indonesia, 306
Industrial Revolution, 229, 300, 323
INFORSE. See International Network for
        Sustainable Energy (INFORSE)
INF Treaty. See Intermediate-Range
        Nuclear Forces (INF) Treaty
Institutional liberalism, 65
Institutions, 55, 176
Instrumentalism, 140–141
Inter-American Commission on Human
        Rights, 331, 336
Inter-American Court of Human Rights,
        326, 331
Inter-American Institute for Cooperation on
        Agriculture, 202
Interdependence, 23, 176
    causes of war and, 133
    integration and, 225
    liberal perspective, 65–66
Interest groups, 89–90
Intergovernmental Panel on Climate
        Change (IPCC), 358, 368
Intermediate-Range Nuclear Forces (INF)
        Treaty, 29, 147, 169–170
Internal balancing, 159
International actors, 22–23
International anarchy. See Anarchy
International Anti-Human Trafficking
        Network, 397
International Association for Maternal and
        Neonatal Health, 347
International Atomic Energy Agency (IAEA),
        45, 263, 395

International Bank for Reconstruction and
        Development, 312
International Bill of Human, 331
International Campaign to Ban Landmines,
        386, 395
International civil society, 344
International Committee of the Red Cross,
        344, 346t
International Conference on Women and
        Conflict Management, 340–341
International Court of Justice. See
        World Court
International courts, 194–196
International Covenant on Civil and Political
        Rights, 331–332
International Covenant on Economic, Social
        and Cultural Rights, 331
International Criminal Court (ICC), 196, 332,
        339, 344, 390, 412
International Criminal Police Organization
        (INTERPOL), 392–393
International development
    distribution of wealth across countries,
        290–292
    distribution of wealth within countries,
        292–295
    Ecuador vs. South Korea, 387
    GDP per capita measure, 289–290, 291m
    IOs and. See International
        organizations (IOs)
    MDG, 308, 310
    north–south divide, 288, 298
    PPP, 290
    2030 Agenda for Sustainable
        Development, 310
    women in, 309
    See also Development theories and
        policies; Economic inequality
International Economy Era, 229
    free trade, 229–231
    to Global Economy Eras, 233–236
    liberalism, 229
    LIEO, 235–237
    Marxism, 232–233
    trade war, 229, 231–232
International Foundation for Electoral
        Systems, 401
International institutions, 65–66
International interactions, complexity of, 9
International Labor Organization, 196
International law, 187–189
    auxiliary source of, 191
    compliance and enforcement, 192–196
    court decisions and, 191
    custom, 190–191
    definition, 188
    for general practice, 191
    horizontal enforcement, 192, 194
    IO decisions and, 191–192
    just war tradition and, 190
    Marshall Islands and, 195
    national enforcement, 192
    nature of, 189
    sources of, 189–192
    treaty, 189
    vertical enforcement, 194–196
    violation of, 193
International level of analysis, 10–11
International Military Education and Training
        program (IMET), 277

International Monetary Fund (IMF), 23, 42, 65, 176, 197–198, 201, 235–236, 268, 290, 307, 310–313, 417
   austerity program, 236, 243
   Bretton Woods system, 201, 235, 310
   HIPC debt relief, 311–312
   success of, 312
   weighted voting, 313
International Network for Sustainable Energy (INFORSE), 397
International norms, 65
International organizations (IOs), 22, 36, 65, 196, 238, 418
   decision processes, 198–200
   and development, 310–315
   environmental protection initiatives and policies, 368–372
   EU. See European Union (EU)
   existence of, 196–197
   FSOs in, 184
   global, 197
   human rights and, 340–344
   IMF. See International Monetary Fund (IMF)
   liberal perspective, 66
   majority decision rule, 198
   power-based explanations, 196
   problem-based explanations, 196–197
   realist perspective, 58–59
   regional, 197–198, 202–203
   roles and functions of, 197
   scope and membership typology, 197–198
   as source of international law, 189, 191–192
   supranational regimes, 45
   types of, 197–200
   UN. See United Nations (UN)
   unit veto decision rule, 199–200
   weighted voting decision rule, 198–199
   World Bank. See World Bank
   in world politics, 201–203
   WTO. See World Trade Organization (WTO)
International Planned Parenthood Foundation, 398
International Red Cross and Red Crescent Movement, 390
International relations
   actors, cooperation challenges of, 7–8
   cooperation dilemmas in, 12–15
   feminist approach, 100–107, 108t
   foreign policy perspective, 84–91, 108t
   levels of analysis in, 10–11
   liberal perspective, 66–69
   Marxist theory and, 92–94, 108t
   money, power and security linkage in, 224–226
   PD and, 13, 15
   realist perspective, 56–63
   security in, 7–8
   stag hunt and, 13, 15
   theory and, 52–56
   women impact on, 100–107
International Republican Institute, 337, 401
International Research and Training Institute for the Advancement of Women (INSTRAW), 342
International security, 7
   challenge of, 148–149
   cooperation for. See Cooperation for peace/security

   dilemma, 148
   geography and, 154–155
   liberal approaches to, 165–176
   managing conflict and, 147–148
   power and, 148–165
   realist approaches to, 149–165
   using military force, 160–165
International Security Assistance Force, 395
International Society of Doctors for the Environment, 400
International system, 408
   anarchy of, 8, 10, 23–24
   causes of war and, 130
   characteristics of, 23
   constructivist perspective, 70–71
   definition, 23
   distributions of power and, 63
   diversity in, 8–9
   as Eurocentric, 25
   history of, 24–45
   interdependence, 23
   liberal perspective, 64–66
   neo-Westphalian, 35–45
   poles/polarity in, 63
   realist perspective, 57–58
   security dilemma, 24–25
   security dimensions and, 22–25
   Westphalian, 26–35
International Telephone and Telegraph Corporation, 300
International Trade Organization, 236
International Tribunal on the Law of the Sea, 196
Internet, 38, 41, 241–242
INTERPOL. See International Criminal Police Organization (INTERPOL)
Interpretivist constructivism, 71
Interstate wars, 36, 116, 141, 160
Intrastate wars, 36
IOs. See International organizations (IOs)
IPCC. See Intergovernmental Panel on Climate Change (IPCC)
Iran, 185, 276, 295, 420
   economic sanctions, 256–257
   Israel and, 24, 74
   Kurds and, 30
   nuclear deal, 68–69, 127–128, 170, 257, 266
   and nuclear proliferation, 170
   security dilemma in, 24
   smart sanctions and, 261–262
   Syrian conflict and, 21–22
   and US conflict, 185, 193–194, 261, 263–264
   women and, 106
Iraq, 135, 263, 266, 278, 303, 343
   al-Qaeda in, 396
   economic sanctions and, 268–269
   Gulf War, 116
   ISIS, 5, 7, 21
   Israel preemptive attacks on, 162, 164
   Kurds, 30–31, 43
   Kuwait invasion, 43, 104, 141, 172, 181, 238
   oil reserve in, 42
   Russia and, 276
   size of military forces, 153
   terrorist attacks in, 123
   US involvement in, 83, 97, 158
Iraq War, 83, 89, 97, 137, 153, 206
Ireland, 203–204

Irish Catholic community, 74
Irish Republican Army (IRA), 74
Irredentism, 138
Irredentist claims, 138
ISI. See Import substitution industrialization (ISI)
ISIS (Islamic State in Iraq and Syria), 5, 7, 21, 66, 120, 395–396
   globalization and, 241
   origins of, 120
   social media use in, 40
   Syrian conflict and, 21–22
Islamic women, 324–325
Israel, 235, 343
   cyberwarfare, 127–128
   Iran and, 24, 74
   Marshall Islands case and, 195
   nationalism issue in, 30
   nuclear weapons, 74, 169
   Palestinian conflict, 415
   preemptive use of force, 162, 164
   preventive use of force, 164
   security dilemma in, 24
   UN peacekeeping mission, 172
   US military aid and, 277
   USS Liberty, 76
Italy, 93, 208
   COVID-19, 210
   in Eurozone, 204
   fascism in, 33
   international trade economy, 237
   Libyan refugees, 410–411
   World Bank voting weight, 201

Jackson-Vanik Amendment, 261
Jaffee, Daniel, 245
Jagger, Mick, 369
Jakobsdóttir, Katrin, 103
Janis, Irving, 89
Japan, 30, 132, 140, 151, 175, 236, 263, 375, 392
   atomic bombing, 153
   as core state, 97, 302
   development aid, 274
   GDP per capita, 289
   geographic location of, 61
   humanitarian aid, 281
   IMF voting weight, 199
   nontariff trade barriers and, 236
   and North Korean threat, 410
   nuclear accidents, 412
   nuclear waste disposal, 355, 364
   pollution problems, 364
   South Korean sex slaves in, 334
   tariff rate, 236, 256
   trade disputes, 238
   trade openness, 246
   trade sanction policies, 260
   UN budget, 215
   World Bank voting weight, 201
   World War II and, 35, 142
JCPOA. See Joint Comprehensive Plan of Action (JCPOA)
Jervis, Robert, 58
Jihad, 396
Johnson, Boris, 95, 223
Johnson, Lyndon, 76, 91, 137
Joint Comprehensive Plan of Action (JCPOA), 170, 257
Joint democracy effect, 136

Jolie, Angelina, 10, 38
Just war tradition, 190

Kaarbo, Juliet, 89
Kant, Immanuel, 64, 173, 234
Kantian anarchy, 70–71
Karic, Dragomir, 390
Karns, Margaret, 203
Karzai, Hamid, 275
Katzenstein, Peter, 72
Kazakhstan, 72, 256
Keck, Margaret, 72
Keegan, John, 114
Kennedy, John, 35, 87
Kennedy, Paul, 289
Kenya, 303, 364, 371
Kenyatta, Uhuru, 339
Keohane, Robert, 65–68
Khmer Rouge government, 344
Khobragade, Devyani, 30
Kim Jong-il, 262
Kim Jong-un, 85, 90, 266, 407, 421
Kirchner, Cristina Fernández de, 334
Knights Templar, 384
Korean War, 35, 172
Kosovo, 130, 141, 172, 235, 338, 343
Kosovo Liberation Army, 394
Kurds, 22, 30–31, 42–43, 321, 338, 373, 415, 418
Kuwait, 30, 83, 104, 141, 172, 181, 238, 296
Kyoto Protocol, 370
Kyrgyzstan, 72, 266

Laqueur, Walter, 119
Lashkar-e-Taiba, 121
La Strada International, 397
Latin American Network for Forced
    Migration, 386
Latvia, 204, 338
Law of the Sea Convention, 182
LDC. See Less-developed country (LDC)
Leader decision making, 86
League of Arab States, 202
League of Nations, 36, 66, 168, 171–172, 190,
    200, 210–211
Lebanon, 21, 24, 235, 395
Lemkin, Raphael, 326
Lenin, Vladimir, 93
Le Pen, Marine, 129
Lesbian, gay, bisexual, transgender, queer,
    and intersex (LGBTQIA). See LGBTQIA
Less-developed country (LDC), 288
Levels of analysis, 10–11
    causes of war and, 131–137
Leviathan (Hobbes), 62
Levy, Jack, 86, 123
Lewinsky, Monica, 90
LGBTQIA, 264–265, 325–326
Liberal approaches to security/conflict, 165
    arms control, 165–169
    collective security, 170–173
    disarmament, 165–166, 169–170
    security communities, 173, 175–176
Liberal economic policy, 229
Liberal feminists, 105
Liberal international economic order (LIEO),
    233–237
Liberalism, 63–64, 229
    of actors, 66–67
    alliances and, 158
    causes of war and, 133–134

central dynamics of international
    relations, 68–69
definition, 12, 63
economic/commercial, 65
institutional, 65
international law and, 188
IOs and, 196
nature of international system, 64–66
political, 65
of power resources, 67–68
in practice, 239–240
realism, constructivism vs., 77t
societal/ideational, 65
variants of, 65
See also Constructivism; Realism
Liberal policies, 419
Liberia, 343
Libertad Act, 262
Libya, 8, 21, 117, 130, 261, 266, 277, 410
Libyan human rights, 343–344
LIEO. See Liberal international economic
    order (LIEO)
Life expectancy, 293–294
Limited wars, 116, 119, 124
Lincoln, Abraham, 199
Linkage strategy, 185–186
Lisbon Treaty, 206
Lithuania, 204, 338
Local actors, 23
Locke, John, 64, 297, 322
Lockean anarchy, 70
The Logic of Political Survival, 90
London Naval Treaty, 169
Lorenz, Konrad, 136
Lukashenko, Alexander, 336–338
Lula da Silva, Luiz Inacio, 334
Luxembourg, 204, 206, 290

Maastricht Treaty, 204
Macedonia, 210
Machiavelli, Niccolò, 56, 101
MAD. See Mutually assured
    destruction (MAD)
Maduro, Nicolás, 276
Magna Carta, 322
Magnitsky, Sergei, 338
Magnitsky Law, 338
Maier, Jürgen, 88
Major armed conflict, 117
Majority rule, 198
Malawi, 265
Malaysia, 306, 326, 374
Maldives, 360
Mali, 371
Malta, 204, 206
Mandela, Nelson, 263
Mao Zedong, 93, 232
Marin, Sanna, 103
Maritime developments, 374–375
Market and government relationship, 226
Marsh, Kevin, 89
Marshall Islands, 195
Marshall Plan, 65
Martínez i Coma, Ferran, 88
Marx, Karl, 91, 232, 323, 401, 420
Marxism/Marxist theory, 12, 84, 91–96, 108t,
    232, 240t, 301, 419
    economics, 232–233, 240t
    international law and, 188
    IOs and, 196

Massachusetts, 360
Massoud, Tansa George, 89
Maternal mortality, 310
Matloff, Judith, 373
May, Theresa, 95, 104, 129, 223
McDermott, Rose, 86–87
McDonald's, 40, 54–55, 234, 300, 418
MDG. See Millennium Development
    Goals (MDG)
Mearsheimer, John, 58, 62–63, 68,
    131–132, 163
Media globalization, 241–242
Medvedev, Dmitry, 76
Meir, Golda, 104
Mejia, Oscar Humberto, 339
Melos, 56
Melting glaciers, 358, 360
Mengistu Haile Mariam, 93
Mercantilism, 226–229, 240t
Merkel, Angela, 10, 85–86, 103–104, 106, 208
Mesopotamia, 25
Metropole, 227
Mexico, 202, 223, 246, 280–281, 294t, 392
    as semi-peripheral state, 97, 303–304
    sustainable economic development, 374
MFN. See Most-favored nation (MFN) status
Microcredit, 309
Microplastics, 371
MID. See Militarized interstate dispute (MID)
Middle East, 427m
    dependency relationship, 94
Middle East Watch, 345
Migrations, 376–377, 386
Militarized interstate dispute (MID), 117
Military and military power
    aid, 276–278
    alliances, 157–159
    arms races, 157
    expenditures, 150–152, 157, 175
    films about, 150
    liberal perspective, 67
    national/international security and, 7
    security, 415–416
    strongest powers in world, 28t, 62t
    technology, 153, 155–157
    US military and global armaments, 29
    weapons and resources, 150–157
    and world politics, 62
Military forces, 152–153, 160
    applying, 160
    compellence, 164–165
    defensive use, 162
    deterrence, 160–162
    preventive and preemptive uses, 162–164
    strategies for linking to security, 160–165
Millennium Development Goals (MDG), 270,
    308, 310, 313, 315, 340, 414
Millennium Ecosystem Assessment,
    390–391
Milosevic, Slobodan, 141, 390
Mingst, Karen, 203
Minor armed conflict, 117
Minority group rights, 324–329
Mintz, Alex, 89
Mitchell, David, 89
Mitchell, Sara McLaughlin, 100
Mitrany, David, 203
Mlambo-Ngcuka, Phumzile, 342
MNCs. See Multinational corporations (MNCs)
Modern economy, 237–240

Modern international politics, 25
Modernization theory, 299–300
Modern trade theory, 229
Moldova, 72, 266
Monarchy system, 25
Money, power and security linkage, 224–226, 255
Mongolia, 363
Monnet, Jean, 203
Monterrey Consensus, 307–308
Montesquieu, Baron de, 63–64
Morell, Michael, 415
Morgenthau, Hans J., 57–60, 101, 113, 131
Morris, Harvey, 373
Most-favored nation (MFN) status, 201–202, 236
Mountain societies, 373
Mubarak, Hosni, 302
Mueller, John, 135
Mujahideen, 39, 116, 231, 276
Multilateral arms control agreement, 166, 168
Multilateral diplomacy, 186
Multinational corporations (MNCs), 23, 36–37, 66, 225, 238, 243–244, 300–301, 418
Multipolar system, 63, 131–132
Murder, 119
Murdie, Amanda, 347
Muslim women, 324–325
Mussolini, Benito, 33
Mutually assured destruction (MAD), 161
Myanmar, 66, 267–268, 336, 339, 383, 413

NAFTA. See North American Free Trade Agreement (NAFTA)
Nai, Allesandro, 88
Narcoterrorism, 121
Narcotics trafficking, 261, 392
Nasser, Gamal Abdel, 273
Nation, 30
National attributes, 134–136
National defense, 7
National Democratic Institute, 337, 401
National Economy Era, 226–229
National Endowment for Democracy, 337, 401
National enforcement, 192
National industrial policy, 239
Nationalism, 30–31, 33
Nationalist terrorists, 121, 394
Nationalization, 301
National level of analysis, 10–11
National missile defense, 163–164
National Oceanic and Atmospheric Administration (NOAA), 353
National security, 7, 9
National Security Agency (NSA), 129
Nation-state, 30, 130
NATO. See North Atlantic Treaty Organization (NATO)
Natural resources and economic development, 295–297
Natural Resources Defense Council, 367
Negative peace, 75
Negotiation, 185
Nelson, Gaylord, 368
Neo-classical realism, 58–59
Neocolonialism, 299
Neo-functionalism, 176, 196
Neoliberal approach, 306

Neo-realism, 58
Neo-Westphalian international system, 35–36, 130, 410
  diplomacy in, 187
  globalization and effects, 40–41
  identity politics, 39–40
  MNCs in 2016, 36–37
  non-state actors, development of, 36
  non-state actors, rise of, 37–40
  sovereignty in, 43–45
  sovereign wealth funds in 2016, 37, 38t
  stresses on states, 41–43
Neo-Westphalian sovereignty, 43–45
Nepal, 324
Netherlands, 204, 208, 210, 264, 303, 325, 338, 344, 360, 368
Network of African People Living with HIV/AIDS, 398
New START Treaty, 29, 169
New world order, 181
New Zealand, 368, 377
NGOs. See Nongovernmental organizations (NGOs)
Nicaragua, 35, 193, 263, 370
Niebuhr, Reinhold, 136
Nigeria, 123, 293–295, 363, 370, 396, 415, 420
Nigerian schoolgirls, 389
Nihilist terrorists, 121, 393
Nike, 245
9/11 terrorist attack. See September 11, 2001 terrorist attack
NOAA. See National Oceanic and Atmospheric Administration (NOAA)
NOAA GFDL CM2.1 Model Simulation, 361f
No Friends but the Mountains: Dispatches From the World's Violent Highlands (Matloff), 373
Nongovernmental organizations (NGOs), 22–23, 36–37, 238
  environmental protection initiatives, 366–368
  and humanitarian intervention, 347
  human rights implementation and enforcement initiatives, 344–348
  liberal perspective, 66
  networks, 384. See also Transnational advocacy networks (TANs)
  for women, 347
Nonproliferation regime, 65
Nonproliferation Treaty, 413
Nonspuriousness, 53
Non-state actors, 3, 22–23
  constructivist perspective, 71–73
  definition, 36
  in global economy, 238–239
  individuals as, 38
  liberal perspective, 66–67
  neo-Westphalian international system, 36–40
  realist perspective, 58–59
  types of, 37t
  in Westphalian international system, 31
Non-state terrorism, 121
Nontariff barrier, 236
Noriega, Manuel, 269
Normal trade relations (NTR), 202, 236
Normative theory, 53
Norms
  cascade, 385
  consequences of violating, 24

definition, 8
  democracy, 31
  internalization, 385
  international law and. See International law
  liberal perspective, 65
  life cycle, 385
  self-help, 23–24
North America, 424m
North American Free Trade Agreement (NAFTA), 223, 246–248
North Atlantic Treaty Organization (NATO), 35, 52, 68, 158, 343, 375, 390, 395, 410–411
Northern Ireland, 74–75, 77
North Korea, 35, 38, 52, 66, 90, 263, 407–408, 410, 415, 421
  cyberwarfare, 128
  economic sanctions and, 62, 266
  global economy, 241
  hacking, 376
  Marshall Islands case and, 195
  nuclear weapons, 155, 163–164, 169, 181, 266
  socialist revolution, 232
  state-sponsored terrorism, 121
  as unitary actor, 59
  and US trade relationship, 266
  in violating rules, 24
North–south divide, 288, 298
Norway, 97, 264, 333, 338
  anti-deforestation efforts, 364
  Gini coefficient, 293
NPT. See Nuclear Nonproliferation Treaty (NPT)
NTR. See Normal trade relations (NTR)
Nuclear deterrence, 161
Nuclear Nonproliferation Regime, 45, 395
Nuclear Nonproliferation Treaty (NPT), 45, 169, 195
Nuclear wastes, 355, 364
Nuclear weapons, 45, 124, 153
  arms control, 14, 29, 165–169
  arms races, 157, 161–162
  constructivist perspective, 73–74
  control agreement, 13–14
  countries using, 156m, 163m
  Cuban Missile Crisis, 35
  digital, 127–128
  disarmament, 7, 165–166, 169–170
  economic sanctions and, 263–264
  Iran nuclear deal, 68–69, 127–128, 170, 257, 266
  nuclear arsenals, 153, 155
  nuclear missiles, 73
  realist approaches to security and, 153, 155–157
  US and global armaments, 29
  warhead inventories, 163m
Nuclear-weapons-free zones, 168
Nye, Joseph, 65–67

OAS. See Organization of American States (OAS)
Obama, Barack, 9, 55, 76, 85, 89, 136, 170, 184, 277, 321, 332–333, 371
Ocean Conservancy, 367
Ocean currents, 360–361
Oceania, 432m

OECD. *See* Organisation for Economic Co-operation and Development (OECD)
Offensive realism, 58
Office of the Special Adviser on Gender Issues and Advancement of Women (OSAGI), 187, 342
Oil and gas resources, 94, 260
Oil and minerals, 295–296
Oneal, John, 65
OneWeb, 376
Online bullying, 376
On the Law of War and Peace (Grotius), 189
Onuf, Nicholas, 69
Open Skies Treaty, 29
Operational code analysis, 86
Operation Eagle Claw, 88
Oppression, 324
Orend, Brian, 190
Organisation for Economic Co-operation and Development (OECD), 270
Organizational politics model, 87–88
Organization of American States (OAS), 195–196, 203, 277, 331, 343
Organization of Monotheism and Jihad, 120. *See also* al-Qaeda
Organized crime TANs, 392–393
Ortega, Daniel, 93
Orthodox liberal, 306
Other-oriented TANs, 395, 400–401
    economic security–oriented, 397–398
    environmental security–oriented, 400
    health security–oriented, 398–400
    personal security–oriented, 395, 397
Outer Space Treaty, 168

P5 (Perm-5), 200, 211, 214
P5+1, 69, 170, 257
Pacific Ocean Garbage Patch, 353
Pact, Kellogg-Briand, 168
Pakistan, 130, 263, 278, 322, 347
    Marshall Islands case and, 195
    nuclear weapons, 155, 163, 169
    polio outbreak in, 383
    security dilemma in, 24
    size of military forces, 152
    state-sponsored terrorism, 121
Palestine, 30, 121, 275
Palestine Liberation Organization (PLO), 395
Palestinian–Israel conflict, 415
Pan-Africanism, 183
Pan-African Parliament, 203
Panama, 263, 269
Pandemic diseases, 377
Paraguay, 305
Paris Agreement, 370–371
Parsimony, 55
Partial Test Ban Treaty, 170
Pashtunistan, 32, 33m
Pathfinder International, 347
Patriarchy, 341
Patronage politics, 296
Paul II, John, 35, 38
PD. *See* Prisoner's dilemma (PD)
Peace
    cooperation for. *See* Cooperation for peace/security
    economic integration and, 224–225
    international trade and, 234–235
    by pieces, 225

Peacekeeping, 172–173, 174m, 277
Peaceland (Autesserre), 281
Peace Research Institute of Oslo (PRIO), 117
Peak oil theory, 420
Peksen, Dursun, 347
Pelosi, Nancy, 102
Penn, Sean, 369
Pérez Alfonzo, Juan Pablo, 295
Peripheral states, 94, 97, 98f, 302–304
Perpetual Peace (Kant), 64
Personality and policymaking, 88
Personality traits, 137
Personal security–oriented TANs, 395, 397
Peru, 198, 362
Philippines, 59, 140, 151, 278, 374–375, 383, 390
Pinochet, Augusto, 191, 339
Plato, 259
Poland, 93, 154–155, 158, 204, 208, 232, 321
Polarity/poles in international system, 63
Policy entrepreneurs, 385
Policymaking, personality and, 88
Policy prescription, theory for, 54
Polio, 383
Political instability, 134–135
Political liberalism, 65
Political sovereignty, 148
Politics Among Nations (Morgenthau), 57
Pollution, 354–355
    deaths, 355m
    economic effects, 355
    nuclear wastes, 355
    Pacific Ocean Garbage Patch, 353
    state actions, 363–364
Polychlorinated biphenyls (PCBs), 372
Polythink, 89
Popular Front for the Liberation of Palestine, 121
The Population Bomb (Ehrlich), 367
Populist movements, 308
Populist revolutions, 335
Portugal, 203–204
Positive peace, 75
Positive-sum, 68, 149
Positivist constructivism, 71
Postmodern constructivism, 71
Poverty, 307
    reduction, 372
    Washington Consensus and, 417
Power
    balance-of-power politics, 63, 159–160, 170
    causes of war and, 131–132
    constructivist perspective, 73–74
    definition, 59
    discursive, 73
    distributions of, 63, 131–132
    fungible, 60
    geography and, 61
    hard, 67
    hierarchical, 60
    ideational aspects of, 73
    international security and, 148–165
    IOs and, 196
    liberal perspective, 67–68
    money, power and security linkage, 224–226, 255
    multidimensional nature, 67
    realist perspective, 59–60
    relative and relational, 59–60

soft, 67, 73
    transition theory, 132
Power and Interdependence (Keohane and Nye), 65, 67
PPP. *See* Purchasing power parity (PPP)
Prediction use of theory, 54
Preemptive use of force, 162–164
Prescription use of theory, 54
Preventive use of force, 162–164
Pre-Westphalian international system, 25, 226–227
Primordialism, 140
Prisoner's dilemma (PD), 12–15
Proletariat, 92
Property rights, 297
Proportional representation, 89
Prospect theory, 86–87
Protection alliance, 158
Protectionism, 227
Prussia, 155, 210
Psychological needs, 137
Public opinion and foreign policy, 90
Punishments, 337–338
Purchasing power parity (PPP), 290
Putin, Vladimir, 10, 72, 76, 85–86, 257, 261, 266, 326, 336

Qatar, 30, 202, 263, 267, 293, 294t
Quality of life, 3, 7–10

R2P. *See* Responsibility to protect (R2P)
Rainbow Warrior, 368
Rainbow Warrior II, 368
Ramaphosa, Cyril, 183
Rational actor model, 84–85, 135
Rational decision makers, 86
Reagan, Ronald, 14, 35, 55, 86, 103, 193, 215, 269, 306, 332
Realism, 56–57
    of actors, 58–59
    causes of war and, 131
    central dynamics of international relations, 60, 62–63
    classical, 58
    defensive, 58
    definition, 12, 56
    international law and, 188
    IOs and, 196
    liberalism, constructivism *vs.*, 77t
    nature of international system, 57–58
    neo-classical, 58–59
    neo-realism, 58
    offensive, 58
    of power resources, 59–60
    variants of, 58
    See also Constructivism; Liberalism
Realist approaches to security/conflict, 149
    alliances, 157–159
    balance-of-power politics, 159–160
    military expenditures, 150–152
    military technology, 153, 155–157
    military weapons and resources, 150–157
    revolution in military affairs, 153, 155–157
    size of military forces, 152–153
    using force, 160–165
Realist policies, 419
Reciprocity, 192
Red Crescent Movement, 66
Red Cross, 22, 66
Refugee Research Network, 66, 386

Refugees, 177, 321–322, 336, 386, 410–411
Regime change, 93
Regime explanations of foreign policy, 90–91
Regional IOs, 197–198
    EU. *See* European Union (EU)
    general, 202–203
    single-issue, 202
Regionalism, 202
Reiter, Dan, 135
Relative deprivation, 137
Relative gains, 60, 62
Republic of Georgia, 288
Resource curse, 295–296
Resource preservation, 374
Responsibility to protect (R2P), 326, 329, 347
Responsible sovereignty, 43–44, 347
Restorative justice, 334–335
The Retreat From Doomsday: The Obsolescence of War (Mueller), 135
Revolutionary terrorists, 121, 395
Revolution in military affairs, 153, 155–157
Rhodesia, 262–263
Ricardo, David, 229, 232, 234, 247
Rice, Condoleezza, 102, 184
Rios Montt, Efrain, 339
The Rise and Fall of the Great Powers (Kennedy), 289
Risse, Thomas, 68
Rohingya refugees, 336
Roman Empire, 25
Romania, 93, 158, 204, 232
Rome Summit, 208
Roosevelt, Franklin D., 211
Roosevelt, Theodore, 44, 186
Rose, Gideon, 58
Rosecrance, Richard, 67
Rouhani, Hassan, 10
Rousseau, Jean Jacques, 13
RPF. *See* Rwandan Patriotic Front (RPF)
Rusk, Dean, 165
Russett, Bruce, 65, 68
Russia, 12, 97, 124, 132, 155, 163, 235, 296, 343, 364, 375, 420
    alliance between France and, 158
    anti-Chechen campaigns, 411
    border conflict, 373
    in Concert of Europe, 210
    constructivist perspective of Russian relations, 71–72, 75–76
    Crimea, 52, 70, 72, 84–85, 157, 194, 257
    CSOs and, 43
    cyberwarfare, 128–129, 376
    economic sanctions, 257
    economic statecraft, 256
    elections, 401
    European Peninsula and, 139m
    France presidential election, interference in, 129
    geographical proximity, 5–6, 139–140, 155
    and geographic neighborhood, 72
    globalization and, 246
    INF Treaty, 147
    international trade economy, 237
    Internet Research Agency, 376
    and Iraq, 276
    Marshall Islands case and, 195
    military aid, 278
    NATO and, 158

nuclear missiles, 147
nuclear waste disposal, 355
nuclear weapons, 13, 29, 157, 163
    in P5, 69, 170, 200
    post–Cold War and, 149
    security and geography, 155
    socialist revolution, 232
    Syrian conflict and, 21–22
    trade disputes, 202
    Ukraine interventions, 10, 52, 70, 72, 76, 84–85, 138, 157, 194, 257, 261
    US presidential election, interference in, 76, 129, 257
    and US relationship, 75–76
    World Bank voting weight, 201
Russian Federation and Central Asia, 431m
Russian Mafia, 388, 390
Rwanda, 43, 75, 77, 93, 141, 172, 244, 328–329, 344, 420
Rwandan Patriotic Front (RPF), 329

Sadat, Anwar, 274
Sagan, Scott, 163
Same-sex relationships, 325, 335t
Sanctions. *See* Economic sanctions
Sandinista regime, 193
Sapolsky, Robert, 101
Satellite television, 41
Saudi Arabia, 21, 201, 230, 234, 263, 277, 296, 321, 334, 372, 420
Schelling, Thomas, 160, 164
Schuman, Robert, 203
Schuman Plan, 203
Schweller, Randall, 58
Scientific Committee on Problems of the Environment (SCOPE), 368
SDG. *See* Sustainable Development Goals (SDG)
Seabed Arms Control Treaty, 168
Sea Shepherd, 369
Second-generation products, 303
Second-generation societal rights, 323–324
Security, 3
    collective, 66, 170–173
    community, 173, 175–176
    definition, 7
    dimensions of, 7–8
    economic, 7
    human, 7
    international, 7, 9
    and money, power linkage, 224–226, 255
    national, 7, 9
    nature of, 7–8
    seeking ways of, 9
    traditional approach to, 113–114
    US presidential approaches, 9
    See also International security
Security dilemma, 24–25
    international security, 148
    liberal perspective, 66, 165
    realist perspective, 57–58
Sederberg, Peter, 119, 121
Selectorate, 90
Self-help, 23–24, 66, 70, 101, 104, 148, 189, 409, 411
Self-oriented TANs, 391, 400–401
    business, 391–392
    organized crime, 392–393
    terrorist, 393–395
Selva, Paul, 147

Semi-peripheral states, 97, 98f, 302–304
Senegal, 338
September 11, 2001 terrorist attack, 39, 83, 118, 121, 127, 238, 385, 395–396
Serbia, 31, 33, 124, 132, 235, 269
Settlement gap, 185
Sex trafficking, 336
Sexual assault, 325
Shanghai, 357
Shang Yang, 56
Sheen, Martin, 369
Sierra Club, 367
Sierra Leone, 199, 343–344
Sikkink, Kathryn, 72
Silent Spring (Carson), 367
Simon, Herbert, 86
Singapore, 305, 326
Single European Act, 204
Six-Day War, 76, 162
Slaughter, Anne-Marie, 187–188
Slavery, 322–323
Slovak Republic, 204, 321
Slovenia, 204
Smart sanctions, 261, 338
Smart weapons, 124
Smith, Adam, 65, 229, 232, 247
Social construction, 70, 73–77, 141. *See also* Constructivism
Socialism
    definition, 93
    Marxist theory and, 93, 232
Socialist revolution, 232
Social media, 40
Societal explanations of foreign policy, 89–90
Societal healing, 335
Societal liberalism, 65
Societal rights, 323–324
Soft power, 67, 73, 340–343
Solar-powered photovoltaic (solar PV), 398
Solberg, Erna, 103
Soleimani, Qassem, 83
Solntsevskaya Bratva, 388
Somalia, 43, 90, 100, 123, 135, 172–173, 281–282, 343
Somoza Debayle, Anastasio, 193
Soros, George, 10, 23, 239
South Africa, 97, 335, 339, 363
    anti-apartheid social movement, 388
    apartheid regime and, 194, 267
    diplomacy in, 183–184
    economic sanctions, 262–263
    Gini coefficient, 293
    NGOs and anti-apartheid efforts, 346
South America, 425m
South Asia, 429m
South China Sea, 374
Southern African Development Community (SADC), 203
South Korea, 164, 247, 278, 287, 335, 377, 410, 415
    GDP per capita, 305
    trade disputes, 238
    women as sex slaves, 334
South Sudan, 22, 290
Sovereignty, 26–27, 189, 348
    definition, 23
    neo-Westphalian, 43–45
    political, 148
    realist perspective, 57

responsible, 43–44
Westphalian, 27, 332
WTO, 248
Sovereign wealth funds, 37
Soviet Union, 10, 33, 155, 257, 261, 273
American U-2 spy plane shot down
incident, 87
arms races, 157
Cold War, 35
consequences of World War II, 141–142
economic collapse, 232–233
invasion of Afghanistan, 116
Marxist theory and, 93
nuclear arms control agreements, 14
nuclear deterrence, 161–162
nuclear disarmament, 169–170
nuclear weapons, 155, 161–162
socialism and, 93
socialist revolution, 232
Space Command, 376
Spain, 262, 338–339
colonization, 227
COVID-19, 210
as EEC member, 203–204
in Eurozone, 204
terrorist attack in, 127
Spanish flu, 377
Special Court for Sierra Leone, 344
Stag hunt, 13–15
Stalin, Joseph, 14, 232
State(s), 22
alliances between, 157–159
causes of war and, 134–136
constructivist perspective, 71–73
cost of "opting out," 249
definition, 26–27
empowerment of, 31, 33, 35
freedom map of, 28m
globalization and, 245–246
government, 27
level of analysis, 10–11
liberal perspective, 66–67
nation-state, 30
of nature, 56–57, 64
realist perspective, 58–59
as unitary actor, 59
in Westphalian international system,
26–30
State-based initiatives, 334–338
State-sponsored terrorism, 120–121
St. Augustine, 136
Steroids, global trade on, 237–238
Strategic Arms Limitation Talks, 169
Strategic Arms Reduction Talks (START), 169
Stratification, 57
Structural adjustment loans, 310
Structural factors, 295
colonial history, 297–299
natural resources, 295–297
Stuxnet, 127–128
Subnational actors, 23, 36
Subsidies, 305
Substate actors, 77
Sudan, 90, 141, 267, 277, 322, 370
Summit meetings, 186
Sumner, Jane Lawrence, 100
Sun Tzu, 56, 259, 263
Support for Eastern European Democracy
(SEED) Act, 55
Supranational organization, 225

Supranational regimes, 45
Sustainable development, 372
Sustainable Development Goals (SDG), 270,
313, 315, 340, 364–365, 372
Sustainable economic development,
372, 374
Sustainable energy, 398
Sweden, 97, 204, 248, 264, 338
Swine flu, 377
Switzerland, 154–155, 290, 338, 373
Syria, 123, 181, 343, 370, 410, 415
Assad regime in, 21–22, 85, 194
chemical weapons use, 8, 21, 85
civil war, 21, 117, 321, 336, 386
conflict and violence, 21–22
consequences of war, 141
development aid, 270, 273
financial sanctions, 261
humanitarian aid, 281
ISIS, 5, 7, 21
Israel preventive attack on, 164
Kurds and, 30
refugee crisis, 321–322
US military intervention, 85
Systemic level of analysis, 10–11
of war, 131–134

Taiwan, 140, 151, 164, 175, 305, 374, 377
Tajikistan, 347
Taliban, 83, 106, 231, 339, 395
Tambovskaya Prestupnaya Grupirovka, 388
TANs. See Transnational advocacy
networks (TANs)
Tanzania, 328–329, 344, 360
Tariffs
definition, 256
GATT, 201–202, 236–237
MFN status, 201–202, 236
nontariff barrier, 236
Taylor, Charles, 344
Technology
communication, 41
diplomacy and, 186
economy era and, 237
globalization and, 40–41, 240–242
Internet, 38, 41, 241–242
military, 153, 155–157
social media, 40
Temer, Michel, 334, 356
Temporal order, 53
Territorial integrity, 148
Terrorism, 118–121, 408
aid sanction and, 261
classification, 121
definition, 119–120
deterrence, 164
globalization and, 241
by means and targets, 119
modern revolutionary, 120
non-state, 121
state-sponsored, 120–121
tactics, 121
terrorist attacks since 1971, 122f
terrorists classification, 121
terrorist TANs, 393–395
in 2018, 123
worldwide incidents, 122t
Terrorist Myths: Illusions, Rhetoric and Reality
(Sederberg), 119
Thaçi, Hashim, 394

Thailand, 5, 242, 245, 306
Thatcher, Margaret, 103–104, 306
Theater missile defense, 163–164
Theories, definition, 11–12, 52
Theories of world politics, 11–12
analytical uses of, 52–53
and causation, 53–54
components of, 53–54
constructivist perspective on, 69–77
description, 54
empirical theory, 53
explanation, 54
foreign policy analysis, 84–91, 108t
and international relations, 52–56
liberal perspective, 63–69
Marxist theory, 91–96, 108t
normative theory, 53
prediction, 54
for prescription, 54
realist perspective, 56–63
WST, 84, 96–98, 108t
Theorizing, 52
Theory in Action, 419–420
arms, arms control and war, 166
democracy promotion, 55
democratic peace, 55, 136
economic sanctions and LGBTQIA
rights, 265
free trade, 230–231
humanitarian interventions, 44
non-state actors in environmental
issues, 367
PD and stag hunt, 14
personality and policymaking, 88
protecting human rights, 347
responsible sovereignty, 44
TANs, 401
US and World Court, 193
women in international development, 309
Therapeutics Research, Education, and
AIDS Training in Asia (TREAT Asia), 398
Third-generation group rights, 324–329
Third-party diplomacy, 186, 187t
Third-party sanctions, 260, 262
Thirty Years' War, 25
Thucydides, 56, 59, 64, 101
Thucydides trap, 113, 132
Tickner, J. Ann, 101
Time horizon problem, 378
Tit-for-tat strategy, 14
Tito, Josip, 93
Tlatelolco Treaty, 168
TNCs. See Transnational corporations (TNCs)
Total sanctions, 262–263
Toyota, 391
TPP. See Trans-Pacific Partnership (TPP)
Track II diplomacy, 187
Trade and trading
barrier, 237
economic security in, 7
fair, 245
GATT, 201–202, 236–237
interdependence and, 225
international peace and, 234–235
liberalization, 236–237
MFN status, 201–202, 236
openness, 244, 246
sanction, 259–260
specialization and, 230–231
on steroids, 237–238

war, 229, 231–233
worldwide, 233f
Trafficking
human, 336, 392, 394, 397
narcotics, 261, 392
sex, 336
The Tragedy of Great Power Politics
(Mearsheimer), 63
Tragedy of the commons, 197, 354, 371
Transatlantic Trade and Investment
Partnership (TTIP), 247
Transnational advocacy networks (TANs),
23, 36, 39, 413–414, 418
boomerang model, 388
business, 391–392
constructivists' view of, 401
definition of, 384
encouraging and enabling cooperation,
390–391
evaluating, 400–401
globalization and, 385
goal of, 387
historical examples, 384–385
home cultures and, 387
and human security, 385–391
influencing states, 387–390
norms life cycle, 385
organized crime, 392–393
other-oriented, 395–400
personal security–oriented, 395, 397
popularizing ideas, 385–387
self-oriented, 391–395
terrorist, 393–395
trends and emerging concerns,
400, 402
Western norms, 387
Transnational corporations (TNCs), 9, 23, 36,
66, 176, 196, 367
Transnational Institute, 400
Trans-Pacific Partnership (TPP), 223, 247
Transplant tourism, 394
Transportation technologies, 40–41, 186
TREAT Asia. *See* Therapeutics Research,
Education, and AIDS Training in Asia
(TREAT Asia)
Treaties of Westphalia, 24–25, 186, 326
Treaty, 189
Treaty of Amity, 194
Treaty of Rome, 203
Treaty of Versailles, 33, 189, 210, 231
Trinidad, 343
Tripolar system, 63
Truman, Harry, 332
Truman Doctrine, 35
Trump, Donald, 9–10, 55, 83, 85–86, 88–89,
147, 158, 194, 223, 247–248, 255, 257,
266, 271, 308, 321, 333, 336, 339, 371
Trusteeship Council, 217
Truth and Reconciliation Commission, 335
Tsai Ing-wen, 103
TTIP. *See* Transatlantic Trade and
Investment Partnership (TTIP)
Tunisia, 21, 118, 120, 266, 324
Turkey, 22, 321–322, 336
CSOs and, 43
Kurds and, 30
Tutsis, 75, 326, 328–329
Twenty Years' Crisis: 1919–1939 (Carr), 57, 64
2030 Agenda for Sustainable Development,
310, 364–365

U-2 spy plane, 87
UDHR. *See* Universal Declaration of Human
Rights (UDHR)
Uganda, 264–265, 322, 328–329, 336, 371
UK. *See* United Kingdom (UK)
Ukraine, 147, 181, 235, 266, 324, 364, 411, 421
ethno-linguistic map, 138m
levels of analysis by Russia, 10
Russia interventions, 10, 52, 70, 72, 76,
84–85, 138, 157, 194, 257, 261
Russia trade disputes, 202
UN. *See* United Nations (UN)
UN Atomic Development Authority
(ADA), 169
Unbalanced multipolar systems, 132
UN Charter, 172–173, 194, 211, 214–215
Article 1, 212
Article 2, 27, 44, 212
UN Conference on the Human
Environment, 368
UN Conference on the Law of the Sea, 375
UN Convention against Illicit Traffic in
Narcotic Drugs and Psychotropic
Substances, 392
UN Convention against Transnational
Organized Crime, 392
Unconventional war, 116–117, 126–129.
See also Terrorism
UN Convention to Combat
Desertification, 365
UN Development Fund for Women
(UNIFEM), 187, 342
UN Development Programme, 333
UN Economic and Social Council
(ECOSOC), 36, 215–216, 340, 342, 397
UN Educational, Scientific and Cultural
Organization (UNESCO), 215–216
Unemployment, 324
UN Environment Programme (UNEP), 368
disasters and conflicts, 370
ecosystem management, 370–371
environmental governance, 371–372
harmful substances, 372
resource efficiency, 372
UN Framework Convention on Climate
Change (UNFCC), 356, 368, 370, 372
UN General Assembly (UNGA), 36, 193–194,
198, 200, 212, 214, 313, 329, 331, 340,
341, 344, 392, 395
UN Human Rights Council, 342–343
UNICEF. *See* United Nations Children's
Fund (UNICEF)
UNIFEM. *See* UN Development Fund for
Women (UNIFEM)
Unilever, 300
Unipolar system, 63
Unitary actor, 59, 84
United Arab Emirates, 202, 263, 321, 420
United Fruit Company, 94, 96, 300
United Kingdom (UK), 97, 127, 132, 155, 158,
206, 321, 375, 395
Brexit, 45, 95, 206, 210, 223, 248–249, 308
colonial history and economic
development, 298
in Concert of Europe, 210
consequences of World War II, 141–142
currency devaluation crisis, 239
cyberwarfare, 128
as EEC member, 203
foreign development aid, 271

foreign trading restrictions, 231
geographic location of, 61
IMF voting weight, 199
international trade economy, 237
Marshall Islands case and, 195
military force, use of, 51
nuclear weapons, 73–74, 155, 163
in P5, 69, 170, 200
size of military forces, 152
trade sanction policies, 260
universal jurisdiction, 338
withdrawal from EU, 223, 247, 249, 421
women, violence against, 106
World Bank voting weight, 201
United Nations (UN), 8, 22–23, 36, 66,
181, 187, 190, 196, 210, 313, 315, 325,
338, 395
Arms Trade Treaty, 182
children and, 340
collective security system, 172
contributions and limits of, 217
economic sanctions, 266–267
environmental protection initiatives and
policies, 368
and global climate change, 368–370
historical foundations, 210–211
and human rights, 329–331, 340–343
MDG, 270, 308, 310, 340
North Korea sanctions, 266
peacekeepers, 343
peacekeeping mission, 172–173, 174m
policy actions of, 52
purposes of, 212
soft-power initiatives, 340–343
as source of international law, 189
structure of, 212–217
Trusteeship Council, 217
2020 budget, 215
UDHR, 330–331, 340, 342
and women's empowerment, 340–342
World Court and, 217
United Nations Children's Fund
(UNICEF), 340
United Nations Entity for Gender Equality
and the Empowerment of Women.
See UN Women
United Nations Truce Supervision
Organization, 172
United States (US), 73–74, 158, 175, 264, 324,
343–344, 369, 375, 385, 395
Agency for International
Development, 337
aid sanction, 261
alliances, 159m
arms races, 157, 161
Baruch Plan, 169
and Canada trade relationship, 244
China and, 113, 266, 337
Civil War, 117
and climate change, 371
Cold War, 35
colonial history and economic
development, 297–298
colonialism, 228
constructivist perspective of Russian
relations, 71–72
as core state, 97, 302
costs of military conflicts, 114
COVID-19, 133, 377
cyberwarfare, 127–129

democracy aid, 278–279
development aid, 271
dominance in international system, 12
economic crises, 5, 243
economic sanctions, 257, 261–263
economic threats in, 42
economy, 420–421
Foreign Service, 184
foreign trading restrictions, 229, 231
free trading, 230–231, 234
FTAs, 247
Fulbright educational exchange
    program, 176
GDP per capita, 289f, 290, 294t
geographic location of, 61
Gulf War, 116
humanitarian aid, 281–282
and human rights, 332–333
human trafficking, 336
Hurricane Katrina, 361
IMF and, 199, 235–236, 313
INF Treaty and, 147
interest groups, 89
as international actors, 23
as international institutions, 65
international trade dependence, 312
international trade economy, 237
and Iran conflict, 83, 97, 185, 193–194,
    261, 263–264
Law of the Sea Convention and, 182
Magnitsky Law, 338
Marshall Islands case and, 195
media globalization, 241
military aid, 277–278
military force, 29, 51–52
military spending, 152
natural resources and development, 295
and Nicaragua, 193
and North Korea trade relationship, 266
nuclear deterrence, 161–164
nuclear disarmament, 169–170
nuclear weapons, 13–14, 29, 73–74, 153,
    155, 157, 161–164
in P5, 69, 170, 200
Paris Agreement, support for, 370
poverty line, 290, 292
presidential security approaches, 9
professional diplomats in, 184
rising sea levels, 360
Russia geographical proximity, 5–6
Russia interference in presidential
    election, 76, 129
and Russia relationship, 75–76
Sierra Club, 367
size of military forces, 152
Space Command, 376
specialization and trading, 230–231
Syria and, 21–22, 85, 321
Thucydides trap, 113
trade disputes, 202, 238
trade sanction policies, 260
trade war, 234, 238, 260
U-2 spy plane shot down incident, 87
UN budget, 215
as unitary actor, 59
withdrawal from Paris Agreement, 371
withdrawal from TPP, 249
World Bank and, 201, 225, 235–236, 313
World Court and, 193–194, 196
world leadership, 410

United States–Mexico–Canada Agreement
    (USMCA), 223, 246
"UNiTE to End Violence Against
    Women," 341
Unit veto, 199–200
Universal Declaration of Human Rights
    (UDHR), 265, 330–331, 340, 342, 412
Universal Human Rights Network
    (Unirights), 397
Universal jurisdiction, 191–192, 338–340
Universal Postal Union, 36
UN Office on Drugs and Crime
    (UNDOC), 341
UNSC. See UN Security Council (UNSC)
UN Secretariat, 36, 214–215
UN Secretary-General, 214
UN Security Council (UNSC), 36, 43,
    172–173, 192–194, 200, 214–215, 217,
    332, 340–341, 343–344, 395, 407
UN Security Council Resolution 688, 43
UN Watch, 390
UN Women, 106, 187, 342, 347
Uppsala Conflict Data Program, 117, 126
US. See United States (US)
US Agency for International Development,
    280, 364
US-based Nuclear Threat Initiative, 395
US Central Intelligence Agency, 415
US Environmental Protection Agency
    (EPA), 248
USMCA. See United States–Mexico–
    Canada Agreement (USMCA)
US National Endowment for
    Democracy, 280
US National Security Agency (NSA), 76, 376
USS Liberty, 76
US Strategic Defense Initiative, 376
USS Vincennes, 193

Vasquez, John, 130
Venezuela, 248, 276, 296, 336, 343, 363, 377
Vertical enforcement, 194–196
Vienna Convention of Diplomatic Relations,
    184, 194
Vienna Convention on the Law of
    Treaties, 189
Vietnam, 35, 68, 97, 141, 151, 232, 245, 303,
    374–375
Vietnam syndrome, 135
Vietnam War, 35, 116, 137, 141–142, 153
Violence, 99–100, 137
    diplomacy and, 185
    in Syria, 21–22
    terrorism, 118–121
    against women, 106, 268
von Clausewitz, Carl, 127, 135

Wag the Dog (film), 90
Walker, Stephen, 86
Wallstrom, Margot, 341
Walt, Stephen, 58
Waltz, Kenneth, 58, 163
War, 62, 114–116, 408
    armed conflict, 114–121
    asymmetric, 117–118
    bargaining theories of, 135
    civil war, 21, 43, 93, 116–117, 118t, 124, 126,
        137–141
    Cold War. See Cold War
    consequences of, 141–142, 386

conventional, 116
Correlates of War, 117
crimes, 332
cyberwarfare, 127–129
cyclical theories of, 132–133
deadliness, increasing, 123
defining empirically, 117
definition, 116
in developing world, 124–126
eras of, 129
evolution of, 121–129
extra-systemic/extra-state, 116
interstate, 36, 116, 141, 160
intrastate, 386
just war tradition, 190
limited, 116, 119, 124
movies about, 123
nature of, 121–129
reparations, 311
rules of, 168
state-centered, 127
trade, 229, 231–233
types of, 116–118
unconventional, 116–117, 126–129
weariness, 135
War, causes of, 129–131
    arms control, 166
    civil war, 137–141
    disarmament, 166
    distributions of power and, 131–132
    factors leading to, 130–131
    feminist perspective, 134
    geography and territory, 130
    individual-level explanations, 136–137
    levels of analysis and, 131–137
    liberal perspective, 133–134
    national attributes and, 134–136
    realist perspective, 131
    state-level explanations, 134–136
    system-level explanations, 131–134
Warsaw Pact, 35
Washington, George, 259
Washington Consensus, 306–307, 309–310
Washington Naval Agreements, 169
Watson, Paul, 369
Wayne, Carly, 89
WBCSD. See World Business Council for
    Sustainable Development (WBCSD)
Wealth gap, 288–295. See also Economic
    inequality
The Wealth of Nations (Smith), 229
Weapons, 150
    arms control, 165–169
    arms races, 157, 161–162
    Arms Trade Treaty, 182
    disarmament, 165–166, 169–170
    expenditures, 150–152
    military aid, 276–278
    technological developments,
        153, 155–157
Weapons of mass destruction (WMD), 83,
    116–117
Weber, Max, 69
Weighted voting system, 198–199, 201, 313
Wendt, Alexander, 69–71
Western Hemisphere, 5
Westphalian international system,
    26, 130, 410
    Cold War, 35
    diplomacy of, 27–28, 30

economy era in, 226–227
evolution of, 31, 33, 35
nations and players, 30–31
non-state actors in, 31
range of states in, 27t
sovereignty in, 27–28
states and characteristics, 26–30
states empowerment, 31, 33, 35
Westphalian sovereignty, 27–28, 332,
    353–354
WHO. *See* World Health Organization
    (WHO)
Why Men Rebel (Gurr), 137
Wick, Katharina, 276
Williams, Jody, 10, 38, 386
Wilson, Edward O., 136
Wilson, Woodrow, 55
Winning coalition, 90
Winterfell, 230
Wittenberg-Cox, Avivah, 103
WMD. *See* Weapons of mass
    destruction (WMD)
Wollstonecraft, Mary, 323
Women
    causes of war and, 134, 137
    difference feminists, 103
    and economic sanctions, 268–269
    female country leaders, 103–104
    feminism, 12, 100–107
    feminist international relations theory, 84
    FSOs, 184
    gender inequality, 106
    globalization and, 106, 243
    human trafficking, 336
    in international development, 309
    liberal feminists, 105
    Muslim, 324–325
    NGOs for, 347
    restrictions, 324
    rights, 323–324, 336, 340, 387
    in Saudi Arabia, 334
    security issues, 417–418
    as sex slaves, 334
    UN Women, 106, 187, 342, 347
    violence, 106, 268, 325, 417
    in workforce, 106
    World Conference on Women, 187, 188t
    and World War C, 103
Women for Women International, 347
Worker Rights Consortium, 245
Working poor, 323
World
    economy, development of, 227f
    economy era. *See* Economy era

fragile and stable states in, 126t
military powers in, strongest, 28t
political map, 6m
trade war, 229, 231–232
World Bank, 23, 176, 201, 225, 235, 275,
    307, 417
    Bretton Woods system, 312
    HIPC debt relief, 311–312
    weighted voting, 313
World Business Council for Sustainable
    Development (WBCSD), 367
World Conference on Women, 187, 188t
World Court, 8, 36, 189–191, 194–195
    Marshall Islands case, 195
    UN and, 217
    US and, 193–194, 196
World Economic Forum, 98
World Future Council, 365
World Health Organization (WHO), 196–197,
    288, 315, 341, 371, 377, 400
World Institute for Nuclear Security, 395
World politics, 3, 6m
    actors, cooperation challenges of, 7–8
    anarchy and, 8, 10, 409–414
    balance-of-power politics,
        63, 159–160, 170
    challenges of, 8–10, 409–414
    complex fields of, 3–7
    complexity of, 9–10, 409–414
    constructivist perspective on, 69–77
    cooperation dilemmas, 12–15
    current trends in, 23
    definition, 3
    diversity and, 8–9, 409–414
    economic security, 416–417
    geography and, 5–6
    how the world works, 408–409
    human security, 417
    at individual level of analysis, 10
    individuals and, 4–5
    international actors in, 22
    IOs in, 201–203
    issues about nature of, 13, 15
    levels of analysis, 10–11
    liberal perspective on, 63–69
    military security, 415–416
    mobile production, sales process
        and, 241
    negotiation in, 183–187
    patterns of, 11–12
    PD and, 13, 15
    Peters projection, 6m
    polar projection, 6m
    realist perspective on, 56–63

security and, 3, 7–8, 414–415
stag hunt and, 13, 15
at state/national level of analysis, 10
at systemic/international level of
    analysis, 10
TANs and, 413–414, 418
theories of. *See* Theories of world politics
trends and emerging concerns,
    418–419
women and children's security issues,
    417–418
World Summit for Children, 340
World systems theory (WST), 84, 96–98,
    108t, 302–304, 419
World Trade Organization (WTO), 45,
    65–66, 192, 196–197, 201–202, 226,
    237–238, 248, 313, 418
World Trade Organization Dispute
    Settlement Body, 196, 202, 237
World War C, 103
World War I, 57, 93, 231
World War II, 35, 43, 57, 92, 132
    causes of, 232
    conflicts after, 126f
    consequences of, 141–142
    contributing factor of, 232
    deaths from war after, 124f
    institution after, 176
    trade war and, 233–234
    World Court after, 195
World War III, 76
Worldwatch Institute, 368
World Wildlife Federation, 356, 367
World Zionist Organization, 384
WST. *See* World systems theory (WST)
WTO. *See* World Trade Organization (WTO)

Xenophobia, 183
Xi Jinping, 10, 85, 266

Yemen, 123, 336, 415
Yugoslavia, 30, 93, 124, 141, 173, 263, 324,
    344, 390
Yunus, Muhammad, 309

Zambia, 265
Zelikow, Philip, 88
Zero-day vulnerabilities/exploits, 128
Zero-sum, 62, 149
Ziehan, Peter, 295
Zimbabwe, 262–263, 324
Zionism, 384
Zionist Organization. *See* World Zionist
    Organization